WEB DESIGN
IN A NUTSHELL

A Desktop Quick Reference

D0071745

WEB DESIGN
IN A NUTSHELL

A Desktop Quick Reference

Jennifer Niederst

O'REILLY®

Beijing · Cambridge · Farnham · Köln · Paris · Sebastopol · Taipei · Tokyo

Web Design in a Nutshell
by Jennifer Niederst

Editor: Richard Koman

Production Editor: Clairemarie Fisher O'Leary

Printing History:

January 1999:   First Edition.

ISBN: 1-56592-515-7   [5/00]
[M]

Table of Contents

Preface .... *xiii*

Part I: The Web Environment

Chapter 1—Designing for a Variety of Browsers *3*

Browsers 3
Design Strategies 9
Writing Good HTML 11
Knowing Your Audience 12
Considering Your Site's Purpose 13
Test! Test! Test! 13

Chapter 2—Designing for a Variety of Displays *14*

Dealing with Unknown Monitor Resolutions 14
Fixed versus Flexible Web Page Design 19
Accessibility 23
Alternative Displays 26

Chapter 3—Web Design Principles
for Print Designers *28*

Color on the Web 28
Graphics on the Web 34
Typography on the Web 41

Chapter 4—A Beginner's Guide to the Server 47

Servers 101 47
Introduction to Unix 50
File Naming Conventions 57
Uploading Documents (FTP) 57
File (MIME) Types 61

Part II: HTML

Chapter 5—HTML Overview 67

HTML Editing Tools 68
WYSIWYG Authoring Tools 68
Document Structure 70
HTML Tags 71
Information Browsers Ignore 73
Tips on Good HTML Style 74
Specifying Color in HTML 75
Character Entities 84
HTML Resources in This Book 89

Chapter 6—Structural HTML Tags 91

Summary of Structural Tags 91
Setting Up an HTML Document 94
Global Settings with the <body> Tag 96
Using <meta> Tags 98

Chapter 7—Formatting Text 102

Summary of Text Tags 102
Working with HTML Text 112
Inline Type Styles 114
The <font> Tag 116
Lists 118
Layout Techniques with HTML 122

Chapter 8—Creating Links 130

Summary of Tags Related to Linking 130
Simple Hypertext Links 133
Linking Within a Document 134
Affecting the Appearance of Links 135

Targeting Windows 137
Imagemaps 137
Non-Web Links and Protocols 143

Chapter 9—Adding Images and Other Page Elements *146*

Summary of Object Placement Tags 146
Horizontal Rules 154
Image Basics 157
The <img> Tag and Its Attributes 158
Adding Java Applets to the Page 164
Adding Plug-in Media with <embed> 165
Adding Media Files with <object> 166

Chapter 10—Tables *168*

Summary of Table Tags 168
Introduction to Tables 176
Basic Table Structure 177
Affecting Table Appearance 181
Table Troubleshooting 187
Tips and Tricks 193
Standard Table Templates 196
Multipart Images in Tables 201

Chapter 11—Frames *206*

Summary of Frame Tags 206
Introduction to Frames 209
Basic Frameset Structure 211
Frame Function and Appearance 214
Targeting Frames 217
Inline (Floating) Frames 219
Frame Design Tips and Tricks 220

Chapter 12—Forms *226*

Summary of Form Tags 226
Introduction to Forms 233
The Basic Form (<form>) 234
Form Elements 236
New Form Attributes (HTML 4.0) 241
Affecting the Appearance of Forms 242
Unconventional Use of Form Elements 246
Demystifying CGI 247

Chapter 13—Server Side Includes *251*

How SSI Is Used 251

SSI and the Server 253

Adding SSI Commands to a Document 253

Using Environment Variables 255

XSSI 255

List of Elements 256

Include Variables 259

Time Formats for SSI Output 260

Part III: Graphics

Chapter 14—GIF Format *265*

GIF87a versus GIF89a 265

Eight-Bit Indexed Color 266

GIF Compression 266

When to Use GIFs 266

Tools Overview 267

Interlacing 268

Transparency 269

Minimizing GIF File Sizes 277

Chapter 15—JPEG Format *283*

24-bit Color 283

JPEG Compression 283

When to Use JPEGs 285

Progressive JPEGs 285

JPEGs in AOL Browsers 286

Creating JPEGs 286

Minimizing JPEG File Size 287

Chapter 16—PNG Format *291*

Platform/Browser Support 292

8-Bit Palette, Grayscale, and Truecolor 293

PNG Compression 293

When to Use PNGs 294

Special Features 295

Creating PNG Files 297

Optimizing PNG File Size 301

Online PNG Resources 302

Chapter 17—Designing Graphics with the Web Palette 303

The Web Palette 303
Other Palettes 305
Image Types 306
Designing with Web-Safe Colors 307
Converting to the Web Palette 309
Survey of Web Graphics Tools 310
Color Blenders 315
Where to Learn More 317

Part IV: Multimedia and Interactivity

Chapter 18—Animated GIFs 321

How They Work 321
Using Animated GIFs 322
Browser Support 322
Tools 323
Creating Animated GIFs 324
Optimizing Animated GIFs 328

Chapter 19—Audio on the Web 330

Copyright Issues 330
Audio Tools Overview 331
Basic Digital Audio Concepts 332
Nonstreaming versus Streaming 333
Nonstreaming (Static) Audio 335
Streaming Audio 341
Bibliography 345

Chapter 20—Video on the Web 347

Tools Overview 347
Basic Digital Video Concepts 348
Compression 349
Video File Formats 351
Streaming Video Technologies 353
Adding Video to an HTML Document 355
Bibliography 358

Chapter 21—Interactivity *359*

    Flash 359

    Shockwave for Director 366

    Java Applets 370

    Interactive Buttons with JavaScript 373

Chapter 22—Introduction to JavaScript *379*

    JavaScript Basics 379

    Sample Scripts 381

    Handling Multiple Browsers 383

    Browser Compatibility 385

Part V: Emerging Technologies

Chapter 23—Cascading Style Sheets *389*

    How Style Sheets Work 391

    Selectors 395

    Specifying Values 398

    Properties 399

    Positioning with Style Sheets 418

    What's New in CSS2 422

    Style Sheet Tips and Tricks 426

    Browser Support Charts 428

Chapter 24—Introduction to DHTML *429*

    Advantages to Using DHTML 430

    Disadvantages 430

    Learning DHTML 431

    Browser Differences 431

    The Document Object Model 431

    DHTML Examples 435

    DHTML Tools 441

    Where to Learn More 443

Chapter 25—Introduction to XML *445*

    Background 445

    Document Type Definition (DTD) 446

    XML Syntax Basics 446

    Examples of XML Technology 448

    Where to Learn More 451

Chapter 26—Embedded Font Technology *453*

Using Embedded Fonts 453
TrueDoc Technology ("Dynamic Fonts") 454
OpenType (for Internet Explorer) 455

Chapter 27—Internationalization *458*

Character Sets 458
HTML 4.0 Language Tags 460
For More Information 463

Part VI: Appendixes

Appendix A—HTML Tags and Elements *467*

Appendix B—List of Attributes *483*

Appendix C—Deprecated Tags *511*

Appendix D—Proprietary Tags *515*

Appendix E—CSS Compatibility *518*

Glossary *527*

Index *535*

Preface

In the beginning, the Web was simple. When I first encountered it in early 1993 (working for O'Reilly's Global Network Navigator, since sold to and put to rest by America Online), there was only one browser for viewing web pages and it ran exclusively on the Unix platform. There were about a dozen tags that made any difference. Designing a web page was a relatively simple task.

It isn't so easy anymore. With the explosion of the Web came an avalanche of new technologies, proprietary tags, and acronyms. Even for someone who is immersed in the terminology and environment on a professional basis, it can be truly overwhelming. You just can't keep all this stuff in your head anymore.

Since leaving O'Reilly's Cambridge, Mass., offices for a freelance career, I never feel more alone than when I get stuck—whether it's because I don't know if it's a good idea to use style sheets for the project I'm designing, or I just can't remember what tag to put that MARGINWIDTH attribute in. And I'm not ashamed to admit that I've been reduced to tears after hours of battling a table that mysteriously refused to behave, despite my meticulous and earnest efforts.

It's at times like these that I wish I could walk down the hall and ask Norm Walsh what the heck is wrong with my table. In his absence, I do the best I can with the volumes of web design information available online (on the Internet, no one knows you have red, puffy eyes). Unfortunately, finding the answer to a specific question is a time-consuming and sometimes equally frustrating process in itself. Deadlines often can't accommodate a two-hour scavenger hunt.

I've often wished there was one place to go to find quick answers to my questions. That's why I wrote this book. It has the useful parts without a lot of fluff, organized so that information can be found quickly. It is based on the wish-lists—and, indeed, the contributions—of both professional and hobbyist web designers.

Contents

This book focuses on the front-end aspects of Web design—HTML authoring, graphics production, and media development. It is not a resource for programming, scripting, or server functions; however, whenever possible, I have tried to provide enough background information on these topics to give designers a level of familiarity with the terminology and technologies. The content in this book is appropriate for all levels of expertise—from professionals who need to look up a particular detail, to beginners who may require full explanations of new concepts and individual tags.

The book is divided into six parts, each covering a general subject area.

Part I, The Web Environment

Part I introduces some broad concepts about the way the Web works, which should orient designers to the peculiarities of the medium. It ends with an introduction to the server and basic Unix concepts.

Chapter 1, *Designing for a Variety of Browsers*, looks at how differing browser capabilities affect design decisions.

Chapter 2, *Designing for a Variety of Displays*, discusses varying monitor resolutions and accessibility issues and their effects on the design process.

Chapter 3, *Web Design Principles for Print Designers*, introduces how the Web deals with color, graphics, and fonts. This is particularly useful for those accustomed to print; however, it is also essential background information for any new web designer.

Chapter 4, *A Beginner's Guide to the Server*, provides a primer on basic server functions, Unix commands, uploading files, and file types.

Part II, HTML

This part focuses on HTML tags and their use. Most chapters begin with a listing of available tags with short descriptions (for easy access), followed by more detailed explanations and practical advice for their use.

Chapter 5, *HTML Overview*, gives a detailed introduction to HTML syntax, including how to specify color and special characters.

Chapter 6, *Structural HTML Tags*, lists the tags used to establish an HTML document and structure its contents, including settings that control or pertain to the whole document.

Chapter 7, *Formatting Text*, lists all tags related to the formatting of text elements in an HTML document.

Chapter 8, *Creating Links*, lists HTML tags related to linking one document to another, including imagemaps.

Chapter 9, *Adding Images and Other Page Elements*, focuses on the tags used for placing objects such as images, rules, or multimedia objects on a web page.

Chapter 10, *Tables*, provides everything you'd ever want to know about tables, including a list of table-related HTML tags, troubleshooting tips, and templates for popular table structures.

Chapter 11, *Frames*, covers the structure and creation of framed documents, including explanations of frame-related HTML tags, as well as tips and tricks.

Chapter 12, *Forms*, lists all tags related to form creation and provides an introduction to working with CGI scripts.

Chapter 13, *Server Side Includes*, provides an overview of Server Side Includes, including their capabilities and listings of the available elements and variables.

Part III, Graphics

The chapters in this part provide background information on web graphics file formats as well as overviews of available tools and practical tips for graphic production and optimization.

Chapter 14, *GIF Format*, describes the popular GIF format and provides tricks for working with transparency and minimizing file sizes.

Chapter 15, *JPEG Format*, describes the JPEG format and provides tips on minimizing file sizes.

Chapter 16, *PNG Format*, introduces this new and powerful graphic file format, discussing its strengths and limitations.

Chapter 17, *Designing Graphics with the Web Palette*, discusses the tools and techniques used in creating graphics with colors from the Web Palette.

Part IV, Multimedia and Interactivity

The chapters in this part focus on the animation, audio, and interactive capabilities of the Web.

Chapter 18, *Animated GIFs*, looks at the creation and optimization of animated GIFs.

Chapter 19, *Audio on the Web*, provides an overview of nonstreaming and streaming audio file formats for web delivery.

Chapter 20, *Video on the Web*, provides an overview of nonstreaming and streaming video file formats.

Chapter 21, *Interactivity*, looks at Macromedia's Flash and Director Shockwave formats as well as Java applets and interactive buttons created with JavaScript.

Chapter 22, *Introduction to JavaScript*, provides a general introduction to JavaScript as well as a number of templates for creating popular effects such as pop-up windows, browser-detection, and status-bar messages.

Part V, Emerging Technologies

This part introduces exciting new technologies that are destined to have an impact on the Web's future but are currently in varying stages of development and are not well supported by current browsers.

Chapter 23, *Cascading Style Sheets*, describes how to use Cascading Style Sheets to control presentation of HTML documents, including detailed explanations of available selectors, properties, and values. It also introduces CSS Level 2 features and provides tips for style sheet use.

Chapter 24, *Introduction to DHTML*, provides a basic overview of Dynamic HTML and related concepts.

Chapter 25, *Introduction to XML*, briefly introduces XML (eXtended Markup Language) and explains why it is significant. This chapter also includes a description of XML-based applications for multimedia and vector graphics.

Chapter 26, *Embedded Font Technology*, introduces two competing technologies, TrueDoc and OpenType, for embedding fonts in web pages.

Chapter 27, *Internationalization*, looks at measures being taken by the World Wide Web Consortium to make the Web multilingual.

Part VI, Appendixes

This section provides lots of useful look-up tables for HTML tags and CSS elements.

Appendix A, *HTML Tags and Elements*, lists all HTML tags as listed in the HTML 4.0 Specification of April 1998. This list also serves as an index to finding full tag explanations throughout the book.

Appendix B, *List of Attributes*, lists all attributes and their respective tags and values.

Appendix C, *Deprecated Tags*, lists all tags that have been "deprecated" (discouraged from use) by the HTML 4.0 Specification.

Appendix D, *Proprietary Tags*, lists tags that work only with Netscape Navigator or Internet Explorer.

Appendix E, *CSS Compatibility*, lists all CSS properties and the browsers that support them, including a handy "safe list."

The *Glossary* defines many of the terms used in the book.

Conventions Used in This Book

The following typographical conventions are used in this book:

`Constant width`
   is used to indicate HTML tags, code examples, and keyboard commands

`Constant italic`
   is used to indicate variable text in code.

Italic

is used to indicate variables, filenames, directory names, URLs, and glossary terms.

 The owl icon designates a note, which is an important aside to its nearby text.

 The turkey icon designates a warning relating to the nearby text.

Request for Comments

We have tested and verified the information in this book to the best of our ability, but you may find that features have changed (or even that we have made mistakes!). Please let us know about any errors you find, as well as your suggestions for future editions, by writing to:

O'Reilly & Associates, Inc.
101 Morris Street
Sebastopol, CA 95472
1-800-998-9938 (in the U.S. or Canada)
1-707-829-0515 (international/local)
1-707-829-0104 (FAX)

You can also send us messages electronically. To be put on the mailing list or request a catalog, send email to:

info@oreilly.com

To ask technical questions or comment on the book, send email to:

bookquestions@oreilly.com

We have a web site for the book, where we'll list examples, errata, and any plans for future editions. You can access this page at:

http://www.oreilly.com/catalog/wdnut/

For more information about this book and others, see the O'Reilly web site:

http://www.oreilly.com

Acknowledgments

A small army of people were instrumental in the writing of this book. First, I'd like to thank my editor, Richard Koman, for his support, vision, and flexibility. On the flip side, I'd also like to thank him for the long leash, the trust in *my* vision, and his appropriate *inflexibility* (the results of which were a better book).

I'd also like to thank Tim O'Reilly for his careful crafting of the "In a Nutshell" series and for giving me the green light on this book.

Thanks also go to Ron Woodall, creator of the HTML Compendium, for his proactive assistance in providing browser support information. I encourage you to check out the Compendium's site (*http://www.htmlcompendium.org*) for a complete list of tags, both current and obsolete, with detailed descriptions; listings and detailed descriptions for all known attributes for each tag; browser support information not listed in this book—such as NCSA Mosaic and earlier versions of the HTML standards; and up-to-date listings and browser compatibility information.

Thanks also to Chris Farnham, for writing chapters on DHTML and XML, as well as for his contribution to the SMIL section of the XML chapter.

Much of the wisdom in this book was culled from web design-related mailing lists such as A List Apart (beautifully maintained by Jeffrey Zeldman), the WebDesign list at Hesketh.com, and most notably, Monkey Junkies (WebMonkey.com's online community). A special "hey" goes out to Taylor.

Also key in the deepening of my understanding of the Web were the works of a number of O'Reilly authors, including: *Webmaster in a Nutshell*, by Valerie Quercia and Stephen Spainhour; *HTML: The Definitive Guide*, by Chuck Musciano and Bill Kennedy; *Learning the Unix Operating System*, by Grace Todino, John Strang, and Jerry Peek; and *Designing with JavaScript*, by Nick Heinle.

I'd like to thank Jim Cline, Dmitry Kirsanov (*www.kirsanof.com*), Chris Maden, Eric Meyer, Dustin Mollo, Greg Porell, and Greg Roelofs for their time and thoughtful review comments.

Thanks to the following people who provided various forms of assistance, information, and tools I required to get my job done: Paul Anderson (Builder.com); Chuck Duff (Digital Frontiers); Brad Ennis and David Lynch (for font research); Chris Florio (for audio and video assistance); Craig Hockenberry (FurboFilters); Andrew King (Webreference.com); Kevin Lynch (Macromedia); Doug Meisner (Adobe Systems, Inc.); and Lynda Weinman (author of a fine set of books).

Thanks also to Clairemarie Fisher O'Leary for her hard work and willingness to make this book "just right," as well as the other folks who helped: Mike Sierra, Edie Freedman, Ellie Cutler, Kim Brown, Chris Reilley, Seth Maislin, and Melanie Wang.

Finally, I'd like to thank my Mom, Dad, and brother Liam, for their unending support and the inspiration they each provide. Thanks to Sifl and Olly for keeping me entertained as my deadline approached. And last, but not least, warm thanks go to Jeff for being there when I needed him.

PART I

The Web Environment

CHAPTER 1

Designing for a Variety of Browsers

Most web authors agree that the biggest challenge (and headache!) in web design is dealing with the variety of browsers and platforms, each with its own support and implementation of HTML and scripting elements. Features and capabilities improve with each new major browser release, but that doesn't mean the older versions just go away. The general public tends not to keep up with the latest and greatest—many are content with what they are given, and many others may be using the computers of a company or institution that chooses a browser for them.

How do you design web pages that are aesthetically and technically intriguing without alienating those in your audience with older browsers? Does a page that is designed to be functional on all browsers necessarily need to be boring? Is it possible to please everyone? And if not, where do you draw the line? How many past versions do you need to cater to with your designs?

This chapter provides background information, statistics, and current wisdom from professional web designers that may help you to make some of these decisions.

There's no absolute rule here. While it's important to make your content accessible to the greatest number of users, experimentation and the real-world implementation of emerging technologies is equally important to keep the medium pushing forward. The key to making appropriate design decisions lies in understanding your audience and considering how your site is going to be used.

Browsers

The browser market is dominated by the two major browsers: Netscape Navigator and Microsoft Internet Explorer. As of this writing, Navigator is in version 4.0 and Internet Explorer is in version 5.0. Together, the "Big Two," including their collective past versions, account for approximately 90% (or more) of browser use today.

The browser landscape has been dominated by these two contenders as they battle it out for market dominance. Their struggle to be cooler than the next guy has resulted in a collection of proprietary HTML tags as well as incompatible implementations of new technologies (most notoriously Dynamic HTML, but also JavaScript and Cascading Style Sheets). On the positive side, the competition between Netscape and Microsoft has also led to the rapid advancement of the medium as a whole.

Netscape publishes information for developers at *http://developer.netscape.com/*. Of particular interest are the documentation pages, including listings of Netscape's HTML tag support at *http://developer.netscape.com/docs/manuals/*.

Microsoft provides a rich resource of developer information at their SiteBuilder Network site, *http://www.microsoft.com/sitebuilder/*, and the SiteBuilder Workshop, *http://www.microsoft.com/workshop/*.

Other Browsers

Most web authors base their designs on the functionality of Navigator and Internet Explorer, since they claim the lion's share of the market; however, there are a number of other browsers you may choose to take into consideration.

Internet Explorer 4.0 on the Macintosh

Not all IE4.0 browsers are created equal! The Macintosh version of IE4.0 lacks significant functionality found in its Windows sibling, so including 4.0-specific features in your site may still leave some users out. As a general guideline, treat Mac IE4.0 like Netscape 3.0.

Some documented shortcomings include:

- No embedded font support
- No support for CSS filters and transitions (visual effects such as "drop shadow" that can be applied to text elements)
- No multimedia controls (animation and transition effects ordinarily created by multimedia authoring software)
- Problematic DHTML implementation: despite the fact that Microsoft claims DHTML is supported on all platforms, it's extremely unreliable on the Mac

Microsoft's official statement on Cross-Platform Functionality can be found at *http://www.microsoft.com/workshop/essentials/versions/xplatform.htm*.

America Online browsers

America Online subscribers use one of seven possible browsers (depending on their platform and version of the AOL software), some of them lacking all but the most minimal HTML support.

The current version of America Online for the PC, 3.0 as of this writing, uses an adaptation of the Microsoft Internet Explorer 3.0 browser; however, you can't always count on it to perform the same as the standard MSIE 3.0 release. (Functionality is particularly limited for Mac users.) Many web designers have been horrified to see their site design (which works perfectly in all the major browsers) once it's been run through the AOL system and spit out in one of their browsers.

The difference is partly due to AOL's reliance on proxy servers and image compression techniques. Their image compression is known to have problems displaying JPEG graphics, resulting in blotchy and color-streaked images (see Chapter 15, *JPEG Format*, for more information). Problems have also been noted in the display of background images.

In addition, some technologies, such as Java and Cascading Style Sheets are not available to users with Windows 3.0 (approximately 40% of AOL's audience). Java-Script (and many other features) will not work for AOL's Macintosh users (approximately 8%).

Fortunately, AOL publishes a site specifically for web developers who want their sites to be accessible and attractive for AOL users. Of particular use is the browser chart, which provides a specific listing of each of its browsers (by release and plat-form), the technologies and features supported, and a breakdown in percentage of users for each browser.

AOL's web developer's site can be found at *http://webmaster.info.aol.com/*.

WebTV

WebTV brings web surfing to the living room with a set-top box, an ordinary tele-vision, and a remote control (an optional keyboard is also available). WebTV uses its own specialized browser for viewing web pages. It does a respectable job of parsing standard HTML 3.2, but is unable to display frames, Java, JavaScript, ActiveX, or any format that requires a plug-in (except Shockwave Flash and RealAudio 3.0, which are built in). They have also created many new proprietary HTML tags for use only with WebTV.

Because WebTV displays web pages on televisions, it introduces new concerns regarding color and screen real estate. This unique browsing environment is discussed further in Chapter 2, *Designing for a Variety of Displays*.

WebTV publishes a developers' resource called "Primetime," where you can find specific information regarding developing sites for WebTV, including a list of the WebTV proprietary tags. WebTV Primetime can be found at *http://www.webtv.net/primetime/*.

A search for "WebTV" on Yahoo (*http://www.yahoo.com*) retrieves a number of other useful WebTV resources.

Opera

Opera is a lean and mean little browser created by Opera Software in Oslo, Norway. It is currently only available for the Windows platform, although a Mac version is in the works. As this book goes to press, Opera costs $35 (that's $35 more than Navigator or Internet Explorer), but it boasts extremely quick down-load times and a small minimal disk requirement (just under 1.2 MB). Opera is respected for its exact compliance with HTML standards. Sloppy tagging that gets by the larger browsers (such as missing closing tags, improper nesting, etc.) will not render correctly in Opera.

Opera 3.0 does not support Java, Cascading Style Sheets, or DHTML, although Java support is promised to be added in version 4.0 (not available as of this printing).

The general public is not likely to flock to Opera, so it may never figure high in browser usage statistics; however, many designers continue to test their sites in Opera to make sure their code is clean.

For more information about Opera, see *http://www.operasoftware.com/*.

Lynx

Last, but not least, is Lynx, a freely distributed text-only browser that offers fast, no-nonsense access to the Web. It has stood proud as the lowest common denominator standard against which web pages can be tested for basic functionality. Lynx may be a simple browser, but it is not stuck in the past. Lynx is constantly being improved and updated to include support for tables, forms, even JavaScript!

People do use Lynx, so don't be surprised if a client demands a Lynx-compliant site design. Lynx is also important to partially sighted users who browse with Lynx and a speech device.

The Extremely Lynx page is a good starting point for finding developer information for Lynx. You can find it at *http://www.crl.com/~subir/lynx.html*.

For information on designing Lynx-friendly pages, see *http://www.crl.com/~subir/lynx/author_tips.html*.

Browser Usage Statistics

Knowing what browsers are most used can be helpful in deciding which technologies to adopt and where to draw the line for backwards compatibility. The most meaningful statistics are those culled from your own site's usage. Server tracking software typically breaks down hits according to the browser making the request, so if you find that only 20% of your visitors are using 4.0 version browsers, for instance, you might not want to switch your site over to style sheets just yet.

Browser usage resources

There are a few browser statistics sites available on the Web. These sites base their statistics on hits to their own pages, which skews the data towards users who care about browser stats—probably not the same section of society using the Web to research a new car purchase or look up television schedules. BrowserWatch provides statistics that are meticulously broken down by version, sub-version, and sub-sub-version for each particular browser.

Because the sampling base is probably not representative of the whole web audience, the statistics on these pages shouldn't be considered as absolute fact, just general guidelines. It's interesting to see the long scrolls of browsers you've never heard of that make up .1 to .5% of overall site usage.

BrowserWatch
   http://browserwatch.internet.com/

Which Browser
   http://www.whichbrowser.com/

BrowserCaps
   http://www.browsercaps.com/

Browser usage overview

As of this writing, the latest trend in browser usage is the closing of the gap between Netscape Navigator and Internet Explorer. In mid-1997, Netscape enjoyed a comfortable 70–80% of the overall browser usage (according to statistic sites such as those listed above). Currently, they are running neck-and-neck at about 40–45% of the market share each (all versions included). This may be due to the fact that IE is so integrated with the Windows operating system that new users are using Internet Explorer by default. It may also reflect consumer approval for the quality of the IE software.

Another trend is that some webmasters are beginning to see WebTV hits increase. Although WebTV is slowly gaining in popularity, it is not making a tremendous impact on browser statistics. It may be difficult to track the WebTV browser, because those users are not likely to ever visit browser statistics sites.

Browser statistics change much faster than book publishing schedules, so the statistics presented below are not necessarily meaningful; however if you are completely unfamiliar with the typical browser breakdowns, these statistics from the BrowserWatch site should give you an idea of who's using what—as of this writing of course. These were the number presented on July 13, 1998. One caution: some of the browsers in this chart are obscure or defunct; don't expect to see them in any sizable numbers.

Netscape Navigator	52.00%
Microsoft Internet Explorer	35.80%
Cyberdog	2.42%
Ibrowse	1.37%
Opera-3.0	1.22%
Lynx	0.93%
Echo	0.68%
MacWeb	0.40%
NEWT ActiveX	0.30%
EmailSiphon	0.27%

As an indication of how statistics can vary, these statistics were taken the same day from the Which Browser site.

Netscape	47.08%
MSIE	51.80%
All Others	1.12%

Again, the most meaningful browser usage statistics will be those gathered from your own site.

Browser Features

Once you've determined the browsers of choice for the majority of your audience, you can make better decisions regarding which HTML tags and web technologies are safe to incorporate into your design. Likewise, you can determine how much of your audience you risk alienating by relying on certain features such as Java or JavaScript.

Every HTML tag in Part II of this book is accompanied by a chart indicating which browsers support it. Exceptional attribute support (or lack thereof) is noted in the descriptions following each tag.

Table 1-1 provides a general listing of popular browsers and the web features and technologies they support.

Table 1-1: Browser Support for Web Technologies

	HTML 3.2	HTML 4.0	Anim. GIFs	Tables	Frames	Plug-ins	Java	Java-Script	Style Sheets
Windows									
Navigator 4.0	yes	partial	yes	yes	yes	yes	yes	yes	yes
Navigator 3.0	yes	—	yes	yes	yes	yes	yes	yes	—
Navigator 2.0	yes	—	yes	yes	yes	yes	yes	yes	—
Navigator 1.0	—	—	—	yes	—	—	—	—	—
Explorer 5.0	yes	yes	yes	yes	yes	yes	yes	yes	yes
Explorer 4.0	yes	partial	yes	yes	yes	yes	yes	yes	yes
Explorer 3.0	yes	—	yes	yes	yes	yes	yes	yes	yes
Explorer 2.0	—	—	—	yes	—	—	—	—	—
Explorer 1.0	—	—	—	yes	—	—	—	—	—
AOL 3.0 (Win95)	yes	—	yes	yes	yes	yes	yes	yes	yes
AOL 3.0 (Win3.0)	yes	—	yes	yes	yes	yes	—	yes	—
Mosaic 3.0	—	—	—	yes	yes	—	—	—	—
Mosaic 1.0	—	—	—	—	—	—	—	—	—
Opera 3.0	mostly	—	yes	yes	yes	—	—	yes	—
Macintosh									
Navigator 4.0	yes	partial	yes	yes	yes	yes	yes	yes	yes
Navigator 3.0	yes	—	yes	yes	yes	yes	yes	yes	—
Navigator 2.0	—	—	yes	yes	yes	yes	—	yes	—
Navigator 1.0	—	—	—	yes	—	—	—	—	—
Explorer 4.0	yes	partial	yes	yes	yes	yes	yes	yes	partial

Table 1-1: Browser Support for Web Technologies (continued)

	HTML 3.2	HTML 4.0	Anim. GIFs	Tables	Frames	Plug-ins	Java	Java-Script	Style Sheets
Explorer 3.0	yes	—	yes	yes	yes	yes	yes	yes	yes
Explorer 2.1	—	—	—	yes	yes	yes	—	—	—
AOL 3.0	yes	—	yes	yes	yes	yes	—	—	—
AOL 2.7	—	—	—	—	—	—	—	—	—
Mosaic 3.0b4	—	—	—	yes	yes	—	—	—	—
Mosaic 2.0	—	—	—	yes	—	—	—	—	—
Mosaic 1.0	—	—	—	—	—	—	—	—	—
Set-top									
WebTV	yes	—	yes	yes	—	—	—	yes	—

Design Strategies

Faced with the dilemma of varying browser capabilities, web designers have developed a variety of design approaches, some more extreme than others. The "correct" way to handle a particular site, of course, depends on its use and audience, but this section should provide a peek into the different positions in the ongoing debate over where to draw the line.

Lowest Common Denominator Design

A minority of web developers adhere to the ideal standards that the Web should be accessible to everyone. They may also maintain that presentation should be in the hands of the end user, not the author. These designers tend to stick with the safest HTML standard (currently HTML 3.2 or even 2.0) and make sure that pages work on all browsers, including Lynx and version 1.0 of the popular browsers.

In web design discussion forums, there is consistently a voice representing the position that all the current embellishments to HTML (Java, JavaScript, style sheets, and DHTML) are unnecessary to successful communication over the Web. Designers who design for the lowest common denominator may choose not to use any of these technologies in their designs.

Current Version Design

Another minority, at the other extreme end of the spectrum, are the web developers who design *only* for the most current version of popular browsers (as of this writing, Navigator 4.0 and Internet Explorer 4.0), with little concern for site performance for other users. The statement "tell them to upgrade—it's *free!*" has often been used in defense of this design tactic. Beyond this, there are even designers who design for only the most current version of one *particular* browser. Note that this approach may be perfectly appropriate for intranet design.

This approach has the obvious disadvantage of alienating a large percentage of the audience. If the functionality of a site depends on a specific trick, for example, if you can't get off the front page without JavaScript, then your site has problems communicating.

On the positive side, these designers tend to be the ones who forge new territories and put new technologies to the test. Creating exciting web features that depend on cutting-edge features does create an incentive for users to keep themselves up-to-date.

Splitting the Difference

Far more commonly, designers take a more balanced approach to web site creation. Designing web pages that "degrade gracefully" is the buzz phrase in web design circles. This design incorporates the cutting-edge web technologies, such as DHTML or JavaScript, but implements them in such a way that the pages are still fully functional on older browsers.

One strategy is to design pages that take advantage of technology supported in the previous version of major browsers. As of this writing, that would be the version 3.0 browsers. So, tables, frames, and JavaScript are fine, but style sheets and DHTML are a problem.

The trick is to code it in a way so that your page degrades well for older or more simple browsers. Simply being careful about always adding alternative text for images with the ALT attribute goes a long way toward making a web page more functional for Lynx users. When tables are used, they can be constructed so they read logically when scanned by a text-only browser.

Once working pages are developed using version 3.0 technologies (while keeping an eye on performance on older browsers), the site can be embellished using the latest techniques and tricks. For instance, it is possible to create a page that looks just fine for all browsers, but that also takes advantage of Cascading Style Sheets for those browsers that can use them. It doesn't hurt the other browsers; the up-to-date users will just get something extra. The same goes for DHTML tricks. They're fine as long as they're not used to carry the crucial message or functionality of the site. Think of these things as icing on the cake.

By being mindful of how well elements degrade, you can construct pages that will wow 'em on the current browsers but not drive them away if they're using an earlier version.

Something for Everyone

Another successful (albeit more labor-intensive) approach is to create multiple versions of your site aimed at different levels of users. One site could incorporate DHTML tricks and JavaScript events. Another could be a solid HTML 3.0-compliant site with images and attractive page layouts, but without the whistles and bells. You could create a text-only version that would serve the folks using Lynx, nonvisual browsers, and browsers on handheld electronic devices. If you were feeling ambitious, you could provide an all-Flash version of your site for those who are interested! In most cases, two carefully planned versions are plenty.

Some sites allow their users to decide which version they'd like to see. It's not uncommon to arrive at a site and be asked to choose between a souped-up version or a text-only version, or to choose between frames or no-frames. This puts the control in the hands of the viewer.

A more sophisticated approach is to automatically serve up an appropriate version of the page for the browser that is making the request. JavaScript is capable of basing actions on the browser being used (see Chapter 22, *Introduction to Java-Script*). Pages can also be assembled on the fly for a particular browser using Server Side Includes (see Chapter 13, *Server Side Includes*). Hotwired's WebMonkey site is a great example of this method in action, *plus* they share their secrets, so check it out at *http://www.webmonkey.com/*.

Of course, this approach takes a bit more time and technical know-how, but it has its rewards.

Writing Good HTML

Whatever your chosen browser, one key to success is to make sure you are writing HTML correctly.

HTML Validation Services

There are a number of online resources that check your web site for various quality issues, including the browser compatibility (or HTML Specification compliance) of your HTML code. There are also HTML validators that check your code for errors.

All will do a certain number of tests for free; however, to get the really good stuff, you generally have to pay for the individual service or a year's subscription for full access to the site. For example, WebSiteGarage provides a nifty (and fee-based) feature called "Browser Snapshot" that will provide up to 18 screenshots of your page on a variety of browsers, including all past versions. This can be a good way to run tests if you don't have access to all of these browsers on your own.

Some of the more popular HTML validation services include:

The World Wide Web Consortium's HTML Validator
http://validator.w3.org/

WebSiteGarage
http://www.websitegarage.com/

NetMechanic
http://www.netmechanic.com/

Doctor HTML
http://www2.imagiware.com/RxHTML/

If these don't suit you, there are a large number of HTML validators listed on Yahoo.

List of Validators on Yahoo
http://www.yahoo.com/Computers_and_Internet/Information_and_Documentation/Data_Formats/HTML/Validation_and_Checkers/

HTML Editors as Validators

Browser compatibility databases and HTML validators are beginning to work their way into HTML authoring tools as well. GoLive Cyberstudio (Mac-only; see *http:// www.golive.com/*) provides a complete database of all the HTML tags and their browser-support information.

Even more useful is Macromedia Dreamweaver's "Check Target Browsers" feature. Authors specify which browsers they are targeting with their site design (Netscape 2.0, 3.0, and 4.0; and Internet Explorer 2.0, 3.0, and 4.0) and Dreamweaver runs a check to see if any tags or attributes in the document are not supported by the target browser(s). For more information on Dreamweaver, see *http://www.macro-media.com/*.

Knowing Your Audience

As with most design challenges, making appropriate decisions regarding which browsers to support and which new technologies to adopt largely depends on knowing your audience. Before designing a new site, be sure to spend plenty of time up front researching the likely platforms, browsers, technical savvy, and connection speeds of the users you are targeting. If you are redesigning an existing site, spend time with the server logs to analyze past site usage.

There are no browser-support guidelines that can anticipate every design situation; however, the following scenarios should start you thinking:

- If you are designing a scientific or academic site, you should probably pay extra attention to how your site functions in Lynx (or other graphics-free browsing environments).

- If your site is aimed at a consumer audience—for instance, a site that sells educational toys to a primarily "mom"-based audience—don't ignore your site's performance and presentation in the AOL browsers.

- If you are designing for a controlled environment, such as a corporate intranet, or even better, a web-based kiosk, you've got it made! Knowing exactly what browser and platform your viewers are using means you can take full advantage of the whistles and bells (and even proprietary features) appropriate to that browser. If you are designing a standalone kiosk, you may even have the luxury of loading the fonts you want to use. Just be sure your design won't crash the browser since there's no one there to restart it for you immediately.

    In these situations, the "current version design" strategy discussed earlier in this chapter is entirely appropriate (just don't get spoiled)!

- If you are designing a computer game site aimed at young gaming geeks, you can probably assume they will have the latest browsers and plug-ins (or will get them if you say they need them).

For most multipurpose web sites, stick with the safer "Splitting the Difference" approach to design, or if you have the resources, create multiple versions and serve them appropriately.

Considering Your Site's Purpose

Another important factor for making web design decisions is knowing how your site is going to be used. Site users tend to fall into two broad categories: those who are on a mission for information, and those who are surfing the Web for entertainment. In general, sites that serve the latter audience have more opportunity to try out cutting-edge or plug-in technologies that improve the overall user experience of the site. For informational sites, you wouldn't want to base the availability of the information on a client-side technology.

Of course, there are plenty of exceptions to this overly generalized rule. For instance, WebMonkey (*http://www.webmonkey.com/*) is an informational site that uses a DHTML-based interface, based on the assumption that its developer audience is using the latest tools. WebMonkey also uses browser detection to serve alternative versions for those without DHTML capabilities. So just because you have a "serious" site doesn't mean you should abandon new technologies entirely.

Another unique case is a site that is *about* the technology being used, such as a VRML environment. In this situation, you have every right to expect users to use the appropriate browser or plug-in to catch up with your content. (Although, it still might be nice to at least provide some screenshots to show the others what they're missing!)

Test! Test! Test!

The final word in the dilemma of designing for a variety of browsers is always TEST! Test your site on as many browsers, browser versions, and platform configurations as you can get your hands on.

Professional web design firms run their sites through a vigorous quality assurance phase before going "live." They generally keep a bank of computers of varying platforms and processing powers that run as many versions of browsers (including Lynx) as possible.

If you do not have the resources to keep a similar set-up on your own, make the site available on a private test site and take a look at it on your friends' computers. You might view it under corporate conditions (a Windows machine with a 4.0 browser, and a T1 connection), then visit a friend at home to see the same site on AOL with a 28.8 modem. (If nothing else, it's a good excuse to get away from your computer and visit your friends!)

Although your pages will certainly look different in different environments, the idea is to make sure that nothing is outright broken and that your content is being communicated clearly.

CHAPTER 2

Designing for a Variety of Displays

One of the most vexing aspects of web design is knowing that your page is at the mercy of the software and hardware configuration of each individual user. A page that looks great on your machine may look radically different, or perhaps even ghastly, when viewed on another user's set-up. This is partly due to the browser's functionality (as discussed in Chapter 1, *Designing for a Variety of Browsers*) and the individual user's preferences (font size, colors, etc.), but the display device itself also plays a large part in the success of the page's design.

This chapter looks at the ways in which design decisions are influenced by the wide range of displays and viewing conditions. For the majority of your audience, the variation in display is a function of the monitor's size (or, more accurately, its resolution) and color capabilities. However, it is important to keep in mind that the diversity does not end there. Some users may be watching your web page on TV. Still others may be viewing it in the palm of their hand on a PDA (personal digital assistant) or cell phone. Sight-impaired users may be listening to your page, not viewing it.

Dealing with Unknown Monitor Resolutions

Browser windows can be resized to any dimension, limited only by the maximum size of the monitor. Designing for an unknown amount of browser real estate is a challenge unique to web design and one that is particularly troublesome for designers who are accustomed to the printed page.

In discussion forums frequented by web design professionals, no topic is more often addressed (nor hotly debated) than the question of which monitor resolution to design for. As with most web design issues, there is no "right" way to design for the Web, and your decisions should always be guided by your knowledge of your target audience and the purpose of your site. Still, it is helpful to understand the environment and to know how others are maneuvering within it.

This section looks at the range of monitor resolutions and presents the current wisdom on making appropriate design decisions. The design advice and "wisdom" presented here has been culled from a number of popular web design mailing lists over the course of nearly half a year.

Standard Monitor Sizes and Resolutions

The first step in determining the likely size of your web page is to look at the maximum amount of space provided by the computer monitor. Computer monitors come in a variety of standard sizes, typically indicated in inches. Some typical monitor sizes are 13", 14", 17", 19", 20", and 21".

The more meaningful measurement, however, is *monitor resolution*—the total number of pixels available on the screen. The higher the resolution, the more detail can be rendered on the screen. When you know the available number of pixels, you can design your graphics (also measured in pixels) and page elements accordingly. Table 2-1 presents a list of some standard monitor resolutions supported by Macintosh and PC platforms. This is not a complete listing, merely the most commonly occurring configurations.

Table 2-1: Common Monitor Resolutions for Personal Computers

Macintosh	PC
512 × 384	640 × 480
640 × 480	800 × 600 (common on laptops)
800 × 600 (common on Powerbooks)	1024 × 870
832 × 624	1280 × 1024
1024 × 768	1600 × 1200
1152 × 870	
1280 × 960	
1280 × 1024	
1600 × 1200	

Resolution is related to but not necessarily determined by monitor size. Depending on the video card driving it, a single monitor can display a number of different resolutions. For instance, a 17" monitor can display 640×480 pixels, 800×600 pixels, or even higher.

It is important to keep in mind that the higher the resolution on a given monitor, the more pixels are packed into the available screen space. The result is smaller pixels, which will make your images and page elements appear smaller as well. If you create graphics and pages on a monitor with a relatively high resolution, say 1280×1024, be prepared for everything to look a lot bigger on standard 14" monitors running at 640×480.

It is for this reason that web measurements are made in pixels, not inches. Something that appears to be an inch wide on your system may look smaller or larger to other users. When you design in pixels, you know how elements measure in proportion to each other. Chapter 3, *Web Design Principles for Print Designers*, further discusses resolution as it applies to graphics.

"Live" Space in the Browser Window

Knowing the size of the monitor is just the beginning . . . the operating system and the browser itself occupy a fair amount of this space. The amount of space that is actually available within the browser window (referred to in this chapter as the browser window's "live" space) is dependent on the computer's operating system, the browser being used, and the individual user's preference settings.

Because so many factors are involved, determining exactly how much live space is available for each monitor resolution is an inexact science.

The information provided in Tables 2-2 through 2-5, on the following pages, should be used as general guidelines, not universal truths. Measurements were taken with the browser maximized to fill the available space in the window. The minimum live space is measured with all possible browser tools (such as buttons, location bars, and scrollbars) visible. The maximum live space is measured with all optional elements hidden, making the browser window as large as it can be for each particular resolution.

Bear in mind that these are theoretical extremes, and actual browser window dimensions will vary. People may have some of the buttons showing, but not all of them. Scrollbars turn on and off automatically, so they are difficult to antici-pate. Users with very high monitor resolutions (1024 pixels wide and higher) do not necessarily open their browser windows to fill the whole area, but may keep several narrow windows open at the same time. Along with these variables are a host of unknowns that can affect browser window size.

The following tables show the minimum (when all browser menus, toolbars, and scrollbars are turned on) and maximum (when they are turned off) live areas for the browsers on both Windows 95 and Macintosh. Absolute pixel values for different monitor resolutions are given. Live areas are shaded gray in the images.

Monitor Color Issues

Monitors also differ in the number of colors they are able to display, if they display colors at all. This is another aspect of the final display that may influence design decisions. Monitors typically display either 24-bit (approximately 17 million colors), 16-bit (approximately 65,000 colors), or 8-bit color (256 colors). Colors taken from the "true" 24-bit color space will *dither* (display with a speckled pattern) when rendered by browsers on 8-bit monitors.

However, there is a set of 216 colors, made up from the cross-section of the Mac and Windows system palettes, that will not dither on Mac and Windows 8-bit displays. This set of colors is known as the Web Palette, among other names. Many designers choose to design web graphics and HTML elements using colors from this palette so the pages look the same for all users. The Web Palette is discussed thoroughly in Chapter 3, and Chapter 17, *Designing Graphics with the Web Palette*.

If you are concerned about users with grayscale or black and white displays, be sure to design high-contrast graphics. When colors are converted to grayscale values (or dithered with black and white pixels), only the brightness of the colors matters. Imagine setting purple text on a teal background; although the colors are

---

Table 2-2: Live area in Netscape Navigator 4.0 on Windows 95

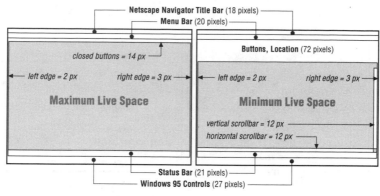

Monitor Resolution	Minimum Live Space	Maximum Live Space
640 × 480	623 × 278	635 × 380
800 × 600	783 × 430	795 × 500
1024 × 768	1007 × 598	1019 × 668
1152 × 870	1135 × 700	1147 × 770
1280 × 1024	1263 × 854	1275 × 924

Table 2-3: Live Area in Internet Explorer 4.0 on Windows 95

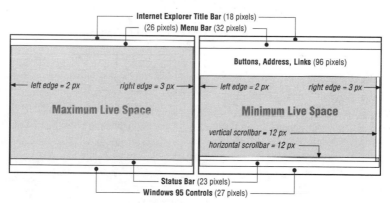

Monitor Resolution	Minimum Live Space	Maximum Live Space
640 × 480	623 × 272	635 × 386
800 × 600	783 × 392	795 × 506
1024 × 768	1007 × 560	1019 × 674
1152 × 870	1135 × 662	1147 × 776
1280 × 1024	1263 × 816	1275 × 930

Table 2-4: Live area in Netscape Navigator 4.0 on Macintosh

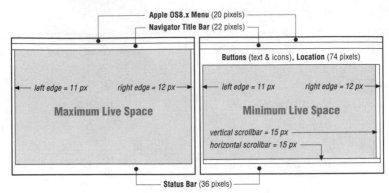

Monitor Resolution	Minimum Live Space	Maximum Live Space
640 × 480	602 × 313	617 × 402
832 × 624	794 × 457	809 × 546
1024 × 768	986 × 601	1001 × 601
1152 × 870	1114 × 703	1129 × 792
1280 × 960	1242 × 793	1257 × 882
1280 × 1024	1242 × 857	1257 × 946

Table 2-5: Internet Explorer 4.0 on Macintosh

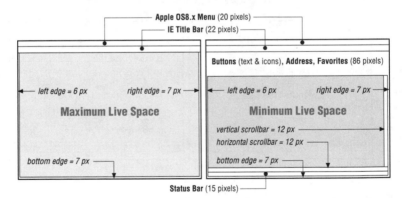

Monitor Resolution	Minimum Live Space	Maximum Live Space
640 × 480	612 × 315	627 × 431
832 × 624	804 × 459	819 × 575
1024 × 768	996 × 603	1011 × 719
1152 × 870	1124 × 705	1139 × 821
1280 × 960	1252 × 795	1267 × 911
1280 × 1024	1252 × 859	1267 × 975

of contrasting hues, they are close enough in overall brightness that the text will be illegible when the colors are displayed on a grayscale monitor.

Monitors also vary in the brightness of their displays, known as the *gamma* value. PC monitors tend to be much darker than Macintosh monitors, so colors that are deep and rich when created on a Mac may look black when displayed on a PC. Likewise, graphics created on a PC may look washed out when viewed on a Mac. Gamma is discussed further in Chapter 3.

Fixed versus Flexible Web Page Design

Closely related to the issue of varying monitor resolutions is the question of whether web pages should be designed to be flexible (resizing and adapting to various window sizes) or fixed at a particular size, (giving the designer more control of the page's dimensions) There are very strong opinions on both sides. Naturally, there are good reasons for and against each approach.

You may find that you choose a fixed structure for some sites and allow others to be flexible. You may find that you have strong convictions that one or the other approach is the only way to go. Either way, it is useful to be familiar with the whole picture and the current opinions of professional web designers. This section attempts to present a balanced overview of the possibilities and the pitfalls.

Flexible Design

Web pages are flexible by default. The text and elements in a straightforward HTML file will flow into the browser window, filling all available space, regardless of the monitor size. When the browser window is resized, the elements reflow to adapt to the new dimensions. This is the inherent nature of the Web. Designers who are initially traumatized by the unpredictability of where the page elements land usually just learn to let go of some control over the page.

Many designers make a conscious decision to construct pages so they can withstand stretching and shrinking web windows. This approach comes with advantages and disadvantages.

Advantages

- The reality is that web pages *will* be displayed on a variety of monitor resolutions and conditions; keeping the page flexible allows it to be "customized" for every display.

- The whole monitor space is filled, without the potentially awkward empty space left over by many fixed-width designs.

- Designing flexible pages is closer to the spirit and the nature of the medium. A "good" web page design by these standards is one that is functional to the greatest number of users.

Disadvantages

- On large monitors, the text line length can get out of hand when the text fills the width of the browser. Long lines of text are particularly uncomfortable to read on a screen, so allowing the text to wrap the full width of the window or frame risks poor reading conditions for some users.

- Elements float around on large monitors, making for a less coherent design that may be more difficult to use. Likewise, in very small monitors, elements get cramped together.
- The results of flexible design are unpredictable, and users will have varying experiences of your page.

Creating flexible pages

As noted above, simple HTML files are flexible by default, so you don't need to do anything special to ensure flexibility. However, you can introduce structure to a flexible document by using tables and frames.

Tables are often used to create columns of text and to divide the web page up into logical sections. By using all relative (percentage) measurements for tables and cells, the table resizes with the browser window; however, the columns and elements remain proportional to one another. For instance, two columns with widths of 25% and 75% always retain those proportions, regardless of the monitor on which they are displayed. Sizing tables is discussed in Chapter 10, *Tables*.

Frames can also be used to add structure to a flexible design. They, too, can be specified with percentage values or to automatically fill any remaining space in the window. The contents within each frame will flow to fill the frame. are discussed in Chapter 11, *Frames*.

Fixed Design

Those who require more control over the layout of a page may opt to design a web page with a fixed width that will stay the same for all users, regardless of their monitor size or how the window is resized. This approach to web design is based on design principles learned in print, such as maintaining a constant grid, the relationship of elements on the page, and comfortable line lengths.

Advantages

- The web page will look the same regardless of the monitor size. This is often crucial for companies interested in presenting a consistent corporate image for every visitor.
- Fixed-width pages and columns provide better control over line lengths. Tables can be used to prevent line lengths from becoming too long when the page is viewed on a large monitor.

Disadvantages

- If the available browser window is smaller than the grid for the page, parts of the page will not be visible and may require horizontal scrolling to be viewed. Horizontal scrolling is nearly universally considered to be a hindrance to ease of use, so it should generally be avoided. One solution is to choose a page size that will serve the most people, as discussed later in this section.

- It is still difficult to control type size in browsers (see Chapter 3 for more information), so elements may still shift unpredictably as a result of larger or smaller type than was used during the design process.

- Trying to absolutely control the display of a web page is bucking the medium. The Web is not like print; it has its own peculiarities and strengths. Advocates of the flexible design strategy will tell you that fixed web page designs are out of place on the Web.

Creating fixed pages

Fixed web page designs are created by putting all the contents of the page in a structural table with absolute measurements specified in pixels. Other tricks, such as sized transparent graphics or Netscape's proprietary <spacer> tag, may also be used to maintain consistent element placement or to hold specific amounts of white space on the page. The positioning elements in Cascading Style Sheets also provide ways to set specific dimensions and placement of web page elements; however, as of this writing they are not well supported by most browsers.

Some visual HTML authoring tools make it easy to create fixed-width designs. Most notably, GoLive Cyberstudio *(www.golive.com)* actually lays out your page on a grid as though it were a page-layout program, then automatically generates the corresponding (and often complicated) table. Macromedia's Dreamweaver achieves fixed page layout via the absolute positioning functions of CSS.

Pop-up windows

Some web sites take advantage of the ultimate in fixed web page design by automatically popping up a new window sized precisely for displaying the contents of the page. The advantage is that all viewers, regardless of their monitor size, will be certain to see the page in a browser window with the proper dimensions. It gives the designer even more control over the presentation of the page.

This trick is achieved using JavaScript to launch a window with specific pixel dimensions, so the obvious disadvantage is that it will not work for users without JavaScript-enabled browsers. Furthermore, many users have a strong adverse reaction to having new windows spontaneously opened for them. It takes control of the presentation—and the entire desktop—away from the end user, which is unacceptable to many web designers. Furthermore, because users have different font settings, text will wrap or be cut off in unpredictable ways for some users. See Chapter 22, *Introduction to JavaScript*, for a window-opening code example.

Combination Pages

Of course, web pages need not be all-fixed or all-flexible. It is certainly possible to create pages that are a combination of the two.

One common technique is to create a fixed page layout using a table, but then to center the table on the page so it is more balanced when displayed on large monitors (avoiding the blank right screen effect). The drawback to this technique is that the table can no longer be precisely placed over a background image. Many sites use a band of color in the background image to reinforce the columns in a fixed page design, but unfortunately, the background image remains in the same place even when the table is allowed to reposition itself on the screen.

Another approach is to use a table or frameset that consists of a combination of absolute and relative sized columns (or frames) measurements. In this way, when the window is resized, one column or frame remains the same width while the rest resizes and reflows to fill the new available space. These techniques are outlined in Chapter 10 and Chapter 11.

Choosing a Page Size

Obviously, if you decide to design a fixed web page you need to make a decision about which screen size you want it to fit. Design common sense dictates that the page should be accessible (and display properly) to the greatest number of people. The idea is to find the most common monitor resolution and design pages that safely fill its live space.

640×480 versus 800×600

Although finding the most common monitor resolution sounds fairly simple, there is currently some controversy over which resolution is the most common. Over the last few years, the most commonly sized PC monitor has increased from 14" to 17". Some surveys show that the majority of users do have 17" monitors, which leads some designers to strongly believe that it is perfectly "safe" to design web pages that fill the 800×600 resolution live space.

Other designers disagree, maintaining that you should take into consideration the millions of 640×480 monitors still in use (particularly by schools, households, or other institutions without the budget to upgrade). Despite the fact that most computers are shipped with 17" monitors, they still display 640×480 pixels by default upon installation, and many users do not know that they can increase the resolution.

The conventional wisdom

As of this writing, the majority of web designers advise that it is still safest to design for 640×480 to prevent users from having to scroll horizontally to view a wider design. Horizontal scrolling is detrimental to the ease of use of a page, so designers draw the line conservatively to avoid it. According to the live space charts above, that means making graphics and tables no wider than 600 pixels. This has the added benefit of keeping text lines at comfortable lengths for reading on the screen.

A growing number of designers declare 800×600 to be the "standard"; however, they are still the minority. Very few design specifically for resolutions higher than that. A few continue to design for display sizes smaller than 640×480.

Of course, your design decision should be guided by the audience for which you are designing. For instance, if you are providing a site of resources for graphic designers, you might reasonably expect that they will have 800×600 resolution monitors and higher and design your pages accordingly. If you are designing a site especially for WebTV or some other display device, you should follow the appropriate guidelines for those devices.

And as always, test your designs in as many monitor configurations as you can get your hands on to see how your page holds up under diverse conditions.

Designing "Above the Fold"

Newspaper editors have always designed the front page with the most important elements "above the fold," that is, visible when the paper is folded and sitting in the rack.

Likewise, the first screenful of a web site's homepage is the most important real estate of the whole site, regardless of whether the page is fixed or flexible. It is here that the user makes the decision to continue exploring the site or to hit the "Back" button and move along. Web designers have adopted the term "above the fold" to apply to the contents that fit in that important first screen. Curiously, my personal experience shows that users tend not to scroll beyond the first page, even when the vertical scrollbar is visible. That places the burden of enticing them to stay on the first screen.

As discussed throughout this chapter, a "screenful" can be quite different depending on the resolution of the monitor. To play it absolutely safe, consider the space available for the lowest common denominator 640×480 monitor—approximately 600×300 pixels. That's not a lot of space!

Some elements you should consider placing above the fold include:

- The name of the site.
- Your primary marketing message.
- Some indication of what the site is about. For instance, if it is a shopping site, you might place the credit card logos or shopping cart in the top corner to instantly communicate that "shopping happens here."
- Navigation to other parts of the site. If the entire navigation device will not fit (such as a list of links down the left edge of the page), at least get it started in the first screenful; hopefully users will scroll to see the remainder. If it is out of sight completely, it is that much more likely to be missed.
- Any other information that is crucial for visitors to the site, such as a toll-free number or a special promotion.

Accessibility

Responsible web design includes making pages accessible even to users with disabilities, such as hearing or sight impairments. The World Wide Web Consortium (W3C) has launched its Web Accessibility Initiative (WAI), which aims to make the Web more universally accessible. The WAI develops technologies, HTML authoring guidelines and tools, and also promotes education and research. The success of the initiative, however, relies on the participation of web developers to build sites according to the proposed guidelines.

Sight-impaired users may simply use a device that magnifies the screen for easier reading, in which case there are no special design requirements. Many vision-impaired users use a text browser (such as Lynx) in conjunction with software that reads the contents of the screen aloud. Some use devices that translate the text into Braille. Either way, there is a greater reliance on the structure and the text within the document. Content in graphics may be completely lost.

Designing Accessible Pages

The following list presents a few simple measures you can take to make your pages more accessible.

- Provide alternative text for all images (via the `<img>` tag's `alt` attribute). Make the alternative text rich and meaningful. Adding `alt` text should be standard procedure for all web page creation; in fact, in the new HTML 4.0 specification, the `alt` attribute is now a *required* part of the `<img>` tag. (See Chapter 9, *Adding Images and Other Page Elements*, for more information.)

- Add periods at the end of `alt` text so a speech device can locate the logical end of the phrase.

- When linking a graphic, provide a caption under it that also serves as a text link.

- Always provide text link alternatives for imagemaps.

- Offer a text-only version of the whole site from the home page.

- Provide transcripts or descriptions of audio clips to make that content accessible to those with hearing impairments.

- Use caution in relying on PDF (Adobe's Portable Document Format) to deliver information. If you are using PDF files, provide an HTML alternative. You may also provide a link to Adobe's site where users can download software tools that convert PDF files to text format for delivery by nonvisual browsers (*http://access.adobe.com*).

- Provide alternative mechanisms for online forms, such as a text-based order form or a phone number for personal assistance.

- Avoid the `<blink>` tag, which is said to wreak havoc with Braille and speech displays.

- Be sure content in tables makes sense when read sequentially in the HTML source.

- Be aware that misuse of HTML structural tags for presentation purposes (such as using the `<blockquote>` tag purely to achieve indents) hinders clear communication via a speech or Braille device.

For a thorough list of guidelines for accessible HTML authoring, visit the W3C's recommendations and checklist at *http://www.w3.org/TR/WD-WAI-PAGEAUTH*.

If you would like to check how accessible your web page is, try running it through a validator, such as Bobby (*http://www.cast.org/bobby/*), that will scan your page and point out accessibility issues.

HTML 4.0 Accessibility Features

The HTML 4.0 specification incorporates a number of new attributes and tags aimed specifically at making Web documents available to a broader audience. This section lists only a broad summary of accessibility features in HTML 4.0. For a more detailed listing, see the Web Accessibility Initiative's review at *http://www. w3.org/WAI/References/HTML4-access*. Or, tackle the HTML 4.0 Specification yourself at *http://www.w3.org/TR/REC-html40/*. Accessibility features of the Spec include:

- Increased distinction between document structure and presentation. HTML 4.0 encourages the use of Cascading Style Sheets for stylistic information.

- Navigational aids such as access keys and tab index for keyboard-only access to page elements.

- A new client-side imagemap recommendation that integrates image and text links.

- Introduction of the `<abbr>` and `<acronym>` tags, which assist speech devices and other agents in the interpretation of abbreviations and acronyms.

- The ability to group table columns and rows logically and to provide captions, summaries, and long descriptions of table contents, thus making the table interpretation easier.

- The ability to group form controls and make long lists of choices easier to comprehend. Form elements are also accessible via tabbing and access keys.

- Improved mechanisms for providing alternative text. The `alt` attribute is now required in the `<img>` tag. The `longdesc` attribute has been introduced to provide a link to longer text explanations of images. The `title` attribute can be added to provide additional information to any element.

CSS2 Accessibility Features

The latest Cascading Style Sheets recommendation, CSS2, also provides mechanisms for improved interpretation by nongraphical and nonvisual devices. The following is just a summary of features. For more information, read the WAI's review at *http://www.w3.org/WAI/References/CSS2-access* or look at the CSS2 Recommendation directly at *http://www.w3.org/TR/REC-CSS2*. Improvements include:

- Mechanisms by which a user-created style sheet can override all the higher style sheets in the cascade, giving the end user ultimate control over display. The user can create a custom style sheet for displaying pages according to special needs.

- Specific support for downloadable fonts—eliminating the tendency to put text in graphics to improve the appearance of the page.

- Positioning and alignment mechanisms that further separate content from presentation. These style sheet rules aim to eliminate the abuse of HTML tags in order to achieve special presentation effects. The HTML tags can be used for the logical structuring of the document, making them more easily interpreted by nonvisual agents.

- A set of controls for the audio rendering of web-delivered information.

- Improved navigation devices such as the ability to add numbered markers throughout a document for orientation purposes.

Where to Learn More

The following resources will help you get started designing accessible pages:

The Web Accessibility Initiative (W3C)
http://www.w3.org/WAI/

> This is the official site of the WAI. It is a good starting point for exploration as it contains a number of excellent links to accessibility-related resources.

Webable! (from the Yuri Rubinsky Insight Foundation)
http://www.yuri.org/webable/

> This is an excellent resource of articles and HTML authoring guidelines. It is the web-specific arm of the Yuri Rubinsky Insight Foundation, which aims to increase access to technology for people with disabilities.

Alternative Displays

The Web isn't just for personal computers anymore! Web browsers are increasingly making their way into our living rooms, briefcases, and cars, in the form of WebTV, handheld PDA devices, and even cellular phones. These extra-small displays introduce new design concerns.

WebTV

WebTV, a device that turns an ordinary television and phone line into a web browser, hit the market in 1996 and is experiencing a slow but steady growth in market share. As of this writing, it is barely a blip on the radar screen of overall browser usage, but because numbers are increasing some developers are taking its special requirements into consideration. Some sites are being developed specifically for WebTV.

WebTV uses a television rather than a monitor as a display device. The live space in the WebTV browser is a scant 544×378 pixels. The browser permits vertical paging down, but not horizontal scrolling, so wider graphics will be partially obscured and inaccessible. Principles for designing legible television graphics apply, such as the use of light text on dark backgrounds rather than vice versa and the avoidance of any elements less than 2 pixels in width.

WebTV publishes a site with guidelines for web developers called Primetime. For more detailed information on the special requirements of WebTV, visit *http://www.webtv.net/primetime/*.

Hand-Held Devices

The increased popularity and usefulness of the Web combined with the growing reliance on hand-held communications devices such as palm-top computers,

PDAs, and cellular telephones has resulted in Web browsers squeezing into the coziest of spaces.

Many of these devices use *thin client* browsers for web content display. A thin client is one that runs with minimal processing requirements on the client side, leaving the bulk of the work to be done by the server.

For instance, HitchHiker is a web browser utility designed to run in the approximately 2-inch square monochrome display of a cellphone. The ProxiWeb browser is another thin client that brings web access to the popular PalmPilot PDA (as well as to the IBM WorkPad and the new Palm III). It works by use of a proxy server that processes web pages for delivery to the handheld device. ProxiWeb even converts graphics to tiny monochrome bitmaps, so some of the original character of the page is maintained (most useful for headlines in graphics). To learn more about ProxiWeb, visit *http://www.proxinet.com/*.

Not many sites are designed specifically for hand-held devices, but as their popularity expands, it will be a more important audience to consider. For the most part, guidelines for making sites accessible to text browsers such as Lynx, including the tips for accessibility listed above, will also apply to making information usable in the limited display area of handheld devices.

CHAPTER 3

Web Design Principles
for Print Designers

If you are accustomed to designing for print, the Web introduces a number of new concepts and new ways of doing things. Part of what makes web design unique is that the pages are displayed on a computer monitor, not paper, requiring familiarity with new color models. In addition, you need to work within the unique environment of the web browser. The HTML markup language brings its own limitations to the mix.

This chapter discusses some basic web design concepts, which may be new for print designers or for anyone who is just getting started in web design. It provides necessary background information about the web environment, including how the browsers deal with color, graphics, and typography, so that you can make design decisions that are appropriate to the medium.

Color on the Web

The Web requires designers to think about color in new ways. In part, it means understanding color in a more technical manner—the appearance of a page can benefit greatly if a designer knows what's going on "under the hood." The peculiarities of working with color in web design are functions of the following simple principles:

*   **Monitors.** Web pages are displayed on computer monitors, therefore the basic rules of how computers and monitors handle color apply to web pages as well.

*   **Browsers.** Because browsers have built-in resources for rendering color when running on systems with limited color display capacity, they can alter the appearance of the colors in your pages.

*   **HTML.** Colors on a web page that are not part of a graphic (for example, background and text colors) need to be properly identified in the HTML tags

of the document. Specifying color in HTML is covered in Chapter 5, *HTML Overview*.

Color on Computer Monitors

Color on monitors is made of light, so traditional systems for specifying color for print (CMYK, Pantone swatches, etc.) do not apply.

RGB color

Computer monitors display colors by combining red, green, and blue light. This color system is known as RGB color.

RGB color is a 24-bit system, with eight bits of data devoted to each of three color channels. Eight bits of data can describe 256 colors. With 256 possible colors in each of the three channels, the total possible number of colors is calculated by multiplying 256×256×256 for a total of 16,777,216. That's more than enough colors to provide stunning representations of artwork and photography.

The problem is that only a small percentage of computers in the world are equipped to display 24-bit color. Many, many more support only 8-bit color; these systems can display only 256 colors at any one time. The good news is that, by using a *color palette*, 8-bit computers can change which 256 colors to display at any one time.

Color Issues on 16-Bit Displays

A phenomenon occurs on 16-bit displays that may cause the colors in your web pages to shift and dither. This includes colors that are "web-safe" on 8-bit displays.

The effect is most noticeable for pages with graphics that are intended to blend seamlessly with a tiled background graphic or specified background color. Despite the fact that the foreground and background elements may have numerically identical RGB values, on 16-bit displays, colors shift and dither in a way that causes the "seams" to be slightly visible. The same page will display perfectly well and without seams on 8-bit and 24-bit monitors.

Which elements shift and which get dithered seems to depend on the browser and operating system combination, so it's difficult to anticipate. If the mismatched colors concern you, making the edges of your graphics transparent instead of a matching color may help eliminate the dithered rectangles on 16-bit displays.

The effect is probably due to the way 24-bit colors are approximated by 16-bit displays using only 65,536 available colors. We welcome more information on why this phenomenon occurs and whether anything can be done to compensate for it. Send submissions to the contact information listed in the *Preface* of this book.

For system-level operations, computers use a specific set of 256 colors called the *system palette*. Macs and PCs use a slightly different set of 256 colors in their system palettes. But specific applications may specify a different palette; for instance, browsers use their own palette, which is substantially different than the Windows system palette (although it's quite similar to the Mac system palette.)

Although all colors on computer monitors are made up of combinations of red, green, and blue light, there are actually a number of numerical systems for identifying colors, including RGB (red, green, and blue values), Lab (lightness, a channel and b channel), and HSB (hue, saturation, brightness).

For purposes of web design, colors are referred to by their numerical RGB values, on a scale from 0 to 255. For instance, the RGB values for a particular dark orange color are R:198, G:83, B:52.

Gamma

Gamma refers to the overall brightness of a computer monitor's display. In more technical terms, it is a numerical adjustment for the nonlinear relationship of voltage to light intensity—but feel free to think of it as brightness. The default gamma setting varies from platform to platform. Images created on a Macintosh will generally look a lot darker when viewed on a PC or Unix terminal. Images created on a PC will generally look washed out when seen on a Mac. The higher the gamma value, the darker the display. Table 3-1 shows the standard gamma settings for the major platforms.

Table 3-1: Common Default Gamma Settings

Platform	Gamma
Macintosh	1.8
PC	2.5
Unix	2.3-2.5

One strategy for designing graphics that look acceptable on all platforms is to calibrate your own monitor to a gamma setting of 2.2, a value that is between Macintosh's 1.8 and the PC's 2.5. Bear in mind that your images will look a bit lighter on most Macs and a bit darker on most PCs and Unix terminals than they appear on your screen, but the jump won't be as drastic as going from one platform to another.

Color in Browsers (The Web Palette)

An interesting problem arises when colors from the full 24-bit color space need to be displayed on an 8-bit display. Rather than relying on the computer's system palette, browsers reduce and remap colors to their own built-in palette. This is a great benefit to web designers because it guarantees that images will look more or less the same on all 8-bit systems. If images were mapped to the various system palettes, they would look quite different on different platforms. (Note that if the browser is running on a 24-bit display, the palette does not come into effect and all colors will be displayed accurately.)

This *Web Palette* consists of the 216 colors shared by the Macintosh and PC system palettes; therefore colors chosen from the Web Palette will render accurately on Mac or PC displays. The Web Palette was optimized for Macs and PCs; Unix machines use a different color model for their system palette, therefore "web-safe" colors may shift or dither when viewed on Unix terminals.

The Web Palette is also known as the Netscape Palette, Netscape 216, Browser-Safe Palette, Web-Safe Palette, Non-dithering Palette, and the 6×6×6 cube. The Web Palette is displayed on the web pages for this book at *http://www.oreilly.com/ catalog/wdnut/*.

The Web Palette in numbers

An important way to look at the Web Palette is by its numerical values. The Web Palette recognizes six shades of red, six shades of green, and six shades of blue, resulting in 216 possible color values (6×6×6 = 216). This is sometimes referred to as the 6×6×6 color cube. Figure 3-1 shows the cubic nature of this palette.

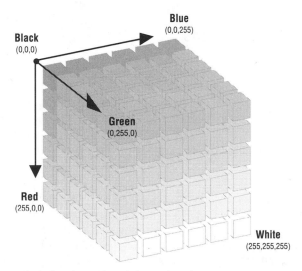

Figure 3-1: The 6×6×6 Color Cube of the Web Palette

There are three systems used for defining RGB values. Which one you use depends on the requirements of your software.

Decimal
Most image editing software displays the RGB value of a color in decimal values, ranging from 0 to 255. A color's decimal RGB value might be 51-51-255, meaning the red value is 51, the green value is 51, and the blue value is 255. Note that these numbers specify one of 256 possible values for each channel; they are not percentage values. Web-safe colors are multiples of 51.

Hexadecimal
HTML and many programming languages require that RGB numbers be specified in the hexadecimal numbering system. Hexadecimal is a base-16 system

that requires only six characters to describe an RGB color. The hexadecimal equivalent of 51-51-255 is 3333FF.

Percentage

The Apple Color Picker specifies colors in percentages, not absolute RGB decimal values. For Macintosh programs that rely on the Apple Color Picker (such as Claris HomePage and Adobe PageMill), you'll need to be able to convert percentage values to true decimal values. The percentage value equivalent of 51-51-255 is 20%-20%-100%.

Table 3-2 shows the decimal, hexadecimal, and percentage values for each of the six component values in the Web Palette.

Table 3-2: Numerical Values for Web Palette Colors

Decimal	Hexadecimal	Percentage
0 (darkest)	00	0%
51	33	20%
102	66	40%
153	99	60%
204	CC	80%
255 (lightest)	FF	100%

Reducing to the Web Palette

Colors on a web page are forced to adapt to the browser's Web Palette. The only way to ensure that all users will see your colors as you intend them is to use web-safe colors when you design the page. (See "Designing with the Web Palette" in this chapter.)

Colors in Images

Browsers attempt to approximate the colors in an image by dithering, mixing pixels of similar colors available in the palette. For photographic images, the effects of dithering are usually not detrimental (and in some cases may be beneficial). However, in areas of flat color (such as in a logo or line-art illustration), the random dot pattern caused by dithering may be undesirable. Chapter 17, *Designing Graphics with the Web Palette*, discusses techniques and tools for applying the palette to graphics during the design and production process.

Colors in the HTML document

Colors specified in the HTML document, such as background and text colors, will usually be replaced by the nearest available Web Palette color (Internet Explorer may dither background colors). This effect is called *color shifting* and it can result in a large discrepancy between how a color (as defined by its RGB values) is rendered on a 24-bit display versus an 8-bit display.

Designing with the Web Palette

While the Web Palette can lead to unpredictable and undesirable effects such as dithering or color shifting on 8-bit monitors, you can also use it to your advantage. Because you know *exactly* which colors will render accurately on Macs and PCs, you can use these colors exclusively when designing your graphics and HTML pages and beat the browser to the task. It requires a little extra effort, but the advantage is that you'll be able to predict what the pages will look like for all users. Using web-safe colors in graphics production is discussed in Chapter 17.

If you choose to add color to the background and text on your web pages, chances are you'll need to do some experimenting with color to get the combinations just right. There are a number of tools and options for selecting web-safe colors and incorporating them into your designs.

Web authoring tools

Many WYSIWYG (What You See Is What You Get) web authoring tools (including Macromedia's Dreamweaver, GoLive Cyberstudio, and Claris HomePage 3.0), allow you to choose from swatches of web-safe colors when applying color to text and backgrounds. You can see the results of your choices immediately in the application window or when previewed in a browser. These tools will automatically generate all the necessary HTML code for you.

Photoshop swatches

If you do not have a web-authoring application, you can experiment with colors in a Photoshop file by loading the web-safe colors into the Swatches palette (see Chapter 17 for instructions on creating a Web Palette CLUT file). Using the eyedropper tool, you can then be sure that the colors you select for backgrounds and text are web-safe. You need to note the RGB values for your final color selections, then convert them to their hexadecimal equivalents for insertion into the HTML color attribute tags in your document.

Online design utilities

There are a number of utilities online that allow you to choose color combinations from the Web Palette and see a sample page with your chosen colors immediately.

ColorMaker (by Sam Choukri)
http://www.bagism.com/colormaker/

This page allows you to set page elements to web-safe colors and automatically displays your color choices in a separate window. It also generates the HTML code for the colors, which you can copy into your document. This tool requires a Java-enabled browser and prefers Netscape Navigator 4.0 or Internet Explorer 4.0.

NED's DynaColor!
http://www.nedesign.com/COLOR/

This is another tool for experimenting with background and text color combinations. You enter your RGB values in either decimal or hex format, and DynaColor! generates a sample page. You can choose to have your color selections shifted to the nearest web-safe color.

System Colors in Web Pages

If an 8-bit display allows 256 colors, and there are 216 colors in the browser's Web Palette, you may be wondering what happens to the other 40 colors. Normally, the browser allows colors from the user's system palette to fill in the extra 40 color slots. These extra colors can go a long way in smoothing out colors that can't be recreated accurately using Web Palette colors alone. This is particularly true for grayscale images, which are difficult to reproduce using only the four web-safe gray tones in the Web Palette.

There is a bug in Netscape 4.0 on the Macintosh that prevents system colors from seeping in to help render images on web pages. This version of the Netscape browser maps everything strictly to the Web Palette, resulting in inferior image quality. This is most noticeable in grayscale images, which shift to the Web Palette's yellow-green and lavender shades in an attempt to display the image accurately. This bug only affects Macintosh users with 8-bit displays using Netscape 4.0 (probably a very small percentage of your audience). For more information on this issue, see *http://www.artware.de/nc4petition/*.

Graphics on the Web

Print designers will need to adapt their graphics production skills for the Web to take into account the peculiarities of graphics that are distributed over a network and displayed on computer monitors.

Graphic File Formats

As of this writing, nearly all of the graphics that you see on the Web are in one of two formats: GIF and JPEG. A third worthy contender, the PNG file, is struggling for browser support and attention. What follows is a very brief introduction to the "big three" of online graphic formats. More detailed descriptions are provided in the chapters dedicated to each format.

The ubiquitous GIF

The GIF (Graphic Interchange Format) file format is the traditional darling of the Web. It was the first file format to be supported by web browsers and it continues to be the format for the vast majority of graphics on the Web today.

GIFs are indexed color files with a maximum 8-bit palette capacity, which means that a GIF can contain a maximum of 256 pixel colors. Because they compress color information by rows of pixels, GIF files are most appropriate for graphics that contain areas of flat color.

See Chapter 14, *GIF Format,* for complete information on the GIF file format.

The handy JPEG

The second most popular graphics format on the Web today is the JPEG (Joint Photographic Experts Group) format. JPEGs contain 24-bit color information that's millions of colors, as opposed to GIF's 256. They use what is called a "lossy" compression scheme, which means that some image information is thrown out

---

the compression process, but in most cases, the degradation of the image is not detrimental or even noticeable.

Photographic images, or any image with subtle gradations of color, are best saved as JPEG files because they offer better image quality packed into a smaller file. JPEGs, however, are not a good solution for flat, graphical images because they tend to mottle colors and the resulting file will generally be a lot larger than the same image saved as a GIF.

See Chapter 15, *JPEG Format,* for complete information on the JPEG file format.

The amazing PNG

There is a third graphic format vying for substantial usage on the Web—PNG (Portable Network Graphic), which, despite some very attractive features has been more or less lurking in the shadows since 1994. It is only recently that browsers have begun supporting PNGs as inline graphics, but PNG is poised to become a very popular web graphic format. For this reason, it is optimistically included here in the "big three."

PNGs can support 8-bit indexed color, 16-bit grayscale, or 24-bit true color images with a "lossless" compression scheme, which means higher image quality, and in some cases, file sizes even smaller than their GIF counterparts. Not only that, PNG files have some nifty features such as built-in gamma control and variable transparency levels (which means now you can have a background pattern show through a soft drop-shadow).

See Chapter 16, *PNG Format,* for complete information on the PNG file format.

Measuring Resolution

Because web graphics exist solely on the screen, it is technically correct to measure their resolution in pixels per inch (ppi). Another resolution measurement, dpi (dots per inch), refers to the resolution of a printed image, dependent on the resolution of the printing device.

In practice, the terms dpi and ppi are used interchangeably. It is generally accepted practice to refer to web graphic resolution in terms of dpi.

Image Resolution

Simply put, all graphics on the Web need to be low-resolution—72ppi (*pixels per inch*). Since web graphics are always displayed on low-resolution computer screens, higher resolution files are unnecessary.

Working at such a low resolution can be quite an adjustment for a designer accustomed to handling the 300ppi images appropriate for print. Most notably, the image quality is lower because there is not as much image information in a given space. This tends to make the image look more grainy or pixelated, and unfortunately, that's just the nature of images on the Web.

Image size

When a graphic is displayed on a web page, the pixels in the image map one-to-one with the display resolution of the monitor. Although 72ppi is the standard, bear in mind that monitor resolutions vary and can run much higher than 72ppi, particularly on higher-end work stations.

A graphic that appears to be about one inch square on your 72ppi monitor may actually appear to be quite a bit smaller on a monitor with a resolution of closer to 100. (See Figure 3-2.)

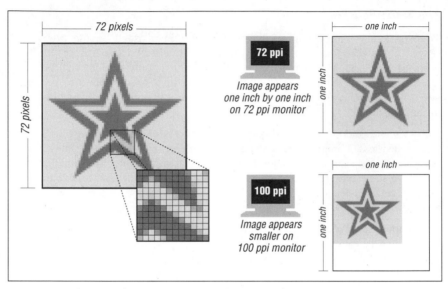

Figure 3-2: The size of an image is dependent on monitor resolution

Good-bye inches, hello pixels

Because the actual dimensions of a graphic are dependent on the resolution of the monitor, the whole notion of "inches" becomes irrelevant in the web environment. The only meaningful unit of measurement is the pixel.

It is a good practice to create your images at 72ppi (it puts you in the ballpark for screen presentation), but to pay attention only to the overall pixel dimensions. You can disregard inches entirely in the web graphics production process. After a while, thinking in pixels comes quite naturally. What's important is the size of the graphic relevant to other graphics on that page and to the overall size of the browser window.

For instance, I know that many users still have 14" monitors with resolutions of 640×480 pixels. To guarantee that my banner graphic will fit in the screen in its entirety, I would make it no more than 600 pixels wide (taking into account some pixels will be used on the left and right for the window and the scrollbar). The size of the remaining buttons and images on my page will be measured in pixels relative to my 600-pixel-wide banner. For more information on designing for standard monitor resolutions, see Chapter 2, *Designing for a Variety of Displays*.

Be Aware of Gamma

The brightness of a monitor is a function of its gamma setting. The standard gamma setting varies from platform to platform, so when you are creating graphics for web pages, bear in mind that some users may be seeing your images much lighter or darker than they appear to you. This can seriously affect the colors you've chosen—the logo you've created in a lovely forest green on your Mac may look pitch black when you view it on a PC.

In general, images created on a Macintosh will look darker when viewed on a PC or Unix terminal. Images created on a PC will generally look washed out when seen on a Mac. This phenomenon is another thing to keep in the back of your mind when you are designing and producing web graphics.

Adjusting gamma with Adobe Photoshop

For the Mac. Adobe Photoshop comes with a Gamma control panel that affects the gamma setting for the whole monitor. To use it:

1. Choose Apple → Control Panels → Gamma to open the Gamma control panel. (If it is not there, drag it from the Photoshop → Goodies → Calibration folder into the System Folder → Control Panels folder.).

2. Turn the panel on using the switch in the lower-left corner.

3. Select 2.2 from the Target Gamma choices. You should see the effect of the gamma change immediately. Close the Gamma control panel.

For Windows. For Windows, Photoshop offers gamma control only within the Photoshop window (it does not affect the monitor globally, as on the Macintosh). To use it:

1. Choose File → Color Settings → Monitor Setup

2. Type a gamma value of 2.2 in the Monitor Setup dialog box. Click OK.

3. You can preview the effects of the gamma setting by clicking Preview in the Calibrate dialog box.

Previewing and adjusting gamma with Adobe ImageReady

ImageReady (a web graphics optimization tool from Adobe) has a function that allows you to preview how your graphic will appear with the gamma setting of an alternate operating system. It also allows you to adjust the gamma value (brightness) of the image to make the image look acceptable for both platforms.

To preview the image, choose View → Windows Gamma/Mac Gamma. The image brightness will adjust to simulate the gamma setting of the specified platform. Choosing it again restores the image to its previous gamma value.

To automatically adjust the gamma in ImageReady:

1. Choose Image → Adjust → Gamma.

2. Select Macintosh-to-Windows to adjust for Windows display, or select Windows-to-Macintosh to adjust for Mac display.

3. Click OK.

You can also apply a manual gamma adjustment by moving the Gamma slider or entering a value in the text box between 0.1 and 9.99.

Images created with Photoshop 4.0 need to have their gamma adjusted for display in Windows because Photoshop 4.0 uses the Mac OS gamma value as its default. Photoshop 5.0, however, uses the Windows gamma value as its default (even when displayed in Mac OS), so graphics created in version 5.0 require no adjustment for proper display in Windows.

Be Aware of File Size

It goes without saying that graphics have made the Web what it is today; however, as a web designer, you should know that many users have a love/hate relationship with graphics on the Web. Remember that graphics increase the time it takes a web page to move across the network; large graphics mean substantial download times, which can try the patience of the reader, particularly one dialing in on a standard modem connection.

Here is the single most important guideline a web designer can follow: *Keep the file size of your graphics as small as possible!* The nature of publishing over a network creates a new responsibility for designers to be sensitive to the issue of download times.

Detailed strategies for minimizing graphic file size for each file format appear in Chapters 14 through 16 in Part III of this book.

Getting correct file sizes on a Macintosh

It is important for web designers to pay attention to file size, measured in bytes or kilobytes (K). On Windows computers, the indication of file size that appears in the directory listing is an accurate measure of the file's actual size. The number the Macintosh Finder shows, however, is almost always inaccurate. This is because of how the Finder displays file sizes and how Macs encode files.

Partition sizes. For one thing, the file size listings in the Finder are measured in even partition units or "blocks," and the larger your hard drive the larger the block. For instance, on a four-gigabyte hard drive, the smallest block size is 65K, so even if a file contains only 1K of information, it will display as 65K in the Finder.

You can use the Finder's Get Info command to get an accurate reading of how many bytes are actually in the file. To open the Get Info box, highlight the file name in the Finder, then select File → Get Info, or use the Command-I keyboard shortcut. The actual number of bytes appears in parentheses next to Size.

This is not the case for all Macintoshes, however. Macs with the newer HFS Plus hard-disk formatting allow variable block sizes, which allow the Finder to indicate file sizes more accurately. Macs shipping with MacOS 8.1 or later may have HFS Plus-formatted drives.

The resource fork. Macintosh files may contain extra Mac-specific code called the *resource fork,* which is used for storing icons, previews, and file type information. Only the actual data (the *data fork*) in the file is readable by other platforms, so the resource fork should be stripped out when the file is uploaded to a server. The size of the data fork is the only number you should consider, as it is the actual number of bytes that will be downloaded by a browser.

Photoshop files. Photoshop usually saves files with an icon and thumbnail views of the image stored in the resource fork. You can turn these off (saving just the data fork) by unchecking the Icon and Thumbnail checkboxes under Image Previews in the Preferences → File Saving dialog box. When you use the GIF89a Export filter to create GIFs, only the data fork is saved, and its file size will be accurate in the Get Info window.

Using Snitch. Unfortunately, there is no way, using the Mac Get Info box alone, to tell how much of the file size is the resource fork and how much is the data fork. Snitch 2.5 is a shareware utility that works like a beefed-up Get Info window. When you select Dates & Sizes in the pop-up menu, Snitch shows you the actual byte sizes of the data and resource forks, as shown in Figure 3-3.

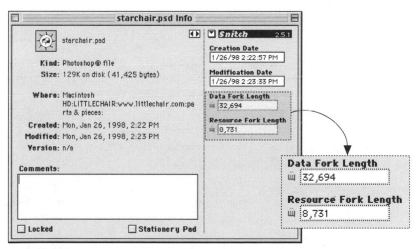

Figure 3-3: Snitch shows the data fork length and resource fork length of Macintosh files

Snitch, written by Mitch Jones, is available for download at *http://www.niftyneato. com* (there is a $20 registration fee if you choose to continue using it). In addition to Dates & Sizes it contains many useful tools for viewing and editing file type information.

Web Graphics Production Tips

The following is a collection of tips for maintaining quality in web graphics.

Work in RGB mode

When you are creating graphics for the Web, it is important to work in the RGB color mode. Because graphics are converted to indexed color mode when saved in the GIF format, you'll often need to make corrections to indexed color images.

If you only need to crop an image or make an adjustment that doesn't require the addition of new colors (such as changing a pixel color to another color in the existing palette), you can work directly in indexed color mode. However, if your changes include resizing, or the addition of new or anti-aliased colors, it is important to convert indexed color images back to RGB before making any changes to the image.

When an image is in indexed color mode, the colors are restricted to those in its defined Color Table and no new colors can be added. This prevents the color blends and adjustments that occur when image elements are transformed (resized, rotated, etc.) or when adding anti-aliased text. When the image is in indexed color mode, any text you add will automatically have aliased (stair-stepped) edges.

The typical steps that should be taken when editing an image are:

1. Open the GIF in the image editing tool.
2. Change it to RGB color mode (in Photoshop, select Image → Mode → RGB Color).
3. Edit the image as necessary.
4. Change it back to indexed color mode, setting the desired palette and bit-depth.
5. Save or export to GIF format.

Resizing tips

The following tips pertain to resizing web graphics:

Convert to RGB Before Resizing
As mentioned earlier, in order to resize an image, Photoshop (or any bitmap image editing tool) needs to create new transitions between areas of color in the image. Indexed color images (such as GIFs) are limited to the colors in the image's color table, which does not give Photoshop enough colors to create convincing "in-between" colors for these transitions.

Don't Resize Larger
As a general rule, it is a bad idea to increase the dimensions of a low-resolution image (such as 72ppi images typically used on the Web). Image editing tools cannot add image information to the file—they can only stretch out what's already there. This results in a pixelated and blotchy image.

Resize Smaller in Increments

Images can be made slightly smaller without much degradation in image quality; however, drastic resizing (making a snap-shot sized image postage-stamp size) will usually result in an unacceptably blurry image. When acquiring an image (whether by scanning or from CD-ROM), it is best to choose an image that is slightly larger than final size. That way, you don't need to make it larger, and you won't have to scale it down too much. If you must make a very large image very small, try doing it in a number of steps, fixing quality at each stage.

Be sure to keep a clean copy of the original image in case you make something too small. Starting over is better than enlarging the image or resizing repeatedly.

Use anti-aliased text

In general, to create professional-looking graphics for the Web you should use anti-aliased text. *Anti-aliasing* is the slight blur used on curved edges to make smoother transitions between colors. Aliased edges, by contrast, are blocky and stair-stepped. Figure 3-4 shows the effect of anti-aliasing (left) and aliasing (right.)

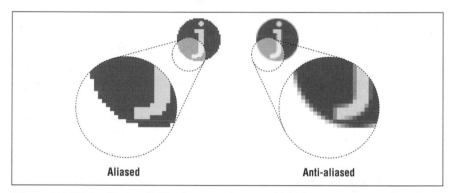

| Aliased | Anti-aliased |

Figure 3-4: With aliasing (left) edges are sharp and blocky; anti-aliasing (right) provides smooth transitions between edges

The exception to this guideline is very small text (10 points or smaller) for which anti-aliased edges blur the characters to the point of illegibility. Text at small sizes may fare much better when it is aliased.

The trade-off for better-looking graphics is file size—anti-aliasing adds to the number of colors in the image and may result in a slightly larger file size. In this case, the improved quality is usually worth a couple of extra bytes.

Typography on the Web

HTML was created with the intent of putting the ultimate control of presentation in the hands of the end-user. This principle makes its most resounding impact when it comes to typography. The stark fact of web design as we know it today is that there is no way of knowing exactly how your text is going to look. Take a look at your browser's preferences and you will find that you (and every other surfer) are able to specify the fonts and sizes that you prefer for online viewing.

For anyone accustomed to designing for other media, this loss of font control is cause for major frustration. From the time they discovered the Web, designers (and their corporate clients) have been pushing for ways to control typography in order to produce attractive and predictable web sites.

Great strides have been made in this effort since the early days of the Web and HTML 1.0; however, as of this writing, the font issue is still unfolding. This section discusses possible strategies and technologies (along with their advantages and disadvantages) for designing type in web documents. It also addresses the issue of using foreign (non-western) characters on web pages.

You Have Two Fonts

About the only thing you can be sure of when you're designing web pages with basic HTML is that you have two fonts to work with: a proportional font, and a fixed-width font. The problem is that you don't know specifically which ones or at what size they will be displayed.

Proportional font

A *proportional font* (called "Variable Width Font" in Netscape Navigator) is one that allots different amounts of space to each character, based on its design. For instance, in a proportional font, a capital "W" takes up more horizontal space on the line than a lowercase "i." Times, Helvetica, and Arial are examples of proportional fonts.

Web browsers use a proportional font for the majority of text in the web page, including body text, headings, lists, blockquotes, etc. In general, proportional fonts are easier to read for large bodies of text.

Because the majority of users do not take the time to change the default font in their browser preferences, you can make a *very* broad assumption that most of the text on your page will be displayed in 10 or 12 point Times (Netscape default) or Helvetica (the default in Microsoft Internet Explorer). Remember, this is only a very general guideline.

Fixed-width font

Fixed-width fonts (also known as "constant-width" or "monospace" fonts) are designed to allot the same amount of horizontal space to all characters in the font. A capital "W" takes up no more space than a lowercase "i." Examples of fixed-width fonts are Courier and Monaco.

Web browsers will use the fixed-width font to render any type within the following HTML tags:

- `<pre>` Preformatted text
- `<tt>` Typewriter text
- `<code>` Code

- <kbd> Keyboard entry

- <samp> Sample text

- <xmp> Example text

Again, because most people do not change the default font settings in their browser preferences, you can make a reasonable guess that text marked with the above HTML tags will be displayed in some variation of Courier.

Text in Graphics

Designers quickly learned that the sure-fire way to have absolute control over font display is to set the text in a graphic. It is common to see headlines, subheads, and call-outs rendered as GIF files. Many web pages are made up exclusively of graphics that contain all the text for the page.

GIF text advantages

The advantage to using graphics instead of HTML text is fairly obvious—control!

- You can specify text font, size, leading, letter spacing, color, and alignment— all attributes that are problematic in HTML alone.

- Everyone with a graphical browser will see your page the same way.

GIF text disadvantages

As enticing as this technique may seem, it comes with many drawbacks. Keep the following disadvantages in mind when deciding whether to use graphics for your text.

- Graphics take longer to download than text. Graphics are likely to be many orders of magnitude larger than HTML text with the same content, and will result in slower downloads.

- Content is lost on nongraphical browsers. People who cannot (or have chosen not to) view graphics will see no content. Alternative text (using the alt attribute) in place of graphics helps, but is limited and not always reliable.

- Information in graphics cannot be indexed or searched. In effect, by putting text in a graphic, you are removing useful pieces of information from your document. Again, the alt attribute helps here.

Why Specifying Type is Problematic

The <font> tag's face attribute and Cascading Style Sheets give web designers an added level of control over typography by enabling the specification of fonts and sizes. Although it is a step in the right direction, using these tags by no means guarantees that your readers will see the page exactly the way you've designed it.

Specifying fonts and sizes for use on web pages is made difficult by the fact that browsers are limited to displaying fonts that are installed on the user's local hard drive. So, even though you've specified text to be displayed in the Georgia font, if users do not have Georgia installed on their machines they will see the text in whatever their default font happens to be. In addition, platforms handle type size display in different ways. Using these tags is more like *recommending* fonts and sizes than actually specifying them.

Type size

Traditionally, type size is specified in points (there are approximately 72 points per inch), but unfortunately, point sizes do not translate well between platforms. In part, this is because their operating systems drive monitors at different resolutions. Typically, Windows uses 96ppi for screen resolution and the Mac OS uses 72ppi, however, multiscan monitors allow higher resolutions.

On a Mac, a font is displayed at roughly the same size at which it would appear in print (e.g., 12pt Times on screen looks like 12pt Times on paper).

Microsoft, however, threw out that convention and chose to display point sizes larger to make it easier to read on a monitor. As a result, 12pt type on a Windows machine is closer to 16pt type in print. To get 12pt print-size type on Windows, you need to specify a point-size of 9 (but then Mac users will see that text at a nearly illegible 6.75pt type).

Selecting fonts for web pages

Each platform has its own set of standard fonts (and font file formats), making it difficult to specify any one font that will be found universally. Although there are many commercial fonts available for both Mac and PC, you can't assume that your audience will have them. The majority of users are likely to be content with the collection of fonts that are installed with their systems or packaged with software such as Internet Explorer, as shown in the following list.

Macintosh	OS 7.0	OS 8.0
	Chicago	Apple Chancery
	Courier	Charcoal
	Geneva	Chicago
	Helvetica	Courier
	Mishawaka	Geneva
	Monaco	Helvetica
	New York	Monaco
	Palatino	New York
	Symbol	Palatino
	Times	Skia
		Symbol
		Times
		Wingdings
Windows	3.1 and 95	NT 3.x
	Arial	Arial
	Courier New	Courier New
	Times New Roman	Times New Roman
	Wingdings	Wingdings
	Symbol	Symbol
	Marlett (Win95 only)	

Unix / Xfree bitmap fonts	charter	lucidatypewriter
	clean	new century schoolbook
	courier	symbol
	fixed	terminal
	helvetica	times
	lucida	utopia
	lucidabright	
Internet Explorer	**3.0 (Windows 95 and NT)**	**4.0 (Windows 95 and NT)**
	Arial Black	Arial Black
	Comic Sans MS	Comic Sans
	Impact	Impact
	Verdana	Verdana
		Webdings

Core fonts for the Web from Microsoft

The problem with reading text on web pages is that many fonts (most notably the ubiquitous Times) are difficult to read at small sizes without the aid of anti-aliasing. The serifs that aid readability in print are actually a hindrance when rendered with a limited number of black and white pixels.

Responding to the need for fonts that are easy to read on the screen, Microsoft has created a collection of TrueType fonts (for both Windows and Mac) that have been specially designed to be optimized for on-screen viewing. They are distributing them for free with the hope that they might grow to be standard and "safe" fonts to specify in web documents. The Microsoft web fonts currently include:

    Arial
    Comic Sans
    Courier New
    Georgia
    Impact
    Times New Roman
    Trebuchet MS
    Verdana
    Webdings (Windows only)

These fonts have generous character spacing, large x-heights and open, rounded features that make them better for online reading. Georgia and Verdana were designed by esteemed type designer Matthew Carter, with hinting provided by Vincent Connare (who also designed Comic Sans and Trebuchet MS).

The complete set of Core Fonts for the Web is available for free download at *http:// www.microsoft.com/typography/free.htm*.

Embedded Fonts

Both Netscape and Internet Explorer support technologies for embedding fonts in a web page, enabling your viewers to see your page exactly as you have designed it. Because the font travels with the HTML file, it is not necessary for the user to have the font installed on the client end in order for specified fonts to display. Not surprisingly, Netscape and Microsoft have lined up with competing technologies.

See Chapter 26, *Embedded Font Technology*, for a more thorough discussion of the creation and implementation of embedded fonts.

CHAPTER 4

A Beginner's Guide to the Server

Even if you focus primarily on what's commonly referred to as "front-end" web development—HTML documents and web graphics—the server and the way it is configured may impact the way you work. In most cases, there is no way to avoid making first-hand contact with the server, even if it's just to upload files.

For this reason, all web designers should have a basic level of familiarity with servers and what they do. At the very least, this will enable you to communicate more clearly with your server administrator. If you have permission for greater access to the server, it could mean taking care of certain tasks yourself without needing to wait for assistance.

This chapter provides an introduction to server terminology and functions, basic Unix commands, and file (MIME) types. It also discusses uploading files and setting permissions, which designers often need to do.

Servers 101

A *server* is any computer running software that enables it to answer requests for documents and other data. The programs that request and display the documents (such as a browser) are called *clients*. The terms "server-side" and "client-side," in regard to specific functions like imagemaps, refer to which machine is doing the processing. Client-side functions happen on the user's machine; server-side functions occur on the remote machine.

Web servers answer requests from browsers (the client program), retrieve the specified file (or execute a CGI script) and return the document or script results. Web browsers and servers communicate via the Hypertext Transfer Protocol (HTTP).

Popular Server Software

As of this writing, the majority of web servers are running on the Unix platform. This is why a lot of Unix terminology is still used in the web world. You may even need to learn a few Unix commands in the course of a job. However, the percentage of Windows NT, Windows 95, and even Macintosh servers is steadily increasing. Some server packages offer a graphical interface as an alternative to Unix command-line controls.

Some popular servers include:

NCSA Server

This is publicly available server software maintained by the National Center for Supercomputing Applications at the University of Illinois at Urbana-Champaign. It runs on the Unix platform.

Apache

A variation of NCSA, Apache has become the most popular web server due to the fact that it is a powerful server and it is available for free. It runs primarily on Unix, but is being released to run on other platforms, including Windows NT.

CERN

This server, maintained by the World Wide Web Consortium, is publicly available from *http://www.w3.org*. It is also Unix-based.

Netscape Servers

Netscape provides a variety of commercial server packages that run on Unix and NT platforms.

Internet Information Server (IIS)

This is Microsoft's server package. It is freely available, easy to install and configure, and runs on Windows NT and 95 platforms.

The majority of servers today (approximately 70%) run Apache or its predecessor, NCSA. The particular brand of server does not impact the majority of things the designer does, such as making graphics or developing basic HTML files. It will certainly influence more advanced web site building techniques such as Server Side Includes (discussed in Chapter 13, *Server Side Includes*), adding MIME types (discussed later in this chapter), and database-driven web pages. Be certain to coordinate with your server administrator if you are using your server in ways beyond simple HTML and graphic files storage.

Basic Server Functions

As a web designer, it is important that you have some level of familiarity with the following elements of the web server.

Root directory

When a browser requests a document, the server locates the document, starting with the document root directory. This is the directory that has been configured to contain all documents intended to be shared via the Web. The root directory does

---

not necessarily appear in the URL that points to the document, so it is important to know what your root directory is when uploading your files.

For example, if the root directory on littlechair.com is */users/httpd/www/* and a browser makes a request for *http://www.littlechair.com/super/cool.html*, the server actually retrieves */users/httpd/www/super/cool.html*. This, of course, is invisible to the user.

Index files

A forward slash (/) at the end of a URL indicates that the URL is pointing to a directory, not a file. By default, servers display the contents of the directory specified in the URL. Most servers are configured, however, to display a specific file, called the *index file*, instead of the directory list. The index file is generally named *index.html*, but on some servers it may be named *welcome.html* or *default.html*. This is another small variation you will need to confirm with your server administrator.

If the server is configured to look for the index file and does not find one, the directory contents may be displayed instead, leaving your files vulnerable to snooping. For this reason, it is a good idea to always name some page (usually the main page) in each directory "index.html" (or an otherwise specified name).

HTTP response header

Once the server locates the file, it sends the contents of that file back to the browser, along with some *HTTP response headers*. The headers provide the browser with information about the arriving file, including its media type (also known as "content type" or "MIME type"). Usually, the server will determine the format from the file's suffix; for example, a file with the suffix .gif is taken to be an image file.

The browser reads the header information and determines how to handle the file, either displaying it in the window or launching the appropriate helper application or plug-in. MIME types are discussed further at the end of this chapter.

CGI scripts

Instead of pointing to an HTML file, a URL may request that a CGI program be run. CGI stands for Common Gateway Interface, and it's what allows the web server to communicate with other programs (CGI scripts) that are running on the server. CGI scripts are commonly written in the Perl, C, or C++ languages.

CGI scripts can be used to perform a wide variety of functions such as searching, server-side imagemap handling, and gaming; however, their most common usage is forms processing. A typical CGI script is examined in Chapter 12, *Forms*.

Most server administrators follow the convention of keeping CGI scripts in a special directory named *cgi-bin* (short for CGI-binaries). Keeping them in one directory makes it easier to manage and secure the server. When a CGI script is requested by the browser, the server performs the function and returns the dynamic content to the browser.

Introduction to Unix

If you work with the Web long enough, chances are you'll run into the need to communicate with a Unix machine. On Macs and PCs, most functions can be performed using tools with graphical interfaces; however, at times there is no substitute for a good old-fashioned *telnet* session. Besides, a little Unix never hurt anyone.

Telnet is a "terminal emulation" protocol that allows you to log in to other computer systems on a network (such as the Internet). It also refers to any application used for communicating with the telnet protocol. A telnet program will give you a character-based terminal window on another system from which you can enter simple command-line instructions. Figure 4-1 shows a typical telnet session.

```
                              Rosetta
***** 28 *** <sierra@rosetta-stone> *** /work/nutshell/webdesign.qref *****
% ls
,ch19.11431      appg         ch18         part1
,ch23.21479      ch00         ch19         part2
,ch24.14385      ch01         ch20         part3
,fwee            ch02         ch21         part4
,fwee~           ch03         ch22         part5
./               ch04         ch23         part6
../              ch05         ch24         pdf/
DIFF             ch06         ch25         ps/
DIFF2            ch07         ch26         schedule.fm
RCS/             ch08         ch27         tbl
SETTABS*         ch09         comma/       temps/
TAGS             ch10         figs/        toc.html
appa             ch11         front/       webdesign.book
appb             ch12         fweeb        webdesignAPL.fm
appb.recover     ch13         fweeb.mif    webdesignIX.fm
appc             ch14         inc/         webdesignLOP.fm
appd             ch15         info.xml     webdesignTOC.fm
appe             ch16         intl/        xrefs
appf             ch17         mif/
***** 29 *** <sierra@rosetta-stone> *** /work/nutshell/webdesign.qref *****
% █
```

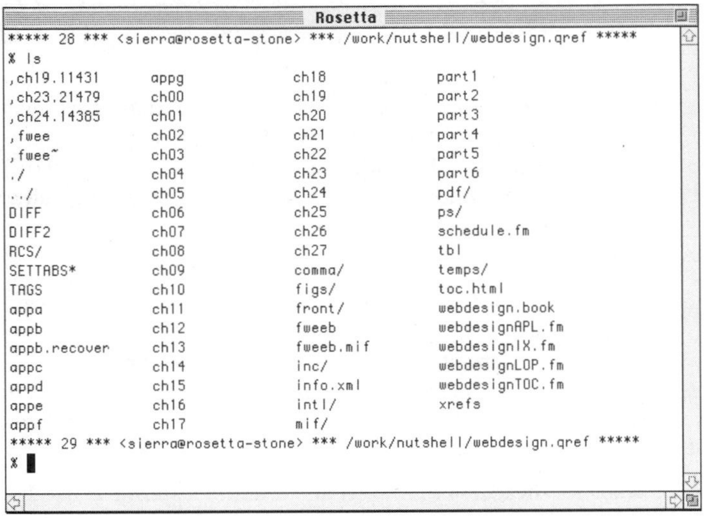

Figure 4-1: Typical telnet session

This section provides a very brief introduction to basic terminology and commands that will enable you to manipulate files and directories on a Unix machine. If you are interested in learning more, read *Learning the Unix Operating System* and *Unix in a Nutshell*, both published by O'Reilly & Associates, Inc.

Logging In

When you open a connection to a remote server with your telnet program, the first thing you see is a prompt to log in to the system. Before you can access the server, the system administrator has to set up a Unix account for you. You will be given a name and password you can enter at the `login:` and `password:` prompts respectively.

When you log in successfully, you will get a Unix system prompt, either a $ or a % (or sometimes #) depending on the flavor of Unix the server is running, which tells you that the system is "ready." At this point, you are using a program called the *shell*, which interprets the commands you type and invokes the programs you ask for. You will automatically be placed in your home directory.

To end the telnet session, simply type "logout" or "exit."

Directory Structures

Because the Web was spawned from the Unix environment, it follows many of the same conventions. For instance, writing correct URL pathnames in hyperlinks relies on an understanding of how directory structures work on the Unix platform.

Directories ("places" to store files) are organized into a hierarchical structure that fans out like an upside-down tree. The top-most directory is known as the *root* and is written as a forward slash (/). The root can contain several directories, each of which can contain subdirectories; each of these can contain more subdirectories, and so on. A subdirectory is said to be the "child" of the directory that holds it (its "parent"). Figure 4-2 shows a system with five directories under the root. The directory *users* has two subdirectories, *jen* and *richard*. Within *jen* are two more subdirectories, *work* and *pers*, and within *pers* is the file *art.html*.

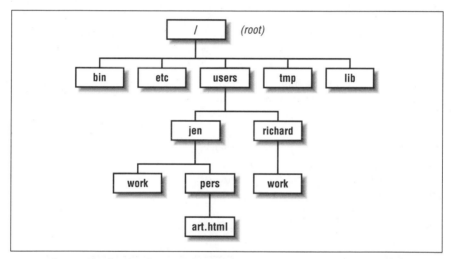

Figure 4-2: Example of a directory hierarchy

A *pathname* is the notation used to point to a particular file or directory; it tells you the path of directories you must travel to get to where you want to go. There are two types of pathnames: *absolute* and *relative*.

Absolute pathnames

An *absolute pathname* always starts from the root directory, which is indicated by a slash (/). So, for example, the pathname for *pers* is */users/jen/pers*, as shown in Figure 4-3. The first slash indicates that we are starting at the root, and is necessary for indicating that a pathname is absolute.

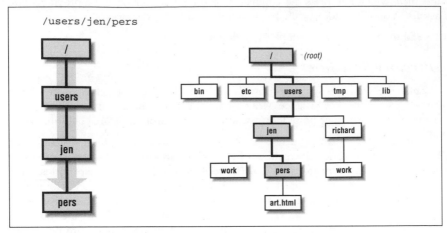

Figure 4-3: Visual representation of the path /users/jen/pers

Relative pathnames

A relative pathname points to a file or directory relative to your current working directory. When building a web site on a single server, relative pathnames are commonly used within URLs to refer to files in other directories on the server.

Unless you specify an absolute name (starting with a slash) the shell assumes you are using a relative pathname. Starting in your current location (your working directory), you can trace your way up and down the directory hierarchy. This is best explained with an example.

If I am currently working in the directory *jen* and I want to refer to the file *art.html*, the relative pathname would be *pers/art.html* because the file *art.html* is in the directory *pers*, which is in the current directory, *jen*. This is illustrated in Figure 4-4.

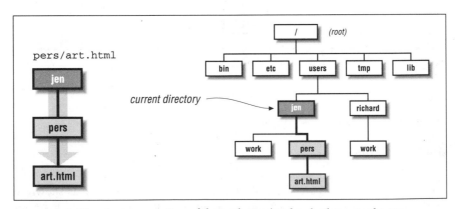

Figure 4-4: Visual representation of the path pers/art.html relative to the jen directory

Going back up the hierarchy is a bit trickier. You go up a level by using the short-hand .. for the parent directory. Again, let's use an example based on Figure 4-2.

If I am currently in the *jen* directory, and I want to refer to the directory *richard/ work*, the pathname would be *../richard/work*. The two dots at the beginning of the path takes us back up one level to the to the *users* directory, and from there we find the directory called *richard* and the subdirectory called *work*, as shown in Figure 4-5.

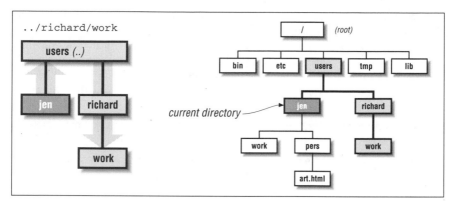

Figure 4-5: Visual representation of the path ../richard/work, relative to the jen directory

If I am currently in my *pers* directory and I want to refer to Richard's *work* directory, I need to go up two levels, so the pathname would be *../../richard/work*, as shown in Figure 4-6.

Note that the absolute path */users/richard/work* accomplishes the same thing. The decision whether to use an absolute versus a relative pathname generally comes down to which is easiest from where you are.

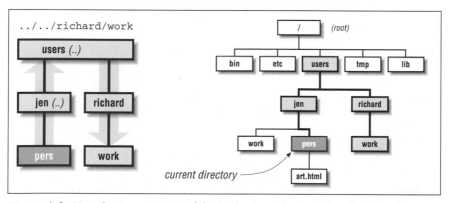

Figure 4-6: Visual representation of the path ../../richard/work, relative to the pers directory

Basic Unix Commands

The general format for Unix commands is:

command *option(s) filename(s)*

The command in bold must be typed in exactly as shown and the values in italics stand for variables that you supply. Some general guidelines for Unix syntax are:

- Commands are entered in lowercase.

- *Options* modify the way in which a command works. They are often single letters prefixed with a minus (-) sign and set off by any number of spaces or tabs. The options listed in this chapter typically can be indicated in one command line by setting them off individually or combining them after a single minus sign. Note: This rule may vary depending on the type of Unix system you are using. Ask your server administrator for help if you run into problems.

- The argument *filename* is the name of a file you want to manipulate in some way.

- Spaces between commands, options, and filenames are important; e.g., "ls -al" works, "ls-al" doesn't.

- The asterisk symbol (*) is a wildcard character that can be used to substitute for any string of characters in a file or directory name. For instance, a search for *.html will retrieve all documents ending in .html.

The following is a brief list of Unix commands that are useful for navigating through directories and managing files.

cd

cd [*pathname*]

This changes your working directory to the specified directory. **cd** alone (without arguments) will take you to your home directory.

cp

cp [*old*] [*new*]

This makes a copy of a file where *old* is a pathname to the original file and *new* is the name you want to give the copy of the file. (This is similar to the "save as" function in an application.) The following sample code makes a copy of the file *art.html* and names the copy *art2.html*.

```
% cp art.html art2.html
```

cp [*file*] [*directory*]

This puts a copy of the original file into an existing directory. The following sample code makes a copy of *art.html* and puts it in Richard's work directory:

```
% cp art.html /user/richard/work
```

ls

`ls [option(s)] [name(s)]`

This gives you a listing of the files and subdirectories (denoted with a slash) in your working directory. Adding a directory name after the options gives you the list of files within the named directory.

Options

-a shows all the files within the directory, including normally hidden files.

-c lists files by creation/modification time.

-l displays long format listing (includes permissions, owner, size, modification time, etc.)

-p marks directories by adding a slash at the end of the name

-x displays the list in rows going across the screen.

Example

A simple listing of names in the current directory:

```
% ls
work
pers
ch01
ch02
ch03
```

List directory contents across the screen with directories indicated with a slash (/):

```
% ls -px
work/     pers/     ch01     ch02     ch03
```

mkdir

`mkdir [dirname]`

This command creates a new directory in the working directory, where *dirname* is the name of the new directory. You must have write permission in the parent directory in order to create a directory.

```
% mkdir nutshell
```

more

`more [filename(s)]`

This displays the contents of a file (or files), one screenful at a time. After each screen is displayed, press RETURN to display the next line or press the spacebar to display the next screenful. Press ? for help with additional commands. Press **q** to quit.

mv

mv [*source*] [*target*]

This basic command moves files and directories around on the system or renames them. Table 4-1 shows the results of various **mv** operations.

Table 4-1: Results of Various mv Operations

Source	Target	Result
File	*name*	Rename file as *name*
File	Existing file	Overwrite existing file with the source file
Directory	*name*	Rename directory as *name*
Directory	Existing directory	Move directory to be a subdirectory of the existing directory
One or more files	Existing directory	Move files to directory

Example

Rename a file:

```
% mv art.html artists.html
```

Move a file from one directory to another:

```
% mv art.html ../richard/work
```

pg

pg [*options*] [*filename*]

This displays the contents of the file on the screen, one page at a time. After each screen is displayed, you are prompted to display the next page by pressing the RETURN key. Press **h** (or ?) for help with additional commands. Press **q** to quit.

Useful pg Commands

-l   Display one more line

n   Move to page *n*

+ or -n
    Move forward or backward by *n* pages

passwd

passwd [*user*]

This creates or changes a password associated with a user name. Only the owner or a privileged user can change a password.

pwd

pwd

This will tell you what directory you are currently in (your *working directory*).

```
% pwd
/user/jen/work
```

rm

rm [*filename*]

rm deletes files (called by name). Be very careful when removing files because it cannot be undone.

rmdir

rmdir [*dirname*]

This allows you to remove a directory (*dirname*) as long as it doesn't contain any files.

File Naming Conventions

In order for your files to traverse the network successfully, you must name them in accordance with established file naming conventions.

*   Avoid character spaces in filenames. Although this is perfectly acceptable for local files on a Macintosh or Windows 95/98/NT machine, character spaces are not recognized by other systems.

*   Avoid special characters such as ?, %, #, etc. in filenames. It is best to limit filenames to letters, numbers, underscores (in place of character spaces), hyphens, and periods.

*   Use proper suffixes. HTML documents require the suffix *.html* (or *.htm* if on a Windows server). GIF graphic files take the suffix *.gif,* and JPEGs should be named *.jpg* or *.jpeg*. If your files do not have the correct suffix, the browser will not recognize them as web-based files. Suffixes for a large number of common file types are listed later in this chapter.

*   Filenames are case-sensitive in HTML. Consistently using all lowercase letters in filenames, while certainly not necessary, may make them easier to remember.

Uploading Documents (FTP)

The most common transaction a web designer will have with a web server is the uploading of HTML documents, graphics, and other media files. Files are transferred between computers over a network via a method called FTP (*File Transfer Protocol*).

If you are working in a telnet session on Unix, you can run the **ftp** program and transfer files with a hefty collection of command-line arguments (not covered in this book).

Fortunately, if you work on a Mac or PC, there are a number of FTP programs with graphical interfaces that spare you the experience of transferring files using Unix command lines. In fact, FTP functions are now built right into most

WYSIWYG HTML editors, such as GoLive Cyberstudio, Claris HomePage, and Dreamweaver, among others. On the Mac, dedicated programs that allow "drag-and-drop" file transfer such as Fetch and Anarchie are quite popular. On the PC, there are numerous simple FTP programs, such as WS_FTP and AceFTP. These (and many others) are available for download at *http://www.shareware.com/* (search for "ftp").

The Netscape Navigator and Internet Explorer browsers also function as simple FTP clients, offering the ability to both download and upload files with a drag-and-drop interface.

The FTP Process

Regardless of the tool you use, the basic principles and processes are the same. Before you begin, you must have an account with permission to upload files to the server. Check with the server administrator to be sure this is set up. (Note: you don't necessarily need an account to upload and download files if the server is set up as an anonymous ftp site.)

1. **Launch the FTP program** of your choice and open a connection with your server. You'll need to enter the exact name of the server, your account name, and password.

2. **Locate the appropriate directory** into which you want to copy your files. You may also choose to create a new directory or delete existing files and directories on the remote server using the controls in your FTP program.

3. **Specify the transfer mode.** The most important decision to make during uploading is specifying whether the data should be transferred in *binary* or *ASCII* mode.

   ASCII files are comprised of alphanumeric characters. Some FTP programs refer to ASCII files as "Text" files. HTML documents should be transferred as ASCII or text.

   Binary files are made up of compiled data (ones and zeros), such as executable programs, graphic images, movies, etc. Some programs refer to the binary mode as "raw data" or "Image." All graphics (*.gif, .jpeg*) and multimedia files should be transferred as "binary" or "Raw Data." Table 4-3 includes a listing of the transfer mode for a number of popular file types.

   In Fetch (Mac), you may see a *MacBinary* option, which transfers the file with its resource fork (the bit of the file containing desktop icons and other Mac-specific data) intact. It should only be used when transferring from one Mac to another. This resource fork is appropriately stripped out of Mac-generated media files when transferred under the standard raw data mode.

   Some FTP programs also provide an *Auto* option, which enables you to transfer whole directories containing files of both types. The program examines each file and determines whether it should be transferred as text or binary information. This function is not 100% reliable on all programs, so use it with caution until you are positive you are getting good results.

4. **Upload your files to the server.** Standard FTP uses the terminology "put" (uploading files from your computer to the server) and "get" (downloading

---

files from the server to your computer), so these terms may be used in your FTP program as well. You can also upload multiple files at a time.

5. **Disconnect.** When you have completed the transfer, be sure to disconnect from the server. You may want to test the files you've uploaded on a browser first to make sure everything transferred successfully.

tting Permissions

ıen you upload files to a web server, you need to be sure that the files' permis- ıs are set so that everyone is able to read your files. *Permissions* control who : read, write (edit), or execute the file (if it is a program), and they need to be ıblished for the owner of the file, the file's group, and for "everyone." When ı create or upload a file, you are automatically the owner, which may mean that y you can set the permissions.

'ith an FTP program

5ome FTP programs enable you to set the default upload permissions via a dialog box. Figure 4-7 shows Fetch 3.0.4's dialog box for doing this. For most web purposes, you want to grant yourself full permissions but restrict all other users to read-only. You may want to confirm that your server administrator agrees with these settings.

Figure 4-7: Standard permissions settings (using Fetch 3.0.4)

The server needs to be specially configured to recognize these permissions commands, so check with your administrator to see if you can use this easy method.

Using chmod in Unix

If you are uploading files and creating directories via an FTP client, your client might not give anyone else in your group the proper permissions. In this case, it may be necessary to open a telnet session and set permissions on files and direc- tories manually using the Unix **chmod** command. Basic **chmod** syntax and examples are discussed in this section, but it is best to check with your server administrator for the correct syntax for your purposes.

From within the telnet session, begin by checking the current permissions and owner of the directories and files. You need to be the owner to change permissions on a directory's contents. At the Unix prompt (% or $), type ls -l to view the contents in the long format. The system returns a listing that looks like this:

```
drwxrwxrwx 2 jen  doc   512 May 19 11:25 chap13
```

The first ten characters reflect the permissions settings. The first character shows the file type (directory, d, or plain file,-). The next three characters show the read (r), write (w), and execute (x) privileges for the owner of the file (in this example, the user *jen* is the owner). The next three characters indicate the same three settings for other members of the file's group. The final three characters show permissions for all other users.

In the example above, all users have complete access to the file. If certain permissions are turned off, the space is held with a dash (-). In the following example, the owner has total access to the file, but the group and other users can only read the file.

```
drwxr--r--
```

A complete explanation of all the finer points of the **chmod** command is beyond the scope of this chapter, but Table 4-2 shows instructions for a few of the most common settings you'll need. Type the **chmod** command and number option as shown, and substitute your directory name for *dirname* (note, you can use a "dot" to indicate the current directory.)

A directory's access permissions help control access to the files in it, such as adding, deleting, and renaming files. The permissions on a file control what can be done to the file's contents, such as reading or editing.

Table 4-2: Common chmod Settings

Type	Permissions	Command	Result
Directory	Allows users in your group to add, delete, and rename files in your directory. All others can only view the directory's contents.	**chmod 775** *dirname*	drwxrwxr-x
Directory	Restricts access to all users except the owner.	**chmod 700** *dirname*	drwx------
File	Allows you and your group to read and edit the file, but allows all other users to read only.	**chmod 664** *filename*	-rw-rw-r--
File	Allows you to edit a file, but allows everyone else on the system to read only.	**chmod 644** *filename*	-rw-r--r--
File	Makes a private file that only you can read or edit.	**chmod 600** *filename*	-rwx------

Chmod syntax also has an alternative letter system. Without going into detail, the command:

```
chmod -R go+rx *
```

is a quick and powerful way to set permissions for the current directory and every directory and file within it (-R). This example gives read (r) and execute (x) privileges to the group (g) and all other users (o).

File (MIME) Types

Servers add a header to each document that tells the browser the type of file it is sending. The browser determines how to handle the file based on that information—whether to display the contents in the window, or to launch the appropriate plug-in or helper application.

The system for communicating media types closely resembles MIME (Multipurpose Internet Mail Extension), which was originally developed for sending attachments in email. The server needs to be configured to recognize each MIME type in order to successfully communicate the media type to the browser.

If you want to deliver media beyond the standard HTML files and graphics (such as a Shockwave Flash movie or an audio file), you should contact your server administrator to be sure the server is configured to support that MIME type. Most common formats are built in to current versions of server software, but if it isn't there already, the administrator can easily set it up if you provide the necessary information.

The exact syntax for configuring MIME types varies among server software; however, they all require the same basic information: type, subtype, and extension. Types are the most broad categories for files. They include text, image, audio, video, application, etc. Within each category are a number of subtypes. For instance, the file type *image* includes the subtypes *gif, jpeg,* etc. The extension refers to the file's suffix, which the server uses to determine the file type and subtype. Not all extensions are standardized.

Table 4-3 lists common media types by extension along with their MIME type/subtype information. The ASCII/Binary information is provided to aid in making upload decisions.

Of course, new technologies and file types are emerging every day, so keep in mind that it is the web designer's responsibility to make sure that for any new media type the appropriate information is communicated to the server administrator.

Table 4-3: MIME Types and Subtypes by Extension

Extension	Type/Subtype	Description	ASCII/ Binary
`.ai`	`application/ postscript`	PostScript viewer	A
`.aif, .aiff`	`audio/x-aiff`	AIFF file	B

Table 4-3: MIME Types and Subtypes by Extension (continued)

Extension	Type/Subtype	Description	*ASCII/ Binary*
.aifc	audio/aifc	Compressed AIFF file	B
.au	audio/basic	μ-law sound file	B
.avi	video/avi or video/x-msvideo	AVI video file	B
.bmp	image/x-MS-bmp	Microsoft BMP file	B
.dcr, .dir, .dxr	application/ x-director	Shockwave files	B
.doc	application/ msword	Microsoft Word document	B
.eps	application/ postscript	Encapsulated Post-Script	A
.exe	application/ x-msdownload	Self-extracting file or executable	B
.gif	image/gif	Graphic in GIF format	B
.gz	application/ x-gzip	Compressed file, use gunzip (Unix decompressor)	B
.hqx	application/ mac-binhex40	Mac BinHex Archive	B
.htm	text/html	HTML document	A
.jpg, .jpeg, .jpe, .jfif, .pjpeg, .pjp	image/jpeg	Graphic in JPEG format	B
.mid	audio/midi or audio/x-midi	MIDI audio file	B
.mov	video/quicktime	QuickTime movie	B
.movie	video/x-sgi-movie	Silicon Graphics movie	B
.mpg, .mpe, .mpeg, .m1v, .mp2, .mp3, .mpa	video/mpeg	MPEG movie	B
.pbm	image/x-portable-bitmap	Portable bitmap image	B
.pcd	image/x-photo-cd	Kodak photo CD image	B
.pdf	application/pdf	Portable Document Format (Acrobat file)	B
.pic	image/x-pict	PICT image file	B
.pl	application/ x-perl	Perl source file	A

Table 4-3: MIME Types and Subtypes by Extension (continued)

Extension	Type/Subtype	Description	ASCII/Binary
.png	image/x-png	Graphic in PNG format	B
.ppt	application/powerpoint	PowerPoint file	B
.ps	application/postscript	PostScript file	A
.qt	video/quicktime	QuickTime movie	B
.ra, .ram	audio/x-pn-realaudio	RealAudio file (and metafile)	B
.rtx	text/richtext	Rich Text Format (Microsoft Word)	A
.rtf	application/rtf	Rich Text Format (MSWord)	A
.sea	application/x-sea	Self-extracting Archive (Stuffit file)	B
.sit	application/x-sit	Stuffit Archive	B
.snd	audio/basic	Digitized sound file	B
.swf	application/x-shockwave-flash	Shockwave Flash file	B
.tar	application/x-tar	Compressed file	B
.tif, .tiff	image/tiff	TIFF image (requires external viewer)	B
.txt	text/plain	ASCII text file	A
.wav	audio/s-wav	Waveform audio file	B
.wrl, .wrz	x-world/x-vrml	VRML 3D file (requires VRML viewer)	B
.xll	application/vnd.ms-excel	Microsoft Excel File	B
.zip	application/x-zip-compressed	Compressed file (decompress using WinZip or Stuffit on Mac)	B

PART II

HTML

CHAPTER 5

HTML Overview

HTML (Hypertext Markup Language) is the language used to create web documents. It defines the syntax and placement of special instructions (tags) that aren't displayed, but tell the browser how to display the document's contents. It is also used to create links to other documents, either locally or over a network such as the Internet.

The HTML standard and all other Web-related standards are developed under the authority of the World Wide Web Consortium (W3C). Standards, specifications, and drafts of new proposals can be found at *http://www.w3.org/*. The most recent work is the HTML 4.0 Specification, which is growing in support by major browsers.

In practice, the HTML "standard" is influenced heavily by the tags that are introduced and supported by the popular browsers, i.e., Microsoft Internet Explorer and Netscape Navigator. These tags may or may not be part of the current HTML specification at any given time.

This chapter provides a basic introduction to the background and general syntax of HTML, including document structure, tags, and their attributes. It also looks briefly at good HTML style and the pros and cons of using WYSIWYG authoring tools.

For a more in-depth study of HTML, I recommend *HTML: The Definitive Guide, Third Edition,* by Chuck Musciano and Bill Kennedy (O'Reilly & Associates, 1998) Another excellent resource for HTML tag information is the HTML Compendium (created by Ron Woodall). The Compendium provides an alphabetical listing of every HTML tag and its attributes, with explanations and up-to-date browser support information for each. The browser support charts accompanying each tag in this book are based on their work. The HTML Compendium can be found at *http://www.htmlcompendium.org/*.

HTML Editing Tools

HTML documents are simple ASCII text files, which means you can use any minimal text editor to write them. Fortunately, there are editing tools designed especially for writing HTML. These save time by providing shortcuts for repetitive tasks like setting up documents, tables, or simply applying styles to text. HTML editors are not the same as WYSIWYG authoring tools (discussed next)—you need to know how to compose HTML by hand; editors just make the process faster and easier.

There are scores of simple HTML editors available, and many of them are free. Just enter "HTML Editor" in the search field of Shareware.com (*http://www.shareware.com/*) and wade through the results. For purposes of brevity, I'm going to cut to the chase.

Windows users should definitely check out HomeSite, a high-powered and inexpensive HTML editor from Allaire Corporation. It, too, has HTML shortcuts and templates, color-coded HTML syntax, an FTP function, spell-checker, HTML syntax checker, and multi-file search-and-replace. In addition, it includes wizards for creating more complex elements (such as frames, JavaScript, and DHTML) and many other attractive features. For more information and to download a demo copy, see *http://www.allaire.com/*.

If you're working on a Macintosh, you want BBEdit, a commercial HTML editor from Bare Bones Software, Inc. It is overwhelmingly the editor of choice among Mac-based web developers. It includes features such as an array of HTML shortcut tools, color-coded HTML syntax, multiple-file search and replace, a built-in FTP function, support for 13 programming languages, a table builder, an HTML syntax checker, and a lot more. For more information and to download a demo, see *http://www.bbedit.com/*.

WYSIWYG Authoring Tools

The last two years have seen an explosion in the web authoring tool market. WYSIWYG (what-you-see-is-what-you-get) HTML editors have graphical interfaces that make writing HTML more like using a word processing or page layout program. In the beginning, their goal was to spare authors from ever having to touch an HTML tag in the way that page layout programs protect designers from typing out PostScript. Today, their role has shifted towards making document production more efficient and automated while still providing access to the HTML source.

Should You Use Them?

These days, nobody pretends that WYSIWYG authoring tools will excuse you from learning HTML completely, but they do provide a considerable head start for many menial tasks. Because these tools are notorious for adding extra code to HTML files, the question of whether or not to use them for web production has become something of a holy war among web developers.

HTML purists insist that hand-writing HTML in a no-frills text editor is the only way to do it "right," and that the HTML documents made by WYSIWYG tools are of unacceptable quality. On the other hand, many developers appreciate being spared the grunt-work of typing every HTML tag and find the WYSIWYG environment useful for viewing the page and making design decisions on the fly.

Of course, there are many reasons both for and against using these tools. The controversy should lessen as the tools, which are currently in their infancy, work out their kinks and start producing clean and robust code. If you do use a WYSIWYG tool, expect to do some manual fine-tuning to the resulting HTML code.

Pros

- They are good for beginners. They can even be useful for teaching HTML because you can lay out the page the way you want, then view the resulting HTML.

- They are good for quick prototyping. Design ideas can be tried out on the fly.

- They provide a good head start for creating complex tables and other advanced functions such as JavaScript and DHTML functions.

Cons

- They are infamous for not generating clean HTML documents. They add proprietary or redundant tags and often take circuitous routes to produce a desired effect. Some may even produce HTML that is incorrect.

- Some editors automatically change an HTML document when you open it in the program. They add their own tags and may strip out any tags they do not recognize.

- The built-in graphics-generating features do not offer much control over the quality or the file size of resulting graphics.

- Software releases tend to lag behind the quickly changing HTML standards, so the HTML you create using the tool may not be completely up-to-date.

- They are expensive. The more powerful packages cost hundreds of dollars up front and additional costs to upgrade.

Some Available Tools

The following is an introduction to a handful of the tools that are popular as of this writing (versions are omitted because of the speed of updates). All are available for both Mac and Windows unless otherwise noted.

Macromedia Dreamweaver

As of this writing, Dreamweaver is emerging as the industry-standard HTML authoring tool due the fact that it produces the cleanest code of any of its competitors. In addition, it provides many shortcuts for creating style sheets, JavaScript, and DHTML functions. It has a fairly steep learning curve. For more information, see *http://www.macromedia.com/*.

GoLive CyberStudio (Mac only)

A powerful HTML editing tool that supports all of the cutting-edge web technologies (JavaScript, ActiveX, WebObjects, style sheets, etc.). It also provides excellent site management tools. Its interface is more difficult to learn than other tools, but it seems to be worth the effort. For more information, see *http://www.golive.com/*.

Microsoft FrontPage (Mac release lags behind Windows release)

This is Microsoft's effort in the web authoring arena. It is easy for beginners to learn and is popular with the business community. On the downside, it generates HTML loaded with Microsoft-specific tags and it will change pre-existing documents as it opens them. FrontPage is closely integrated with Microsoft's Internet Information Server (IIS), so check with your ISP for possible conflicts. For more information, see *http://www.microsoft.com/frontpage/*.

FileMaker Claris Home Page

This HTML editor is good for beginners and adequate for noncommercial web page production. It features a simple interface, easy access to web-safe colors, a library for storing elements that can be used repeatedly, and much more. It is guilty of generating redundant HTML full of proprietary tags and it will change pre-existing HTML documents. For more information, see *http://www. filemaker.com/*.

Adobe PageMill

PageMill was the first WYSIWYG editor out of the gate in 1995, but it has since been eclipsed by more powerful packages in the professional web authoring world. It is still adequate for personal web page production and is easy to learn and use. It lacks an easy method for accessing the HTML code and is also guilty of adding proprietary tags to the document. For more information, see *http://www.adobe.com/*.

Document Structure

An HTML document contains text (the contents of the page) with embedded tags, which provide instructions for the structure, appearance, and function of the contents.

An HTML document is divided into two major portions: the head and the body. The head contains information about the document, such as its title and "meta" information describing the contents. The body contains the actual contents of the document (the part that is displayed in the browser window).

The following example shows the tags that make up the standard skeletal structure of an HTML document:

```
<HTML>
<HEAD>
<TITLE>Document Title</TITLE>
</HEAD>
<BODY>
Contents of Document
</BODY>
</HTML>
```

HTML Tags

Every HTML tag is made up of a tag *name*, sometimes followed by an optional list of attributes, all of which appears between angle brackets < >. Nothing within the brackets will be displayed in the browser. The tag name is generally an abbreviation of the tag's function (this makes them fairly simple to learn). Attributes are properties that extend or refine the tag's function.

The name and attributes within a tag are not case sensitive. <BODY BGCOLOR=white> will work the same as <body bgcolor=white>. However, values for particular attributes may be case sensitive, particularly URLs and filenames.

Containers

Most HTML tags are containers, meaning they have a beginning (also called "opener" or "start") tag and an end tag. The text enclosed within the tags will follow the tag's instructions, as in the following example:

    The weather is <I>gorgeous</I> today.

Result: The weather is *gorgeous* today.

An end tag contains the same name as the start tag, but it is preceded by a slash (/). You can think of it as an "off" switch for the tag. End tags never contain attributes.

For some tags, the end tag is optional and the browser determines when the tag ends by context. This practice is most common with the <p> (paragraph) tag. Browsers have supported the <p> tag without its end tag, so many web authors take advantage of the shortcut. Not all tags allow this, however, and not all browsers are forgiving, so when in doubt include the end tag. This is especially important when using Cascading Style Sheets (discussed in Chapter 23, *Cascading Style Sheets*) with your document.

In the HTML charts that appear in this book, container tags are indicated with the syntax < >...</>. If the end tag is optional, it will be so noted in the tag's explanation.

Standalone Tags

A few tags do not have end tags because they are used to place standalone elements on the page. The image tag (<img>) is such a tag and it simply plops a graphic into the flow of the page. Other standalone tags include the linebreak (<br>), horizontal rule (<hr>), and tags that provide information about a document and don't affect its displayed content, such as the <meta> and <base> tags.

Attributes

Attributes are added within a tag to extend or modify the tag's actions. You can add multiple attributes within a single tag. Tag attributes, if any, belong after the tag name, each separated by one or more spaces. Their order of appearance is not important.

Most attributes take *values*, which follow an equal sign (=) after the attribute's name. Values are limited to 1024 characters in length and may be case sensitive.

Sometimes the value needs to appear in quotation marks (double or single). Here's how to determine if you need quotation marks around a value:

- If the value is a single word or number, and contains only letters (a-z), numbers (0-9), or the special characters period (.) or hyphen (-), then it is OK to place it directly after the equal sign without quotation marks.

- If the value contains several words separated by commas or spaces, or if it contains any special characters besides a period or hyphen, then it needs to be contained within quotation marks. For example, URLs require quotation marks because they contain the characters ".//". Likewise, quotation marks are required around color specifications that take the syntax "#*rrggbb*".

 Be careful not to leave out the closing quotation mark, or all the content from the opening quotation mark until the browser encounters a subsequent quotation mark will be interpreted as part of the value, and won't display in the browser. This is a simple mistake that can cause hours of debugging frustration.

If you are still unsure, using quotation marks consistently for all values will work just fine and is probably a good idea anyway.

The following are examples of tags that contain attributes:

```
<IMG SRC="graphics/pixie.gif" ALIGN=right WIDTH=45 HEIGHT=60>
<BODY BGCOLOR="#000000">
<FONT FACE="Trebuchet MS, Arial, Helvetica" SIZE=4>
```

Nesting HTML Tags

HTML tags can be applied to content containing other HTML tags for multiple tag effects on a single element. This is called *nesting*, and to do it properly, both the beginning and end tags of the enclosed tag must be completely contained within the beginning and end tags of the applied tag, as follows:

```
The weather is <B><I>gorgeous</I></B> today.
```

Result: The weather is *gorgeous* today.

```
This links to <A HREF="document.html">a really <B>cool</B>
page</A>.
```

Result: This links to a really cool page.

A common mistake is simply overlapping the tags. Although some browsers display content marked up this way, other browsers will not allow the violation, so it is important to nest tags correctly. The following example shows incorrect nesting of tags (note that the <B> tag is closed before the <I>):

```
The weather is <B><I>gorgeous</B></I> today.
```

Information Browsers Ignore

Some information in an HTML document, including certain tags, will be ignored when the document is viewed in a browser. These include:

Line breaks

Line returns in the HTML document are ignored. Text and elements will wrap continuously until they encounter a `<p>` or `<br>` tag within the flow of the document text. Line breaks are displayed, however, when text is tagged as preformatted text (`<pre>`).

Tabs and multiple spaces

When a browser encounters a tab or more than one consecutive blank character space in an HTML document, it will display it as a single space. So, if the document contains:

```
far,            far                away
```

the browser will display:

far, far away

Extra spaces can be added within the flow of text by using the nonbreaking space character entity (` `). Multiple spaces will be displayed, however, when text is tagged as preformatted text (`<pre>`).

Multiple `<p>` tags

A series of `<p>` (paragraph) tags with no intervening text is interpreted as redundant by all browsers and will display as though it were only a single `<p>` tag. Most browsers will display multiple `<br>` tags as multiple line breaks.

Unrecognized tags

A browser simply ignores any tag it doesn't understand or that was incorrectly specified. Depending on the tag and the browser, this can have varied results. Either the browser will display nothing at all, or it may display the contents of the tag as though it were normal text.

Text in comments

Browsers will not display text between the special `<!--` and `-->` elements used to denote a *comment.* Here is a sample comment:

```
<!-- This is a comment -->
<!-- This is a
multiple line comment
that ends here. -->
```

There must be a space after the initial `<!--` and preceding the final `-->`, but you can put nearly anything inside the comment otherwise. You cannot nest comments. Microsoft Internet Explorer has its own proprietary way of indicating comments with `<comment>` ... `</comment>` tags. This markup is not supported by any other browser.

Tips on Good HTML Style

This section offers some guidelines for writing "good" HTML—code that will be supported by a wide variety of browsers, that will be easily handled by applications expecting correct HTML, and that will be extensible to emerging technologies built on the current HTML specification.

Follow HTML syntax as described by the current available W3C specification

Writing HTML "correctly" may take extra effort, but it ensures that your document will display the way you intend it on the greatest number of browsers. Some browsers are quite lax in the way they parse HTML. For instance, if you omit a closing `</table>` tag, Internet Explorer will display the contents of the table just fine. Netscape Navigator will leave that portion of your web page completely blank.

Some browsers, particularly Opera, are very strict. Simple slips or shortcuts that slide right by Navigator or Internet Explorer may cause your whole web page to self-destruct. If you are careful in the way you write your HTML (minding your `<p>`s and `<q>`s!), you will have more success on more browsers.

To be absolutely sure how you're doing, you should run your HTML code through one of the many available online HTML validation services, such as the one at the W3C (*http://www.validator.w3.org/*). Other HTML validators are listed in Chapter 1, *Designing for a Variety of Browsers*.

Follow code-writing conventions to make your HTML document easier to read

Although not a true programming language, HTML documents bear some resemblance to programming code in that they are usually long ASCII documents littered with tags and commands. The overall impression can be chaotic, making it difficult to find the specific element you're looking for. The following conventions serve to make your document easier to read when viewed in a simple text editor.

Capitalize tags and attributes

Tags and their attributes are not case-sensitive, so capitalizing them consistently in a document makes them stand out from the rest of the content on the page.

Use line breaks and tabs for legibility

Because browsers ignore line breaks, tabs, and extra spaces in an HTML document, you can use them to give your document structure. For instance, you can add extra lines between the head and body of the document or tabs before the items in a list. The white space will help differentiate elements on the page.

Adding character spaces and returns will add to the size of your HTML file, so if you are extremely concerned about download times, keep your HTML compact. A new utility called Mizer from Antimony Software strips out all the unnecessary characters, making HTML files 10–15% smaller and allowing the browser to display the page up to 30% faster. For more information, see *http://www.antimony.com/*.

Avoid adding extra or redundant tags

Extra and redundant HTML tags add unnecessary bytes to the size of your HTML file causing slightly longer download times. They also make the browser work harder to parse the file, further increasing display times. One example of redundant tagging is multiple and identical <font> tags within a sentence, a common side effect created after making small edits with a WYSIWYG authoring tool.

Name your files according to the following guidelines:

- Use proper suffixes. HTML documents require the suffix *.html* (or *.htm* if on a Windows server). Suffixes for a number of common file types can be found in Table 4-3.

- Avoid spaces and special characters such as ?, %, #, etc. in file names. It is best to limit file names to letters, numbers, underscores (in place of spaces), hyphens and periods.

- File names are case-sensitive in HTML. Consistently using all lowercase letters in file names, while certainly not necessary, may make them easier to remember.

Mind your line endings.

Although not mandatory, it is accepted practice to keep your line lengths to under 80 characters to make the document easier to view on a wide variety of platforms.

In addition, you should be certain that you set your HTML editor to use Unix-style Line Feed (LF) line endings, particularly if you have a Unix server.* Other line ending possibilities are Carriage Returns (CR) used by Macintosh, and Carriage Return + Line Feed (CR+LF) used by PCs. Some editors, such as BBEdit, allow you to set the line feed style under the Save Options.

 Line breaks and extra spaces can create unwanted white space in certain contexts. For instance, if you have a string of graphics that should abut seamlessly, adding a line break or a space between the <img> tags will introduce extra space between the graphics (even though, technically, it shouldn't). In addition, extra spaces within and between table cells (<td> tags) can add unwanted (and mysterious) spaces in your table. This is discussed further in Chapter 10.

Specifying Color in HTML

You can specify the color of certain page elements using HTML tags. There are two methods for specifying colors in web documents: by RGB values and by color name.

---

* This tip taken from *Creative HTML Design*, by Lynda Weinman and William Weinman, published by New Riders Publishing.

Specifying Color by RGB Values

The most common and precise way to specify a color in HTML is by its numerical RGB values. For an explanation of RGB color, see "Color on the Web" in Chapter 3, *Web Design Principles for Print Designers*.

Once you've identified the red, green, and blue values of your chosen color, you'll need to translate them to their *hexadecimal* equivalents in order to enter them into the HTML color tag. These values are written in HTML with the following syntax:

```
"#RRGGBB"
```

where RR stands for the hexadecimal red value, GG stands for the hexadecimal green value, and BB stands for the hexadecimal blue value. Using these values, you can specify any color from the "true color" space (millions of colors).

Let's look at an example to put this in context. To set the background color of a document to dark olive green, the complete HTML tag would look like this:

```
<BODY BGCOLOR="#556B2F">
```

The hexadecimal system

The hexadecimal numbering system is base-16 (as opposed to base-10 for decimal numbers). It uses the following 16 characters:

```
0, 1, 2, 3, 4, 5, 6, 7, 8, 9, A, B, C, D, E, F
```

A through F represent the decimal numbers 10 through 15.

Converting decimal to hexadecimal

You can calculate hex values by dividing your number by 16 to get the first digit, then using the remainder for the second digit. For example, dividing the decimal number 203 by 16 yields 12 with a remainder of 11. The hexadecimal value of 12 is C; the hex value of 11 is B. Therefore, the hexadecimal equivalent of 203 is CB.

Fortunately, there are more simple methods for converting numbers to hexadecimal:

- Use the conversion chart in Table 5-1, which translates decimal values from 0 to 255.

- Use a hexadecimal calculator. On the Macintosh, you can download a copy of a utility called Calculator II (*ftp://ftp.amug.org/pub/mirrors/info-mac/sci/calc/calculator-ii-15.hqx*). Windows users will find a hexadecimal calculator in the "Scientific" view of the Windows' standard calculator.

- Use online resources. There are several resources online for calculating hexadecimal equivalents. Some allow you to enter all three values for red, green,

---

Table 5-1: Decimal to Hexadecimal Equivalents

dec = hex	dec = hex	dec = hex	dec = hex	dec = hex	dec = hex
0 = 00	51 = 33	102 = 66	153 = 99	204 = CC	255 = FF
1 = 01	52 = 34	103 = 67	154 = 9A	205 = CD	
2 = 02	53 = 35	104 = 68	155 = 9B	206 = CE	
3 = 03	54 = 36	105 = 69	156 = 9C	207 = CF	
4 = 04	55 = 37	106 = 6A	157 = 9D	208 = D0	
5 = 05	56 = 38	107 = 6B	158 = 9E	209 = D1	
6 = 06	57 = 39	108 = 6C	159 = 9F	210 = D2	
7 = 07	58 = 3A	109 = 6D	160 = A0	211 = D3	
8 = 08	59 = 3B	110 = 6E	161 = A1	212 = D4	
9 = 09	60 = 3C	111 = 6F	162 = A2	213 = D5	
10 = 0A	61 = 3D	112 = 70	163 = A3	214 = D6	
11 = 0B	62 = 3E	113 = 71	164 = A4	215 = D7	
12 = 0C	63 = 3F	114 = 72	165 = A5	216 = D8	
13 = 0D	64 = 40	115 = 73	166 = A6	217 = D9	
14 = 0E	65 = 41	116 = 74	167 = A7	218 = DA	
15 = 0F	66 = 42	117 = 75	168 = A8	219 = DB	
16 = 10	67 = 43	118 = 76	169 = A9	220 = DC	
17 = 11	68 = 44	119 = 77	170 = AA	221 = DD	
18 = 12	69 = 45	120 = 78	171 = AB	222 = DE	
19 = 13	70 = 46	121 = 79	172 = AC	223 = DF	
20 = 14	71 = 47	122 = 7A	173 = AD	224 = E0	
21 = 15	72 = 48	123 = 7B	174 = AE	225 = E1	
22 = 16	73 = 49	124 = 7C	175 = AF	226 = E2	
23 = 17	74 = 4A	125 = 7D	176 = B0	227 = E3	
24 = 18	75 = 4B	126 = 7E	177 = B1	228 = E4	
25 = 19	76 = 4C	127 = 7F	178 = B2	229 = E5	
26 = 1A	77 = 4D	128 = 80	179 = B3	230 = E6	
27 = 1B	78 = 4E	129 = 81	180 = B4	231 = E7	
28 = 1C	79 = 4F	130 = 82	181 = B5	232 = E8	
29 = 1D	80 = 50	131 = 83	182 = B6	233 = E9	
30 = 1E	81 = 51	132 = 84	183 = B7	234 = EA	
31 = 1F	82 = 52	133 = 85	184 = B8	235 = EB	
32 = 20	83 = 53	134 = 86	185 = B9	236 = EC	
33 = 21	84 = 54	135 = 87	186 = BA	237 = ED	
34 = 22	85 = 55	136 = 88	187 = BB	238 = EE	
35 = 23	86 = 56	137 = 89	188 = BC	239 = EF	
36 = 24	87 = 57	138 = 8A	189 = BD	240 = F0	
37 = 25	88 = 58	139 = 8B	190 = BE	241 = F1	
38 = 26	89 = 59	140 = 8C	191 = BF	242 = F2	
39 = 27	90 = 5A	141 = 8D	192 = C0	243 = F3	
40 = 28	91 = 5B	142 = 8E	193 = C1	244 = F4	
41 = 29	92 = 5C	143 = 8F	194 = C2	245 = F5	
42 = 2A	93 = 5D	144 = 90	195 = C3	246 = F6	
43 = 2B	94 = 5E	145 = 91	196 = C4	247 = F7	
44 = 2C	95 = 5F	146 = 92	197 = C5	248 = F8	
45 = 2D	96 = 60	147 = 93	198 = C6	249 = F9	
46 = 2E	97 = 61	148 = 94	199 = C7	250 = FA	
47 = 2F	98 = 62	149 = 95	200 = C8	251 = FB	
48 = 30	99 = 63	150 = 96	201 = C9	252 = FC	
49 = 31	100 = 64	151 = 97	202 = CA	253 = FD	
50 = 32	101 = 65	152 = 98	203 = CB	254 = FE	

and blue, and convert to hexadecimal while showing you a sample of your chosen color immediately. Examples of online calcualtions include:

Mediarama's Color Page Builder
http://www.inquisitor.com/hex.html

Plug in your decimal RGB values for page elements, and this page will automatically generate a sample page with your color selections and the HTML code for the <BODY> tag.

URL Univox Internet: RGB 2 Hex
http://www.univox.com/rgb2hex.html

This is a stripped-down, no-frills tool for converting decimal RGB values to their hex equivalients.

Hexadecimal values for Web Palette colors

All colors in the 216-color Web Palette are made up of combinations of the following six hexadecimal values:

```
00,    33,    66,    99,    CC,    FF
```

Specifying Colors by Name

Colors can also be identified by one of 140 color names originally developed for the X Window System. The complete list appears in Table 5-2 (alphabetically with numerical values) and Table 5-3 (by hue). You can also view samples of each color on the web page for this book (*http://www.oreilly.com/catalog/wdnut/*).

To set the background color to a dark olive green using a color name, the complete HTML tag would look like this:

```
<BODY BGCOLOR="darkolivegreen">
```

Color name cautions

There are several pitfalls to using color names instead of numerical color values, as outlined below.

Browser Support
Color names are only supported by Navigator versions 2.0 and higher and Internet Explorer versions 3.0 and higher. Internet Explorer 2.0 supports the following 16 color names:

aqua	gray	navy	silver
black	green	olive	teal
blue	lime	purple	white
fuschia	maroon	red	yellow

These are also the colors specified by the W3C in the HTML 4.0 Specification.

Color Shifting
Of the 140 color names, only 10 represent nondithering colors from the Web Palette. They are: aqua, black, blue, cyan, fuschia, lime, magenta, red, white, and yellow.

When viewed on an 8-bit display, the remaining 130 colors will shift to their nearest Web Palette equivalent (or System Palette color). In many cases, the difference is drastic. Many of the pastels shift to solid white.

The "Nearest Web-safe Color" column in Table 5-2 lists the color that will actually be displayed for each color name on an 8-bit display.

Table 5-2: Color Names with their Numeric Values

Color Name	RGB Values	Hexadecimal	Nearest Web-safe Color
aliceblue	240 - 248 - 255	F0F8FF	FFFFFF
antiquewhite	250 - 235 - 215	FAEBD7	FFFFCC
aqua	0 - 255 - 255	00FFFF	00FFFF
aquamarine	127 - 255 - 212	7FFFD4	66FFCC
azure	240 - 255 - 255	F0FFFF	FFFFFF
beige	245 - 245 - 220	F5F5DC	FFFFCC
bisque	255 - 228 - 196	FFE4C4	FFFFCC
black	0 - 0 - 0	000000	000000
blanchedalmond	255 - 255 - 205	FFEBCD	FFFFCC
blue	0 - 0 - 255	0000FF	0000FF
blueviolet	138 - 43 - 226	8A2BE2	9933FF
brown	165 - 42 - 42	A52A2A	993333
burlywood	222 - 184 - 135	DEB887	CCCC99
cadetblue	95 - 158 - 160	5F9EA0	669999
chartreuse	127 - 255 - 0	7FFF00	66FF00
chocolate	210 - 105 - 30	D2691E	996600
coral	255 - 127 - 80	FF7F50	FF6666
cornflowerblue	100 - 149 - 237	6495ED	6699FF
cornsilk	255 - 248 - 220	FFF8DC	FFFFCC
crimson	220 - 20 - 60	DC143C	CC0033
cyan	0 - 255 - 255	00FFFF	00FFFF
darkblue	0 - 0 - 139	00008B	000099*
darkcyan	0 - 139 - 139	008B8B	009999
darkgoldenrod	184 - 134 - 11	B8860B	CC9900
darkgray	169 - 169 - 169	A9A9A9	999999*
darkgreen	0 - 100 - 0	006400	006600
darkkhaki	189 - 183 - 107	BDB76B	CCCC66
darkmagenta	139 - 0 - 139	8B008B	990099
darkolivegreen	85 - 107 - 47	556B2F	666633
darkorange	255 - 140 - 0	FF8C00	FF9900
darkorchid	153 - 50 - 204	9932CC	9933CC
darkred	139 - 0 - 0	8B0000	990000*
darksalmon	233 - 150 - 122	E9967A	FF9966

Table 5-2: Color Names with their Numeric Values (continued)

Color Name	RGB Values	Hexadecimal	Nearest Web-safe Color
darkseagreen	143 - 188 - 143	8FBC8F	99CC99
darkslateblue	72 - 61 - 139	483D8B	333399
darkslategray	47 - 79 - 79	2F4F4F	333399*
darkturquoise	0 - 206 - 209	00CED1	00CCCC
darkviolet	148 - 0 - 211	9400D3	9900CC
deeppink	255 - 20 - 147	FF1493	FF0099
deepskyblue	0 - 191 - 255	00BFFF	00CCFF
dimgray	105 - 105 - 105	696969	666666
dodgerblue	30 - 144 - 255	1E90FF	0099FF
firebrick	178 - 34 - 34	B22222	CC3333
floralwhite	255 - 250 - 240	FFFAF0	FFFFFF
forestgreen	34 - 139 - 34	228B22	339933
fuchsia	255 - 0 - 255	FF00FF	FF00FF
gainsboro	220 - 220 - 220	DCDCDC	CCCCCC*
ghostwhite	248 - 248 - 255	F8F8FF	FFFFFF
gold	255 - 215 - 0	FFD700	FFCC00
goldenrod	218 - 165 - 32	DAA520	CC9933
gray	128 - 128 - 128	808080	999999*
green	0 - 128 - 0	008000	009900
greenyellow	173 - 255 - 47	ADFF2F	99FF33
honeydew	240 - 255 - 240	F0FFF0	FFFFFF
hotpink	255 - 105 - 180	FF69B4	FF66CC
indianred	205 - 92 - 92	CD5C5C	CC6666
indigo	75 - 0 - 130	4B0082	330099
ivory	255 - 240 - 240	FFF0F0	FFFFFF
khaki	240 - 230 - 140	F0D58C	FFCC99
lavender	230 - 230 - 250	E6E6FA	FFFFFF*
lavenderblush	255 - 240 - 245	FFF0F5	FFFFFF
lawngreen	124 - 252 - 0	7CFC00	00FF00
lemonchiffon	255 - 250 - 205	FFFACD	FFFFCC
lightblue	173 - 216 - 230	ADD8E6	99CCFF
lightcoral	240 - 128 - 128	F08080	FF9999
lightcyan	224 - 255 - 255	E0FFFF	FFFFFF
lightgoldenrodyellow	250 - 250 - 210	FAFAD2	FFFFCC
lightgreen	144 - 238 - 144	90EE90	99FF99
lightgrey	211 - 211 - 211	D3D3D3	CCCCCC*
lightpink	255 - 182 - 193	FFB6C1	FFFFCC
lightsalmon	255 - 160 - 122	FFA07A	FF9966

Table 5-2: Color Names with their Numeric Values (continued)

Color Name	RGB Values	Hexadecimal	Nearest Web-safe Color
lightseagreen	32 - 178 - 170	20B2AA	33CC99
lightskyblue	135 - 206 - 250	87CEFA	99CCFF
lightslategray	119 - 136 - 153	778899	669999
lightsteelblue	176 - 196 - 222	B0C4DE	CCCCCC
lightyellow	255 - 255 - 224	FFFFE0	FFFFFF
lime	0 - 255 - 0	00FF00	00FF00
limegreen	50 - 205 - 50	32CD32	33CC33
linen	250 - 240 - 230	FAF0E6	FFFFFF
magenta	255 - 0 - 255	FF00FF	FF00FF
maroon	128 - 0 - 0	800000	990000*
mediumaquamarine	102 - 205 - 170	66CDAA	66CC99
mediumblue	0 - 0 - 205	0000CD	0000CC
mediumorchid	186 - 85 - 211	BA55D3	CC66CC
mediumpurple	147 - 112 - 219	9370DB	9966CC
mediumseagreen	60 - 179 - 113	3CB371	33CC66
mediumslateblue	123 - 104 - 238	7B68EE	6666FF
mediumspringgreen	0 - 250 - 154	00FA9A	00FF99
mediumturquoise	72 - 209 - 204	48D1CC	33CCCC
mediumvioletred	199 - 21 - 133	C71585	CC0066
midnightblue	25 - 25 - 112	191970	000066*
mintcream	245 - 255 - 250	F5FFFA	FFFFFF
mistyrose	255 - 228 - 225	FFE4E1	FFFFFF*
moccasin	255 - 228 - 181	FFE4B5	FFFFCC
navajowhite	255 - 222 - 173	FFDEAD	FFCC99
navy	0 - 0 - 128	000080	009999*
oldlace	253 - 245 - 230	FDF5E6	FFFFFF
olive	128 - 128 - 0	808000	999900
olivedrab	107 - 142 - 35	6B8E23	669933
orange	255 - 165 - 0	FFA500	FF9900
orangered	255 - 69 - 0	FF4500	FF3300
orchid	218 - 112 - 214	DA70D6	CC66CC
palegoldenrod	238 - 232 - 170	EEE8AA	FFFF99
palegreen	152 - 251 - 152	98FB98	99FF99
paleturquoise	175 - 238 - 238	AFEEEE	99FFFF
palevioletred	219 - 112 - 147	DB7093	CC6699
papayawhip	255 - 239 - 213	FFEFD5	FFFFCC
peachpuff	255 - 218 - 185	FFDAB9	FFCCCC
peru	205 - 133 - 63	CD853F	CC9933

Table 5-2: Color Names with their Numeric Values (continued)

Color Name	RGB Values	Hexadecimal	Nearest Web-safe Color
pink	255 - 192 - 203	FFC0CB	FFCCCC
plum	221 - 160 - 221	DDA0DD	CC99CC
powderblue	176 - 224 - 230	B0E0E6	CCFFFF
purple	128 - 0 - 128	800080	990099
red	255 - 0 - 0	FF0000	FF0000
rosybrown	188 - 143 - 143	BC8F8F	CC9999
royalblue	65 - 105 - 225	4169E1	3366FF
saddlebrown	139 - 69 - 19	8B4513	993300
salmon	250 - 128 - 114	FA8072	FF9966
sandybrown	244 - 164 - 96	F4A460	FF9966
seagreen	46 - 139 - 87	2E8B57	339966
seashell	255 - 245 - 238	FFF5EE	FFFFFF
sienna	160 - 82 - 45	A0522D	996633
silver	192 - 192 - 192	C0C0C0	CCCCCC
skyblue	135 - 206 - 235	87CEEB	99CCFF
slateblue	106 - 90 - 205	6A5ACD	6666CC
slategray	112 - 128 - 144	708090	669999
snow	255 - 250 - 250	FFFAFA	FFFFFF
springgreen	0 - 255 - 127	00FF7F	00FF66
steelblue	70 - 130 - 180	4682B4	3399CC
tan	210 - 180 - 140	D2B48C	CCCC99
teal	0 - 128 - 128	008080	009999
thistle	216 - 191 - 216	D8BFD8	CCCCCC*
tomato	253 - 99 - 71	FF6347	FF6633
turquoise	64 - 224 - 208	40E0D0	33FFCC
violet	238 - 130 - 238	EE82EE	FF99FF
wheat	245 - 222 - 179	F5DEB3	FFCCCC
white	255 - 255 - 255	FFFFFF	FFFFFF
whitesmoke	245 - 245 - 245	F5F5F5	FFFFFF
yellow	255 - 255 - 0	FFFF00	FFFF00
yellowgreen	154 - 205 - 50	9ACD32	66CC33

* These color names shift to the nearest Mac system palette color when viewed on a Macintosh using any browser except Netscape Navigator 4.0 (which shifts it to the nearest Web Palette color).

Table 5-3: Web Color Names by Hue

black
white

Neutrals—cool

darkgray
darkslategray
dimgray
gainsboro
ghostwhite
gray
lightgray
lightslategray
silver
slategray
snow

Neutrals—warm

antiquewhite
cornsilk
floralwhite
ivory
linen
oldlace
papayawhip
seashell

Browns/Tans

bisque
beige
blanchedalmond
brown
burlywood
chocolate
khaki
moccasin
navahowhite
peru
rosybrown
sandybrown
sienna

tan
wheat

Oranges

darkorange
orange
orangered
peachpuff

Yellows

darkgoldenrod
gold
goldenrod
lemonchiffon
lightgoldenrodyellow
lightyellow
palegoldenrod
yellow

Greens

aquamarine
chartreuse
darkgreen
darkkhaki
darkolivegreen
darkseagreen
forestgreen
green
greenyellow
honeydew
lawn green
lightgreen
lime
limegreen
mediumseagreen
mediumspringgreen
mintgreen
olive
olivedrab
palegreen

seagreen
springgreen
yellowgreen

Blue-greens

aqua
cyan
darkcyan
darkturquoise
lightcyan
lightseagreen
mediumaquamarine
mediumturquoise
paleturquoise
turquoise

Blues

aliceblue
azure
blue
cadetblue
cornflowerblue
darkblue
darkslateblue
deepskyblue
dodgerblue
indigo
lightblue
lightskyblue
lightsteelblue
mediumblue
mediumslateblue
midnightblue
navy
powderblue
skyblue
slateblue
steelblue

Table 5-3: Web Color Names by Hue (continued)

Purples		
blueviolet	palevioletred	lightsalmon
darkmagenta	plum	magenta
darkorchid	purple	mistyrose
darkviolet	thistle	pink
fuchsia	violet	salmon
lavender		
lavenderblush	**Pinks**	**Reds**
mediumorchid	coral	crimson
mediumpurple	darksalmon	darkred
mediumvioletred	deeppink	firebrick
orchid	hotpink	indianred
	lightcoral	maroon
	lightpink	red

Coloring Page Elements

Table 5-4 lists the HTML elements for which you can specify a color. Each tag's use is further explained in Chapters 6, 7, and 10 of this book.

Table 5-4: Summary of HTML Tags with Color Attributes

Tag	Attribute	Description
`<BODY>`	`BGCOLOR=color`	Document background
`<BODY>`	`TEXT=color`	Regular text
`<BODY>`	`LINK=color`	Hypertext link
`<BODY>`	`VLINK=color`	Visited link
`<BODY>`	`ALINK=color`	Active link
`<FONT>`	`COLOR=color`	Colors a selection of text
`<BASEFONT>`	`COLOR=color`	Colors the following block of text (IE only)
`<TR>`	`BGCOLOR=color`	Table row background
`<TD>`	`BGCOLOR=color`	Table cell background
`<TH>`	`BGCOLOR=color`	Table header background

Character Entities

Characters not found in the normal alphanumeric character set, such as © or &, must be specified in HTML using *character entities*. Using keyboard commands (such as Option-g for the © symbol) within your HTML document will not produce the character when the document is rendered in a browser (in fact, the browser will generally display the numeric entity for the character).

Character entities can be defined by name (`&name;`) or by numeric value (`&#nnn;`). The browser interprets the string to display the proper character. Named entities are preferable because numeric values may be interpreted differently on different platforms.

Table 5-5 presents the defined standard, proposed, and several nonstandard, but generally supported, character entities for HTML. Not all 256 characters in the ISO character set appear in the table. Missing ones are not recognized by the browser as either named or numeric entities.

Entities for which the conformance column is blank are part of the HTML 2.0 and later standards and will work with nearly all available browsers. Characters whose conformance column contains "4.0" are supported in the HTML 4.0 Specification only. As of this writing, they are supported by versions 4.0 of Netscape Navigator and Internet Explorer. An "N" in the conformance column indicates that the character is a nonstandard entity.

Table 5-5: Character Entities

Number	Name	Symbol	Description	Conformance
				Horizontal tab	

			Line feed	

			Carriage return	
 			Space	
!		!	Exclamation point	
"	"	"	Quotation mark	
#		#	Hash mark	
$		$	Dollar sign	
%		%	Percent sign	
&	&	&	Ampersand	
'		'	Apostrophe	
(		(	Left parenthesis	
)		)	Right parenthesis	
*		*	Asterisk	
+		+	Plus sign	
,		,	Comma	
-		-	Hyphen	
.		.	Period	
/		/	Slash	
0–9		0-9	Digits 0-9	
:		:	Colon	
;		;	Semicolon	
<	<	<	Less than	
=		=	Equal sign	
>	>	>	Greater than	
?		?	Question mark	
@		@	Commercial at sign	
A–Z		A – Z	Letters A – Z	

Table 5-5: Character Entities (continued)

Number	Name	Symbol	Description	Conformance
[		[	Left square bracket	
\		\	Backslash	
]		]	Right square bracket	
^		^	Caret	
_		_	Underscore	
`		`	Grave accent	
a–z		a-z	Letters a – z	
{		{	Left curly brace	
|		|	Vertical bar	
}		}	Right curly brace	
~		~	Tilde	
‚		,	Comma	N
ƒ		ƒ	Florin	N
„		„	Right double quote	N
…		…	Elipsis	N
†		†	Dagger	N
‡		‡	Double dagger	N
ˆ		ˆ	Circumflex	N
‰		‰	Permil	N
Š		_	Underscore	N
‹		<	Less than sign	N
Œ		Œ	Capital OE ligature	N
‘		'	Left single quote	N
’		'	Right single quote	N
“		"	Left double quote	N
”		„	Right double quote	N
•		•	Bullet	N
–		–	En dash	N
—		—	Em dash	N
˜		~	Tilde	N
™		™	Trademark	N
š		_	Underscore	N
›		>	Greater than sign	N
œ		œ	Lowercase oe ligature	N
Ÿ		Ÿ	Capital Y, umlaut	N
			Nonbreaking space	4.0
¡	¡	¡	Inverted exlamation mark	4.0
¢	¢	¢	Cent sign	4.0

Table 5-5: Character Entities (continued)

Number	Name	Symbol	Description	Conformance
£	£	₤	Pound sign	4.0
¤	¤	¤	General currency symbol	4.0
¥	¥	¥	Yen sign	4.0
¦	¦	¦	Broken vertical bar	4.0
§	§	§	Section sign	4.0
¨	¨	¨	Umlaut	4.0
©	©	©	Copyright	4.0
ª	ª	ª	Feminine ordinal	4.0
«	«	«	Left angle quote	4.0
¬	¬	¬	Not sign	4.0
­	­	–	Soft hyphen	4.0
®	®	®	Registered trademark	4.0
¯	¯	¯	Macron accent	4.0
°	°	°	Degree sign	4.0
±	±	±	Plus or minus	4.0
²	²	2	Superscript 2	4.0
³	³	3	Superscript 3	4.0
´	´	´	Acute accent	4.0
µ	µ	µ	Micro sign (Greek mu)	4.0
¶	¶	¶	Paragraph sign	4.0
·	·	·	Middle dot	4.0
¸	¸	¸	Cedilla	4.0
¹	¹	1	Superscript 1	4.0
º	º	º	Masculine ordinal	4.0
»	»	»	Right angle quote	4.0
¼	¼	1/4	Fraction one-fourth	4.0
½	½	1/2	Fraction one-half	4.0
¾	¾	3/4	Fraction three-fourths	4.0
¿	¿	¿	Inverted question mark	4.0
À	À	À	Capital A, grave accent	
Á	Á	Á	Capital A, acute accent	
Â	Â	Â	Capital A, circumflex accent	
Ã	Ã	Ã	Capital A, tilde accent	
Ä	Ä	Ä	Capital A, umlaut	
Å	&Aring	Å	Capital A, ring	
Æ	Æ	Æ	Capital AE ligature	
Ç	Ç	Ç	Capital C, cedilla	
È	&Egrave	È	Capital E, grave accent	

Table 5-5: Character Entities (continued)

Number	Name	Symbol	Description	Conformance
É	É	É	Capital E, acute accent	
Ê	Ê	Ê	Capital E, circumflex accent	
Ë	Ë	Ë	Capital E, umlaut	
Ì	Ì	Ì	Capital I, grave accent	
Í	Í	Í	Capital I, acute accent	
Î	Î	Î	Capital I, circumflex accent	
Ï	Ï	Ï	Capital I, umlaut	
Ð	Ð	Ð	Capital eth, Icelandic	
Ñ	Ñ	Ñ	Capital N, tilde	
Ò	Ò	Ò	Capital O, grave accent	
Ó	Ó	Ó	Capital O, acute accent	
Ô	Ô	Ô	Capital O, circumflex accent	
Õ	Õ	Õ	Capital O, tilde accent	
Ö	Ö	Ö	Capital O, umlaut	
×	×	×	Multiply sign	4.0
Ø	Ø	Ø	Capital O, slash	
Ù	Ù	Ù	Capital U, grave accent	
Ú	Ú	Ú	Capital U, acute accent	
Û	Û	Û	Capital U, circumflex	
Ü	Ü	Ü	Capital U, umlaut	
Ý	Ý	Ý	Capital Y, acute accent	
Þ	Þ	Þ	Capital Thorn, Icelandic	
ß	ß	ß	Small sz ligature, German	
à	à	à	Small a, grave accent	
á	á	á	Small a, acute accent	
â	â	â	Small a, circumflex accent	
ã	ã	ã	Small a, tilde	
ä	ä	ä	Small a, umlaut	
å	å	å	Small a, ring	
æ	æ	æ	Small ae ligature	
ç	ç	ç	Small c, cedilla	
è	è	è	Small e, grave accent	
é	é	é	Small e, acute accent	
ê	ê	ê	Small e, circumflex accent	
ë	ë	ë	Small e, umlaut accent	
ì	ì	ì	Small i, grave accent	
í	í	í	Small i, acute accent	

Table 5-5: Character Entities (continued)

Number	Name	Symbol	Description	Conformance
î	î	î	Small i, circumflex accent	
ï	ï	ï	Small i, umlaut	
ð	ð	∂	Small eth, icelandic	
ñ	ñ	ñ	Small n, tilde	
ò	ò	ò	Small o, grave accent	
ó	ó	ó	Small o, acute accent	
ô	ô	ô	Small o, circumflex accent	
õ	õ	õ	Small o, tilde	
ö	ö	ö	Small o, umlaut	
÷	÷	÷	Division sign	4.0
ø	ø	ø	Small o, slash	
ù	ù	ù	Small u, grave accent	
ú	ú	ú	Small u, acute accent	
û	û	û	Small u, circumflex accent	
ü	ü	ü	Small u, umlaut	
ý	ý	ý	Small y, acute accent	
þ	&thorn	þ	Small thorn, Icelandic	
ÿ	&yuml	ÿ	Small y, umlaut	

HTML Resources in This Book

In addition to the detailed descriptions of HTML tags and their use in the following eight chapters, there are several appendixes at the end of the book that provide a quick reference for the entire set of HTML tags, sliced a number of different ways.

Appendix A, *HTML Tags and Elements*

> This is an alphabetical listing of all the currently available HTML tags mentioned in this book. It includes all the tags listed in the HTML 4.0 Specification (including the complete list of attributes for each tag), tags in current use that are not specifically mentioned in the 4.0 Spec, and all browser-specific tags and attributes. It also provides chapter and page references so you can look up the detailed information for each tag quickly.

Appendix B, *List of Attributes*

> This is a listing of every available attribute as published by the HTML 4.0 Specification. It indicates in which tags the attribute can be used, whether it is optional or required, and whether it has been deprecated by the HTML 4.0 Specification.

Appendix C, *Deprecated Tags*

> This appendix lists all of the tags and attributes that have been officially deprecated by the W3C in the HTML 4.0 Specification. Deprecated tags are still supported by browsers for backward-compatibility, but are discouraged from use. Most attributes are deprecated in favor of style sheet controls. The table also lists recommended substitutes when noted by the W3C.

Appendix D, *Proprietary Tags*

Here's where you'll find the list of tags supported only in Internet Explorer or Netscape Navigator.

Appendix E, *CSS Compatibility*

This appendix lists all elements in the Cascading Style Sheets specification and notes how well Navigator and Internet Explorer support them.

CHAPTER 6

Structural HTML Tags

This chapter looks at the subset of HTML tags that is used primarily to give the document structure. It also discusses tags that are used for providing information about the document and those used for controlling its appearance or function on a global level.

Summary of Structural Tags

In this section, browser support for each tag is noted to the right of the tag name. Browsers that do not support the tag are grayed out. Browsers that deprecate the tag are noted with a superscript D. Tag usage is indicated below the tag name. A more thorough listing of attributes for each tag, according to the HTML 4.0 Specification, appears in Appendix A, *HTML Tags and Elements*.

<base>   NN: 2, 3, 4 - MSIE: 2, 3, 4, 5 - HTML 4 - WebTV - Opera3

```
<base>
```

Specifies the base URL for all relative URLs in the document. Place this within the `<head>` of the document.

Attributes

`href=url`
> Specifies the URL to be used.

`target=name`
> Defines the default target window for all links in the document. Often used to target frames. *This attribute is not supported in MSIE 2.0*

```
<body>...</body>
```

Defines the beginning and the end of the document body. The body contains the content of the document (the part that is displayed in the browser window). Attributes to the <body> tag affect the entire document.

Attributes

alink="#*rrggbb*" or *color name*
> Sets the color of active links (i.e., the color while the mouse button is held down during a "click"). Color is specified in hexadecimal RGB values or by standard web color name. Chapter 5, *HTML Overview*, explains how to specify color in HTML.

background=*url*
> Provides the URL to a graphic file to be used as a tiling graphic in the background of the document.

bgcolor="#*rrggbb*" or *color name*
> Sets the color of the background for the document. Color is specified in hexadecimal RGB values or by standard web color name.

link="#*rrggbb*" or *color name*
> Sets the default color for all the links in the document. Color is specified in hexadecimal RGB values or by standard web color name.

text="#*rrggbb*" or *color name*
> Sets the default color for all the text in the document. Color is specified in hexadecimal RGB values or by standard web color name.

vlink="#*rrggbb*" or *color name*
> Sets the color of the visited links for the document. Color is specified in hexadecimal RGB values or by standard web color name.

Netscape Navigator 4.0 only

marginwidth=*number*
> Specifies the distance (in number of pixels) between the left browser edge and the beginning of the text and graphics in the window.

marginheight=*number*
> Specifies the distance (in number of pixels) between the top edge of the browser and the top edge of text or graphics in the window.

Internet Explorer only

bgproperties="fixed"
> When set to "fixed," the background image does not scroll with the document content.

leftmargin=*number*
> Specifies the distance (in number of pixels) between the left browser edge and the beginning of the text and graphics in the window.

`topmargin=number`

Specifies the distance (in number of pixels) between the top edge of the browser and the top edge of text or graphics in the window.

<head>   NN: 2, 3, 4 · MSIE: 2, 3, 4, 5 · HTML 4 · WebTV · Opera3

`<head>...</head>`

Defines the head (also called "header") portion of the document that contains information about the document. The `<head>` tag has no attributes, but serves only as a container for the other header tags, such as `<base>`, `<meta>`, and `<title>`.

<html>   NN: 2, 3, 4 · MSIE: 2, 3, 4, 5 · HTML 4 · WebTV · Opera3

`<html>...</html>`

Placed at the beginning and end of the document, this tag tells the browser that the entire document is composed in HTML.

<link>   NN: 2, 3, 4 · MSIE: 2, 3, 4, 5 · HTML 4 · WebTV · Opera3

`<link>`

Defines a relationship between the current document and another document. This tag goes within the `<head>` portion of the document. It is often used to refer to an external stylesheet.

Attributes

`href=url`

Identifies the target document.

`methods=list`

Specifies a browser-dependent list of comma-separated display methods for this link. It is not commonly used.

`rev=relation`

Specifies the relationship from the target document to the source.

`rel=relation`

Specifies the relationship from the current source document to the target.

`rel=stylesheet`

This attribute is used within the `<link>` tag to create a relationship with an external stylesheet.

`title=text`

Provides a title for the target document.

`type=resource`

Shows the type of an outside link. The value `text/css` indicates that the linked document is an external cascading style sheet.

urn=*urn*

Defines a location-independent Universal Resource Name (URN) for the referenced document. The actual syntax of the URN has not been defined, making this more of a placeholder for future versions of HTML.

<meta> NN: 2, 3, 4 · MSIE: 2, 3, 4, 5 · HTML 4 · WebTV · Opera3

`<meta>`

Provides additional information about the document. It should be placed within the `<head>` tags at the beginning of the document. It is commonly used for making documents searchable (by adding keywords) and may be used for client-pull functions. Meta tags are discussed at the end of this chapter.

Attributes

content=*text*

Specifies the value of the meta tag and is always used in conjunction with name= or http-equiv=.

http-equiv=*text*

Specifies information to be included in the HTTP header that the server appends to the document. It is used in conjunction with the name attribute.

name=*text*

Specifies a name for the meta information.

scheme=*text*

Provides additional information for the interpretation of meta data. This is a new attribute introduced in HTML 4.0.

<title> NN: 2, 3, 4 · MSIE: 2, 3, 4, 5 · HTML 4 · WebTV · Opera3

`<title>...</title>`

Specifies the title of the document. The title generally appears in the top bar of the browser window.

Setting Up an HTML Document

The standard skeletal structure of an HTML document is as follows:

```
<HTML>
<HEAD><TITLE>Document Title</TITLE></HEAD>
<BODY>Contents of Document</BODY>
</HTML>
```

The HTML standard requires that the entire document appear within the `<html>` container, however, most browsers can properly display the contents of the document even if these tags are omitted. All HTML documents are made up of two main structures, the *head* (also called the "header") and the *body*. The exception to this rule is when the document contains a *frameset* in place of the body. For more information, see Chapter 11, *Frames.*

The Document Header

The header, delimited by the `<head>` tag, contains information that describes the HTML document. The head tag has no attributes of its own, but merely serves as a container for other tags that help define and manage the document's contents.

Titles

The most commonly used element within the header is the document title (within `<title>` tags, as shown in the example above), which provides a description of the page's contents. The title is also used as the name of the link as displayed in a user's bookmarks or "hot list." Search engines rely heavily on document titles as well. For all these reasons, it is important to provide thoughtful and descriptive titles for all your documents and avoid vague titles such as "Welcome," or "My Page."

Other header elements

Other useful HTML elements are also placed within the `<head>` tags of a document:

`<base>`

> This tag establishes the document's base location, which serves as a reference for all the links in the document. For more information, see Chapter 8, *Creating Links*.

`<link>`

> This tag defines the relationship between the current document and another document. Although it can signify relationships such as index, next, and previous, it is most often used today to link a document to an external style sheet (see Chapter 23, *Cascading Style Sheets*).

`<meta>`

> "Meta" tags are used to provide information about a document, such as keywords or descriptions to aid search engines. It may also be used for client-pull functions. The `<meta>` tag is discussed later in this chapter.

`<script>`

> JavaScripts and VBScripts may be added to the document within its header.

`<style>`

> Embedded style sheets must be added to the document header by placing the `<style>` element within the `<head>` container. For more information, see Chapter 23).

The Document Body

The document body, delimited by `<body>` tags, contains the contents of the document—the part that you want to display in the browser window.

The body of an HTML document might consist of just a few paragraphs of text, a single image, or a complex combination of text, images, tables, and multimedia objects. What you put on the page is up to you.

Global Settings with the \<body> Tag

The \<body> tag, originally designed to delimit the body of the document, has been extended to include controls for the backgrounds and text colors of a document. These settings are global, meaning they will apply to the entire document.

Colors

You can use the \<body> tag to set colors for the background and text elements (see Table 6-1). Specified link colors apply to linked text, but also to the border around linked graphics. (To learn how to specify color in HTML, see Chapter 5.)

Table 6-1: Attributes for Specifying Colors with the \<body> Tag

Page Element	HTML TAG	Description
Background color	`<BODY BGCOLOR="color">`	Sets the color for the background of the entire page.
Regular text	`<BODY TEXT="color">`	Sets the color for all the regular text in the document. The default color for text is black.
Links	`<BODY LINK="color">`	Sets the color for hyperlinks. The default color for links is blue.
Visited link	`<BODY VLINK="color">`	Sets the color for links that have already been clicked. The default color for visited links is purple.
Active link	`<BODY ALINK="color">`	Sets the color for a link while it is in the process of being clicked. The default color for an active link is red.

A single \<body> tag can contain a number of specific attributes, as shown here:

```
<BODY BGCOLOR="color" TEXT="color" LINK="color" VLINK="color"
ALINK="color">
```

Tiling Background Graphics

You've probably seen web pages that have a graphic image repeating behind the text. These are called *background tiles*, or *tiling graphics*, and they are added to the document via the \<body> tag using the `background` attribute and the URL of the graphic as follows:

```
<BODY BACKGROUND="background.gif">
```

Any web-based graphic file format (such as GIF or JPEG) can be used as a background tile (some new browsers even support animated GIFs in the background). Following are a few guidelines and tips regarding the use of background tiles:

- Use graphics that won't interfere with the legibility of the text over it.

- Keep file sizes small. As usual for the web, it is important to keep the file size as small as possible for background graphics, which often lag behind the display of the rest of the page. Effective stripe effects can be created by repeating a graphic that is very wide, but only one pixel high (or vice versa).

- Provide a background color specification in the <body> tag that will display while the background image downloads. In some cases, the background graphic may be the last element to display on the page while background colors display almost instantly. It is a nice trick to specify a background color that matches the overall intensity and hue of your background graphic, to at least set the mood while users wait for the background image to load. This is particularly useful if you've got light-colored text or graphics matched to the background graphic which will look unreadable or just ugly against the interim default gray browser background.

- If you want the color of the background image to match other graphics positioned inline in the web page, be sure that they are saved in the same graphic file formats. Because browsers interpret colors differently for JPEGs and GIFs, the file formats need to match in order for the colors to match seamlessly (GIF with GIF, JPEG with JPEG).

- Non-web-safe colors (colors not found in the Web Palette) are handled differently for background images than they are for foreground images when the page is displayed on an 8-bit monitor. This makes it very difficult to match inline images to the background seamlessly, even when the graphics use the exact same color (or even when using the same graphic in both places).

  To make matters worse, the way they are handled differs from browser to browser. For instance, on the Mac, Netscape dithers the foreground graphic but shifts the background graphic to its nearest Web Palette value. In Internet Explorer, just the opposite happens: the background image dithers and the foreground image shifts. If you are trying to create a seamless effect, either make your foreground images transparent or stick diligently to the colors in the Web Palette.

  The Web Palette is explained in the section "Color in Browsers—The Web Palette" in Chapter 3, *Web Design Principles for Print Designers*, and further in Chapter 17, *Designing Graphics with the Web Palette*.

Adjusting Browser Margins

By default, browsers allow a margin of 10 to 12 pixels (depending on the browser and platform) between the browser window and the document's contents. It is possible to add attributes to the <body> tag to increase or decrease the margin width. The margin may be removed completely, allowing objects to sit flush against the window, by setting the attribute values to 0.

The drawback is that Internet Explorer and Netscape Navigator use different attributes to control margins. In addition, Netscape's tags only work with version 4.0 and higher. If you want to reach a broader audience, you can use frames for a similar effect (see "Frame Margins" in Chapter 11).

IE uses the attributes `leftmargin` (affects space on left and right) and `topmargin` (affects space on top and bottom). Navigator 4.0 uses the more standard `margin-width` and `marginheight` for the same measurements, respectively. To set margins for both browsers, it is necessary to use all four attributes. In the following example, the margins are turned off for both browsers by setting the margins to 0:

```
<BODY MARGINWIDTH=0 MARGINHEIGHT=0 LEFTMARGIN=0 TOPMARGIN=0>
```

Using <meta> Tags

The `<meta>` tag has a wide variety of applications, but is primarily used to include information about a document, such as the creation date, author, or copyright information. The data included in a `<meta>` tag is useful for servers, web browsers, and search engines but is invisible to the reader. It must always be placed within the `<head>` of the document.

A document may have any number of `<meta>` tags. There are two types of `<meta>` tags, using either the `name` or `http-equiv` attribute. In each case, the `content` attribute is necessary to provide a value (or values) for the named information or function. The examples below show basic `<meta>` tag syntax. In the following sections, we will look at each type of meta tag and its uses.

```
<META HTTP-EQUIV="name" CONTENT="content">
<META NAME="name" CONTENT="content">
```

The http-equiv Attribute

Information provided by an `http-equiv` attribute is added to the HTTP response header. The HTTP header contains information the server passes to the browser just before it sends the HTML document. It contains MIME type information and other values that affect the action of the browser. Therefore, the `http-equiv` attribute provides information that somehow affects the way the browser handles your document.

There are a large number of predefined `http-equiv` types available. This section will look at just a few of the most useful. For a complete listing, see the Dictionary of HTML META Tags at *http://vancouver-webpages.com/META/*.

Meta tags for client-pull

Client-pull refers to the ability of the browser (the client) to automatically request (pull) a new document from the server. The effect for the user is that the page displays, and after a period of time, automatically refreshes with new information or is replaced by an entirely new page. If you string documents with client-pull instructions and set very short time intervals, you can create a sort of slide show effect. Client-pull was once used for rudimentary animation in the early days of the Web, but now that there are better alternatives the client-pull method is rarely used for animation. Client-pull is still a handy technique for redirecting old URLs to new ones. If you retire content at a given URL, you may want to redirect users to a different page, rather than just allowing a 404 error.

Client-pull uses the **refresh** attribute value, first introduced by Netscape. It tells the browser to wait a specified number of seconds (indicated by an integer in the content attribute) and then load a new page. If no page is specified, the browser will just reload the current page. The following example instructs the browser to reload the page after 15 seconds (we can assume there's something fancy happening on the server side that puts updated information in the HTML document):

```
<META HTTP-EQUIV="refresh" CONTENT="15">
```

To reload a different file, provide the URL for the document within the content attribute as shown below:

```
<META HTTP-EQUIV="refresh" CONTENT="1; URL=http://nextdocument.
html">
```

Note that there is only a single set of quotation marks around the value for **content**. Although URLs usually require their own quotation marks, these are omitted within the context of the content attribute.

To create a slide-show effect, add a **meta refresh** tag in the <head> of each document that points to the next HTML document in the sequence. You can set the time interval to as many seconds as you like; setting it to 0 will trigger the next page as soon as the current page has downloaded. Bear in mind, however, the actual amount of time the page takes to refresh is dependent on complex factors of file size, server speed, and general web traffic.

In the following example, three files are coded to loop endlessly at five-second intervals:

Document *1.html* contains:

```
<META HTTP-EQUIV="refresh" CONTENT="5; URL=2.html">
```

Document *2.html* contains:

```
<META HTTP-EQUIV="refresh" CONTENT="5; URL=3.html">
```

Document *3.html* contains a tag which points back to *1.html*:

```
<META HTTP-EQUIV="refresh" CONTENT="5; URL=1.html">
```

Other uses

expires

Indicates the date and time after which the document should be considered expired. Web robots may use this information to delete expired documents from a search engine index.

```
<META HTTP-EQUIV="expires" CONTENT="July 16, 1998 06:27:00
EST">
```

content-type

The content-type **text/html** is automatically added to the HTTP header for HTML documents, but this attribute can be extended to include the character set for the document. This causes the browser to load the appropriate character set before displaying the page.

This is part of the HTML 4.0 measures to internationalize the Web. You can read more about identifying character sets in Chapter 27, *Internationalization*.

```
<META HTTP-EQUIV="content-type" CONTENT="text/html;
charset=SHIFT_JIS">
```

content-language

This may be used to identify the language in which the document is written. Like the character set extension mentioned above, it is part of the ongoing effort to internationalize the Web. The browser can send a corresponding "Accept-Language" header, which causes the server to choose the document with the appropriate language specified in its <meta> tag.

For more information on internationalization, as well as for a listing of 2-letter language codes, see Chapter 27.

This example tells the browser that the document's natural language is French:

```
<META HTTP-EQUIV="content-language" CONTENT="fr">
```

Inserting Meta-Information with the name Attribute

The name attribute is used to insert hidden information about the document that does not correspond to HTTP headers. For example:

```
<META NAME="author" CONTENT="Jennifer Niederst">
<META NAME="copyright" CONTENT="1998, O'Reilly & Associates">
```

You can make up your own <meta> names, or use one of the names put forth by search engine and browser companies for standardized use. Just a few of the accepted and more useful <meta> names are discussed in the following sections. For a complete listing of possible name types, see the Dictionary of HTML META Tags at *http://vancouver-webpages.com/META/*.

Meta tags for search engines

The popular search engines Infoseek and AltaVista introduced several <meta> names that aid their search engines in finding pages. Note that not all search engines use meta data, but adding them to your document won't hurt. There is a blurry distinction between name and http-equiv, so most of these meta names will also work as http-equiv definitions.

description

This provides a brief, plain-language description of the contents of your web page, which is particularly useful if your document contains little text, is a frameset, or has extensive scripts at the top of the HTML document. Search engines that recognize the description may display it in the search results page. Some search engines use only the first 20 words of descriptions, so get to the point quickly.

```
<META NAME="description" CONTENT="Jennifer Niederst's resume
and web design samples">
```

keywords

You can supplement the title and description of the document by providing a list of comma-separated keywords that would be useful in indexing your document.

```
<META name="keywords" content="designer, web design, training,
interface design">
```

author

Identifies the author of the web page.

```
<META NAME="author" CONTENT="Jennifer Niederst">
```

copyright

Identifies the copyright information for the document.

```
<META NAME="copyright" CONTENT="1998, O'Reilly & Associates">
```

robots

This tag was created as an alternative to the *robots.txt* file and is mainly used as a way to prevent your page from being indexed by search engine "spiders." It is not well supported, but some people like to include it anyway. The content attribute can take the following values: index (the default), noindex (prevents indexing), nofollow (prevents the search engine from following links on the page), and none (the same as setting "noindex, nofollow").

```
<META NAME="robots" CONTENT="noindex, nofollow">
```

Other uses

rating

This provides a method of rating the content of a web page to indicate its appropriateness for kids. The four available ratings are general, mature, restricted, and 14 years.

```
<META NAME="rating" CONTENT="general">
```

generator (or formatter for FrontPage)

Many HTML authoring tools add an indication of the name and version of the creation tool. This is used by tools vendors to assess market penetration.

```
<META NAME="generator" CONTENT="Adobe PageMill">
```

Structural Tags

CHAPTER 7

Formatting Text

Designers accustomed to desktop publishing programs are usually shocked to find how little control HTML offers over the display of the page. Before you get too frustrated, bear in mind that HTML was not developed as a method for dictating presentation, but rather as a means of marking the structure of a document.

In fact, the tags that do provide specific display information (`<center>`, for example) are usually just bastardizations of the pure HTML concept. One day, we'll put all of our style and presentation information in style sheets and leave HTML markup to work as originally designed. But that's another story (one told in Chapter 23, *Cascading Style Sheets*).

This chapter looks at the nature of text in web pages and reviews the HTML tags related to the display of text elements.

Summary of Text Tags

This section is a listing of tags used for formatting text. It is divided into the following subgroups:

- Paragraphs and Headings (Block-Level Elements)
- Text Appearance (Inline Styles)
- Spacing and Positioning
- Lists

Browser support for each tag is noted to the right of the tag name. Browsers that do not support the tag are grayed out. Browsers that deprecate the tag are noted with a superscript D. Tag usage is indicated below the tag name. A more thorough listing of attributes for each tag, according to the HTML 4.0 Specification, appears in Appendix A, *HTML Tags and Elements*.

Paragraphs and Headings (Block-Level Elements)

Block-level elements are always formatted with a line-break before and after, with most adding some amount of additional space above and below as well. The most commonly used block elements are paragraphs (`<p>`), headings (`<h1...h6>`), and blockquotes (`<blockquote>`).

Lists and list items are also block-level elements, but they have been grouped in their own section below.

<address>   NN: 2, 3, 4 · MSIE: 2, 3, 4, 5 · HTML 4 · WebTV · Opera3

`<address>...</address>`

Identifies ownership or authorship information, typically at the beginning or end of a document. Addresses are generally formatted in italic type with a line break (but no extra space) above and below.

<blockquote>   NN: 2, 3, 4 · MSIE: 2, 3, 4, 5 · HTML 4 · WebTV · Opera3

`<blockquote>...</blockquote>`

Enclosed text is a blockquote, which is generally displayed with an indent on the left and right margins and added space above and below the paragraph.

Note that:

- Some older browsers display blockquote material in italic, making it difficult to read.

- Browsers are inconsistent in the way they display images within blockquotes. Some align the graphic with the indented blockquote margin; others align the image with the normal margin of paragraph text. It is a good idea to test on a variety of browsers.

<div>   NN: 2, 3, 4 · MSIE: 2, 3, 4, 5 · HTML 4 · WebTV · Opera3

`<div>...</div>`

Denotes the beginning and end of a division of the page. First introduced in HTML 3.2 as a way to define a unique style for each division, only the alignment function (using the `align` attribute) was implemented by the major browsers.

The `<div>` tag has proven itself enormously valuable, however, when used in conjunction with style sheets (see Chapter 23).

Attributes

`align=center|left|right`
    Aligns the text within the tags to the left, right, or center of the page.

<h1> through <h6>   NN: 2, 3, 4 · MSIE: 2, 3, 4, 5 · HTML 4 · WebTV · Opera3

`<hn>...</hn>`

Specifies that the enclosed text is a heading. There are six different levels of headings, from `<h1>` to `<h6>`, with each subsequent level displaying at a smaller size. `<h5>` and `<h6>` usually display smaller than the surrounding body text.

Attributes

`align=center|left|right`

> Used to align the header left, right, or centered on the page. *Microsoft Internet Explorer 3.0 and earlier do not support right alignment.*

<p>   NN: 2, 3, 4 · MSIE: 2, 3, 4, 5 · HTML 4 · WebTV · Opera3

`<p>...</p>`

Denotes the beginning and end of a paragraph when used as container. Many browsers will also allow the `<p>` tag to be used without a closing tag to start a new paragraph. The container method is preferred, particularly if you are using Cascading Style Sheets with the document.

Attributes

`align=center|left|right`

> Aligns the text within the tags to the left, right, or center of the page.

Text Appearance (Inline Styles)

The following tags affect the appearance of text. With the exception of `<basefont>`, all of the tags listed in this section define inline styles, meaning they can be applied to a string of characters within a block element without introducing line breaks. (`<basefont>` is used to specify the appearance of type for a whole document or for a range of text.)

<abbr>   NN: 2, 3, 4 · MSIE: 2, 3, 4, 5 · HTML 4 · WebTV · Opera3

`<abbr>...</abbr>`

Identifies the enclosed text as an abbreviation. It has no inherent effect on text display, but can be used as an element selector in a style sheet.

Attributes

`title=string`

> Provides the full expression for the abbreviation. This may be useful for non-visual browsers and search engines.

Example

```
<ABBR TITLE="Massachusetts">Mass.</ABBR>
```

<acronym>

```
<acronym>...</acronym>
```

Indicates an acronym. It has no inherent effect on text display, but can be used as an element selector in a style sheet.

Attributes

`title=string`
> Provides the full expression for the acronym. This may be useful for non-visual browsers and search engines.

Example

```
<ACRONYM TITLE="World Wide Web">WWW</ACRONYM>
```

<b>

```
<b>...</b>
```

Enclosed text is rendered in bold.

<basefont>

```
<basefont>
```

Specifies certain font attributes for text following the tag. It can be used within the <head> tags to apply to the entire document, or within the body of the document to apply to the subsequent text. This tag is not part of the HTML standard.

Attributes

`color="#rrggbb" or name`
> *MSIE 3.0+ only.* Sets the color of the following text using hexadecimal RGB values.

`face=font`
> *MSIE 3.0+ only.* Sets the font for the following text.

`size=value`
> Sets the basefont size using the HTML size values from 1 to 7 (or relative values based on the default value of 3). Subsequent relative size settings will be based on this value.

<big>

```
<big>...</big>
```

Sets the type one font size larger than the surrounding text. It is equivalent to <font size="+1">.

<blink>

```
<blink>...</blink>
```

Causes the contained text to flash on and off.

<cite>
NN: 2, 3, 4 · MSIE: 2, 3, 4, 5 · HTML 4 · WebTV · Opera3

`<cite>...</cite>`

Denotes a citation—a reference to another document, especially books, magazines, articles, etc. Browsers generally display citations in italic.

<code>
NN: 2, 3, 4 · MSIE: 2, 3, 4, 5 · HTML 4 · WebTV · Opera3

`<code>...</code>`

Denotes a code sample. Code is rendered in the browser's specified monospace font (usually Courier).

<del>
NN: 2, 3, 4 · MSIE: 2, 3, 4, 5 · HTML 4 · WebTV · Opera3

`<del>...</del>`

Indicates deleted text. It has no inherent style qualities on its own, but may be used to hide deleted text from view or display it as strike-through text via style sheet controls. It may be useful for legal documents and any instance where edits need to be tracked. Its counterpart is *inserted* text (`<ins>`). Both can be used to indicate either inline or block-level elements.

<em>
NN: 2, 3, 4 · MSIE: 2, 3, 4, 5 · HTML 4 · WebTV · Opera3

`<em>...</em>`

Indicates emphasized text. Nearly all browsers render emphasized text in italic.

<font>
NN: 2, 3, 4 · MSIE: 2, 3, 4, 5 · HTML 4D · WebTV · Opera3

`<font>...</font>`

Used to affect the style (color, typeface, and size) of the enclosed text.

Attributes

`color="#rrggbb"`
> Specifies the color using a hexadecimal RGB value.

`face=typeface (or list of typefaces)`
> Specifies a typeface for the text. The specified typeface will be used only if it is found on the user's machine. You may provide a list of fonts (separated by commas) and the browser will use the first available in the string.

`size=value`
> Sets the size of the type to an absolute value on a scale from 1 to 7 (3 is the default), or using a relative value +n or −n (based on the default or `<basefont>` setting).

<i>
NN: 2, 3, 4 · MSIE: 2, 3, 4, 5 · HTML 4 · WebTV · Opera3

`<i>...</i>`

Enclosed text is displayed in italic.

<ins> NN: 2, 3, 4 - **MSIE:** 2, 3, **4, 5** - **HTML 4** - WebTV - Opera3

`<ins>...</ins>`

Indicates text that has been inserted into the document. It has no inherent style qualities on its own, but may be used to indicate inserted text in a different color via style sheet controls. It may be useful for legal documents and any instance in which edits need to be tracked. Its counterpart is deleted text (`<del>`). Both can be used to indicate either inline or block-level elements.

<kbd> NN: 2, 3, 4 - **MSIE:** 2, 3, **4, 5** - **HTML 4** - **WebTV** - **Opera3**

`<kbd>...</kbd>`

Indicates text that is typed on a keyboard. It is displayed in the browser's monospace font (usually Courier). Some browsers also display it in bold.

<q> NN: 2, 3, 4 - **MSIE:** 2, 3, **4, 5** - **HTML 4** - WebTV - Opera3

`<q>...</q>`

Delimits a short quotation that can be included inline, such as "to be or not to be." It differs from `<blockquote>`, which is for longer quotations set off as a separate paragraph element. It may be rendered with quotation marks.

Attributes

`cite=url`
> Designates the source document from which the quotation was taken.

<s> NN: 2, 3, 4 - **MSIE:** 2, 3, **4, 5** - **HTML 4**D - **WebTV** - **Opera3**

`<s>...</s>`

Enclosed text is displayed as strike-through text (same as `<strike>` but introduced by later browser versions).

<samp> NN: 2, 3, 4 - **MSIE:** 2, 3, **4, 5** - **HTML 4** - **WebTV** - **Opera3**

`<samp>...</samp>`

Delimits sample output from programs, scripts, etc. Sample text is generally displayed in a monospace font.

<small> NN: 2, 3, 4 - **MSIE:** 2, 3, **4, 5** - **HTML 4** - **WebTV** - **Opera3**

`<small>...</small>`

Renders the type one font size smaller than the surrounding text. It is equivalent to `<font size="-1">`.

Formatting Text

<span> — NN: 2, 3, **4** - MSIE: 2, 3, **4, 5** - **HTML 4** - WebTV - Opera3

`<span>...</span>`

This is a null text container used for identifying a span of inline characters. It has no inherent style effect on its own, but can be used in conjunction with Style Sheets to apply styles to any span of text. (See Chapter 23.)

<strike> — NN: 2, **3, 4** - MSIE: **2, 3, 4, 5** - **HTML 4D** - WebTV - Opera3

`<strike>...</strike>`

Enclosed text is displayed as strike-through text (crossed through with a horizontal line).

<strong> — NN: **2, 3, 4** - MSIE: **2, 3, 4, 5** - **HTML 4** - WebTV - Opera3

`<strong>...</strong>`

Enclosed text is strongly emphasized. Nearly all browsers render `<strong>` text in bold.

<sub> — NN: **2, 3, 4** - MSIE: 2, **3, 4, 5** - **HTML 4** - WebTV - Opera3

`<sub>...</sub>`

Formats enclosed text as subscript.

<sup> — NN: **2, 3, 4** - MSIE: 2, **3, 4, 5** - **HTML 4** - WebTV - Opera3

`<sup>...</sup>`

Formats enclosed text as superscript.

<tt> — NN: **2, 3, 4** - MSIE: **2, 3, 4, 5** - **HTML 4** - WebTV - Opera3

`<tt>...</tt>`

Formats enclosed text as typewriter text. The text enclosed in the `<tt>` tag will be displayed in a monospaced font such as Courier.

<u> — NN: **2, 3, 4** - MSIE: **2, 3, 4, 5** - **HTML 4D** - WebTV - Opera3

`<u>...</u>`

Enclosed text will be underlined when displayed.

<var> — NN: **2, 3, 4** - MSIE: **2, 3, 4, 5** - **HTML 4** - WebTV - Opera3

`<var>...</var>`

Indicates an instance of a variable or program argument (usually displayed in italic).

Spacing and Positioning

The following tags give authors control over the line breaks, alignment, and spacing within an HTML document. Tables (discussed in Chapter 10, *Tables*) and style sheets (Chapter 23) offer better control over spacing and positioning than the minimal controls listed here.

*
*   NN: 2, 3, 4 · MSIE: 2, 3, 4, 5 · HTML 4 · WebTV · Opera3

`<br>`

Breaks the text and begins a new line, but does not add extra space as the <p> tag does.

Attributes

`clear=all|left|right`
> Breaks the text flow and resumes the next line after the specified margin is clear. This is often used to start the text below an aligned image (preventing text wrap).

<center>   NN: 2, 3, 4 · MSIE: 2, 3, 4, 5 · HTML 4D · WebTV · Opera3

`<center>...</center>`

Centers the enclosed text horizontally on the page (same as `<DIV align=center>`.

<multicol>   NN: 2, 3, 4 · MSIE: 2, 3, 4, 5 · HTML, 4 · WebTV · Opera3

`<multicol>...</multicol>`

Netscape only. Displays enclosed text in multiple columns of approximately the same length.

Attributes

`cols=number`
> Specifies the number of columns (mandatory).

`gutter=number`
> Specifies the amount of space (in pixels) to maintain between columns.

`width=number`
> Specifies the width of the columns in pixels. All columns within `<multicol>` are the same width.

<nobr>   NN: 2, 3, 4 · MSIE: 2, 3, 4, 5 · HTML 4 · WebTV · Opera3

`<nobr>...</nobr>`

Text (or graphics) within the "no break" tags will always display on one line, without allowing any breaks. The line may run beyond the right edge of the browser window, requiring horizontal scrolling.

\<pre\>

```
<pre>...</pre>
```

Delimits preformatted text, meaning that lines are displayed exactly as they are typed in, honoring multiple spaces and line breaks. Text within <pre> tags will be displayed in a monospace font such as Courier.

Attributes

width=*value*
> This optional attribute determines how many characters to fit on a single line within the <pre> block.

\<wbr\>

```
<wbr>
```

Indicates a potential word break point. The <wbr> tag works only when placed within <nobr>-tagged text and causes a line break only if the current line already extends beyond the browser's display window margins.

Lists

The following is a collection of tags used for formatting a number of different types of lists in HTML. Any list can be nested within another list.

\<dir\>

```
<dir>...</dir>
```

Creates a directory list consisting of list items <li>. Directory lists were originally designed to display lists of files with short names, but they have been deprecated with the recommendation that unordered lists (<ul>) be used instead. Most browsers render directory lists the same as unordered lists (with bullets), although some will use a multicolumn format.

\<dl\>

```
<dl>...</dl>
```

Indicates a definition list, consisting of terms (<dt>) and definitions (<dd>).

Attributes

compact
> Makes the list as small as possible. Few browsers support the compact attribute.

\<dd\>

```
<dd>...</dd>
```

Denotes the definition portion of an item within a definition list. The definition is usually displayed with an indented left margin. The closing tag is commonly omitted, but should be included when applying style sheets.

\<dt\>

```
<dt>...</dt>
```

Denotes the term portion of an item within a definition list. The closing tag is normally omitted, but should be included when applying style sheets.

\<li\>

```
<li>...</li>
```

Defines an item in a list. It is used within the <dir>, <ol>, and <ul> list tags.

Attributes

The following attributes have been deprecated by the HTML 4.0 Specification in favor of style sheet controls for list item display.

type=*format*
> Changes the format of the automatically generated numbers or bullets for list items.
>
> Within unordered lists (<ul>), the type attribute can be used to specify the bullet style (disc, circle, or square) for a particular list item.
>
> Within ordered lists (<ol>), the type attribute specifies the numbering style (see options under <ol> listing below) for a particular list item.

value=*number*
> Within ordered lists, you can specify the number (*n*) of an item. Following list items will increase from the specified number.

\<menu\>

```
<menu>...</menu>
```

This indicates the beginning and end of a menu list, which consists of list items <li>. Menus are intended to be used for a list of short choices, such as a menu of links to other documents. It is little used and has been deprecated in favor of <ul>.

Attributes

compact
> Displays the list as small as possible (not many browsers do anything with this attribute).

type=disc|circle|square
> Defines the shape of the bullets used for each list item.

`<ol>...</ol>`

Defines the beginning and end of an ordered list, which consists of list items `<li>`.

Attributes

`compact`
>   Displays the list as small as possible (not many browsers do anything with this attribute).

`start=number`
>   Starts the numbering of the list at *n*, instead of 1.

`type=1|A|a|I|i`
>   Defines the numbering system for the list as follows:

Type Value	Generated Style	Sample Sequence
1	Arabic numerals (default)	1, 2, 3, 4...
A	Uppercase letters	A, B, C, D...
a	Lowercase letters	a, b, c, d...
I	Uppercase Roman numerals	I, II, III, IV...
i	Lowercase Roman numerals	i, ii, iii, iv...

The `type` attribute has been deprecated by the HTML 4.0 Specification in favor of style sheet controls for list item display.

`<ul>...</ul>`

Defines the beginning and end of an ordered list, which consists of list items `<li>`.

Attributes

`compact`
>   Displays the list block as small as possible. Not many browsers support this attribute.

`type=disc|circle|square`
>   Defines the shape of the bullets used for each list item.

Working with HTML Text

Formatting web page text is unlike formatting text for print. In print, you have the luxury of knowing that text will stay where you put it. Web text, on the other hand, is more fluid. Many aspects of presentation are determined when the document flows into each user's browser window.

A good place to begin formatting a web document is to establish the general structure of the document by adding HTML tags that create paragraphs and heading levels in the raw text.

Paragraphs and Line Breaks

Line breaks that occur in the HTML source document are ignored when rendered by a web browser. HTML text wraps text automatically to fill the width of the browser window (or table cell). When the window is resized, the text is reflowed to fill the new width. Lines will break in different places (with fewer words per line) for a user who has the default type size set very large than for a user with small default type.

In HTML, you must deliberately specify where you want a line to break. This is most often done by indicating paragraphs and headings (both are examples of *block-level* elements), which automatically add line breaks with extra white space above and below. If you want to break a line but not add any extra space, insert a line break with the <br> tag.

The following two figures show the difference between lines broken with a <p> tag and a <br>. In Figure 7-1, the line is broken by a <p> and extra space is introduced. In Figure 7-2, the <br> tag breaks the line but does not add space.

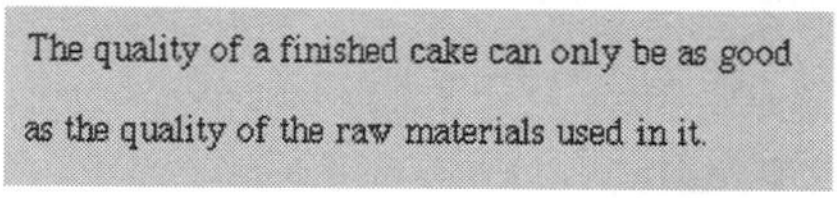

The quality of a finished cake can only be as good

as the quality of the raw materials used in it.

```
<P>The quality of a finished cake can only be as good
<P>as the quality of the raw materials used in it.
```

Figure 7-1: Breaking text with the <p> tag adds vertical spacing

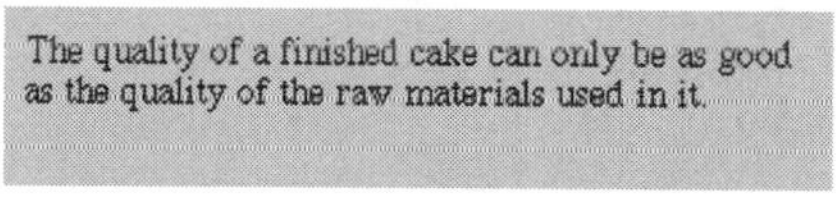

The quality of a finished cake can only be as good
as the quality of the raw materials used in it.

```
<P>The quality of a finished cake can only be as good
<BR>as the quality of the raw materials used in it.
```

Figure 7-2: Breaking text with the <br> tag doesn't add vertical spacing

Most elements on a web page are contained within paragraphs, which, according to the HTML standard, should be enclosed in the <p> and </p> tags. However, because browsers are clever enough to infer that a new opening tag indicates the end of the previous paragraph, many web authors leave off the closing </p> tag and insert <p>s as though they were line spaces.

This is fine for most current web purposes, but it should be noted that lax coding may not be as tolerated in future web page description languages or for browsers such as Opera that adhere to HTML standards strictly. It is already important to tag paragraphs properly for use with Cascasding Style Sheets. XML promises to be quite particular about closing tags as well. It's probably not a bad idea to get into the habit of closing all the tags you once left hanging.

Headings

Headings are displayed in bold text with automatic line breaks and extra space above and below. There are six levels of HTML headings, ranging from <h1> (the top-level heading) to <h6> (lowest priority). Browsers display headings with a diminishing font size so that <h1>s are the largest possible font and <h6> are the smallest.

In fact, <h5> and <h6> are generally sized even smaller than the default body text, making them not very commanding as headings. Some web authors use the fifth and sixth level headings for the "small type" elements such as copyright information at the bottom of the page. Figure 7-3 shows the relationship of the six heading levels as displayed in a browser.

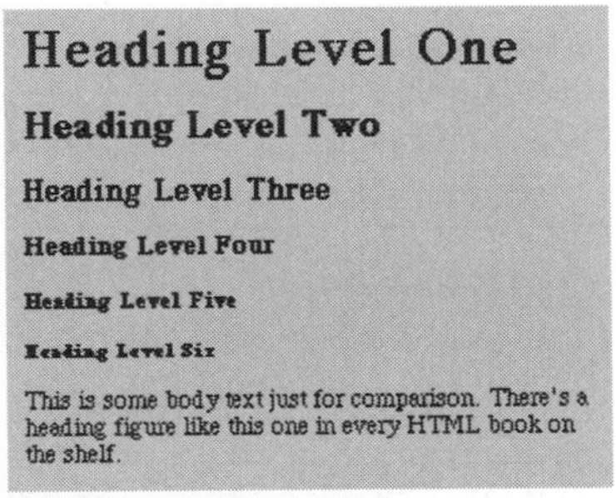

Figure 7-3: Results of the six heading tags, with regular body text for comparison

Legal HTML syntax requires that headings appear in order (i.e., an <h2> cannot precede an <h1>), for proper document structure. In practice, however, designers typically pick and choose from heading levels to create desired presentation effects. For instance, a top-level <h1> heading, although it may make sense for the structure of the document, may look too large and clunky for the page, so an <h2> or <h3> might be used instead. Because browsers do not enforce correct structural hierarchies, web page authors have gotten away with these techniques.

Now that HTML has been extended to provide more fine-tuned controls over font display, headings have become less popular as text-formatting tools. In fact, now the other extreme is common, in which pages are coded purely for presentation (for instance, with the <font> tag) without providing any indication of the document's structure.

Style sheets, once they are fully supported, will be a welcome solution to this dilemma, making it possible to structure documents with heading levels according to legal HTML syntax while offering precise control over their presentation. For more information, see Chapter 23.

Inline Type Styles

Most HTML text tags indicate style or structural information for *inline* elements (strings of characters within the flow of text). Inline style tags affect the appearance of the enclosed text without adding line breaks or extra space. Closing tags are required for inline style tags in order to turn "off" the style attribute.

HTML styles fall into two conceptual categories: *logical* (or "content-based") styles and *physical* styles. This distinction is purely intellectual and does not affect the way you use the tags in an HTML document. However, in the movement toward removing style information from the content revived by the introduction of style sheets, logical tags are the more "pure" way to go.

Logical Styles

Logical or content-based styles describe the enclosed text's meaning, context, or usage and leave the specific rendering of the tag to the discretion of the browser. Using logical tags, you may indicate that a selection of text should be emphasized or displayed as code. Fortunately, browsers adhere to conventions for the display of logical styles; for instance, you can be pretty certain that emphasized text will be rendered in italics, and that code will appear in a monospaced font.

Table 7-1 gives a list of logical inline style tags. Refer to the "Summary of Text Tags" at the beginning of this chapter for complete browser-support information.

Table 7-1: Logical Inline Style Tags

Tag	Description	Usually Displayed as:
`<abbr>`	Abbreviation	Body text (requires style sheets for style information)
`<acronym>`	Acronym	Body text (requires style sheets for style information)
`<cite>`	Citation	Italic
`<code>`	Code	Monospace font
`<del>`	Deleted text	Body text (requires style sheets for style information)
`<div>`	Division	Body text (requires style sheets for style information)
`<em>`	Emphasized	Italic
`<ins>`	Inserted text	Body text (requires style sheets for style information)
`<kbd>`	Keyboard text	Monospace font
`<q>`	Inline quotation	Italic (newer browsers only)
`<samp>`	Sample text	Monospace font
`<span>`	Span	Body text (requires style sheets for style information)
`<strong>`	Strong	Bold
`<var>`	Variable	Monospace oblique font

Formatting Text

Physical Styles

Physical styles provide specific display instructions, such as "italic" or "strikethrough." Some physical styles control the size of the text, such as "big" or "small." Once style sheets are universally supported they will be the preferred method for specifying precise display information, so these physical tags may fall by the wayside.

Table 7-2 lists the available physical inline style tags with their uses. Refer to the "Summary of Text Tags" at the beginning of this chapter for complete browser-support information.

Table 7-2: Physical Inline Style Tags

Tag	Description	Function
<b>	Bold	Displays text in bold type
<big>	Big	Displays type one size larger than the surrounding text (equivalent to size="+1")
<blink>	Blink	Makes the text flash on and off (*Netscape Navigator only*)
<font>	Font	Specifies the font face, size, and color (discussed in "The <font> Tag" section later in this chapter)
<i>	Italic	Displays text in italic type
<s>	Strike-through	An alternative tag for <strike> (newer browsers only)
<small>	Small	Displays type one size smaller than the surrounding text (equivalent to size="-1")
<strike>	Strike-through	Displays strike-through text (crossed through with a horizontal line)
<sub>	Subscript	Displays the text at a smaller size, slightly below the baseline of the surrounding text
<sup>	Superscript	Displays the text at a smaller size, slightly above the baseline of the surrounding text
<tt>	Teletype	Displays the text in the user's default mono-spaced font
<u>	Underline	Underlines the text

The <font> Tag

The <font> tag is an inline style tag used to specify the size, color, and font face for the enclosed text using the size, color, and face attributes, respectively. A single <font> tag may contain all of these attributes as shown:

```
<FONT FACE="sans-serif" COLOR="white" SIZE="+1">
```

For an explanation of acceptable values for the color attribute, refer to "Specifying Colors in HTML" in Chapter 5, *HTML Overview*.

It should be noted that the <font> tag with all its attributes has been deprecated by the World Wide Web Consortium due to the fact that style sheets are now available and are considered superior for controlling presentation. It is still supported, but may become obsolete in future versions of HTML.

Specifying Size with <font>

You can use the `size` attribute within the <font> tag to adjust type size. This attribute is supported by versions 1.1 and higher of both Navigator and Internet Explorer.

Browsers measure type on a relative scale from 1 to 7, where 3 is the default and will be displayed at the size specified by the user's preferences. These "virtual" sizes are relative, meaning they do not signify actual pixel or point adjustments. Each size is successively 20 percent smaller or larger than the default size, 3.

The size value can be specified as an absolute value from one to seven or as a relative value by means of a plus or minus sign. When relative values are given, the default value (which is 3, unless otherwise specified with a <basefont> tag) is increased or decreased by that relative amount. Type will never be displayed larger than 7 or smaller than 1, even if the relative size results in such a value.

Absolute value	1	2	3	4	5	6	7
Relative value	-2	-1	-	+1	+2	+3	+4

Therefore, `<font size="4">`*block of text*`</font>` is the same as `<font size="+1">`*block of text*`</font>`, and both will result in a block of text that is 20 percent larger than the default text size.

It is interesting to note that when <font> tags are nested, the effects of their relative sizes are not cumulative, but rather are always based on the default or basefont size of the text. Therefore, if the default text size for a document is 3, any text in that document that is enclosed in `<font size="+1">` will result in text with a size of 4, even if that text is nested within a paragraph with `<font size=5>`.

<font size> advantage

*   **Gives designers some control over type size** without resorting to inappropriate tags (such as Heading) to adjust size.

<font size> disadvantage

*   **Overrides viewers' preference for comfortable on-screen reading.** By changing sizes, you risk some viewers seeing type that is illegibly small or ridiculously big.

Recommendations

*   Limit the use of `<font size>` to small blocks of text, such as copyright information, rather than applying a size adjustment to an entire page.

*   If your content needs to be found by search engines that look for heading information, do not use the `<font size>` tag as a substitute for HTML heading tags, which are weighted more heavily.

Specifying Fonts with <font>

Internet Explorer 1.0 introduced the proprietary `face="value"` attribute to the `<font>` tag, which allows you to specify specific fonts for selected text. This attribute was adopted by Navigator in versions 3.0 and higher (note, it does not work in Navigator 2.0 or earlier).

The face attribute does not guarantee that the user will see your text in your specified font. Consider it merely a recommendation. Read "Why Specifying Type is Problematic" in Chapter 3, *Web Design Principles for Print Designers*, before gleefully sprinkling the `<font>` tag throughout your documents.

The quote-enclosed value of `face` is one or more display font names separated by commas as follows:

```
<FONT FACE="Verdana, Arial, sans-serif">block of text</FONT>
```

The browser looks at the string of font names until it finds one that is installed on the system and can be used for display. If none of the suggested fonts are installed, the default font will be used instead.

You can include a generic font family (`serif`, `sans-serif`, `monospace`, `cursive`, or `fantasy`) as the last choice in your list, which allows the browser to choose any available font within that class should your named fonts not be found. It's sort of a last-ditch effort to get something like the font you want, without leaving it entirely to chance.

<font face> advantages

- **Gives designers some influence over font selection.**

- **Degrades acceptably.** If the suggested fonts are not found (or if the tag is not supported), the text will simply be displayed in the browser's default font specified by the user.

<font face> disadvantages

- **Font specification (and other stylistic control) is better handled by style sheets.** Because it flagrantly links style information with content, this tag has been deprecated by the HTML 4.0 Specification and may be obsolete in future versions of HTML.

- **Not viable for specifying non-western fonts.** `<font face>` uses simple mapping to match identifying character set numbers to character shapes ("glyphs") that may not translate correctly for the font you select.

Lists

The original HTML specification included tags for five different types of lists: numbered lists (called ordered lists), bulleted lists (called unordered lists), definition lists, menus, and directory lists. Since then, directory lists and menus have been "deprecated" with the recommendation that unordered lists be used for the same effect. In this section, we'll look at the structure of each type of list in current use.

Lists and the items within them are block-level elements, meaning that line spaces will automatically be added before and after them. Extra space may be added above and below the entire list element but, in general, if you want to add space between individual list items, you need to insert a <p> tag between them (although, technically, that is not good HTML form).

Unordered (Bulleted) Lists

An unordered list is used for a collection of related items that appear in no particular order. List items are displayed on an indent with a bullet preceding each list item. The bullet shape is automatically inserted by the browser when it encounters the list item, so you do not need to type a bullet character into your HTML source code.

An unordered list is delimited by the <ul>...</ul> tags, with each item indicated by an <li> tag. The closing </li> tag is usually omitted, but it should be included if you are using Style Sheets to control list item display.

Figure 7-4 shows the structure and display of a simple unordered list.

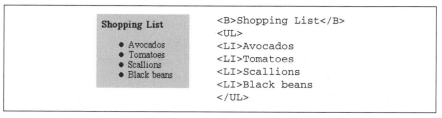

Figure 7-4: A simple unordered list

Changing the bullet shape

HTML provides only a minimal amount of control over the appearance of bullets. You can change the shape of the bullets for the whole list by using the **type** attribute within the <ul> tag. The **type** attribute allows you to specify one of three shapes: disc (the default), square, or circle. Figure 7-5 shows discs (left), circles (center), and squares (right).

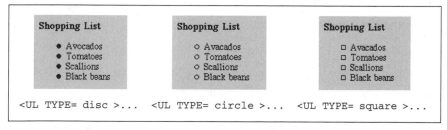

Figure 7-5: Bullet types changed with the TYPE attribute

The **type** attribute can be applied within a list-item tag (<li>) to change the shape of the bullet for that particular item. Figure 7-6 shows this effect.

Formatting Text

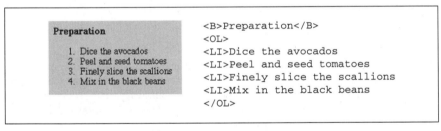

```
Shopping List        <B>Shopping List</B>
                     <UL>
  ● Avocados         <LI TYPE=disc>Avocados
  ○ Tomatoes         <LI TYPE=circle>Tomatoes
  □ Scallions        <LI TYPE=square>Scallions
                     </UL>
```

Figure 7-6: Changing the bullet type within list items

If you want to use your own graphic as the bullet for a list, you would need to simulate a list using a table for alignment, since the HTML list tags provide no way to turn off the automatic bulleting or to introduce custom characters. (See Chapter 10.)

Ordered (Numbered) Lists

Ordered lists are used when the sequence of the items is important. They are displayed on an indent, with a number (automatically inserted by the browser) preceding each list item. You do not type the numbers into your HTML source code.

Ordered lists follow the same basic structure as unordered lists: the entire list is contained within the <ol> and </ol> tags and each individual list item is indicated with an <li> tag.

Figure 7-7 shows the structure and display of a simple ordered list.

```
Preparation              <B>Preparation</B>
                         <OL>
  1. Dice the avocados   <LI>Dice the avocados
  2. Peel and seed tomatoes  <LI>Peel and seed tomatoes
  3. Finely slice the scallions  <LI>Finely slice the scallions
  4. Mix in the black beans  <LI>Mix in the black beans
                         </OL>
```

Figure 7-7: A simple ordered list

Changing the numbering scheme

The type attribute can be used within ordered lists to specify the style of numbering. There are five possible values: 1 (numbers), A (uppercase letters), a (lowercase letters), I (uppercase roman), and i (lowercase roman). The value "1" is the default and is shown in Figure 7-7. Figure 7-8 shows the code and displays of the other four settings.

As with unordered lists, you can use the type attribute within individual <li> tags to mix-and-match styles within a list.

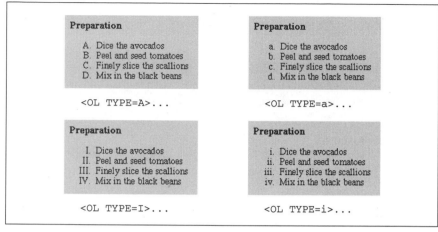

Figure 7-8: Changing the numbering style with the TYPE attribute

Setting the first number

If you want the list to start with some number (or letter value) other than 1, use the start attribute to specify the first number, as shown in Figure 7-9.

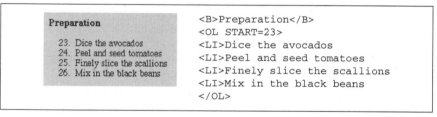

Figure 7-9: Setting the first number in the list with the START attribute

Definition Lists

The third type of list supported by HTML is the definition list, which follows a different structure than the other two. Definition lists consist of terms and definitions (any amount of descriptive text to be associated with the term) as in a glossary. In general, terms are positioned against the left edge of the page and definitions are positioned on an indent.

Terms and definitions are block-level items, so line breaks will be added around them, however, if you want extra space between terms and definitions, you must insert <p> tags between them.

A definition list is designated by the <dl>...</dl> tags. Within the list, each term is indicated with a <dt> and its definition is marked with a <dd>. Closing </dt> and </dd> tags may be safely omitted if style sheets are not in use. Figure 7-10 shows the display of a basic definition list and the code that created it.

```
                Poaching
                        Cooking food partially or completely submerged
                        in simmering liquid.
                Baking
                        Cooking food in the indirect, dry heat of an oven.
                        The food may be covered or uncovered.
                Broiling
                        Cooking food a measured distance from the direct,
                        dry heat of the heat source.

<DL>
<DT>Poaching
<DD>Cooking food partially or completely submerged in
simmering liquid.
<DT>Baking
<DD>Cooking food in the indirect, dry heat of an oven.
The food may be covered or uncovered.
<DT>Broiling
<DD>Cooking food a measured distance from the direct,
dry heat of the heat source.
</DL>
```

Figure 7-10: Simple definition list

Nesting Lists

Any list can be nested within another list. For instance, you could add a bulleted list item under an item within a numbered list; numbered lists can be added within a definition; and so on. Lists can be nested several layers deep; however, since the left indent is cumulative, it doesn't take long for the text to end up pressed against the right margin.

It is helpful to use indents in your HTML source document to keep nesting levels clear. Be careful to close all of the lists you start!

Nesting unordered lists

When unordered lists are nested within each other, the browser automatically displays a different bullet for each consecutive level, as shown in Figure 7-11.

Nesting ordered lists

It would be nice if nested ordered lists automatically displayed in standard outline format, but unfortunately, browsers do not have the capacity to automatically change numbering schemes. By default, every level within a nested numbered list will display with numbers (arabic numerals). If you want standard outline format, you need to label each list manually with the type attribute, as shown in Figure 7-12.

Layout Techniques with HTML

First, let it be stated that "layout techniques with HTML" is an oxymoron. HTML was specifically designed to pass off all layout functions to the end user. The

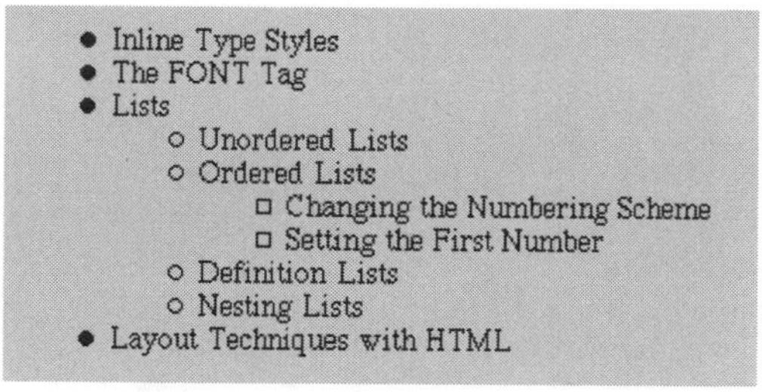

```
<UL>
<LI>Inline Type Styles
<LI>The FONT Tag
<LI>Lists
    <UL>
    <LI>Unordered Lists
    <LI>Ordered Lists
        <UL>
        <LI>Changing the Numbering Scheme
        <LI>Setting the First Number
        </UL>
    <LI>Definition Lists
    <LI>Nesting Lists
    </UL>
<LI>Layout Techniques with HTML
</UL>
```

Figure 7-11: Nested unordered list

controls over presentation listed here are the result of either extensions to the original HTML standard or a "creative use" (or misuse, depending who you ask) of an existing tag.

Ideally, presentation should be controlled using style sheets; however, they are not supported in enough browsers to be considered reliable. In the meantime, tables may offer more precise control over positioning than can be achieved using text-related HTML tags. (See Chapter 10 for more information on formatting with tables.)

Preformatted Text

Preformatted (<pre>) text is unique in that it is displayed exactly as it is typed in the HTML source code—including all line returns and multiple character spaces (in all other HTML text, returns and consecutive spaces are just ignored). Preformatted text is always displayed in a monospace font, which allows columns of characters to line up correctly.

The same block of source text was coded as <pre> text and as teletype (<tt>), another method for specifying a monospace font. The difference is obvious, as shown in Figures 7-13 and 7-14.

The <pre> tag is the only HTML tag that lets you know *exactly* how your text will line up when displayed in a browser. For this reason, it was adopted early on as a

```
    A. Inline Type Styles
    B. The FONT Tag
    C. Lists
            1. Unordered Lists
            2. Ordered Lists
                    a. Changing the Numbering Scheme
                    b. Setting the First Number
            3. Definition Lists
            4. Nesting Lists
    D. Layout Techniques with HTML
```

```
<OL TYPE=A>
<LI>Inline Type Styles
<LI>The FONT Tag
<LI>Lists
    <OL TYPE=1>
    <LI>Unordered Lists
    <LI>Ordered Lists
        <OL TYPE=a>
            <LI>Changing the Numbering Scheme
            <LI>Setting the First Number
        </OL>
    <LI>Definition Lists
    <LI>Nesting Lists
    </OL>
<LI>Layout Techniques with HTML
</OL>
```

Figure 7-12: Nested ordered list

```
                Calories   Carb(g)   Fat(g)
French Fries      285        38        14
Fried Onion Rings 550        26        47
Fried Chicken     402        17        24
```

```
<PRE>
                Calories   Carb(g)   Fat(g)
French Fries      285        38        14
Fried Onion Rings 550        26        47
Fried Chicken     402        17        24
</PRE>
```

Figure 7-13: Preformatted text

favorite cheat for controlling alignment in web pages. The downside is that all the text will be displayed in Courier.

Note that <pre> is a block element, meaning that it will always be preceded and followed by a line break (some browsers will also add extra space above and below the block). For this reason, it is not possible to set text within a paragraph

```
Calories Carb(g) Fat(g) French Fries 285 38 14 Fried
Onion Rings 550 26 47 Fried Chicken 402 17 24


<TT>
                      Calories    Carb(g)    Fat(g)
French Fries            285         38         14
Fried Onion Rings       550         26         47
Fried Chicken           402         17         24
</TT>
```

Figure 7-14: Teletype text

as preformatted. If you need a number of blank spaces within a sentence, use
nonbreaking space characters ( ) instead.

Preventing Line Breaks

Text and graphics that appear within "no-break" (<nobr>) tags always display on
one line, and are not wrapped in the browser window. If the string of characters
or elements within <nobr> tags is very long, it continues off the browser window
and users need to scroll horizontally to the right to see it, as shown in Figure 7-15.

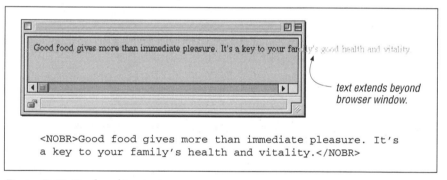

```
<NOBR>Good food gives more than immediate pleasure. It's
a key to your family's health and vitality.</NOBR>
```

Figure 7-15: Nonbreaking text

The <nobr> tag can be used to hold together a row of graphics, such as the
buttons of a toolbar, so they will always display as one piece.

Adding a <br> within <nobr> tagged text will cause the line to break.

The word-break (<wbr>) is an esoteric little tag that can be used in conjunction
with the no-break tag. <wbr> is used to indicate a potential word break point
within <nobr> tagged content. When the "no-break" segment extends beyond the
browser window, the <wbr> tag tells it exactly where it is permitted to break the
line, as shown in Figure 7-16. It keeps line lengths from getting totally out of hand.

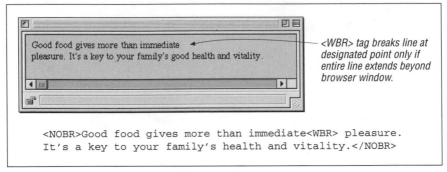

```
<NOBR>Good food gives more than immediate<WBR> pleasure.
It's a key to your family's health and vitality.</NOBR>
```

Figure 7-16: Use of the <wbr> tag within <nobr> text

Centering Text Elements

There are two methods for centering text elements horizontally on a page: the <center> tag, and the align attribute. Bear in mind that these tags have been deprecated by the HTML 4.0 Specification in favor of style sheet controls (although browsers will continue to support them for a while).

The align attribute

The preferred way to center elements is to use the block-level tags' align attribute with its value set to center. The align attribute can be added to the paragraph tag (<p>), any heading tag (<h1> through <h6>), or a page division (<div>). Be sure to close the tags at the end of the element.

In Figure 7-17, each element is centered individually using align=center.

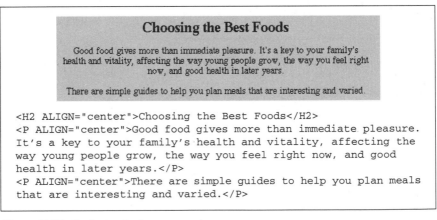

```
<H2 ALIGN="center">Choosing the Best Foods</H2>
<P ALIGN="center">Good food gives more than immediate pleasure.
It's a key to your family's health and vitality, affecting the
way young people grow, the way you feel right now, and good
health in later years.</P>
<P ALIGN="center">There are simple guides to help you plan meals
that are interesting and varied.</P>
```

Figure 7-17: Centering text

As an alternative, you could enclose all three elements in a <div> tag with align=center. Unfortunately, the align attribute in a <div> tag is only recognized by Internet Explorer version 3.0 and higher and by Navigator version 4.0, so it is not a universal solution. The following code creates the same effect shown in Figure 7-17:

```
<DIV ALIGN="center">
<H2>Choosing the Best Foods</H2>
<P>Good food gives more than immediate pleasure. It's a key to
your family's health and vitality, affecting the way young
people grow, the way you feel right now, and good health in
later years.</P>
<P>There are simple guides to help you plan meals that are
interesting and varied.</P>
</DIV>
```

The <center> tag

An extension to HTML, the <center> tag is extremely straightforward to use (and for that reason, it is used commonly)—just place the <center> and </center> tags around sections of the page you would like to be centered, as shown in the following code. You could place your whole page within <center> tags, if you'd like, or just apply it to certain paragraphs. The <center> tag can only be applied to block-level elements since it is illogical to center text within the flow of left-aligned text.

```
<CENTER>
<H2>Choosing the Best Foods</H2>
<P>Good food gives more than immediate pleasure. It's a key to
your family's health and vitality, affecting the way young
people grow, the way you feel right now, and good health in
later years.</P>
<P>There are simple guides to help you plan meals that are
interesting and varied.</P>
</CENTER>
```

The <center> tag has been deprecated by the HTML 4.0 Specification in favor of <DIV align=center>.

Right and Left Alignment

The align attribute is also used for specifying left alignment and right alignment by setting its value to left or right, respectively. The alignment will remain in effect until the browser encounters another alignment instruction in the source. Figure 7-18 shows the effects of setting the attribute to left or right.

Text aligned with the align attribute will override any centering set with the <center> tag.

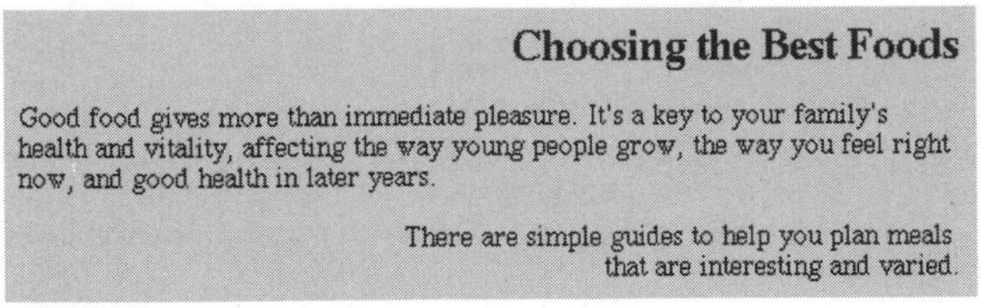

```
<H2 ALIGN="right">Choosing the Best Foods</H2>
<P ALIGN="left">Good food gives more than immediate pleasure. It's
a key to your family's health and vitality, affecting the way
young people grow, the way you feel right now, and good health
in later years.</P>
<P ALIGN="right">There are simple guides to help you plan meals
<BR>that are interesting and varied.</P>
```

Figure 7-18: Left and right alignment

Creating Indents with HTML

Unfortunately, there is no specific function for creating indented text in HTML, so it has become common for web designers to make do with existing tags that provide automatic indenting.

This section looks at the more popular "cheats" for indenting text using only text-formatting tags. More refined (and less "kludgey") indenting effects can be achieved using tables (see Chapter 10) and style sheets (Chapter 23). Some designers use transparent graphics to hold white space within the text flow.

<blockquote>

The blockquote element has been a long-time favorite for adding white space along the left and right margins of a block of text. Browsers generally add approximately 40 pixels of space between the browser margin (*not* its window border) and the left and right edges of a blockquote element, as shown in Figure 7-19.

There are a few points you should know when using blockquotes. Some browsers display blockquote material in italic, making it nearly impossible to read on the screen. Also, if you plan on placing aligned images in a blockquote, keep in mind that browsers are inconsistent in the way they display images within blockquotes. Some align the graphic with the indented blockquote margin; others align the image with the normal margin of paragraph text. It is a good idea to test on a variety of browsers.

Creating indents with list elements

Some web authors (and WYSIWYG authoring tools) take advantage of the automatic indentation that takes place when you specify text as a list. The two following methods are both syntactically incorrect and ought to be avoided, however, they can be used in a pinch to create an indent from the left margin of

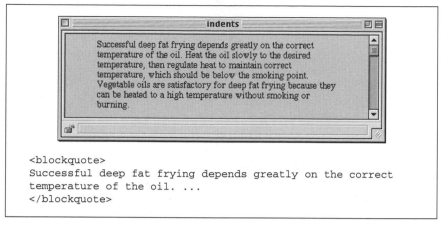

```
<blockquote>
Successful deep fat frying depends greatly on the correct
temperature of the oil. ...
</blockquote>
```

Figure 7-19: Setting off text with <blockquote>

the browser window. Either approach will produce the result shown in
Figure 7-20.

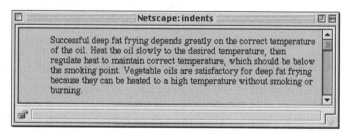

Figure 7-20: Indented text

A <ul> with no items

Marking a text element as an unordered list will set the text on a left-indent.
As long as you don't add any list items (<li>) within the list, no bullets will
appear.

```
<UL>
Successful deep fat frying depends greatly on the correct
temperature of the oil. ...
</UL>
```

A <dd> without its term

A definition (<dd>) within a definition list (<dl>) will also be set with the
standard left indent. It's fine to omit the term from the list. I've seen definition
lists set within definition lists to create deeper levels of indent (it's not pretty,
but it works).

```
<DL>
<DD>Successful deep fat frying depends greatly on the correct
temperature of the oil. ...
</DD>
</DL>
```

CHAPTER 8

Creating Links

This chapter focuses on the HTML tags related to linking one document to another, including uses for the anchor tag, linking with imagemaps (both client- and server-side), affecting the appearance of hyperlinks, and creating links with non-Web protocols.

Summary of Tags Related to Linking

In this section, browser support for each tag is noted to the right of the tag name. Browsers that do not support the tag are grayed out. Browsers that deprecate the tag are noted with a superscript D. Tag usage is indicated below the tag name. A more thorough listing of attributes for each tag, according to the HTML 4.0 Specification, appears in Appendix A, *HTML Tags and Elements*.

<a>   NN: 2, 3, 4 · MSIE: 2, 3, 4, 5 · HTML 4 · WebTV · Opera3

`<a>...</a>`

Defines an *anchor* within the document. An anchor is used to link to another document. It can also serve to label a fragment within a document (also called a *named anchor*), which is used as a reference for linking to a specific point in an HTML document.

Attributes

`href=url`
Specifies the URL of the target destination.

`method=value`
Specifies a list of names, each representing a particular document-processing method, usually an application name. It is browser-dependent and is rarely used in practice.

`name=text`

> Places a fragment identifier within an HTML document. Fragments are discussed further in the "Linking within a Document" section of this chapter.

`rel=relationship`

> *Not supported by Netscape Navigator or Opera.* Establishes a relationship between the current document and the target document. Common relationships include: `next`, `prev`, `head`, `toc`, `parent`, `child`, `index`, and `glossary`.

`rev=relationship`

> *Not supported by Netscape Navigator or Opera.* Specifies the relationship from the target back to the source (the opposite of the `rev` attribute).

`title=text`

> Specifies a title for the target document.

`target=text`

> *Not supported by WebTV or Internet Explorer 2.0 and earlier.* Specifies the name of the window or frame in which the target document should be displayed. For more information, see "Targeting Windows" in this chapter and "Targeting Frames" in Chapter 11, *Frames*.

`urn=urn`

> Specifies a Universal Resource Name (URN) for the referenced document. URN syntax is currently not defined so this attribute has no practical use.

New in HTML 4.0 Specification

`accesskey=character`

> Assigns an access key (shortcut key command) to the link. Access keys are also used for form fields. The value is a single character.

`charset=charset`

> Specifies the character encoding of the target document.

`coords=x,y coordinates`

> Specifies the x,y coordinates for a clickable area in an imagemap. HTML 4.0 proposes that client-side imagemaps could be replaced with an `<object>` tag containing the image and a set of anchor tags defining the "hot" areas (with shapes and coordinate attributes). This system has not yet been implemented by browsers.

`hreflang=language code`

> Specifies the base language of the target document.

`shape=shape name`

> Defines the shape of a clickable area in an imagemap. This is only used in the `<a>` tag as part of HTML 4.0's proposal to replace client-side imagemaps with a combination of `<object>` and `<a>` tags. This system has not yet been implemented by browsers.

`tabindex=number`

> Specifies the position of the current element in the tabbing order for the current document. The value must be between 0 and 32767. It is used for tabbing through the links on a page (or fields in a form).

Creating Links

type=*MIME type*
> Specifies the content type (MIME type) of the defined content.

Link Examples

To a local file:

```
<A HREF="filename.html">...</A>
```

To an external file:

```
<A HREF="http://server/path/file.html">...</A>
```

To a named anchor:

```
<A HREF="http://server/path/file.html#fragment">...</A>
```

To a named anchor in the same file:

```
<A HREF="#fragment">...</A>
```

To send an email message:

```
<A HREF="mailto:username@domain">...</A>
```

To a file on an FTP server:

```
<A HREF="ftp://server/path/filename">...</A>
```

<area>   NN: 2, 3, 4 - MSIE: 2, 3, 4, 5 - HTML 4 - WebTV - Opera3

```
<area>
```

The **area** tag is used within the <map> tag of a *client-side imagemap* to define a specific "hot" (clickable) area. Client-side imagemaps are discussed later in this chapter.

Attributes

coords=*values*
> Specifies a list of comma-separated pixel coordinates that define a "hot" area of an imagemap. The specific syntax for the coordinates varies by shape (see the "Imagemaps" section later in this chapter).

href=*url*
> Specifies the URL for a specific area.

nohref
> Defines a "mouse-sensitive" area in an imagemap for which there is no action when the user clicks in the area.

shape=rect|rectangle|circ|circle|poly|polygon
> Defines the shape of the clickable area.

<map>   NN: 2, 3, 4 - MSIE: 2, 3, 4, 5 - HTML 4 - WebTV - Opera3

```
<map>...</map>
```

Encloses client-side image map specifications. Client-side imagemaps are discussed later in this chapter.

`name=text`

> Gives the image map a name that is then referenced within the `<img>` tag. This attribute is required.

Simple Hypertext Links

The anchor (`<a>`) tag is used to identify a string of text or an image that serves as a hypertext link to another document. In its simplest incarnation, it looks like this:

```
I'm <A HREF="link.html">linking</A> to you!
```

To make an image a link, enclose the image tag within the anchor tags as follows:

```
<A HREF="link.html"><IMG SRC="pixie.gif"></A>
```

The URL is the name of the document you want to link to. URLs can be absolute or relative.

Absolute URLs

An *absolute URL* is made up of the following components: a protocol identifier, a host name (the name of the server machine), the pathname (if there is one), and the specific file name. When you are linking to documents on other servers, you need to use an absolute URL. The following is an example of a link with an absolute URL:

```
<A HREF="http://www.littlechair.com/web/index.html">...</A>
```

Here the protocol is identified as *http* (the standard protocol of the Web), the host is *www.littlechair.com* and *web/index.html* is the pathname leading to the particular file.

Relative URLs

A *relative URL* provides a pointer to another document relative to the location of the current document. The syntax is based on relative pathname structures in the Unix operating system, which are discussed in Chapter 4, *A Beginner's Guide to the Server.* When you are pointing to another document within your own site (on the same server), it is usually best to use relative URLs.

For example, if I am currently in *jcc.html* (identified here by its absolute pathname):

```
www.littlechair.com/web/samples/jcc.html
```

and I want to put a link on that page to *talk.html,* which is in the same directory:

```
www.littlechair.com/web/samples/talk.html
```

I could use a relative URL within the link as follows:

```
<A HREF="talk.html">...</A>
```

Using the same example, to link to the file *index.html* in a higher level directory (*web*), I could use the relative pathname to that file as shown:

```
<A HREF="../index.html">
```

This relative URL is the equivalent to the absolute URL *http://www.littlechair.com/web/index.html*.

Linking Within a Document

By default, when you link to a page, the browser displays the top of that page. To aid in navigation, you can use the anchor tag to link to a specific point or section within a document. This is a two-step process.

Naming a fragment

First, you need to identify and name the portion of the document (called a fragment) that you want to link to. The fragment is marked using the anchor (<a>) tag with its name attribute, giving the document fragment a name that can be referenced from a link.

To illustrate, let's set up a named fragment within a sample document called *dailynews.html* so users can link directly to the Stock Quotes section of the page. The following anchor tag marks the Stock Quotes title as a fragment named "stocks."

```
<A NAME="stocks">Daily Stock Quotes</A>
```

Linking to a fragment

The second step is to create a link to the fragment using a standard anchor tag with its href attribute. Fragment identifiers are placed at the end of the pathname and are preceded by the hash (#) symbol.

To link to the "stocks" fragment from within *dailynews.html*, the link would look like this:

```
<A HREF="#stocks">Check out the Stock Quotes</A>
```

Linking to a fragment in another document

You can create a link to a named fragment of any document on the Web by using the complete pathname. (Of course, the named anchors would have to be in place already.) To link to the stocks section from another document in the same directory, use a relative pathname as follows:

```
<A HREF="dailynews.html#stocks">Go to today's Stock Quotes</A>
```

Use an absolute URL to link to a fragment on another site, as in the following example:

```
<A HREF="http://www.webreview.com/style.html#fragment">
```

Using named anchors

Named anchors are most often used as a navigational aid by creating a hyperlinked table of contents at the top of a very long scrolling web page. Users can see the major topics at a glance and quickly get to the portions that interest them.

When linking down into a long page, it is generally a good idea to add links back to the top of the page or to the table of contents.

Note that the HTML 4.0 Specification allows any element on a web page to be targeted by its ID value just as though it were a named anchor. The first line demonstrates a heading that includes an ID identifier. The second line is a link on the same page to that particular heading.

```
<H2 ID="intro">Introduction</H2>
Return to the <A HREF="#intro">Introduction</A>
```

Affecting the Appearance of Links

As we all by now know, linked text is blue and underlined by default and graphics are identified by blue borders (unless you turn them off). But it doesn't have to be that way! Changing the color of links is easy with HTML, so you can make your links more coordinated with your chosen site palette. Style sheets offer even more control over the appearance of links.

You should exercise some caution in changing link appearance. The blue text and underlines have become a strong visual clue for "click here," so altering this formula may confuse your users. Use your knowledge of the savvy of your target audience to guide your design decisions.

Setting Colors in <body>

Link color specifications in the <body> tag are applied to the whole document.

Links	`<BODY LINK="color">`	Sets the color for hyperlinks. The default color for links is blue.
Visited links	`<BODY VLINK="color">`	Sets the colors for links that have already been clicked. The default color for visited links is purple.
Active links	`<BODY ALINK="color">`	Sets the color for a link while it is in the process of being clicked. The default color for an active link is red.

Specifying Color for a Specific Link

You can override the color of a specific link by placing <font> tags *within* the anchor tags. There is no way to set the visited link and active link colors for specific links. This feature is supported by versions 3.0 and 4.0 of Internet Explorer, but only version 4.0 of Netscape Navigator.

```
<A HREF="document.html"><FONT COLOR=aqua>Specially colored
link</FONT></A>
```

Setting Global Link Colors with Style Sheets

You can apply almost any style sheet property to a link by using the anchor tag (<a>) as a selector. However, CSS1 introduced a group of pseudo-classes (link,

visited, and active) that replicate the function of the <body> tag attributes listed in
the section "Setting Colors in <body>" earlier in this chapter. The syntax for specifying colors with anchor pseudo-classes is as follows.

To specify a color for links:

```
A:link { color: "#rrggbb" or colorname }
```

To specify a color for visited links:

```
A:visited { color: "#rrggbb" or colorname }
```

To specify a color for active links:

```
A:active { color: "#rrggbb" or colorname }
```

The advantage to setting colors this way is that you separate style information
from content. The major disadvantage is that style sheets (and particularly pseudo-
classes) are currently poorly supported by browsers, so you risk a significant
portion of your audience not seeing your page as you intend.

See Chapter 23, *Cascading Style Sheets*, for a better understanding of style sheet
syntax and usage.

Turning Off Underlines

The `text-decoration` style sheet property can be used to turn off the underlines for all the links in a document (it is supported by all browsers that support
style sheets). Use this with caution, however, since most users rely on the under-
line to indicate what is "clickable," particularly now that brightly colored HTML
text is more prevalent. Be sure that your interface and system of visual cues is
clear enough that links are still evident.

The style sheet rule for turning off underlines is as follows:

```
A { text-decoration: none }
```

To turn off underlines for specific links, label them with a CLASS attribute:

```
<A CLASS="internal" HREF="linkypoo.html">Go to another page</A>
```

and include the class in the selector of the style sheet rule as follows:

```
A.internal { text-decoration: none }
```

Changing Status Bar Text with JavaScript

By default, when you position the mouse over a link, the browser displays the
target URL in the status bar at the bottom of the browser. Use the following Java-
Script command in an anchor tag to change the status bar message to whatever
text you specify. In this example, the phrase "Samples of my web design work"
would be displayed in the browser's status bar.

```
<A HREF="web.html" onMouseOver="window.status='Samples of my
web design work'; return true;">The Web Lounge</A>
```

Be aware that many users value the ability to see the URL for a link, so if you are
going to change the message, make sure that you substitute worthwhile and
descriptive messages. Otherwise, you risk making your site less pleasant to use.

Targeting Windows

The problem with the hypertext medium is that when a user clicks on an interesting link on your page, he might never come back! One currently popular solution to this problem is to make the target document display in a second browser window. In that way, your page is still readily available.

Use the `target` attribute of the anchor tag to launch a new browser window for the linked document. Setting the `target="_blank"` attribute causes the browser to open a fresh browser window. For example:

```
<A HREF="http://www.webreview.com/" TARGET="_blank">...</A>
```

If you set every link on your page to target a `_blank` window, every link will launch a new window, potentially leaving your user with a mess of open windows.

A better method, especially if you have more than one link, is to give the targeted window a specific name, which can then be reused by subsequent links. The following link will open a new window called "display":

```
<A HREF="http://www.webreview.com/" TARGET="display">...</A>
```

If you target every link on that page to the "display" window, each targeted document will open in the same second window.

The `target` attribute is most often used in conjunction with framed documents. The syntax and strategy for using the target attribute with framed documents is discussed in Chapter 11.

Some browsers do not support the `target` attribute (including WebTV and MSIE2.0 and earlier). Furthermore, Netscape Navigator 4.0 has a bug that prevents the new named window from coming to the front. To the user, this looks as though the link did not work since the target document loads into a browser window that is stuck behind the current window.

Imagemaps

Ordinarily, placing a graphic within anchor tags will make the entire image a link to a single document, regardless of where the user clicks on the image. It is also possible (and quite common) to create multiple links, or "hot spots," within a single graphic. These graphics are called *imagemaps*. The effect is created with HTML tags and/or text files and scripts on the server; the graphic itself is an ordinary graphic that just serves as a backdrop for the pixel coordinates.

There are two types of imagemaps: *client-side* and *server-side*. For client-side imagemaps, the coordinate and URL information necessary to create each link is contained right in the HTML document. The process of putting the pieces together happens in the browser on the user's machine (thus, client-side). For server-side imagemaps, as the name suggests, the map information resides on the server and is processed by the server or a separate CGI script.

Client-side imagemaps are a slightly newer technology and are not universally supported by all browsers (although the majority of current browsers know what to do). For this reason, many web developers create redundant imagemaps (both client- and server-side) so that if the browser doesn't recognize the client-side map, the server's imagemap processor can take over.

Creating Imagemaps

The key to making imagemaps work is a map, based on the image, that associates pixel coordinates with URLs. This map is handled differently for client-side and server-side (as we will outline below), but the outcome is the same. When the user clicks somewhere within the image, the browser passes the coordinates of the mouse pointer to the map, which, in turn, generates the appropriate link.

Available tools

Although it is possible to put together imagemap information manually, it is much easier to use a tool to do it for you. There are many imagemap creation tools available as shareware for both Windows and the Mac. Be sure to look for one that is capable of outputting both client- and server-side map information, such as the following:

Mac

> MapMaker 1.1.2 by Frederic Eriksson available at *http://www.kickinit.com/ mapmaker/*

Windows

> MapEdit by Tom Boutell available at *http://www.boutell.com/mapedit/*

If you have one of the popular WYSIWYG HTML editors, chances are there's an imagemap creation tool built right in.

Creating the map

Regardless of the tool you're using, and regardless of the type of imagemap you're creating, the process for creating the map information is basically the same. Read the documentation for your imagemap tool to learn about features not listed here.

1. Open the image in your imagemap program.

2. Define areas within the image that will be clickable by using the appropriate shape tools: rectangle, circle, or polygon (for tracing irregular shapes).

3. While the outline of the area is still highlighted, enter a URL for that area in the text entry field provided, as shown in Figure 8-1.

4. Continue adding shapes and their respective URLs for each clickable area in the image.

5. For server-side imagemaps, you also need to define a default URL, which is the page that will display if users click outside a defined area. Many tools

have a prominent field for entering the default URL, but on others you may
need to look for it under a pull-down menu.

6. Select the type of imagemap (client- or server-side) you want to create.

7. Save or export the map information. Server-side imagemaps are saved in a
   map definition file (*.map*) that will reside on the server. Client-side
   imagemaps are embedded directly in the HTML file.

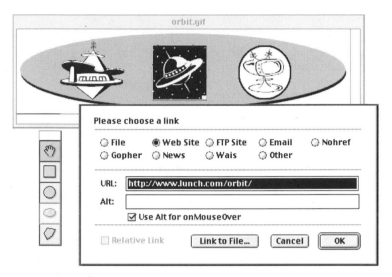

Figure 8-1: Creating map information (shown in MapMaker 1.1.2)

If you do not have an imagemap tool, it is possible to write out the map information by hand following the examples in this chapter. Simply note the pixel
coordinates as indicated by your image editor and type them into the appropriate
place in the map file. For instance, Photoshop's Info palette gives pixel coordinates as you move the mouse around the image.

Client-Side Imagemaps

Client-side imagemaps have three components:

- An ordinary graphic file (*.gif, .jpeg,* or *.png*)

- A map delimited by <map> tags containing the coordinate and URL information for each area

- The usemap attribute within the image tag (<img>) that indicates which map
  to reference

There are many advantages to using client-side imagemaps. They are self-
contained within the HTML document and do not rely on a server to function. This
means you can test the imagemap on your local machine or make working site
demos for distribution on disk. It also cuts down on the load on your server and
improves response times. In addition, they display complete URL information in

the status bar when the user mouses over the area (server-side imagemaps display only coordinates).

The only disadvantage is that because it is slightly newer technology, they are not universally supported. Netscape Navigator 1.0 and Internet Explorer 2.0 do not support client-side imagemaps. Experimental or obscure browser programs may not either. Fortunately, these browsers make up a tiny portion of the current browser population.

Sample client-side imagemap

Figure 8-2 shows a sample imagemapped graphic. Example 8-1 gives the HTML document that contains the client-side imagemap.

Example 8-1: HTML for Client-Side Image Map

```
      <HTML>
      <HEAD><TITLE>Client-side Imagemap Sample></TITLE></HEAD>
      <BODY>
A     <MAP NAME="spacey">
B     <AREA SHAPE="RECT" COORDS="203,23,285,106"
      HREF="http://www.lunch.com/orbit/">
C     <AREA SHAPE="CIRCLE" COORDS="372,64,40" HREF="mypage.html">
D     <AREA SHAPE="POLY"
      COORDS="99,47,105,41,94,39,98,34,110,35,115,28,120,35,133,38,13
      3,42,124,42,134,58,146,56,157,58,162,63,158,67,141,68,145,72,15
      5,
      73,158,75,159,80,148,83,141,83,113,103,87,83,72,83,64,80,64,76,
      68,73,77,72,79,63,70,59,67,53,68,47,78,45,89,45,99,47"
      HREF="yourpage.html">
      </MAP>
E     <IMG SRC="orbit.gif" WIDTH=500 HEIGHT=125 BORDER=0
      USEMAP="#spacey">
      </BODY>
      </HTML>
```

A   This marks the beginning of the map. You must give the map a name. Within the <map> there are <area> tags for each hotspot within the image.

B   Each area tag contains the shape identifier (**shape**), pixel coordinates (**coords**), and the URL for the link (**href**). In this case, the shape is the rectangle (both **rect** and **rectangle** are acceptable) that corresponds to the black square in the center of the image.

C   This area corresponds to the circular area on the right of the image in Figure 8-2. Its shape is **circle** (**circ** is also acceptable). For circles, the coordinates identify the position of the center of the circle and its radius in pixels (**coords=x,y,r**).

Example 8-1: HTML for Client-Side Image Map (continued)

D   This is the area tag for the irregular (polygon) shape on the left of the image in Figure 8-2. For polygons, the coordinates are pairs of x,y coordinates for each point or vertex along the path that surrounds the area (`coords=x1,y1,x2,y2,x3,y3...`). At least three pairs are required to define a triangle; complex polygons generate a long list of coordinates.

E   The USEMAP attribute is required within the image tag to indicate that this graphic is an imagemap that uses the <map> named "spacey."

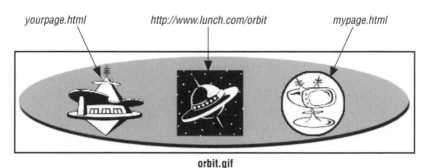

Figure 8-2: Imagemapped graphic

Server-Side Imagemaps

Server-side imagemaps will work with all browsers, but they are a bit more involved to create. In addition, they rely on the server, which makes them less portable than their client-side counterparts and increases the load on the server.

Server-side imagemaps have four elements:

- An ordinary graphic file (*.gif*, *.jpeg*, or *.png*)

- HTML tags in the document: the ISMAP attribute within the graphic's <img> tag and an anchor tag that links the graphic to the *.map* file on the server

- A map definition file (*.map*) containing the pixel coordinate and URL information for each clickable area; the *.map* file resides on the server and the format is server-dependent

- A CGI script that runs on the server (or a built-in function of the server software) that interprets the *.map* file and sends the correct URL to the HTTP server

Because server-side imagemaps are so dependent on the configuration of the server, you need to coordinate with your server administrator if you plan on implementing them. You'll need to find out which flavor of *.map* file to create (NCSA or CERN) as well as the pathname to which the imagemapped graphic should be linked (this usually includes a *cgi-bin* directory).

Sample map definition file (.map) file

Example 8-2 shows a server-side image map (called *spacey.map*) for the imagemapped graphic shown in Figure 8-2. Let's look at its component parts:

Example 8-2: Server-Side Image Map

```
A  default index.html
B  rect http://www.lunch.com/orbit/ 203,23 285,106
   circle mypage.html 372,64 412,104
   poly yourpage.html 99,47 105,41 94,39 98,34 110,35 115,28 120,35
   133,38 133,42 124,42 134,58 146,56 157,58 162,63 158,67 141,68
   145,72 155,73 158,75 159,80 148,83 141,83 113,103 87,83 72,83
   64,80 64,76 68,73 77,72 79,63 70,59 67,53 68,47 78,45 89,45 99,47
```

A This establishes the default URL, whish is what the browser will display if the user clicks outside one of the clickable areas. Set this to the current document if you want the impression that the click has no effect.

B Each hot area in the image is defined by a shape name (`rect`, `circle`, `poly`), a URL, and a set of pixel coordinates. The syntax for the coordinates varies by shape and is generally the same as explained for client-side imagemaps above. The syntax for some shapes may vary from server to server. In this .map file, the coordinates are defined for use by an NCSA server. Note that the coordinates defining the circle are different than in the client-side example. NCSA's syntax for defining a circle is "`x1,y1,x2,y2`," which corresponds to the x,y coordinates of the circle's center point followed by the x,y coordinates for the bottom-right point of the square that would enclose the circle.

The HTML document

Within the HTML file, the image is treated as shown here:

```
<HTML>
<HEAD><TITLE>Server-side Sample</TITLE></HEAD>
<BODY>
<A HREF="/cgi-bin/imagemap/spacey.map">
<IMG SRC="orbit.gif" ISMAP></A>
</BODY>
</HTML>
```

The anchor tag links the whole graphic to the map definition file (*spacey.map*) which is located within the *cgi-bin* directory on the server. This is a typical configuration; however, you should follow your server administrator's instructions.

The `ismap` attribute within the image tag tells the browser that the graphic is an imagemap.

When Not to Use Imagemaps

Imagemaps are not always the best solution and are actually waning somewhat in popularity as web design evolves. Slicing up a large image and holding the pieces together with a table often offers functionality that an imagemap can't match. This technique is so popular that it is built into web graphics tools such as Macromedia Fireworks and Adobe ImageReady. There is also a demonstration in Chapter 10, *Tables*.

Providing complete alternative text

When a user cannot view images (or has chosen to turn them off), the browser displays the text specified by the alt attribute within the <img> tag. Unfortunately, for each imagemap graphic you only get one alternative text message. This means all the links within the imagemap are unavailable to users without graphics.

One common solution to this is to provide a redundant set of links in HTML text somewhere else on the page so that users who cannot view graphics can still navigate the site.

If the image is divided into pieces, you can provide alternative text for each linked piece, which alleviates the need to add the extra line of linked text to your HTML page. The disadvantage, of course, is that this is really only ideal for graphics that neatly fit into rectangles.

Rollover buttons

Rollover buttons (graphics that change when the user mouses over them) are popular effects that use the power of JavaScript. Although it is possible to have an entire imagemap graphic change based on mouse-over cues, it is more efficient to break the image into pieces and swap out only the small portion that needs to change with the mouseover. You decrease the download time by only pre-loading the necessary small graphics. See Chapter 21, *Interactivity*, for sample JavaScript code for creating rollover effects.

Non-Web Links and Protocols

Linking to other web pages using the HTTP protocol is by far the most common type of link; however, there are several other types of transactions that can be made using other standard Internet protocols.

Mail Link (mailto)

The mailto protocol can be used in an anchor tag to automatically send an email message to the recipient from within the browser. Note that the browser must be configured to support this tag, so it will not work for all users. The mailto protocol has the following components:

    mailto:*username@domain*

A typical mail link might look like this:

    <A HREF="mailto:jen@oreilly.com">Send Jennifer email</A>

You can also experiment with adding information within the mailto URL that automatically fills in standard email fields such as Subject or cc:. As of this writing, these additional functions are only supported by Netscape 4.0, so use them with caution and do lots of testing:

    mailto:username@domain?subject=subject
    mailto:username@domain?cc=person1

```
mailto:username@domain?bcc=person2
mailto:username@domain?body=body
```

Additional variables are appended to the string with a & as follows:

```
mailto:username@domain?subject=subject&cc=person1&body=body
```

Spaces within subject lines need to be written as %20 (the space character in hexadecimal notation). The following is a sample mail link employing these additions:

```
<A HREF="mailto:jen@oreilly.com?subject=Like%20your%20book">
Email for Jen</A>
```

FTP Link (ftp://)

You can link directly to a file on an FTP server. When the user clicks on the link, the file will automatically download using the browser's built-in FTP functions and will be saved on the user's machine. If the document is on an anonymous FTP server (i.e., no account name and password are required), the FTP link is simple:

```
<A HREF="ftp://server/pathname">...</A>
```

If you are providing a link to an FTP server that requires the user to log in, the format is:

```
<A HREF="ftp://user:password@server/pathname">...</A>
```

It is highly recommended that you never include both the user name and password to a server within an HTML document. If you use the syntax user@server/path, the user will be prompted to enter his or her password in a dialog box.

By default, the requested file is transferred in binary format. To specify that the document should be transferred as an ASCII file, add ;type=a to the end of the URL:

```
<A HREF="ftp://user:password@server/pathname;type=a">...</A>
```

The variable type=d identifies the pathname as a directory and simply displays its contents in the browser window.

Following are some examples of FTP links:

```
<A HREF="ftp://pete@ftp.someserver.com/program.exe">...</A>
<A HREF="ftp://ftp.superwarehouse.com/games;type=d">...</A>
```

Other Links

The following URL types are not as well known or as useful as mailto: or ftp://, but they are available. As with other links, place these URLs after the HREF attribute within the anchor tag.

Type	Syntax	Use
File	file://server/path	Specifies a file without indicating the protocol. This is useful for accessing files on a contained site such as a CD-ROM or kiosk application, but is less appropriate over networks (such as the Internet).

Type	Syntax	Use
News	news:newsgroup news:message_id	Accesses either a single message or an entire newsgroup within the Usenet news system. Some browsers do not support news URLs so you should avoid using them.
NTTP	nntp://server:port/ newsgroup/article	Provides a complete mechanism for accessing Usenet news articles. The article will only be served to machines that are allowed to retrieve articles from this server, so this URL has limited practical use.
Telnet	telnet://user:pass- word@server:port/	Opens a telnet session with a desired server. The **user** and **password@** elements are optional and follow the same rules as described for `ftp://`.
Gopher	gopher:// server:port/path	Accesses a document on a gopher server. The gopher document retrieval system was eclipsed by the World Wide Web, but some gopher servers are still operating.

CHAPTER 9

Adding Images and Other Page Elements

This chapter focuses on the HTML tags available for placing elements such as rules, images, or multimedia objects on a web page. It also includes nondisplaying elements that are inserted as units into the HTML document such as style sheets and scripts.

Summary of Object Placement Tags

In this section, browser support for each tag is noted to the right of the tag name. Browsers that do not support the tag are grayed out. Browsers that deprecate the tag are noted with a superscript D. Tag usage is indicated below the tag name. A more thorough listing of attributes for each tag, according to the HTML 4.0 Specification, appears in Appendix A, *HTML Tags and Elements*.

<applet>   NN: 2, 3, 4 - MSIE: 2, 3, 4, 5 - HTML 4D - WebTV - Opera3

`<applet>...</applet>`

This tag, introduced by Netscape Navigator 2.0, is used to place a Java applet on the web page.

Attributes

`align=center|left|right`
> Aligns the applet and allows text to wrap around it (same as image alignment).

`alt=text`
> Provides alternate text if the applet cannot be displayed.

`code=class`
> Specifies the class name of the code to be executed (required).

`codebase=url`
> URL from which the code is retrieved.

`height=number`
> Height of the applet window in pixels.

`hspace=number`
> Holds *n* pixels space clear to the left and right of the applet window.

`name=text`
> Names the applet for reference elsewhere on the page.

`vspace=number`
> Holds *n* pixels space clear above and below the applet window.

`width=number`
> Width of the applet window in pixels.

<bgsound>
NN: 2, 3, 4 **- MSIE: 2, 3, 4, 5 -** HTML 4 - WebTV - Opera3

`<bgsound>`

Plays an audio file automatically in the background when the document loads in the browser. This tag is discussed in Chapter 19, *Audio on the Web.*

Attributes

`src=url`
> This mandatory attribute provides the URL of the audio file to be downloaded and played.

`loop=number|infinite`
> Sets the number of times the sound file should play. The value can be a number or set to `infinite`.

<embed>
NN: 2, 3, 4 **- MSIE:** 2, 3, 4, 5 - HTML 4 **- WebTV - Opera3**

`<embed>...</embed>`

Embeds an object into the web page. Embedded objects are most often multimedia files that require special plug-ins to display. Specific media types and their respective plug-ins may have additional proprietary attributes for controlling the playback of the file. Many of these are outlined in Chapters 19, 20, and 21 of this book. The closing tag is not always required, but is recommended.

Attributes

`align=left|right|top|bottom`
> *NN 4.0 and MSIE 4.0 only.* Controls the alignment of the media object relative to the surrounding text. `Top` and `bottom` are vertical alignments. `Left` and `right` position the object on the left or right margin and allow text to wrap around it.

`height=number`
> Specifies the height of the object in number of pixels. Some media types require this attribute.

`hidden=yes|no`
> Hides the media file or player from view when set to `yes`.

`hspace=`*number*

> *NN 4.0 and IE 4.0 only.* Used in conjunction with the `align` attribute, this attribute specifies in number of pixels the amount of space to leave clear to the left and right of the media object.

`name=`*name*

> Specifies a name for the embedded object. This is particularly useful for referencing the object from a script.

`palette=foreground|background`

> *NN 4.0 and MSIE 4.0 only.* This attributes applies to the Windows platform only. A value of `foreground` makes the palette used by the plug-in the foreground palette. Similarly, a value of `background` makes the plug-in use the background palette, which is also the default.

`pluginspage=`*url*

> *NN 4.0 and MSIE 4.0 only.* Specifies the URL for information on installing the appropriate plug-in.

`src=`*url*

> Provides the URL to the file or object to be placed on the page. This is a required attribute.

`units=pixels|en`

> Defines the measurement units used by height and width. The default is pixels. En units are half the point size of the body text.

`vspace=`*number*

> *NN 4.0 and MSIE 4.0 only.* Used in conjunction with the `align` attribute, this attribute specifies (in pixels) the amount of space to leave clear above and below the media object.

`width=`*number*

> Specifies the width of the object in number of pixels. Some media types require this attribute.

Internet Explorer only

`alt=`*text*

> Provides alternative text when the media object cannot be displayed (same as for the `<img>` tag).

`code=`*filename*

> Specifies the class name of the Java code to be executed.

`codebase=`*url*

> Specifies the base URL for the application.

Netscape Navigator only

`border=`*number*

> Specifies the width of the border (in pixels) around the media object.

`frameborder=yes|no`

> Turns the border on or off.

`pluginurl=url`
> Specifies a source for installing the appropriate plug-in for the media file. Netscape recommends that you use `pluginurl` instead of `pluginspage`.

`type=MIME type`
> Specifies the MIME type of the plug-in needed to run the file. Navigator uses either the value of the TYPE attribute or the suffix of the filename given as the source to determine which plug-in to use.

*
* — NN: 2, 3, 4 · MSIE: 2, 3, 4, 5 · HTML 4 · WebTV · Opera3

`<hr>`

Adds a horizontal rule to the page.

Attributes

`align=center|left|right`
> If the rule is shorter than the width of the window, this tag controls horizontal alignment of the rule. The default is `center`.

`noshade`
> This displays the rule as a solid (non-shaded) bar.

`size=number`
> Specifies the thickness of the rule in pixels.

`width=number or %`
> Specifies the length of the rule in pixels or as a percentage of the page width. By default, rules are the full width of the browser window.

<img> — NN: 2, 3, 4 · MSIE: 2, 3, 4, 5 · HTML 4 · WebTV · Opera3

`<img>`

Places a graphic on the page.

Attributes

`align=type`
> Specifies the alignment of an image using one of the following attributes:

Type	Resulting Alignment
absbottom	*Navigator 3.0 & 4.0 and Internet Explorer 4.0 only.* Aligns the bottom of the image with the bottom of the current line.
absmiddle	*Navigator 3.0 & 4.0 and Internet Explorer 4.0 only.* Aligns the middle of the image with the middle of the current line.
baseline	*Navigator 3.0 & 4.0 and Internet Explorer 4.0 only.* Aligns the bottom of the image with the baseline of the current line.
bottom	Aligns the bottom of the image with the text baseline. This is the default vertical alignment.
center	According to the W3C Spec, this centers the image horizontally on the page; however, in reality, browsers treat it the same as `align=middle`.

Type	Resulting Alignment
left	Aligns image on the left margin and allows subsequent text to wrap around it.
middle	Aligns the text baseline with the middle of the image.
right	Aligns image on the right margin and allows subsequent text to wrap around it.
texttop	*Navigator only.* Aligns the top of the image with the ascenders of the text line.
top	Aligns the top of the image with the top of the tallest object on that line.

alt=*text*
> Provides a string of alternative text that appears when the image is not displayed.

border=*number*
> Specifies the width (in pixels) of the border that surrounds a linked image. It is standard practice to set **border=0** to turn the border off.

height=*number*
> Specifies the height of the image in pixels. It is not required, but recommended to speed up the rendering of the web page.

hspace=*number*
> Used in conjunction with the **align** attribute, this attribute specifies in number of pixels the amount of space to leave clear to the left and right of the image.

ismap
> Indicates that the graphic is used as the basis for a server-side imagemap (an image containing multiple hypertext links). See Chapter 8, *Creating Links*, for more information on server-side imagemaps.

longdesc=*url*
> New in HTML 4.0 Specification. Specifies a link to a long description of the image or an imagemap's contents. This is used to make information about the image accessible to nonvisual browsers.

lowsrc=*url*
> *Netscape Navigator (all versions) and Internet Explorer 4.0 only.* Specifies an image (usually of a smaller file size) that will download first, followed by the final image specified by the **src** attribute.

src=*url*
> Provides the URL of the graphic file to be displayed.

usemap=*url*
> Specifies the map containing coordinates and links for a client-side imagemap (an image containing multiple hypertext links).

vspace=*number*
> Used in conjunction with the **align=left** or **right** attribute, this attribute specifies in number of pixels the amount of space to leave clear above and below the image.

`width=number`
Specifies the width of the image in pixels. It is not required, but recommended to speed up the rendering of the web page.

Internet Explorer's DYNSRC attribute

Internet Explorer versions 2.0 and later use the `<img>` tag to place a video on the page using the `dynsrc` attribute. The following attributes are related to the `dynsrc` function and work only with Internet Explorer:

`controls`
Adds playback controls for the video.

`dynsrc=url`
Provides the URL for the video file to be displayed on the page.

`loop=number|infinite`
Sets the number of times to play the video. It can be a number value or set to `infinite`.

`start=fileopen|mouseover|fileopen, mouseover`
Specifies when to play the video. By default, it begins playing as soon as it's downloaded (`fileopen`). You can set it to start when the mouse pointer is over the movie area (`mouseover`). If you combine them (separated by a comma), the movie plays once it's downloaded, then again every time the user mouses over it.

<marquee>   NN: 2, 3, 4 **- MSIE: 2, 3, 4, 5 -** HTML 4 **- WebTV -** Opera3

`<marquee>...</marquee>`

Creates a scrolling-text marquee area.

Attributes:

`align=top|middle|bottom`
Aligns the marquee with the top, middle, or bottom of the neighboring text line.

`behavior=scroll|slide|alternate`
Specifies how the text should behave. `Scroll` is the default setting and means the text should start completely off one side, scroll all the way across and completely off, then start over again. `Slide` stops the scroll when the text touches the other margin. `Alternate` means bounce back and forth within the marquee.

`bgcolor="#rrggbb"` or *color name*
Sets background color of marquee.

`direction=left|right`
Defines the direction in which the text scrolls.

`height=number`
Defines the height in pixels of the marquee area.

`hspace=number`
Holds *n* pixels space clear to the left and right of the marquee.

Images & Objects

`loop=`*number*`|infinite`
Specifies the number of loops as a number value or infinite.

`scrollamount=`*number*
Sets the number of pixels to move the text for each scroll movement.

`scrolldelay=`*number*
Specifies the delay, in milliseconds, between successive movements of the marquee text.

`vspace=`*number*
Holds a number of pixels space clear above and below the marquee.

`width=`*number*
Specifies the width in pixels of the marquee.

<noembed>   NN: 2, 3, 4 · MSIE: 2, 3, 4, 5 · HTML 4 · **WebTV** · **Opera3**

`<noembed>...</noembed>`

The text or object specified by `<noembed>` will appear when an embedded object cannot be displayed (e.g., when the appropriate plug-in is not available). This tag is placed within the `<embed>` container tags.

<noscript>   NN: 2, 3, 4 · MSIE: 2, 3, 4, 5 · **HTML 4** · **WebTV** · **Opera3**

`<noscript>...</noscript>`

Provides alternate content for when the script is not executed (either because the browser does not recognize the `<script>` tag, or because it has been configured not to run scripts).

<object>   NN: 2, 3, 4 · **MSIE: 2, 3, 4, 5** · **HTML 4** · WebTV · Opera3

`<object>...</object>`

Places an object (such as an applet, media file, etc.) on a web page. It is similar to the `<embed>` tag. The `<object>` tag often contains information for retrieving ActiveX controls that Internet Explorer on Windows uses to display the object.

Attributes

`align=baseline|center|left|middle|right|textbottom|`
`   textmiddle|texttop`
Aligns object with respect to surrounding text.

`border=`*number*
Sets the width of the border in pixels if the object is a link.

`classid=`*url*
Identifies the class identifier of the object. The syntax depends on the object type.

`codebase=`*url*
Identifies the URL of the object's codebase. Syntax depends on the object.

`codetype=codetype`
> *MSIE 3.0/4.0 and HTML 4.0 Spec only.* Specifies the media type of the code.

`data=url`
> Specifies the URL of the data used for the object. The syntax depends on the object.

`declare`
> *MSIE 3.0 and HTML 4.0 Spec only.* Declares an object without instantiating it.

`height=number`
> Specifies the height of the object in pixels.

`hspace=number`
> Holds *n* pixels space clear to the left and right of the object.

`name=text`
> Specifies the name of the object to be referenced by scripts on the page.

`shapes`
> *MSIE 3.0 and HTML 4.0 Spec only.* Indicates that the object contains an imagemap.

`standby=message`
> *MSIE 3.0 and HTML 4.0 Spec only.* Specifies message to display during object loading.

`type=type`
> Specifies the media type for the data.

`usemap=url`
> Specifies image map to use with the object.

`vspace=number`
> Holds *n* pixels space clear above and below the object.

`width=number`
> Specifies the object width in pixels.

<param>
NN: 2, 3, 4 - MSIE: 2, 3, 4, 5 - HTML 4 - WebTV - Opera3

`<param>...</param>`

Supplies a parameter within the `<applet>` or `<object>` tag.

Attributes

`name=text`
> Defines the name of the parameter.

`value=text`
> Defines the value of the parameter.

`valuetype=type`
> *Internet Explorer only.* Indicates the type of value: `data` indicates that the parameter's value is data (default); `ref` indicates that the parameter's value is a URL; `object` indicates that the value is the URL of another object in the document.

`type=type`
> *Internet Explorer only.* Specifies the media type.

```
<script>...</script>
```

Adds a script that is to be used in the document. See Chapter 22, *Introduction to JavaScript*, for demonstrations of the use of the <script> tag.

Attributes

type=*content type*
> Specifies the language of the script. Its value must be a media type (ex. text/javascript). This attribute is required by the HTML 4.0 specification and is a recommended replacement for the "language" attribute.

language=*language*
> Identifies the language of the script, such as JavaScript or VBScript. This attribute has been deprecated by the HTML 4.0 Spec in favor of the "type" attribute.

src=*url*
> *Netscape only.* Specifies the URL of an outside file containing the script to be loaded and run with the document.

```
<spacer>
```

Holds a specified amount of blank space within the flow of a page. It is often used to maintain space within table cells for correct display in Navigator.

Attributes

type=vertical|horizontal|block
> Specifies the type of spacer: vertical inserts space between two lines of text, horizontal inserts space between characters, and block inserts a rectangular space.

size=*number*
> Specifies a number of pixels to be used with a vertical or horizontal spacer.

height=*number*
> Specifies height in number of pixels for a block spacer.

width=*number*
> Specifies width in pixels for a block spacer.

align=*value*
> Aligns block spacer with surrounding text. Values are the same as for the <img> tag.

Horizontal Rules

The simplest element you can add to a web page is a horizontal rule, plopped into place with the <hr> tag. In most browsers, horizontal rules display by default as an "embossed" shaded rule that extends across the full width of the browser window (or available text space). Horizontal rules are used as simple dividers, breaking an otherwise long scroll into manageable chunks.

Since it is a block-level element, a horizontal rule will always create a line break above and below. If you want additional space between the rule and the surrounding elements, insert <p> tags above and/or below the <hr>, as shown in Figure 9-1.

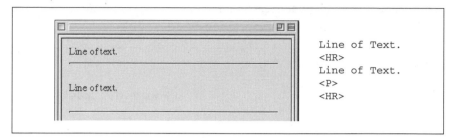

Figure 9-1: Inserting a <p> tag adds vertical space above or below a horizontal rule

There are a few attributes for the <hr> tag that allow authors to "design" rules more to their liking. They allow you to change the width, height, alignment of the rule. You can also opt to turn off the 3-D shaded effect using the noshade attribute.

Specifying Thickness

The size attribute controls the thickness or weight of the rule. Size is specified in number of pixels. See Figure 9-2

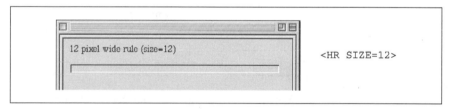

Figure 9-2: A 12-pixel rule

Specifying the Rule Length

Somewhat counterintuitively, the length of the rule is controlled by the width attribute (corresponding to the width of the page, I suppose). The value for the rule width can be provided as a specific pixel length by entering a number, or as a percentage of the available page width. See Figure 9-3.

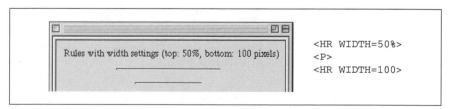

Figure 9-3: Rules set to 50% of page width (top) and 100 pixels (bottom)

Rule Alignment

If you've specified a length of a rule (using the **width** attribute) that is shorter than the width of the page, you can also decide how you would like the rule aligned: left, right, or centered. Like all other elements, horizontal placement is controlled using the **align** attribute and the values **left**, **right**, or **center**. See Figure 9-4.

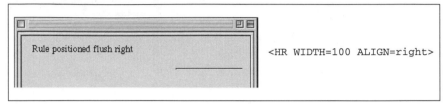

Figure 9-4: Rule positioned flush right

Turning Off 3-D Shading

The **noshade** attribute allows you to turn off the 3-D shading for horizontal rules. This will cause the rule to display as a solid black line. See Figure 9-5.

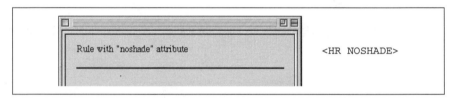

Figure 9-5: Rule with 3-D shading turned off

Creative Combinations

By using the available attributes in combination, you can get a little bit creative with horizontal rules. The most common trick is to set the width and size to the same value, creating a little embossed square that can be centered on the web page. Unfortunately, rules cannot be placed next to each other on a line. See Figure 9-6.

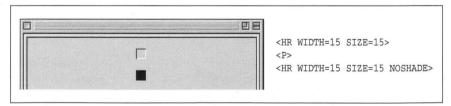

Figure 9-6: A 15-pixel-thick, 15-pixel-wide rule

Image Basics

Before jumping into the finer points of the `<img>` tag, let's back up and consider general graphics usage issues.

How Graphics Can Be Used

The overwhelming majority of graphics on the Web are used as inline images, graphics that are displayed in the browser window as part of the flow of the HTML document. Banners and buttons are examples of inline images. Inline images, which are placed on the page with the `<img>` tag, can serve a variety of functions as listed below. (Note that images may also be used as background tiles or viewed externally with a helper application).

As a Simple Graphic

A graphic can be used on a web page much as it is used in print—as a static image that adds decoration or information, such as a company logo or an illustration.

As a Link

A graphic can also be used to link to another document as an alternative to text links. Linking graphics are discussed later in this chapter.

As an Imagemap

An imagemap is a single graphic with multiple "hotspots" that link to other documents. There is nothing special about the graphic itself; it is an ordinary inline image. The "magic" is the result of special coding and map files that link pointer coordinates with their respective URLs. The `usemap` or `ismap` attribute within the `<img>` tag indicates to the browser that the graphic is used as a client-side or server-side imagemap (respectively).

A full explanation of how imagemaps work and how to create them appears in Chapter 8.

As Spacing Devices

Because web pages are difficult for designers to control with HTML alone, many designers use transparent graphics to invisibly control the alignment of text or the behavior of tables. David Siegel introduced the convention of using a single transparent pixel that can be resized to create any amount of white space on the page. Although it is one solution for arranging elements on the page, it isn't necessarily good HTML form.

Netscape's solution for holding extra space on a web page is its proprietary `<spacer>` tag. Spacers can be used to hold a specified amount of horizontal space, vertical space, or a "block" of space with width and height measurements. The `<spacer>` tag and its attributes are listed earlier in this chapter. Because this is a proprietary tag and because it adds presentation information throughout the HTML document, the use of the `<spacer>` tag is generally considered to be poor HTML form.

Acceptable Graphics Formats

A graphic needs to be in either GIF or JPEG format to be displayed as an inline image by the vast majority of browsers. Furthermore, the files need to be named with the proper suffixes—*.gif* for GIF files; *.jpeg* or *.jpg* for JPEG—in order to be recognized by the browser.

There is a third format, PNG (pronounced "ping"), which was designed specifically with web distribution in mind; however, only the very latest browser versions support PNG files (suffix *.png*) as inline graphics, and they don't support all of PNG's most attractive features. Until PNG gains better support, stick with either GIF or JPEG.

These graphics file formats, as well as other requirements for putting graphics online, are discussed in detail in the chapters of *Part III: Graphics*.

The *<img>* Tag and Its Attributes

The `<img>` tag inserts a graphic image into the document's text flow. Unlike horizontal rules, it doesn't create any paragraph breaks, so you can place graphics inline with the text. By default, the bottom of an image will align with the baseline of surrounding text (ways to alter this will be discussed later).

There are over a dozen attributes that can be added within the `<img>` tag to affect its display, but the only required attribute is `src`, which provides the URL of the graphic. The minimal HTML tag for placing an image on the page looks like this:

```
<IMG SRC="url of graphic">
```

Figure 9-7 shows an inline image and its HTML source.

```
<P>Star light <IMG SRC="star.gif"> Star bright.</P>
```

Figure 9-7: A graphic placed within a line of text

Linking Graphics

To make a graphic a link, place anchor tags around the image tag just as you would around any string of text characters:

```
<A HREF="document.html"><IMG SRC="picture.gif"></A>
```

When a graphic is linked, the browser displays a 1-pixel-wide border around the image in the same color as the text links on the page (usually a bright blue). In most cases, this blue border is unacceptable, particularly around a graphic with transparent edges, but it is quite simple to turn it off using the `border` attribute.

The `border` attribute specifies the width of the border in number of pixels. Specifying a value of zero turns the borders off, as shown in the following example. Of

---

course, if you are fond of the blue borders, you could just as easily make them really wide by setting a higher number value.

```
<A HREF="document.html"><IMG SRC="picture.gif" BORDER=0></A>
```

Alternative Text

If a graphic cannot be displayed (either because the file is corrupted or cannot be found), the browser displays a generic broken graphic icon in its place. The browser will also display a generic graphic icon when the user has chosen to turn graphics off for faster browsing (and a lot of users do). The alt attribute allows you to specify a string of alternative text to be displayed in place of the graphic when the graphic is unavailable, as shown in Figure 9-8. It is also what non-graphical browsers will display in place of images.

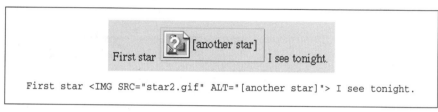

```
First star <IMG SRC="star2.gif" ALT="[another star]"> I see tonight.
```

Figure 9-8: Alternative text is displayed when graphics are unavailable

When alternative text is provided in the image tag, users at least know what they're missing. This is particularly important when graphics are links that make up the main navigation of the site. Readers can follow a link if they know where it goes, even if the graphic isn't visible. Without the alternative text, the page would be a big dead end.

Taking the extra time to provide alternative text for your images is the simplest way to make your page accessible to the greatest number of readers. In fact, the HTML 4.0 Specification has declared alt to be a required attribute within the <img> tag (although browsers are not currently enforcing it).

Specifying Width and Height

Although src is the only truly required attribute in the <img> tag, a few others come strongly recommended. The first is alt, discussed in the previous section. width and height are the others. The width and height attributes simply indicate the dimension of the graphic in pixels, such as:

```
<IMG SRC="star.gif" WIDTH=50 HEIGHT=50>
```

With this information the browser can lay out the page before the graphics download. Without width and height values, the page is displayed and then when the graphics finally arrive, the whole page is displayed a second time with the graphics in place (this process may actually take place in a series of passes depending on how it is constructed). It is worthwhile to take the time to include accurate width and height information in the image tag.

Resizing images

If the values specified in the width and height attributes are different than the actual dimensions of the graphic, the browser will resize the graphic to match the specified dimensions. If you specify a percentage value for width and height, the browser will resize the image to the desired proportions.

Although this effect can certainly be used strategically, as for resizing a single pixel graphic to hold a certain amount of space, it usually just results in a pixelated, poor image quality, as shown in Figure 9-9. It is better to resize images in a graphics program than to leave it up to the browser.

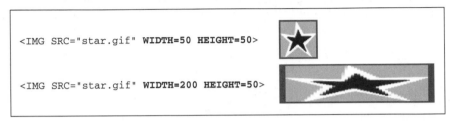

Figure 9-9: Scaling an image with width and height attributes

Using width and height to preload images

Preloading images refers to methods used for downloading images and storing them in cache before they actually need to be displayed on the page. One trick for preloading is to place the graphic on a page that will be accessed first (such as a home page), but set the width and height attributes to one pixel. This will cause the image to download with the rest of the page, but the only thing that will be visible is a one-pixel dot (which can be tucked away in a inconspicuous place).

```
<IMG SRC="bigpicture.gif" WIDTH=1 HEIGHT=1>
```

Ideally, the image will have finished downloading quietly while the user is still reading the first page and will pop into view instantly when the user links to the page where the image is displayed at its full size.

Vertical Alignment

The align attribute is used to control how the graphic is positioned in relation to the flow of the text.

Vertical alignment controls the placement of the graphic in relation to points in the surrounding text (usually the baseline). The default alignment is bottom, which aligns the bottom of the image with the baseline of the surrounding text (shown in Figure 9-10).

Figure 9-10: Default (bottom) alignment of image with text

The universally supported values for vertical alignment are top, middle, and bottom. Netscape Navigator introduced another (somewhat more subtle) set, which was then picked up for support in Internet Explorer 4.0. These are absbottom, absmiddle, texttop, and baseline (the same as bottom).

Figure 9-11 demonstrates the intended effects of each of these alignment values. The reality is slightly different. The absbottom value, for instance, seems to render the same as bottom, even in Navigator.

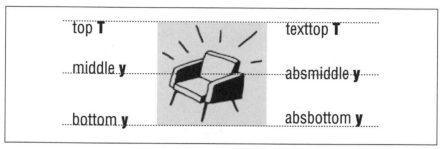

Figure 9-11: Vertical alignment values

Horizontal Alignment

The align attribute can be used to align a graphic horizontally on a page using the values left or right.

When a graphic is aligned left, it is placed along the left margin of the page and text is allowed to flow around it. Likewise, a right-aligned graphic is placed against the right margin, with text wrapping around it. Figure 9-12 shows how images are displayed when set to align to the left or right.

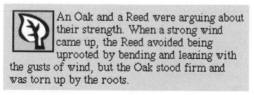

Figure 9-12: Text wraps around images when they are aligned to the left or right

Adding space around aligned images

When text flows around a graphic, it tends to bump right up against the graphic's edge. Usually, it is preferable to have a little space between the graphic and the surrounding text. In HTML, this is provided by using the vspace and hspace attributes within the <img> tag.

The vspace attribute holds a specified number of pixels space above and below an aligned graphic. Space to the left and the right is added with hspace. Note that space is always added symmetrically (both top and bottom, or on both sides), and it is not possible to specify an amount of space along a particular side of the graphic. Figure 9-13 shows an image aligned with the hspace attribute set to 12.

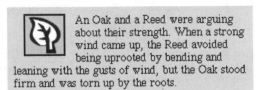

```
<IMG SRC="leaf.gif" ALIGN="left" HSPACE=12><P>An Oak and a Reed...
```

Figure 9-13: Image alignment with horizontal spacing

Stopping text wrap

Text will automatically wrap to fill the space along the side of an aligned graphic. If you want to stop the wrap and have the text resume below the image, insert a line break tag (<br>) with a clear attribute.

The clear attribute has three possible values: left, right, and all. It tells the browser to skip down on the page until the specified margin is clear (i.e., no graphics) and begin flowing the text at that point.

If your graphic is aligned right, insert <br clear=right> to begin the text below the graphic. For left-aligned graphics, use <br clear=left>. The <br clear=all> tag starts the text after the graphics on both margins (see Figure 9-14), so it may be the only value you'll ever need.

Tips for Placing Graphics

These are a few tips for graphics use that may not be obvious from simply looking at HTML code.

Link to large images

Remember that when designing for the Web, you must always consider the time it takes to download files. Images are particularly bandwidth-hungry, so you should use them inline with care. One successful strategy for providing access to very large images (with correspondingly large file sizes) is to provide a postage-stamp-size preview graphic that links to the full-size graphic.

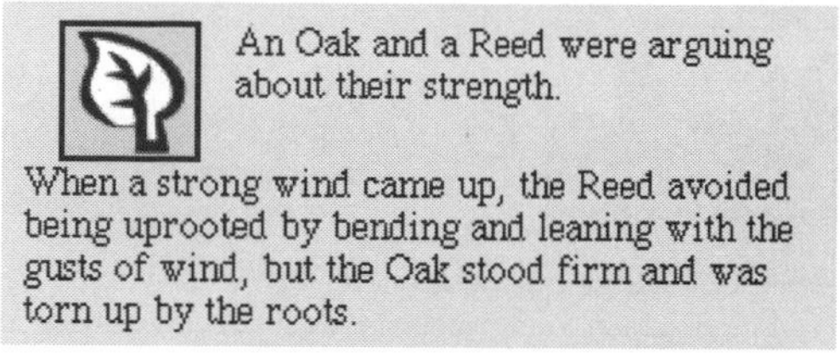

An Oak and a Reed were arguing about their strength.

When a strong wind came up, the Reed avoided being uprooted by bending and leaning with the gusts of wind, but the Oak stood firm and was torn up by the roots.

```
<IMG SRC="leaf.gif" ALIGN="left" HSPACE=12><P>An Oak and a Reed
were arguing about their strength.<BR CLEAR=all>When a strong...
```

Figure 9-14: Effect of the clear=all attribute

The preview could be a reduction of the whole image or just an alluring fragment. Be sure to provide information necessary to help users decide whether they want to spend the time clicking the link, such as a description of what they're going to get and the file size of the image (so they can make an estimate of how long they'll need to wait).

Reuse images whenever possible

When a browser downloads a graphic, it stores it temporarily in the disk cache (a space for temporarily storing files on the hard disk). That way, if it needs to redisplay the page, it can just pull up a local copy of the HTML and graphics files without making a new trip out to the remote server.

When you use the same graphic repetitively in a page or a site, the browser only needs to download the graphic once. Every subsequent instance of the graphic is grabbed from the local cache, which means less traffic for the server and faster display for the end user.

The browser recognizes a graphic by its entire pathname, not just the file name, so if you want to take advantage of file caching, be sure that each instance of your graphic is pointing to the same graphic on the server (not multiple copies of the same graphic in different directories).

The lowsrc trick

Large graphics may take a long time to download via slow connection speeds, which means your viewers may spend moments staring at an empty space on the screen. The `lowsrc` attribute for the `<img>` tag (first introduced by Netscape) provides one way to quickly give users some indication of the image to come while the "real" graphic is still downloading.

The `lowsrc` attribute provides the URL for an image file that the browser loads and displays when it first encounters the `<img>` tag. Then, once the document has completely loaded, the browser goes back and retrieves the image specified by the `src` attribute, as shown in Figure 9-15.

Figure 9-15: Code and images for using the lowsrc trick

To use this the way it was intended, the `lowsrc` image should contain the same image as the final graphic, but in a format that compresses to a much smaller file size. For instance, an image made up of only black and white pixels could stand in for a full-color JPEG.

Some web authors use `lowsrc` to simulate a two-frame animation effect, such as having some element appear in the second pass that wasn't in the initial `lowsrc` version. Bear in mind that the effect only works the first time the page is down-loaded, and depending on the way the images are cached, the `lowsrc` image may not show up again just by reloading the page. Also, on a very good connection, the `lowsrc` image may flash so quickly that users may miss it entirely.

Adding Java Applets to the Page

Java applets are self-contained programs written in the Java programming language, that can be placed inline on a web page just like a graphic. There are lots of Java applets available on the Web for free from Java library sites such as the JavaBoutique *(http://javaboutique.internet.com)*.

Most Java applet instructions require that you add the applet to the page using the handy `<applet>` tag (made just for the job!). However, the HTML 4.0 Spec recommends that applets be added using the `<object>` tag instead, although this is problematic in that some browsers don't recognize the `<object>` tag when used with Java. In this section, we will focus on the `<applet>` method.

The `<applet>` tag is a container for any number of parameter (`<param>`) tags. The following is an example of how an `<applet>` tag for a game might look:

```
<APPLET CODEBASE=class CODE="Wacky.class" WIDTH=300 HEIGHT=400>
<PARAM NAME="Delay" VALUE="250">
<PARAM NAME="Time" VALUE="120">
<PARAM NAME="PlaySounds" VALUE="YES">
</APPLET>
```

The opening applet tag contains a number of standard attributes:

code
> Tells the browser which applet will be used. Applets end with the suffix `.class` or `.jar`. This attribute is required.

codebase
> This tells the browser in which directory to find the applets. If the applets are in the same directory as the page, the `codebase` attribute is not necessary.

width and **height**
> These specify the pixel dimensions of the "window" the applet will occupy. These attributes are required for the Java applet to function properly.

The `<applet>` tag can also take many of the same attributes used for images, such as `alt` (for providing alternative text if the applet can not be displayed), `align` (for positioning the applet in the flow of text), and `hspace/vspace` (used in conjunction with `align`).

Special parameters for the applet are provided by any number of parameter tags (sometimes there are none). The `<param>` tag always contains the name of the parameter (`name=`) and its value (`value=`). Parameters provide special settings and controls that are specific to the particular applet, so you need to follow the parameter coding instructions provided by the programmer of the applet.

Adding Plug-in Media with <embed>

The `<embed>` tag places a media object, such as a Flash movie or the controls for a RealAudio track, on a web page. It displays the media object in a rectangular area that behaves much like an inline image in terms of positioning in the flow of the text. The `<embed>` tag was originally created by Netscape for use with plug-in technologies. It is currently supported by both browsers; however, the HTML 4.0 Specification prefers the use of the all-purpose `<object>` tag for the placement of multimedia elements.

When the browser encounters the `<embed>` tag, it matches the suffix of the file name (Netscape also looks for the value of the `type` attribute) with the appropriate plug-in.

The following is a very simple example of the `<embed>` tag:

```
<EMBED SRC="url" HEIGHT="165" WIDTH="250" ALIGN="right"
HSPACE="6">
</EMBED>
```

The `src` attribute is required to tell the browser the location of the media file to be played. Many media types require that the `width` and `height` values (the dimensions of the plug-in element in pixels) be specified in order for the plug-in to function.

If you are triggering plug-in functions from a script, you will need to give the element a name using the `name` attribute.

Like images, media objects can be positioned using the `align` attribute and its related `hspace` and `vspace` settings. In Internet Explorer, you can also specify alternative text with the familiar `alt` attribute.

There are a few special attributes that are only supported by version 4.0 browsers that you might also want to include. To hide the media file or object from view, use the `hidden` attribute with a value of "yes." The `pluginspage` attribute provides the URL of a page where the user can download information for the required plug-in should it not be found on the client machine. Netscape 4.0 introduced the `pluginurl` attribute, which specifies a link to a function that installs the plug-in automatically.

The complete list of attributes for the `<embed>` tag is detailed in the "Summary of Object Placement Tags" section earlier in this chapter.

Plug-in-Specific Attributes

In addition to these standard attributes, the embed tag may also contain plug-in-specific attributes for controlling the function of the player. The attributes `loop`, `autostart`, `autoplay`, and `volume` are examples of media-specific controls. Complete `<embed>` tags with their respective attributes are listed for several media types in Chapters 19, 20, and 21 of this book.

<noembed>

The `<noembed>` tag provides alternative content that displays if the browser cannot display the specified media file. In the following example, the browser would display the contents of the GIF file in place of the media object.

```
<EMBED SRC="url" HEIGHT="165" WIDTH="250"    ALIGN="right"
HSPACE="6">
<NOEMBED><IMG SRC="needplugin.gif"></NOEMBED>
</EMBED>
```

Adding Media Files with <object>

The `<object>` tag is an all-purpose object-placer. It can be used to place a variety of object types, such as ActiveX controls, plug-in media, Java applets, images, and more. The following shows the syntax of a simple `<object>` tag:

```
<OBJECT CLASSID="url" CODEBASE="url" DATA="url" TYPE="mimetype"
ID="name">
```

The `classid` is the URL of the object's implementation (the program). It has the same function as the `code` attribute of the `<applet>` tag when used for Java applets. When used for a plug-in media type, `classid` functions like `<embed>`'s `pluginurl` attribute, which points to the place where the appropriate plug-in can be found and automatically installed.

`Codebase` provides the URL for the plug-in and functions, the same as the `code-base` attribute in the `<applet>` tag. For plug-ins, `codebase` is the same as the `pluginspage` attribute.

The `data` attribute represents the URL of the object itself. It is equivalent to the `src` attribute for the `<embed>` tag. The `type` attribute provides the MIME type of the media object.

Objects placed with the `<object>` tag can be positioned with the standard `align` attribute, which has the same values as for the `<img>` tag. If the object is a plug-in, the `width` and `height` attributes may be required for the plug-in to function.

When using `<object>` for Java applets, the object tag may contain a number of parameter (`<param>`) tags, the same as for the `<applet>` tag. Unfortunately, as of this writing, Netscape 4.0 does not support `<param>` tags within the `<object>` tag, so it may not play applets correctly if placed this way.

A complete list of attributes for the `<object>` tag is detailed in the "Summary of Object Placement Tags" section earlier in this chapter.

CHAPTER 10

Tables

HTML tags for creating tables were originally developed for presenting rows and columns of tabular data, however, designers quickly co-opted them as a valuable tool for controlling the layout of web pages. Tables allow you to create columns of text, hold white space between elements, and constrict the dimensions of the page's content in ways other HTML formatting tags won't.

The HTML 4.0 Specification on tables is a great deal more complex than the previous 3.2 standard. It makes an effort to bring context and structure to table data as well as provide systems for incremental display and display on non-visual display agents (such as speech- and Braille-based browsers). Of course, this is just in its proposal stage as of this writing, so it will take a while to see how browsers will adopt the standards in practical use. To read what the HTML 4.0 Specification has to say about tables, see the W3C's site at *http://www.w3c.org/TR/REC-html40/ struct/tables.html.*

Summary of Table Tags

In this section, browser support for each tag is noted to the right of the tag name. Browsers that do not support the tag are grayed out. Browsers that deprecate the tag are noted with a superscript D. Tag usage is indicated below the tag name. A more thorough listing of attributes for each tag, according to the HTML 4.0 Specification, appears in Appendix A, *HTML Tags and Elements*.

<caption>   NN: 2, 3, 4 · MSIE: 2, 3, 4, 5 · HTML 4 · WebTV · Opera3

`<caption>...</caption>`

Provides a brief summary of the table's contents or purpose. According to the W3C HTML 4.0 Specification, if used, the caption must immediately follow the `<table>` tag and precede all other tags. The width of the caption is determined by the width of the table. The caption's position as displayed in the browser can be controlled with the `align` attribute (or `valign` in MSIE).

Attributes

`align=top|bottom|left|right|center`
Positions the caption relative to the table. This attribute has been deprecated by the W3C 4.0 Spec in favor of style sheet positioning.

`summary=text`
W3C 4.0 Specification only. Used to provide a longer description of the table's contents that could be used by a speech- or Braille-based web browser.

`valign=top|bottom`
Internet Explorer 3.0 and higher only. Positions the caption above or below the table (`top` is the default).

<col> NN: 2, 3, 4 **· MSIE:** 2, 3, **4, 5 · HTML 4 ·** WebTV **·** Opera3

`<col>`

Specifies properties for a column (or columns) within a *column group* (`<colgroup>`). Columns can share attributes (such as text alignment) without being part of a formal structural grouping.

Column groups and columns were introduced by Internet Explorer 3.0 and are now proposed by the HTML 4.0 Specification as a standard way to label table structure. They may also be useful in speeding the table display (i.e., the columns can be displayed incrementally without waiting for the entire contents of the table).

Attributes

`align=left|right|center`
Specifies alignment of text in the cells of a column.

`char=character`
Specifies a character along which the cell contents will be aligned. The default character is a decimal point (language-appropriate).

`charoff=length`
Specifies the distance to the first alignment character (`char`) on each line. If a line doesn't use an alignment character, it should be horizontally shifted to end at the alignment position.

`span=number`
Specifies the number of columns "spanned" by the `<col>` element (which shares its attributes with all the columns it spans).

`valign=top|middle|bottom|baseline`
Specifies the vertical alignment of text in the cells of a column.

`width=pixels, percentage, n*`
Specifies the width (in pixels, percentage, or relative) of each column spanned by the `<col>` element. It overrides the width attribute of the containing `<colgroup>` element.

`<colgroup>...</colgroup>`

Creates a *column group*, a structural division within a table that can be appointed attributes with style sheets or HTML. A table may include more than one column group. The number of columns in a group is specified either by the value of the **span** attribute or by a tally of columns `<col>` within the group. Its end tag is optional.

Column groups and columns were introduced by Internet Explorer 3.0 and are now proposed by the HTML 4.0 Specification as a standard way to label table structure. They may also be useful in speeding the table display (i.e., the columns can be displayed incrementally without waiting for the entire contents of the table).

Attributes

`align=left|right|center`
> Specifies the alignment of text in the cells of a column group.

`char=character`
> Specifies a character along which the cell contents will be aligned. The default character is a decimal point (language-appropriate).

`charoff=length`
> Specifies the distance to the first alignment character (**char**) on each line. If a line doesn't use an alignment character, it should be horizontally shifted to end at the alignment position.

`span=number`
> Specifies the number of columns in a column group. If span is not specified, the default is 1.

`valign=top|middle|bottom|baseline`
> Specifies the vertical alignment of text in the cells of a column group.

`width=pixels, percentage, n*`
> Specifies a default width for each column in the current column group. Width can be measured in pixels, percentages, or defined as a relative size (*). For example, 2* sets the column two times wider than the other columns; 0* sets the column width at the minimum necessary to hold the column's contents.

<table>   NN: 2, 3, 4 · MSIE: 2, 3, 4, 5 · HTML 4 · WebTV · Opera3

`<table>...</table>`

Defines the beginning and end of a table. The end tag is required, and its omission may cause the table not to render in some browsers.

Attribute

`align=left|right|center`
> Aligns the table within the text flow (same as align in the `<img>` tag). The default alignment is `left`. The *center* value is not universally supported, so it is more reliable to center a table on a page using tags outside the table (such

as <center> or <div>). This attribute has been deprecated by the W3C 4.0 Specification in favor of style sheet positioning.

background=*url*

Specifies a graphic image to be tiled in the background of the table. In Internet Explorer 3.0 and higher, the image tiles behind the entire table. In Netscape Navigator 4.0, the tile repeats in each individual frame (although its support is not officially documented).

bgcolor= "*#rrggbb*" or *color name*

Specifies a background color for the entire table. Value is specified in hexadecimal RGB values or by color name (see Chapter 5, *HTML Overview*, for more information on specifying colors in HTML).

border=*number*

Specifies the width (in pixels) of the border around the table and its cells. Set it to **border=0** to turn the borders off completely. The default value is 1. Adding the word **border** without a value results in a 1-pixel border.

cellpadding=*number*

Sets the amount of space, in number of pixels, between the cellborder and its contents. The default value is 1. For more information, see the "Space Between Cells" section in this chapter.

cellspacing=*number*

Sets the amount of space (in number of pixels) between table cells. The default value is 2. For more information, see the "Space Between Cells" section in this chapter.

frame=void|above|below|hsides|lhs|rhs|vsides|box|border

Tells the browser where to draw borders around the table. The values are as follows:

void	the frame does not appear (default)
above	top side only
below	bottom side only
hsides	top and bottom sides only
vsides	right and left sides only
lhs	left-hand side only
rhs	right-hand side only
box	all four sides
border	all four sides

When the border attribute is set to a value greater than zero, the frame defaults to **border** unless otherwise specified. This attribute was introduced by Internet Explorer 3.0 and now appears in the HTML 4.0 Specification. It is not supported by Netscape as of this writing.

height=*number, percentage*

Specifies the height of the entire table. It can be specified in a specific number of pixels or by a percentage of the browser window.

hspace=*number*

Holds a number of pixels space to the left and right of an aligned table (same as **hspace** in the <img> tag).

`rules=all|cols|groups|none|rows`

Tells the browser where to draw rules within the table. Its values are as follows:

none   no rules (default)
groups   rules appear between row groups (thead, tfoot, and tbody) and column groups
rows   rules appear between rows only
cols   rules appear between columns only
all   rules appear between all rows and columns

When the border attribute is set to a value greater than zero, rules default to "all" unless otherwise specified.

This attribute was introduced by Internet Explorer 3.0 and now appears in the HTML 4.0 Specification. It is not supported by Netscape as of this writing.

`summary=text`

Provides a summary of the table contents for use with non-visual browsers.

`vspace=number`

Holds a number of pixels space above and below an aligned table (same as vspace in the <img> tag).

`width=number, percentage`

Specifies the width of the entire table. It can be specified in a specific number of pixels or by percentage of the browser window.

Internet Explorer 2.0 and higher only

`bordercolor="#rrggbb"` or *color name*

Specifies the color of the main center portion of a table border. (Table borders are rendered using three color values to create a 3-D effect.)

`bordercolorlight="#rrggbb"` or *color name*

Specifies the color of the light shade used to render 3-D-looking table borders.

`bordercolordark="#rrggbb"` or *color name*

Specifies the color of the dark shade used to render 3-D-looking table borders.

\<tbody\>   NN: 2, 3, 4 · **MSIE:** 2, 3, **4, 5** · **HTML 4** · WebTV · Opera3

`<tbody>...</tbody>`

Defines a row or group of rows as the "body" of the table. It must contain at least one row (`<tr>`). The end tag is optional.

"Row group" tags (tbody, thead, and tfoot) were introduced by Internet Explorer and are part of the HTML 4.0 Specification, but all attributes may not be fully supported. The system could speed table display and provide a mechanism for scrolling the body of a table independently of its head and foot. It could also be useful for printing long tables for which the head information could be printed on each page.

Attributes

`align=left|center|right|justify|char`
> Specifies horizontal alignment (or justification) of cell contents.

`char=character`
> Specifies a character along which the cell contents will be aligned. The default character is a decimal point (language-appropriate).

`charoff=length`
> Specifies the distance to the first alignment character (`char`) on each line. If a line doesn't use an alignment character, it should be horizontally shifted to end at the alignment position.

`valign=top|middle|bottom|baseline`
> Specifies vertical alignment of cell contents.

<td>   NN: 2, 3, 4 · MSIE: 2, 3, 4, 5 · HTML 4 · WebTV · Opera3

`<td>...</td>`

Defines a table data cell. The end tag is not required, but may prevent unpredictable table display, particularly if the cell contains images. A table cell can contain any content, including another table.

Attributes

`align=left|center|right`
> Aligns the text (or other elements) within a table cell. The default value is `left`. This attribute has been deprecated by the W3C 4.0 Spec in favor of positioning with style sheets.

`background=url`
> Specifies a graphic image to be used as a tile within the cell. Netscape's documentation does not cover this tag, but it is supported by version 4.0.

`bgcolor="#rrggbb"` or `color name`
> Specifies a color to be used in the table cell. A cell's background color overrides colors specified at the row or table levels.

`colspan=number`
> Specifies the number of columns the current cell should span. The default value is 1. According to the W3C 4.0 Specification, the value zero ("0") means the current cell spans all columns from the current column to the last column in the table; in reality, however, this feature is not supported in currently available 4.0 browsers.

`height=number, percentage`
> Specifies the height of the cell in number of pixels or by a percentage value relative to the table height. The height specified in the first column will apply to the rest of the cells in the row. The height values need to be consistent for cells in a particular row. This attribute has been deprecated in the W3C 4.0 Specification.

`nowrap`

Disables automatic text wrapping for the current cell. Line breaks must be added with a `<p>` or `<br>`. This attribute has been deprecated by the W3C 4.0 Spec in favor of style sheet controls.

`rowspan=`*number*

Specifies the number of rows spanned by the current cell. The default value is 1. According to the W3C 4.0 Spec, the value zero ("0") means the current cell spans all rows from the current row to the last row; in reality, however, this feature is not supported in currently available 4.0 browsers.

`valign=top|middle|bottom|baseline`

Specifies the vertical alignment of the text (or other elements) within the table cell. The default is *middle*.

`width=`*number*

Specifies the width of the cell in number of pixels or by a percentage value relative to the table width. The width specified in the first row will apply to the rest of the cells in the column and the values need to be consistent for cells in the column. This attribute has been deprecated in the W3C 4.0 Specification.

Internet Explorer 2.0 and higher only

`bordercolor="#`*rrggbb*`"` or *color name*

Defines the border color for the cell.

`bordercolorlight="#`*rrggbb*`"` or *color name*

Defines the dark shadow color for the cell border.

`bordercolordark="#`*rrggbb*`"` or *color name*

Defines the light highlight color of the cell border.

New in HTML 4.0 Specification

`abbr=`*text*

Provides an abbreviated form of the cell's content.

`axis=`*text*

Places a cell into a conceptual category, which could then be used to organize the table in different ways.

`headers=`*id reference*

Lists header cells (by "id") that provide header information for the current data cell. This is intended to make tables more accessible to non-visual browsers.

`scope=row|col|rowgroup|colgroup`

Specifies groups of data cells for which the current header cell is applicable. This is intended to make tables more accessible to non-visual browsers.

<tfoot>   NN: 2, 3, 4 · **MSIE:** 2, 3, **4, 5** · **HTML 4** · WebTV · Opera3

`<tfoot>...</tfoot>`

Defines the foot of a table and should contain information about a table's columns. It is one of the "row group" tags introduced by Internet Explorer and proposed in the W3C 4.0 Specification (see <tbody>) and must contain at least one row (<tr>). Its end tag is optional.

Attributes

align=left|center|right|justify|char
> Specifies horizontal alignment (or justification) of cell contents.

char=*character*
> Specifies a character along which the cell contents will be aligned. The default character is a decimal point (language-appropriate).

charoff=*length*
> Specifies the distance to the first alignment character (char) on each line. If a line doesn't use an alignment character, it should be horizontally shifted to end at the alignment position.

valign=top|middle|bottom|baseline
> Specifies vertical alignment of cell contents.

<th>   **NN: 2, 3, 4 - MSIE: 2, 3, 4, 5 - HTML 4 - WebTV - Opera3**

<th>...</th>

Defines a table header cell. Table header cells function the same as table data cells (<td>). Browsers generally display the content of table header cells in bold text centered horizontally and vertically in the cell (although some browsers vary). The end tag is optional.

Attributes

> The <th> tag uses the same attributes as the <td> tag. See listing under <td>.

<thead>   NN: 2, 3, 4 - **MSIE:** 2, 3, **4, 5 - HTML 4 -** WebTV - Opera3

<thead>...</thead>

Defines the head of the table and should contain information about a table. It must contain at least one row (<tr>). <thead> is one of the "row group" tags introduced by Internet Explorer and proposed in the W3C 4.0 Specification (see <tbody>). Its end tag is optional.

Attributes

align=left|center|right|justify|char
> Specifies horizontal alignment (or justification) of cell contents.

char=*character*
> Specifies a character along which the cell contents will be aligned. The default character is a decimal point (language-appropriate).

charoff=*length*
> Specifies the distance to the first alignment character (char) on each line. If a line doesn't use an alignment character, it should be horizontally shifted to end at the alignment position.

valign=top|middle|bottom|baseline
> Specifies vertical alignment of cell contents.

<tr>...</tr>

Defines a row of cells within a table. A table row as delimited by <tr> tags contains no content other than a collection of table cells (<td>). The end tag is optional.

Attributes

align=left|center|right
>   Aligns the text (or other elements) within the cells of the current row. This attribute has been deprecated by the W3C 4.0 Spec in favor of positioning with style sheets.

bgcolor="#rrggbb" or color name
>   Specifies a color to be used in the row. A row's background color overrides the color specified at the table level.

valign=top|middle|bottom|baseline
>   Specifies the vertical alignment of the text (or other elements) within cells of the current row.

Internet Explorer 2.0 and higher only

background=url of image file
>   Specifies a graphic image to be used as a tile within the row.

bordercolor="#rrggbb" or color name
>   Defines the border color for the row.

bordercolorlight="#rrggbb" or color name
>   Defines the dark shadow color for the row border.

bordercolordark="#rrggbb" or color name
>   Defines the light highlight color of the row border.

Introduction to Tables

Although there are no true classifications, tables can be used in the following general ways:

Table Usage	Illustration
Data Table This is a table at its most basic (and as the creators of HTML intended)—rows and columns of textual data. Of course, data tables can be much larger and more complex than shown in this example.	Values that Make Up the Web Palette

Decimal	Hexidecimal	Percentage
0	00	0%
51	33	20%
102	66	40%
153	99	60%
204	CC	80%
255	FF	100%

Text Alignment
Tables are often used to clean up the display of text by creating effects common to print, such as columns, hanging indents, and extra white space.

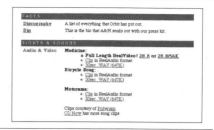

Page Template
Many web designers use a large table as a container to give structure to a page. One common configuration is to create narrow columns for navigational items as shown in this example. A template for a two-column table follows in the "Templates" section of this chapter.

Multipart Image Container
Tables can be used to hold together a large graphic that has been divided into separate sections to accommodate animations, rollovers, etc. In the example at right, the border was turned on to reveal the individual sections. Holding images together with tables is discussed at the end of this chapter.

The HTML 4.0 Specification proposal discourages the use of tables for page layout, favoring Cascading Style Sheets with absolute positioning instead. But until style sheets are more universally and consistently supported by the browsers in current use, tables remain a designer's most reliable tool for constructing complex page layouts.

Basic Table Structure

At their most basic, tables are made up cells, arranged into rows and columns. You can control display characteristics for the whole table level, the row level, and for individual cells (there are currently no supported methods for controlling columns as a group).

Rows and Cells

The bare minimum tags for describing a table are `<table>`, `<tr>`, and `<td>`. The following HTML shows the basic structure for a four-cell table:

```
<TABLE>
<TR>
     <TD>cell 1</TD><TD>cell 2</TD>
</TR>
<TR>
     <TD>cell 3</TD><TD>cell 4</TD>
</TR>
</TABLE>
```

The `<table>` tag defines the contents of the table. Each row is defined by `<tr>` tags, and is made up of a number of data (or header) cells. The number of columns is defined by the number of cells in a row. Data cells are indicated by the `<td>` tag. A table cell may contain any data that can be displayed in an HTML document (formatted text, images, multimedia elements, and even other tables).

Figure 10-1 gives a visual representation of this concept. The image on the left shows that the table consists of two rows and that each consists of two cells. The image on the right shows just how the HTML describes the rows and cells.

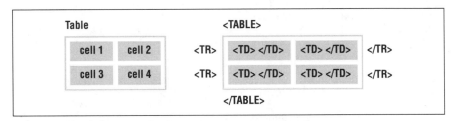

Figure 10-1: HTML tables are divided into rows and cells, as shown at left. The <tr> tag creates rows and the <td> tag creates cells, as shown at right.

Header cells use the `<th>` tag and function the same as data cells but are displayed in bold centered text. You may also add a caption to the table (using the `<caption>` tag), which provides a title or brief description of the table. The `<caption>` tag should be placed before the first row of the table; be sure that it is outside the row containers. Because tables are so often used as layout devices only, the caption feature is less used than the other main table components.

Table level controls

At the table level (using attributes within the `<table>` tag outlined above), you can control:

- the width of the table and its position on the page
- the color of all its cells
- the thickness of the border
- the spacing within and between cells (using cellpadding and cellspacing, respectively)

Row level controls

For each row (using attributes within the <tr> tag), you can control only:

- the vertical and horizontal alignment of the cells' contents

- backround colors for all the cells contained in that row

Row settings override table-level settings. Note that table row tags are merely containers for cell tags and contain no actual data themselves.

Cell level controls

Much of a table's structure and appearance is controlled at the individual cell level using <td> or <th> attributes. Within cells, you can control:

- the vertical and horizontal alignment of the cell's contents

- the color of the cell background

- the height and width of the cell (and the row and column that contain it)

- whether the cell should span over more than one cell space in the table grid

Alignment and color specifications at the cell level will override settings made at the row and table level.

Spanning Rows and Columns

Cells in a table can occupy the space of more than one cell in a row or column. This behavior is set within the <th> or <td> tags using the colspan and rowspan attributes.

Column span

In Figure 10-2, <td colspan=2> tells the browser to make "cell 1" occupy the same horizontal space as two cells. The resulting spanned cell is indicated in the figure on the left. Note that the row containing the spanned cell now only has one set of <td> tags instead of two.

Setting the colspan to a number greater than the actual number of columns (such as "colspan=4" in the following example) may cause some browsers to add empty columns to the table, possibly throwing your elements out of alignment. For example, in Netscape 4.5 and earlier, additional collapsed columns appear as an extra-wide border on the right of the table. The HTML 4.0 Specification requests that empty cells not be added.

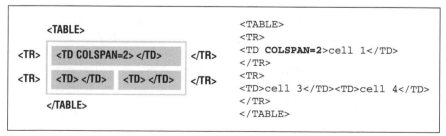

Figure 10-2: The colspan attribute spans cells horizontally.

Row span

Similar to `colspan`, the `rowspan` attribute stretches a cell to occupy the space of cells in rows below. Include the `rowspan` attribute in the row where you want the cell to begin and set its value equal to the number of rows you want it to span.

In Figure 10-3, note that the bottom row now only contains one cell (the other one has been incorporated into the vertical spanned cell). The resulting spanned cell is illustrated in the figure on the left. The browser ignores over-extended `rowspan` values.

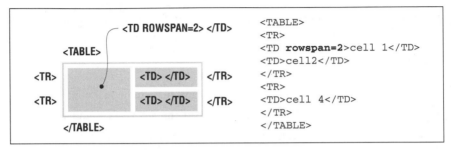

Figure 10-3: The rowspan attribute spans cells vertically

 You may combine `colspan` and `rowspan` attributes to create a cell that spans both rows and columns.

Row and Column Groups

Internet Explorer 3.0 introduced a system for grouping rows and columns so they can be treated as units by style sheets or other HTML formatting tags. The system is now reflected in the W3C 4.0 Specification for tables, so it bears mentioning here. However, support for row and column groups is far from universal as of this writing (in fact, Navigator 4.0 doesn't recognize them at all), so keep them in mind, but use them with caution.

Row groups

Rows can be classified into a table head (`<thead>`), a table foot (`<tfoot>`), and one or more table body (`<tbody>`). The head and foot should contain information about the document and may someday be used to display fixed elements while the body scrolls independently. It is recommended by the W3C that the foot (if there is one) appear before the body of the table so the table can render the foot before downloading all of the (potentially numerous) rows of data.

The `rules` attribute in the table tag may use row group information for placing rules within a table.

Column groups

Column groups create structural divisions within a table. This allows the columns created with <td> and <th> tags to be addressed as a group, usually for style and formatting purposes.

The <colgroup> tag delimits a conceptual group of columns. The number of columns included in the group is indicated with the span attribute. You can set the width of every column in the group (using pixel measurements, percentages, or relative values) with the width attribute.

The <col> element is used to apply attribute specifications across several tables without actually grouping them together structurally or conceptually. Like <colgroup>, you can specify the span (number of affected columns) and width (in pixels, percentages, or relative values) within the <col> tag.

Sample HTML

The following is a bare-bones example of how row and column groups would be integrated into the HTML table structure (with its resulting table display in a browser). Figure 10-4 shows the result. Note again that proper support for row and column groups and their attributes is rare as of this writing, however, it may be useful to be familiar with this structure in the future.

```
<TABLE BORDER=1>
<CAPTION>Table Description</CAPTION>
<COLGROUP width=100>
    <COL>
    <COL>
</COLGROUP>
<COLGROUP width=50>
<THEAD valign="top">
<TR>
    <TH>Heading 1</TH><TH>Heading 2</TH><TH>Heading 3</TH>
</TR>
</THEAD>
<TFOOT>
<TR>
    <TH>Footer 1</TH><TH>Footer 2</TH><TH>Footer 3</TH>
</TR>
</TFOOT>
<TBODY>
<TR>
    <TH>Cell Data 1</TH><TH>Cell Data 2</TH><TH>Cell Data 3</TH>
</TR>
</TBODY>
</TABLE>
```

Affecting Table Appearance

The HTML table standard provides many tags for controlling the display of tables. Bear in mind that, as with most formatting tags, browsers have their own way of interpreting your instructions, so results may vary among browser releases and

Table Description		
Heading 1	**Heading 2**	**Heading 3**
Cell Data 1	Cell Data 2	Cell Data 3
Footer 1	Footer 2	Footer 3

Figure 10-4: This table uses the column and row groups to organize structure

platforms. This is particularly true of tables since the standard is still being nailed down. As always, it is best to do a lot of testing in a variety of viewing environments.

It is important to note that many of the tags that affect appearance (align, valign, and bgcolor) have been deprecated by the HTML 4.0 Specification in favor of achieving the same effects with style sheets. Expect the major browsers, however, to continue supporting the following methods until style sheets are universally supported.

Borders

You can add a shaded border around the table and its cells by adding the border attribute within the <table> tag. If no value is indicated, the border attribute indicates a width of one pixel, as shown in Figure 10-5.

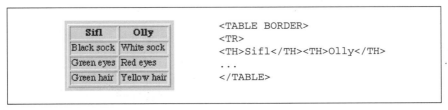

```
<TABLE BORDER>
<TR>
<TH>Sifl</TH><TH>Olly</TH>
...
</TABLE>
```

Figure 10-5: Table with a one-pixel border

Specifying a higher number for the border will add a thicker beveled border around the outside edges of the table, as shown in Figure 10-6. Thicker lines between cells are created with cellspacing, described later.

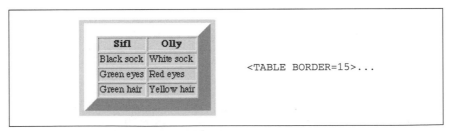

`<TABLE BORDER=15>...`

Figure 10-6: Table with a 15-pixel border

Even if you don't want a table to display with a border in your final design, turning the border on during the design process can help in visualizing the table structure; it is particularly useful for debugging problematic tables. Just remember to turn it off again before uploading.

Positioning a Table on the Page

On current browsers (Navigator and IE versions 3.0 and higher), tables behave the same as images when it comes to placing them in the flow of the page. Use the `align` attribute in the `<table>` tag to position the table against the left or right margin and allow text to flow around it. Like images, you can specify a number of pixels to hold clear to the left and right of the table using the `hspace` attribute. `vspace` holds space above and below the table.

Centering tables

The 4.0 browsers allow you to center a table on the page by setting the `align` attribute to equal `center`. Unlike left or right margin alignments, this setting does not allow text to flow around the table.

Because this attribute is not universally supported, it is best to center a table using HTML tags outside the table, such as `<center>` or `<div>`.

Aligning Text in Cells

By default, the text (or any element) in a data cell will be positioned flush left and centered vertically within the available height of the cell, as shown in Figure 10-7. 

Name	History
Chester	Born in Las Vegas on a craps table, **Chester** met Sifl in 1985 while touring the gardens of the Captain Crunch factory.
Stealth	**Stealth**'s vendetta against Olly started 15 years ago when Olly (a waiter at the time) served Stealth scrambled eggs with plastic dinosaurs in them.

Figure 10-7: Default placement of data within a cell.

Table header text (`<th>`) is generally displayed in bold text centered horizontally and vertically in the cell. You can override these defaults by using the `align` and `valign` attributes at either the row or cell level.

Row Settings

Alignment settings specified within the `<tr>` tag affect all the table cells (`<td>` or `<th>`) within that row. This makes it easy to apply alignment changes across multiple cells.

Cell Settings

Alignment attributes within a cell (<td> or <th>) apply to the current cell. Cell settings will override row settings. Furthermore, alignment settings within the contents of the cell (e.g., <p align=right>) take precedence over both cell and row settings.

Horizontal alignment is specified with the align attribute, which takes the standard left, right, or center values. These values work the same as regular paragraph alignment.

Vertical alignment is controlled using the valign attribute, which can be set to top, middle (the default), bottom, or baseline ("first text line appears on a baseline common to all the cells in the row").

By default, the text in a cell will automatically wrap to fill the allotted space. To keep text on one line (unless broken by a <br> or <p>), use the nowrap attribute within the table cell (<td> or <th>). This should be done with caution because the text in the cell may render larger for some users and will run out of room in the table cell.

Sizing Tables

You can control the size of the entire table as well as the size of rows and columns. By default, a table (and its rows and columns) will be sized automatically to the minimum dimensions required to fit their contents. In many cases, it is desirable to assign a table or column a specific size (especially when using the table to build a page structure).

If the contents require a width greater than the specified size, the table will generally resize to accommodate the contents. Size specifications are treated as suggestions that will be followed as long as they don't conflict with other display directions. In effect, by specifying the size of a table you are merely specifying the minimum size.

Table sizes can be unpredictable even when specified, because they vary from browser to browser. For instance, Netscape 3.0 will preserve the specified width of the cell even if its contents are wider, resulting in items hanging outside the table or into neighboring cells. It is best to specify ample room to accommodate the contents of the cells.

Table dimensions

The width attribute is used within the <table> tag to specify the width of the table. You can specify an absolute value (measured in pixels) or a relative value (a percentage of the available width of the screen) as shown in the following table:

Style	Sample HTML	Result
Absolute value	<TABLE WIDTH=600>	Makes the table 600 pixels wide
Relative value	<TABLE WIDTH=80%>	Makes the table 80% of the screen width

To make a table fill the browser width, set the width to 100%.

Table height can be specified using the height attribute, which can also be defined by absolute or relative values. By default, the table will end after the longest column of data, but you can force it to be longer or to always fill the screen (height=100%).

Cell dimensions

Similarly, you can use the width and height attributes within a cell tag (<td> or <th>) to specify the dimensions of that cell. A cell's width setting will affect the width of the entire column it occupies, therefore, column widths can be specified by setting the width of just one cell in the column (generally those in the top row); the remaining cells will follow.

Likewise, the cell's height may determine the height of all the cells in that row, so row height can be set using just one cell in each row.

Height and width values can be absolute measurements in pixels, or percentages relative to the dimensions of the table.

Table Cell Spacing

There are two types of space that can be added in and around table cells: cell padding and cell spacing. The cellpadding and cellspacing attributes are used within the <table> tag and apply to the whole table.

cellspacing
    Cell spacing, which is controlled by the cellspacing attribute within the <table> tag, refers to the space between the cells (see the left image in Figure 10-8). Values are specified in number of pixels. Increasing the cell spacing results in wider shaded borders between cells. In the left image in Figure 10-8, the gray areas indicate the 10 pixels of cell spacing added between cells. The default value for cellspacing is 2, therefore, if no cell-spacing is specified, browsers will automatically place 2 pixels of space between cells.

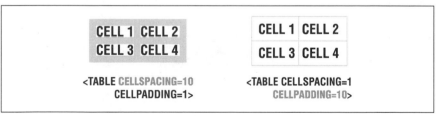

Figure 10-8: Cell spacing versus cell padding

cellpadding
    Cell padding refers to the amount of space between the cell's border and its contents (as indicated in the right image in Figure 10-8). It is specified using the cellpadding attribute within the <table> tag. Values are specified in number of pixels; the default value is 1. Relative values (percentages of available space) may also be used.

Different effects can be created using different combinations of spacing and padding. If you want your table to be seamless, as when it is holding together an image, be sure to set the border, cellspacing, and cellpadding to 0, as follows:

```
<TABLE BORDER=0 CELLPADDING=0 CELLSPACING=0>
```

Coloring Tables

You can specify a background color for the entire table (<table>), selected rows (<tr>), or individual cells (<td> or <th>) by placing the bgcolor attribute in the appropriate tag. The bgcolor attribute is recognized by MSIE versions 2.0 and higher and Navigator versions 3.0 and higher.

Color values can be specified either by their hexadecimal RGB values or by a standard color name. For more information on specifying color in HTML, see Chapter 5, *HTML Overview*.

Color settings in a cell will override settings made at the row level, which override settings made at the table level. To illustrate, in the following example, the whole table is set to light gray, the second row is set to medium gray, and the furthest right cell in that row is set to dark gray. Figure 10-9 shows the results.

```
<TABLE BORDER=1 BGCOLOR="#CCCCCC">
<TR>
<TD></TD><TD></TD><TD></TD>
</TR>
<TR BGCOLOR="#999999">
<TD></TD><TD></TD><TD BGCOLOR="#333333"></TD>
</TR>
<TR>
<TD></TD><TD></TD><TD></TD>
</TR>
<TR>
<TD></TD><TD></TD><TD></TD>
</TR>
</TABLE>
```

Figure 10-9: Effects of setting background colors at cell, row and table levels

Netscape Navigator and Internet Explorer treat background colors at the table level differently. Navigator fills every cell in the table with the specified color, but the border picks up the color of the document background. IE fills the entire table area, including the borders, with the specified color for a more unified effect. Background colors at the row and cell level are treated consistently by the two browsers (although Navigator uses the document background color for empty cells).

Table Troubleshooting

Despite the control they offer over page layout, tables are also notorious for causing major headaches and frustrations. This is partly due to the potential complexity of the code—it's easy to miss one little character that will topple a table like a house of cards. Another source of chaos is that browsers are inconsistent and sometimes quirky in the way they interpret table code. It is not uncommon to spend several careful hours crafting a table that looks perfect in browsers X and Y, but crumbles into a little ball in browser Z. Or it may look great with one user's settings, but unacceptable with another's.

Although not every problem can be anticipated, there are a number of standard places tables tend to go wrong. HTML tables have some inherent peculiarities that can make them frustrating to work with, but knowing about the potential pitfalls up front can make the design process go more smoothly. As always, it is necessary to test your designs on as many browser and platform configurations as possible.

Text in Tables

When designing tables that contain text, remember that text size can vary greatly from user to user. This adds an inherent level of unpredictability to the way your tables display.

Not only does text display larger on PCs than on Macs, each individual can set the font size for text display. So although you've put a nice, tidy column of options in a table cell, for the user whose font is set to 16 points, the text may get some extra line breaks and stretch off the screen.

In general, variable text sizes affect the height of cells and tables as the cells stretch longer to accommodate their larger contents (particularly if the width has been specified with an absolute pixel value). If you have HTML text in a cell, particularly if the cell needs to be displayed at specific pixel dimensions within the table, be sure to give it lots of extra room and test your page with different browser font settings.

If you are using style sheets, you can control the size of the text by setting it to a specific pixel height; bear in mind, however, that many users still use browsers that do not support style sheets.

Form Elements in Tables

Like text, the way form elements display in a browser is dependent on the size of the default monospace (or constant width) font that is specified in the user's browser preferences. If the user has his monospace font set to 24 points (or to "largest" in Internet Explorer), your form elements (particularly text fields) will resize larger accordingly.

In the real-world example in Figure 10-10, I used a table to hold together a badge illustration, which contained a form for entering a name and password. In testing, we found that the target audience generally had their browser fonts set to 18 points (they were working on very high-resolution monitors), which caused the form text fields to resize and break the table apart. Making the badge image larger and incorporating lots of extra space was the solution in this case.

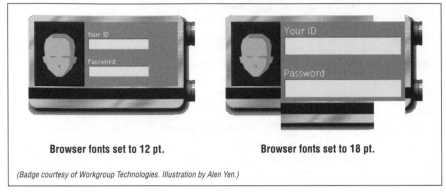

| Browser fonts set to 12 pt. | Browser fonts set to 18 pt. |

(Badge courtesy of Workgroup Technologies. Illustration by Alen Yen.)

Figure 10-10: The badge looks fine when browser fonts are set to 12 points, but falls apart at 18 points

Unwanted White Space

It is common for extra white space to creep between table cells (or between the cells and the border). When you are trying to create a seamless effect with colored cells or hold together pieces of a larger image, this extra space is unacceptable.

Returns and spaces within <td>s

The problem most often lies within the cell (<td>) tag. Some browsers will render any extra space within a <td> tag, such as a character space or a line return, as white space in the table. This can occur when the cell contains text; however, the effect is most noticeable when the contents are images.

 Because <table> and <tr> tags are regarded as only containers for other tags, not as containers for actual content or data, spaces and returns within these tags are ignored.

If you want a seamless table, begin with the border, cellpadding, and cellspacing all set to zero (0) in the <table> tag. In the code in Figure 10-11, a graphic is divided into four parts and held together with a table. The goal is to hold the graphic together seamlessly. As shown in the figure, the returns and extra spaces within the <td> tags add white space in each cell

To keep out unwanted white space, be sure that the enclosing <td> and </td> tags are flush against the content of the cell, with no extra spaces or returns. In Figure 10-12, I've kept the <td> tags and their contents on one line, and the problem goes away.

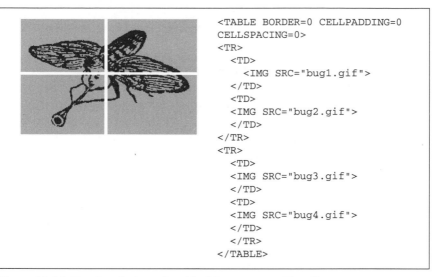

```
<TABLE BORDER=0 CELLPADDING=0
CELLSPACING=0>
<TR>
  <TD>
    <IMG SRC="bug1.gif">
  </TD>
  <TD>
  <IMG SRC="bug2.gif">
  </TD>
</TR>
<TR>
  <TD>
  <IMG SRC="bug3.gif">
  </TD>
  <TD>
  <IMG SRC="bug4.gif">
  </TD>
  </TR>
</TABLE>
```

Figure 10-11: Line breaks in code add white space to table cells

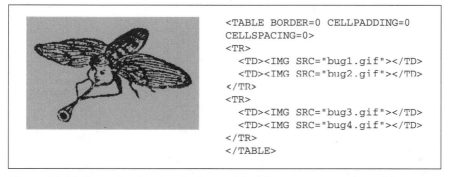

```
<TABLE BORDER=0 CELLPADDING=0
CELLSPACING=0>
<TR>
  <TD><IMG SRC="bug1.gif"></TD>
  <TD><IMG SRC="bug2.gif"></TD>
</TR>
<TR>
  <TD><IMG SRC="bug3.gif"></TD>
  <TD><IMG SRC="bug4.gif"></TD>
</TR>
</TABLE>
```

Figure 10-12: Removing line breaks from table cells creates a seamless table

Missing end tags

In most cases, closing cell tags (</td>) are optional, however, omitting them may add extra white space to the cell. The principle is the same as in Figure 10-11—the line break to the next starting <td> tag is rendered as extra space. For seamless tables, it is necessary to use end tags within tables as shown in Figure 10-12. The code below results in the effect shown in Figure 10-11.

```
<TABLE BORDER=0 CELLPADDING=0 CELLSPACING=0>
<TR>
  <TD><IMG SRC="bug1.gif">
  <TD><IMG SRC="bug2.gif">
<TR>
  <TD><IMG SRC="bug3.gif">
  <TD><IMG SRC="bug4.gif">
</TABLE>
```

Cellspacing in Netscape Navigator*

According to the HTML Specification, if you set `cellspacing=0` within the `<table>` tag, there should be no extra space between cells. There is a bug in Netscape's table implementation, however, that causes extra space to be added even when the cellspacing is set to 0. To eliminate all extra space for Netscape, you must explicitly include the `border=0` attribute in the `<table>` tag as well.

The default value of the `border` attribute should be 0, but in Netscape it takes up space (even though it doesn't draw a shaded line) unless you explicitly set it to 0.

Collapsing Cells in Netscape

As of this writing, all versions of Netscape will collapse empty cells and will not render a background color in a collapsed cell. For that reason, all cells in a table need to contain *something* in order for it to render properly and with its background color. There are a number of options for filling cells for display in Netscape.

Nonrendering text

Sometimes, adding a simple nonbreaking space (` `) or a single line break (`<br>`) within a cell is enough for it to be recognized and displayed properly in Netscape. Neither of these text strings renders visibly when the table is displayed in the browser.

The single-pixel trick

Another popular work-around is to place a transparent one-pixel GIF file in the cell and set its width and height dimensions to fill the cell. If you choose this method, be sure to set both the `height` and the `width` attributes. If you set only one, many browsers will resize the image proportionally (into a big square), which may not be appropriate for the table.

One drawback to this method is that a missing graphic icon will appear in the cell if the graphic doesn't load properly or if the viewer has the graphics turned off in the browser.

Using <spacer>

Table cells can also be held open with a `<spacer>` tag, which is Netscape's proprietary method for adding blank space on a web page. Set the spacer type to "block" and specify the width and height measurements as follows:

```
<TD><SPACER TYPE=block WIDTH=n HEIGHT=n></TD>
```

Although the `<spacer>` tag is Netscape-specific, the whole issue of collapsing cells is Netscape-specific as well, making spacers a good solution in this situation (although they're best avoided for general use). Browsers that don't understand

---

* This tip taken with permission from *Creative HTML Design*, by Lynda Weinman and William Weinman, published by New Riders Publishing, 1998.

---

the `<spacer>` element will just ignore it, but chances are they won't need it to render the table properly anyway.

Restraining Row Heights*

You might guess that the following code would create the table shown in Figure 10-13:

```
<TABLE CELLSPACING=0 CELLPADDING=0 BORDER=1>
<TR>
  <TD ROWSPAN=2><IMG SRC="red.gif"
   WIDTH=50 HEIGHT=150></TD>
  <TD HEIGHT=50><IMG SRC="blue.gif"
   WIDTH=100 HEIGHT=50></TD>
</TR>
<TR>
  <TD ALIGN=center>extra space</TD>
</TR>
</TABLE>
```

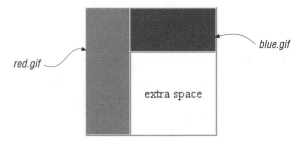

Figure 10-13: This is the table we're trying to create

However, what actually happens is that the bottom cell shrinks to fit the text it contains, and the cell containing the darker graphic on the right—despite being set to `height=50`—is stretched vertically, as shown in Figure 10-14.

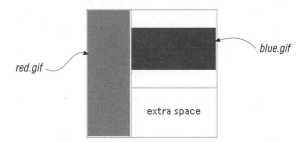

Figure 10-14: The actual result of the code

---

* This tip courtesy of Builder.com. It first appeared in the Builder.com article "Advanced HTML Tips," by Paul Anderson. It is reprinted here with permission of Builder.com and CNET. See *http://builder.com/Authoring/AdvHtml/index.html* for the complete article.

The problem is that the `height` attribute specifies a minimum, not a maximum, and a row defaults to the height of its tallest cell (determined either by the cell's contents or its height value). That's why the table doesn't work as intended—the text in the last cell isn't tall enough to force the desired effect. Since we can determine the exact height that we want in that last cell (by subtracting the height of *blue.gif* from the column height), giving it a `height=100` attribute will make it the proper height.

If you don't know the exact height—say, because other columns contain text—you may be better off removing the `rowspan` attributes and using a nested table instead. The nested table will size its rows based on their content only.

Column Span Problems*

If you want to create a table with multiple column spans, yet accurately control the width of each column, it is necessary to specify a width for at least one cell in each column. To be really safe, take the time to specify a width for every cell in the table. When column spans overlap, it is easy to get unpredictable results.

The goal was to create a table 600 pixels wide with three columns of 200 pixels each. In each row, there is a 400-pixel-wide graphic that should straddle neatly over two columns, as shown in Figure 10-15.

Figure 10-15: The target layout: getting two graphics to span two columns

The first (failed) attempt at coding set the table to a specific width and provided column spans for the graphics, as shown in the following code:

```
<TABLE BORDER=1 CELLPADDING=0 CELLSPACING=0 WIDTH=600
BGCOLOR="#FFFFFF">
<TR>
    <TD COLSPAN=2><IMG SRC="2col.gif" ALIGN=top WIDTH="400"
    HEIGHT="50" BORDER="0"></TD>
    <TD ALIGN=center>text cell<BR>(should be 200 pixels)</TD>
</TR>
<TR>
    <TD ALIGN=center>text cell<br>(should be 200 pixels)
    </TD>
    <TD COLSPAN=2><IMG SRC="2col.gif" ALIGN=TOP WIDTH="400"
    HEIGHT="50" BORDER="0"></TD>
</TR>
</TABLE>
```

---

* This tip courtesy of Builder.com. It first appeared in the Builder.com article "Advanced HTML Tips," by Paul Anderson. It is reprinted here with permission of Builder.com and CNET. See *http://builder.com/Authoring/AdvHtml/index.html* for the complete article. The solution shown here was submitted by Steven Masters.

This code, however, doesn't give the browser enough information, particularly about the middle column, to accurately render the table. The unsuccessful result of this first code attempt is shown in Figure 10-16. The problem is that the center column is not defined anywhere.

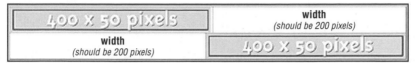

Figure 10-16: Since the middle column was not defined, the table is rendered with two 400-pixel-wide columns

The solution

The solution in this case, because the middle cell is eaten up by column spans in both rows, is to create a dummy row (shown in bold) that establishes the width of the three columns as intended (in 200-pixel increments). This row will not render in the browser. In addition, the absolute width for every cell must be specified.

The following code produces the desired effect on all browsers that support tables—and on all platforms.

```
<TABLE BORDER=1 CELLPADDING=0 CELLSPACING=0 WIDTH=600
BGCOLOR="#FFFFFF">
<TR>
    <TD WIDTH="200" HEIGHT="0"></TD>
    <TD WIDTH="200" HEIGHT="0"></TD>
    <TD WIDTH="200" HEIGHT="0"></TD>
</TR>
<TR>
    <TD colspan=2 WIDTH="400"><IMG SRC="2col.gif" WIDTH="400"
    HEIGHT="50" BORDER="0"></TD>
    <TD WIDTH="200" ALIGN=CENTER>text cell<BR>(should be 200
    pixels)</TD>
</TR>
<TR>
    <TD WIDTH="200" ALIGN=center>text cell<br>(should be 200
    pixels)</TD>
    <TD colspan=2 WIDTH="400"><IMG SRC="2col.gif" WIDTH="400"
    HEIGHT="50" BORDER="0"></TD>
</TR>
</TABLE>
```

Tips and Tricks

This section provides a few tricks of the trade for working with tables.

<font> and Tables

Unfortunately, placing <font> tags around a table will not affect the font of all the text contained within the table. You need to repeat the <font> tag and its attributes around the content in every cell of the table. For complex tables with lots of cells, the repetitive <font> tags can actually add significantly to the size of the HTML file (not to mention the visual clutter).

Style sheets are a much more efficient way to apply style information to the contents of a table (and they are the W3C's method of choice for all your font styling needs).

Waiting for Tables to Display

With current technology and HTML standards, the browser must wait until the entire contents of a table have downloaded before it can begin rendering the page. Any text and graphics *outside* the table will display quickly while the browser works on the table.

You can use this phenomenon to your advantage by placing outside the table elements you want your viewers to see first (can anybody say "banner ads"?).

Baseline Alignment Trick*

If you want to align the first lines of text by their baselines across a row, you should be able to use `valign=baseline`; in reality, this setting is too unpredictable across browsers to be used reliably. A trick for achieving the same result is to add a nonbreaking space (` `) in each first line that is set the same size as the largest character. That way, you can set `valign=top`, and the baselines will all line up.

First look at simple top alignment. As shown in Figure 10-17, the top of the text is aligned, but the baselines are off.

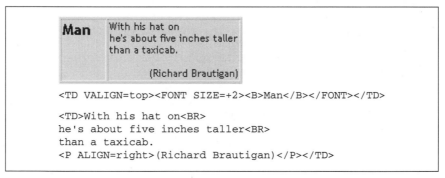

Figure 10-17: With top alignment, the baselines of the text don't line up

By adding a non-breaking space at the larger text size (in bold), the baselines align neatly, as shown in Figure 10-18.

---

* This tip courtesy of Builder.com. It first appeared in the Builder.com article "Advanced HTML Tips," by Paul Anderson. It is reprinted here with permission of Builder.com and CNET. See *http://builder.com/Authoring/AdvHtml/index.html* for the complete article.

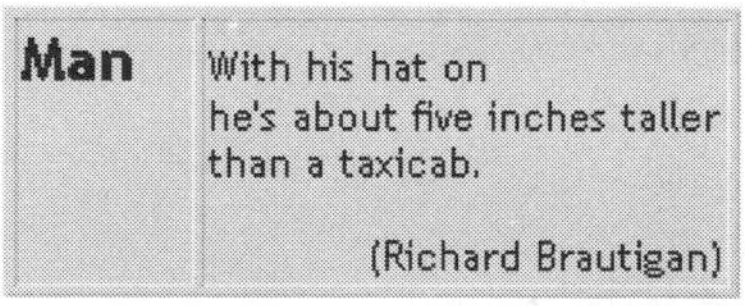

```
<TD VALIGN=top><FONT SIZE=+2><B>Man</B></FONT></TD>

<TD>With his hat on<FONT SIZE=+2><B> </B></FONT><BR>
he's about five inches taller<BR>
than a taxicab.
<P ALIGN=right>(Richard Brautigan)</P></TD>
```

Figure 10-18: With a non-breaking space set at the same font size as the "Man" text, the baselines line up

Rowspans Made Easy*

HTML 3.2 specifies that if a cell's colspan implies more columns than have been created up to that point in the table, the browser should create the additional columns. With rowspan, however, the specification states that browsers shouldn't create any extra rows. The existing browsers follow both of these rules.

So if you have a cell that spans vertically to the bottom of the table, past rows that might vary in number or are too numerous to easily count, just give it a rowspan that you know is excessively high.

In Figure 10-19, we've set rowspan to 99. Even though there are only seven rows in the actual table, your browser won't generate any extra rows.

```
<TABLE BGCOLOR="#ffff99" BORDER=1>
 <TR>
  <TD WIDTH=10 ROWSPAN=99
   BGCOLOR="#cc3333"> </TD>
  <TD>It</TD></TR>
 <TR><TD>doesn t</TD></TR>
 <TR><TD>matter</TD></TR>
 <TR><TD>how</TD></TR>
 <TR><TD>many</TD></TR>
 <TR><TD>rows</TD></TR>
 <TR><TD>are</TD></TR>
 <TR><TD>here</TD></TR>
</TABLE>
```

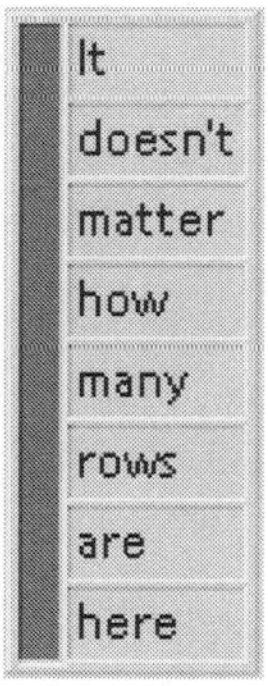

Figure 10-19: Although rowspan is set to 99, the table only contains the actual number of rows needed

---

* This tip courtesy of Builder.com. It first appeared in the Builder.com article "Advanced HTML Tips," by Paul Anderson. It is reprinted here with permission of Builder.com and CNET. See *http://builder.com/Authoring/AdvHtml/index.html* for the complete article.

Standard Table Templates

Ever look at a table and say "how'd they do that?" This section provides templates that give you shortcuts for creating standard table effects.

A Simple Announcement Box

Figure 10-20 depicts a simple one-cell table containing text. By setting the background to a bright color, it can be used as an effective attention-getting device for a special announcement. It could also be used as an alternative to a graphical headline for a page.

Of course, you can specify any background color you choose. Try playing with the border and cell padding for different effects. You can use width and height attributes to make the bar any size. Remember, placing the bgcolor within the cell will render differently than placing it in the <table> tag in Internet Explorer, so experiment and test to see what you like the best. 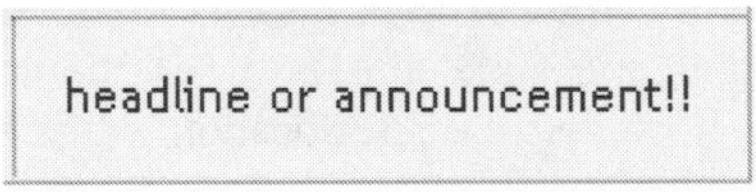

```
<TABLE BGCOLOR="#CCFF99" BORDER=2 CELLPADDING=12 CELLSPACING=0>
<TR>
   <TD ALIGN=center VALIGN=middle>headline or announcement!!</TD>
</TR>
</TABLE>
```

Figure 10-20: Announcement box

Centering an Object in the Browser Window

The table in the following code and in Figure 10-21 can be used to center an object in a browser window regardless of how the window is resized. It uses a single cell table with its size set to 100%, then centers the object horizontally and vertically in the cell.

```
<HTML>
<BODY>
<TABLE WIDTH=100% HEIGHT=100% BORDER=0 CELLSPACING=0
CELLPADDING=0>
<TR>
   <TD align=center valign=middle>your object here</TD>
</TR>
</TABLE>
</BODY>
</HTML>
```

Creating a Vertical Rule

This sample table creates a vertical rule between columns that resizes with the height of the table. The trick is to create an extra column only one pixel wide (or

Figure 10-21: Centering an object

the desired thickness of the vertical rule) and fill it with a background color. This cell is indicated in bold. The result is shown in Figure 10-22.

The cell cannot be totally empty or it will collapse in Netscape and its background color won't display, so I've added a `<br>`. For this to display correctly, the cell padding must remain at zero or the 1-pixel wide column will plump up with extra space. Add space between columns with the `cellspacing` attribute instead.

```
this

is

some

content

<TABLE BORDER=0 CELLPADDING= 0  CELLSPACING= 10>
<TR ALIGN=LEFT VALIGN=TOP>
   <TD width=50><BR></TD>
   <TD width=1 BGCOLOR= darkred ><BR></TD>
   <TD>
       <P>this
       <P>is
       <P>some
       <P>content
   </TD>
</TR>
</TABLE>
```

Figure 10-22: A vertical rule that resizes with the depth of the table

Creating a Box Rule

Although Microsoft Internet Explorer recognizes the proprietary `bordercolor`, `bordercolorlight`, and `bordercolordark` attributes, there is no method for specifying border colors using standard HTML for all browsers.

To create a colored rule around a box of text using standard HTML, place one table within another as shown in Figure 10-23. To nest tables, place the entire contents of one table within a <td> of the other.

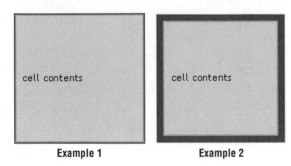

Example 1   **Example 2**

Figure 10-23: Two examples of creating box rules with nested tables

In Example 1 in Figure 10-23, cell width and height are set in the interior table. In the exterior table, a cell padding of 0 results in a one-pixel rule around the table. You can increase the thickness of the rule by increasing the cellpadding value. Note, however, that this will also increase the overall dimensions of the table. The color of the rule is specified by the bgcolor attribute in the <table> tag for the exterior table:

```
<TABLE CELLPADDING=0 BORDER=0>
<TR>
   <TD BGCOLOR="#333333" ALIGN=center VALIGN=center>
      <TABLE BORDER=0 WIDTH=200 HEIGHT=200 CELLPADDING=10>
      <TR><TD BGCOLOR="#999999">cell contents</TD></TR>
      </TABLE>
   </TD>
</TR>
</TABLE>
```

In Example 2 in Figure 10-23, to restrict the dimensions of the table, set specific dimensions for the exterior table and set the dimensions of the interior table slightly smaller (to a difference twice the desired rule thickness). In this example, the desired rule thickness is 10, so the interior table's dimensions are 20 pixels less than the exterior table's dimensions.

```
<TABLE WIDTH=200 HEIGHT=200 cellpadding=0 border=0>
<TR>
   <TD BGCOLOR="#333333" ALIGN=center VALIGN=center>
      <TABLE BORDER=0 WIDTH=180 HEIGHT=180 CELLPADDING=10>
      <TR><TD BGCOLOR="#999999">cell contents</TD></TR>
      </TABLE>
   </TD>
</TR>
</TABLE>
```

Two-Column Page Layouts

Many sites use a two-column table to lay out the structure of their pages. This grid creates a narrow column on the left for navigational options and a wider column on the right for the page's contents, as shown in Figure 10-24. These sample tables can be used to provide a basic structure to the page; you can place any elements (including other tables) within either table cell to create more complex layouts.

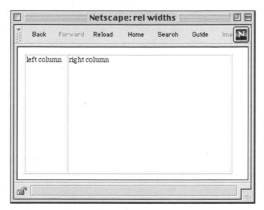

Figure 10-24: Typical two-column layout

First, a word about browser margins

When using a table to lay out the structure of a page, bear in mind that it will be placed in the page against the normal browser margins, not flush against the top and left edge of the browser window. The width of the margin varies from browser to browser (and platform to platform), but it generally ranges from 8 to 12 pixels. You should take this blank space into account when choosing measurements for your table and its column widths.

The only way to get rid of the margins for most browsers is to put the whole page in a framed document, which offers margin controls (see Chapter 11, *Frames*). If you are designing exclusively for Internet Explorer, you can take advantage of Microsoft's proprietary `topmargin` and `leftmargin` attributes, which can be used to set these margins to 0 pixels. For Netscape 4.0, use the corresponding `margin-height` and `marginwidth` attributes. Or if you are using style sheets, add the following rule:

```
BODY { margin:0; padding:0; }
```

Fixed-width columns

If it's predictability and control you're after, then fixing the width of your table and its columns is the way to go. As long as the contents fit in the cells entirely, the table will hold its dimensions regardless of browser window size. If contents (such as graphics) are wider than the cell, the cell will usually expand to accommodate them.

Of course, you can change the specific width values to any pixel value you choose, however, it is important that the total of the cell widths equals the width set for the entire table. If the values are different, browsers maintain the width setting for the table and resize all the columns proportionately within the allotted space. As a result, none of the column widths will display at the number of pixels specified.

Note that the border in each of the following examples has been set to 1 but you can change it to any other value. Starting with the border set to 1 (as shown in Figure 10-24) makes it easier to see how the table is behaving. Once you get the table working properly, get rid of the border by setting the value to 0.

```
<HTML>
<BODY>
<TABLE BORDER=1 WIDTH=600>
<TR>
    <TD VALIGN=top WIDTH=150>left column</TD>
    <TD VALIGN=top WIDTH=450>right column</TD>
</TR>
</TABLE>
</BODY>
</HTML>
```

Relative column widths

Using relative values for the width of your table allows your page to resize itself to fill the browser window. Many designers prefer this method because it is more flexible and suits any monitor configuration. Although the actual column widths will change when the browser window resizes (and their contents will rewrap), they will remain in proportion to one another.

Again, you can turn the border off by setting the value to zero. You may change the width values for the cell in each column, but be sure that they total 100%.

```
<HTML>
<BODY>
<TABLE BORDER=1 WIDTH=100%>
<TR>
    <TD VALIGN=top WIDTH=20%>left column</TD>
    <TD VALIGN=top WIDTH=80%>right column</TD>
</TR>
</TABLE>
</BODY>
</HTML>
```

Combination

At times, you may want to restrict the width of the left column, but allow the right column to resize with the page—if you want the contents of the left column to stay aligned over a colored background image, for instance. Set the width of the left column to any pixel value you choose and do not specify a width for the right column.

This technique is not guaranteed to keep the width of the "fixed" column at its specified width. If the browser window is resized to be very narrow, the fixed column will be resized smaller and its contents will wrap.

```
<HTML>
<BODY>
<TABLE BORDER=1 WIDTH=100%>
<TR>
    <TD VALIGN=top WIDTH=150>left column</TD>
    <TD VALIGN=top>right column</TD>
</TR>
</TABLE>
</BODY>
</HTML>
```

Multipart Images in Tables

There are a number of reasons why you may want to slice a large image into pieces and use a table to reconstruct it seamlessly on a web page:

Rollovers

If you want portions of the image—but not the whole image—to respond to the mouse passing over them (mouseover events or rollovers), it is more efficient to swap out just the bits that change instead of reloading the whole image.

Animations

Similarly, if you want to add animation to small areas within an image, it is better to break up the image and animate just the portions that move. This will result in smaller files to download.

Better Optimization

At times, you may find that an image contains distinct areas of flat color and distinct areas of soft or photographic images. Breaking the image into sections allows you to save some sections as GIF (the flat color areas) and others as JPEG (for graduated tones), to achieve better optimization and image quality overall. For more information on optimizing images, see Chapter 14, *GIF Format*, and Chapter 15, *JPEG Format*.

Imagemaps

Break the image into separated linked images instead of using an imagemap. This allows linking to work offline, as well as provides alternative (ALT) text for each graphical element. This makes the page more accessible for people using non-graphical or speech-based browsers.

In Figure 10-25, I've divided the image into sections so I can save the television image as a JPEG and the rest as GIFs (since they are flat, graphical images). Also, I use rollover events to replace the television image based on which section icon the user mouses over. The table on the right has its border set to 1 to reveal the individual graphics that make up the image. When the border is set to zero, the effect is seamless, as shown on the left.

Figure 10-25: A multipart image held together by a table

Slicing & Dicing Tools

Multipart images in tables have been growing in popularity in recent years. Not surprisingly, software companies are responding with tools that make the production process much easier than the previous method of splitting the graphic manually and writing the table code in an HTML editor. (This manual method is outlined below.)

Both Macromedia Fireworks and Adobe ImageReady include functions that export an image as many individually numbered graphics (based on the position of guidelines) and automatically write the table code that holds them all together.

You can copy and paste the table code into your HTML file. One caution: you will need to adjust the pathnames if your graphics are to reside in a different directory than your HTML files. The automatically generated code writes relative pathnames assuming everything will be in the same directory. A simple find-and-replace should take care of this quickly.

Macromedia Fireworks

To export a multipart image and its respective HTML file:

1. Open the image (it can be a layered Photoshop file). Use the Slice tool on the URLs toolbar to define rectangular segments in the image. Note, if you place a rectangular slice in the middle of a graphic, Fireworks will automatically slice the remainder of the image into the fewest number of segments to contain the specified slice.

2. Set the default export settings for the entire image (file format, bit depth, dithering, etc.). These settings will be applied to each resulting slice after export (all portions will share the same color palette).

3. You can override the default settings for an individual slice, for instance, reducing its palette, or making it a JPEG among GIFs. Start by selecting the slice object and opening its Object Properties dialog box, selected via Modify → Object Properties or by using the options pop-up menu (the arrow on the far right of the URLs toolbar).

4. Among the options on the Object Properties dialog box are the Slice Export Settings. Select Custom and either one of the palette options from the pop-up menu, or select the continue button (indicated by ellipses "...") to get an Export Preview dialog box for that particular slice. From there you can fine-tune the optimization of the slice.

5. Once you have your slices chosen and configured, choose File → Export Slices. Type a name for the HTML file (the table that holds the pieces together), choose its location, and decide if you'd like your graphic pieces saved in a subfolder.

6. Click Export. You can now copy the table code from the generated HTML file and paste it into your final document.

7. Turn rulers on (View → Rulers). Drag guidelines from the rulers into the image area at the points where you want the image to be divided.

For more information about Fireworks, see *http://www.macromedia.com/software/fireworks*.

Adobe ImageReady

To create a multipart image and HTML file in ImageReady:

1. Open the image. Select View → Rulers if the rulers are not already visible. Drag guides from the rulers into the image area where you want the image divided.

2. Select the format and optimization values with the Optimize palette and Optimize preview.

3. When you are ready, save the file using File → Save Optimized As (saving the original is not the same thing). This gives you the Save As dialog box in which you can check the boxes next to Save HTML File and Slice Along Guides.

4. ImageReady creates a series of graphics numbered by row and column as well as an HTML file containing the table that holds the graphics together.

For more information about Adobe ImageReady, see *http://www.adobe.com/imageready*.

Producing Images in Tables Manually

If you do not have Macromedia Fireworks or Adobe ImageReady, it is certainly possible to create the effect by hand. First you need to divide the image into separate graphic files using an image processor such as Photoshop or Paint Shop Pro. Then, write the HTML for the table using whichever HTML editor pleases you. These methods are demonstrated below.

Dividing an image with Photoshop 4.0

When dividing an image with Photoshop, it is important to set the guide preferences in a way that enables easy and accurate selections without redundant or overlapping pixels between image sections. This is illustrated in steps 2 and 3 and shown in Figure 10-26.

1. Open the image in Photoshop. Make sure the rulers are visible by selecting View → Show Rulers.

2. Set your preferences to use pixels as the unit of measurement by selecting File → Preferences → Units & Rulers. Select "pixels" from the pop-up menu and hit OK.

3. Select View → Snap to Guides. This will snap your selection to the precise location of the guide.

4. Use the rectangle marquee (make sure feathering and anti-aliasing options are turned off) to select each area of the image. You can use the Info palette (Window → Show Info) to get accurate pixel measurements for each section as you select it. This information will be needed when you create the HTML file.

5. Copy and paste each section into a new file. Flatten the image and save it as a GIF or a JPEG. You may want to develop a numbered naming scheme to keep the pieces organized.

Figure 10-26: Splitting up an image with Photoshop

Creating the table in HTML

Following is the HTML code that is used to hold together the Sifl & Olly image from Figure 10-25:

```
<TABLE BORDER="0" CELLPADDING="0" CELLSPACING="0" WIDTH="333">
  <TR>
  <TD><IMG SRC="part_1.gif" WIDTH="56" HEIGHT="92" BORDER="0"></TD>
  <TD><IMG SRC="part_2.gif" WIDTH="169" HEIGHT="92" BORDER="0"></TD>
  <TD><IMG SRC="part_3.gif" WIDTH="108" HEIGHT="92" BORDER="0"></TD>
  </TR>
  <TR>
  <TD><IMG SRC="part_4.gif" WIDTH="56" HEIGHT="133" BORDER="0"></TD>
  <TD><IMG SRC="part_5.gif" WIDTH="169" HEIGHT="133" BORDER="0"></TD>
  <TD><IMG SRC="part_6.gif" WIDTH="108" HEIGHT="133" BORDER="0"></TD>
```

```
  </TR>
  <TR>
  <TD><IMG SRC="part_7.gif" WIDTH="56" HEIGHT="82" BORDER="0"></TD>
  <TD><IMG SRC="part_8.gif" WIDTH="169" HEIGHT="82" BORDER="0"></TD>
  <TD><IMG SRC="part_9.gif" WIDTH="108" HEIGHT="82" BORDER="0"></TD>
  </TR>
  </TABLE>
```

There is no difference between writing a table for piecing together graphics and writing any other kind of table; however, you should pay careful attention to the following settings if you want the image to piece back together seamlessly on all browsers.

- In the `<table>` tag, set the following attributes to zero: `border=0`, `cellpadding=0`, `cellspacing=0`.

- In the `<table>` tag, specify the width of the table with an absolute pixel value. Be sure that the value is exactly the total of the widths of the component images. You may also add the height attribute for thoroughness' sake, but it is not required.

- Don't put extra spaces or line returns between the `<td>` and the `<img>` tags (extra space within `<td>`s causes extra space to appear when the image is rendered). Keep them flush together on one line. If you must break the line, break it somewhere within the `<img>` tag.

- Set the `width` and `height` values in pixels for every image. Be sure that the measurements are accurate.

- Set the `border=0` for every image.

- Specify the `width` and `height` pixel values for every cell in the table, particularly if it contains colspans and rowspans. Be sure that they match the pixel values set in the `<img>` tag and the actual pixel dimensions of the graphic. For simple grid-like tables (such as the one in Figure 10-25), you may not need to give individual cell dimensions since the enclosed images will force each cell to the proper dimensions.

- Sometimes it is preferable to keep the table simple. For instance, the sample graphic could have been divided into just five portions (a top graphic, three middle graphics, and a bottom graphic) and held together with a table made up of three rows with a single cell each. These decisions are a matter of judgment and obviously depend on the individual project.

CHAPTER 11

Frames

Frames are a method for dividing the browser window into smaller sub-windows, each displaying a different HTML document. This chapter covers the structure and creation of framed documents, controls for affecting their display and function, as well as some advanced tips and tricks.

Summary of Frame Tags

In this section, browser support for each tag is noted to the right of the tag name. Browsers that do not support the tag are grayed out. Browsers that deprecate the tag are noted with a superscript D. Tag usage is indicated below the tag name. A more thorough listing of attributes for each tag, according to the HTML 4.0 Specification, appears in Appendix A, *HTML Tags and Elements*.

<frame>   NN: 2, 3, 4 · MSIE: 2, 3, 4, 5 · HTML 4 · WebTV · Opera3

```
<frame>
```

Defines a single frame within a `<frameset>`.

Attributes

`bordercolor="#rrggbb"` or `color name`
    Sets the color for frame's borders (if the border is turned on). Support for this attribute is limited to Netscape Navigator 3.0 and higher and Internet Explorer 4.0.

`frameborder=1|0` *(IE 3+ and W3C 4.0 Spec.)*; `yes|no` *(NN 3+ and IE 4.0)*
    Determines whether there is a 3-D separator drawn between the current frame and surrounding frames. A value of 1 (or **yes**) turns the border on. A value of 0 (or **no**) turns the border off. You may also set the frameborder at the frameset level, which may be more reliable.

Because Netscape and Internet Explorer support different values, you may need to specify the frameborder twice within `<frame>` to ensure full browser compatibility, as follows:

```
frameborder=yes frameborder=1 ...
```

longdesc=*url*
> Specifies a link to a document containing a long description of the frame and its contents. This addition to the HTML 4.0 Specification may be useful for non-visual web browsers.

marginwidth=*number*
> Specifies the amount of space (in pixels) between the left and right edges of the frame and its contents. The minimum value according to the HTML Specification is 1 pixel. Setting the value to 0 (zero) in order to place objects flush against the edge of the frame will work in Internet Explorer, however, Netscape will still display a 1-pixel margin space.

marginheight=*number*
> Specifies the amount of space (in pixels) between the top and bottom edge of the frame and its contents. The minimum value according to the HTML Specification is 1 pixel. Setting the value to 0 (zero) in order to place objects flush against the edge of the frame will work in Internet Explorer, however, Netscape will still display a 1-pixel margin space.

name=*text*
> Assigns a name to the frame. This name may be referenced by targets within links to make the target document load within the named frame.

noresize
> Prevents users from resizing the frame. By default, despite specific frame size settings, users can resize a frame by clicking and dragging its borders.

scrolling=yes|no|auto
> Specifies whether scrollbars appear in the frame. A value of **yes** mean scrollbars always appear; a value of **no** means scrollbars never appear; a value of **auto** (the default) means scrollbars appear automatically when the contents do not fit within the frame.

src=*url*
> Specifies the location of the initial HTML file to be displayed by the frame.

<frameset>   NN: 2, 3, 4 - MSIE: 2, 3, 4, 5 - HTML 4 - WebTV - Opera3

```
<frameset>...</frameset>
```

Defines a collection of frames or other framesets.

Attributes

border=*number*
> Sets frame border thickness (in pixels) between all the frames in a frameset (when the frame border is turned on).

`bordercolor=#rrggbb"` or `color name`
> Sets a border color for all the borders in a frameset. Support for this attribute is limited to Netscape Navigator 3.0 and higher and Internet Explorer 4.0.

`cols=list`
> Establishes the number and sizes of columns in a frameset. The number of columns is determined by the number of values in the list. Size specifications can be in absolute pixel values, percentage values, or relative values (*) based on available space.

`frameborder=1|0` *(IE 3+ and W3C 4.0 Spec.)*; `yes|no` *(NN 3+ and IE 4.0)*
> Determines whether 3-D separators are drawn between frames in the frameset. A value of 1 (or **yes**) turns the borders on; 0 (or **no**) turns the borders off.
>
> Because Netscape and Internet Explorer support different values, you may need to specify the frameborder twice within `<frame>` to ensure backwards compatibility, as follows:
>
> `frameborder=yes frameborder=1 ...`

`framespacing=number` *(IE only)*
> *Internet 3.0 and higher only.* Adds additional space (in pixels) between adjacent frames.

`rows=list (number, percentage,` or `*)`
> Establishes the number and sizes of rows in the frameset. The number of rows is determined by the number of values in the list. Size specifications can be in absolute pixel values, percentage values, or relative values (*) based on available space.

<iframe>

NN: 2, 3, 4 - **MSIE:** 2, **3, 4, 5** - **HTML 4** - WebTV - Opera3

`<iframe> ... </iframe>`

Defines a floating frame within a document with similar placement tags to `<img>`. This element requires a closing tag. Introduced by Microsoft Internet Explorer 3.0, inline frames are now part of the W3C 4.0 HTML Specification. As of this writing, however, they are only supported by Internet Explorer.

Attributes

`align=top|middle|bottom|left|right`
> Aligns the inline frame on the page within the flow of the text. Left and right alignment allows text to flow around the frame.

`frameborder=1|0`
> Turns on or off the displaying of a 3-D border for the frame. The default is 1, which inserts the border.

`height=number`
> Specifies the height of the frame in pixels or as a percentage of the window size.

`hspace=number`

Used in conjunction with left and right alignment, this attribute specifies the amount of space (in pixels) to hold clear to the left and right of the frame.

`marginheight=number`

Specifies the amount of space (in pixels) between the top and bottom edges of the frame and its contents.

`marginwidth=number`

Specifies the amount of space (in pixels) between the left and right edges of the frame and its contents.

`name=text`

Assigns a name to the frame to be referenced by targeted links.

`noresize`

Prevents users from resizing the frame. By default, despite specific frame size settings, users can resize a frame by clicking and dragging its borders.

`scrolling=yes|no|auto`

Determines whether scrollbars appear in the frame (see explanation in `<frame>` earlier in this chapter).

`src=url`

Specifies the URL of the HTML document that will initially display in the frame.

`vspace=number`

Used in conjunction with left and right alignment, this attribute specifies the amount of space (in pixels) to hold clear above and below the frame.

`width=number`

Specifies the width of the frame in pixels or as a percentage of the window size.

<noframes>   NN: 2, 3, 4 · MSIE: 2, 3, 4, 5 · HTML 4 · WebTV · Opera3

`<noframes> ... </noframes>`

Defines content that will be displayed by browsers that cannot display frames. Browsers that do support frames will ignore the content between `<noframes>` tags.

Introduction to Frames

Frames allow you to divide the browser window into smaller sub-windows, each of which displays a different HTML document. Introduced by Netscape Navigator 2.0, frame support was soon added by other popular browsers. The basic frame specification works with Netscape Navigator 2.0 and higher as well as Microsoft Internet Explorer 3.0 and higher. As of this writing, frames have found their way into the World Wide Web Consortium's HTML 4.0 Specification.

Despite the advanced navigational functionality that frames offer, they do present certain problems and peculiarities that have lead to their currently controversial status. In fact, they've become so notorious that it is not uncommon for web developers to encounter clients who, despite not knowing a lick of HTML themselves, will strongly proclaim "NO FRAMES! FRAMES BAD!" at the beginning of a project.

Like most things, frames are neither all good nor all bad. It is your responsibility to be familiar with both sides of the coin so you can help present the best solution for your clients' needs.

Advantages

- The main advantage to frames is that they enable parts of the page to remain stationary while other parts scroll. This is useful for elements you may not want to scroll out of view, such as navigational options or banner advertising.

- Frames unify resources that reside on separate servers. For instance, you may use frames to combine your own material (and navigation graphics) with threaded discussion material generated by software on a vendor's server.

- With the <noframes> tag, you can easily add alternative content for browsers that do not support frames. This degradability is built into the frames system.

Disadvantages

- Frames are not supported by older browsers. (<noframes> may address this problem.)

- Frames may make site production more complicated because you need to produce and organize multiple files to fill one page.

- Navigating through a framed site may be prohibitively challenging for some users.

- Users cannot bookmark individual pages nested within a framed document. Bookmarks only identify the top-level framed document in its initial state; there is currently no way to track the states of a frameset, therefore no way to bookmark individual states. There are workarounds in 4.0 browsers, however, such as opening the contents of the frame in a new window and bookmarking that page.

- A large number of frames on a page may significantly increase the load on the server because so much of the load on a server is initial document requests. Four requests for 1K files (the frameset and the contents of three frames) is more work for your server than a single request for a 4K document.

- Framed documents can be a nuisance for search engines. Content-level documents may be missed in searches. If a contained document is found by a search engine, it is likely it will be displayed out of context of its frameset, potentially losing important navigational options. For more information on searching framed documents, see "Helping Search Engines" later in this chapter.

- It is more difficult to track actual page (or ad) impressions when the pages are part of a framed document.

Basic Frameset Structure

A web page that is divided into frames is held together by a top level *frameset* document.

A frameset document contains a standard header portion (as indicated with the <head> tag). However, unlike standard HTML documents, frameset documents do not have a <body>—instead, they contain a <frameset> tag, which is used to define columns and rows of individual frames (each indicated with a <frame> tag). Figure 11-1 shows the structure of a basic frameset document that creates two frames, occupying two columns of equal width.

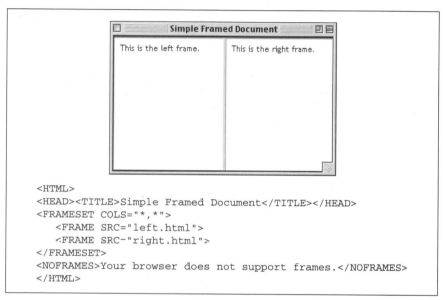

```
<HTML>
<HEAD><TITLE>Simple Framed Document</TITLE></HEAD>
<FRAMESET COLS="*,*">
    <FRAME SRC="left.html">
    <FRAME SRC-"right.html">
</FRAMESET>
<NOFRAMES>Your browser does not support frames.</NOFRAMES>
</HTML>
```

Figure 11-1: Basic frameset document

The contents of framed documents come from separate HTML files that are displayed within each frame. For example, in Figure 11-1, the content that appears in the left frame is actually a standard HTML file called *left.html.* The samples throughout this chapter reference simple HTML documents similar to this one:

```
<HTML>
<HEAD><TITLE>Left Frame Contents</TITLE></HEAD>
<BODY BGCOLOR="white">
This is the left frame.
</BODY>
</HTML>
```

At the *frameset* level (i.e., within the <frameset> opening tag), you establish the rows and columns and decide if you want borders to display between each frame (borders are discussed later in this chapter.)

At the *frame* level (within the <frame> tag), you identify the URL of the document to display in that frame and give the frame a name for future reference. You also have control over whether the frame has scrollbars, whether it can be resized by the user, and what its margins should be (if any). Each of these controls are discussed later in this chapter.

<noframes> content

Frameset documents may also have content contained within the optional <noframes> tag. Browsers that do not understand frames display the contents within <noframes> as though it were normal text. For instance, in non-frames browsers, the document in Figure 11-1 would simply display the text "Your browser does not support frames."

To treat the alternative content like a regular document, you may include the <body>...</body> tags within <noframes> (although, technically, it is not kosher HTML coding). This will allow you to specify attributes such as document background color and text color for the page.

Establishing Rows and Columns

Rows and columns are established within the <frameset> tag, using the rows and cols attributes, respectively. These attributes divide the frameset in a grid-like manner. Frames are filled from left-to-right for columns and top-to-bottom for rows.

The size of each row (or column) is specified in a quote-enclosed, comma-separated list of values after the attribute. The number of values listed determines the number of rows (or columns). Figure 11-2 shows the most simple division of a framed document into two equal-sized rows (on the left) and columns (right).

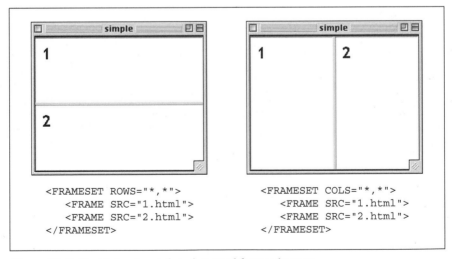

```
<FRAMESET ROWS="*,*">          <FRAMESET COLS="*,*">
    <FRAME SRC="1.html">           <FRAME SRC="1.html">
    <FRAME SRC="2.html">           <FRAME SRC="2.html">
</FRAMESET>                    </FRAMESET>
```

Figure 11-2: Simple horizontal and vertical frames layouts

Specifying sizes

Frame size can be listed in one of three ways:

Absolute pixel values
> The browser will interpret an integer as an absolute pixel value. The frameset `<frameset cols="150,450">` will create two columns, one exactly 150 pixels wide, and the other exactly 450 pixels wide. If the browser window is larger than the total specified pixels, it will enlarge each frame proportionally to fill the window.

Percentages
> Percentages are based on the total width of the frameset. The total should add up to 100%. The frameset `<frameset rows="25%,50%,25%">` creates three rows; the top and bottom frames will each always occupy 25% of the height of the frameset and the middle row will make up 50%, regardless of how the browser window is resized.

Relative values
> Relative values, indicated by the asterisk (*) character, are used to divide up the remaining space in the frameset into equal portions. For instance, the frameset `<frameset cols="100,*">` creates two columns—the first will be 100 pixels wide, the second will fill whatever portion is left of the window.
>
> You can also specify relative values in multiples of equal portions and combine them with other measurement values. For example, the frameset defined by `<frameset cols="25%,2*,*">` divides the window into three columns. The first column will always occupy 25% of the window width. The remaining two will divide up the remaining space; however, in this case, the middle column will always be 2 times as big as the third. (You may notice that this results in the same division as the percentages example.)

Combining rows and columns

You can specify both rows and columns within a single frameset, creating a grid of frames, as shown in Figure 11-3. When both `cols` and `rows` are specified for a frameset, frames are created left-to-right in each row, in order. Rows are created top-to-bottom. The order of appearance of `<frame>` elements within the `<frameset>` does make a difference in where their contents display. The order in which documents are displayed is demonstrated in Figure 11-3.

Nesting Frames

It is possible to nest a frameset within another frameset, which means you can take one row and divide it into several columns (or conversely, divide a column into several rows), as shown in Figure 11-4. Nesting gives you more page layout flexibility and complexity than simply dividing a frameset into a grid of rows and columns.

In Figure 11-4, the top-level frameset contains one frame (100 pixels wide) and one frameset that occupies the remainder of the window. That frameset creates three rows; the last row is divided by another nested frameset into two columns. There is no limit on the number of levels frames can be nested. If you are nesting

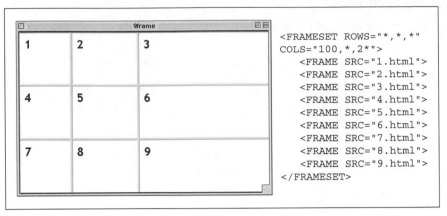

Figure 11-3: Frameset with rows and columns

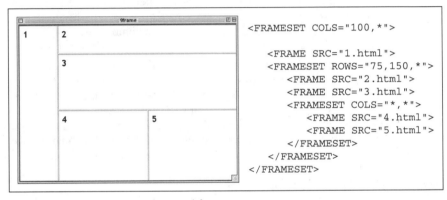

Figure 11-4: Document with nested framesets

frames, be careful to close each successive frameset or the document will not display correctly.

Frame Function and Appearance

By default, your frames will be separated by borders with 3D beveled edges and each frame will be given a scrollbar if its contents do not fit in their entirety. This section looks at the attributes that give you greater control over the display and function of frames.

Frame Borders and Spacing

Borders can be manipulated using attributes within the <frameset> tag. Unfortunately, as of this writing borders are handled inconsistently between browsers, which makes specifying borders frustrating and sometimes unpredictable.

According to the documentation, you should be able to apply frame border attributes within the <frame> tags to adjust the borders for individual frames. Although frame settings should override frameset-level border settings, I have yet to see this handled successfully in any browser.

Borders for Netscape

For Netscape, use the `frameborder` attribute to turn borders off (no) or on (yes). You can set the color of the borders using the `bordercolor` attribute with an RGB or standard color name. The `border` attribute sets the thickness of the borders (in pixels) when the `frameborder` attribute is turned on, so you can set the borders as thick as you like. To turn the borders off entirely, set the `frameborder=no` and `border=0`.

Borders for Internet Explorer

Internet Explorer also uses the frameborder attribute to turn borders off and on, however, it supports the values 0 and 1, respectively (these are the values documented in the HTML 4.0 Specification). IE 4.0 will also accept no and yes values with `frameborder`. Only version 4.0 will recognize the `bordercolor` attribute noted above. In the <frameset> tag, you set the amount of space between frames (in pixels) with the `framespacing` attribute. To turn borders off for Internet Explorer, set `framespacing=0` and `frameborder=0`.

Turning borders off for both browsers

The vast majority of times designers exert control over borders is to turn them off entirely to give a framed page a smooth and seamless appearance. In order to turn borders off for all browsers, it is necessary to load the <frameset> tag with redundant information, as follows:

```
<FRAMESET FRAMEBORDER=0 FRAMESPACING=0 FRAMEBORDER=no BORDER=0>
```

Scrolling

The `scrolling` attribute within the <frame> tag controls whether scrollbars appear within the frame, regardless of the frame's contents.

The default setting is auto, which behaves like any browser window—no scrollbars display unless the contents are too big to fit entirely within the frame.

To make scrollbars always appear, even for mostly empty frames, set `scrolling=yes` (see Figure 11-5).

To make sure scrollbars never appear, such as when a frame is filled entirely by a graphic and it's OK if the edges are slightly obscured, set `scrolling=no`. In Figure 11-5, the top frame (as shown in the figure on the left) only has a scrollbar because it was specified in the HTML source.

When scrollbars are visible, they take up some of the width of the current frame, so figure in the width of a scrollbar when calculating frame sizes in precise pixel measurements. On a Macintosh, both Navigator and Internet Explorer render scrollbars 15 pixels wide. On the PC, scrollbars are 12 pixels wide.

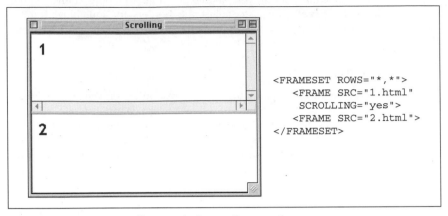

```
<FRAMESET ROWS="*,*">
    <FRAME SRC="1.html"
    SCROLLING="yes">
    <FRAME SRC="2.html">
</FRAMESET>
```

Figure 11-5: Setting scrollbars with the scrolling attribute

Disabling Resize

By default, any user can resize your frames—overriding your careful size settings—simply by clicking and dragging on the border between frames. You can prevent them from doing that (and messing up your cool design) by adding the noresize attribute within the <frame> tag.

Be careful that you're not disabling functionality the user needs, though; if the frame contains text, chances are good that some users may need to resize.

Frame Margins

As you probably already know, browsers hold a margin space on all borders of the browser window, preventing a document's contents from displaying flush against the edge of the browser. The width of the margin varies from browser to browser. In 4.0 browsers, the margin can be adjusted using attributes in the <body> tag (see Chapter 6, *Structural HTML Tags*), but that is a somewhat limited audience.

Frames have margin attributes that allow you to control (or remove) the margins on any frame-enabled browser. The good news is that you can finally position objects right up against the edges of the frame. The (slightly) bad news is that Netscape (as of this writing) will always display at least a 1-pixel margin, even if you set the margin to 0. There's not much you can do about it except camouflage it with a matching background color or image.

To adjust the top and bottom margins of a frame, specify a number of pixels for the marginheight attribute. Use the marginwidth attribute to specify the amount of space for the left and right margins. They can be combined as shown in the example in Figure 11-6.

Figure 11-6 shows the same HTML document (containing only a graphic) loaded into two frames within a frameset. The left frame has specific margins specified. The right frame has its margins set to zero. Because this sample is shown in

Internet Explorer, the image on the right rests flush against the frame borders (again, Netscape would display this frame with a margin of 1 pixel).

```
<FRAMESET COLS="*,*">
    <FRAME SRC="bug.html" marginheight="20" marginwidth="12">
    <FRAME SRC="bug.html" marginheight="0" marginwidth="0">
</FRAMESET>
```

Figure 11-6: Effects of setting frame margins (left) and not (right).

Targeting Frames

One of the challenges of managing a framed document is coordinating where linked documents display. By default, a linked document loads into the same frame as the link; however, it is often desirable to have a link in one frame load a page into a different frame in the frameset. This is the case when a list of links in a narrow frame loads content into a larger main frame on the page.

This is done by using the `target` attribute in the anchor (`<a>`) tag to specify the target frame by name. First, of course, it is necessary to assign a name to the frame using the `name` attribute in the `<frame>` tag as follows:

```
<FRAME SRC="original.html" NAME="main">
```

Now any link can load a document into that frame by specifying its name as the target window, as shown in this link example:

```
<A HREF="new.html" TARGET="main">
```

In the above example, the document *new.html* would load into the frame named "main" (replacing *original.html*).

If a link contains a target name that does not exist, a new browser window is opened to display the document, and that window is given the target's name. Subsequent links targeted to the same name will load in that window.

The <base> tag

If you know that you want all the links in a given document to load in the same frame (such as from a table of contents into a main display frame), you can set the target once in the `<base>` tag instead of for every link in the document (saving a lot of typing and extra characters in the HTML document).

Placing the <base> tag in the <head> of the document, with the target frame specified by name, will cause all the links in the document to load into that frame. The following is a sample targeted base tag:

```
<HEAD>
<BASE TARGET="main">
</HEAD>
```

Targets in individual links will override the target set at the document level via the <base> tag.

Reserved target names

There are four standard target names for special redirection actions. Note that all of them begin with the underscore (_) character. You should avoid naming your frames with a name beginning with an underscore as it will be ignored by the browser. The four reserved target names are:

_blank
A link with target="_blank" opens a new, unnamed browser window to display the linked document. Each time a link that targets _blank is opened, it launches a new window, potentially leaving the user with a mess of open windows.

_self
This is the default target for all <a> tags; it loads the linked document into the same frame or window as the source document. Because it is the default, it is not necessary to use with individual <a> tags; however, it may be useful within the <base> tag of the document.

_parent
A linked document with target="_parent" will load into the parent frame (one step up in the frame heirarchy). If the link is already at the top-level frame or window, it is equivalent to _self. Figure 11-7 demonstrates the effects of a link targeting the parent frame.

Figure 11-7: In nested framesets, the _parent target links to the parent frameset

The _parent target name only works when the nested framesets are in separate documents. It does not work for multiple nested framesets within a single frameset document (such as the example shown under "Nesting Frames" earlier in this chapter).

_top

This causes the document to load at the top-level window containing the link, replacing any frames currently displayed. A linked document with target= "_top" "busts out" of its frameset and is displayed directly in the browser window, as shown in Figure 11-8.

Figure 11-8: Linking with the _top target replaces the entire frameset

Inline (Floating) Frames

Microsoft Internet Explorer 3.0 introduced a feature called inline frames, which are identified with the <iframe> tag. They enable a scrollable frame to be placed anywhere within the flow of an HTML document, much like an image.

Although, as of this writing, inline frames are still only supported by Internet Explorer (limiting their practicality), the <iframe> tag and its attributes currently appears in the W3C's HTML 4.0 Specification. With the W3C's thumbs-up, we may see more browsers supporting this nifty feature in future versions. See "Faking an <iframe>" later in this chapter for an example of how to create a similar effect in a way that works in Netscape Navigator, too.

Placing an inline frame is like placing an image on a page. As shown in the following code, within the <iframe> tag, specify the width and height of the frame and the HTML file you want it to display. As with images, you can align the frame on the page and specify hspace and vspace. As with frames, you can specify margins within the frame and border display. Figure 11-9 shows the results.

```
<HTML>
<HEAD><TITLE>IFRAME</TITLE></HEAD>
<BODY BGCOLOR="black" TEXT="white">

<H2>Inline (Floating) Frames</H2>
```

```
<IFRAME SRC="scrolly.html" WIDTH=200
HEIGHT=100 ALIGN=left HSPACE=12></IFRAME>

Microsoft Internet Explorer 3.0 introduced a feature called
inline frames...
</BODY>
</HTML>
```

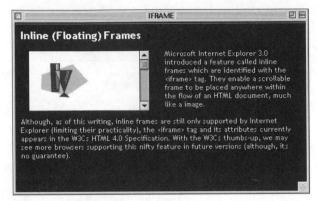

Figure 11-9: Inline frame with IE's <iframe> tag

Frame Design Tips and Tricks

Using frames effectively requires more than just knowing the HTML tags. This section provides a few pointers and tricks for framed documents.

All-Purpose Pages

Just because you design a web page to be part of a framed document doesn't necessarily guarantee that it will always be viewed that way. Keep in mind that some users might end up looking at one of your pages on its own, out of the context of its frameset (this is possible if a search engine returns the URL of the content). Since frames are often used for navigation, this orphaned content page could be a big fat dead-end for a user.

For that reason, you should try to design your content pages so that they stand up on their own. Adding a small amount of redundant information to the bottom of each page can make a big difference in usability. First, indicate the name of the site with a link to its home page on each content document. This will help to orient a newcomer who may have just dropped in from a search engine.

It is important to pay particular attention to the navigational options that are available on content pages when viewed without their frameset. At the very least, provide a small link to the top level of your site on every page that points users back to a more appropriate (and framed) starting point. Be sure to set the target="_top" attribute so if a framed user clicks on it, it won't load the home page frameset within the current frameset.

Helping Search Engines

Search engines all work differently, but they pretty much uniformly do not understand frames or any content within a `<frameset>` or `<frame>` tag. This means search engines will not find any links that require burrowing through a site for indexing purposes, and all the content of your site will be missed.

There are a few measures you can take that will make your site more friendly to search engines:

- **Include content in the frameset document**. Search engines will read content within the <noframes> tag, so it is a good idea to make it as descriptive as possible, so search engines have something to index (instead of just "you need frames to see this site"). Adding a link within the noframes text to the HTML file containing all of your navigational links will help search engines (and humans!) get to the content of your site without relying on the frameset.

- **Use descriptive titles**. Titles are the most important things that search engines index, so use descriptive titles on all content documents. Document titles do not display when the document is loaded into a frame, so it doesn't affect your frame design.

- **Use <meta> tags**. Although not all search engines use <meta> tag information, they can be a useful tool for those that do. If your top-level frameset document contains limited content within the <noframes> tag, you can add a site description and keywords to the page via <meta> tags for the search engine to index. The following is a sample of standard <meta> tags used to aid search engines:

```
<HEAD>
<TITLE>Littlechair Studios</TITLE>
<META name="description" content="Jennifer Niederst's resume
and web design samples.">
<META name="keywords" content="designer, web design, training,
interface design">
</HEAD>
```

For more information about search engines and how they work, see the Search Engine Watch site at *http://www.searchenginewatch.com* (from which the above information was gathered).

Loading Two Frames from One Link

Ordinarily, a link can target only one frame, but there are a few options for creating links that change the contents of two frames at once. One involves simple HTML and the other use JavaScript controls.

Loading a framed document

Using HTML to make a single link change two frames, you can create separate documents containing the frames you want to change, instead of nesting them into the top-level document.

For instance, the following code creates a frameset with two frames: a narrow "top" frame and a "main" bottom frame. The document containing this frameset will be called *top.html*.

```
<FRAMESET ROWS=50,*>
<FRAME SRC="toolbar.html" NAME="top">
<FRAME SRC="first_two_frames.html" NAME="main">
</FRAMESET>
```

The bottom frame is to be divided into two frames, but instead of nesting frames directly within the *top.html* frameset, you can create a number of separate two-frame documents, as shown:

```
<FRAMESET COLS=250,*>
<FRAME SRC="left.html" NAME="leftframe">
<FRAME SRC="right.html" NAME="rightframe">
</FRAMESET>
```

That way, a link within the "top" frame can target just one frame ("main"), but will load a new two-frame document, essentially changing the contents of two frames at once.

Of course, this method will only work for frames that are right next to each other.

Loading two frames with JavaScript*

Adding an onClick JavaScript command within the link allows the browser to load documents into two frames based on one mouse click. For this example, imagine a document that contains two frames, a list of options on the left and the contents in the main window on the right. We want a link in the left frame to change the contents on the right, but also to load a new list of options (perhaps with the current choice highlighted) into the left frame. The code is quite simple:

```
<A HREF="content.html" onClick="window.self.location='newlist.
html'" TARGET="display">Chocolate</a>
```

The text in bold is the JavaScript line that tells the browser to load *newlist.html* into the same window/frame as the link. The remaining code is the standard HTML link that will load *content.html* into the display frame on the right.

Another (and more robust) method for changing two frames with one click uses a function that changes the contents of two frames (named "toolbar" and "main"), as shown in this sample code:

```
<SCRIPT LANGUAGE="JavaScript">
<!--
function changePages (toolbarURL, mainURL) {
parent.toolbar.location.href=toolbarURL; parent.main.location.
href=mainURL;
}
-->
</SCRIPT>
```

---

* This tip was gathered from WebMonkey—*http://www.webmonkey.com.*

Within the anchor tag, the additional code provides the URLs for the documents that will be used in the script (and loaded into the respective frames), as shown in the following example:

```
<A HREF="javascript:changePages('toolbar_document2.html','main_
document 2.html');">
```

Faking an <iframe>

Inline (floating) frames are really cool, but unfortunately, as of this writing, they only work on Internet Explorer. The following code gives the effect of an inline frame using standard frames tags (but, of course, without all the cool text-wrap functionality). It creates a scrolling frame that will always be centered in the browser window, regardless of how the window is resized, as shown in Figure 11-10.

```
<FRAMESET COLS="*,130,*" NORESIZE BORDER=0 FRAMEBORDER=0
FRAMEBORDER=no FRAMESPACING=0>
    <FRAME SRC="black.html" SCROLLING=no>
    <FRAMESET ROWS="*,90,*"  NORESIZE BORDER=0 FRAMEBORDER=0
     FRAMEBORDER=no FRAMESPACING=0>
        <FRAME SRC="black.html" SCROLLING=no>
        <FRAME SRC="pix.html" SCROLLING=auto MARGINWIDTH=0
         MARGINHEIGHT=0>
        <FRAME SRC="black.html" SCROLLING=no>
    </FRAMESET>
    <FRAME SRC="black.html" SCROLLING=no>
</FRAMESET>
```

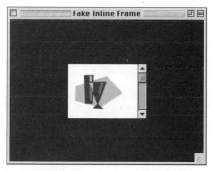

Figure 11-10: Scrolling frame centered in the browser window

The middle column setting in the first <frameset> is the width of the window in pixels. The middle row setting in the nested <frameset> gives the window's height. You can change the size of the window by adjusting these settings. You can also set the scrolling function of the frame within its <frame> tag.

In this example, all of the remaining frames are filled with an HTML file with no contents and a black background. Of course, these frames could contain actual contents as well.

Frame-Proof Your Site

Some sites may link to your site and load it into a single frame in their interface. If you really don't want to see your site squished into someone else's frame, you can add this tricky (yet simple) JavaScript to the <head> of your document, which will make your page always load into the top level of the browser window: This script will work for Netscape Navigator 3.0 and higher and Internet Explorer 3.0 and higher.*

```
<SCRIPT LANGUAGE="JAVASCRIPT"><!-- Hide from old browsers
if (top != self)
top.location.href = location.href;
// Stop hiding from old browsers -->
</SCRIPT>
```

Preloading Images with Hidden Frames

Preloading images refers to methods used for downloading images and storing them in cache before they actually need to be displayed on the page. One method for doing this is to place all the images you'd like to download in a framed document that is hidden from view. The images download and are cached when the first frameset is loaded, but they won't be seen until the user links to a visible page that includes them.

The trick is to create a frameset with two rows (or columns). Set the size of the first row to 100%—this is the frame that will be used to display your first page. In the second row, the one that gets squeezed out of existence, specify the document that contains your images.

```
<FRAMESET ROWS="100%,0" NORESIZE BORDER=0 FRAMEBORDER=0
FRAMEBORDER=NO FRAMESPACING=0>
    <FRAME SRC="firstpage.html">
    <FRAME SRC="thepictures.html">
</FRAMESET>
```

You can put a bunch of images there, but keep in mind that it's not a free download, just a predownload, so all the same rules about minimizing file sizes apply. There's always the chance that the user might click before they've all arrived.

Getting Rid of Page Margins

Unfortunately, there is no method in standard HTML for universally getting rid of the margins that are automatically inserted between the sides of the browser and the contents of a page. Style sheets offer margin controls, but they are not well enough supported to be relied upon. There are also <body> tag attributes that can remove margins in 4.0 version browsers (see Chapter 6).

Web authors who must have the contents of their page nestle in right against the edges of the browser have the marginheight and marginwidth attributes of the

---

* Thank you to Vince Heilman for contributing this script.

`<frame>` tag at their disposal. This will produce the margin-free effect for a much wider audience of all frame-enabled browser users.

The trick is to put the entire page in a frame that is specified to fill 100% of the available window space. The frameset code looks like this:

```
<FRAMESET ROWS="100%,0" NORESIZE BORDER=0 FRAMEBORDER=0
FRAMEBORDER=NO FRAMESPACING=0>
    <FRAME SRC="entirepage.html" MARGINHEIGHT=0 MARGINWIDTH=0>
</FRAMESET>
```

Be aware, however, that even if you set the margins to zero, Netscape Navigator will still display it with a one-pixel margin. The gap can often be disguised with a background color or a background graphic.

Frames

CHAPTER 12

Forms

Forms provide a method for true interaction between users and the publisher of a web site in a way that could never be done in print. With forms, you can use input from a user to provide a customized response on-the-fly or just collect the data for later use. Forms can be used for simple functions like surveys and guest-books, and they are the element that makes a complex online commerce system possible.

This chapter provides a detailed review of the available form elements and how to use them. It also provides a brief introduction to CGI for those who may still be intimidated by making forms work.

Summary of Form Tags

In this section, browser support for each tag is noted to the right of the tag name. Browsers that do not support the tag are grayed out. Browsers that deprecate the tag are noted with a superscript D. Tag usage is indicated below the tag name. A more thorough listing of attributes for each tag, according to the HTML 4.0 Specification, appears in Appendix A, *HTML Tags and Elements*.

<button> NN: 2, 3, **4** - MSIE: 2, 3, **4, 5** - HTML **4** - WebTV - Opera3

```
<button> ... </button>
```

Defines a "button" that functions similar to buttons created with the input tag, but allows for richer rendering possibilities. Buttons can contain content such as text and images.

Attributes

name=*text*
> Assigns the control name for the element.

value=*text*
> Assigns the initial value to the button.

type=submit|reset|button
> Identifies the type of button: submit button (default value), a reset button, or a custom button (used with JavaScript), respectively.

<fieldset>   NN: 2, 3, 4 - **MSIE:** 2, 3, **4, 5** - **HTML 4** - WebTV - Opera3

<fieldset> ... </fieldset>

> Groups related controls and labels. The proper use of this tag should make documents more accessible to nonvisual browsers. It is similar to <div> but is specifically for grouping fields.

<form>   **NN: 2, 3, 4 - MSIE: 2, 3, 4, 5 - HTML 4 - WebTV - Opera3**

<form> ... </form>

Indicates the beginning and end of a form. There can be more than one form in an HTML document; however, forms cannot be nested and it is important that they do not overlap.

Attributes

action=*url*
> Specifies the URL of the application that will process the form (required). This is most often a pointer to a CGI script on the server. The default is the current URL.

enctype=*encoding*
> Specifies how the values for the form controls are encoded when they are submitted to the server. The default is the Internet Media Type (application/x-www-form-urlencoded). The value multi-part/form-data should be used in combination with the file input element.

method=get|post
> Specifies which HTTP method will be used to submit the form data (required). With get (the default), the information is appended to and sent along with the URL itself. The post method puts the form information in a separate part of the body of the HTTP request. post is the preferred method according to the W3C specification.

HTML 4.0 Specification attributes

accept=*content-type-list*
> Specifies a comma-separated list of file types (MIME types) the server will accept and is able to process. Browsers may one day be able to filter out unacceptable files when prompting a user to upload files to the server.

accept-charset=*charset list*
> Specifies the list of character encodings for input data that must be accepted by the server in order to process the current form. The value is a space- and/ or comma-delimited list of charset values. The default value is unknown.

Internet Explorer 3.0 and higher only

target=*name*
> Specifies a target window for the results of the form submission to be loaded. The special target values _bottom, _top, _parent, and _self may be used.

<input type=button>   NN: 2, 3, 4 · MSIE: 2, 3, 4, 5 · HTML 4 · WebTV · Opera3

`<input type=button>`

Creates a customizable "push" button. Customizable buttons have no specific behavior but can be used to trigger functions created with JavaScript controls.

Attributes

name=*string*
> Assigns a name to the form element to be passed to the forms processing application.

value=*string*
> Specifies the initial value for the parameter.

<input type=checkbox>   NN: 2, 3, 4 · MSIE: 2, 3, 4, 5 · HTML 4 · WebTV · Opera3

`<input type=checkbox>`

Creates a checkbox input element within a `<form>`. Checkboxes are like on/off switches that can be toggled by the user. When a form is submitted, only the "on" checkboxes submit values to the server.

Attributes

checked
> When this attribute is added, the checkbox will be checked by default.

name=*text*
> Assigns a name to the checkbox to be passed to the form-processing application if selected. Giving several checkboxes the same name creates a group of checkbox elements, allowing users to select several options with the same property.

value=*text*
> Specifies the initial value of the control that is passed on to the server. If not defined, a value of "on" is sent.

<input type=file>   NN: 2, 3, 4 · MSIE: 2, 3, 4, 5 · HTML 4 · WebTV · Opera3

`<input type=file>`

Allows users to submit external files with their form submission. It is accompanied by a "browse" button when displayed in the browser.

accept=*MIME type*
> Specifies a comma-separated list of content types that a server processing the form will handle correctly. It can be used to filter out nonconforming files when prompting a user to select files to send to the server.

name=*text*
> Assigns a name to the control.

value=*text*
> Specifies the initial filename to be submitted.

<input type=hidden>   NN: 2, 3, 4 - MSIE: 2, 3, 4, 5 - HTML 4 - WebTV - Opera3

```
<input type=hidden>
```

Creates an element within a `<form>` that does not display in the browser. Hidden controls can be used to pass special form-processing information along to the server that the user cannot see nor alter.

name=*text*
> Specifies the name of the parameter that is passed to the form-processing application for this input element (required).

value=*text*
> Specifies the value of the element that is passed to the form-processing application.

<input type=image>   NN: 2, 3, 4 - MSIE: 2, 3, 4, 5 - HTML 4 - WebTV - Opera3

```
<input type=image>
```

Allows an image to be used as a substitute for a submit button.

Attributes

align=top|middle|bottom
> Aligns the image with respect to the surrounding text lines.

name=*text*
> Specifies the name of the parameter to be passed along to the form-processing application.

src=*url*
> Provides the URL of the image (required).

<input type=password> NN: 2, 3, 4 - MSIE: 2, 3, 4, 5 - HTML 4 - WebTV - Opera3

```
<input type=password>
```

Creates a text-input element (like text) but the input text is rendered in a way that hides the characters, such as displaying a string of asterisks (*) or bullets (•). Note this does *not* encrypt the information and should not be considered as a real security measure.

Attributes

`maxlength=`*number*
> Specifies the maximum number of characters the user can input for this element.

`name=`*text*
> Specifies the name of this parameter to be passed to the form-processing application for this element (required).

`size=`*number*
> Specifies the size of the text-entry box (measured in number of characters) to be displayed for this element. Users can type entries that are longer than the space provided, causing the field to scroll to the right.

`value=`*text*
> Specifies the value that will initially be displayed in the text box.

<input type=radio>   NN: 2, 3, 4 - MSIE: 2, 3, 4, 5 - HTML 4 - WebTV - Opera3

`<input type=radio>`

Creates a radio button that can be turned on and off. When a group of radio buttons share the same control name, only one button within the group can be "on" at one time and all the others will be turned "off." This makes them different from checkboxes, which allow multiple choices to be selected within a group.

Attributes

`checked`
> Causes the radio button to be in the "on" state when the form is initially displayed.

`name=`*text*
> Specifies the name of the parameter to be passed on to the forms-processing application if this element is selected (required).

`value=`*text*
> Specifies the value of the parameter to be passed on to the forms-processing application.

<input type=reset>   NN: 2, 3, 4 - MSIE: 2, 3, 4, 5 - HTML 4 - WebTV - Opera3

`<input type=reset>`

Creates a reset button that clears the contents (or sets them to their default values) of the elements in a form.

Attributes

`value=`*text*
> Specifies alternate text to appear in the button (it will say "Reset" by default).

<input type=submit> NN: 2, 3, 4 · MSIE: 2, 3, 4, 5 · HTML 4 · WebTV · Opera3

```
<input type=submit>
```

Creates a submit button that sends the information in the form to the server for processing.

Attributes

`value=text`

Specifies alternate text to appear in the button (it will say "Submit" by default).

<input type=text> NN: 2, 3, 4 · MSIE: 2, 3, 4, 5 · HTML 4 · WebTV · Opera3

```
<input type=text>
```

Creates a text input element. This is the default input type and certainly the most useful and common.

Attributes

`maxlength=number`

Specifies the maximum number of characters the user can input for this element.

`name=text`

Specifies the name of this parameter to be passed to the form-processing application for this element (required).

`size=number`

Specifies the size of the text-entry box (measured in number of characters) to be displayed for this element. Users can type entries that are longer than the space provided, causing the field to scroll to the right.

`value=text`

Specifies the value that will initially be displayed in the text box.

<isindex> NN: 2, 3, 4 · MSIE: 2, 3, 4, 5 · HTML 4D · WebTV · Opera3

```
<isindex>
```

Marks the document as searchable. The server on which the document is located must have a search engine that supports this searching. The browser will display a text entry field and a generic line that says "This is a searchable index. Enter search keywords." This method is outdated—more sophisticated searches can be handled with form elements and CGI scripting.

<label> NN: 2, 3, 4 · MSIE: 2, 3, 4, 5 · HTML 4 · WebTV · Opera3

```
<label>...</label>
```

Used to attach information to controls. Each `label` element is associated with exactly one form control.

for=*text*
> Explicitly associates the label with the control by matching the value of the for attribute with the value of the id attribute within the control element.

Example

```
<LABEL for="lastname">Last Name: </LABEL>
<INPUT type="text" id="lastname" size="32">
```

<legend>   NN: 2, 3, 4 **- MSIE:** 2, 3, **4, 5 - HTML 4 -** WebTV - Opera3

```
<legend>...</legend>
```

Assigns a caption to a <fieldset>. This improves accessibility when the fieldset is rendered nonvisually.

<optgroup>   NN: 2, 3, 4 **-** MSIE: 2, 3, 4, 5 **- HTML 4 -** WebTV - Opera3

```
<optgroup>...</optgroup>
```

Defines a logical group of <options>. This could be used by browsers to display hierarchical cascading menus. <optgroups> cannot be nested.

Attributes

label=*text*
> Specifies the label for the option group (required).

<option>   NN: 2, 3, 4 **- MSIE:** 2, 3, 4, 5 **- HTML 4 - WebTV - Opera3**

```
<option> ... </option>
```

Defines an option within a select element (a multiple-choice menu or scrolling list). The end tag, although it exists, is usually omitted.

Attributes

selected
> Makes this item selected when the form is initially displayed.

value=*text*
> Returns a specified value to the forms-processing application instead of the <option> contents.

<select>   NN: 2, 3, 4 **- MSIE:** 2, 3, 4, 5 **- HTML 4 - WebTV - Opera3**

```
<select> ... </select>
```

Defines a multiple-choice menu or a scrolling list. It is a container for one or more <option> tags.

Attributes

multiple
> This allows the user to select more than one <option> from the list.

name=*text*

Defines the name for selected <option> values that, if selected, are passed on to the forms-processing application (required).

size=*number*

Controls the display of the list of options. When size=1 (and multiple is not specified), the list is displayed as a pull-down menu. For values higher than 1, the options are displayed as a scrolling list with the specified number of options visible.

<textarea>　　　　NN: 2, 3, 4 - MSIE: 2, 3, 4, 5 - HTML 4 - WebTV - Opera3

<textarea>...</textarea>

Defines a multiline text-entry control. The text that is enclosed within the <textarea> tags will be displayed in the text-entry field when the form initially displays.

cols=*number*

Specifies the visible width of the text-entry field, measured in number of characters (required). Users may enter text lines that are longer than the provided width, in which case the entry will scroll to the right (or wrap if the browser provides some mechanism for doing so).

name=*text*

Specifies a name for the parameter to be passed to the form-processing application (required).

rows=*number*

Specifies the height of the text-entry field in numbers of lines of text (required). If the user enters more lines than are visible, the text field scrolls down to accommodate the extra lines.

wrap=off|virtual|physical

Internet Explorer 4.0 and Netscape Navigator 2.0 and higher only. Sets word wrapping within the text area.

off turns word wrapping off; users must enter their own line returns.

virtual displays the wrap, but the line endings are not transmitted to the server.

physical displays and transmits line endingsto the server.

soft is the same as virtual.

hard is the same as physical.

Introduction to Forms

HTML form tags merely provide an interface and controls for gathering information. The real work is done by forms-processing applications, usually CGI scripts, behind the scenes. CGI (Common Gateway Interface) is the interface between HTTP (the program responsible for web transactions) and other programs on the server.

A CGI program (or script) can be written in a number of programming languages. It doesn't matter to the server which one, as long as it can retrieve data and send data back. On Unix, the most popular language is Perl, but C, C++, Tcl, and Python are also used. On Windows, programmers write scripts in Visual Basic, Perl, and C/C++. On the Mac, AppleScript and C/C++ are common.

If you are coming at web design from a designer's point of view (or even just as a novice to web design), chances are you will be handling the HTML form elements and leaving the programming to trained programmers. Often, ISPs will provide a few canned CGI scripts, such as a guestbook or mailing function, that you can point to from within your form, but if you want something customized for your site, I recommend you hire a professional programmer to write it for you.

CGI programming is certainly beyond the scope of this book, but if you are interested in reading more, try *CGI Programming for the World Wide Web*, by Shishir Gundavaram (O'Reilly & Associates). For information on customizing existing scripts, see the section "Demystifying CGI" at the end of this chapter.

The Basic Form (<form>)

The <form> tag, which is used to designate a form, contains the information necessary for interacting with the CGI program on the server. A form is made up of a number of control elements (text-entry fields, buttons, etc.) used for entering information. When the user has completed the form and presses the "submit" button, the entered data is passed to the CGI program specified by the action attribute.

You can have several forms within a single document, but they cannot be nested and you must be careful they do not overlap.

Figure 12-1 shows a very simple form and its <form> tag.

The action attribute

The action attribute in the <form> tag provides the URL of the program to be used for processing the form. By convention, CGI programs are usually kept in a directory called *cgi-bin*. In the example in Figure 12-1, the form information is going to a Perl script called *mailform.pl* which resides in the *cgi-bin* directory of the current server.

The method attribute

The method attribute specifies one of two ways, either get or post, in which the information from the form can be transmitted to the server. Form information is transferred in a series of *name=value* pairs, separated by the ampersand (&) character.

Let's take into consideration a simple form with two fields: one for entering a name, and the other for entering a nickname. If a user enters "Josephine" in the first field and "Josie" in the second, that information is transmitted to the server in the following format:

```
name=Josephine&nickname=Josie
```

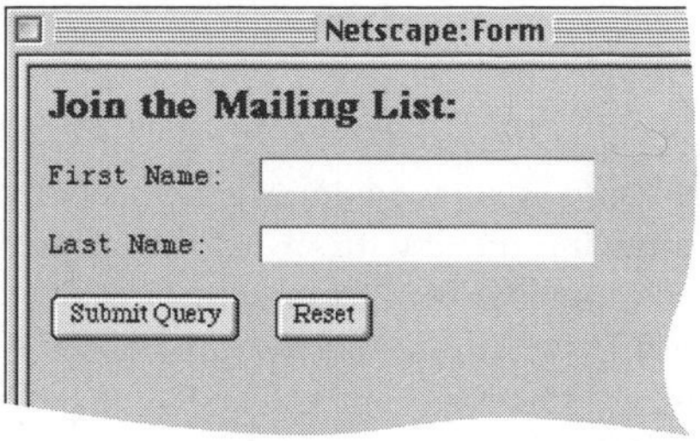

```
<H2>Join the Mailing List:</H2>

<FORM ACTION="/cgi-bin/mailform.pl" METHOD=GET>
<PRE>
First Name: <INPUT TYPE="text" NAME="first">
Last Name:  <INPUT TYPE="text" NAME="last">
<INPUT TYPE="submit">  <INPUT TYPE="reset">
</PRE>
</FORM>
```

Figure 12-1: A simple form

With the get method, the browser transfers the data from the form as part of the URL itself (appended to the end). The information gathered from the nickname example would be transferred via the get method as follows:

```
GET http://www.oreilly.com/cgi-bin/
guestbook.pl?name=Josephine&nickname=Josie
```

The post method transmits the form input information after the URL and certain header information. When the server sees the word POST at the beginning of the message, it stays tuned for the data. This is the preferred transfer method according to the W3C. The information gathered with the name and nickname form would read as follows using the post method:

```
POST http://www.oreilly.com/cgi-bin/guestbook.pl HTTP1.0
... [more headers here]
name=Josephine&nickname=Josie
```

Encoding

Another behind-the-scenes step that happens in the transaction is that the data gets encoded using standard URL encoding. This is a method for translating spaces and other characters not permitted in URLs (such as slashes) into their hexadecimal equivalents. For example, the space character translates to %20, the slash character is transferred as %2F.

The default encoding format, the Internet Media Type (application/x-www-form-urlencoded), will do for most forms. If your form includes a file input type (for uploading documents to the server), you may need to use the enctype attribute to set the encoding to its alternate setting, multipart/form-data.

In general, you will need to communicate with your server administrator to get all the necessary settings for the <form> tag to enable your form to function properly.

Form Elements

There are variety of elements (also sometimes called "controls" or "widgets") that can be used for gathering information from a form. This section looks at each control and its specific attributes. Every form control (except submit and reset) requires that you give it a name (using the name attribute) so the form-processing application can sort the information. The value of the name must not have any spaces (use underscores instead).

Input Controls: <input>

The following controls are entered as attribute options within the <input> tag.

Text entry

The simplest type of form element is the text entry field, which is the default setting for the <input> element. This field allows the user to enter a single word or a line of text. By default, the browser displays a box that is 20 characters wide, but you can set it to be any length using the size attribute.

The user can type an unlimited number of characters into the field (the display will scroll to the right if the text exceeds the width of the supplied box), but you can set a maximum number of characters using the maxlength attribute.

Use the value attribute to specify text to appear when the form is loaded. This can be changed by the user. If you have a form that consists of only one text input element, hitting the Enter key will submit the form without requiring a specific Submit button in the form. The following code creates a text field with a size of 15 characters, a maximum length of 50 characters, and the text "your first name" displayed in the field.

```
What is your name?<P>
<INPUT TYPE="text" NAME="name"  SIZE="15" MAXLENGTH="50"
VALUE="your first name">
```

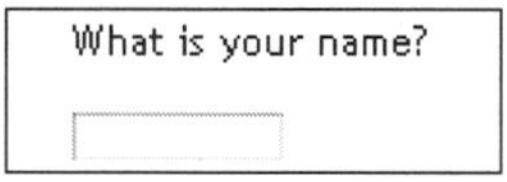

What is your name?

Figure 12-2: Text entry input

Password text entry

A password field works just like text entry, except the characters are obscured from view using asterisk (*) or bullet (•) characters. Although the characters are not displayed in the browser, the actual characters are available in the form data, so this is not a secure system for transmitting passwords. For example, the following code text reveals the actual characters in the default value.

```
What is your password?<P>
```

```
<INPUT TYPE="password" NAME="password"   SIZE="8" MAXLENGTH="8"
VALUE="abcdefg">
```

```
What is your password?

••••••••
```

Figure 12-3: Password input

Hidden entry

This input type adds to the form a control that isn't displayed in the browser. It is
useful for sending information to be processed along with the user-entered data,
such as labels used by the script to sort forms. Some CGI scripts require that
certain hidden fields be added to the form in order to function properly. Here is a
hidden element:

```
<INPUT TYPE="hidden" NAME="extra_info" value="important">
```

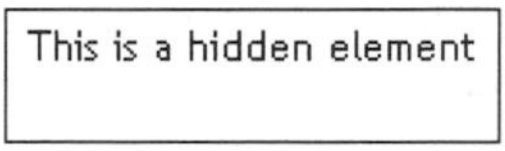

```
This is a hidden element
```

Figure 12-4: Hidden input

Checkbox

Checkboxes are typically used for multiple-choice questions. They work best
when more than one answer is acceptable. When the box is checked, the corresponding value is transmitted with the form to the processing program on the
server.

Checkboxes can be used individually to transmit specific name/value coordinates
to the server when checked. To make an option already checked when the page
loads, add the **checked** attribute to the **input** tag.

If you assign a group of checkboxes the same name, they behave like a multiple-
choice list in which the user can select more than one option for a given property, as shown in the following code and in Figure 12-5.

```
Which of the following operating systems have you used?<P>
<INPUT TYPE="checkbox" NAME="os" VALUE="Unix" CHECKED> Unix
<INPUT TYPE="checkbox" NAME="os" VALUE="Win95"> Windows 95
<INPUT TYPE="checkbox" NAME="os" VALUE="WinNT"> Windows NT
<INPUT TYPE="checkbox" NAME="os" VALUE="Mac" CHECKED> Macintosh
8.0
```

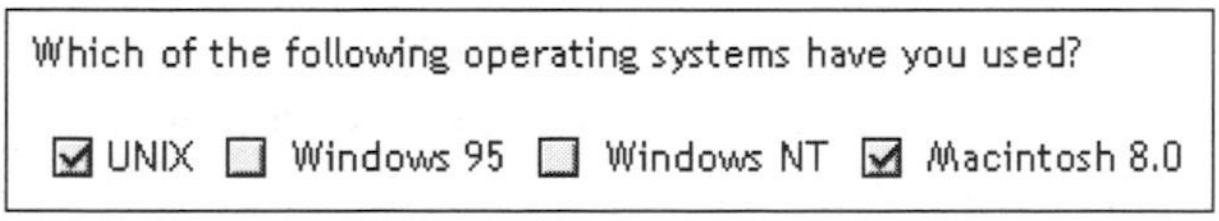

```
Which of the following operating systems have you used?

☑ UNIX   ☐ Windows 95   ☐ Windows NT   ☑ Macintosh 8.0
```

Figure 12-5: Multiple checkboxes with the same name

Radio button

Radio buttons are used to toggle between choices. When a radio button is checked, its corresponding value will be sent to the server for processing. Radio buttons are different than checkboxes in that when several radio buttons are grouped together by the same name, only one radio button can be selected at one time, as shown in the following code and in Figure 12-6. If no button is marked as checked when the form loads, the first button in the group will be selected.

```
Which operating system do you like the best?<P>
<INPUT TYPE="radio" NAME="os" VALUE="Unix"> Unix
<INPUT TYPE="radio" NAME="os" VALUE="Win95"> Windows 95
<INPUT TYPE="radio" NAME="os" VALUE="WinNT"> Windows NT
<INPUT TYPE="radio" NAME="os" VALUE="Mac" CHECKED> Macintosh 8.0
```

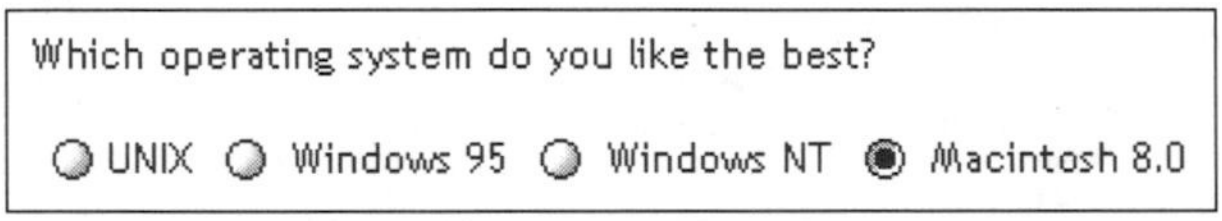

Which operating system do you like the best?

◯ UNIX   ◯ Windows 95   ◯ Windows NT   ◉ Macintosh 8.0

Figure 12-6: Only one radio button in a group can be selected

Submit and reset buttons

Every form (unless it consists of exactly one text field) needs a submit process to initiate the transmission of information to the server. By default, the submit button will say "Submit" or "Submit Query," but you can change it by adding your own text after the value attribute.

The reset button reverts all forms back to the state they were in when the form loaded (either blank or with default values). Its default value is "Reset," but like the submit button, you can change its text by specifying its value, as shown in Figure 12-7.

```
You have completed the form.<P>
<INPUT TYPE="submit"><INPUT TYPE="reset" VALUE="Start Over">
```

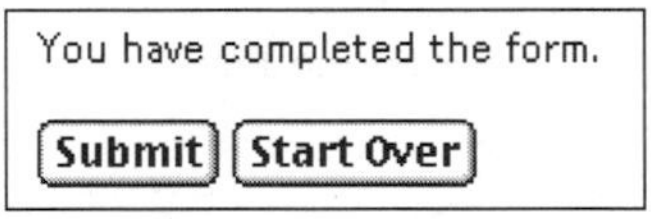

You have completed the form.

[Submit] [Start Over]

Figure 12-7: Submit and reset buttons

Custom button

This button doesn't have any predefined function, but rather is a generic tool that can be customized with JavaScript. Use the value attribute to write your own text on the button, as shown in the following code and in Figure 12-8. It is only supported on 4.0 version browsers.

```
This does something really exciting.<P>
<INPUT TYPE="button" VALUE="Push Me!">
```

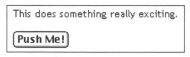

Figure 12-8: Custom button

Image button

You can replace the submit button with a graphic of your choice by using the image type, as shown in the following code and in Figure 12-9. Clicking on the image will return the coordinates of the mouse click to the server. You must provide the URL of the graphic with the src attribute. The name attribute, in this case, is optional.

```
<INPUT TYPE="image" SRC="graphics/sendme.gif">
```

Figure 12-9: Using an image for a button

File selection

The file-selection form field lets users select a file stored on their computer and send it to the server when they submit the form. It is displayed as a text entry field with an accompanying "Browse" button for selecting the file, as shown in the following code and in Figure 12-10. Like other text fields, you can set the size and maxwidth values as well as the default text in the field.

When using the file input type, you should specify enctype="multi-part/form-data" in the <form> tag. Ask your server administrator to confirm this setting.

```
Send this file with my form information:<P>
<INPUT TYPE="file" SIZE="28">
```

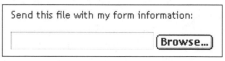

Figure 12-10: The file-selection form field

Text Area: <textarea>

The <textarea> tag creates a multiline, scrollable text entry box that allows users to input extended text entries, as shown in the following code and in Figure 12-11. When the form is transmitted, the browser sends the text along with the name specified by the required name attribute.

Specify the number of lines of text the area should display using the rows attribute. The cols attribute specifies the width (measured in characters). Scrollbars are provided if the user types more text than will fit in the allotted space.

Normally, the text is submitted just as it is typed in, with line returns only where the user presses the Enter key. However, you can use the **wrap** attribute to control text wrapping. When **wrap** is set to **virtual** or **soft**, the text wraps in the user's display. **Physical** or **hard** wrap settings transmit every new line with a hard-coded line return. When wrap is set to **off**, the default setting, the lines do not wrap. The wrap functions are browser-dependent.

The text that appears between **<textarea>** and its end tag **</textarea>** will be the initial contents of the text entry window when the form is displayed.

```
What did you dream last night?<P>
<TEXTAREA NAME="dream" ROWS="4" COLS="45">Tell us your dream in
100 words or less</TEXTAREA>
```

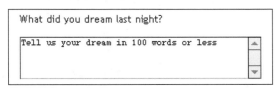

Figure 12-11: The text area form field

Creating Menus with the <select> tag

The **<select>** tag creates a menu of options that is more compact than groupings of checkboxes or radio buttons. A menu displays as either a pop-up menu or as a scrolling list of choices, depending on how the size is specified. The **<select>** tag works as a container for any number of **<option>**s.

The text between the opening and ending **<option>** tags is the value that will be sent to the server. If you want to send a value for that choice that is not displayed in the list, use the **value** attribute within the **<option>** tag.

Pull-down menus

The **<select>** element displays as a pull-down menu of options when no size specification is listed (the default) or when **size=1**. In a pull-down menu, only one item may be selected at a time. (Note: adding the **multiple** attribute turns the menu into a scrolling list, as described in the next section). By default, the first **<option>** in the list displays when the form loads, but you can preselect another option by adding **selected** within its **<option>** tag.

```
What is your favorite ice cream flavor?<P>
<SELECT NAME="ice_cream">
<OPTION>Rocky Road
<OPTION>Mint Chocolate Chip
<OPTION>Pistachio
<OPTION SELECTED>Vanilla
<OPTION>Chocolate
<OPTION VALUE="swirl">Fudge Ripple
<OPTION>Praline Pecan
<OPTION>Bubblegum
</SELECT>
```

In a select form, the item with the selected attribute is displayed as the default value. Clicking on the arrows brings up the full list, as shown in Figure 12-12.

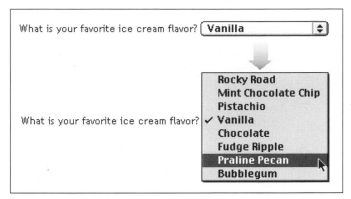

Figure 12-12: Items in a select menu can be set to display after the menu is collapsed

Scrolling menus

To make the menu display as a scrolling list, simply specify the number of lines you'd like to be visible in the list using the `size` attribute or add the `multiple` attribute to the `<select>` tag, as shown in the following code and in Figure 12-13. The `multiple` attribute makes it possible for users to select more than one option from the list.

```
What are your favorite ice cream flavors?<P>
<SELECT NAME="ice_cream" SIZE=6 MULTIPLE>
<OPTION>Rocky Road
<OPTION>Mint Chocolate Chip
<OPTION>Pistachio
<OPTION SELECTED>Vanilla
<OPTION>Chocolate
<OPTION VALUE="swirl">Fudge Ripple
<OPTION>Praline Pecan
<OPTION>Bubblegum
</SELECT>
```

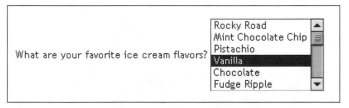

Figure 12-13: Use the size attribute to display a select menu as a scrolling list

New Form Attributes (HTML 4.0)

The HTML 4.0 Specification introduced a number of new attributes that make form elements more accessible and easier to use. Some can be used with Dynamic

HTML to make form elements turn on and off, or become hidden or visible based on user input. Table 12-1 lists the new attributes along with the form elements to which they can be applied.

Table 12-1: New Form Attributes in HTML 4.0

Attribute	Description	Related Tag(s)
accept-charset	Specifies the list of character encodings (character sets) that must be accepted by the server processing the form. It is part of the W3C's internationalization efforts requiring alternative character sets to represent non-Western writing systems.	<FORM>
accesskey	Assigns an access key (keyboard shortcut) to an element for quicker access.	<BUTTON> <INPUT> <LABEL> <LEGEND> <TEXTAREA>
disabled	Disables the control for user input.	<BUTTON> <INPUT> <OPTGROUP> <OPTION> <SELECT> <TEXTAREA>
read-only	Prevents the user from changing the text in a field.	<INPUT type=text> <INPUT type=password> <TEXTAREA>
tabindex	Specifies position in the tabbing order. Tabbing navigation allows the user to cycle through the active fields using the Tab key.	<BUTTON> <INPUT> <SELECT> <TEXTAREA>

Affecting the Appearance of Forms

Form elements are automatically rendered by the browser, giving the designer little control over the appearance of the controls themselves. Not surprisingly, the same element may be rendered slightly differently on different browsers and platforms (see Table 12-2).

To make things even more interesting, Netscape will resize form elements containing text (text fields, text areas, and scrolling lists) when the constant width font is resized in the browser preferences. So, if a user's fonts are set to 18 points, a <textarea> could suddenly become huge, and exceed the space you've allotted. Like many things on the Web, the way your forms will look is somewhat unpredictable.

Table 12-2: The Appearance of Form Elements on Major Browsers

	Netscape 4.0 Macintosh	Netscape 4.0 Windows 95	Internet Explorer 4.0 Macintosh	Internet Explorer 4.0 Windows 95
Text Entry `<INPUT type="text">`	your name here	your name here	your name here	your name here
Password Entry `<INPUT type="file">`	••••••	*******	••••••	••••••
Checkbox (left) `<INPUT type="checkbox">`	☒	☑	☑	☑
Radio Button `<INPUT type="radio">`	○ ⦿	○ ⦿	⦿ ○	○ ⦿
Submit Button `<INPUT type="submit">`	Submit Query Reset	Submit Query Reset	Submit Reset	Submit Query Reset
Reset Button `<INPUT type="reset">`				
File Selection Entry `<INPUT type="file">`	Browse...	Browse...	Browse...	Browse...
Text Area `<TEXT AREA COLS=20 ROWS=30>`	Default text here.	Default text here.	Default text here.	Default text here
Select Menu (pop-up) `<SELECT SIZE=1>`	Option 1	Option 1	Option 1	Option 1
Select Menu (scrolling list) `<SELECT SIZE=4>`	Option 1 / Option 2 / Option 3 / Option 4	Option 1 / Option 2 / Option 3 / Option 4	Option 1 / Option 2 / Option 3 / Option 4	Option 1 / Option 2 / Option 3 / Option 4

Aligning Form Elements

A page with lots of form elements can get real ugly in a hurry. The best favor you can do for a form is to align the elements in some orderly fashion. There are two methods for doing this: using the <pre> tag and using a table.

The <pre> tag

Unlike standard HTML body text, preformatted text (delimited by <pre> tags) is displayed exactly as it is typed in, honoring multiple character spaces and line breaks. Using characters wrapped in <pre> tags has been a long-time favorite cheat for aligning elements on a web page, going back to the Web's infancy.

If you put your entire form within <pre> tags, you can align the elements by columns of characters. The drawbacks to this method are that it does not offer much flexibility for page design and it may be tedious work. The advantage is that it will be viewed the same way by all viewers, even those using browsers that don't support forms in tables (early browser versions, especially early versions of the AOL browser).

Using tables for form alignment

Tables are really the best tool available for tidying messy form elements. There is nothing special about tables used for forms; the same principles and guidelines outlined in Chapter 10, *Tables*, apply for this use. However, there are a few points to keep in mind for better results:

- Form elements tend to be rendered with extra space above and below. This can be problematic when trying to fit a form into a tight table cell. If you want to lay out a form with a table, it is better to put the <table> element within the <form> element instead of the other way around. Forms can contain all sorts of page elements, so it is not a problem for one to span over more of the page than just the form element. If you must put a form within a table, be sure to give it plenty of space.

- Remember that form elements that contain text (text entry fields, text areas, and scrolling lists) will resize in Netscape relative to the constant-width font size as set in the browser preferences. This is especially treacherous when form elements are placed in a meticulously sized table, as shown in Figure 12-14.

Figure 12-14: Netscape expands forms to accommodate user-defined font sizes

Working with Menus

As mentioned earlier, browsers automatically generate form elements such as pull-down and scrolling menus; however, there are a few ways in which you can tweak their appearance.

First, your page may look neater overall if your menu elements are all the same width so they align nicely. The width of a menu element is automatically determined by the item with the most number of characters in the list. (The size attribute affects only the list's height.)

One way to give your lists the same width is to create a dummy option item (<option>) within each list and make it the desired width by filling it with a number of nonbreaking spaces ( ) or hypens (-).

A dummy option item containing only a number of hyphens can also be used as a divider within the list. Select menus can not contain horizontal rules (<hr>), so adding a row of hyphens is the closest you can get to dividing the list items visually into groups, as shown in Figure 12-15.

Figure 12-15: A row of hyphens serves as a divider in a select menu

The trick to doing this successfully is to make sure that if the user selects your dummy row (and there's nothing that can prevent users from doing so), the information will not be transferred to the server. The desired effect is to make it seem like nothing happens. This can be accomplished with a JavaScript such as the following one contributed to this book by Martin Burns of Edinburgh, Scotland:

```
<SCRIPT>
function checker(selector) {
  if(selector.options[selector.selectedIndex].text = '---------
------') {
    selector.options.selectedIndex = selector.options.
defaultIndex
  }
}
</SCRIPT>
<SELECT name="brand" size=1 onChange="checker(this)">
  <OPTION selected value="">Arugula
  <OPTION>Romaine
  <OPTION>Spinach
  <OPTION>Swiss Chard
  <OPTION>---------------
  <OPTION>Acorn Squash
```

```
<OPTION>Butternut Squash
<OPTION>Spaghetti Squash
</SELECT>
```

Unconventional Use of Form Elements

In the spirit of using HTML tags in a way they were never intended (*a la* tables for page layout), feel free to experiment with using form elements creatively. Remember that forms do not require CGI scripts to in order to display on a web page—scripts are required only to retrieve and process information. This means you can create nonfunctioning form elements to take advantage of the ways they display information.

The most flexible of these are selection menus. A pop-up menu can contain sidebar information embedded in the flow of text. Before there were inline frames (`<iframe>`) there were scrolling selection menus, which can be used to present a little scrolling thought or story (just put a few words of text in each `<option>`). Both of these display alternatives force the user to interact with your content in a more active way than just reading text on the page.

One of the first sites to push forms to their limits was Word (*http://www.word.com/*), a publication featuring original writing and other expressive works. In Figure 12-16, an entire story is contained in a pop-up menu on the Word site.

Figure 12-16: Strange forms: this pop-up menu contains a whole story

If you do choose to use form elements in unconventional ways, be sure that it suits the tone and nature of your content. Cute gimmicks may not be appropriate for business-oriented sites or sites on which you would expect to find functional forms (such as e-commerce sites).

Demystifying CGI

Often designers assume that *cgi-bin* contains things beyond our comprehension. It's time to look behind the curtain! Although it is true that creating Perl and C scripts from scratch requires programming experience, you can still take advantage of the power of scripts by using one that is already made.

Many web-hosting services offer a library of standard CGI scripts that are already installed on their servers. In that case, all you may need to do is point to the script from your page. Some hosting providers will also allow you to upload scripts of your own.

There are a number of great resources for CGI scripts on the Web, including scripts that process forms and send their contents in formatted email messages. Many of them are available for free and include exhaustive documentation that leads even a novice through the process of customizing and installing the script on the server. Some of the more popular CGI archives include:

Matt's Script Archive

http://www.worldwidemart.com/scripts/

A collection of free and useful scripts written by Matt Wright (including Form-Mail discussed later in this chapter) with excellent documentation for configuring.

The CGI Resource Index

http://www.cgi-resources.com/

A complete index of over 1200 CGI-related resources. This site is compiled by Matt Wright of Matt's Script Archive.

Selena Sol's Public Domain CGI Script Archive

http://www.extropia.com/Scripts/

"A public service website developed out of the late-night scripting expeditions of Selena Sol and Gunther Birznieks."

Freescripts.com

http://www.freescripts.com/

Like the name says, this is another site providing useful and free customizable CGI scripts.

Ask Your Server Administrator

Because adding scripts and programs to your web site relies heavily on your server and its configuration, you'll need to work with your server administrator to get things set up. Before you start, you should ask your administrator the following questions:

- **Does your web site-hosting package include access to CGI scripts?** Not all web site hosting services provide access to CGI scripts and functions.

- **Does the server have a script available that does what you're looking for?** Many web site-hosting services have standard scripts available for their customers' use. If there's one already installed, it may save you some time in development.

- **Can you upload your own scripts to the server?** Again, depending upon your arrangement for web site-hosting, you may not be permitted to upload your own scripts to the server, particularly if you are sharing a server with other sites.

- **Do you have upload privileges to the cgi-bin directory?** Assuming you can upload your own scripts to the server, you will need to make sure that you have write privileges to the directory where the scripts are stored (usually called cgi-bin). Your administrator may need to set up an account for you that gives you access to the directory and allows you to make your scripts readable and executable by other users.

- **On what kind of server is your site hosted? What server software is it running?** Scripts are usually written to perform on a particular platform and web server software configuration. Before you spend time customizing a script, be sure that it can be run on your server.

- **What is the exact pathname to the script (once installed)?** You will need to include this in the action setting in a <form>, or wherever you need to reference the script.

In addition, there will usually be a few questions specific to your chosen script that will need to be answered by your administrator. For instance, in order to run a Perl script, the basic Perl interpreter needs to be installed on the server. Or if you want a script that automatically takes the contents of a form and sends it in an email message, you may need to know the exact pathname of the sendmail program on the server (as we'll see in the following example). You should also ask whether to use the post or get method for transmitting form information.

Using Available Scripts

Let's take a look at the process for customizing a free script found on one of the CGI script archives. The purpose of this tutorial is to give you an idea of what to expect and to show that you don't need specific programming skills to do it.

In the following example, we use the FormMail script (written by Matt Wright), which takes the contents of a form and sends it to a specified user in a formatted email message. Although the script in its entirety (about nine book pages worth) is not shown here, you can easily download it from Matt's Script Archive (*http://www.worldwidemart.com/scripts/*).

1. First, make all the necessary arrangements with your server administrator as outlined in the previous section. You should have an understanding of how your particular server and account handle CGI scripts before proceeding.

2. Download the script. Upon downloading, you are given the script as well as a very complete ReadMe file that outlines step-by-step the process for using the script. Read the documentation carefully.

3. Configure the script. You may need to make changes within the script itself to customize it for your use. Following is a sample of the FormMail script. (Note

that certain portions of this script have been omitted where indicated for purposes of fitting it in this chapter).

The FormMail program only requires three variables to be changed (highlighted in bold type in this example):

— the pathname of the Perl interpreter on your server (in the first line of script)

— the pathname of your server's sendmail program (after $mailprog in the sample below)

— the list of domains on which you will allow forms to reside and use your FormMail script (following @referers in the sample below).

These variables are clearly explained in the ReadMe file and are presented with labels in the beginning of the script for ease of customization. Furthermore, each section of the script is clearly labeled as to its function, if you are interested.

[full copyright notice omitted]

```perl
########################################################################
# Define Variables                                                     #
#        Detailed Information Found In README File.                    #

# $mailprog defines the location of your sendmail program on your unix #
#          system.                                                     #

$mailprog = '/usr/lib/sendmail';

# @referers allows forms to be located only on servers which are       #
# defined in this field.  This security fix from the last version      #
# which allowed anyone on any server to use your FormMail script on     #
# their web site.                                                      #

@referers = ('worldwidemart.com','206.31.72.203');

# Done                                                                 #
########################################################################
```

[section omitted]

```perl
sub check_url {

    # Localize the check_referer flag which determines if user is valid.#
    local($check_referer) = 0;

    # If a referring URL was specified, for each valid referer, make    #
    # sure that a valid referring URL was passed to FormMail.           #
if ($ENV{'HTTP_REFERER'}) {
        foreach $referer (@referers) {
            if ($ENV{'HTTP_REFERER'} =~ m|https?://([^/]*)$referer|i) {
                $check_referer = 1;
```

```
                last;
        }
    }
}
else {
    $check_referer = 1;
}

    # If the HTTP_REFERER was invalid, send back an error.
#
    if ($check_referer != 1) { &error('bad_referer') }
}
```
[remaining script omitted]

4. Add mandatory controls to the form. The FormMail script relies on the following hidden input control, which must be included in the form. It tells the script who to mail the form results to.

```
<INPUT TYPE=hidden NAME="recipient" VALUE="email@your.host.
com">
```

5. Add optional controls to the form. The FormMail documentation also provides a listing of other form controls you might include in your form and the exact HTML for creating them. The following is an example taken from the documentation that describes how to specify the "subject" field of an email message generated by the script:

Field:
> subject

Description:
> The subject field allows you to specify the subject you wish to appear in the e-mail sent to you after this form has been filled out. If you do not have this option turned on, the script will default to a message subject: WWW Form Submission

Syntax:
> If you wish to choose what the subject is:
>
> ```
> <INPUT TYPE=hidden NAME="subject" VALUE="Your Subject">
> ```
>
> To allow the user to choose a subject:
>
> ```
> <INPUT TYPE=text NAME="subject">
> ```

6. Upload the script, following the instructions of your server administrator. Be sure that you have included the proper pathname to the script with the action attribute in the <form> tag.

CHAPTER 13

Server Side Includes

In layperson's terms, Server Side Includes (SSI) are special placeholders in an HTML document that the server will replace with actual data just before sending the final document to the browser. By the time the document gets to the browser, it looks just like any other HTML page (even if someone happens to "view source"), as though you typed the data into the HTML source by hand.

When the server looks through the file for placeholders (SSI commands), it is said to *parse* the file. The server then inserts the requested data, which could be anything from the current date and time to other HTML documents to the results of a CGI script. (The complete list of information available via Server Side Includes is listed later in this chapter.)

How SSI Is Used

SSI allows you to create the framework for pages that will be dynamically generated by the server. For the web author, this can be a powerful tool for managing site production and increasing efficiency. The following are just a few examples of the ways SSI can be used:

- Placing elements that you use over and over again. If you have an element that appears on every page of your site, such as a complex navigational header, you can place a single SSI command that just sources it in instead. If you make changes to the header, such as changing a URL or a graphic, you only need to make the change once, and it will be updated automatically on all pages of your site.

- Place a constantly changing element on your page with a single line. For example, if you maintain a homepage that has a message that changes every day, use a Server Side Include command (and a script on the server) to replace the message automatically. You never need to touch the source code for the home page—you just let the server do the work.

251

- Show the date and time the page was last updated.

- Allow multiple users to submit content for inclusion on a web page without giving them access to the HTML source. For example, staff members could send in weekly updates via email. The server could run a script that turns the email into a text file, which is then inserted into the web page via an SSI command.

- Serve an appropriate web page based on the browser making the request. You can even serve documents based on the user's domain name. (Note: not all servers can perform conditional functions. This is discussed later in this chapter.)

Obviously, these are just a handful of possibilities, but they demonstrate the sorts of tasks Server Side Includes are good for.

Advantages

Server Side Includes offer the following advantages:

- It's easy to learn the basic SSI syntax and start implementing simple SSI.

- Most servers provide support for SSI or can add it quickly (check with your server administrator first).

- Pages can be dynamically generated, including up-to-the-second information and content served based on information about the users' viewing environment.

- It isn't browser-dependent like JavaScript, so will work for everyone (as long as it works on your server).

- The commands don't display in the browser, so your methods are invisible to the user.

- It's less work for the server than processing CGI programs for the same functions.

Disadvantages

There are few disadvantages:

- Parsing a file and adding information requires slightly more work for the server than serving a straight HTML document.

- Enabling Server Side Includes on the server may pose a security risk. Talk to your server administrator to find out the policy for SSI on your server.

Getting the Most Out of SSI

The examples in this chapter illustrate the basic form and function of SSI commands. On their own, Server Side Includes provides some useful, although limited, tools for dynamic page generation. The real power of Server Side Includes comes in the combination of SSI commands with CGI scripts running on the server. The CGI programs do the necessary processing before the information is ready to be placed in the HTML page.

If you focus on front-end web design, you can get started right away using the elements and variables listed in this chapter, however, you may need to consult a CGI programmer to design the back-end for more advanced SSI solutions.

SSI and the Server

It should come as no surprise that the function of SSI depends heavily on the configuration of the server. This is another instance in which you need to communicate with your system administrator to find out whether your server supports SSI and, if so, which syntax to follow.

The instructions in this chapter use SSI commands that work for NCSA HTTPd Server Side Includes, and, specifically, those documented in the Apache server's `mod_include` module. Apache is a freely distributed and highly sophisticated server software package that makes up a large percentage of servers on the Web. NCSA, Netscape, and WebSite server software also support SSI without significant configuration changes. The instructions and examples shown in this chapter may not work with your server, so be sure to check with an administrator first.

Adding SSI Commands to a Document

Server Side Include commands have the following format:

```
<!--#element attribute="value" -->
```

The `element` is one of the predefined functions that Server Side Includes can perform, such as `include` or `echo` (we'll talk more about specific elements later).

The command also includes one or more `attribute/value` pairs that provide the specific parameters to the function.

There are a few important things to note about SSI command syntax:

- The whole command must be enclosed within comment indicators (`<!--` ... `-->`).

- The comment terminator (`-->`) must be preceded by a space to make it clear it is not part of the SSI information.

- Keep the whole command on one line (line breaks between the comment tags may cause the SSI not to function).

- The # symbol is an important part of the command and must not be omitted.

Example: Virtual Includes

The simplest type of Server Side Include is a "virtual include," which tells the server to add information to a file before sending it to the browser.

In this example, let's take a page from within a web site that uses a standard navigational toolbar held together with a table. Instead of placing the table in the HTML source for every web page in the site, we could just insert it into each document as follows:

```
<HTML>
<HEAD><TITLE>News</TITLE></HEAD>
```

```
<BODY>
<!--#include virtual="navtable.html" -->
<H1>Today's Headlines</H1>
... page contents...
</BODY>
</HTML>
```

Documents that contain SSI commands should be saved with an identifying suffix, which indicates to the server that the file should be parsed before being sent to the browser. In most cases, the suffix is *.shtml* (the default), however, this can be configured to be any suffix, so check with your server administrator first.

The command in the above example uses the `include` element, which inserts the text of another document into the parsed file. The `include` element uses the `virtual` parameter to specify the URL of the document to be inserted, in this case, *navtable.html*. The following shows the entire contents (simplified for sake of space) of *navtable.html*:

```
<TABLE>
<TR><TD><IMG SRC="toolbar.gif"></TD></TR>
...complicated toolbar stuff...
</TABLE>
```

Technically, this is just a fragment of an HTML document because the structural tags (<html>, <head>, and <body>) have been omitted. This is one way to ensure the final document doesn't end up with a double (and conflicting) set of structural tags. If you leave them in, be sure they match the parsed document exactly, and keep in mind that double <body> tags aren't received well by some browsers.

Many web masters (including the folks at HotWired) label these fragments with the *.htmlf* suffix to keep them distinct from normal HTML documents, although it's not necessary.

The server puts the fragment in the spot indicated by the virtual include command. When the document is sent to the browser, the source looks like this:

```
<HTML>
<HEAD><TITLE>News</TITLE></HEAD>
<BODY>
<TABLE>
<TR><TD><IMG SRC="toolbar.gif"></TD></TR>
...complicated toolbar stuff...
</TABLE>
<H1>Today's Headlines</H1>
... page contents...
</BODY>
</HTML>
```

The `include` element is just one of the elements available through SSI. The full list of Apache 1.3 elements appears in the "List of Elements" section later in this chapter.

Using Environment Variables

In the example in the previous section, the information placed in the document was prepared ahead of time and saved in a file on the server for future use.

Another type of information that can be used by an SSI element is *environment variables*. These are bits of information that the operating system (or the HTTP server) always keeps track of and makes available for use by CGI programs and SSI. The current date and time, the modification times of local files, and the user's browser version are all examples of environment variables. To use one in an SSI, call it by its specific variable name (DATE_LOCAL, LAST_MODIFIED, and HTTP_USER_AGENT, respectively, for the above examples) in the command. Note that variable names vary for different server software.

Example: Printing the Date and Time

Let's look at a very simple example of how environment variables work. In the following example, we'll display the current date and time on the web page using the echo element (which prints a specified variable to the screen) and the DATE_LOCAL variable. If I put the following SSI command in my HTML source:

```
<!--#echo var="DATE_LOCAL" -->
```

the server will print the following in its place:

```
Thursday, 02-Jul-98 20:10:24 EST
```

> If the date and time format looks a little dry to you, you can change it using the config element and SSI time formats as explained later in this chapter.

XSSI

If your server is running Apache Version 1.2 or higher, you can take advantage of XSSI (eXtended Server Side Includes), which provides more advanced command functions (and, consequently, uses code that is a bit more complicated for non-programmer-types.)

This section presents a brief overview of features unique to XSSI. For the nitty-gritty how-to information, see the Apache 1.3 mod_include documentation at *http://www.apache.org/docs/mod/mod_include.html*. There are several good articles on XSSI available on the WebMonkey site (*http://www.webmonkey.com*—look for "backend"), which provide good explanations and examples of real-world implementations of XSSI.

Flow Control Elements

Flow control elements are a set of if/else commands (similar to if statements used in a programming language) that allow authors to create conditional commands. Using flow control elements, authors can make documents display differently based on specific variables (the "test conditions"). For instance, you could publish one version of your page for users accessing it with the Netscape browser and another for Internet Explorer users.

The basic flow elements are:

```
<!--#if expr="test_condition" -->
<!--#elif expr="test_condition" -->
<!--#else -->
<!--#endif -->
```

The first command contains the `if` statement that causes the server to test for a condition (e.g., if the browser is Netscape). If it is found to be true, the server prints the text or executes any SSI commands immediately following the `if` command. If the test condition is false, the `elif` or `else` statements are used to output specified text or commands. The `endif` element ends the `if` element and is required.

In the following example, a greeting is customized based on the user's browser:

```
<!--#if expr="\"$HTTP_USER_AGENT\" = \"Mozilla\"" -->
Welcome Netscape User!
<!--#elif expr="\"$HTTP_USER_AGENT\" = "\"Explorer\"" -->
Welcome Internet Explorer User!
<!--#else -->
Welcome!
<!--#endif -->
```

As you can see, this is where a little programming knowledge comes in handy for getting the most out of SSI.

Setting Variables

The standard available environment variables were introduced earlier in this chapter. XSSI adds the capability to create your own variables using the `set` element as follows:

```
<!--#set var="category" value="help" -->
```

Your customized variables can then be used as test conditions using the flow control elements listed earlier.

List of Elements

The following is a list of the primary Server Side Includes and their respective attributes.

config

```
config errmsg|sizefmt|timefmt="string"
```

This controls various aspects of SSI.

errmsg

> Defines the default message sent if an error occurs while parsing the document.
>
> ```
> <!-- #config errmsg="Error: File not found" -->
> ```

sizefmt

> Sets the format to be used when displaying the size of the file. Valid values are **bytes** or **abbrev**, which rounds the size up to the nearest kilobyte.
>
> ```
> <!-- #config sizefmt="abbrev" -->
> ```

timefmt

> Sets the format for dates and times. The full range of formats and examples are provided in the section "Time Formats for SSI Output."

echo

```
echo var="environment or set variable"
```

Prints (displays in the document) the value of the variable.

Attributes

var

> The value is the name of the variable to print.
>
> ```
> <!--#echo var="DATE_GMT" -->
> ```

exec

```
exec cmd|cgi-"string"
```

Executes external programs and inserts the output in the current document.

Attributes

cgi

> Provides the relative URL path to the CGI script.
>
> ```
> You are visitor number <!--#exec cgi="/cgi-bin/counter.pl" -->
> ```

cmd

> Specifies any shell program on the server. The SSI variables are available to the command.
>
> ```
> <!--#exec cmd="/bin/finger $REMOTE_USER@$REMOTE_HOST" -->
> ```

fsize

```
fsize file|virtual="path"
```

Inserts the file size of a specified file. The size follows the **sizefmt** format configuration.

`file`

>   Specifies the location of the file as a pathname relative to the directory of the document being parsed.

`virtual`

>   Specifies the URL path relative to the current document being parsed. If it does not begin with a slash (/) it is taken to be relative to the current document.
>
>   `The size of this file is <!--#fsize file="thisfile.html" -->`

flastmod

`flastmod file|virtual ="path"`

Inserts the last modification date of a specified file. The date follows the `timefmt` format configuration.

Attributes

`file`

>   Specifies the location of the file as a pathname relative to the directory of the document being parsed.

`virtual`

>   Specifies the URL path relative to the current document being parsed. The URL cannot contain a scheme or hostname, only a path (and optional query string). If it does not begin with a slash (/) it is taken to be relative to the current document.
>
>   `That file was last modified on`
>   `  <!--#flastmod virtual="/mydocs/thatfile.html" -->`

include

`include file|virtual = "path"`

Inserts the contents of another document or file into the parsed file.

Attributes

`file`

>   Specifies a path relative to the directory of the parsed file (i.e., it cannot include ../ nor can it be an absolute path). The virtual attribute should always be used in preference to this one.

`virtual`

>   Specifies a URL relative to the document being parsed. The URL cannot contain a scheme or hostname. If it does not begin with a slash (/) it is taken to be relative to the current document.

printenv

```
printenv
```

Apache 1.2 and higher only. Prints out a listing of all existing variables and their values.

```
<!--#printenv -->
```

set

```
set
```

Apache 1.2 and higher only. Sets the value of a variable.

Attributes

`var`
> The name of the variable to be set.

`value`
> The value given to the variable.

```
<!--#set var="password" value="mustard" -->
```

Include Variables

These variables are available to the **echo** command, `if`, `elif`, and to any program on the server invoked with the **exec** command.

`DATE_GMT`
> The current date in Greenwich Mean Time

`DATE_LOCAL`
> The current date in the local time zone

`DOCUMENT_NAME`
> The name of the current file (excluding directories)

`DOCUMENT_URI`
> The (%-decoded) URL path of the current file

`LAST_MODIFIED`
> The last modification date and time for the current file

`QUERY_STRING_UNESCAPED`
> Undecoded query string with all shell metacharacters escaped with a back-slash (\)

Other Available Variables

The following are just a few of the many standard Unix environment variables available to both CGI programs and Server Side Includes:

`HTTP_ACCEPT`
> A list of the media types the client can accept

HTTP_REFERER

The URL of the document the client points to before accessing the CGI program

HTTP_USER_AGENT

The browser the client is using to issue the request

REMOTE_ADDR

The remote IP address from which the user is making the request

REMOTE_HOST

The remote hostname from which the user is making the request (can be useful for detecting top level domain suffixes such as .com, .edu, etc.)

Time Formats for SSI Output

SSI provides a rich set of date and time formats that can be used with the `timefmt` attribute of the `config` command. To format the date, insert the code for the format, separated by commas as you intend it to display in the inserted text:

```
<!--#config timefmt="%A, %B %e, %Y" -->
Good morning! It is now <!--#echo var="DATE_LOCAL" -->
```

would result in the date and time displayed in this manner:

```
Good morning! It is now Friday, July 3, 1998
```

As you can see, `%A` specifies the full day name, `%B` specifies the full month name, etc. Commas placed within the list will display in the inserted date and time.

Table 13-1 provides the standard SSI time format codes and their meanings.

Table 13-1: SSI Time Formats

Status Code	Meaning	Example
%a	Day of the week abbreviation	Sun
%A	Day of the week	Sunday
%b	Month name abbreviation (also %h)	Jan
%B	Month name	January
%d	Date	01
%D	Date as "%m/%d/%y"	07/19/65
%e	Date	1 (*not* 01)
%H	24-hour clock hour	13
%I	12-hour clock hour	01
%j	Decimal day of the year	148
%m	Month number	11
%M	Minutes	08
%p	AM | PM	AM
%r	Time as "%I:%M:%S %p"	01:50:40 AM
%S	Seconds	09
%T	24-hour time as "$H:%M:%S"	20:15:30

Table 13-1: SSI Time Formats (continued)

Status Code	Meaning	Example
%U	Week of the year (also %W)	37
%w	Day of the week number (starting with Sunday=0)	2
%y	Year of the century	98
%Y	Year	1998
%Z	Time zone	EST

PART III

Graphics

CHAPTER 14

GIF Format

GIF (Graphic Interchange Format) was the first graphic file type to be displayed by early web browsers, and it remains the most popular and versatile format for distributing color images on the Web to this day. Any image type can be saved as a GIF, but they excel at condensing graphical images with areas of flat color.

GIFs are completely platform independent, meaning a GIF created on any platform can be viewed and edited on any other platform. They were originally developed by CompuServe to distribute images over their network to a variety of platforms (this is why you sometimes see GIFs referred to as "CompuServe GIF").

It is also the only graphic file format that is universally supported by all graphical browsers, regardless of version. If you want to be absolutely sure everyone will see your graphic, make it a GIF.

GIF87a versus GIF89a

There are technically two types of GIF file: the GIF87a and the newer, improved GIF89a. Both are fully supported on most browsers, and both use .gif as their file name suffix.

GIF87a is the original format for indexed color images. It uses LZW compression and has the option of being interlaced.

GIF89a is the same, but also includes transparency and animation capabilities. If you want to add these features to your graphic, you'll need to create the graphic with a tool that supports the GIF89a format. These features have become so popular with web developers that this format has become the *de facto* standard on the Web today. Detailed descriptions of each feature appear in the following sections of this chapter.

Eight-Bit Indexed Color

GIF files are indexed color images that can contain a maximum of 8-bit color information (they can also be saved at lower bit rates). This means they can contain up to 256 colors—the maximum number that 8 bits of information can define (2^8 = 256). Lower bit-depths result in fewer colors and may also reduce file size. This is discussed in "Minimizing GIF File Sizes" at the end of this chapter.

"Indexed color" means that the set of colors in the image, its *palette*, is stored in a color table. Each pixel in the image contains a reference (or "index") to a table cell containing the color for that pixel. In Photoshop, you can view the table for an indexed color image by selecting Image → Mode → Color Table.

When you convert a 24-bit (millions of colors) image to GIF, it is necessary to first convert the image to Indexed Color mode, and as part of that process, reduce the number of colors to a palette of 256 or fewer colors. The image editing tool does its best to approximate the full color range by using the most appropriate colors to approximate the image (an "adaptive" palette). You can specify an alternate set of colors to use in this process, such as the Web Palette.

GIF Compression

There are two main things to know about GIF compression. First, it is a "lossless" compression, meaning no image information is lost in the compression process, and the decompressed image will be identical to the original. (Note that some information may be lost in the conversion process from RGB to GIF format, but once it is converted, the compression itself is lossless.)

Second, GIF uses LZW (Lempel-Zev-Welch) compression, which takes advantage of repetition in data streams. Translated into graphic terms, this means that LZW compression is extremely efficient at condensing rows of pixels of identical color. To use a simplified example, when the compression scheme hits a row of 15 identical blue pixels, it can store the information as "15 blue," but when it encounters a row that has a gentle gradation from blue to black, it needs to store a description for every pixel along the way, therefore requiring more data. This is why GIFs are efficient at storing simple graphical images; the areas of flat color take advantage of the LZW compression.

On a historical note, Unisys, the company that holds the patent on LZW compression, caused quite a stir on the Internet in 1994 when they announced that it would begin charging licensing fees to developers incorporating GIF compression into their products. In the face of fees and legal hassles, the Internet population rushed to find nonproprietary alternatives to the GIF format, leading to the development of PNG (see Chapter 16, *PNG Format*). Unisys does enforce its patent and charges software companies fees for including GIF support, but GIF shows no sign of disappearing any time soon.

When to Use GIFs

GIF is a versatile format for condensing color images for use on the Web. It is particularly well-suited for any image with areas of flat color, such as logos, line art, icons, cartoon-like illustrations, etc. It will compress them cleanly (since it is a lossless compression) and efficiently (LZW compression looks for repetition of pixel colors).

You will also need to use GIF format if you want a portion of the image to be transparent, since it is the only format universally supported by browsers. PNG files can contain transparency information (actually, in a more sophisticated way than GIF), but as of this writing, browser support is too spotty to use them confidently.

GIF is also a good option for adding simple animation to your page without relying on plug-in technology, Java programming, or server-intensive methods. Most browsers display an animated GIF as easily as any other GIF. See Chapter 18, *Animated GIFs*, for more information on GIF animation.

GIFs are not particularly good for photographic images. With the 8-bit limit, true color information is lost and the subtle gradations of tone become pixilated when the image is reduced to 256 colors. The quality of the image may be greatly reduced. In addition, GIF is not able to condense photo-realistic image content efficiently.

In many cases (especially for very small images), GIF will work just fine for all image types, but you will get much better image quality and smaller file sizes if you save photographs and continuous-tone images as JPEGs (*see* Chapter 15, *JPEG Format*, for more information).

Tools Overview

GIFs can be created with a wide variety of graphics programs and utilities.

Image-editing Software

There are many tools available for creating GIF files. The professional industry standard remains Adobe Photoshop (version 5 is now available), a full-featured image editing application. However, if you work on a PC, you may want to try Paint Shop Pro, which has some of the same features for a fraction of the cost. You can download a demo at *http://www.jasc.com/*.

Web Graphics Tools

Two new tools have shown up on the scene that have been designed from the ground up to address the special requirements of Web graphics.

Macromedia Fireworks 1.0 combines a vector drawing application with a bitmap editing program. Among its many impressive features are editable text, "live" effects that can be edited at any time, side-by-side export previews, animation features, rollover buttons, advanced image slicing tools, and much more. It alleviates the need to switch between drawing programs, bitmap programs, and specialized web utilities. For more information, see Macromedia's site at *http://www.macromedia.com/*.

Adobe ImageReady 1.0 is a web graphic optimization tool that shares many interface features with its sibling, Photoshop. It provides editable text, optimization previews, interactive palettes, and animation tools, among other convenient features. For more information, see Adobe's site at *http://www.adobe.com/*.

GIF

Both Macromedia Fireworks 1.0 and Adobe ImageReady 1.0 provide GIF creation capabilities along with many fine-tuning controls over bit-depth, dithering, and palette selection, which standard image editing programs lack, and both programs condense GIF files very efficiently. Specific features are discussed in the "Minimizing GIF File Sizes" section of this chapter.

Vector Drawing Programs

With the growing demand for web graphics, many vector-based drawing applications now offer the ability to save bitmapped GIF files without exporting the files and opening them in a program such as Photoshop (a big time saver). In addition, simple graphics with solid fills, which are typical of images created in vector-based drawing tools, are ideal for GIF compression. Vector drawing tools such as Macromedia Freehand (versions 7 and higher), Adobe Illustrator (version 7), Corel Draw, and Corel Xara offer GIF creation capabilities.

Plug-ins

There are also a host of third-party plug-ins that can enhance the functionality of Photoshop and other software that supports Photoshop plug-ins. The most notable of these are PhotoGIF from BoxTop Software (*http://www.boxtopsoft.com/*) and HVS ColorGIF from Digital Frontiers (*http://www.digfrontiers.com/*). Each provides tools that exceed Photoshop's built-in features for fine-tuning GIFs. Specific features are highlighted in the "Minimizing GIF File Sizes" section of this chapter.

Shareware Utilities

In addition, there are dozens of utilities for both Mac and PC that perform simple and specialized tasks. These utilities can be downloaded for free and can be registered for a very modest fee. One example is GifConverter, which will convert most existing graphic formats into GIF, and also allows you to add interlacing. Another is Ulead GifSmartsaver, a very nice standalone GIF optimization utility. Shareware.com is a valuable resource for finding such utilities (search for "gif" at *http://www.shareware.com/*).

Interlacing

Normal GIFs are either displayed one row of pixels at a time, from top to bottom, or they wait until the entire file has downloaded before the image appears. On slow connections, this can mean potentially long waits with empty space and generic graphic icons on the screen.

As an alternative, you can save a GIF87a or 89a with interlacing. An interlaced GIF is displayed in a series of four passes, with the first hint of the upcoming image appearing after only 1/8th (12.5%) of the file has downloaded. The first pass has the appearance of a blurry mosaic; as more data flows in, the blurred areas are filled in with real image information and the image becomes more defined. The three subsequent passes fill in 25%, 50%, and 100% of the image information, respectively.

Graphics programs that support the GIF format will provide an interlacing option (usually a checkbox) in the Save as or Export dialog box. Simply turn the interlacing on or off when you save the GIF.

Advantages

The advantage to using interlacing is that it quickly gives the viewer some idea of the graphic to come. This peek may be enough to make some important decisions. For instance, if the graphic is a familiar imagemap, the user can use the link to go to another page before the entire image has downloaded. In some cases, the partially downloaded image might be enough for the viewer to decide that she doesn't want to wait for the rest.

Disadvantages

The main trade-off in choosing to make a GIF interlaced is it will slightly increase the file size of the resulting graphic. There are also aesthetic considerations involved that come down to a matter of personal taste. Some viewers would rather see nothing at all than look at the temporary visual chaos an interlaced GIF creates. For these reasons, you may choose to limit interlacing to instances when it makes sense, such as for large imagemaps, instead of using it for every small graphic on a page.

Transparency

The GIF89a format introduced the ability to make portions of graphics transparent. Whatever is behind the transparent area (most likely the background color or pattern) will show through. With transparency, graphics can be shapes other than rectangles!

To understand how transparency works, you need to start with the color table (the table that contains the palette) for the indexed color image. In transparent GIFs, one position in the color table is designated as "transparent," and whatever pixel color fills that position is known as the Transparency Index Color (usually gray by default). All pixels in the image that are painted that color will be transparent when viewed in a browser.

In most graphics tools, the transparent area is specified by selecting a specific pixel color in the image with a pointer or eyedropper tool (in Paint Shop Pro, it needs to be specified numerically). All pixels in the image that are the selected colors (corresponding to the same position in the color table) will be replaced with the Transparency Index Color and therefore transparent when they are rendered in a browser.

Let's look at three techniques for working with transparent GIFs. Most of these techniques use Adobe Photoshop for its layering features. The first provides strategies for getting rid of "halos" (or fringe) around transparent graphics. The next gives pointers for preventing unwanted transparency within your image. Finally, there is a demonstration of how transparency can be edited using the Alpha Channel for the image.

Preventing "Halos"

Far too often, you see transparent graphics on the Web with light-colored fringe around the edges that doesn't blend into the background color.

This effect is the result of anti-aliasing, the slight blur used on curved edges to make smoother transitions between colors. Aliased edges, by contrast, are blocky and stair-stepped. In Figure 14-1, the circle on the right has both anti-aliased edges and an anti-aliased "j." The circle on the left has all aliased edges. (Note: the images below have been enlarged to make pixel-level detail more prominent.)

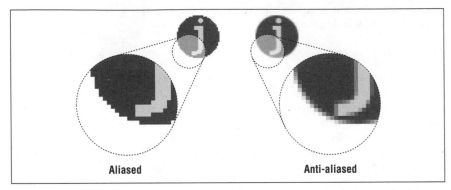

Figure 14-1: The figure on the right has anti-aliased edges; the figure on the left is aliased

Figure 14-2 illustrates that when the color around an anti-aliased edge is made transparent, the blur along the edge is still intact, and you can see all those shades of gray between the graphic and the darker background.

Figure 14-2: A "halo" effect created by anti-aliased edges in a transparent graphic

This "halo" effect makes graphics look messy and unprofessional, but it is easily prevented.

Use aliased edges

The easiest way to avoid anti-aliased fringe around your images is to keep your image and text edges aliased (as shown in Figure 14-3). That way there are no stray pixels between your image and the background color.

Figure 14-3: Transparent graphic with aliased edges (no halo effect)

In Photoshop, the marquee, lasso, and magic wand selection tools all have the option of turning off anti-aliasing in their respective Option palettes. You can also choose to turn off anti-aliasing when creating text.

The advantages to aliased edges are that you avoid halos, and they require fewer pixel colors and will compress more efficiently. The disadvantage is that the blocky edges often just look bad.

Anti-alias to a colored background layer

Transparency can still be used successfully with smooth, anti-aliased edges, as long as they are anti-aliasing to a color similar to the final background color of the page.

For this technique to work, you need to start with a layered Photoshop file with the image sitting in its own layer. If you are starting with a flattened image, such as from a CD-ROM or scan, you first need to use a selection tool to cut the image from the background (using an anti-aliased selection tool) and paste it on a layer of a new Photoshop file.

1. In your layered file, create a new layer at the bottom of the "stack."

2. Fill the whole layer with a color that is the same as, or as close as possible to, the background color of your web page. If you are using a tiled background pattern, choose a color that approximates its dominant color value. If you cannot select the exact color, it is better to guess a little darker.

3. When the layers are flattened as a result of converting to Indexed Color, the anti-aliased text and other soft edges will blend into the color of the bottom layer. The transition pixels will be the appropriate color and will not stand out when placed against the background color on your web page.

Using Adobe ImageReady 1.0

ImageReady, because it was designed specifically for web graphics, has methods for preventing halos integrated into its interface design, making it simple to prepare transparent GIFs the "right" way.

Transparency controls are accessed in the Optimize Palette when GIF is selected from the Format menu. When the Transparency checkbox is checked, the transparent areas of the final GIF are determined by the transparent areas of the layers (the areas that the checkerboard pattern shows through).

To prevent anti-aliased edges from forming "halos," specify a "Matte" color that matches the background color of your page. ImageReady blends the anti-aliased edges with your chosen Matte color while preserving the transparent areas of the image. When the GIF is saved and displayed in a browser, the blurred edges blend into the background seamlessly.

Preventing Unwanted Transparent Areas

When you select a color to be made transparent, pixels of that color in the entire graphic will turn transparent, including all occurrences within the image area that you may want to remain visible. The trick to preventing this is to fill the area to be transparent with a color you are certain does not appear anywhere else in the image.

For this example, consider an image that has a white background, but also white text within the image area. The goal is to turn the white pixels around the image transparent, but to keep the white text visible.

Creating a distinct color for transparency

1. Flatten your image so any anti-aliased edges will merge with your chosen background color (see "Anti-alias to a colored background layer," earlier in this chapter). If you are starting with an Indexed Color image, change it to RGB so you can add a color to its palette.

2. Using the Magic Wand tool with the tolerance set to 1 and anti-aliasing turned *off* (these settings are important!), select the areas in the image that you'd like to be transparent. Holding down the Shift key allows you to add to your selection. (Note, don't use "Select Similar" or you will select *all* the pixels in the image, which is what you're trying *not* to do!)

3. Fill your selection with a distinct color that does not appear anywhere in the image (one of the obnoxious bright colors usually works well). Be sure to choose a web-safe color if you are converting to the Web Palette in order to avoid dithering.

4. Check the image to be sure that all areas you wish to be transparent are filled with the distinct color.

5. Now you can convert the image to Indexed Color, save as GIF format, and select the distinct color to be transparent as you would normally.

Changing the distinct color without losing transparency

The following is an additional (and entirely optional) step to the preceding technique. If for some reason you are unhappy with the new color in your file, or if you worry that it will be visible if transparency isn't supported (not as likely as it used to be), you can turn the new color back to its original color value (white in our example) while keeping it distinct from nontransparent pixels sharing that color (the white in the text areas).

1. Create a distinct color for the transparency.

2. After the image has been converted to Indexed Color, open the Color Table (Image → Mode → Color Table).

3. Find the new, distinct color in the Color Table (if you made it obnoxious enough, it should be easy to find), and click on it.

4. Edit the RGB values in the dialog box to set the color back to the color it was before (white in our example). By doing this, you are assigning that color to two positions in the Color Table; one will be made transparent, the other will remain visible.

5. For some transparent-GIF creation tools, it will be important to know the position of the new white in the Color Table, so you may want to pay attention to the neighboring colors in the table.

6. Once the color is changed, close the dialog boxes and Export to GIF89a, selecting the background area to be transparent. You'll know you've selected the correct white because the areas will be filled with the Transparency Index Color in the preview.

Editing Transparency with the Alpha Channel

Although there isn't an independent transparency channel stored as part of the GIF code structure, Adobe Photoshop translates the transparency information for an image into a sort of picture or map, which can be viewed as an Alpha Channel.

Figure 14-4 shows a graphic (on the left) with the background (in this case, black) showing through its transparent areas. The image on the right shows the corresponding alpha channel for the transparent areas of the graphic as it appears in Photoshop. To access the transparency information, open the GIF file in Photoshop and select Channel Number 2 in the Channels Palette. Areas of the image corresponding to the black pixels in the Alpha Channel will be transparent; areas of the image under white pixels will be visible. There can be no shades of gray in the GIF transparency Alpha Channel.

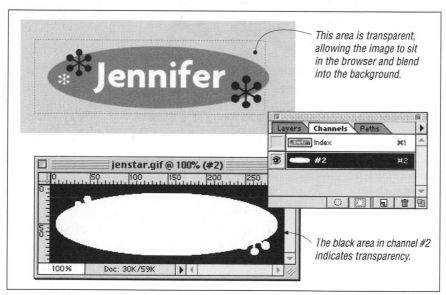

Figure 14-4: Transparent graphic and its corresponding alpha channel in Photoshop

Adding transparent areas

You can edit the channel, thus affecting the transparency information for the image, using any of the selection and painting tools. If you add black pixels to the Alpha Channel, the corresponding pixels in the image will become transparent when the image is saved again as a GIF and viewed in a browser. You can edit the channel using any aliased fill or paint tool (just be sure anti-aliasing is turned off).

Figure 14-5 illustrates how adding a black stroke in the Alpha Channel results in corresponding transparent areas in the GIF file, allowing the background (in this case, black) to show through.

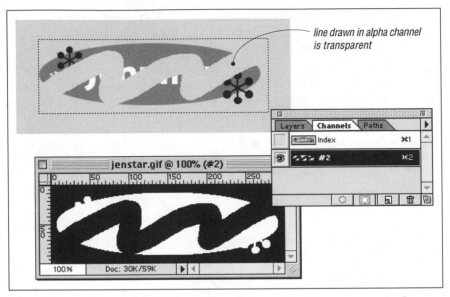

Figure 14-5: Editing the alpha channel results in new transparent areas in the graphic

The following technique is another alternative for removing fringe and unwanted pixels around transparent images by carefully adding transparent pixels to the Alpha Channel.

1. Open a GIF89a file that has transparency information.

2. View the Alpha Channel by selecting Windows → Show Channels, and turning on the eye icon in the left column. If the eye icon is activated for both channels, the image will show through and the channel will appear as a translucent mask.

3. Click on Channel #2 and activate it in order to edit the transparency information.

4. In most cases, you'll only be fine-tuning, so the pencil tool set to a 1- or 2-pixel wide brush will do the trick.

5. When you've made the desired changes to the channel, simply save the GIF file. If you choose to export the file, select "#2" from the "Transparency From:" pop-up menu.

Making transparent areas visible again

In a limited way, you can use the Alpha Channel information to reverse transparency as well; however, once image information is erased, you can never truly get it back again. When you change pixels in the Alpha Channel from black (transparent) back to white (visible), what appears is the Transparency Index Color, not the area's original color.

So for instance, in the graphic used in the previous example, once I scribble through my name in the graphic, it can never be restored to its original state just by "undoing" the transparency (i.e., erasing the black pixels in the alpha channel). Instead of being transparent, the areas appear in the default Transparency Index Color, as shown in Figure 14-6.

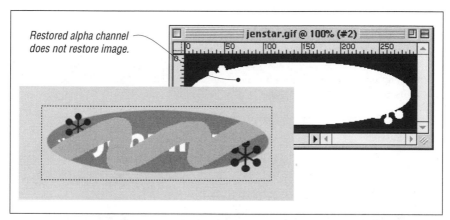

Figure 14-6: Restoring alpha channel does not restore original image

In spite of the crudeness of the above example, when planned properly the Alpha Channel can be used to remove unwanted transparency from pixels within an image (an alternative to the "Creating a distinct color for transparency" technique discussed earlier).

For this example, consider an image that has a white background but also white text. The goal is to turn the white pixels around the image transparent but to keep the white text visible. Simply making white transparent turns the white text transparent as well, as shown in Figure 14-7.

Figure 14-7: All white areas turn transparent when white background is selected as transparent

To make only the background transparent, follow these steps:

1. Before exporting to GIF89a, make a note of the RGB values of the color that is shared by the background area and the image elements. In our example, that color is white (255, 255, 255). This is the color that will appear when transparency is "undone."

2. When exporting to GIF89a (File → Export → GIF89a), use the eyedropper to make the background area transparent. Remember that all the pixels of this color in the image will also become transparent.

3. Change the Transparency Index Color from its default gray to the desired color (white) by clicking on the swatch and filling in the RGB values in the Color Picker. Click OK.

4. Export the image by clicking OK.

5. Open the exported GIF file, and activate Channel #2 in the Channels palette.

6. Wherever you want transparency to be removed (such as the text areas within the image), change the black pixels to white using the eraser tool (shown in the Figure 14-8), pencil tool, or filled selections. These areas will no longer be transparent.

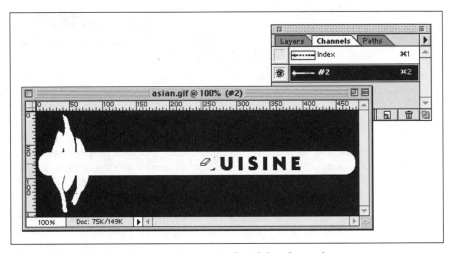

Figure 14-8: Erasing transparent areas in the alpha channel

7. Save the file, or export to GIF89a, selecting "#2" from the "Transparency From:" pop-up menu. The formerly transparent text is restored to the Transparency Index Color, which is now our desired white color, as shown in Figure 14-9.

Copying transparency information

As with any channel in Photoshop, you can copy a transparency Alpha Channel from one document to another.

Figure 14-9: Type is restored to Transparency Indexed Color (which has been set to white)

This may be useful for instances when you want identical transparent areas for a group of graphics, such as a set of buttons. It is particularly useful if you've somehow edited the Alpha Channel and want to apply that change repeatedly.

1. Open the file that contains the "master" transparency alpha channel (the one you want to apply to many graphics). Also open any files you want to copy this information into ("copy" files).

2. In the master file, activate Channel #2 in the Channels Palette.

3. Using the pop-up menu from the arrow in the upper right, select "Duplicate Channel."

4. In the Duplicate Channel dialog box, you have the option of naming the channel as it will appear in the target files. If you leave the field blank, the channel will be named "#2" automatically, which is fine.

5. Choose a destination document from the pull-down menu. The menu gives you a list of open files. Once you've selected a file, click OK.

6. The "copy" file now has an alpha channel you can use for transparency. Export the file to GIF89a (File → Export → GIF89a) and select "#2" (or the name you gave the channel) from the "Transparency From:" pop-up menu. Click OK.

Minimizing GIF File Sizes

When you are designing and producing graphics for the Web, it is of utmost importance to keep your file sizes as small as possible. The standard guideline for estimating download time over a modem is 1 second per kilobyte. Of course, actual download times will vary widely, but it at least gives you a ballpark number to use for comparisons.

There are a few simple strategies you can follow to minimize the size of your GIF files.

Design Strategies

You can help keep file size under control by the design decisions you make. After a while, designing for the Web becomes second nature.

Limit dimensions

Though it may seem obvious, the easiest way to keep file size down is to limit the dimensions of your graphic. There aren't any numerical guidelines here; just don't make graphics larger than they need to be.

- Scale large images down (see "Resizing tips" in Chapter 3, *Web Design Principles for Print Designers*).

- Crop out any extra space around the important areas of your image.

- Avoid large graphics if they are not absolutely necessary.

Design with flat color

You can make design decisions that will take advantage of the way GIF compresses files. If you design your graphics with flat color from the beginning, you are basically giving the LZW compression the kind of file it likes—rows of repetitive pixel colors.

- Fill areas with solid colors rather than gradients (fades from one color to another).

- Limit the amount of photographic material in your GIFs (use JPEGs for photo images).

- Favor horizontal fields of color in your designs when applicable; for example, horizontal stripes will condense better than vertical stripes.

- Turn off anti-aliasing when it isn't necessary. The blur that makes smooth (not stair-stepped) contours also adds to the number of colors in the image.

Reduce Bit-Depth/Number of Colors

Although GIF format can support 8-bit color information with a maximum of 256 colors, you don't necessarily have to use all of them. In fact, you can reduce the size of a file considerably by saving it with a lower bit-depth, which corresponds to fewer number of colors (see Table 14-1).

Table 14-1: Color Depth Equivalents for Bit-Depths

Bit depth	Number of colors
1-bit	2 (black and white)
2-bit	4
3-bit	8
4-bit	16
5-bit	32
6-bit	64
7-bit	128
8-bit	256

The goal is to find the minimum bit-depth that still maintains the integrity and overall character of the image. You may be surprised to find how many images survive a reduction to 5-bit color (just 32 pixel colors). Of course, the bit-depth at which the image quality becomes unacceptable depends on the specific image and on your personal preferences.

Reducing the number of colors actually works in two ways. First, clusters of similarly colored pixels suddenly become the same color, creating more pockets of repeating pixels for LZW compression to work on. For that reason, fewer image colors take better advantage of GIF's compression scheme, resulting in smaller files.

Also, lower bit depths require less actual data to describe the colors in the image. Even if no pixels change color, a 5-bit graphic file will be smaller than an 8-bit version of the same image.

Limit Dithering

When a true color image is reduced to an Indexed color palette of only 256 colors, dithering usually occurs. *Dithering* is the random dot pattern that results when colors are approximated by mixing similar and available colors from a limited palette. Dithering is relevant to GIF file size because it interrupts the clean areas of flat color that are conducive to efficient LZW compression, and can make the file size larger than it needs to be.

Bear in mind, however, that dithering also enables you to maintain image quality and character at lower bit depths, and in this respect can be considered an efficient optimization tool. Lower bit depths generally result in smaller file sizes.

If you are serious about optimizing your GIFs, you can approach the challenge at the pixel level and control the dithering in your image. Dithering options are addressed where applicable in the following tools section.

Tools for Optimizing GIFs

Although Adobe Photoshop offers basic controls for minimizing GIF files, a new breed of tools has arrived that have been built specifically for the creation of web graphics. Not surprisingly, optimization is a key feature of each of them. This section looks at some available techniques and tools for slimming your GIFs with special attention paid to reducing bit-depth and adjusting dithering.

Adobe Photoshop (4.0 and 5.0)

Photoshop allows you to reduce the bit-depth (number of colors) in the Adaptive Palette only, at which time it gives you the option of 2- through 8-bit encoding. Once a custom palette is specified (such as the Web Palette), the bit-depth control is disabled.

This trick for reducing the number of colors in a Web Palette image requires three steps:

1. Convert the file to Indexed Color using the Web Palette, thus ensuring that all the colors in the image are browser-safe.

2. Convert the image to RGB format.

3. Convert the image to Indexed Color again, only this time, choose an Exact palette that reduces the number of colors in the Color Table from 216 to just the number of colors that are actually used. This can significantly reduce file size, depending on the image.

When converting to Indexed Color, Photoshop limits your control over dithering to either None (no dithering) or Diffusion (dithering). This "on" or "off" approach to dithering doesn't allow you as much opportunity to reduce file size as is possible with other tools (discussed below).

Macromedia Fireworks 1.0

In Fireworks, optimization controls are accessed via the Export Preview dialog box (File → Export) shown in Figure 14-10. It provides a number of palette options to choose from, and once in a given palette, the actual number of colors may be reduced to reduce the size of the file. There is also a sliding scale for precisely controlling the amount of dithering. Higher percentages allow for more dithering. When you reduce the dithering amount, areas of the image simplify and LZW compression can work more efficiently (resulting in smaller files).

At very low dithering rates, your image may look posterized. If this is not the effect you want, experiment with the point at which you get the greatest reduction in file size while maintaining image quality. This point depends on the content of the image—dithering is most acceptable in photographic images and least acceptable in areas of flat color.

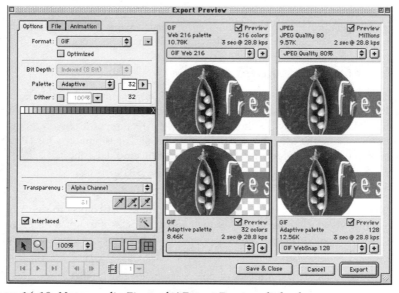

Figure 14-10: Macromedia Fireworks' Export Preview dialog box

The Export Preview allows you to view up to four different versions side-by-side, along with their corresponding file sizes and typical download times, so you can get instant feedback on the effects of your settings and choose the best configuration. Settings can be named and saved for future use.

Adobe ImageReady 1.0

The Optimize Palette with GIF selected in the Formats menu (Figure 14-11) contains all the controls over image optimization.

Figure 14-11: Adobe ImageReady's Optimize dialog box

ImageReady defaults to a Perceptual Palette that is made up of the best colors in the image by giving priority to the colors for which the human eye has greater sensitivity. This palette usually produces images with the best image integrity. To the right of the palette menu is the Colors control where you can select from a list of standard color-depths (8, 16, 32, etc.) or set it to Auto to capture the exact number of colors in the image.

Dithering is controlled by a sliding scale from 0 to 100%. Higher numbers result in more dithering and higher file sizes. Reducing the amount of dithering increases the efficiency of the LZW compression on the image. As mentioned above, you need to make the decision at which point the loss in image quality outweighs the file size savings. The slider makes it possible to make more fine-tuned decisions.

Like other web-specific design tools, ImageReady provides a preview of the image that reflects the changes of your settings in real time. It also shows the effects of your changes on the file size and approximate download time. Settings can be saved as "Droplets" and used for batch processing by dragging and dropping files onto the Droplet icon.

HVS ColorGIF 2.0 (Digital Frontiers Software)

HVS ColorGIF 2.0 plug-in from Digital Frontiers is in a class by itself when it comes to GIF optimization. In all the tests I've run, HVS ColorGIF's compression algorithms produce the smallest GIFs while maintaining the highest image quality compared to other optimizing tools.

It can be used with Photoshop, ImageReady, Fireworks, Paint Shop Pro, or any graphics application that supports plug-ins. ColorGIF is available for both Mac and PC; you can download a demo from Digital Frontier's web site at *http://www. digfrontiers.com/*.

ColorGIF is accessed as a Filter. Its dialog box (Figure 14-12) is packed with features. Like the previous two programs, it offers a preview of the effects of the settings, although, unlike the others, you can only view one preview at a time.

There is a list of standard Palette options to choose from, and once in a palette, you can further reduce the bit-depth of the image. It was the first tool to provide fine-tuning control over the amount of dithering in an image. In addition, there are white and black threshold settings that can simplify portions of your image and allow it to be compressed even further.

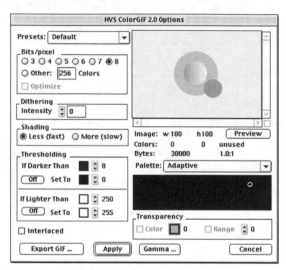

Figure 14-12: HVS ColorGIF 2.0 dialog box

CHAPTER 15

JPEG Format

JPEG (which stands for Joint Photographic Experts Group, the standards body that created it) is a compression algorithm used by files in the JFIF format, commonly referred to as "JPEG files."

Like any graphics file format to find widespread use on the Web, JPEGs are platform-independent. In addition, JPEGs are fully supported for use as inline images in versions 2.0 and higher of Netscape Navigator and Microsoft Internet Explorer, as well as in most other current browsers (see the "JPEGs in AOL Browsers" section in this chapter).

24-bit Color

JPEG images contain 24-bit RGB color information, which means they are comprised from the true color space of millions of colors. JPEG files can also carry grayscale images. This results in higher image quality and more rich and subtle color variations. Unlike GIF files, JPEGs do not use palettes for referencing color information.

Bear in mind, however, that when JPEGs are displayed on a system that only supports 8-bit color, the browser will reduce the colors in the image to the Web Palette, and some dithering will occur. In general, however, dithering is more acceptable in photographic image areas than in areas of flat color. For an explanation of the Web Palette, see Chapter 3, *Web Design Principles for Print Designers*, and Chapter 17, *Designing Graphics with the Web Palette*.

JPEG Compression

JPEG uses what is known as a "lossy" compression scheme, meaning that some color information is actually thrown out in the compression process. Fortunately, for photographic images at most compression levels, this loss is not discernible to the human eye, particularly when the image is being displayed on a monitor at screen resolution (and even less so for images saved at print resolutions).

Using "lossy" compression algorithms, JPEG is able to achieve 10:1 to 20:1 data-compression ratios without visible loss in quality. Of course, the savings in file size at any given compression is dependent on the content of the specific image and results will vary. If maintaining high image quality is not a priority, these ratios can go even higher.

The efficiency of JPEG compression is based on the *spatial frequency*, or concentration of detail, of the image. Image areas with low frequency (smooth gradients, like a blue sky) are compressed much further than areas with higher frequency (lots of detail, like blades of grass). Even a single sharp color boundary, although not giving "lots of detail," represents a surge in spatial frequency and therefore poses problems for JPEG compression.

The compression algorithm samples the image in 8×8-pixel squares then translates the relative color and brightness information into mathematical formulas. These sampling squares may become visible when images are compressed with the highest compression ratios (lowest quality settings).

It is perhaps most meaningful to compare JPEG compression on photographic images to that of GIF. A detail-rich photographic image that takes up 85K of disk space as a GIF image would require only 35K as a JPEG. Again, the rate of compression depends on the specific image, but in general, a JPEG will compress a photographic image two to three times smaller than GIF. For flat-color graphics, however, GIF is far more efficient than JPEG.

JPEG Decompression

JPEGs need to be decompressed before they can be displayed; therefore, it takes a browser longer to decode and assemble a JPEG than a GIF of the same file size. Bear in mind that a small portion of the download time-savings gained by using a JPEG instead of a GIF is lost to the added time it takes to display. (Not much though, so don't sweat it.)

Variable Compression Levels

One advantage to JPEGs is that you can control the degree to which the image is compressed. The higher the quality, the larger the file. The goal is to find the smallest file size that still maintains acceptable image quality.

The quality of a JPEG image is denoted by its "Q" setting, usually on a scale from 1 to 100. In nearly all programs, the lower numbers represent lower image quality but better compression rates (and smaller files). The higher numbers result in better image quality and larger files.

For the most part, the Q setting is an arbitrary value with no specific mathematical significance. It is just a way to specify the image quality level you'd like to maintain. When JPEG compression goes to work, it will compress as much as it can while maintaining the targeted Q setting. The actual compression ratio depends on the content of the individual image.

The scales for specifying Q-settings (or "Quality") vary among tools that create JPEGs. For example, Photoshop uses a scale from 0 to 10 (an improvement over 3.0's options of "low, medium, or high"), but it should be noted that its highest level of compression (0) corresponds to a Q-factor of approximately 30 on the standard scale.

Image Loss

Be aware that once image quality is lost in JPEG compression, you can never get it back again. Loss in image quality is also additive, meaning you lose a little bit more information each time you decompress and compress an image, so each time you edit a JPEG and resave it—even if it's just to crop the image—you degrade the image further. Not only that, you may introduce new artifacts to the image that prevent the second compression from working as efficiently as the first, resulting in higher file sizes.

It is a good idea to hang on to one copy of the original digital image if you anticipate having to make changes, so your final image only goes through the compression process once. You should also start from an original image each time to experiment with different compression levels.

When to Use JPEGs

As mentioned earlier, JPEGs, with their 24-bit color capacity and specialized compression scheme are ideal for photographic and other continuous-tone images, such as paintings, watercolor illustrations, and grayscale images with the 256 shades of gray.

JPEGs are notably *not* good at compressing graphical images with areas of solid color, such as logos, line art, type, and cartoon-like illustrations. JPEG's lossy compression makes flat colors blotchy and pixilated, resulting in unacceptable loss of quality in some cases. Not only that, the files will generally be quite a bit larger than a GIF file of the same image. JPEG compression is also not good at sharp edges or typography since it tends to leave artifacts that "ripple" the edges.

It is generally best to let JPEGs handle photographic material and to leave the graphics to GIF.

Progressive JPEGs

Progressive JPEGs are just like ordinary JPEGs except they display in a series of passes (like interlacing in the GIF format), each pass containing more detailed information until the whole image is rendered clearly. Graphics programs allow you to specify the number of passes it takes to fill in the final image (3, 4, or 5 scans). Bear in mind that over a fast Internet connection, the image may load and render so quickly the user may not see any passes at all.

Advantages

One advantage to using Pro-JPEGs is that like using interlaced GIFs, they provide some indication of the full image for the reader to look at without having to wait for the entire image to download. Progressive JPEGs are also generally slightly smaller than standard JPEG files.

Disadvantages

One disadvantage to Progressive JPEGs is that they require more processing power to display. The higher the specified number of passes, the more power it takes the user's machine to render them.

The other disadvantage is that they are not supported on older browser versions. Netscape Navigator 2.0 and Internet Explorer 2.0 display Pro-JPEGs inline, but may not support the progressive display. Pro-JPEGs are fully supported by versions 3.0 and higher of both Netscape and MSIE. If a browser cannot identify a Pro-JPEG, it will display a broken graphic image.

JPEGs in AOL Browsers*

The America Online 3.0 software uses a version of the Internet Explorer browser that is integrated with Johnson & Grace compression technology for faster image downloads. Unfortunately, the J&G compression has trouble rendering JPEGs created with Photoshop 4.0 because of problems locating the header information in the file. As a result, JPEG image quality gets mangled, displaying a blurry image, sometimes with green, streaky artifacts.

Although users can turn off the "Use Compressed Graphics" option in their Preferences, you can't count on them to do so. AOL's recommendation is to use Photoshop 3.0 instead. Some web developers have found that Photoshop 3.0-created Progressive JPEGs survive their journey through the AOL grinder more successfully, maintaining image quality closer to the original. (Note that Netscape 1.0 users and users with AOL 2.7 on the Mac platform will not be able to see Pro-JPEGs in their AOL browser; however, they make up only 1% of AOL's audience as of this writing.) This problem is rumored to be fixed in the upcoming 4.0 version of the AOL software.

If you want to be absolutely certain your images look perfect for AOL users, stick to GIF format.

Creating JPEGs

Because JPEG is a standard file format, it is supported by all the popular graphics tools. Adobe Photoshop, JASC Paint Shop Pro, Adobe ImageReady, and Macromedia Fireworks all provide similar options for saving JPEGs.

Each tool provides sliders for controlling quality/compression ratios, although they use different numbering systems. Adobe products use a 0–10 compression scale, with the lowest setting corresponding to around 30 on the standard scale of 1–100. Paint Shop Pro uses a scale from 1 to 100; however, it works as the inverse of the standard scale with lower numbers corresponding to higher image quality and less compression. Fireworks uses a percentage value from 1 to 100%.

---

* Thanks for to Max Leach for his assistance with this topic.

All of these products provide the ability to save images in Progressive JPEG format with a checkbox control. Special features for optimizing JPEGs for web delivery are discussed in the following section, "Minimizing JPEG File Size."

There are also plug-in utilities especially for JPEG creation, such as ProJPEG from Boxtop Software (*www.boxtopsoft.com/*) and HVS JPEG 2.1 from Digital Frontiers (*www.digfrontiers.com/*). These plug-ins work with all of the programs mentioned here and are discussed further in the following section.

Regardless of the tool you use, the following guidelines apply:

- Make sure your file is in RGB or grayscale format. You can apply JPEG compression to CMYK files in some applications, but these files are not compatible with web browsers.

- If you are working in Adobe Photoshop, whether with its native JPEG tools or with plug-ins, all layers will need to be flattened before you can save it in JPEG format.

- Name your file with the suffix *.jpg* or *.jpeg*. This is necessary for the browser to recognize it as a readable JPEG file type.

Minimizing JPEG File Size

As for all files intended for Web delivery, it is important to optimize JPEGs to make them as small as possible. Because JPEGs are always 24-bit by nature, reducing bit-depth is not an option. For the most part, all you have to play with is the quality setting, however, it is possible to prepare an image prior to compression. There are a number of specialized tools available for making JPEGs as small as they can be while letting you make decisions about image quality.

Aggressive Compression Ratios

If your image has a lot of continuous tone or gradient colors, you can be pretty aggressive with the compression level and not worry too much about loss of quality in the resulting JPEG. Even at some of the lowest quality settings, (0 or 1 in Photoshop, 20–30 on the standard scale) the image quality is still suitable for viewing on web pages.

Of course, this depends on the individual image. Photoshop's low-quality setting will result in a blocky or blotchy effect in areas of flat color, which may be unacceptable to you. You may need to do some testing to find the compression level that works best. Be sure to save a copy of the original image so you can do a fresh JPEG compression with each test.

ImageReady, Fireworks, ProJPEG, and HVS JPEG provide previews of the effects of your compression settings, both as an image preview and its corresponding file size. This makes it easier to experiment with compression ratios before saving the JPEG. With Photoshop and Paint Shop Pro, you need to save the file and open it again in the program or a browser to see the effects of your compression selection.

JPEG

"Optimized" JPEGs

Standard JPEGs use a precalculated, general purpose compression table (called the Huffman table) for compressing an image. Some tools offer the ability to create an "optimized" compression table that is customized for the particular image. This results in better color fidelity and slightly smaller file sizes. This format is supported on current browsers, however some (mostly older) browsers may have trouble displaying optimized JPEGs.

The optimization option is presented differently in each tool:

Photoshop (4.0 and 5.0)
Select the *Baseline (Optimized)* option in the JPEG dialog box.

ImageReady 1.0
Check the "Optimized" checkbox in the Optimize palette.

Pro-JPEG (BoxTop Software)
Check the "Optimize Huffman Codes" checkbox in the Pro-JPEG dialog box.

HVS JPEG (Digital Frontiers)
In addition to optimizing Huffman Codes, HVS JPEG utilizes a different (and unique) method of optimization that, according to Digital Frontiers, uses a proprietary algorithm to base compression rates on a spatial frequency analysis of the image.

These optimization controls are grouped under the "Q-Table" options in the dialog box (see Figure 15-1). "General" uses the standard compression table. "Generate Optimized Q-Table" creates a customized table for the image.

In addition to these, HVS JPEG provides two predefined tables for optimizing certain image types. "Portraits" is best used on images with smooth tones. "Textured" is for images where it is important to preserve detail and texture.

Precompression Image Preparation

Simple JPEG compression does an admirable job of condensing photographic images without requiring much extra attention. However, if you are serious about making your JPEGs as compact as possible, you may want to maximize JPEG compression's strengths by feeding it the kind of image it likes—an image with subtle gradations, fewer details, and no hard edges.

Preparing an image for better compression is a matter of adding blur effects to the image prior to compression. This can be done manually in a general-purpose program like Photoshop, or by using a built-in prefilter in a web-based graphics tools. Both techniques are discussed below.

Using Adobe Photoshop (4.0 and 5.0)

Adding a slight Gaussian blur to an image—as small as .5 pixels—may result in a 10 to 15% reduction in file size. Of course, just how much blur you can safely add without image degradation and how much file savings will result will vary by image.

You may also use a selection tool to apply the blur to just those areas of your image in which fine detail is not important, such as a sky or a curtain behind the main subject. When you run the image through JPEG compression, it can store those areas with the minimum amount of information, and you're the one that's made the decision of which details to sacrifice.

Using Macromedia Fireworks 1.0

Fireworks provides a "smoothing" prefilter in its JPEG Export Preview dialog box. The smoothing filter blurs hard edges across the whole image. Select the amount of smoothing on a scale of 1 to 8, with the higher numbers producing more blurring and potentially smaller files.

Using HVS JPEG plug-in

Once again, HVS JPEG offers functionality you can't get anywhere else. The Edge-Preserving Detail Filter (in the upper-left corner of the dialog box shown in Figure 15-1) smoothes out texture detail while working to maintain the edges. This results in higher compression with better overall image quality and without edge artifacts.

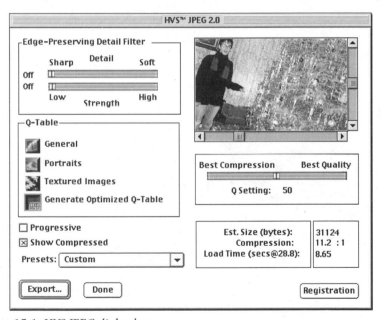

Figure 15-1: HVS JPEG dialog box

If you have an image that has a lot of detail, position the Detail slider towards the left. If your image is soft, you can slide the Detail slider to the right for a more aggressive application of the prefilter. Note that if either of the edge-preserving sliders is positioned all the way to the left, no prefilter will be applied.

Once you've set the Detail slider to match the general quality of the image, you can experiment with various amounts of blur using the Strength slider. This is not a scientific process—it's a matter of finding the point at which you are comfortable with the image quality while minimizing the file size.

Always apply the prefilters first (that's why they're called "pre" filters), because the optimization tables and compression ratios will be based on these settings. After applying the filters and optimization, you may be able to reduce the compression Q-setting a bit without noticeable change in image quality.

CHAPTER 16

PNG Format

The *Portable Network Format* (PNG for short—pronounced "ping") is a versatile and full-featured graphics file format poised to make a big wave on the Web . . . it's just taking its time doing so.

PNG was developed in January and February 1995 as an effort to find a non-proprietary alternative to GIF when Unisys threatened to enforce its patent on LZW compression and collect licensing fees from developers of GIF-supporting programs. This caused a flurry of outrage and activity on the Internet.

Days after the announcement, Thomas Boutell posted the first draft of the PNG specification to the *comp.graphics* newsgroup. A community of programmers then quickly cooperated in specifying and implementing an impressive list of features:

- 8-bit palette support (like GIF) and support of 16-bit grayscale, and up to 48-bit truecolor (RGB) support

- A lossless compression scheme and better compression than GIF for indexed color (palette) images

- Two-dimensional progressive display that is more sophisticated than GIF's 1-dimensional interlacing

- An alpha channel that can contain 8-bit or 16-bit transparency information, which means pixels can have up to 65,000 shades of transparency (not just "on" or "off" like GIF); 8-bit (256 shades of transparency) is far more common

- Gamma correction information to make the PNG display with its intended brightness regardless of platform

- Several methods for checking file integrity and corruption

- Text storage capabilities, for keyword information such as copyright

- Nonpatented compression free from licensing restrictions

Despite this list of attractive capabilities, and despite an official W3C recommendation, PNGs have been the source of a lot of talk and relatively little action on the part of developers. The real foil to an all-out PNG explosion has been the lack of browser support. Fortunately, that picture is slowly changing, and hopefully PNGs will have their day.

Platform/Browser Support

PNG was designed to be network-friendly, so naturally it is recognized and supported on all platforms. PNG does not enjoy universal support by browsers, however, particularly by the Big Two. Initially, in Navigator and Internet Explorer, PNGs could only be handled as embedded objects (placed with the `<embed>` tag) and viewed with plug-ins such as PNG Live. Eventually, PNGs became supported as inline images (placed with the `<img>` tag, like any other web graphic) in Navigator 4.04 and IE 4.0, however, they do not support alpha channel transparency or gamma correction without an additional plug-in.

There are a handful of lesser-known browsers that do offer PNG support in all its glory. However, at the time of this writing, because of PNG's lack of browser support, they are not yet viable options for use on standard commercial web pages. All indications show that support is growing, and PNG could become the web standard it was designed to be. Table 16-1 indicates PNG support as of this writing by a number of popular browsers (plus Arena, which has exceptional PNG support, but is not in widespread use).

Table 16-1: Browser Support for PNG (as of October, 1998)

Browser	Plat-form	View PNGs	Progressive Display	Gamma Correction	Alpha-Channel Transparency
Netscape Navigator 4.04	Mac	X	X	—	—
Netscape Navigator 4.04	PC	X	X	—	With PNG Live 2.0 plug-in
Microsoft Internet Explorer 4.0	Mac	—	—	—	—
Microsoft Internet Explorer 4.0	PC	X	X	—	With PNG Live 2.0 plug-in
Microsoft Internet Explorer 5.0b1	PC	X	X	Not known as of this writing	(Alpha-transparency support is promised, but it is not available in current beta)
Arena		X	X	X	X

It should be noted that although Netscape Navigator 4.0 does not natively support alpha-channel transparency, it does currently support binary transparency (the same as that used for GIFs), and full alpha support is slated for version 5.0.

Updated browser support information can be found at the PNG Home Page maintained by Greg Roelofs (*http://www.cdrom.com/pub/png/pngapbr.html*).

8-Bit Palette, Grayscale, and Truecolor

PNG was designed to replace GIF for online purposes and the inconsistently implemented TIFF format for image storage and printing. As a result, there are three types of PNG files: indexed color (palette images), grayscale, and truecolor.

8-Bit Palette Images

Like GIFs, PNGs can be saved as 8-bit indexed color. This means they can contain up to 256 colors, the maximum number that 8 bits of information can define. Indexed color means the set of colors in the image, its palette, are stored in a color table. Each pixel in the image contains a reference (or "index") to its corresponding color and position in the color table.

Although 8-bit is the maximum, PNGs may be saved at lower bit-depths (1-, 2-, and 4-bit, specifically) as well, thus reducing the maximum number of colors in the image (and the file size).

Grayscale

PNGs can also support 16-bit grayscale images—that's as many as 65,536 shades of gray (2^{16}), enabling black and white photographs and illustrations to be stored with enormous subtlety of detail. This is useful for medical imaging and other types of imaging where detail must be maintained, but it is not much of an advantage for images intended for web delivery. Grayscale images are also supported at 1-, 2-, 4-, and 8-bit depths as well.

Truecolor

PNG can support 24-bit and 48-bit truecolor images. "Truecolor" refers to the full color range (millions of colors) that can be defined by combinations of red, green, and blue (RGB) light on a computer monitor. Truecolor images do not use color tables and are limited only by the number of bits available to describe values for each color channel. In PNG format, each channel can be defined by 8-bit or 16-bit information.

PNG Compression

The most notable aspect of PNG compression is that it is "lossless," meaning no information is lost in the compression process. A decompressed PNG image will be identical to the original.

PNGs use a "deflate" compression scheme. Like GIFs, PNG's compression works on rows of pixels, taking advantage of repetition in bytes of information. By use of filters (discussed in the next section), it can take advantage of some vertical patterns as well; however, filters are not recommended for use with palette images. PNG's compression engine typically compresses images 5–25% better than GIF.

Filters

Before PNG compresses an image, it first runs the image data, row by row, through one of five filters. What follows are brief descriptions of each filter that may aid in making a filter selection in an image-editing tool such as Adobe Photoshop. Although these filters are available, the only two methods that should be used are None (for indexed-color images) and Adaptive (for everything else).

Full technical descriptions of each filtering algorithm appear in the PNG Specification (*http://www.w3.org/TR/PNG-Filters.html*).

None

As it implies, this option applies no filter before compression. The PNG Specification recommends that the filter be set to "None" for flat, indexed color images.

Sub

This filtering algorithm analyzes relationships of image information in rows of pixels. It may be appropriate for images with horizontal color gradients (from Lynda Weinman's *Designing Web Graphics*, Second Edition, New Riders Publishing).

Up

This algorithm looks for relationships in columns of pixels. It may be appropriate for images with vertical color gradients (also from *Designing Web Graphics*).

Average

This algorithm uses an average of the horizontal and vertical relationships for each pixel.

Paeth

This is a complex filter developed by Alan W. Paeth that uses the best prediction based on samples from three directional relationships (left, above, and upper right).

Adaptive

This filtering method applies each of the above filters to every individual row of pixels, then chooses the algorithm that works best for that row, resulting in the best compression for that particular image overall. So, if you can't decide which filter to use, you can let "Adaptive" try them all for you. The PNG Specification recommends using the "Adaptive" method for continuous tone images.

When to Use PNGs

Unfortunately, the answer to this question is "when a higher percentage of browsers in use support them." As of this writing, there is too great a risk that most of your audience won't see your PNG at all, or will see it without the features that make it worth using.

But in a perfect world, where PNG is fully implemented on all browsers, PNG is capable of supporting both indexed and truecolor image types, so there's no bitmapped graphic it can't handle.

Not a JPEG Substitute

Although PNG does support 24-bit color and higher, its lossless compression scheme will nearly always result in larger files than JPEG's lossy compression applied to the same image. The high bit-depth support was developed so PNGs could take the place of TIFF files for saving highly detailed images where loss of image information is unacceptable (such as medical images). For Web purposes where every byte counts, photographic and continuous tone images are still best saved as JPEGs.

A Good GIF Substitute

PNGs are recommended for the type of image that would typically be saved as a GIF (graphics with areas of flat color or sharp edges). PNG's better compression engine can result in a file size that is smaller than a GIF compression of the same image. Bear in mind, however, that the efficiency of compression largely depends on how well the PNG format is implemented in the graphics program being used. PNG also has a more sophisticated interlacing technique than GIF and starts displaying the image in 1/8th the time.

Special Features

You may choose to use a PNG (in that perfect world) for some of its advanced features that no other graphic offers, such as variable transparency levels and full color management systems for automatic image correction, including gamma and color balance corrections.

Interlacing (Progressive Display)

Like GIFs, PNGs can be encoded for interlaced display. When this option is selected, the image will display in a series of passes, the first displaying after only a portion of the file has been downloaded, and each subsequent pass increasing in detail and clarity until the whole image is rendered.

Interlaced PNGs display over a series of seven passes (using a method known as "Adam7," named for its creator, Adam Costello). The first rendering of the image appears after only 1/64 of the file has downloaded (that's eight times faster than GIF). Unlike GIF, which fills in horizontal rows of information, PNGs fill in both horizontally and vertically.

Gamma Correction

Briefly stated, *gamma* refers to the brightness setting of a monitor (for more information on gamma, see Chapter 3, *Web Design Principles for Print Designers*). Because gamma settings vary by platform (and even by manufacturer), the graphics you create may not look the way you intend. In general, graphics created on Macs look dark on PCs and graphics created on PCs will look washed out on Macs.

PNGs can be tagged with information regarding the gamma setting of the platform on which they were created. This information can then be interpreted by software on the user's end to make appropriate gamma compensations. When this is implemented on both the creator and end-user's side, the PNG will retain its intended brightness and color intensity.

Transparency

Both 24-bit and 8-bit indexed color PNGs can have variable levels of transparency. This sophisticated transparency function allows for smooth transitions between foreground and background elements. Grayscale images can also have variable transparency.

As of this writing, the only common tools that allow you to create transparency information in PNGs are Adobe Photoshop (4.0 and higher), Adobe ImageReady, Macromedia Fireworks, the GIMP (an image editing tool for Unix, Linux, and OS/2), and PaintShop Pro (4.0 and higher). Photoshop currently only supports 24-bit transparency, which results in unacceptably large files. ImageReady and Fireworks both support the more complicated 8-bit, palette-based transparency.

Transparency techniques are discussed in the "Creating PNG Graphics" section of this chapter.

Bear in mind that even if you manage to make a PNG file with transparency, it may be a challenge finding a browser to display it. Full alpha-channel transparency is currently supported in browsers only with the help of the PNG Live 2.0 plug-in (PC-only); however, full support is promised for the near future.

Alpha channel

In addition to the standard channels for RGB color values for truecolor images, PNGs may contain an additional alpha channel used for transparency information. Each pixel is then defined by its RGBA values. For 24-bit images, the alpha channel can contain up to 8 bits of information for 256 levels of transparency for every pixel in the image (a great improvement over GIFs, which have two transparency levels: transparent or not transparent). Keep in mind, however, that an RGB PNG file with alpha channels will be about 20% larger than one without.

48-bit PNGs may contain an alpha-channel with 16 bits of information—that's over 65,000 levels of transparency! 24-bit images, however, are far more prevalent and are adequate for most purposes.

In practical terms, this means you can create glows and soft drop shadows that allow background patterns and underlying images to show through in a realistic manner. Figure 16-1 illustrates the effect of graphics showing through areas with variable levels of transparency.

8-bit transparency

Indexed color PNGs can also contain variable levels of transparency (up to 256 levels); however, this information is not handled in a distinct alpha channel as for 24-bit images. Instead, transparency information for each color occupies positions in the color table. So, if you have a red area that fades out using eight levels of transparency, that red would be present in eight slots in the color table, each with its own transparency setting. Other than adding to the number of pixel colors in

Figure 16-1: Variable transparency allows PNGs to blend with background patterns

the Color Table, adding transparency to an 8-bit PNG does not significantly increase its file size.

Embedded Text

PNGs also have the ability to store strings of text. This is useful in permanently attaching text to an image, such as a description of what is in the image or copyright information. Unfortunately, this is another one of PNG's finer capabilities that is not supported by creation tools nor browsers.

Creating PNG Files

The good news is that there are quite a few tools out there for both PCs and Macs that can save files in PNG format. The bad news is that a precious few support special features such as alpha channel transparency or gamma correction (and even then, it's a struggle finding a browser to view them). Furthermore, some programs that create PNG files do not compress them as well as they could (including Adobe Photoshop 4.0 and PaintShop Pro).

Table 16-2 lists PNG feature support in a number of popular graphics tools. For a more comprehensive list of image editing tools and graphics file converters that support PNG compression, see *http://www.cdrom.com/pub/png/pngapps.html.*

*Table 16-2: Graphics Applications that Support PNG Format
(as of October, 1998)*

Application	Read/Write	Compression Filter Options	Alpha-Channel Transparency	8-bit Transparency	Gamma Correction
Adobe Photoshop 4.0/5.0[1]	X	X	X	—	—
PaintShopPro 4.0[2]	X	—	X	—	—
Adobe ImageReady 1.0	X	—	X	X	X
Macromedia Fireworks 1.0[3]	X	—	X	X	—
Macromedia Freehand 7.0[4] and higher	X	—	X	—	—

PNG

Table 16-2: Graphics Applications that Support PNG Format
(as of October, 1998) (continued)

Application	Read/Write	Compression Filter Options	Alpha-Channel Transparency	8-bit Transparency	Gamma Correction
Adobe Illustrator 7.0 and higher	X	—	—	—	—
CorelDRAW	X	—	—	—	—

1 Photoshop's inclusion of individual filter options is not necessarily a beneficial feature, since only two are useful and the rest are confusing. Photoshop stores both gamma and chrominance information, although gamma is only correct in 4.0 if the ambient is "medium"; in 5.0, gamma is reportedly always incorrect.

2 PaintShop Pro 3.0 reportedly creates unnecessarily large palette files. This may be fixed in versions 4.0 and later.

3 PNG is the native file format for Macromedia Fireworks.

4 Freehand preserves Alpha Channel information when 32-bit depth and Save Alpha Channel options are selected during export. It does not provide a way to create an Alpha Channel.

Adobe Photoshop (4.0 and higher)

Photoshop supports the PNG format, but it is notoriously inefficient at compressing files. In most cases, PNG files will be larger than a GIF file of the same image. It does offer alpha channel transparency (for 24-bit RGB images only) and some gamma support, but gamma handling appears to be implemented incorrectly.

Saving as a PNG

To save a file in PNG format, select PNG from the Format pop-up menu when doing a "Save As." The PNG Options dialog box (shown in Figure 16-2) allows you to turn on or off interlacing. You can also select a compression filter from the following choices (descriptions of each appear earlier in this chapter): None, Sub, Up, Average, Paeth, or Adaptive. If your image is an RGB or grayscale image, "Adaptive" may be the best selection for optimum compression. If your image is an Indexed Color image, it is recommended that you set the filter to "None."

Adding transparency

Transparency information is indicated by an Alpha Channel, which you will need to create manually (unlike with GIF files, for which Photoshop generates an alpha channel automatically based on a pixel color selection).

The parts of the image corresponding to black areas in the channel will be totally transparent when the image is viewed in a browser. Remember PNG supports variable shades of transparency, so you can make selections with feathered edges and use gradient fills. Shades of gray in the alpha channel correspond to differing amounts of transparency (the darker, the more transparent).

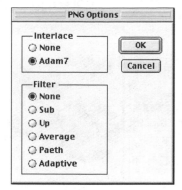

Figure 16-2: PNG options in Adobe Photoshop 4.0 and higher

There are two ways to create an alpha channel:

- **Save a selection.** Select the area of the image that you'd like to remain visible. Save the selection to a channel (Select → Save Selection).

- **Create a new channel.** Activate the Channels Palette by selecting Windows → Show Channels. Select "New Channel..." from the pop-up menu in the upper-right corner. Make sure that "Color Indicates" is set to "Masked Areas."

You can use any of the image-editing tools (paintbrushes, selections, fills) to edit the alpha channel information. When all channels are visible, the channel will act as a mask and your image will show through.

When you are finished creating the Alpha Channel, save the PNG file with a *.png* suffix.

Macromedia Fireworks 1.0

Macromedia Fireworks uses PNG as its native file format because of its lossless compression. It also allows you to export PNG files, including both Alpha Channel and 8-bit varible transparency.

The various PNG settings are accessed in the Export Preview dialog box (File → Export) by selecting PNG from the Format menu (see Figure 16-3). Choose either "Indexed (8-bit)," "Millions (24-bit)," or "Millions + Alpha (32-bit)" from the Bit Depth menu.

When 8-bit is selected, controls similar to those for GIFs appear for setting the palette, number of colors, and dither amount. There are no extra controls for a straightforward 24-bit or 32-bit export.

To add variable levels of transparency to a 24-bit image, simply select "Millions + Alpha (32-bit)" from the pull-down menu and your work is done.

For 8-bit images, there are three transparency options:

None
This option adds no transparency information to the PNG image.

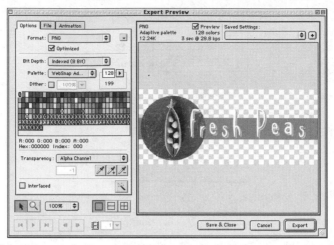

Figure 16-3: Macromedia Fireworks' Export Dialog box showing PNG options

Index Color

For this method, use the eyedropper tool to select the pixel color (or colors) you want to be transparent, the same as you would for a transparent GIF file. The chosen color will appear with an "X" in the Color Table. This method does not allow for variable levels of transparency—pixels are transparent or not, as in transparent GIFs.

Alpha Channel

Fireworks uses the transparency information in the layered image (fades, anti-aliased edges, opacity settings, etc.) to automatically generate variable levels of transparency for each affected pixel color. Each level for each color occupies a slot in the Color Table and is indicated with an "X," as shown in Figure 16-3. If you want a filled object to be 50% transparent, create the object and set its opacity to 50% using the slider tool *before* exporting. Under the Alpha Channel transparency method, the transparency level will be preserved.

Despite its name, this method does not actually use an alpha channel to store transparency information. The transparency information is stored in the color table.

When you are finished with the Export settings, click "Export" and save the file with the *.png* suffix.

Adobe ImageReady 1.0

To create a PNG file in ImageReady, select PNG-8 (8-bit indexed PNGs) or PNG-24 (24-bit PNGs) from the file formats menu in the Optimize Palette (Figure 16-4). The Optimize Palette provides interlacing and transparency controls as well, that change according to which file format is selected. The Optimize Palette for the PNG-8 format (on the left in Figure 16-4) includes the same controls used for GIF files for making decisions regarding palette, the amount of allowable dither, and the color-depth for the image.

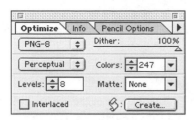 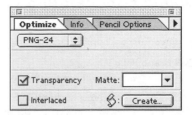

Figure 16-4: Adobe ImageReady Optimize dialog box for PNG-8 (left) and PNG-24 (right)

To create a 24-bit PNG with variable transparency, check the Transparency checkbox and make sure the Matte menu is set to "No Matte." 24-bit PNGs are automatically saved with 256 levels (8-bit) transparency.

For 8-bit PNGs, variable transparency is handled differently, so you must specify the number of levels of transparency you'd like the image to have (between 1 and 256). If your image contains a gradient, the number of levels of transparency can control banding effects in the transparency. (Note, Fireworks does not offer a control for setting the number of levels of transparency.)

Each transparency level for each affected color occupies a slot in the image Color Table. The transparency information is based on the information in the layered image. Therefore, if you know you want an object or layer to have a specific transparency level, set the opacity of the layer in the original image before optimizing.

When you are finished with the Optimize settings, choose "Save Optimized" from the File menu and name the file with the *.png* suffix.

Optimizing PNG File Size

Unfortunately, at the time of this writing, PNGs are so poorly supported by both browsers and production tools that there isn't enough practical experience available to suggest any optimizing strategies.

For Web use, PNGs will be an alternative for indexed color images, and we may find that following some of the same image-creation guidelines used for GIFs may aid in minimizing PNGs as well.

24-bit RGB images are best saved in JPEG format for use online, but if you are saving them as PNGs and are interested in keeping them as small as possible, you are basically limited to selecting the best compression filter. Greg Roelofs, one of the developers of the PNG format, describes this process as "more of a black art than a science." As mentioned earlier, the recommended filter choices are None for indexed-color images and Adaptive for everything else. Use "level 9" (or "max") compression regardless, and don't use interlacing if you want maximal compression. Adding interlacing to any PNG will increase its file size.

If you are serious about optimizing PNGs, you should download Glenn Randers-Pehrson's *pngcrush* application ($7 shareware, available at *http://www.netgsi.com/ ~glennrp/pngcrush/*). It is a command-line DOS application, but it can run in batch mode. This tool comes highly recommended by Greg Roelofs.

Online PNG Resources

If you are interested in learning more about the PNG format, there are several good resources available online.

PNG Home Page

http://www.cdrom.com/pub/png/

This site is written and maintained by Greg Roelofs, one of the creators of the PNG format. It contains a complete history of PNG's birth, descriptions of its features, and up-to-date lists of applications that support the new format. It also includes a copy of the PNG Specification and the official PNG extensions documents (as well as the draft MNG Spec). All of it is written with so much enthusiasm that you can't help but become a PNG fan! It is the source of much of the information in this chapter.

PNG Specification

http://www.w3.org/TR/png.html

This is the complete PNG specification published at the W3C web site. For a technical document, it is very user-friendly to nonprogrammers and offers detailed information on how PNGs work, as well as some useful background information and tutorials.

CHAPTER 17

Designing Graphics with the Web Palette

When images with colors from the full 24-bit color space are displayed on 8-bit monitors (capable of displaying only 256 colors), browsers do the best they can to render the image using colors in their own built-in Web Palette. (Note that if the browser is running on a 24-bit display, the Web Palette does not come into effect and all colors will be displayed accurately.)

Remapping images to the Web Palette can result in unpredictable and undesirable dithering. Not only that, sometimes flat colors shift to the nearest web-safe colors without dithering. The algorithm for deciding which colors to shift and which to dither (as well as choosing *where* to shift) differs depending on the browser brand and version.

But because you know *exactly* which colors will not dither, you can use the Web Palette to your advantage by choosing these colors in the image creation process. It requires a little extra effort, and an adjustment to a limited color choice, but the payoff is that you get to see your image the way everyone else will, with fewer surprises. It gives you, not the browser, control over whether and how the image will dither.

If you don't care about dithering or how your graphics appear on 8-bit monitors, then this chapter is not for you.

The techniques in this chapter apply to graphics that use 8-bit palettes such as GIF or PNG. Because PNG is not widely supported at this time, GIF is featured in the following examples.

The Web Palette

The Web Palette consists of the 216 colors capable of being displayed by both Macintosh and Windows systems. Therefore colors chosen from the Web Palette will render accurately on Mac or PC displays (although they may still shift or dither on low-end Unix displays).

The Web Palette is also known as the Netscape Palette, Web 216, Netscape 216, Browser-Safe Palette, Web-Safe Palette, Nondithering Palette, and the 6×6×6 cube.

Colors in the Web Palette are defined by their numerical values. The Web Palette recognizes six shades of red, six shades of green, and six shades of blue, resulting in 216 possible color values (6 × 6 × 6 = 216). This is sometimes referred to as the 6×6×6 color cube. It's easy to recognize a web-safe color because it will consist of combinations of only six possible values (shown in Table 17-1).

There are three systems used for defining RGB values, which are used in different situations:

Decimal

RGB values are identified by their decimal values in the color pickers of image-editing software such as Photoshop. Web-safe values are multiples of 51, ranging from 0 to 255.

Hexadecimal

This is the base-16 numbering system used in programming languages and in HTML. (See Chapter 5, *HTML Overview.*)

Percentage

In some instances, you will need to identify web values by their percentage equivalents. Some Macintosh applications rely on the Apple Color Picker, which lists RGB values by percent. Web-safe values are multiples of 20%.

Table 17-1 shows the decimal, hexadecimal, and percentage values for each of the six shades in the Web Palette. Depending on the software you are using to create graphics, colors may be identified using any (or all) of these numbering systems.

Web Palette on 16-Bit Displays

Because 16-bit displays must approximate colors from the true color space, slight color shifting and dithering may occur even if you choose colors from the "safe" web palette.

This is most noticeable for pages with graphics that are intended to blend seamlessly with a tiled background graphic or specified background color. Although the foreground and background elements may have identical web-safe RGB values, on 16-bit displays, colors shift and dither in a way that causes the "seams" to be slightly visible.

Which elements shift and which get dithered seems to depend on the browser and operating system combination, so it's difficult to anticipate. If the mismatched colors concern you, making the edges of your graphics transparent instead of a matching color may help eliminate the dithered rectangles on 16-bit displays.

Table 17-1: Equivalent Values of Web Palette Shades

	Decimal	Hexadecimal	Percentage
(darkest)	0	00	0%
	51	33	20%
	102	66	40%
	153	99	60%
	204	CC	80%
(lightest)	255	FF	100%

Other Palettes

All 8-bit Indexed Color images (such as GIF or PNG-8) use a palette of colors to define the colors in the image. The Web Palette is just one of infinite palette possibilities. However, there are several standard palettes you can choose from within popular graphics programs. This section defines the common palette choices that will be referred to throughout this chapter.

Exact

If the image contains fewer than 256 colors, choosing the Exact palette option makes a palette out of the actual colors that are found in the image.

Adaptive

This is a custom palette generated using the most commonly used pixel colors in the image. Less commonly used colors are approximated by the most commonly used colors. It allows for color-depth reduction while preserving the original character of the image. Because the number of colors is being reduced, some dithering and color-shifing will occur.

System (Mac/Windows)

Choosing either system palette will convert the image to the palette of 256 colors as defined by each operating system.

Uniform

This palette contains an evenly stepped sampling of colors from the RGB spectrum.

Custom

This allows you to load in a palette that was previously saved and apply it to the current image.

Perceptual (Adobe ImageReady only)

This creates a custom palette by giving priority to colors for which the human eye has greater sensitivity. Unlike Adaptive, it is based on algorithms, not just a pixel count. It generally results in images with better color integrity than adaptive palette images.

WebSnap Adaptive (Macromedia Fireworks only)

An adaptive palette in which colors that are near in value to Web Palette colors are converted to the closest Web Palette color.

The following list shows the palettes that popular web graphics tools make available when you convert graphics to Indexed Color mode.

Adobe Photoshop (4.0 and 5.0)
Exact, System (Mac), System (Windows), Web, Uniform, Adaptive, Custom, Previous

Adobe ImageReady
Perceptual, Adaptive, Web, MacOS, Windows

Macromedia Fireworks
Adaptive, Web-Snap Adaptive, Web 216, Exact, Macintosh, Windows, Grayscale, Black & White, Uniform, Custom

PaintShop Pro
Indexing is automatic; no palette options are offered

Image Types

Before jumping into specific graphic production tools and techniques, let's first look at the different types of images and how the Web Palette applies to each of them.

Photographic Images

Images made up entirely of photographic material will dither when converted from RGB mode to Indexed Color mode. In most cases, dithering is acceptable, or at least less obvious, in areas with a lot of photographic detail.

You have a number of options for dealing with purely photographic images. The first (and probably the best) is to save it as a JPEG, which will probably result in a smaller file size and will allow any user with a 24-bit display to see it in its original true-color glory. If you must convert it to Indexed Color, an Adaptive palette (or Perceptual if you're using ImageReady) will preserve the original colors and character of the image. You can allow the browser to do the dithering for 8-bit displays, but the image will look much better for users with 24-bit displays.

The only advantage to converting photographic material to the Web Palette is that you can see exactly how the image will appear on 8-bit displays and you will know that the image will look exactly the same for all users.

Flat Graphics

Dithering is most distracting and unacceptable in areas of flat color within a graphic, particularly if that area contains small text. The restricted number of colors in the Web Palette has its largest influence on graphics where dithering might be a problem, such as logos, line-art illustrations, and graphical headlines. You should pay particular attention to the Web Palette for these types of images.

Your best bet is to design the graphic using colors from the Web Palette right from the beginning instead of converting it after the fact. Another alternative is to convert to the Web Palette and severely restrict the amount of dithering, which will force the image to use Web colors and make the file size smaller, but may also result in ugly banding and posterization in gradient and blurred areas.

Combination Images

Images that contain combinations of photographic and flat web-safe colors are a bit more challenging. Simple graphics with blends or gradients of colors also fall into this category.

The trick is to allow the photographic portion of the image (where dithering isn't such an issue) to keep its adaptive palette while mapping the remainder of the image to the Web Palette. This was problematic for Photoshop alone; however, newly available tools designed specifically for creating web graphics have powerful features for dealing with just these issues. These tools will be discussed later in this chapter.

Another option is to break these images into separate graphics and optimize each part appropriately—perhaps even saving photographic pieces as JPEG files. The pieces can be held together using an HTML table as discussed at the end of Chapter 10, *Tables*.

Designing with Web-Safe Colors

If you are creating graphics from scratch, especially graphics such as logos or simple illustrations that contain areas of flat color, why not use nondithering colors right from the start? In this way, you can be certain that your graphics will look the same for all users. The major drawback to this is that with only 216 colors to choose from (a good 30 of which you'd never be caught dead using for anything), the selection is extremely limited. (See the "Color Blenders" section of this chapter for one approach to overcoming the limited choice of colors.)

The trick is to have the Web Palette colors available in a Swatches palette or in whatever device your graphics program uses for making colors handy. You should be aware, however, that even if you select web colors for fills, the shades of colors created by soft drop shadows or anti-aliased edges between areas of color will probably not be web-safe.

Tools with Built-in Web Palettes

Not surprisingly, with the explosion of the Web's popularity, the Web Palette is finding its way into many commercial graphics tools.

Adobe Photoshop 5.0

Version 5 ships with the Web Safe Colors CLUT file (see the following section) in its Color Palettes directory. These can be easily loaded into the Swatches palette by selecting Replace Swatches or Load Swatches from the Swatches pop-up menu.

Adobe ImageReady 1.0

ImageReady was created specifically for the optimization of web graphics, so it's not surprising that the Web Palette comes preloaded in the Swatches palette.

Macromedia Fireworks 1.0

As a tool designed for the creation of web graphics, Fireworks has the Web Palette available in its Swatches palette by default.

Adobe Illustrator 7.0

Version 7.0 of Adobe Illustrator introduces the ability to work within the RGB color space (instead of being limited to CMYK as in previous versions), so you can color your graphics and even export them directly to GIF format. To select colors from the 216 web-safe colors, select Windows → Swatch Libraries → Web.

Macromedia Freehand 7.0 and higher

You can select colors from the Websafe Color Library, under Options on the Color Palette. Colors appear with their decimal and hexadecimal RGB values.

Macromedia Director 5.0 and higher

You can find the Web Palette under the Xtras pull-down menu. Look for the palette called "Netscape."

Macintosh System OS8

MacOS8 comes with an HTML Color Picker in addition to the standard Color Picker. This tool makes selecting web-safe colors extremely easy via slider bars that snap into place at the safe color values. It also translates the colors into the hexadecimal values that HTML and browsers understand. (See Chapter 5 for more information on hexadecimal numbering.)

Pantone ColorWeb Pro

ColorWeb Pro is a Mac-only product that enables designers to select web-safe colors via an addition to the Macintosh Color Picker. It also has printed swatch books that provide Pantone color equivalents for the Web Palette when you need to coordinate your web page with a printed piece. Another swatch book lists traditional Pantone ink colors, but lists their digital equivalents in decimal and hexadecimal RGB values.

Color Look-Up Tables (CLUT Files)

Photoshop and some other graphics tools save palettes in files called CLUTs (Color Look-Up Table). To make the Web Palette available in the Swatches palette, you need to load the appropriate Web CLUT file using the Load Swatches... or Replace Swatches... function (in Photoshop) or some equivalent command.

Creating a CLUT file in Photoshop 4.0

Photoshop 5.0 ships with the Web Safe Colors CLUT file in its Color Palettes folder, however, Photoshop 4.0 does not. If you are using version 4.0, it's easy enough to create one as follows:

1. Convert any RGB image to Indexed Color.

2. In the Indexed Color dialog, select Web from the Palette pop-up menu. Click OK.

3. Select Image → Mode → Color Table. Although the Table pop-up lists Custom as the current option, the table itself contains the 216 browser-safe RGB values.

4. Click the Save button, and save the color palette. Name it descriptively and save it into Photoshop's Color Palettes folder.

5. Load these colors into the Swatches Palette by choosing Replace Swatches from the Swatches Palette submenu.

Now you can select from swatches of web-safe colors to fill areas of your graphic. If you don't want to create the CLUT file yourself, you can download it from Lynda Weinman's FTP site, as explained in the following section.

CLUT files for other graphics programs

Many commercial tools that don't ship the Web Palette in its color selector tools (including Photoshop) will allow you to load in palette files. Lynda Weinman, author of a well-known series of books on web design, has created a collection of browser-safe palette files that can be loaded into the following software packages:

Software Package	CLUT File Name
Adobe Photoshop	bclut2.aco
Paint Shop Pro	netscape.pal
Photo-Paint	216clut.cpl
MetaCreations Painter	clut (in Painter folder)

All of these files can be downloaded from Lynda's FTP site: *ftp://luna.bearnet.com/ pub/lynda/*.

Converting to the Web Palette

Regardless of the tools you use to create web graphics, when you convert to Indexed Color there are a number of issues to keep in mind that should guide the decisions you make along the way. This section takes a look at some of those decisions, particularly regarding the use of the Web Palette. Individual tools and their features will be discussed in the section "Survey of Web Graphics Tools."

Selecting a Palette

The first thing you should decide is which palette to apply to the image. Standard palette choices were defined earlier in this chapter. Your palette choice should be appropriate to the image. Use Adaptive (or ImageReady's Perceptual) when the image contains photographic material or lots of blends and gradients in the graphic. If you've created your graphic using web-safe colors and you want to be certain they stay that way, or if you just want the image to look the same for all users, choose the Web Palette.

Reducing the Number of Colors

As stated throughout this book, it is always important to keep graphic file sizes as small as possible for web delivery. One way to reduce the file size is to reduce the number of colors the graphic contains. When you convert to the Web Palette, the Color Table for the graphic will contain all 216 colors, even if just a few of them actually appear in the image. Stripping away the unused colors can reduce file size significantly (depending on the image) without altering the appearance of the image. Specific techniques for reducing the number of colors while maintaining web-safe colors are discussed in the section "Survey of Web Graphics Tools."

Shifting to the Nearest Web-Safe Color

As an alternative to dithering, you may want to try shifting certain colors in your image to their nearest web-safe equivalents. This is especially useful for images that contain combinations of photographic and flat color areas—you can shift the flat color to a color in the Web Palette and let the rest continue to dither.

The new web graphics tools provide many "web-snap" functions that give you more control over the quality of your image on 8-bit displays.

Survey of Web Graphics Tools

Each of the tools in this section (with the exception of the WebScrubber plug-in filter) are multifaceted programs with lots of nifty features. The following descriptions focus on how each tool handles the Web Palette. By no means are they intended as reviews of each tool's full capabilities.

Adobe Photoshop (4.0 and 5.0)

Adobe Photoshop has grown to be the *de facto* standard for creating web graphics. Although all the basic functionality for creating web-safe GIF and PNG files is included, it wasn't until plug-in utilities and full-scale tools created specifically for web graphics arrived that it became obvious how limited Photoshop is for creating web-appropriate graphics.

To save a graphic with the Web palette, simply select Image → Mode → Indexed Color and flatten the layers. Select Web from the menu of palette choices. At this point, you can decide whether you want the image to dither (Diffusion) or not (None). When you are finished, you can either Save As or Export to GIF format.

Reducing color depth

When you choose the Web Palette, the Color Table is filled with 216 colors, regardless of whether they are used in the image. Unfortunately, there is no way to reduce color depth in Photoshop once a specific palette has been applied. The only way to reduce the number of web colors involves three steps:

1. Convert to Indexed Color using the Web Palette option.
2. Revert back to RGB color mode by selecting Image → Mode → RGB.
3. Immediately change the image back to Indexed Color, this time selecting Exact from the Palette options. The image will be saved with only the colors that actually appear in the image.

Caution: Photoshop 4.0 shifts colors in adaptive palettes

When Photoshop 4.0 converts images to Indexed Color using an Adaptive Palette, a phenomenon occurs that slightly shifts the RGB values for colors. So, even though you've filled the background of your graphic with a web-safe blue with the

RGB values 51, 51, 153, if you convert it using the Adaptive Palette option, these values may shift to 49, 49, 156—a color that *will* dither on 8-bit displays.

Some other drawing programs, notably Corel Draw, will also shift colors when exporting to GIF format. Do some tests by opening the exported images in an image-editing program and check your RGB values to determine whether there is a problem.

Preventing color shift. Using Photoshop 4.0 alone, the only way to ensure that your colors will stay web-safe is to choose Web from the Palette options when converting to Indexed Color. Although this is a perfect solution for graphical images made up of flat colors, the quality of photographic images may suffer as a result of a simple Web Palette conversion. You can reduce the number of colors in the palette as outlined above.

If you are using Photoshop 5.0, checking the box next to Preserve Exact Colors will prevent the colors from shifting from their web-safe settings when converting to Indexed Color with an Adaptive Palette.

Fixing Color Shift. If your image is very simple, made up of just a few dominant flat colors, you can easily make them web-safe again by manually editing their RGB values in the Color Table:

1. Open the GIF file. You can check for color shift quickly by placing your cursor over the color and checking the RGB values in the Info Palette. Combinations of 0, 51, 102, 153, 204, and 255 are web safe.

2. If the values have shifted, view the Color Table (Open Image → Mode → Color Table).

3. Find the color in the grid (it may be tricky to find the right color if the Color Table is full). Double-click on the color, and type in the correct RGB values.

As you might guess, this process can become quite tedious if you have more than one or two colors to adjust. For complex images, consider using the Web Scrubber filter or a tool like ImageReady to correct the colors for you.

Adobe ImageReady 1.0

ImageReady has many fine web-specific tools and features, however, palette control (with a special regard for the Web Palette) is one of its specialties. Image-Ready offers unprecedented control over palette colors and makes it easy to select nondithering colors.

Converting to Indexed Color

Before saving an image as an 8-bit GIF or PNG, you can first manipulate it in the Optimize Palette. Here you select the palette to which you would like the image to be reduced. The default is Perceptual (the best 256 colors based on human visual perception of color), but other choices include Adaptive and Web.

The number of colors can be reduced easily by selecting one of the common bit-depths from the Colors pop-up menu. Selecting "Auto" strips out unused colors and reduces the palette to just the necessary colors.

The Optimized Colors Palette

The real fun comes in with ImageReady's Optimized Colors Palette, shown in Figure 17-1. Once a palette has been chosen for the image in the Optimize Palette (or for images that were opened as Indexed Color), the color table for the image is displayed in the Optimized Colors Palette. You can use the palette to make changes to colors in the image. Colors can be added, deleted, locked, or shifted to their nearest web-safe color.

Figure 17-1: Adobe ImageReady's Optimized Colors Palette and options

To select a color in the table, either click on it directly or use the Eye-dropper tool to select the color from within the optimized image. You can lock the color by clicking on the Lock icon at the bottom of the palette window. This is useful if you have a color you want to be certain stays in the palette, even if the image changes or the number of colors is drastically reduced. Locked colors have a small square in the bottom right corner of the swatch.

You can also easily shift a color to its nearest web-safe color by clicking on the cube icon at the bottom of the palette window. This will change all the corresponding pixels in the image to the new web-safe color. Web-safe colors in the palette are indicated with a small diamond-shaped mark in the center of the swatch.

The pop-up menu in the top-right corner of the palette offers the ability to undo color locking and shifting for individual colors or for all the affected colors at once. It also gives you the ability to sort the colors in the palette according to Hue, Luminance, and Popularity.

This tool allows you to carefully target portions of the image that you want to use Web Palette colors (such as flat color areas) while maintaining the integrity of more subtle areas of the image.

The Web Shift slider

Another Web Palette tool tucked away is the Web Shift slider. You access it in the pop-up menu in the top-right corner of the Optimize palette (different than the Optimize Colors palette). When you select Show Options, the palette expands to include the Web Shift slider (shown in Figure 17-2).

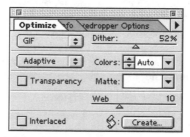

Figure 17-2: Web Shift slider visible in ImageReady's Optimize Palette

The slider is used to shift a range of colors to their nearest Web Palette colors. The slider specifies a tolerance level (from 0 to 30) for colors to be shifted to the closest Web Palette equivalents. The higher the value, the more colors that will shift.

Macromedia Fireworks 1.0

Fireworks is another tool that was designed from the ground up specifically for the creation of web graphics. It, too, offers a number of features that allow web designers to keep file sizes as small as possible while using web-safe colors.

The Swatches panel contains the Web Palette by default, and it is particularly easy to create graphics from scratch using Fireworks vector drawing tools. Vector tools make it easy to draw simple text and objects filled with flat web-safe colors—the type of images that compress efficiently when converted to GIF format for web distribution.

To convert an image to the Web Palette, select File → Export and make your adjustments in the Export Preview dialog box (Figure 17-3).

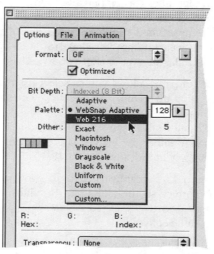

Figure 17-3: Palette options in Fireworks' Export Preview dialog box

Among the palette choices are Web 216 and WebSnap Adaptive. Web 216 is the standard Web Palette. Clicking the "Optimize" checkbox just below the format menu will strip any unused colors from the color table, keeping the file size as small as possible. You can set the color depth in the Number of Colors pop-up menu. The number below the entry field is the actual number of colors used in the image. Severely limiting the amount of dithering while in the Web 216 Palette pushes colors to their nearest web-safe values.

The WebSnap Adaptive Palette shifts colors that are near in value to browser-safe colors to their closest browser-safe color. WebSnap Palettes will snap a color to web safe if its RGB values are within 7 bits of a colorcube value (e.g., 57-57-57 will snap to 51-51-51, while 60-57-57 will not). There is no way to adjust this tolerance as there is in ImageReady and Web Scrubber.

Web Scrubber Plug-in Filter (Furbo Filters)

If you haven't yet invested in a web-graphics tool such as ImageReady or Fireworks, you can lay out a smaller chunk of change for special web utilities that work as plug-ins for Photoshop, PaintShop Pro, or any program that accepts Photoshop-compatible plug-ins.

Web Scrubber from Furbo Filters is particularly good at optimizing images that contain a combination of photographic imagery and areas of flat-web-safe color. It provides "web-snap" abilities similar to ImageReady and allows you to reduce the number of colors in a paletted image (something Photoshop can't do on its own).

As of this writing, Web Scrubber is available only for the Mac as part of Furbo Filters' Webmaster series of plug-ins. These plug-ins are available at *http://www.furbo-filters.com/*. They are working on a similar set for Windows, but in the meantime, Windows users may download the WebScrub filter for free from David Siegel's site at *http://www.verso.com/agitprop/dithering/*.

Web Scrubber uses an algorithm (developed by Todd Fahrner and Philip Gwyn) that works like a snap-to device for colors. As stated in the documentation, "colors that are nearly web safe are shifted so that they use one of the 216 colors. Colors that aren't close to being web safe are left alone to dither when displayed in the browser." You can control the amount of shift you would like to occur.

The Web Scrubber control panel allows you to select the number of colors in the image with the Colors pop-up menu. Use the Red, Green, and Blue sliders to control how much color shift you want to allow. The higher the number, the more colors will be forced to shift to the nearest web-safe color. The lower the number, the more the browser may dither the image. The effects of your changes appear immediately in the preview window. (See Figure 17-4.)

If you've used Photoshop 4.0's Adaptive Palette to convert your image, you can use Web Scrubber to correct all the shifted RGB values. Generally, Photoshop doesn't shift values more than five units, so a slider setting of 5 in Web Scrubber should clean colors up sufficiently.

Settings higher than 10 tend to affect the quality of the image, particularly at lower bit depths. You can experiment with different values and see how they affect file

Figure 17-4: WebScrubber filter dialog box

size. In general, with Web Scrubber you will find that you can maintain higher quality at a lower bandwith.

When you are done "scrubbing" an image, convert it to Indexed Color using the Exact palette and Save As or Export to GIF format.

Color Blenders

The problem with the Web Palette is that it only has 216 colors to choose from (and they probably wouldn't be your first choices). If you are bored with your color options, you may want to try a new type of graphics utility called a *color blender*. Color blenders approximate any RGB color by mixing two colors from the Web Palette in a tiny checkerboard pattern. You can use these "hybrid colors" to fill areas of graphics or to create a background tile.

Two color blender tools exist as of this writing: ColorSafe from BoxTop Software (*http://www.boxtopsoft.com/*) and DitherBox from RDG Tools (*http://www.dith-erbox.com/*). Their features and interface are nearly identical, but DitherBox is somewhat less expensive. DitherBox is also now included as part of Adobe Imag-eReady 1.0. You can download free demo versions for either the Mac or Windows at their respective sites.

The Pros and Cons of Color Blenders

No technology is either all good or all bad, so let's look at the ups and downs of color blenders:

Color blender advantages

* They allow you to choose colors off the beaten path of the 216-color web-safe palette, yet still be certain they will look the same on 24- and 8-bit moni-tors.

Disadvantages

- The controlled dither can add to the file size if used as a fill for large areas of the graphic.

- It is more difficult to get inline images to blend seamlessly over a background tiled with a hybrid color. For instance, an image with a hybrid blue background may not line up correctly with the same hybrid blue in the browser background. For best results, create the original image with a background that is similar to the hybrid blue, and use transparency.

Using ColorSafe

ColorSafe from BoxTop Software is demonstrated here, but the interface is nearly exactly the same as that of DitherBox. Figure 17-5 shows the options in the Color-Safe dialog box.

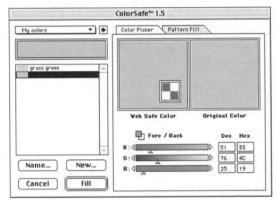

Figure 17-5: ColorSafe dialog box for mixing colors from two web-safe colors

Color Picker

The Color Picker is where you create "hybrid colors" from two web-safe colors. RGB sliders allow you to choose any RGB color combination and see the immediate results in the preview boxes.

If you have a specific color you'd like to convert, load it as the foreground color before launching the ColorSafe filter. When you click the "Fore/Back" icon, your color will be translated into its nearest hybrid. The controls on the left allow you name your hybrid colors and save whole lists of names for future use.

The "Fill" button will automatically fill the selected area in your image. Note: ColorSafe will not open if your image is empty and no areas are selected.

Pattern Fill

The Pattern Fill function allows you to create custom patterns out of colors in the Web Palette (or whatever palette you choose to load) up to 8×8 pixels in size. These patterns can be used wherever pattern fills are used in Photoshop.

Creating Background Tiles with Hybrid Colors

When creating a background tile filled with hybrid colors, the key is to set the width and height to an even number of pixels so the pattern will repeat correctly. You can make the tile quite small (10 or 12 pixels square) to limit file size.

1. Create a new graphic in Photoshop and fill the whole area with the color you'd like your background to be. (Neither ColorSafe nor DitherBox will open if the image is completely empty.)

2. Select a color blender filter (ColorSafe or DitherBox) from the Filters menu. You can adjust the color using the RGB controls.

3. Fill your image with the new hybrid color.

4. Convert the image to Indexed Color using the Exact Palette and either Save as or Export to GIF format.

5. Insert your graphic into the HMTL document by adding the `background` attribute identifying your tile to the `<body>` tag as follows:

```
<BODY BACKGROUND="tilegraphic.gif">
```

Where to Learn More

The champion of the Web Palette is undeniably Lynda Weinman, author of many fine books on web design. Her book *Designing Web Graphics*, Second Edition (New Riders Publishing) includes samples and instructions for working with the browser-safe palette. For a more in-depth look at the palette as well as suggestions on hundreds of pleasing combinations that can be created with it, check out Lynda's book *Coloring Web Graphics* (New Riders Publishing).

PART IV

Multimedia and Interactivity

CHAPTER 18

Animated GIFs

These days, it's just about impossible to browse the Web without seeing the flashing, bouncing, and wiggling of GIF animation. The animated GIF is ubiquitous, and there are many good reasons fueling its popularity.

- **Users need no special software or plug-in.** All they need is a browser that supports animation—which is fortunately the overwhelming majority of browsers in use as of this writing.

- **GIF is the standard file format for the Web.** Animated GIFs are not a unique file format in themselves, but merely take advantage of the full capabilities of the original GIF89a specification. Even if a browser cannot display all of its frames, the GIF will still be visible as a static image.

- **They're easy to create.** There are scores of GIF animation tools available (some are built into larger web graphics applications), and they're simple to learn and use.

- **They require no server configurations.** Because they are standard GIF files, you do not need to define a new file type on the server.

- **They use streaming technology.** Users don't need to wait for the entire file to download to see something. Each frame displays as soon as it downloads.

The only drawbacks to animated GIFs are that they can contain no sound, no interactivity (you can't make different parts respond to mouse actions), and they may cause some extra work for your hard disk to keep refreshing the images.

How They Work

Animated GIFs work a lot like traditional cell animation. The file contains a number of frames layered on top of each other. In simple animations, each frame is a complete scene. In more sophisticated animations, the first frame provides the background and subsequent frames just provide the changing portion of the image.

The GIF animation consists of a number of images and a set of instructions that specify the length of delay between frames, as well as other attributes like transparency and palettes.

Using Animated GIFs

Nowhere has GIF animation made a larger impact than in banner advertising. Ad agencies aren't stupid . . . they know that adding motion and flashing to a web page is a sure-fire way to attract attention. And it's true—adding animation is a powerful way to catch a reader's eye.

But beware that this can also work against you. Many users complain that animation is *too* distracting, making it difficult to concentrate on the content of the page. Although it adds a little "pizzazz" to the page, overall, too much animation can actually spoil the user's enjoyment of your page.

Use animated GIFs wisely. A few recommendations:

- Avoid more than one animation on a page.

- Use the animation to communicate something in a clever way (not just as gratuitous flashing lights).

- Avoid animation on text-heavy pages that might require concentration to read.

- Consider whether the extra bandwidth to make a graphic "spin" is actually adding value to your page.

- Decide if your animation needs to loop continuously.

- Experiment with timing. Sometimes a long pause between loops can make an animation less distracting.

Browser Support

Versions 2.0 and higher of both Netscape Navigator and Microsoft Internet Explorer have some degree of support for GIF animation, with the implementation improving with each subsequent release. Still, there are a few specific aspects of animation that prove to be particularly problematic for some early-version and lesser-known browsers.

If your animation uses one of the following, you may want to do some cross-browser, cross-platform testing:

Looping
> Very early browsers do not support looping at all. More commonly, looping is supported, but settings for a specific number of loops may be ignored. If you specify the number of repetitions, be aware that some users will experience nonstop looping instead. Internet Explorer versions 2 and 3 support only one-loop animation.

Revert to Previous
> This disposal method does not work on Netscape 2.0, 3.0, and the Mac version of 4.0 (it treats it as "do not dispose.") (See the "Disposal Methods" section later in this chapter.) Revert to Previous is supported only by Internet Explorer versions 3.0 and higher. Although it can result in slightly smaller file

sizes, it is recommended to avoid this setting. This and other disposal methods are more thoroughly discussed later in this chapter.

Browsers that do not support GIF animation will display a static image. The problem is that some browsers display the first frame and others display the last frame. If possible, it is advisable to make both your first and last frames meaningful (particularly if it contains important information like the name of your company).

Tools

You don't need to search very far to find a GIF animation tool—there seem to be scores of them available. Regardless of the tool you choose, the interface is basically the same. Tools tend to differ somewhat in the degree to which they are able to optimize (shrink the file size of) of the resulting graphic. The following sections provide an overview of the most popular and/or recommended tools.

GIF Animation Utilities

These are useful tools dedicated to the creation of animated GIF files.

GifBuilder 0.5 (Mac only)

GifBuilder, developed by Yves Piguet, is the old standby for creating animated GIFs on the Macintosh. It's freeware that's easy and intuitive to use. Its method of optimization, although adequate, is not as efficient as some other programs. It is available for download at *http://www.pascal.com/mirrors/ gifbuilder/*.

GIF Movie Gear (Windows only)

GIF Movie Gear lets you view thumbnails of all frames at a glance and directly manipulate them. Includes drag-and-drop functionality, real-time previewing of palette and compression options, and support for AVI, BMP, Photoshop files, JPEG, as well as GIF. GIF Movie Gear offers pixel-level optimization. You can download a trial version from *http://www.gamani.com*. Registration is $30.

Ulead GIF Animator 2.0 (Windows only)

Ulead's GIF Animator features wizards for quickly and easily constructing animations, 200 levels of undo, pixel-level optimization, built-in transition and animation effects, a plug-in architecture for adding new animation modules, and support for AVI and QuickTime videos and layered Photoshop files. Download a preview copy from *http://www.ulead.com*. Registration is $39.95.

GIFmation 2.1 (Mac and Windows)

This is commercial software from BoxTop Software that comes highly recommended by web developers. It features a more visual interface than GIFBuilder, sophisticated palette-handling options, and a bandwidth simulator. It also uses the efficient "frame differencing" method (discussed later in this chapter) for optimizing animations significantly better than its competition. GIFmation costs $49.00 (as of this writing) and is available at *http://www. boxtopsoft.com/*.

GifGifGif (Mac and Windows)

Although not full-featured like other GIF animation utilities, this tool offers the unique ability to automatically capture screen activity for use as an animated GIF. This is useful for illustrating software demos. GifGifGif is from Pedagoguery Software (*http://www.peda.com/*).

Applications that Include GIF Animation Tools

GIF animation tools are now being built-in or bundled with many popular graphics applications, eliminating the need to jump between different software packages.

Macromedia Fireworks (Mac and Windows)

Macromedia Fireworks was designed specifically for the creation of web graphics. It supports multiple layers that can be converted to multiple animation frames. Among other features are automatic super-palette optimization and the ability to perform LZW optimization. In animated GIF optimization tests run by WebReference.com, Fireworks created the smallest animation files (see *http://www.webreference.com/dev/gifanim/results.html*). For more information, see Macromedia's site at *http://www.macromedia.com/software/fireworks/*.

Adobe ImageReady (Mac and Windows)

Adobe ImageReady is a tool for preparing and optimizing graphics for the Web. It includes a GIF animation tool that converts layers into frames, and allows easy layer editing. For more information see Adobe's site at *http://www.adobe.com/*.

Animation Shop & Paint Shop Pro 5.0 (Windows only)

Animation Shop is a tool that comes bundled with the latest version of Paint Shop Pro, an inexpensive and powerful graphics creation application from JASC Software Inc. For more information, see JASC's web site at *http://www.jasc.com/*.

Creating Animated GIFs

Regardless of the tool you choose, the process of creating an animated GIF is about the same and involves making decisions about a standard set of features and options. Some of the following descriptions use some of GIFBuilder's terminology, but the concepts and settings are consistent across tools.

Frame Delay

Also called "interframe delay," this setting sets the amount of time between frames. Frame delays are measured in 1/100ths of a second. You can apply a different delay time to each frame in the animation to create pauses and other timing effects. This differs from digital video formats, in which the delay between all frames is consistent.

Transparency

You can set transparency for each frame within an animation. Previous frames will show through the transparent area of a later frame—if disposal methods are set correctly.

If the background frame is made transparent, the browser background color or pattern will show through.

 There is a bug in early versions of Netscape in which transparency only works with background patterns, not colors specified in HTML.

Don't be surprised if the transparent areas you specified in your original graphics are ignored when you import them into a GIF animation utility. You may need to set transparency in the animation package. GIFBuilder offers the following options:

None
> No transparency.

White
> All the white pixels in the image will become transparent.

Based on first pixel
> The color of the "first pixel"—that is, the top left pixel, the one at coordinates 0,0—is transparent. This is a handy option since you'll often have an image in the center and the four corners will be transparent.

Other
> This option lets you select one of the palette colors as transparent.

Disposal Methods

Disposal method gives instructions on what to do with the previous frame once a new frame is displayed.

Most GIF animation utilities offer "optimization," a file-size reducing process that takes advantage of the fact that previous frames will "show through" transparent areas of a later frame. In order for this process to work, disposal method must be set to Do Not Dispose (or Leave Alone, Leave As Is, etc.). With this method, areas of previous frames continue to display unless covered up by an area in a succeeding frame. The four choices are:

Unspecified (Nothing)
> Use this option to replace one full-size, nontransparent frame with another.

Do Not Dispose (Leave As Is)
> In this option, any pixels not covered by the next frame continue to display. Use this when you want a frame to continue to show throughout the animation.

Restore to Background

> The background color or background tile shows through the transparent pixels of the new frame (replacing the image areas of the previous frame).

Restore to Previous

> This option restores to the state of the previous, undisposed frame. For example, if you have a static background that is set to Do Not Dispose, that image will reappear in the areas left by a replaced frame.

> This disposal method is not correctly supported in Netscape Navigator (it is treated like Do Not Dispose), leading to all the frames being visible and stacking up. Although it can produce better optimized animation files, it is safest not to use it.

The effects of each of these disposal methods are compared in Figure 18-1.

Color Palette

Animated GIFs, like static GIF files, use a list of up to 256 colors that can be used in the image. They can have multiple palettes (one for each frame) or one global palette. The palette choice affects how well the images will appear on the inevitable variety of systems and monitor set-ups.

One problem with using multiple, frame-specific palettes is they can cause a flashing effect on some early versions of Netscape (it cannot load the frames and their respective palettes in synch). In any case, multiple palettes dramatically increase file size. It is recommended you use one global palette for the whole animation. GIFmation allows you to easily create a customized global palette. In fact, any image editor can be used to create a global palette. Just place all images to be used in one document, then index the document. The resulting palette will be a global palette for the entire animation. DeBabelizer could be used for this as well, but it's not as straightforward.

Other palette options include:

System Palette

> You can apply the Mac or Windows system palettes to your animation if you know it will be viewed exclusively on one platform.

Grayscale

> This will convert your image to 256 shades of gray. Keep in mind, however, that browsers running on 8-bit monitors will try to convert the various shades of gray to the web palette. Since there are only a few true grays in the web palette, a grayscale image may not look very good on those monitors.

Adaptive Palette

> Either ask your utility to create a global palette from the colors in the animation, or import one you created in another program. For most animations, this is your best bet.

Web Palette (6×6×6 palette)

> Use the web palette if your animation is composed largely of flat colors.

Disposal Methods

Unspecified

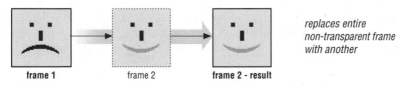

replaces entire non-transparent frame with another

Do Not Dispose

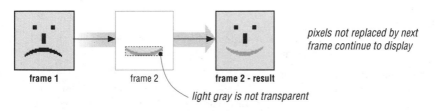

pixels not replaced by next frame continue to display

light gray is not transparent

Restore to Background

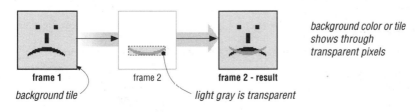

background color or tile shows through transparent pixels

background tile   light gray is transparent

Restore to Previous *(supported by Microsoft Internet Explorer 3.0 or greater)*

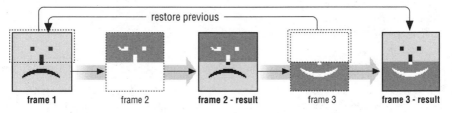

Figure 18-1: Disposal method comparison

Other Options

The following are descriptions of other aspects of animated GIF files that can be set within most animation programs.

Loop

You can specify the number of times an animation repeats—none, forever, or a specific number. As noted earlier, not all browsers will support a specific number of loops (it will either loop or not). One workaround to this problem is to build looping right into a file by repeating the frame sequence a number of times; of course, this increases the file size and download time.

Interlaced

Like ordinary GIF89a graphics, animated GIFs can be set to be interlaced, which causes them to display in a series of passes (starting blocky, finishing clear). It is recommended that you leave the interlacing option set to "no" or "off" because each frame is on the screen for a short amount of time.

Depth

This option allows you to limit the bit depth of the image to some number less than 8 (the default for GIF). Bit depth and its effect on file size is discussed in detail in Chapter 14, *GIF Format*. Note, if you select the Netscape (6×6×6) palette, you will need to keep the bit depth set to 8.

Dithering

Dithering is a way to simulate intermediate color shades. It should be used with continuous-tone images.

Background Color

Regardless of what color you select in the background color option, Netscape and Internet Explorer display the background color or image you specify in your HTML page. So, this option doesn't affect the display of the GIF in a browser, only within the tool itself.

Starting Points

These settings are a good starting point for creating full-frame animations:

Color Palette: Global, adaptive palette
Interlacing: Off
Dithering: On for photographic images, Off for drawings with few colors
Image Size: Minimum Size
Background Color: Black
Looping: None or Forever
Transparency: Off
Disposal Method: Do Not Dispose

Optimizing Animated GIFs

As with any file served over the Web, it is important to keep animated GIFs as small as possible. I recommend reading "Optimizing Animated GIFs," an article and tutorial by Andrew King that appeared in WebReference.com in 1997, and from which many of the following tips were summarized (with permission). You can find it at *http://www.webreference.com/dev/gifanim/index.html*.

Image Compression

Start by applying the same file-size reduction tactics used on regular, static GIF files to the images in your animation frames. For more information, see "Minimizing GIF File Sizes" in Chapter 14. These measures include:

- Eliminating unnecessary dithering

- Removing stray pixels from otherwise solid areas

- Reducing the number of colors

- Reducing the bit depth

Optimizing Methods

In addition to the standard image-compressing methods, GIF animation tools optimize animations by eliminating the repetition of pixels in unchanging image areas. Only the pixels that change are recorded for each frame. Different tools use different optimizing methods, which are not created equal in terms of efficiency. These methods, in order from least to most compression, include:

Minimum Bounding Rectangle

In this method, the changed portion of the image is saved, but it is always saved in the smallest rectangular area necessary to contain the changed pixels.

Frame Differencing

In frame differencing, *only* the individual pixels that change are stored for each frame. This is a more efficient method than Minimum Bounding Rectangle, which includes a lot of unnecessary pixel information to make up the rectangle. Of the tools listed above, only GIFmation, GMG, and Ulead GIF Animator use the Frame Differencing method for optimization.

LZW Interframe Optimization

This optimization method uses the LZW compression scheme to minimize the frequency of changes in pixel patterns between frames. This compression method, when used in conjunction with frame difference, is capable of producing the smallest possible file sizes. Macromedia Fireworks is currently the only commercial product that takes advantage of LZW compression for animations (the GIF Wizard online service also uses it).

GIF Wizard

GIF Wizard is an online service that evaluates and optimizes graphics on users' web sites, using compression techniques created by Tom Kirchman. Notably, GIF Wizard is the only current compression product that takes advantage of all three of the above-mentioned optimization methods. The LZW compression support enables GIF Wizard to compress animations smaller than any other utility currently available.

GIF Wizard is located at *http://www.gifwizard.com/*. You can upload your animation for a free demo of its powers. GIF Wizard instantly evaluates your graphic and provides several alternative versions, each with a report of the percentage of bytes saved.

GIF Wizard can also do an evaluation of your entire site. There are annual fees for access to its full range of optimization and link-checking services.

CHAPTER 19

Audio on the Web

Simple audio files found their way onto the Web in its earliest days. The problem with audio is that the files are generally quite large and may take a prohibitively long time to download. The introduction of streaming audio (files that play while they download) finally made quality audio and even live broadcasts distributed via web pages a reality.

Obviously, audio, even specialized for the Web, is a rich and complex topic that cannot be thoroughly treated in a single chapter of a Nutshell reference book. If you are interested in reading about all the ins and outs of creating professional-quality audio for a web site, there are many books that provide in-depth looks at developing audio for the Web (see the bibliography at the end of this chapter). There are also some fine tutorials in the multimedia section of the WebMonkey site (*http://www.webmonkey.com/*).

If you need to put professional-quality audio on your site, consider outsourcing the work to professionals, or bring in a consultant to help you get set up properly.

This chapter provides an overview of basic audio terminology and file formats as well as an introduction to the many options for adding audio to a web site.

Copyright Issues

Like images, there are a number of sources for acquiring audio files to use on a web site. Be aware, however, simply posting somebody else's music or recordings from a CD is a copyright violation. Record companies and entertainment corporations are taking measures to crack down on the illegal use of copyrighted material. Even collections of silly sound effects that seem like they were designed for multiple uses may be protected. Be sure to read the fine print for terms of use.

Royalty-Free Audio Resources

Fortunately, collections of prerecorded sound effects and music are available for multimedia and Internet use. Many are royalty-free, meaning once you've purchased the package of sounds, you can use them however you wish and pay no licensing fees.

Some collections include:

- Microsoft Sounds Gallery: *http://www.microsoft.com/gallery/files/sounds/*
- Digital Kitchen: *http://www.dkitchen.com/*
- DXM Production's Earshot SFX Library: *http://www.earshotsfx.com/*
- Creative Support Services: *http://www.cssmusic.com/*

Record It Yourself

The safest way to avoid possible copyright infringement is to record your own material. The final product may be anything from a simple personal greeting to a live concert broadcast.

As with most things, with sound quality, you get what you pay for. It is possible to capture sound using available resources (like the microphone that came with your computer), but the quality will not be appropriate for a professional site. The cost of recording equipment escalates quickly for each level of sound quality, which may make it more cost-effective for a small business to hire the services of a professional studio.

Although this may be a good choice for a small business, it may be too expensive for many hobbyists and garage bands. Depending on how well the studio is equipped, it can cost from $30 to $250 per hour, and up. About $3000 to $5000 investment in equipment (not counting the computer) is enough to get started on a home (or small business) studio. It's sort of a "sweat equity" arrangement though, since a lot of effort is required to get that home studio going.

Audio Tools Overview*

There is a wide gamut of software for audio editing and format conversion. The software ranges from single-purpose utilities available via free download to professional digital-audio editing suites costing thousands of dollars. The following list is culled from somewhere in the middle—high-powered tools with accessible prices. The U.S. dollar amounts given reflect those at the time of this writing and are subject to change. In most cases, they should be used as guidelines only.

One of the most popular commercial audio editing tools for the Mac is SoundEdit 16 from Macromedia (*http://www.macromedia.com/*). On the PC the standard audio editor is Sound Forge from Sonic Foundry (*http://www.sonicfoundry.com/*).

Since Windows machines don't have the same basic audio features that Macs have, PC users may need to invest in some costly audio hardware to do true multitrack

---

* A big thank you goes to Chris Florio for compiling this list of audio tools.

recording. Once the hardware is added however, there are a number of good software packages from Cakewalk and other companies to record and process audio and MIDI.

QuickTime 3.0 (Mac and PC)

The first essential audio/video tool for all web designers or multimedia producers on both Mac and PC is QuickTime 3.0. This is the first release of QuickTime to be fully functional on Windows. QT 3.0 comes with the tools for creating streaming video and audio for the Web. QuickTime supports dozens of file formats and there are a number of new codecs that come with QT that are ideal for the Internet (see Qcomp, next). QuickTime also comes with a built-in software-only MIDI synthesizer. This synth includes hundreds of instruments that can be used to make high-quality MIDI soundtracks that take only a few kilobytes of space and sound the same on all Macs and PCs. Best of all, QuickTime 3.0 is free from Apple (*http://www.apple.com/quicktime/*). A professional version of QuickTime can be licensed for $29.95.

Qcomp, from Qdesign Corporation (Mac and PC)

The Qcomp audio compressor that comes free with QuickTime 3.0 is of particular interest to web designers. Qcomp, from QDesign Corporation (*http://www.Qdesign.com/*), is one of the best ways to put high-quality music on the Web. CD-quality (16-bit, 44k) stereo audio files can be played in real time when compressed with Q-comp, and they sound excellent compared with other types of compression. Qcomp's pro version, which lets you optimize your files and speed up the process, is $399.

Peak, from Bias (Mac only)

The most versatile and fun audio-editing software on the Mac is called Peak, from Bias (*http://www.bias-inc.com/*). Peak can do more things to an audio file than you will ever need and outputs to most audio formats including AIFF, WAV, QuickTime, and RealAudio.

Metro, from Cakewalk (Mac only)

For Mac users who want to record their own music a program from Cakewalk called Metro (*http://www.cakewalk.com/*) will let you record as many tracks of digital audio as your computer can handle. Metro also comes with a very good MIDI sequencer. The MIDI and audio tracks can be processed, edited, and mixed within Metro. This is a great package for less than $200.

Media Cleaner Pro, from Terran Interactive (Mac and PC)

One last package that is useful for optimizing audio and video files for the web is Media Cleaner Pro from Terran Interactive (*http://www.terran.com/*). This program is designed to get the best quality files at the smallest size in whatever format you choose. MediaCleaner works all of the QuickTime compressors as well as RealAudio and RealVideo. Media Cleaner also does batch compressing. The program sells for $359 and is available bundled with the Qcomp and Sorenson pro packages.

Basic Digital Audio Concepts

In order to distribute recorded speech or music over the Internet, the analog audio must be converted to a digital format (described by bits and bytes). This process is called *encoding*. It is analogous to scanning a photograph to a digital bitmap format, and many of the same concepts regarding quality and file size apply.

Sampling Rate

To convert an analog sound wave into a digital description of that wave, samples of the wave are taken at timed intervals. The number of samples taken per second is called the *sampling rate*. The more samples taken per second, the more accurately the digital description can recreate the original shape of the sound wave, and therefore, the better the quality of the digital audio.

Sample rates are typically measured in kilohertz (KHz). On the high end, CD-quality audio has a sampling rate of 44.1 KHz. On the low end, 8 KHz produces a thin sound quality that is equivalent to AM radio. Some standard sampling rates include: 8 KHz, 11.025 KHz, 11.127 KHz, 22.05 KHz, 44.1 KHz, and 48 KHz. The higher the sampling rate, the more information is contained in the file, and therefore the larger the file size.

Bit Depth

Like images, audio files are also measured in terms of their bit depth (also called sampling resolution or word length). The more bits, the better the quality of the audio, and of course, the larger the resulting audio file.

Some common bit depths are 8-bit (which sounds thin or tinny, like a telephone signal) and 16-bit, which is required to describe music of CD quality.

Channels

Audio files can support from one to six separate channels of audio information. The most familiar of these are mono (1 channel) and stereo (2 channels), but some formats can support 3-channel, quadraphonic, and 4- or 6-channel surround sound.

Compression

Some audio file formats (such as MPEG and AIFF/C) are compressed using a specialized audio compression algorithm in order to save disk space. MPEG uses a lossy compression scheme (it strips out sounds that are not discernible to the human ear) to achieve very high compression ratios (from 4:1 to 12:1) while maintaining near-original sound quality.

Nonstreaming versus Streaming

Audio formats served via the Web fall into two general categories. Nonstreaming audio files need to be downloaded to the user's hard disk before they can begin playing. Streaming audio files begin playing almost immediately and continue playing as they are downloading. The following is a brief introduction to each approach as well as its advantages and disadvantages. A more detailed discussion of specific streaming and nonstreaming audio formats follows.

Nonstreaming Audio

When nonstreaming audio files (also called "static" audio) are retrieved from the server, they must download to the hard disk *in their entirety* before they can begin playing on the client end. Unfortunately, audio files are often quite large and require a long time to download, particularly over dial-up modem connections. For instance, a 1-minute WAVE file of CD-quality audio requires over 10 MB of disk space! (Of course, this can be reduced by sacrificing sound quality, as discussed later.)

How it works

Static audio files tend to be in common audio formats, and are transferred via a simple FTP transaction like any other web file.

When the user's browser detects the audio file, it will either launch an external player or use a plug-in to play the audio. Which player it uses depends on the platform, the browser, its version, and its configuration, therefore the web site designer cannot directly control which player will be used.

Some common Macintosh external players include SoundMachine and SoundApp. MediaPlayer is a common player on the Windows operating system. Internet Explorer versions 3 and higher can play many audio file formats natively. Netscape Navigator 3.0 and higher uses the LiveAudio plug-in to play most audio files. The QuickTime player is available for both platforms and as a plug-in to both browsers.

Advantages

- It doesn't require special server software.

- It is simple to create audio files in standard formats.

Disadvantages

- Large file sizes can result in unacceptably long waits for the files to download and begin playing.

- Because the audio file is copied to the hard drive, it is more difficult for artists and publishers to limit distribution and protect copyrights.

Streaming Audio

Streaming audio technology was developed to address the problem of unacceptable download times. Streaming media (be it audio or video) begins playing almost immediately after the request is made, and continues playing as the audio data is being transferred. Some vendors offer live broadcast capabilities.

In some streaming solutions, such as those from RealNetworks and Xing Technology's Streamworks, the server holds open a special connection (UDP) through which it pushes data continuously. In this method, the source audio file itself is never transferred to the user's machine. Others, such as QuickTime 3.0 and Shockwave, do load files into the user's cache, but have players that allow playback after only a fraction of the total data is loaded.

Streaming Audio Components

Streaming media technology involves several software components:

- The *encoder* is a piece of proprietary software that converts audio to the streaming format (also proprietary). The source can be an existing audio file in one of the standard static formats, or it might be taken from a direct audio signal, as is the case in live broadcast.

- A *player* is required on the user's end to play the audio content. Vendors distribute their players for free. These are generally also available as browser plug-ins.

- Many streaming audio file formats require special audio *server software*. Streaming media companies make their money by selling the server software and often licensing a certain number of streams (the number of connections that can happen concurrently). This software is usually quite costly.

Advantages

- Audio begins playing soon after the stream begins.
- Sound quality doesn't need to be as severely sacrificed.
- Artists and publishers can control distribution and protect copyright because the user never gets a copy of the audio file.

Disadvantages

- Potentially high cost of server software.
- Requires a dedicated or preconfigured server, which may be problematic with some hosting services.
- Sound quality and stream may be adversely affected by low speed or inconsistent Internet connections.

Which Should You Choose?

As noted above, there are benefits and drawbacks to each of these approaches to web audio. As a general rule, if you want to add audio to your web site that is professional-quality and more than one minute in length (music, in particular), you should consider investing in one of the streaming media solutions. If you are building a web site that is based on your audio offerings and expect a fair amount of traffic, you should consider a separate server machine dedicated to audio.

If you have a personal or small commercial web site and would like to add a greeting or some other small audio sample, making simple audio files available for download is a fairly easy task.

Nonstreaming (Static) Audio

This section looks at static audio file formats, tips for optimizing audio files for download, and how audio files can be linked to HTML documents.

File Formats

A multitude of audio file formats exist for use on computers today. The following list represents just those that are widely used on the Web because of their cross-platform and cross-browser support.

WAVE (.wav)

The Waveform Audio File Format was originally developed as the standard audio format for the Microsoft Windows operating system, however, it is now supported on the Macintosh as well. WAVE files can support arbitrary sampling rates and bit depths, although 8 KHz and 11.025 KHz at 8- or 16-bit are most common. Its performance is similar to AIFF.

AIFF (.aif, .aiff)

The Audio Interchange File Format was developed as the standard audio format for the Macintosh platform, however, it is now supported by Windows and other platforms. It can support up to six channels and arbitrary sampling rates and bit depths, with 8 KHz and 11.127 KHz at 8-, 16- and 32-bits being the most common. Its performance is similar to WAVE.

μ-LAW (.au)

-Law (pronounced *myoo-law*) is the Unix standard audio format. *.au* files support mono or stereo channels, variable bit depths, and the following sampling rates: 8.013, 22.05, and 44.1 KHz. Its popularity as an Internet file format is waning because Unix platforms have become a small minority on the Web and because other cross-platform audio formats offer better sound quality.

MPEG (.mpa, .mp2, .mp3)

MPEG is actually a family of multimedia standards created by the Moving Picture Experts Group. It supports three types of information: video, audio, and streaming (which is synchronized video and audio). MPEGs can also be used as a streaming audio format, as in Xing's Streamworks technology.

MPEG audio files maintain pristine sound quality at compression rates as high as 10:1. They do this by using a lossy compression scheme that strips out sounds that are not discernible to the human ear.

There are a number of MPEG standards: MPEG-1 was originally developed for video transfer at VHS quality; MPEG-2 is a higher-quality standard that was developed for television broadcast; other MPEG specs that address other needs (such as MPEG-4 and -7) are currently in development. MPEGs can be compressed using one of three schemes: Layer-I, -II, or -III. The complexity of the coding (and therefore the processor power needed to encode and decode) increases at each level. Due to this complexity, you need special encoding tools to produce MPEG audio files.

On the Web, the most popular MPEG formats are MPEG-2, using compression Layers II and III (with the suffixes *.mp2* and *.mp3*, respectively). The suffix *.mpa* denotes a file that is audio only.

Netscape Navigator and Internet Explorer may support MPEG audio via the use of the QuickTime Plug-in. Or you could configure your browser to use one of the many available MPEG players, such as maplay or WinAMP (Windows) or SoundApp or MPEG Audio Player (Mac).

To learn more about MPEG, visit the MPEG Web Site (*http://www.mpeg.org/*).

MIDI (.mid)

MIDI (which stands for Musical Instrument Digital Interface) is a different breed of audio file format. It was originally developed as a standard way for electronic musical instruments to communicate with each other.

A MIDI file contains no actual audio information (the digital representation of analog sound), but rather a set of mathematical commands that describe a series of notes. These notes are played by a MIDI player using the available "instrument" sounds on a computer's sound card. MIDIs are to other audio formats what vector graphics are to bitmaps—just mathematical formulas for creating the final product on the other end.

As a result, MIDI files are incredibly compact. They are capable of packing a minute of music into just 10K, which is 1,000 times smaller than a one-minute WAVE file (approximately 10.MB).

The drawback to MIDI files is that they can only contain notes, not real sounds, so they are only useful for synthesizer-sounding music. You cannot reproduce the sound of a human voice or any organic sounds using MIDI. Despite this limitation, MIDIs are an extremely attractive alternative for adding instrumental music to your web site with very little download time.

Optimizing Audio Files for Download

There are ways to reduce the size of an audio file so it is appropriate for downloading via a web page. Not surprisingly, this usually requires sacrificing quality. Reducing file size (and quality) is not such an issue if you are using one of the streaming audio technologies. The aspects of the audio file you can control are:

Length of the audio clip

It might seem obvious, but you should keep the audio sample as short as possible. For example, consider providing just part of a song rather than the whole thing. If you are recording a greeting, make it short and sweet.

Number of channels

A mono audio file requires half the disk space of a stereo file and is recommended for web audio.

Bit depth

Audio files for the Web are most often saved at 8 bits, which will result in a file that is half the size of a 16-bit file.

Sampling rate

Cutting the sampling rate in half will cut the file size in half (e.g., a sampling rate of 22.05 KHz requires half the data than one of 44.1 KHz). As a general guideline, audio files that are voice-only can be reduced down to 8 KHz. Sound effects will work at 8 Khz or 11.025 KHz. Music will sound acceptable at 22 Khz.

Using these guidelines, if we start with a one-minute music sample at CD quality (10MB), and change it to a mono, 8-bit, 22 Khz WAVE file, its size is reduced to 1.25 MB, which is much more reasonable for downloading.

Obviously, just how stingy you can be with your settings while retaining acceptable quality depends on the individual audio file. You should certainly do some testing to see how small you can make the file without sacrificing essential audio detail.

Adding Nonstreaming Audio to an HTML Document

This section looks at the many ways audio files can be accessed by an HTML document. You can link to an audio file using an anchor (<a>) or embed the plug-in player in the flow of the page with the <embed> tag. Sounds can also be used as backgrounds that begin playing automatically when the page downloads. This section provides one technique for triggering a sound using JavaScript.

A simple link

You can use a simple anchor tag (<a>) to link to an audio file from a web page, as follows:

```
<a href="audio/song.wav">Play the song.</a>
```

When the reader clicks on the linked text (you could also use a graphic as the link) the browser will retrieve the file from the server and launch a helper application (or plug-in, if so configured) to play the file.

If the browser uses an external player, a new small window will open with the controls for playing the audio. If the browser is configured to use a plug-in player (such as the popular QuickTime plug-in), a control panel may load right in the browser window, replacing the original web page! You may want to advise readers to use the Back button to return to the original page should this happen.

It is also good web design form to warn readers of the size of an audio file so they can make informed decisions whether they want to spend the time downloading.

<embed> for use with plug-ins

When you use the <embed> tag, the browser places the plug-in controls in the flow of the text like an image. Although it was created by Netscape, Internet Explorer began supporting the <embed> tag with version 3.0, making it a relatively safe way to add audio (or any media) to your page. Note that when you use a plug-in, the audio will stop playing when the user leaves the page.

In Navigator, the <embed> tag works with the LiveAudio plug-in to play audio files. You have the option of putting a small control panel inline on the web page that allows the user to start and stop the audio, as well as affect its volume.

The following <embed> tag places a control panel on the page that will play the audio file when the user presses the Play button:

```
<EMBED SRC="audio/song.mid" CONTROLS="console" HEIGHT=60
WIDTH=145 AUTOSTART="false"></EMBED>
```

The LiveAudio plug-in `<embed>` tag can take a number of attributes:

src=*URL*
> Defines the URL of the audio file

controls=console|smallconsole|playbutton|pausebutton|
stopbutton|volumelever
> console places a control panel with play, stop, pause, and volume controls. smallconsole places a smaller version with just play, stop, and a volume control. The default setting is console. See Figure 19-1 (taken from a Macintosh display).

console (144 x 60 pixels)

smallconsole (144 x 15 pixels)

Figure 19-1: Live Audio's console (left) and small console (right) controls

height=*number*
width=*number*
> Width and height tags are required by the `<embed>` tag. In the case of audio files, the width and height measurements correspond to the size of the console in pixels. Gray space will be added around the control if measurements larger than the console's maximum dimensions are specified.

loop=true|false|*number*
> When set to true, the audio file will play continuously. When set to false (the default), the audio plays through just once. You can also specify a numerical value for the number of times you want the audio to play in a row.

autostart=true|false
> When this is set to true, the audio clip starts playing as soon as it loads. When false, the audio will begin playing when the user clicks Play in the console.

hidden=true
> This attribute, when set to true, causes the console to be hidden from view. Note that combined with autostart=true, this can create the same effect as `<bgsound>`.

volume=(*0-100*)
> This allows you to set the volume for the sound when it begins playing. It is based on a percentage scale from 1 to 100. If it is not specified, the audio file will be played at the default system volume.

```
align=left|right
hspace=number
vspace=number
```
> These attributes allow the console to be positioned against the left or right margin (with horizontal and vertical gutter space) and allows text to wrap around it. These work the same as within the `<img>` tag.

```
starttime=minutes:seconds
```
> *Supported only by Mac, Windows 95, and NT.* Specifies at what point in the audio file the playback should begin.

```
endtime=minutes:seconds
```
> *Supported only by Mac, Windows 95 and NT.* Specifies at what point in the audio file the playback should end. Minutes and seconds are indicated with two digits (e.g., 02:15 for 2 minutes, 15 seconds).

```
mastersound
```
> Indicates which `<embed>` element contains the link to the audio file. Required when grouping audio controls (using the NAME attribute).

```
NAME=text
```
> This is used to group individual controls for use with a single audio file.

Background sound

There are several ways (mostly browser-specific) to make an audio file start playing automatically when a web page loads. Note that the disadvantage of using background sounds is that the user has no way of turning the sound off if she does not like it. Also, if it is a large file, you are forcing a potentially lengthy download on the user.

- For Internet Explorer 2.0+ (no other browsers support this tag) use the `<bgsound>` tag, as follows:

  ```
  <BGSOUND SRC="audio/song.mid" LOOP=3>
  ```

  where `src` gives the URL for the audio file and `loop` is the number of times you want the audio to play (this attribute can be set to "infinite"). WAVE, AIFF, and MIDI sound files can be played as background sounds using this method.

- To set a background sound that will work with both Netscape Navigator and Internet Explorer, use a combination of the background sound tag and an `<embed>` tag that hides the control panel, as follows:

  ```
  <EMBED SRC="audio/song.mid" autostart=true hidden=true></EMBED>
  <NOEMBED><BGSOUND="audio/song.mid"></NOEMBED>
  ```

- For Netscape Navigator and later versions of MSIE, you can make audio play automatically with client-pull by using the `<meta>` tag as follows:

  ```
  <META http-equiv="refresh" content="1;url=audio/song.mid">
  ```

  which causes the page to refresh (and the audio to play) after 1 second.

Streaming Audio

Since RealAudio came on the scene in 1994, there has been a stampede of competitors. As of this writing, RealNetworks continues to dominate the market due to the ubiquitous distribution of its player and its proven track record. However, some competitors offer niche products that may better suit your particular need.

There are many other streaming audio formats, some of which are targeted at optimizing voice-only sound samples. This area of technology is developing quickly, and companies come and go quickly. For a current list of contenders, you can check the plug-in list on Netscape's web site (*http://www.netscape.com/comprod/ products/navigator/version_2.0/plugins/audio-video.html*).

Available Technologies

The following list represents just a few of the options for adding streaming audio to your Web site. The web sites listed with each technology provide complete information on how the system works, pricing structures, and the required software components.

RealAudio (RealNetworks)

Progressive Networks (now RealNetworks) was a pioneer in producing a viable technology for bringing streaming audio to the Web. Despite heavy competition, it leads the pack in terms of widespread use and popularity, and has grown to be the standard for putting audio online.

RealAudio is a server-based streaming audio solution with a special emphasis on optimizing audio for 14.4 and 28.8 connections. To listen to RealAudio files, users must download and install RealPlayer, which is available for Windows 95, NT, Mac, and Unix platforms.

RealAudio is just part of a complete line of products for delivering audio, video, and interactive media. The wide distribution of its player and a proven track record makes RealAudio an attractive solution to organizations interested in putting streaming media on the Web.

For more information, visit RealNetworks site at *http://www.real.com/*.

Liquid Music System (LiquidAudio)

As stated on their web site, LiquidAudio specifically targets the needs of the music industry by "providing labels and artists with software tools and technologies to enable secure online preview and purchase of CD-quality music."

LiquidAudio delivers CD-quality audio and is the only streaming format that offers Dolby encoding. Audio files can be watermarked with copyright, owner, and purchaser information, discouraging piracy and copyright violation.

The player, Liquid MusicPlayer CD, is unique in that it can offer views of album graphics, lyrics, credits, and up-to-date promotions or announcements (such as tour dates). The player works with the Liquid MusicServer (which is easily tied into SQL databases) to enable individual tracks or entire CDs to be purchased online.

For more information, see the LiquidAudio web site at *http://www.liquidaudio.com/*.

Streamworks (Xing Technologies)

Xing Technologies was another early player in the streaming audio arena. Their Streamworks technology, which offers audio and video delivery, is aimed at high-speed networks (although it can be encoded to serve 28.8 bps modem connections).

Streamworks' claim to fame is that it is the only format based entirely on the industry-standard MPEG specification, offering MPEG-1 and MPEG-2, Layer-3 audio. This is especially powerful for distributing video, however, it can also be used for audio only.

The high data rate required to deliver CD-quality audio and TV-quality video makes Streamworks most appropriate to intranet and extranet applications, such as training or distance learning. For more information on this product, visit the Xing Technologies web site at *http://www.xingtech.com/*.

Shockwave Audio (Macromedia)

Macromedia originally developed its Shockwave technology to deliver interactive Director movies to the Web, however, many web developers are using the technology for its audio capabilities alone. Shockwave is discussed in more depth in Chapter 21, *Interactivity*.

Shockwave Audio is attractive because it offers highly compressed, high-quality streaming audio without requiring special server software (desirable if you have a limited budget). The drawback is that it lacks the advanced controls and usage tracking that the commercial server products offer.

You can convert an existing audio file to Shockwave format using the Shockwave Audio Xtras in Director or SoundEdit 16, Version 2. The file is then saved in Shockwave format (with the suffix *.swa*).

Shockwave audio is played using the standard Shockwave plug-in for Netscape Navigator or Internet Explorer on the Windows 3.1/95/NT and Mac platforms.

For more information on using Shockwave for audio, see Macromedia's web site at *http://www.macromedia.com/support/director/how/shock*.

QuickTime Audio (Apple)

Although QuickTime is best known as a video technology, it is also possible to create audio-only QuickTime Movies (*.mov*). QuickTime audio supports 8- to 16-bit format and variable sampling rates and comes highly recommended by audio experts as a reliable audio format for web purposes.

Although the QuickTime system extension is needed to play a *.mov* file, it is widely distributed and available for both Windows and Macintosh. In addition, recent versions of both Netscape Navigator and Internet Explorer come with the QuickTime Plug-in so QuickTime audio can be embedded right on the page.

The QuickTime player can begin playing the audio as the data is downloading. However, because it is reading it from the user's cache, it is only a partially streaming media.

Many multimedia authoring tools support the QuickTime format and can be used for converting audio files to the *.mov* format. MoviePlayer Pro 3.0 (part of the QuickTime Pro 3.0 release) allows you to create, edit, and convert media files to QuickTime format. The Qdesign audio codec (compression/decompression algorithm) is recommended for audio files formatted for QuickTime 3.0 playback.

For more information on QuickTime, see *http://www.apple.com/QuickTime.*

Adding Streaming Audio to an HTML Document

As with static audio files, there are two methods for adding streaming audio to a page—via a link or using an <embed> tag. Using the <embed> option will put the controls for the streaming audio inline on the Web page. Embedding the controls allows for the design of custom interfaces, but it should be noted that the audio will stop playing when the user leaves the page.

Each technology's plug-in has its own set of attributes that can be added to the <embed> tag. We will look at the options for using the <embed> tag with Quick-Time and RealAudio later in this chapter.

Linking to streaming audio

Some plug-ins require that links be made to special go-between files instead of to the streaming audio file itself. These reference files (optionally) reside in the same directories as the HTML documents. When they are accessed via a hyperlink, they pass the URL of the actual media file to the appropriate plug-in, which in turn requests the audio stream from the server.

For example, RealAudio's reference files are called "metafiles" (suffix *.ram*). In HTML, the link is made to the metafile (*.ram*), not the RealAudio file itself, as follows:

```
<A HREF="song.ram">Link to the song</A>
```

The metafile contains the URL that points to the RealAudio file (suffix *.ra*):

```
pnm://[ip.address]/song.ra
```

It may also include an optional set of parameters for controlling starting, stopping, and information about the audio file.

Metafiles are useful for maintenance and control purposes. To change the audio, all you have to do is change the tiny metafile, rather than having to dig through HTML source code. You can also do things like calling multiple streaming media files from one metafile. One link to the metafile plays all the files.

Each streaming audio solution works differently, so refer to the documentation on each vendor's web site for specific instructions.

Linking to Shockwave and QuickTime audio

Because Shockwave and QuickTime files are transferred like any other file from an HTTP server, you can link them to the Web the same as downloadable media. The difference is that audio will start playing more quickly because the player does not need to wait for the entire file to download. It will begin playing once the buffer is filled and will continue playing as the remainder of the file is being transferred.

```
<A HREF="song.dcr">Link to Shockwave Audio</A>
```

Many streaming audio files that have dedicated server solutions may also be accessed via standard HTTP connections. This generally lowers performance.

<embed> attributes for QuickTime plug-in

src=*URL*
> The URL for the *.mov* file.

controller=true|false
> This provides a control strip that allows the user to start and stop the audio and adjust its volume. The controls will appear by default.

autoplay=true|false
> When set to true, the audio file will begin playing automatically. This is equivalent to the autostart attribute used with many other plug-in players.

loop=true|false|palindrome
> To play the audio just once, set loop to false. If you want it to repeat infinitely, set it to true. The palindrome setting will play the audio file through, then play it in reverse when it gets to the end, and then play it through again.

href=*URL*
> This makes the control strip (or movie frame for a video) a link to another web page.

width=*value*
height=*value*
> These values define the dimensions of the control panel area (it is more useful for videos where it also defines window size)

<embed> attributes for the RealAudio plug-in

The three primary attributes for embedding RealAudio are:

src=*URL*
> The URL to the RealAudio file (.ra)

autostart=true|false
> When set to true, the RealAudio file will begin playing automatically.

width=*value*
height=*value*
> Sets the size for the control panel.

In addition, you can use multiple <embed> statements to create a custom interface made up of individual controls. Each <embed> tag takes a controls attribute with one of the following control elements:

```
controls=all|ControlPanel|InfoVolumePanel|InfoPanel|
StatusBar|PlayButton|StopButton|VolumeSlider|Position
Slider|Position Field|StatusField
```

Streaming Audio Summary

Table 19-1 lists statistics for popular streaming audio solutions as of this writing. Because web audio technology changes so quickly, I encourage you to check the sites listed to get updated information.

Bibliography

I recommend the following books for a good starter course on web audio. Although some of the specifics are dated, they provide thorough and clear explanation of audio issues (these books helped me immensely in the writing of this chapter).

WebsiteSOUND, Patrick Seaman and Jim Cline (New Riders Publishing, 1996), ISBN 1-56205-626-3.

Designing Multimedia Web Sites, Stella Gassaway, Gary Davis, and Catherine Gregory (Hayden Books, 1996), ISBN 1-56830-308-4.

Many other promising books are being published as I'm writing. The following look worthy of checking out:

The IUMA Guide to Creating Audio on the Web, Marjorie Baer (editor), Jeff Patterson, and Ryan Melcher (Peachpit Press, 1998), ISBN 0-20169-613-4.

RealMedia Complete: Streaming Audio and Video Over the Web, Jonathan Angel (1998), ISBN 0-07913-727-X.

Table 19-1: Streaming Audio Summary

Technology	File Type	Reference File Type	Live Broadcast	Video	Player	Encoder	Server	Delivery[1]	Bandwidth Options
RealAudio RealNetworks *www.real.com* RealNetworks has announced its new G2 system; it was not available as of this writing.	.ra	.ram	yes	yes	RealPlayer 5.0 (free) or RealPlayer Plus (commercial product) *(Windows 3.1/95/ NT, Mac)*	RealEncoder or Adobe Premier Plug-in *(Windows 95/NT, Mac)*	RealNetworks Basic Server 5.0 (free) and Basic Server Plus 5.0 (full-featured commercial product) *(Win 95/NT, most Unix)*	UDP or HTTP	Optimized for 14.4 and 28.8 Separate files are required for specific bit rates.
Liquid Music System LiquidAudio *www.liquidaudio. com*	.lqt	n/a	no	no	Liquid Music Player CD *(Windows 95/NT, Mac)*	LiquifierPro *(Windows)* or *Liquifier Plug-in for Pro-Tools (Mac)*	Liquid MusicServer 3.0 *(NT, Sun, Solaris, SGI)*	UDP	Multiple bit rates can be stored in one file.
Streamworks Xing Technologies *www.xingtech. com*	.mp2 .mpa	.xsm *(embedded)* .xdm *(non-embedded)*	yes	yes	Streamworks Player *(Windows 95/NT, Mac)*	Xing MPEGEncoder *(Windows 95/NT)* This is a commercial product	Streamworks Server *(NT, Linux, Solaris, Irix, HP-UX, Unix)*	UDP, TCP, HTTP	Aimed at 250kbps and higher; files can be "thinned" to serve multiple bandwidths, but separate rate files are recommended for specific bit rates.
Shockwave Audio Macromedia *www.macro-media.com*	.dcr	n/a	no	no[2]	Shockwave Plug-in to NN 2.0+, IE 3.0+3, AOL 3 *(Windows 3.1/95/ NT,Mac)*	with Shockwave Audio Xtras in Director 5.0, 6.0, or Sound Edit 16, version 2.	n/a	HTTP	14.4 through T1; separate files are required for specific bit rates.
QuickTime Audio Apple *www.quicktime. com*	.mov	n/a	no	yes	QuickTime Plug-in to NN3.0+ and IE3.0+ *(Windows 95/NT, Mac)*	Many tools available, including MoviePlayerPro (part of Quick-Time 3.0 upgrade)	n/a	HTTP	n/a

1 UDP continuously pushes data through an open connection stream; however, UDP connections are problematic for some firewall configurations. Some vendors have responded by adding the capacity to revert to HTTP delivery if the UDP connection fails.
2 The filetype fully supports interactive multimedia presentations.
3 Shockwave Plug-in for Internet Explorer does not operate on the Mac platform.

CHAPTER 20

Video on the Web

Like audio, video clips were linked to web pages in the Web's earliest days. Delivering video via the Web is especially problematic because video files require huge amounts of data to describe the video and audio components, making for extremely large files. Few people will sit and wait an hour for a couple of minutes of video fun.

Many of the same technologies that have been applied to improve the experience of receiving audio over the Web have been applied to video as well. As with audio, you have the option of simply linking a video to your web page for download and playback, or you can choose from a number of streaming solutions. "Streaming" means the file begins playing almost immediately after the request is made, and continues playing as the file is transferred to the player. For a more complete description of streaming versus nonstreaming media, see Chapter 19, *Audio on the Web*.

This chapter will introduce you to basic video technology, concepts, and file formats (including several streaming options). If you are interested in learning how to produce video files for the web, the books listed in the bibliography at the end of this chapter are a great start. There are also some excellent tutorials on producing multimedia at WebMonkey's site (*http://www.webmonkey.com/*).

Tools Overview*

Newer Macs like the 8500, 8600, and the G3 Macs come with video hardware, but otherwise, if you wish to digitize video to put on your website you will probably need to add some video hardware to your computer.

The best software packages on both the Mac and PC for creating and editing video are from Adobe (*http://www.adobe.com/*). AfterEffects is a terrific package for

---

* Thanks go to Chris Florio for compiling this tools overview.

creating video effects and compositing (think animated Photoshop). Premiere is an extremely powerful video-editing tool that can also can create many special effects. Premiere also has strong sound capabilities.

The following packages are also noteworthy. The U.S. dollar amounts given reflect those at the time of this writing and are subject to change. In most cases, they should be used as guidelines only.

QuickTime 3.0 (Mac and PC)

The first essential A/V tool for all web designers or multimedia producers on both Mac and PC is QuickTime 3.0. This is the first release of QuickTime to be fully functional on Windows. QT 3.0 comes with the tools need to create streaming video and audio for the web. QuickTime supports dozens of file formats and there are a number of new codecs that come with QT that are ideal for the Internet (see Sorenson, next). Best of all, QuickTime 3.0 is free from Apple. (*http://www.apple.com/QuickTime*). A pro version of QuickTime can be licensed for $29.95.

Sorenson (Mac and PC)

A compression technology called Sorenson from Sorenson Vision, Inc. (*http://www.s-vision.com/*) is fast becoming the standard on the Web. Sorenson was originally created for medical imaging and delivers much higher quality images than Cinepak or Indeo at the equivalent file sizes. The basic Sorenson codec comes free with QuickTime 3.0, but a pro package is available for $499.

Media Cleaner Pro (Mac and PC)

One last package useful for optimizing sound and video files for the web is Media Cleaner Pro from Terran Interactive (*http://www.terran.com/*). This program is designed to get the best quality files at the smallest size in whatever format you choose. MediaCleaner works all of the QuickTime compressors as well as RealAudio and RealVideo. Media Cleaner also does batch compressing. The program sells for $359 and is available bundled with the Qcomp and Sorenson pro packages.

Basic Digital Video Concepts

The following is a list of aspects of digital video that can be manipulated with standard video-editing software. It is important to be familiar with these terms so you can create video optimized for web delivery.

Movie Length

It's a simple principle—limiting the length of your video clip will limit its file size. Videos longer than a minute or two may create prohibitive download times. If you must serve longer videos, consider one of the streaming video solutions.

Frame Size

Obviously, the size of the frame will have an impact on the size of the file. "Full-screen" video is 640×480 pixels. The amount of data required to deliver that size image would be prohibitive for most web applications. The most common frame size for web video is 160×120 pixels. Some producers will go as small as 120×90 pixels. It is not recommended that you use a frame size larger than 320×240 with current technology. Actual size limits depend mostly on CPU power and bandwidth of your Internet link.

Frame Rate

The frame rate is measured in number of frames per second (fps). Standard TV-quality video uses a frame rate of 30 frames per second to create the effect of smooth movement. For the Web, a frame rate of 15 or even 10 fps is more appropriate, and is still capable of producing fairly smooth video playback. For "talking head" and other low-motion subjects, even lower frame rates may be useful. Commercial Internet broadcasts are routinely done at 0.5, 0.25, or even 0.05 frames per second.

Quality

Many video-editing applications allow you to set the overall quality of the video image. The degree to which the compression algorithms crunch and discard data is determined by the target quality setting. A setting of Low or Medium results in fairly high compression, and is appropriate for Web delivery. Frame rate and quality are often traded off, depending on the application, to reduce bandwidth requirements.

Color Bit Depth

The size of the video is affected by the number of pixel colors in each frame. Reducing the number of colors from 24- to 8-bit color will drastically reduce the file size of your video, just as it does for still images. Of course, you will also sacrifice image quality.

Data Rate

This is the rate at which data must be transferred in order for the video to play smoothly without interruption. The data rate (also called "bit rate") for a movie is measured in kilobytes per second (K/sec or kbps). It can be calculated by dividing the size of the file (in K) by the length of the movie (in seconds). So, for example, a highly compressed movie that is 1900K (1.9 MB) and 40 seconds long has a data rate of 47.5K/sec.

For streaming media in particular, a file's data rate is more important than its total size. This is due to the fact that the total bandwidth available for delivery may be severely limited, particularly over a dial-up connection. For example, even an ISDN line at 128kbps offers a capacity to deliver only 16K of data per second.

Compression

Digital video wouldn't be possible without methods for compressing the vast amounts of data necessary to describe sound and frame images. Video files can be compressed in a number of different ways. This section looks at a variety of compression schemes and introduces the methods they use for achieving compression rates.

Lossless versus Lossy Compression

Compression can be "lossless," which means no information is lost and the final file is identical to the original.

Most codecs use forms of *lossy compression*. Lossy compression sacrifices some data from the file to achieve much higher compression rates. Lossy compression schemes, such as MPEG, use complicated algorithms that toss out data for sound and image detail that is not discernible to the human ear or eye. The decompressed file is extremely similar in character to the original, yet is not identical. This is similar to the way JPEG handles still images.

Spatial versus Temporal Compression

Spatial (or *intraframe*) *compression* takes place on each individual frame of the video, compressing the pixel information as though it were a still image.

Temporal (also called *interframe*) *compression* happens over a series of frames and takes advantage of areas of the image that remain unchanged from frame to frame, throwing out data for repeated pixels.

Temporal compression relies on the placement of *key frames* placed throughout the frames sequence. The key frames are used as masters against which the following frames (called delta frames) are compared. It is recommended that a key frame be placed once every second; therefore, if you have a frame rate of 15 fps, set your key frame rate once every 15 frames.

Videos without a lot of motion, such as talking head clips, take the best advantage of temporal compression. Videos with pans and other motion are compressed less efficiently.

Video Codecs

There are a number of *codecs* (compression/decompression algorithms) that can be used to compress video files for the Web. Many of these codecs can be applied to several different file formats (discussed in the next section of this chapter).

Video-editing software packages often offer a long list of codecs in their compressor list options. Here we focus on just those that are relevant to video intended for web delivery.

Radius Cinepak

Cinepak is the most highly recommended codec for the Web. It provides one of the highest possible compression/decompression rates and it is compatible with both QuickTime or AVI formats. It employs both spatial and temporal compression and a lossy compression scheme at lower quality levels. Low to medium quality settings will produce acceptable quality video.

Intel Indeo

The Indeo codec provides compression rates similar to Cinepak by the use of spatial and temporal compression, with lossy compression at low quality levels. Its drawbacks are that it does not maintain quality at data rates as low as Cinepak and it requires high-end machines to perform at its best. Unfortunately, new incompatibilities with QuickTime 3.0 have made it impossible to use the Indeo codec to create a QuickTime movie viewable on both Mac and PCs, making Indeo a less attractive option for Web use.

Animation

If your video clip is all computer-generated graphical imagery (i.e., not sourced from videotape), you may want to try the Animation compressor. Depending on the type of image, the Cinepak codec may work just as well (or better) for these types of files.

MPEG

The MPEG codec can only be used when the final video file will be in MPEG format (it is not compatible with other file types). It uses a lossy compression scheme (although it may be lossless at high-quality settings) and spatial and temporal compression. MPEG offers the best compression possible, however, MPEGs are not yet as widely supported on the Web as other formats.

Sorenson

QuickTime 3.0 (released in early 1998) introduced the impressive new Sorenson codec, which has promised to emerge as the new standard for video compression.

Sorenson Video codec was designed for low-bandwidth applications and is capable of producing files with lower data rates (if you select the Limit Data Rate option) than Cinepak. As of this writing, its disadvantage is that users must have QuickTime 3.0 installed in order to view videos compressed with Sorenson, so it may take a while before it is a risk-free codec choice.

Video File Formats

As for still images, there is a wide variety of formats for video material; however, not all of them are appropriate for the Web. This section looks at the three primary video file formats used for web distribution: *.mov*, *.avi*, and *.mpg*.

QuickTime Movie (.mov)

QuickTime, a system extension that makes it possible to view audio/video information on a computer, was introduced by Apple Computer in 1991. Although developed for the Macintosh, it is also supported on PCs via QuickTime for Windows. QuickTime 3.0 allows Windows users to both view and create QuickTime movies. In the last seven years, QuickTime has grown to be the industry standard for multimedia development, and most hardware and software offer QuickTime support.

Both Netscape Navigator 3.0+ and Internet Explorer 3.0+ come with QuickTime plug-in players, so the majority of web readers are able to view QuickTime movies right in the browser. The most recent version of the QuickTime plugin (as of this writing) is Version 2.0 (a little confusing since it works with the features of Quick-Time 3.0). It is installed as part of QuickTime 3.0 installation.

QuickTime movies (which may also contain audio-only information) are very popular for distribution via the Web due to their superior compression rates (meaning smaller files and shorter download times) and cross-platform, cross-browser support. In fact, the QuickTime format has been adopted by the ISO

(International Standards Organization) as the starting point for the development of a unified digital media storage format for the MPEG-4 specification.

Multiplatform QuickTime movies

If you're creating QuickTime movies on a Macintosh, your movies must be "flattened" before they can be played on multiple platforms. Macintosh files have two forks, a resource fork and a data fork, but other platforms only recognize single-fork files containing the data fork alone. Flattening a movie is the process in which the movie resource is moved out of the resource fork, creating a single-fork, self-contained movie that can be played on all platforms.

In QuickTime's MoviePlayer utility, click "Make playable on non-Macintosh computers" or "Make movie self-contained" when saving. Users of earlier versions of QuickTime will need to use an additional flattening utility such as FlattenMooV (available at *ftp://ftp.utexas.edu/pub/mac/graphics/flattenmoov.hqx*).

Streaming QuickTime movies

QuickTime 2.5 introduced Apple's "Fast Start" technology, which turns QuickTime movies into a streaming format (meaning that they begin playing immediately and continue to play as they download). QuickTime 3.0 will create flattened and streaming movies automatically, without any extra steps (making Apple's Internet Movie Tool obsolete).

Reference movies

Another interesting feature of version 2.0 of the QuickTime plug-in is its support for reference movies. Reference movies are used as pointers to alternate versions (or "tracks") of a movie, each optimized for a different connection speed. When a user downloads the reference movie, the plug-in ensures that the best track for the current connection speed is played.

You can also save a version of your movie that doesn't use the Sorenson codec in the reference file. This movie will play for users who don't have the latest plug-in version, ensuring backwards compatibility.

Media Cleaner Pro 3.0 from Terran Interactive (*http://www.terran-int.com/*) makes it easy to create reference and alternative movies.

For more information

For general information on QuickTime, see Apple's site at *http://www.apple.com/quicktime/*.

For information of particular interest to web developers, check out this page at the Apple site: *http://www.apple.com/quicktime/authors/webmas.html*.

Another great resource for QuickTime information is the QuickTime FAQ at *http://www.quicktimefaq.org/*.

AVI (.avi)

AVI (which stands for Audio/Video Interleaved) was introduced by Microsoft in 1992 as the standard movie format to work with its "Video for Windows (VFW)" multimedia architecture for Windows 95. In AVI files, the audio and video information is interleaved every frame, which in theory produces smoother playback.

As of this writing, AVI remains the standard for multimedia authoring on the Windows platform due to the fact that it comes with the operating system. It can be used as a basis for converting to most of the streaming media formats discussed in this chapter.

Macintosh users must install Video for Windows Apple Macintosh Utilities in order to view AVI movies directly, or use a tool to convert the file to QuickTime format.

MPEG (.mpg)

MPEG is a set of multimedia standards created by the Moving Picture Experts Group. It supports three types of information: video, audio, and streaming (which is synchronized video and audio). MPEG was initially popular as a web format because it was the only format that could be produced on the Unix system.

MPEG files offer extremely high compression rates with little loss of quality. They accomplish this using a lossy compression technique that strips out data that is not discernible to the human ear or eye.

There are a number of MPEG standards: MPEG-1 was originally developed for video transfer at VHS quality; MPEG-2 is a higher-quality standard that was developed for television broadcast; other MPEG specs that address other needs (such as MPEG-4 and -7) are currently in development. MPEGs can be compressed using one of three schemes, Layer-I, -II, or -III. The complexity of the coding (and therefore the processor power needed to encode and decode) increases at each level. Due to this complexity, you need special encoding tools to produce MPEG videos.

To learn more about MPEG, visit the MPEG Web Site *(http://www.mpeg.org/)*.

Streaming Video Technologies

As with audio, the competition is fierce in the streaming video arena. Not surprisingly, we see many of the same players as in the audio line-up. New technologies come and go weekly, so for a current list of contenders, see Netscape's plug-in page at *http://www.netscape.com/comprod/products/navigator/version_2.0/plugins/audio-video.html*.

As of this writing, RealNetworks continues to dominate the market due to the ubiquitous distribution of its player and its proven track record. However, some competitors offer niche products that may better suit your particular needs. Bear in mind that QuickTime 3.0 movies will stream without the use of a proprietary server package.

The following list represents just a few of the options for adding streaming video to your web site. The web sites listed with each technology provide complete information on how the system works, pricing structures, and the required software components.

RealVideo (RealNetworks)

RealNetworks (which used to be Progressive Networks) launched its streaming video capabilities in version 3.0 of its RealMedia line of products (of which RealAudio is the star component). As of this writing, RealNetworks' acquisition of VivoActive, a leader in streaming video technology, affirms their commitment to video delivery.

RealVideo can be optimized to stream over 14.4, 28.8, 56, and 112 kbps (ISDN or T1 connection). It uses the same RealServer software as RealAudio, and is capable of distributing live video broadcasts.

The RealVideoEncoder (available for Win 95/NT and Mac) has many predefined templates that make it easy to optimize video files appropriately for your purposes. It can process a new signal or convert an existing *.avi* or *.mov* (Quick-Time) movie.

The wide distribution of its player and a proven track record have made RealNetworks' products the *de facto* standard for adding streaming media to a web site.

For more information, visit the RealNetworks site at *http://www.real.com/*.

NetShow (Microsoft)

NetShow is Microsoft's ambitious effort to develop a streaming technology solution capable of delivering video, audio, and "illustrated audio" (audio synchronized with images, like a slide show presentation). It is based on the Advanced Streaming Format (*.asf*), which Microsoft is pushing as the new multimedia standard to succeed the current AVI standard.

As of this writing, the NetShowTools, a collection of conversion and video-editing tools, was only available for Windows 95 and NT platforms. However, if NetShow is adopted as a standard, expect to see the *.asf* format appear as an option in many multimedia tools available on both platforms.

NetShow delivery requires the NetShow Server, which is free via download, and runs only on the Windows NT 4.0 platform. Microsoft recently announced "NetShow with RealAudio and RealVideo," which provides full compatibility for creating, serving, and playing RealAudio/RealVideo content with the NetShow package.

Microsoft also offers the NetShow Theater Server (a commercial product), aimed at providing streaming multimedia presentations over dedicated high-bandwidth networks such as intranets. It is aimed at the training and educational market.

For general information, see Microsoft's NetShow site *at http://www.microsoft.com/ netshow/*. For practical how-to information on developing streaming media for NetShow, see *http://www.microsoft.com/workshop/author/streaming/*.

Streamworks (Xing Technology)

Streamworks' claim to fame is it is the only format based entirely on the industry-standard MPEG specification, offering MPEG-1 and MPEG-2, Layer-3 audio. This format uses a lossy compression capable of extremely high compression rates while maintaining excellent quality.

Despite the magic of MPEG, the high data rate required to deliver CD-quality audio and TV-quality video makes Streamworks most appropriate to intranet and extranet applications, such as training or distance learning. It is possible to encode a Streamworks file for delivery over 28.8 kbps connections, but Streamworks is aiming at high-bandwidth delivery of 250 kbps and up.

For more information, visit the Xing Technology web site at *http://www.xingtech.com/.*

Streaming Video Summary

Table 20-1 lists information for popular streaming audio technolgies. Because these technologies change so rapidly, I encourage you to visit the web pages listed for up-to-date information about the various software packages and their capabilities.

Adding Video to an HTML Document

This section looks at the ways video files can be linked to or embedded within an HTML document.

With a Simple Link

Video files can be linked to HTML documents using the standard link tag around a string of text or a graphic as follows:

```
<A HREF="video.mov"> Check out the video (1.3MB)</A>
```

When the user clicks on the link, the browser looks at the file type (as defined in the filename suffix) and launches a player application to play the movie. Which player it uses depends on how that user has the browser configured, so it is out of the control of the web page designer.

In most cases, the movie will open in a separate window with start and stop controls. Be aware that if the browser is configured to use a plug-in for the specified file type, the movie may load in the browser window, replacing the original web page.

If you are linking to a file that will need to be downloaded before it can be played, it is a good idea to print the size of the file so the user can make the decision whether to start the download.

If you are linking to a streaming format, you may need to link to a reference file (such as a *.ram* metafile for RealVideo) instead of to the actual video file. (Reference files are discussed in more detail in Chapter 19.) Carefully follow the vendor's instructions for adding their streaming media to your page.

Table 20-1: *Streaming Video Summary*

Technology	File Type	Reference File Type	Live Broadcast	Player	Encoder	Server	Delivery[1]	Bandwidth Options
RealVideo RealNetworks *www.real.com* RealNetworks has announced its new G2 system; it was not available as of this writing.	.rm	.rpm	yes	RealPlayer 5.0 (free) or RealPlayer Plus (commercial product) *(Windows 3.1/95/NT, Mac)*	RealVideoEncoder or Adobe Premier Plug-in *(Windows 95/ NT, Mac)*	RealNetworks Basic Server 5.0 (free) and Basic Server Plus 5.0 (full-featured commercial product) *(Win 95/NT, most Unix)*	UDP and HTTP	Optimized for 14.4 and 28.8. Separate files are required for specific bit rates.
NetShow Microsoft *www.microsoft. com/netshow*	.asf	.asx	yes	NetShow Player *(Windows 3.1/95/NT, Mac, Unix)*	NetShow Tools *(Windows 95/ NT only)*	NetShow Server *(Windows NT 4.0)*	UDP, TCP, and HTTP	Separate files required for each bitrate (28, 56, 128, etc.) as of this writing. Scaling will certainly be added to a future version.
Streamworks Xing Technologies *www.xingtech. com*	.mpg	.xsm— embedded .xdm— non-embedded	yes	Streamworks Player *(Windows 95/NT, Mac)*	Xing MPEGEncoder *(Windows 95/ NT)* This is a commercial product	Streamworks Server *(NT, Linux, Solaris, Irix, HP-UX, Unix)*	UDP and HTTP	Aimed at high bandwidths (250kbps and higher); files can be "thinned" to serve multiple bandwidths, but separate files are recommended for specific bit rates.

1 UDP continuously pushes data through an open connection stream; however, UDP connections are problematic for some firewall configurations. Some vendors have responded by adding the capacity to revert to HTTP delivery if the UDP connection fails.

The <embed> Tag

When you add a video file to your page with an <embed> tag, the browser will look for the appropriate plug-in and display the movie with its player inline on the web page. The <embed> tag was introduced by Netscape Navigator, but it is supported by Internet Explorer 3.0 and higher, making it a safe way to put a video right on a page.

A typical <embed> tag would look like this:

```
<EMBED SRC="cool.mov" AUTOPLAY=false WIDTH=160 HEIGHT=120>
</EMBED>
```

Each plug-in has its own set of attributes that can be added to the <embed> tag. The following list of attributes work with the popular QuickTime plug-in, which now comes bundled with Navigator and IE.

src=URL

> This points to the video file you want to play. It is a mandatory attribute.

width=number
height=number

> These set the width and height in number of pixels for the video frame. These settings are mandatory.

autoplay=true|false

> The video will start playing automatically if this attribute is set to true. The default is false (meaning the user will have to start the video with the Play button).

controller=true|false

> A control bar for the video will be visible when this is set to true (or by default). Although it is possible to turn off the controls, it is usually advisable to leave them visible and available for use.

loop=true|false|palindrome

> true causes the video to loop continuously. false (the default) causes the video to play through once. palindrome makes the video play through, then play in reverse, then play through, continuously.

playeveryframe=true|false

> When set to false (the default), you allow the video to skip frames in order to ensure smooth playback. Do not set this attribute to true if you have audio with your movie.

href=url

> This attribute makes your movie a link to another page.

pluginspage=url

> This provides a link to a source to acquire the plug-in if the browser can't find it on the system.

The dynsrc Attribute

This is Internet Explorer's attribute for embedding a video inline on a page. Note: This tag does not work with any version of Netscape Navigator, so using it may alienate a large portion of your audience.

You place this tag on a page like any other image, and you can add the same attributes to it that you could add to an <img> tag, such as alignment, horizontal and vertical gutter space, etc., as follows:

```
<IMG DYNSRC="waycool.mov" ALIGN=right HSPACE=12>
```

The <img dynsrc> tag can also take a number of specialized attributes for controlling video display:

controls
   Adds playback controls for the video.

dynsrc=*url*
   Provides the URL for the video file to be displayed on the page.

loop=*value*
   Sets the number of times to play the video. It can be a number value or set to infinite.

start=fileopen, mouseover
   Specifies when to play the video. By default, it begins playing as soon as it's downloaded (fileopen). You can set it to start when the mouse pointer is over the movie area (mouseover). If you combine them (separated by a comma), the movie plays once it's downloaded, then again every time the user mouses over it.

Bibliography

The following books were instrumental in writing this chapter. Both are excellent resources for further study.

Designing Multimedia Web Sites, Stella Gassaway, Gary Davis and Catherine Gregory (Hayden Books, 1996), ISBN 1-56830-308-4.

Publishing Digital Video, Second Edition, Jan Ozer (Academic Press, 1997), ISBN 0-12-531942-8.

CHAPTER 21

Interactivity

The Web, built on the concept of hyperlinking from document to document, is an interactive medium by nature. However, the vast majority of documents are modeled after static, print layouts.

"Interactivity," as used in this chapter, refers to ways to make a web page less like a printed page and more like a CD-ROM or kiosk interface. Some features that set these media apart from print are:

- motion

- integrated sound effects

- elements (such as buttons) that respond to the position of the cursor

- the ability for the user to manipulate what is on the screen

- animation and video

This chapter looks at some available technologies and techniques for adding enhanced interactivity to web pages. It begins with overviews of two plug-in technologies, the Flash and Shockwave players, both from Macromedia. Next, it discusses adding Java applets to web pages. Finally, it provides two JavaScripts for making graphics interactive with "rollover" effects.

Dynamic HTML (DHMTL), another increasingly popular alternative for adding motion and interactivity to web pages, is discussed in Chapter 24, *Introduction to DHTML*, in Part V of this book.

Flash

Flash is a ground-breaking multimedia format developed by Macromedia. Flash gives you the ability to create full-screen animation, interactive graphics, and integrated audio clips, all at remarkably small file sizes. Its magic lies in that it is a vector-based format (rather than bitmap), resulting in extremely compact files well-suited for web delivery. Vector graphics define objects with mathematical formulas that require far less data than describing each individual pixel of a bitmap image.

359

For more information (and to download a demo copy), visit Macromedia's site at *http://www.flash.com/*. Be sure to visit the gallery for examples of Flash used as navigation interfaces, interactive buttons, and even games.

Advantages

Many aspects of the Flash file format make it ideal for adding interactive content to web pages:

Small file size
As mentioned above, Flash's vector format means small files and quick downloads.

Scalable
Flash images and animations can be resized with no loss of detail, making it easy to fill the whole browser window with a Flash interface without adding to the file size. Flash can be used to create static images, such as maps, where zooming into finer detail is desirable.

High image quality
Real-time anti-aliasing smoothes the edges of graphics and text, regardless of the display size. Users can zoom in on vector graphics with no loss of image quality.

Streaming technology
Flash files start playing quickly and continue to play as they download. There is no special server software required.

Integrated sound
Flash is a good way to bring background sound and user-triggered sound effects to a web site. RealFlash (introduced below) enables Flash animation to be synchronized with high-quality streaming audio.

Interactivity
Incorporating interactivity into a Flash file is done without scripting. Designers can easily create their own navigation interfaces and interactive graphics and animations without prior knowledge of programming languages.

Well-supported format
The Flash player required to play Flash files is available for Windows 3.1/95/98/NT and MacOS platforms. The Flash format is also natively supported by WebTV. Alternatively, Flash content can be played via ActiveX controls (for IE on Windows 95/98/NT) or with the Flash Player Java Edition (on any Java-enabled browser). All future versions of the Netscape browser, from version 4.06 and beyond, will contain the Flash player.

Scriptable
You can use JavaScript commands to control a Flash element on your page. The following are just a few of the Flash functions that can be called from JavaScript:

Play() starts playing the animation.
StopPlay() stops the animation.
Rewind() goes to the first frame.
GotoFrame(intframeNum) goes to a specific frame of the movie.

`PercentLoaded()` returns the percent of the *.swf* file that has streamed into the browser.

In addition, you can activate JavaScript commands from within the Flash file. Note that to use JavaScript to call methods in a Flash file, your `<embed>` and `<object>` tags must have a `name` or `id` attribute (respectively).

For more information and instruction on using JavaScript with Flash, see Macromedia's Flash Technotes online at *http://www.macromedia.com/support/flash/*.

Disadvantages

And on the downside . . .

Plug-in player required

Standard Flash files require the Shockwave Essentials or Flash players to be installed on the user's machine. Although this may seem like a small hurdle, particularly since the Shockwave and Flash players are some of the most popular and universally available plug-ins, the words "plug-in required" are enough to make many clients say "no way" without a second thought.

To its credit, Macromedia has anticipated such resistance and has responded with some alternative strategies. Flash Player Java Edition enables Flash files to play on any Java-enabled browser. (Note that currently its performance is dependent on Java and somewhat unreliable, but Macromedia is continually working on providing optimized players.) The Flash authoring tool also allows you to export your animation as a GIF, although you may need to optimize it in a dedicated GIF animation utility.

In addition, they provide assistance in generating plug-in detection by providing the Aftershock utility that ships with Flash 3. This utility will automatically detect the browser configuration and will serve the appropriate media whether it is native Flash, Java, or animated GIF. There are additional JavaScript filters available at *http://www.macromedia.com/support/flash/how/subjects/javaplugs/javaplugs.html*.

Content is lost on nongraphical browsers

Using Flash movies for document headlines and navigation introduces the same problems as using static graphics in place of text. People who cannot view your Flash animation (or even an alternative GIF image) will not be able to read your content. `alt` text helps, but is limited and not always reliable. In addition, information in a Flash movie cannot be indexed or searched.

No support for Unix

Unix users currently cannot view nor create Flash movies. Macromedia is evaluating various Unix playback strategies to support their open file format initiative.

Expensive authoring software required

You currently need Macromedia's Flash software to create Flash files. Flash 3 costs US$299 in retail boxes or US$269 from electronic software download (ESD) as of this writing.

Proprietary format

Although Macromedia is working to get Flash established as an open vector format for the Web, as of this writing it is a proprietary format controlled by Macromedia.

Creating Flash Content for the Web

You need to purchase Macromedia's Flash 3 software to create Flash files. You can download a free demo from the Macromedia site at *http://www.flash.com/*. Obviously, it is beyond the scope of this book to teach the Flash software interface, so I recommend using the tutorials that come with the software as well as support documents provided by Macromedia (*http://www.macromedia.com/support/flash/*).

Flash is comprised of a full set of vector drawing tools (like Freehand or Illustrator) and animation tools. Note that although Flash is vector-based, it supports bitmap image information in JPEG, GIF, or PNG form (using bitmaps greatly increases file size, however).

Even if you have no animation experience, Flash makes it easy to create motion and morphing effects because it can generate "in-between" frames automatically. Flash 3.0 adds some basic sound-editing capabilities, so you can make your sound files as compact and efficient as possible.

When your Flash image or movie is done, choose File → Export → Shockwave Flash to create a Flash file (be sure to name it with the suffix *.swf*) to make it optimized for file size and data streaming over the Web. In order to update an existing Flash file, edit the original Flash movie file (FLA file) and re-export it.

Configuring the Server

Although no special server software is necessary to serve standard Flash files, you will need to configure your server to recognize a new MIME type. The specific syntax for configuration varies for different servers, so coordinate with your system administrator and see Macromedia's site for further support information. The following information will suit the needs of most servers:

Type/subtype
    application/x-shockwave-flash

File extension for Flash
    .swf

Adding Flash to an HTML Document

Flash images and movies are placed in HTML documents using the <embed> or <object> placement tags. <embed> was developed by Netscape and works with Netscape 2.0 and later, Internet Explorer 3.0+ for the Mac, and other plug-in compatible browsers.

Internet Explorer versions 3 and higher use the <object> tag, which enables them to automatically download the ActiveX controls for playing Flash media.

To code your page so it is accessible to the maximum number of users, use a combination of the <embed> and <object> tags. Explanations of each of these options follow. Note that technologies change quickly and Macromedia revises their tagging instructions from time to time. Consult the Macromedia support pages online for updates.

The <embed> tag

The standard tag is as follows:

```
<EMBED SRC="path/file.swf" WIDTH=x HEIGHT=x
PLUGINSPAGE="http://www.macromedia.com/shockwave/download/
index.cgi?P1_Prod_Version=ShockwaveFlash">
</EMBED>
```

The width and height values are mandatory and specify the dimensions of the image or movie in pixels. Note that you can also specify the dimensions in percentages (corresponding to the percentage of the browser window the movie fills). The pluginspage attribute provides a URL to the page where the user can download the Flash player if it is not found on the user's computer (use the exact URL shown in the above code). It is a recommended attribute, but not mandatory.

Netscape 2.0 does not support the <embed> tag within a table cell. It is supported properly only in NN3.0+ and IE3.0+, so use caution when formatting Flash content with tables.

There are a number of Flash-specific attributes that can be added within the <embed> tag:

NAME=*text*
> This assigns a name to the movie, which is necessary if it is going to be called from a JavaScript or within a form.

QUALITY=low|autolow|autohigh|high
> This attribute controls the anti-aliasing quality. autolow (the default) starts the animation at normal quality (aliased) and switches to high quality (anti-aliased) if the user's computer is fast enough. Conversely, autohigh starts the animation in high quality mode and reverts to normal quality if the computer is too slow. high anti-aliases the animation regardless of computer speed. low uses normal display quality (recommended for animations that must display quickly).

LOOP=true|false
> Specifies whether the movie plays in a continuous loop. The default is true.

PLAY=true|false
> If play is set to true, the movie will begin playing automatically. A setting of false requires the user to initiate the movie. The default is true.

BGCOLOR=*rrggbb*
> Use this setting to override the background color of the Flash movie, for instance, to make it match the background color of a web page. The value is a hexadecimal RGB value (see Chapter 5, *HTML Overview*, for an explanation of specifying RGB colors in HTML).

SCALE=showall|noborder|exactfit

This is used in conjunction with percentage width and height values for defining how the animation fits in the frame. showall (the default) fits the movie into the frame while maintaining the image proportion (note, the frame background may be visible along one or two edges of the movie). noborder scales the movie to fill the frame while maintaining the aspect ratio of the movie (note, one or two edges might get cut off). exactfit fits the image into the frame exactly, but may result in image distortion.

SALIGN=l|r|t|b

This attribute positions the movie within the frame. The letters l, r, t, b correspond to left, right, top, and bottom, respectively. You can use any combination of l or r with t or b; for example, lt aligns the movie to the top-left corner of the browser window. If the showall attribute is selected, the leftover space would appear below and to the right of the movie.

BASE=url

Sets the base URL and directory that is used for relative path names within the Flash movie.

MENU=true|false

Right-clicking in Windows or Control-clicking on a Mac on a Flash movie brings up a pop-up menu of playback controls. Setting MENU to false disables the choices in the pop-up menu.

The <object> tag

The <object> tag gives the direction to the browser to download and install the particular ActiveX player for Flash files. It is used only by Internet Explorer versions 3.0 and higher. The following is an example of the basic <object> tag:

```
<OBJECT CLASSID="clsid:D27CDB6E=AE6D-11cf-98B8-444553540000"
    CODEBASE="http://active.macromedia.com/flash2/cab5/swflash.
    cab" width=300 height=150>
    <PARAM NAME="MOVIE" value="moviename.swf">
</OBJECT>
```

The classid parameter identifies the particular ActiveX control, and codebase provides the browser with its location for downloading. It is important that the values for these parameters appear in your code *exactly* as they are printed here.

You need to specify the width and height dimensions in pixels or in percentage of the browser window. The first parameter establishes the name and location of your Shockwave Flash file.

The same additional controls as outlined for the <embed> tag (quality, loop, play, etc.) can be used with the <object> tag as well, however, they appear as additional parameters within the <object> tags using the following tag structure:

```
<PARAM NAME="PLAY" value="true">
<PARAM NAME="LOOP" value="false">
```

The <noembed> tag

The <noembed> tag is used to provide an alternative image or text message for browsers that do not recognize the <embed> tag (at this point, only Netscape 1.0 and Internet Explorer 1.0 and 2.0).

Browsers that do understand the <embed> tag will always ignore the contents of <noembed>, even if the media file is unable to play due to a missing plug-in. For this reason, it is not appropriate to include directions specific to the Flash player (or any plug-in) in the <noembed> element. It is merely a courtesy for the few users who view the Web with extremely outdated browsers.

The <noembed> tag is placed after the <embed> tag and looks like this:

```
<EMBED>...</EMBED>
<NOEMBED><IMG SRC="image.gif" width=300 height=150></NOEMBED>
```

Putting it together for all browsers

To make your Flash content available to the maximum number of users, it is recommended that you use both the <embed> and <object> tags. It is important to keep the <embed> and <noembed> tags within the <object> tags so Internet Explorer users don't get two copies of your movie.

Do not use quotation marks within the <embed> tag when it is placed within an <object> tag. The quotation marks will cause the <object> tag to choke.

The following sample code places an anti-aliased animation on the page that plays and loops automatically:

```
<OBJECT CLASSID="clsid:D27CDB6E=AE6D-11cf-98B8-444553540000"
 CODEBASE="http://active.macromedia.com/flash2/cab5/swflash.
 cab" width=300 height=145 NAME="animation">

<PARAM NAME="MOVIE" value="animation.swf">
<PARAM NAME="PLAY" value="true">
<PARAM NAME="LOOP" value="true">
<PARAM NAME="QUALITY" value="autohigh">

    <EMBED SRC=animation.swf WIDTH=300 HEIGHT=145
    PLUGINSPAGE=http://www.macromedia.com/shockwave/download/
    index.cgi?P1_Prod_Version=ShockwaveFlash NAME=animation
    PLAY=true LOOP=true QUALITY=autohigh>
    </EMBED>

<NOEMBED>This content requires a plug-in compatible browser.
</NOEMBED>
</OBJECT>
```

Additional Flash Products

RealFlash

This collaborative effort between Macromedia and RealNetworks (the company behind RealAudio and RealVideo), RealFlash is the integration of Flash media into RealNetworks' RealSystem. This enables true streaming of Flash animation synchronized with high-quality streaming audio.

For more information, visit *http://www.real.com/devzone/flash/* and check out the FAQ and tutorial.

Generator

Generator is a server-side product that enables Flash and other bitmap graphics to be generated on-the-fly based on database information or form-generated content. With it, you can create Flash quality graphics and animations that update in real time, such as breaking news headlines, charts, interactive maps, etc.

For more information, see *http://www.macromedia.com/software/generator/*.

Shockwave for Director

Macromedia's Director software (which significantly predates the Web) has become the industry standard for creating multimedia presentations appropriate for CD-ROMs and kiosk displays. Director movies incorporate images, motion, sound, interactive buttons, and even QuickTime movies. In 1996, Macromedia introduced the Shockwave system that enabled Director movies to be played directly on web pages, expanding the possibilities of what a web "page" is all about.

Advantages

Shockwave has a number of attractive features:

Lingo programming

Because Shockwave can be customized with Lingo programming, it offers functionality, such as the ability to remember user position, keep scores, "know" correct answers, and other games-related functions, that cannot be achieved with Flash.

Good compression

The Shockwave file format offers efficient compression ratios, compressing Director movies to 1/3 to 1/2 of their original size.

Full-featured interactivity

Brings full CD-ROM-like interactivity to web pages.

Streaming

Shockwave movies begin playing very quickly and continue playing as they download. There is no special server software required.

Well-supported format

The Shockwave plug-in required to play Flash files is available for Windows 3.1/95/NT and Mac platforms. It is one of the most popular and widely distributed plug-ins.

Scriptable

Shockwave movies can be controlled by basic JavaScript commands such as `Play()` and `Stop()`. Other JavaScript interactions can be set with Lingo programming within the Shockwave movie. For more information, see Macromedia's Director support pages at *http://www.macromedia.com/support/director/how/shock/*.

Disadvantages

And on the down side . . .

Larger file size

Despite impressive compression, some Director Shockwave movies (particularly those containing sound and video content) may still be quite large for transferring over network connections. Depending on the nature of the content, Shockwave may be overkill for simple effects (such as an interactive button) that may be more efficiently handled by Flash.

Plug-in required

As mentioned in the Flash section of this chapter, users need to have the Shockwave plug-in installed in order to view your Director movies. Despite the popularity of the Shockwave plug-in, many clients still see this as a prohibitive disadvantage.

Larger plug-in footprint

The plug-in required for playing Shockwave files is about 1MB in size and requires more system resources to run.

Expensive authoring tool

In order to create Shockwave movies, you need Macromedia Director, which costs approximately US$995 as of this writing.

Difficult to author

Director, with its Lingo programming language, has a steep learning curve. However, with behaviors, it's fairly easy for beginners to jump in and accomplish some sophisticated stuff within a short period of time.

Proprietary format

Shockwave movies are in a propriety format that can only be authored in Macromedia's Director program.

Creating Shockwave Movies

Shockwave movies must be created using Macromedia Director. Director is a powerful multimedia authoring environment. Although learning the basics of the software itself is not too daunting, to make Director movies do the really cool interactive stuff, you must learn Lingo, Director's proprietary programming language. Lingo, although simple by programming standards, can still take a long time to master, which is why many designers hire Director and Lingo specialists.

That said, a lesson in Director and Lingo is beyond the scope of this book. If you're interested in learning Director, I recommend you spend time with the manual and other available tutorial books. Also, be sure to take advantage of the excellent support material and resources on the Macromedia web site. Pay special attention to tips for optimizing file size and preparing files for streaming.

Once you've created a movie in Director, you must save it in Shockwave format to make it play over the Web. The directions for doing this are slightly different for Director versions 5 and 6.

Director 5

In Director 5, you need to use the Afterburner Xtra (available for download on Macromedia's site) to compress the movie and save it in the Shockwave format. Open your movie in Director and choose Xtras → Afterburner. Name the file (remember to use the suffix *.dcr*) and save it. It is ready to be uploaded to the server.

Director 6

You can save a movie in Shockwave format directly in version 6. Just choose File → Save As Shockwave. Be sure to name the file with the suffix *.dcr.*

Configuring the Server

Although you don't need special server software to handle Shockwave files, the server must be configured to recognize the new MIME type. The specific syntax for configuration varies for different servers, so coordinate with your system administrator. The following provides the standard necessary elements:

Type/subtype

    application/x-director

File extensions for Director Shockwave

    .dcr (also .dir and .dxr)

Adding Shockwave Files to an HTML Document

Like Flash, Director Shockwave files are added to an HTML document with the `<embed>` or `<object>` tags. `<embed>` was developed by Netscape and works with Netscape 2.0 and later, Internet Explorer 3.0+ for the Mac, and other plug-in compatible browsers.

Internet Explorer versions 3 and higher use the `<object>` tag, which enables them to automatically download the ActiveX controls for playing Shockwave media.

To code your page so it is accessible to the maximum number of users, use a combination of the `<embed>` and `<object>` tags. Explanations of each of these options follows. Note that technologies change quickly and Macromedia revises their tagging instructions from time to time. Consult the Macromedia support pages online for updates.

The <embed> tag

The standard tag is as follows:

```
<EMBED SRC="path/file.dcr" WIDTH=x HEIGHT=x
PLUGINSPAGE="http://www.macromedia.com/shockwave/">
</EMBED>
```

The width and height values are mandatory and specify the dimensions of the movie in pixels. The pluginspage attribute provides a URL to the page where the user can download the Shockwave plug-in if it is not found on the user's computer (the URL shown in the previous example will work). It is a recommended, but not mandatory, attribute.

 Netscape 2.0 does not support the <embed> tag within a table cell. It is supported properly only in NN3.0+ and IE3.0+, so use caution when using tables.

The following additional attributes, which are specific to controlling Director Shockwave movies, can be added to the <embed> tag:

NAME=text

This assigns a name to the movie, which is necessary if it is going to be called from a JavaScript or within a form.

PALETTE=background|foreground

This determines how the movie's palette affects the user's system when Shockwave plays the movie. Background uses the viewer's system palette and is recommended for most movies. Foreground causes the movie's palette to take over the user's system (it is not supported by Internet Explorer).

BGCOLOR=#rrggbb

Defines the color of the movie rectangle before the movie appears. The value is specified in hexadecimal RGB values and can be set to match the background color of the web page (see Chapter 5, *HTML Overview*, for an explanation of this color-naming system).

The <object> tag

The <object> tag gives the direction to the browser to download and install the particular ActiveX player for Shockwave Flash files. It is used only by Internet Explorer versions 3.0 and higher. The following is an example of the basic <object> tag:

```
<OBJECT CLASSID="clsid:166B1BCA-3F9C-11CF-8075-444553540000"
CODEBASE="http://active.macromedia.com/director/cabs/sw.
cab#version=6,0,0,0" WIDTH="450" HEIGHT="280" NAME="MovieName">
    <PARAM NAME="SRC" VALUE="movie.dcr">
</OBJECT>
```

The classid parameter identifies the particular ActiveX control and codebase provides the browser with its location for downloading. It is important that the values for these parameters appear in your code *exactly* as they are printed here (see code in bold).

You need to specify the width and height in pixels of the exact dimensions of your Director movie stage.

The `bgcolor` parameter as described earlier can also be used with the `<object>` tag, however, it is formatted as follows and added within the `<object>` tags:

```
<PARAM NAME="BGCOLOR" value="#33CC00">
```

The <noembed> tag

As mentioned in the Flash section, the `<noembed>` tag is used to provide an alternative image or text message for browsers that do not recognize the `<embed>` tag (at this point, that's only Netscape 1.0 and Internet Explorer 1.0 and 2.0). The vast majority of browsers in use today will ignore the contents of the `<noembed>` tag entirely, without basing it on the availability of a specific plug-in.

If you choose to include it, the `<noembed>` tag is placed after the `<embed>` tag and looks like this:

```
<EMBED>...</EMBED><NOEMBED>This material requires a plug-in
capable browser.</NOEMBED>
```

Putting it together for all browsers

To make your Shockwave movie available to the maximum number of users, it is recommended that you use the `<embed>` and `<object>` tags. It is important to put the `<embed>` and `<noembed>` tags within the `<object>` tags so that Internet Explorer users don't get two copies of your movie.

 Do not use quotation marks within the `<embed>` tag when it is placed within an `<object>` tag. The quotation marks will cause the `<object>` tag to choke.

The following code places a Shockwave movie on a web page:

```
<OBJECT CLASSID="clsid:166B1BCA-3F9C-11CF-8075-444553540000"
CODEBASE="http://active.macromedia.com/director/cabs/sw.
cab#version=6,0,0,0" WIDTH="300" HEIGHT="150" NAME="MovieName">
<PARAM NAME="SRC" VALUE="movie.dcr">

<EMBED SRC=movie.dcr WIDTH=300 HEIGHT=150 PLUGINSPAGE=http://www.
macromedia.com/shockwave/>
</EMBED>
<NOEMBED> This material requires a plug-in capable browser.
</NOEMBED>
</OBJECT>
```

Java Applets

Java is an object-oriented programming language developed by Sun Microsystems (*http://www.sun.com*). It should be noted that it is not related to JavaScript, which is a scripting language developed by Netscape Navigator to run within an HTML document in a browser. Because Java is a full programming language (like C or C++), it can be used to create whole applications.

Java's primary contribution to the Web, however, has been in the form of Java *applets*, self-contained mini-executable programs. These programs, named with the .*class* suffix, can be placed right on the web page, like a graphic.

Advantages and Disadvantages

Applets are ideal for web distribution for the following reasons:

- They are platform-independent.

- They download completely and run on the client-side, so there is no continued burden on the server.

- Applet files are generally quite compact and download quickly.

- They don't require a proprietary plug-in to be installed. All the major browsers are now Java-enabled, which means chances are good that users will be able to view the applet.

Of course, every utopian technology has its darker side, and unfortunately, in the real world, browsers can be temperamental in the way they handle Java applets. Browsers are notorious for crashing in the presence of a computation-hungry applet. In general, it takses browsers a long time to initialize Java, which tends to chase users away. There was a great buzz amongst web developers when Java applets first hit the scene, but since then enthusiasm has waned in the face of performance issues and the development of other web multimedia solutions.

What Applets Can Do

What *can't* applets do?! Java applets are used for everything from simple animations to flight simulators. Because Java allows for computations on-the-fly, they are useful for programs that interact with user input. Not surprisingly, a large percentage of Java applets are games, but applets are also used for more practical purposes, such as calculators and spreadsheets. More interestingly, they can serve live data (news headlines, stock quotes, sports scores, etc.) and let users navigate through complex data relationships.

There are probably thousands of Java applets out there. The following is just a smattering of the types of things they can do:

- **Utilities**—calculators, calendars. clocks, spreadsheets, etc.

- **Text effects**—scrolling marquees, wiggling text, flashing colored text messages, etc.

- **Audio effects** —digital "guitars," radio buttons, etc.

- **Games**—Asteroids, crosswords, Hangman, Minesweeper, etc.

- **Miscellaneous** — biorhythm charts, flight simulators, daily quotes, etc.

Where to Get Applets

If you need a customized applet for your site, your best bet is to hire a programmer to create one to your specifications. However there are a number of applets available for free or for a licensing fee that you can download from libraries on the Web.

A good place to start is the applets section of Sun's Java site at *http://java.sun.com/applets/*. This page provides a list of links to applet-related resources.

If you are looking for cool applets you can use right away, try the JavaBoutique at *http://javaboutique.internet.com/*. Here you will find hundreds of applets available for download as well as clear instructions for their use. It's a great way to add interactivity to your site without learning any programming.

In addition to these, there are a number of small businesses with Java applet packages for sale or available for a nominal licensing fee. Because the list is constantly changing, I recommend doing a search for "Java Applets" on Yahoo (*http://www.yahoo.com*) or your favorite search engine.

Adding an Applet to a Page

It is fairly easy to download an applet and add it to a web page. The steps below follow the instructions provided by the JavaBoutique for downloading applets from their site, but they can be used for applets from any resource.

1. Download the *.class* file along with any associated image or audio files. (Note, there is a bug in Netscape 4.0 that requires you to hold the Shift key before clicking the link for the *.class* file). In some cases, you may be given the raw Java code, in which case you would need to compile it using Sun's Java Developer Kit.

2. The *.class* file should be saved in the same directory as the HTML file unless otherwise noted by the codebase attribute in the associated <applet> tag (this attribute gives the path for the applet). If the applet requires additional resources (such as image or audio files), be sure to save them in the same directory structure you found them (or follow the directions provided with the applet).

3. When getting an applet from a library such as JavaBoutique, the required HTML source is made available with the download, so you can just copy and paste it into your HTML document and adjust the parameters as necessary.

   Applets are generally placed on web pages using the <applet> tag. Some applets also require that parameters be set or customized with <param> tags, which are placed within the opening and closing <applet> tags. The <applet> tag and all its attributes are discussed in detail in Chapter 9, *Adding Images and Other Page Elements*. The following shows two typical <applet> tags.

   The first is quite simple and contains only the required attributes:

   ```
   <APPLET CODE=Hangman.class WIDTH=300 HEIGHT=150>
   </APPLET>
   ```

   The second contains additional parameters :

   ```
   <APPLET CODE="GifCraps.class" ALIGN="baseline" WIDTH="400"
   HEIGHT="280">
   <PARAM NAME="r-value" VALUE="150">
   ```

```
<PARAM NAME="g-value" VALUE="150">
<PARAM NAME="b-value" VALUE="255">
<PARAM NAME="pauseTime" VALUE="25">
</APPLET>
```

The W3C's HTML 4.0 Specification recommends that the all-purpose <object> tag be used to place Java applets on web pages instead of the <applet> tag. Unfortunately, as of this writing, Netscape Navigator has problems recognizing Java applets placed with the <object> tag, and in particular, doesn't recognize the <param> tag when used within <object> tags. Until browser support catches up with the W3C's recommendations, the <applet> tag is still the safest way to go, however, you should at least be aware of the changing tides.

4. Test the applet in a browser or applet viewer. Because applets run client-side, you don't need a server to do your testing.

5. Last, but not least, it is good form to credit the author of the applet as well as the online resource. The JavaBoutique provides a discreet logo you can place on the page with the applet.

Troubleshooting

Most problems with applets are due to elements not being in the right places. Make sure that your *.class* file is in the directory noted by the **codebase** attribute or within the same directory as the HTML file if no **codebase** is specified. Also be sure that your supporting resource files are in their correct directories and that everything is named correctly (remember that names in Java code are case-sensitive).

Troubles may arise in setting all the parameters correctly, but these problems can not be anticipated and need to be solved on a per-applet basis.

Interactive Buttons with JavaScript

An interactive button, also called a "rollover," changes when the cursor or pointer is positioned over it. By making a button light up (or otherwise call attention to itself), you provide a stronger visual signal that the area is clickable than with a static flat graphic. Rollovers can also be used to pop up a graphic with additional information about the link. Whether it is because rollovers recreate the feel of CD-ROM interfaces or just because they're fun, audiences seem to enjoy the effect.

Rollovers are created by placing a JavaScript in the HTML file with instructions displaying different versions of a graphic based on the position of the mouse. For instance, when the mouse pointer is over graphic "X," the JavaScript runs a function to display the glowing version of the graphic ("glowing X"). JavaScript is discussed further in the next chapter, Chapter 22, *Introduction to JavaScript*.

There are many variations on the JavaScript used for creating simple rollovers. The following were written by Nick Heinle, author of *Designing with JavaScript* (O'Reilly & Associates, Inc., 1997) and creator of WebCoder.com (*www.webcoder. com*), both excellent resources for learning JavaScript.

Simple Rollovers

The first step is to create two versions of each button, one in an "on" state, and one in an "off" state. Make sure that they have exactly the same pixel dimensions or one will be resized and distorted. Note also the naming scheme.

Example 21-1 creates a simple image swap when the cursor is over each button. It works with Netscape Navigator 3.0 and higher and Internet Explorer 3.01 (for Macintosh only) and Internet Explorer 4.0 (all platforms). We'll begin by listing the script in its entirety, then we'll take a look at the individual components.

Example 21-1: Simple JavaScript Rollover Code

```
   <HTML>
   <HEAD><TITLE>Four Rollover Buttons</TITLE>
A  <SCRIPT LANGUAGE = "JavaScript">
B  <!--
C  if (document.images) {

D  img1on = new Image();              // Active images
   img1on.src = "image1on.gif";
   img2on = new Image();
   img2on.src = "image2on.gif";
   img3on = new Image();
   img3on.src = "image3on.gif";
   img4on = new Image();
   img4on.src = "image4on.gif";

E  img1off = new Image();             // Inactive images
   img1off.src = "image1off.gif";
   img2off = new Image();
   img2off.src = "image2off.gif";
   img3off = new Image();
   img3off.src = "image3off.gif";
   img4off = new Image();
   img4off.src = "image4off.gif";
   }

F  function imgOn(imgName) {
           if (document.images) {
                document[imgName].src = eval(imgName + "on.src");
           }
   }

G  function imgOff(imgName) {
           if (document.images) {
                document[imgName].src = eval(imgName + "off.src");
           }
   }

   //-->
```

Example 21-1: Simple JavaScript Rollover Code (continued)

```
</SCRIPT>
</HEAD>

<BODY BGCOLOR="#FFFFFF">
```
H `<A HREF = "page1.html"`
I   `onMouseOver = "imgOn('img1')"`
J   `onMouseOut = "imgOff('img1')">`
```
<IMG NAME = "img1" BORDER=0 HEIGHT=20 WIDTH=125 SRC="image1off.
gif"></A>

<A HREF = "page2.html"
 onMouseOver = "imgOn('img2')"
 onMouseOut = "imgOff('img2')">
<IMG NAME = "img2" BORDER=0 HEIGHT=20 WIDTH=125 SRC="image2off.
gif"></A>

<A HREF = "page3.html"
 onMouseOver = "imgOn('img3')"
 onMouseOut = "imgOff('img3')">
<IMG NAME = "img3" BORDER=0 HEIGHT=20 WIDTH=125 SRC="image3off.
gif"></A>

<A HREF = "page4.html"
 onMouseOver = "imgOn('img4')"
 onMouseOut = "imgOff('img4')">
<IMG NAME = "img4" BORDER=0 HEIGHT=20 WIDTH=125 SRC="image4off.
gif"></A>
</BODY>
</HTML>
```

A This simply starts the script within the <head> portion of the document and defines it for the browser as "JavaScript."

B JavaScript code is placed within the comment tags (<!-- ... //-->) so that browsers that do not recognize JavaScript will keep the code hidden.

C This line detects whether the user's browser supports the **images** object, which is a prerequisite for dynamic images to work. All the functions in this script are contingent on the browser recognizing the **images** object. If it is not recognized, the browser will not display the rollover effect.

D All of the graphics in the "on" state in this section are preloaded into memory and an image object is created for them.

E All of the graphics in the "off" state in this section are preloaded and an image is created for each. To add more buttons, simply follow the naming scheme for adding an "on" and "off" state for each button. The name of the GIF file does not need to be exactly the same as the image object name shown in this example.

F This is the function that activates the button graphic. When the mouse is put over the graphic, the MouseOver event handler passes the image name to this function, which adds the "on" suffix to it. This sources in the "on" state GIF file.

Example 21-1: Simple JavaScript Rollover Code (continued)

G This is the function that returns the graphic to its "off" state. It does this by attaching the "off" suffix, and sourcing in the appropriate graphic.

H This is the HTML for one of the buttons within the <body> of the document. There are actually two things happening here. First, the button is assigned a name within the <img> tag. JavaScript uses this name to refer to this particular graphic slot. The actual JavaScript commands, called event handlers, need to go within the anchor <A> tag.

I This portion says to perform the "imgOn" function when the mouse is over the graphic and it passes the image name to that function.

J This portion says to perform the "imgOff" function when the mouse leaves the area of the graphic.

Multiple Rollovers

You can also have a single MouseOver event change more than one graphic. With this technique, not only does your button light up when you roll the pointer over it, but a graphic containing an explanation of the link appears in a separate image area on the page.

The following example has two buttons (links to the "jukebox" and "videos" sections of a site). When the user mouses over either of the buttons, the Java-Script turns that button "on" and also displays an informational graphic in a third image area that has been named "holder."

The code for multiple rollovers is the same as the single rollover example in Example 21-1, but with a few additions to establish and display the additional graphic (in this case, the information graphic). An explanation of these additions follows Example 21-2.

Example 21-2: JavaScript Code for Multiple Rollovers

```
       <HTML>
       <HEAD>
       <TITLE>Multiple Rollovers</TITLE>
       <SCRIPT LANGUAGE = "JavaScript">
       <!--

       if (document.images) {
               img1on = new Image();
               img1on.src = "jukeboxon.gif";      // Active Images
               img2on = new Image();
               img2on.src = "videoson.gif";

               img1off = new Image();
               img1off.src = "jukeboxoff.gif";    // Inactive Images
               img2off = new Image();
               img2off.src = "videosoff.gif";

A              img1ad = new Image();
```

Example 21-2: JavaScript Code for Multiple Rollovers (continued)

```
                img1ad.src = "jukeboxinfo.gif";        // Information
                                                       // Images
                img2ad = new Image();
                img2ad.src = "videosinfo.gif";
         }

   // Function to 'activate' images.
   function imgOn(imgName) {
          if (document.images) {
                 document[imgName].src = eval(imgName + "on.src");
B                document["holder"].src = eval(imgName + "ad.src");
          }

   }

   // Function to 'deactivate' images.
   function imgOff(imgName) {
          if (document.images) {
                 document[imgName].src = eval(imgName + "off.src");
C                document["holder"].src = "clear.gif";
          }

   }

   // -->
   </SCRIPT>
   </HEAD>
   <BODY BGCOLOR = "#FFFFFF">

   <!-- 1st Rollover  -->
   <A HREF = "jukebox.html"
    onMouseOver = "imgOn('img1')"
    onMouseOut = "imgOff('img1')">
   <IMG NAME= "img1" BORDER = 0 HEIGHT = 24 WIDTH = 100 SRC =
   "jukeboxoff.gif"></A>

   <!-- 2nd Rollover -->
   <A HREF = "videos.html"
    onMouseOver = "imgOn('img2')"
    onMouseOut = "imgOff('img2')">
   <IMG NAME= "img2" BORDER = 0 HEIGHT = 24 WIDTH = 100 SRC =
   "videosoff.gif"></A>

   <!-- Additional Image -->
D  <IMG NAME = "holder" HEIGHT = 100 WIDTH =100 SRC = "clear.gif">
   </BODY>
   </HTML>
```

A This portion preloads the information graphics and creates an image object for each of the "on" and "off" graphics before it.

Example 21-2: JavaScript Code for Multiple Rollovers (continued)

B The function for activating the rollover buttons (turning them to their "on" state) now includes an additional line that changes the image in the "holder" graphic to one of the informational graphics.

C Similarly, the deactivate function in the JavaScript now contains a line that returns the "holder" graphic back to its "off" state (displaying "clear.gif").

D This is the `IMG` tag named `holder` where the information graphics will appear. It contains a graphic called "clear.gif" when neither button is activated.

CHAPTER 22

Introduction to JavaScript

JavaScript is a client-side scripting language that adds interactivity and conditional behavior to web pages. With JavaScript, you can do such things as display additional information about links, create mouse rollover effects, change the contents of pages based on certain conditions, randomly display content on a page, load content in new browser windows and frames, and (with some help from CSS) move elements around the page.

This chapter is derived from material and code by Nick Heinle, author of *Designing with JavaScript*, (O'Reilly & Associates, 1997). For more tutorials on writing JavaScript, see Nick's pages at *webcoder.com*. For a more advanced reference, see *JavaScript: The Definitive Guide*, Third Edition, by David Flanagan (O'Reilly & Associates, 1998). Also note that for simple functionality, you may not need to write your own JavaScript at all; software like Macromedia's Dreamweaver can do your coding for you.

JavaScripts are usually placed directly in the HTML document. They can go either in the head or the body and there can be numerous scripts in a single HTML document. Here's the syntax:

```
<SCRIPT LANGUAGE="JavaScript">
script goes here
</SCRIPT>
```

JavaScript Basics

There are two parts to most JavaScript applications: the functions that tell the browser what to do, and references to these functions. Let's take the example of a simple web page that displays a linked document in a second window:

```
<HTML>
<HEAD>
<SCRIPT LANGUAGE="JavaScript">
<!--
```

```
function openWin(URL) {
aWindow=window.open(URL,"thewindow","toolbar=no,width=350,
height=400,status=no,scrollbars=yes,resize=no,menubar=no");
}
//-->
</SCRIPT>
</HEAD>
<BODY>
<P><A HREF="javascript:openWin('mozart.html');">Mozart</A></P>
<P><A HREF="javascript:openWin('beethoven.html');">Beethoven
</A></P>
<P><A HREF="javascript:openWin('wagner.html');">Wagner</A></P>
</BODY>
</HTML>
```

The JavaScript inside the <script> tags defines a function, called openWin(), that tells the browser what to do when the function is called. Now look at the body of the document. The openWin() function is being called from the anchor tags. Let's take a look at one of those lines:

```
<A HREF="javascript:openWin('mozart.html');">Mozart</A>
```

The line starts off as a normal <a href> tag. But the value of href is not a standard URL; it's a call to a JavaScript function. The word javascript: tells the browser that this will be a JavaScript link. Next, the openWin() function, which was defined up in the head of the document, is called. Since the JavaScript call is in a link, the function will run when the user clicks on the link (the word "Mozart"). The content in parentheses—('mozart.html');—specifies a value that will be passed to the openWin() function. We'll see what passing is all about when we look at the function. The rest of the line is a standard link—the hypertext and the closing anchor tag.

Now let's look at the openWin() function:

```
function openWin(URL) {
aWindow=window.open(URL,"thewindow","toolbar=no,width=350,
height=400,status=no,scrollbars=yes,resize=no,menubar=no");
}
```

The first line of code "declares" a new function with the name openWin(). The set of parentheses indicates that the function can take "arguments" or "parameters." Arguments are conditions that affect the way the function runs. In this example, we are going to pass a URL to the function, which will open a new window with that URL.

After the function declaration comes an opening curly bracket ({). You'll see the closing curly bracket on the last line. Everything in between these curly brackets is the code that will run.

The two lines of code are actually one line that runs longer than the printable area of this page. The line starts by creating a new *variable*. A variable is a container, a place to put things. In this case we're putting the window-opening code into the variable called aWindow. More commonly, variables are used to store information about the current state of the page or the user environment.

The window opening code uses the `window.open` method, which is a standard way of controlling windows, specifying a bunch of information about the window to be opened. There are three parameters for `window.open`: the URL to be displayed in the window, the name of the window, and the characteristics of the window. In this function, we're not specifying a single URL; we're asking to have a URL passed to the function when it is run. That's what's happening when we give the URL *mozart.html* in the anchor tag; we're "passing" that URL to the `openWin()` function.

The text `thewindow` gives the name of the window. The final parameter gives the characteristics of the window: 350×400, with scrollbars, no toolbar, no status bar, no menu bar, and it can't be resized by the user. Note that in the final set of quotes, no spaces or carriage returns are permitted.

Now that we understand all the code here, let's review what happens when the user clicks on the links. When the Mozart link is clicked, the `openWin()` code is run, passing the URL *mozart.html* to the function, which opens a new 350×400 window displaying that URL. When the Beethoven link is clicked, the same function is run, but *beethoven.html* is passed to the function and displayed in the window.

Now that we've covered the basic terms and concepts of JavaScript, let's look at some scripts that will enhance the functionality of your pages.

Sample Scripts

How about some useful scripts to get you started? This section offers several scripts you can copy into your web pages.

Status Line Messages

Probably the simplest JavaScript you can add to your site is a message that appears in the status bar (the bar at the bottom that shows URLs or says "Document: Done"). You can use this bar to display a message when the user places the mouse over a link. To do this simply add a little JavaScript to a standard anchor tag. You don't even need to declare a script. Non-JavaScript-compatible browsers will simply ignore the code. Here's how you do it:

```
<A HREF="mozart.com" onMouseOver="window.status='A study of
Mozart's operas'; return true;">Mozart</A>
```

The above code displays the text "A study of Mozart's operas" when the user puts the cursor over the Mozart link. To use this code on your site, just replace the text between the single quotes (and the URL and hypertext, of course).

Opening a New Window

We detailed the code for opening a new window earlier in the chapter, so we'll just take a quick look here at which code needs to be replaced to use this script on your site. The code again:

```
<HTML>
<HEAD>
```

```
<SCRIPT LANGUAGE="JavaScript">
<!--
function openWin(URL) {
aWindow=window.open(URL,"thewindow","toolbar=no,width=350,
height=400,status=no,scrollbars=yes,resize=no,menubar=no");
}
//-->
</SCRIPT>
</HEAD>
<BODY>
<P><A HREF="javascript:openWin('mozart.html');">Mozart</A></P>
<P><A HREF="javascript:openWin('wagner.html');">Wagner</A></P>
<P><A HREF="javascript:openWin('beethoven.html');">Beethoven</A>
</P>
</BODY>
</HTML>
```

The code in bold indicates the parts you should alter for your site. Give the new window a name, if you wish, by replacing the text "thewindow." Specify the settings for the window by changing the values of toolbar, status, scrollbars, resize, and menubar from no to **yes** (or vice versa). Set the width and height appropriately. Remember not to put any spaces or linebreaks in this code.

Note that you can hardwire the function by replacing the text "URL" with a specific URL, such as *mozart.html*. If you do this, you simply call the function without passing the URL to the function, as follows:

```
<A HREF="javascript:openWin();">Mozart</A></P>
```

Managing Frames

Another popular job for JavaScript is loading content into frames, particularly loading several different frames with one click. Here is the code for a function that changes the contents of both a toolbar frame and a main frame with a single click. This code assumes that the toolbar frame has been named *toolbar* and the main frame has been named *main*.

```
function changePages (toolbarURL, mainURL) {
parent.toolbar.location.href=toolbarURL;
parent.main.location.href=mainURL;
}
```

The actual anchor tag looks like this:

```
<A HREF="javascript:changePages('toolbar_document2.html',
'main_document2.html');"Change Pages</A>
```

If you use the frame names *toolbar* and *main* you can use this code as is—just change the URLs you pass to the function. If you change the frame names to say *left* and *right*, your function would look like this:

```
function changePages (leftURL, rightURL) {
    parent.left.location.href=leftURL;
    parent.right.location.href=rightURL;
}
```

Handling Multiple Browsers

Unlike with CGI scripts, which run on the server and don't require any particular intelligence on the part of the browser, JavaScript code is completely dependent on browser support. If you put a JavaScript on your page, browsers that don't understand JavaScript won't know what to do with it. These browsers will interpret the code as straight text and the result will be rather unpleasant.

Not as unpleasant, however, as if your code isn't completely understood by a JavaScript-aware browser. Unfortunately JavaScript support is not an on-or-off option; Netscape has released several different versions of JavaScript with varying levels of support in each browser. To make matters worse, Microsoft's support for JavaScript has at times lagged behind Netscape's, sometimes outpaced it, and sometimes it's just been different. Fortunately, JavaScript provides ways to hide scripts from non-supporting browsers and to target the browsers that understand specific JavaScript elements.

Hiding JavaScript from Old Browsers

It's quite simple to hide JavaScript from old browsers: simply comment out the script, as shown:

```
<SCRIPT LANGUAGE=JavaScript>
<!--
JavaScript code here
// -->
</SCRIPT>
```

It's important that the comment codes (`<!--` and `//-->`) be on their own lines. If you put the comment code on the same line as some code, that line will be commented out and the script won't work.

Checking for Browsers

If you have a script that you know works in Netscape 4 but doesn't work in any other browser, you may want to check browser versions and serve your script to Netscape 4 users and some straight HTML to other browsers. The first step is to check the browser's name and number and to assign that information to a variable:

```
<HTML>
<HEAD>
<TITLE>A Page</TITLE>
<SCRIPT LANGUAGE = "JavaScript">
<!--

bName = navigator.appName;
bVer = parseInt(navigator.appVersion);

if      (bName == "Netscape" && bVer >= 4) br = "n4";
else if (bName == "Netscape" && bVer == 3) br = "n3";
else if (bName == "Netscape" && bVer == 2) br = "n2";
```

```
else if (bName == "Microsoft Internet Explorer" && bVer >= 4)
br = "e4";
else if (bName == "Microsoft Internet Explorer") br = "e3";
else br = "n2";
```

This code puts the name of the browser in a variable called bName and the version number in a variable called bVer. Depending on the name and number in these variables, the variable br is assigned a value corresponding to the different browsers. Thus, if the browser is Netscape 4, br is set to n4; if the browser is IE 4, br is set to e4. After the browser identity has been assigned to this variable, you use if/else statements to write the code:

```
if br=n4 {
//Netscape 4-specific JavaScript goes here
}

else if br=e4 {
//IE-4 specific code goes here
}
//-->
</SCRIPT>
</HEAD>
```

In this code, the first if statement checks to see if the browser is Netscape 4; if it is, it runs the Netscape-4 specific code. If it's not Netscape 4, the code checks for IE4; if it's IE4, the appropriate code is run. If it's neither of these browsers, no script is run and the body of the HTML document is displayed normally.

```
<BODY>
//Standard HTML code goes here
</BODY>
</HTML>
```

Of course in most JavaScript documents, the script is invoked within the HTML. For instance, an anchor tag may invoke a JavaScript when the mouse is placed over a link:

```
<HTML>
<HEAD>
<TITLE>A Page</TITLE>
<SCRIPT LANGUAGE="JavaScript">
<!-
bName=navigator.appName;
bVer=parseInt(navigator.appVersion);
if ((bName=="Netscape" && bVer>=3) ||
(bName=="Microsoft Internet Explorer" && bVer>=4)) br="n3";
else br="n2";
//-->
</SCRIPT>
</HEAD>
<BODY BGCOLOR="#FFFFFF">
<A HREF="home.html" onMouseOver="document.home.src='home_on.gif';">
<IMG BORDER=0 HEIGHT=35 WIDTH=111 NAME="home" SRC="home_off.gif"></A>
</BODY>
</HTML>
```

This code changes the image from *home_off.gif* to *home_on.gif* when the mouse is placed over the graphic, but Netscape 1.0 and 2.0 and IE 1, 2 and 3 don't understand this code. Fortunately, an `if` statement can be placed right in the anchor tag so the JavaScript will only be used by appropriate browsers. Replace the bold lines in the above code with these lines:

```
<A HREF=home.html onMouseOver="if (br=='n3') document.home.
src='home_on.gif';">
<IMG BORDER=0 HEIGHT=35 WIDTH=111 NAME="home" SRC="home_off.
gif"></A>
```

Here the mouseover effect is conditional on the browser being Netscape 3 or IE 4 or higher.

Browser Compatibility

As noted earlier, varying levels of JavaScript support have been built into browsers since Netscape 2.0. The following table, by Nick Heinle, shows which browsers support which JavaScript objects. For an online version of the table, see *http://webcoder.com/reference/2/index.html*.

JavaScript Features	Nav 2	Nav 3	Nav 4	IE 3	IE 4
Applets	No	Yes	Yes	Yes[1]	Yes[1]
Areas	No	Yes	Yes	No	Yes
Array	No	Yes	Yes	Yes	Yes
CSS	No	No	Yes[2]	No	Yes
Cookie	Yes	Yes	Yes	Yes[3]	Yes
Date	Yes	Yes	Yes	Yes	Yes
Event	No	No	Yes[4]	No	Yes[4]
External scripts	No	Yes	Yes	No[5]	Yes
Forms	Yes[6]	Yes	Yes	Yes[3,6]	Yes
Frames	Yes	Yes	Yes	Yes	Yes
History	Yes	Yes	Yes	Yes[3]	Yes
Images	No	Yes	Yes	No[7]	Yes
JavaEnabled	No	Yes	Yes	No	Yes
Links	Yes	Yes	Yes	Yes	Yes
Location	Yes[8]	Yes	Yes	Yes[3,8]	Yes
Math	Yes	Yes	Yes	Yes	Yes
Navigator	Yes	Yes	Yes	Yes	Yes
MimeTypes	No	Yes	Yes	No	No
Options	No	Yes	Yes	No	No
String	Yes	Yes	Yes	Yes	Yes
Window	Yes[9,10]	Yes[10]	Yes	Yes[3,9,10]	Yes[10]
Write	Yes[3]	Yes[3]	Yes	Yes	Yes

[1] Allows access to ActiveX too, but no Java API calls.
[2] Navigator only allows predisplay control, except with positioning.

3 Implementation is buggy or incomplete: see the bugs table at *http://webcoder.com/reference/2/index.html*.

4 The event model is improved, but it's different in IE and Navigator.

5 External scripts are supported in IE 3.01, but not 3.0.

6 No support for `reset()`.

7 IE3 for the Mac supports the image object.

8 No support for `replace()`.

9 No support for `scroll()`, `focus()`, or `blur()`.

10 No support for `moveTo()`, `moveBy()`, `resizeTo()`, or `resizeBy()`.

PART V

Emerging Technologies

CHAPTER 23

Cascading Style Sheets

For those frustrated with the limited control over document presentation provided by straight HTML markup, Cascading Style Sheets are a welcome advance in web design. Like their counterparts in desktop publishing page-layout programs, style sheets in HTML allow authors to apply typographic styles and spacing instructions for elements on a page. The word *cascading* refers to what happens when several sources of style information vie for control of the elements on a page—style information is passed down from higher-level style sheets (and from parent to child element within a document) until it is overridden by a style command with more weight. (The cascading rules are discussed in detail later in this chapter.)

This comes as good news for both designers who want more control over presentation, and for HTML purists who stand by the principle that style should be separate from content and structure. Style sheets make both these dreams possible.

Advantages

- **Greater typography and page layout controls**. With style sheets, you can specify traditional typography attributes such as font size, line spacing, and letter spacing. It also offers methods for specifying indents, margins, and element positioning. It even uses terminology from traditional and desktop publishing such as points and em spaces.

CSS

- **Style is separate from structure**. HTML is designed for indicating the structure of a document, to which presentation is applied by the end user's browsing device. Over recent years, however, HTML has been extended to provide greater control over presentation (the `<font>` tag being the most infamous example). Style sheets, when done correctly, mark the return to the original intention of HTML by removing presentation instructions from HTML and placing them in a separate, optional area.

- **Potentially smaller documents**. Placing font specifications once at the beginning of the document instead of using a `<font>` description for every individual element can drastically cut down on the number of characters in the document, and thus its file size. As always with the Web, it is desirable to keep file sizes (and download times) as small as possible.

- **Easier site maintenance**. It is possible to link multiple HTML pages to a single style sheet, which means you can make style changes to hundreds or thousands of web pages by editing a single file.

Disadvantages

As of this writing, there is one major drawback to implementing style sheets: *Browser support!* First, style sheet information is not supported in browser versions earlier than Microsoft Internet Explorer 3.0 or Netscape Navigator 4.0. That is not as frustrating as the inconsistency of support among browsers and versions that claim they *do* support CSS.

The World Wide Web Consortium first published its recommendation for style sheets in 1996 and they were first implemented by Internet Explorer 3.0. Since then, as usual, Microsoft and Netscape have chosen diverging paths in the properties their browsers support and the way those properties are presented. And, of course, each browser's support varies, making universal and browser-safe style sheet implementation a near impossibility at this time.

The browser-support charts in Appendix E, *CSS Compatibility*, are evidence of the gap in style sheet implementations. Unfortunately, this means that style sheets cannot be relied upon for crucial display instructions for web sites with a general audience, who are likely to still be using older browser versions.

Strategies for Using Style Sheets Today

The browser-support problem is a major impediment to implementing style sheets on a wide-scale basis, especially for commercial or consumer-oriented sites. However, that does not mean that you should abandon them completely. There are ways to take advantage of style sheets today, or at least prepare for a time when they can be relied upon completely.

- **Include end tags**. While current browsers don't mind if you leave off the `</p>` or `</li>` tag, style sheets (and other advanced web technologies such as XML) do mind. It is necessary to have clearly defined text elements, including both tags. If you think you may be adding style sheet functionality to your site in the future, get ready by closing all your tags today.

- **Use style sheets as "icing."** One way to create a site that degrades well to any browser is to first create a style-sheet-free site that is acceptable on all browser and platform configurations. Once you are happy with it, add style sheet information that will not affect the display in older browsers (such as <div> and <span>, and the class attribute). Choosing properties that are fully supported by the major browsers (see Appendix E) will broaden the chances your design will be seen as you intend it. For a "safe" list of CSS elements, see *http://style.webreview.com/safegrid.html.*

  You can improve the sophistication of the typography and other presentation for those whose browsers support styles, and still keep the site clear and fully functional for all others.

- **Use browser-detection scripts.** Another approach is to develop two style sheets—one that is formatted to work well in Netscape, and another custom-tailored for Internet Explorer. Serve up the appropriate style sheet using a simple browser-detect JavaScript. (For more information on this technique, see "Serving the Right Style Sheet" by Rob Falla on WebReview, *http://webreview.com/wr/pub/98/05/15/coder/index.html.*)

- **Use style sheets for Intranets.** If you have the good fortune to be designing a site for which you know the exact browser/platform configuration for all of your users (such as a corporate Intranet or a self-contained kiosk display), feel free to use the supported style sheets to their limits.

The Future of Style Sheets

Despite a bumpy start, style sheets still hold great promise as the preferred method for specifying page presentation. In 1998, the W3C published its second style sheet proposal (CSS2), which includes additional properties and advanced methods for absolute positioning that could make tables and frames as layout devices a thing of the past. Style sheets are also a key component to programming dynamic effects with DHTML.

Ironically, both Netscape and Microsoft are promising support of CSS2 elements, although they do not yet fully support the CSS1 specification in a bug-free manner. Hopefully, the bugs and inconsistencies will be ironed out and Version 2 and 3 browsers will fade into distant memory, taking style sheets out of the realm of the theoretical into the essential.

How Style Sheets Work

Rule Syntax

Style sheets consist of one or more rules for describing how a page element should be displayed. The following sample contains two rules. The first makes all the H1s in a document red; the second specifies that paragraphs should be set in 12pt. Verdana or some sans-serif font:

```
H1 { color: red }
   P { font-size: 12pt;
       font-face: Verdana, sans-serif;
   }
```

A rule is a declaration of how a page element (whether it is a heading, a block-quote, or a paragraph) should be displayed. Figure 23-1 shows the components of a style sheet rule.

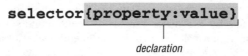

declaration

Figure 23-1: Parts of a style-sheet rule

The two main sections are the *selector* (which identifies the element to be affected) and the *declaration* (the style or display instructions to be applied to that element). In the sample code above, H1 and P are the selectors. The different types of selectors that may be used are discussed in the "Selectors" section of this chapter.

The declaration, enclosed in curly brackets, is made up of a *property* and its *value*. Properties are separated from their values by the colon (:) character followed by a space. A property is a stylistic parameter that can be defined, such as color, font-family, or line-height.

A declaration may contain several property/value pairs. Multiple properties must be separated by semicolons (;).

Values are dependent on the property. Some properties take measurements, some take color names, and others have a predefined list of accepted values. The syntax for measurement and color values are discussed later in this chapter.

Adding Styles to an HTML Document

Rules (and sets of rules) can be applied to HTML documents in three ways: as inline style directions, as a style element embedded at the top of the HTML file, and as an external file that can be either linked to or imported into the document.

Inline styles

Style information can be added to an individual element by adding the `style` attribute within the HTML tag for that element. The value of the style attribute is one or more standard style declarations, as shown here:

```
<H1 STYLE="color: red">This Heading will be Red</H1>

<P STYLE="font-size: 12pt; font-face: Verdana, sans-serif">
This is the content of the paragraph to be set with the
described styles.</P>
```

Although a perfectly valid use of style information, inline styles are equivalent to the <font> tag in that they "pollute" the document with presentation information. Style information is still tied to each individual content element and any changes would need to be made in every tag, in every file, rather than globally. Inline styles are best used to occasionally override higher-level rules.

Embedded style sheet

A more compact method for adding style sheets is to embed a style block in the top of the HTML document using the `<style>` element. The following example shows our sample rules embedded in a simple HTML document:

```
<HTML>
<HEAD>
<STYLE TYPE="text/css">
<!--
    H1 { color: red}
    P { font-size: 12pt;
        font-face: Verdana, sans-serif;
        }
-->
</STYLE>
<TITLE>Style Sheets</TITLE>
</HEAD>
...
</HTML>
```

The `<style>` element must be placed within the `<head>` tags in the document. In addition, it is usually necessary to place HTML comment tags (`<!--` and `-->`) around the `<style>` contents. This hides the style information from browsers that don't understand the `<style>` tag (otherwise, they could display the rules as text in the browser window).

Currently, cascading style sheets are the only style sheet language, but the W3C has prepared for the possibility of additional languages to be added in the future by providing the `type` attribute within the `<style>` element. The only viable style type as of this writing is `text/css`. If the `type` attribute is omitted, some browsers may ignore the entire style sheet.

External style sheet

The most powerful way to use styles is to collect them all in a separate text document and create links to that document from all the HTML pages in a site. In this way, you can make stylistic changes consistently across a whole site by editing the style information in a single document. This is a powerful tool for large-scale sites.

There are two ways to refer to external style sheets (which must be named with the *.css* suffix) from within an HTML document.

Linking. The most standard and best-supported method is to create a link to that document using the `<link>` tag in the `<head>` of the document as shown here:

```
<HEAD>
<LINK REL="STYLESHEET" HREF="/pathname/stylesheet.css"
TYPE="text/css">
</HEAD>
```

The `rel` attribute defines the linked document's relation to the current document—a "stylesheet." The `href` attribute provides the URL to the file containing the style sheet information.

The style sheet document is a simple text document that contains a collection of style sheet rules. It may not contain HTML tags, particularly the structural tags that set up an HTML document (<html>, <head>, and <body>).

Importing. An alternative to linking is to import external style sheets into the <style> element using the @import function as shown:

```
<STYLE>
    @import url(http://pathname/stylesheet.css);
</STYLE>
```

@import commands must come *before* any style rules.

The advantage to importing is that multiple style sheets can be applied to the same document (only one stylesheet can be "linked" to a document). When additional @import functions are added within the <style> element, the style information from the last file read (the one at the bottom of the list) will take precedence over the previous ones. The major drawback to @import is limited browser support (it is currently only supported by Internet Explorer 4.0).

Inheritance

An important feature of style sheets is the concept of inheritance, in which style properties are passed down from an element (the parent) to any element contained within it (the child). An element is said to *inherit* properties applied to elements higher in the HTML hierarchy.

For instance, any style applied to a list will be inherited by every list item (<li>) within that list. If you specify that all the text in the <body> of a document should be red, all text elements contained in the body of the document will be red (unless specified otherwise).

Styles applied to specific elements will override settings higher in the hierarchy. With planning, inheritance can be used to make style specification more efficient. For example, if you'd like all the text on the page to be blue except for list items, you can set the color property at the <body> level to apply to the whole document and then use another rule to make <li>s another color. The more specific rules override more general rules.

If two rules of equal weight are listed in a style sheet, whichever one is later in the style sheet will apply.

Conflicting Style Sheets: The Cascade

Style sheets are said to be cascading because more than one type of style sheet (inline, embedded, or external) can simultaneously affect the presentation of a single document. For example, it is possible to add inline styles to a document that is already linked to an external style sheet.

With several styles applied to a document, conflicts are certain to arise. For example, when an inline style says the paragraph should be maroon, but the external style sheet says all paragraphs are blue, which style gets used?

The W3C anticipated this situation and devised a hierarchical system that assigns different weights to each type of style information. This cascade order provides a set of rules for resolving conflicts between different style sheets. Styles with more weight (those defined at the more specific level) will take precedence over styles set in a higher-level style sheet.

As in inheritance, more specific rules override more general rules. This allows you to design a general style for a whole site, then modify it for particular pages or elements, alleviating redundancy.

The following list shows the hierarchy of style instructions from general to specific, such that elements lower in the list have more weight and will override styles above them.

- Browser default settings

- User style settings (set in browser)

- Linked external style sheet

- Imported style sheets; when multiple styles are imported, the commands from the last file read will take precedence over the first ones listed

- Embedded style sheets (rules within the `<style>` element); later rules have greater weight than earlier rules

- Inline style information

- HTML tag attributes, which override all style information defined anywhere

Selectors

Selectors are the parts of the rule that identify the element (or elements) to which the style will be applied. There are several methods for identifying elements.

Type Selector

The simplest type of selector calls an HTML element by its tag, as shown:

```
H1 { color: blue }
H2 { color: blue }
P { color: blue }
```

Type selectors can be grouped into comma-separated lists so a single property will apply to all of them. The following code has the same effect as the previous code:

```
H1, H2, P { color: blue }
```

<div> and <span>

Two HTML elements, div and span, were especially created for use with style sheets. They have no inherent properties of their own, but can be used to designate elements on a web page that should be affected by style sheet instructions. They will be ignored by browsers that do not understand them.

The `<div>` tag is used to delimit block-level tags and can contain other HTML elements within it.

```
<DIV STYLE="color: blue">
<H1>Headline!</H1>
```

```
<P>This is a whole paragraph of text.</P>
</DIV>
```

The `<span>` tag is used inline to change the style of a set of characters:

```
<P>This is a paragraph and <SPAN STYLE="color: blue">this area
will be treated differently</SPAN> from the rest of the
paragraph</P>
```

When used with the CLASS and ID attribute selectors (discussed later in this chapter), these tags can be used to create custom-named elements, sort of like creating your own HTML tags.

Deleted and inserted text

Deleted text (`<del>`) and inserted text (`<ins>`) are two new logical elements introduced by the HTML 4.0 Specification. They have no inherent style information and rely on style sheets (not the browser) for text display instructions. They are used when it is important to track edits to a document, such as in legal contracts.

For instance, deleted text might be hidden from view or displayed in strike-through text. Inserted text might be displayed in bold or in a different color from the original document.

```
DEL { text-decoration: line-through }
INS { color: red }
```

Contextual Selectors

You can also specify style attributes for HTML elements based on the context in which they appear.

As we've seen already, a simple selector specifies that all emphasized text within a document should be red.

```
EM { color: red }
```

Using a contextual selector (written as a list of simple selectors separated by white space) you can specify that only the emphasized text that appears within a list item will be green:

```
LI EM { color: green }
```

In other words, this affects emphasized text when it appears *in the context of* a list item element. If both of these rules for emphasized text were to appear in the same document, the contextual selector (because it is more specific) would take precedence over the simple selector.

Several contextual selectors can be grouped together in comma-separated lists. The following code makes bold (`<B>`) text red when it appears in the context of a heading:

```
H1 B, H2 B, H3 B { color: red }
```

CLASS and ID Attribute Selectors

Attribute selectors allow web page authors to apply style rules based on special identifying attributes placed within HTML element tags. There are currently two available attribute selectors: CLASS and ID.

CLASS selector

You can classify elements by adding a CLASS attribute to the HTML element tag. Elements in a class can then be modified with a single style rule. For instance, you can identify all the items in the HTML document that you classify as "important":

```
<H1 CLASS="important">Attention!</H1>
<P CLASS="important">Your account is past due.</P>
```

To specify the styles for elements of a particular class, add the class name to the HTML selector, separated by a period (.). Note: CLASS names cannot contain spaces; use hyphens or underscores instead if necessary.

```
H1.important { color: red }
P.important { color: red }
```

To apply a property to all the elements of the same class, omit the tag name in the selector (be sure to leave the period—it is the character that indicates a class):

```
.important { color: red }
```

ID selector

The ID attribute is used similarly to CLASS, however, it is used for targeting specific elements rather than classifying them. If you have several elements that need treatment, use CLASS. If you have a specific element that must be uniquely treated, you can give it an ID:

```
<P ID="061998">New item added today</P>
```

ID selectors are indicated by the hash (#) symbol within the style sheet as follows:

```
P#061998 { color: red }
```

Omit the HTML tag name to apply properties to all elements with a given ID:

```
#061998 { color: red }
```

Pseudo-Selectors

The CSS1 Specification provides several pseudo-elements and pseudo-classes that are not based on structural elements of a document. They can be used as selectors, but the code does not appear in the HTML source, rather, they are interpreted by the browser based on context and function. Pseudo-selectors are indicated by the colon (:) character. Unfortunately, as of this writing, 4.0-version browsers do not support pseudo-selectors.

Pseudo-elements

In CSS1, the pseudo-elements (sub-parts of existing elements) are first-line and first-letter. They can be used to apply styles to the first line or letter of an HTML element as it is displayed in the browser window. The following code adds extra letter spacing in the first line of text for every paragraph:

```
P:first-line { letter-spacing: 6pt }
```

Pseudo-elements can be combined with class information, so you can apply first-line or -letter effects to only a certain class of element. The following sample makes the first letter of any paragraph classified as "opener" big and red:

```
P.opener:first-letter { font-size: 300%; color: red }
```

Pseudo-classes

CSS1 provides pseudo-classes, which can be applied to the anchor (<a>) tag: `link`, `visited`, and `active` (referring to the various link states as interpreted by the browser). These do not apply to named anchors, only those containing the HREF attribute.

```
A:link { color: red }
A:visited { color: blue }
A:active { color: maroon }
```

This style information provides the same functionality as specifying link colors in the <body> of a document, however, it has the advantages that style sheets provide. Netscape's support for pseudo-classes is pretty buggy.

Specifying Values

It is important to use the proper syntax for specifying length and color values in style sheet rules.

Length Units

Table 23-1 lists units of measurements that can be specified in style sheet values.

Table 23-1: Units of Measurements for Style Sheet Values

Code	Unit	Description
px	Pixel	Pixel units are relative to the monitor resolution.
pt	Point	A traditional publishing unit of measurement for type. There are approximately 72 points in an inch.
pc	Pica	A traditional publishing unit of measurement equal to 12 points (or 1/6 of an inch).
em	Em	A relative unit of measurement that traditionally equals the width of the capital letter M in the current font. In practical terms, it is equal to the point size of the font (e.g., an em space in 24pt type is 24 points long).
ex	Ex	A relative unit of measurement which is the height of the letter "x" for that font (approximately half the length of an Em).
in	Inches	Standard unit of measurement in the U.S.
mm	Millimeters	Metric measurement.
cm	Centimeters	Metric measurement.

Some values can be specified as percentages that are relative to the font size or bounding box of the element. The following example makes the line height 120% of the element's font size:

```
P { line-height: 120% }
```

Specifying Color

As in HTML tags, there are two methods for specifying color in style sheets: by name and by numerical values.

By name

You can specify color values by name as follows:

```
H1 { color: olive }
```

The CSS1 Specification specifically lists only 16 color names that can be used in style sheets; they are:

aqua	gray	navy	silver
black	green	olive	teal
blue	lime	purple	white
fuchsia	maroon	red	yellow

Other names from the complete list of color names may be supported by some browsers. For the complete list, see "Specifying Color in HTML" in Chapter 5, *HTML Overview*).

By RGB values

Within style sheets, RGB colors can be specified in any of the following methods:

```
H1 { color: #0000FF }
H1 { color: #00F }
H1 { color: rgb(0,0,255) }
H1 { color: rgb(0%, 0%, 100%) }
```

The first method uses three two-digit hexadecimal RGB values (for a complete explanation, see "Specifying Color in HTML" in Chapter 5). The second method uses a three-digit syntax, which is essentially converted to the six-digit form by replicating each digit (therefore, 00F is the same as 0000FF).

The last two methods use a functional notation specifying RGB values as a comma-separated list of regular values (from 0 to 255) or percentage values (from 0 to 100%). Note that percentage values can use decimals, e.g., `rgb(0%, 50.5%, 33.3%)`.

Properties

The real meat of style sheets lies in the collection of properties that can be applied to selected elements. The properties reviewed in this chapter reflect those provided in the CSS Level 1 specification (CSS1). The CSS Level 2 specification, released in May 1998, contains many additional properties and additional values for existing properties (see "What's New in CSS2" later in this chapter). However, because current browsers are still struggling with bug-free and consistent support of CSS1, these properties should be enough to give you a good start in working with style sheets.

First, a disclaimer—the explanations provided here describe how each property ought to work according to the specification. Most of these will work differently on different browsers and many are not supported at all. For a listing of which browsers support which properties, see the charts in Appendix E.

Type-Related Properties

Style sheets offer controls for type presentation similar to those found in desktop publishing. The following group of properties affects the way type is displayed, both in terms of font and text spacing.

font-family

Values:

family name, generic family name

Example:

P { font-family: "Trebuchet MS", Verdana, sans-serif }

Applies to:

All elements

Inherited:

Yes

You can specify any font (or list of fonts, separated by commas) in the font-family property. Bear in mind, however, that the font needs to be present on the user's machine in order to display, so it is safest to stick with common fonts.

You may (and it is advisable) include a generic font family as the last option in your list so that if the specific fonts are not found, a font that matches the general style of your choices will be substituted. The five possible values are:

- serif (e.g., Times)
- sans-serif (e.g., Helvetica or Arial)
- monospaced (e.g., Courier or New Courier)
- cursive (e.g., Zapf-Chancery)
- fantasy (e.g., Western, Impact, or some display-oriented font)

Note that in the example, the first font is enclosed in quotes. Font names that contain character spaces must be enclosed in quotation marks (single or double). Generic family names must never be enclosed in quotation marks.

font-style

Values:

normal|italic|oblique

Example:

H1 { font-style: italic }

Applies to:

All elements

Inherited:

Yes

The font-style property selects between normal (the default) and italic or oblique faces within a font family. Oblique type is just a slanted version of the normal face. Italic is usually a separate face design with more curved characters. Note that bold is part of font-weight, not font-style in style sheet syntax.

font-variant

Values:

normal|small-caps

Example:

P:first-line { font-variant: small-caps }

Applies to:

All elements

Inherited:

Yes

Use the font-variant property to specify that an element display in small caps. If a true small caps font face is not available, the browser may simulate true small caps by displaying all caps at a reduced size. More values may be supported for this property in future style sheet versions.

font-weight

Values:

normal|bold|bolder|lighter|100|200|300|400|500|600|700|800|900

Example:

STRONG { font-weight: 700 }

Applies to:

All elements

Inherited:

Yes

The font-weight property specifies the weight, or boldness, of the type. It can be specified either as a descriptive term (normal, bold, bolder, lighter) or as one of the nine numeric values listed above. The default font weight is normal, which corresponds to 400 on the numeric scale. Typical bold text corresponds to 700 on the numeric scale. There may not be a font face within a family that corresponds to each of the nine levels of boldness (some may come in only normal and bold weights).

Unfortunately, the current browsers are inconsistent in support of the font-weight property.

font-size

Values:
> absolute size|relative size|length|percentage

Applies to:
> All elements

Inherited:
> Yes

As the name suggests, the font-size property specifies the size of the text element. There are four methods for specifying font size:

Absolute sizes
> Values: xx-small|x-small|small|medium|large|x-large|xx-large

Example: H1 { font-size: x-large }

Absolute sizes are descriptive terms that reference a table of sizes kept by the browser.

Relative sizes
> Values: larger|smaller

Example: H1 { font-size: larger }

These values specify the size of the type relative to the parent object.

Length sizes
> Values: *number* + em|ex|px|pt|pc|mm|cm|in

Example: H1 { font-size: 24pt }

You can also specify font size using any of the length values described in the "Length Units" section earlier in this chapter.

Percentage sizes
> Values: *n*%

Example: H1 { font-size: 125% }

This specifies font size as a percentage of the inherited size. For instance, in this example the H1 will be 125% larger than the size of regular body text.

font

Values:

> *font-style| font-variant| font-weight| font-size|*
> *line-height| font-family*

Examples:

> EM { font: 12pt Times, serif }
>
> H1 { font: oblique bolder 18pt Helvetica, sans-serif }

Applies to:

> All elements

Inherited:

> Yes

The font property is a shorthand property for specifying all the available font controls in a single rule. Values should be separated by character spaces. The font property must contain a size attribute before the font name. In this property, the order of the enclosed values is important (although not every value needs to be present) and must be listed as follows:

> { font: weight style variant size/line-height font-name(s) }

color

Values:

> *color name| RGB color value*

Examples:

> BLOCKQUOTE { color: navy }
>
> H1 { color: #666633 }

Applies to:

> Block-level elements

Inherited:

> Yes

This property is used to describe the text (a.k.a. "foreground") color of an element. For an explanation of specifying color values, see the "Color Values" section earlier in this chapter.

line-height

Values:

> normal | number | length | percentage

Example:

> P { line-height: 1.2 }
>
> P { line-height: 1.2em }
>
> P { line-height: 120% }

Applies to:

All elements

Inherited:

Yes

The `line-height` property sets the distance between the baselines of adjacent lines of text. In traditional publishing, this measurement is called "leading" and can be used to create different effects by adding white space to the block of text.

The default value is `normal`, which corresponds to 100–120% depending on the browser's interpretation of the tag. When a number is specified alone, that number will be multiplied by the current font size to calculate the `line-height` value. Line-heights can also be specified using any of the length units described earlier. Percentage values relative to the current (inherited) font size may also be used.

These examples demonstrate three alternative methods for the same amount of line spacing. For example, if the point size is 12 pt, the resulting line-height for each of the examples listed would be 14.4 pts.

word-spacing

Values:

`normal|length`

Example:

`H3 { word-spacing: .5em }`

Applies to:

All elements

Inherited:

Yes

This property specifies an additional amount of space to be placed between words of the text element. Note that when specifying relative lengths (such as em, which is based on font size), the *calculated* size will be passed down to child elements, even if they have a smaller font size than the parent.

letter-spacing

Values:

`normal|length`

Example:

`P.opener:firstline { letter-spacing: 2pt }`

Applies to:

All elements

Inherited:

Yes

This property specifies an amount of space to be added between characters. Note that when specifying relative lengths (such as em, which is based on font size), the *calculated* size will be passed down to child elements, even if they have a smaller font size than the parent.

text-decoration

Values:

    none|underline|overline|line-through|blink

Example:

    A: link, A:visited, A:active { text-decoration: underline }

Applies to:

All elements

Inherited:

No, but browsers should display elements as matching their parents

This applies a "decoration" to text such as underlines, overlines (a line over the text), strike-throughs, and the ever-beloved blinking effect.

vertical-align

Values:

    baseline|bottom|middle|sub|super|text-bottom|text-top|
    top|percentage

Example:

    IMG.capletter { vertical-align: text-top }

The vertical-align property, as it sounds, affects the vertical alignment of an element. The possible values are as follows:

baseline

Aligns the baseline (or bottom) with the baseline of the parent element (this is the default)

bottom

Aligns the bottom of the element with the lowest element on the line

middle

Aligns the "vertical midpoint of the element (typically an image) with the baseline plus half the x-height of the parent" (in the words of the CSS1 Specification)

sub

Makes the element a subscript

super

Makes the element a superscript

text-bottom

Aligns the bottom of the element with the bottom of the parent element's font (its descenders)

text-top
:   Aligns the top of the element with the top of the parent element's font (its ascenders)

top
:   Aligns the top of the element with the tallest element on the line

Percentage values refer to the value of the line-height property of the element.

text-transform

Values:
:   none|capitalize|lowercase|uppercase

Example:
:   H1.title { text-transform: capitalize }

Applies to:
:   All elements

Inherited:
:   Yes

This property affects the capitalization of the element. The possible values are as follows:

none
:   Displays the element as it is typed in the HTML source and neutralizes any inherited value

capitalize
:   Displays the first letter of every word in uppercase characters

lowercase
:   Displays the whole element in lowercase characters

uppercase
:   Displays the whole element in uppercase characters

text-align

Values:
:   center|justify|left|right

Example:
:   DIV.center { text-align: center }

Applies to:
:   Block-level elements

Inherited:
:   Yes

This affects the horizontal alignment of the contained text elements. The possible values are center, left, right, and justify (aligns both the left and right margins).

text-indent

Values:

> length|percentage

Example:

> P.first { text-indent: 3em }

Applies to:

> Block-level elements

Inherited:

> Yes

This property specifies an amount of indentation (from the left margin) to appear in the first line of text in an element. The value of text-indent may be negative to create hanging-indent effects, although this feature is poorly supported. Values can be specified in any available unit of length or as a percentage of the line length.

Box Properties

Style sheets treat each element on a page as though it were contained within a box (imagine four lines drawn against the edges of this paragraph). More accurately, each element is in a series of containing boxes (see Figure 23-2), beginning with the content itself, surrounded by padding, then the border, which is surrounded by the margin.

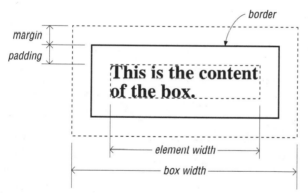

Figure 23-2: The box formatting model for page elements.

The content itself is the element width. A background applied to an element will extend into the padding, but not beyond the border. The box width extends to the outside edges of the margin. The boundary of the margin is not visible but is a calculated amount.

The CSS1 provides many properties for controlling the presentation of an element's box, including setting the amount of padding and margin, the appearance of the borders, and the background color (discussed in the next section). The box model is also the basis for absolute positioning (discussed later in this chapter), so it is important to get a feel for how they work. For more information on how box elements are formatted and interact with each other, see Section 4, "Formatting Model" in the CSS specification online at *http://www.w3.org/TR/REC-CSS1*.

margin-top, margin-right, margin-bottom, margin-left

Values:

   length|percentage|auto

Example:

   IMG { margin-top: 0px }

   IMG { margin-right: 12px }

   IMG { margin-bottom: 0px }

   IMG { margin-left: 12px }

Applies to:

   All elements

Inherited:

   No

These properties specify the amount of margin on specific sides of the element (as called by name). Values can be specified in length units, as a percentage based on the size of the element's overall box width, or as auto, which automatically fills in a margin amount based on other elements on the page.

margin

Values:

   length|percentage|auto

Example:

   IMG { margin: 20px }

   IMG { margin: 0px 12px 0px 12px }

   IMG { margin: 0px 12px }

Applies to:

   All elements

Inherited:

   No

This is a shorthand property for specifying all the margins of an element. Values can be entered as length units, as a percentage based on the size of the element's overall box width, or as auto, which automatically fills in a margin amount based on other elements on the page.

If a single value is given, as in the first example, that value will apply to the margins on all four sides of the box.

You can combine values for each of the four sides in a list, as shown in the second example. It is important to note that the values always follow a clockwise order, as follows:

```
{ margin: top right bottom left }
```

(Note that the second example duplicates the four separate rules illustrated for the margin-top, etc. properties.)

When you specify three values, the second value will apply to both the right and left margins:

```
{ margin: top right/left bottom }
```

Two values, as shown in the third example, are interpreted as follows:

```
{ margin: top/bottom right/left }
```

(Note that the third example has the same effect as the second example.)

If the browser doesn't find a value for the left margin, it just duplicates the value for the right; if the bottom margin value is missing, it duplicates the value for the top.

padding-top, padding-right, padding-bottom, padding-left

Values:
> length|percentage

Example:
> P.sidebar { padding-top: 1em }

Applies to:
> All elements

Inherited:
> No

These properties specify an amount of padding to be added around the respective sides of an element's contents (as called by name). Values are the same as explained for the margin property.

padding

Values:
> length|percentage

Example:
> P.sidebar { padding: 1em }

Applies to:
> All elements

Inherited:
> No

This is a shorthand property for specifying the padding for all sides of an element. A single value will apply the same amount of padding on all sides of the content. More than one value will be interpreted the same as described for the `margin` property (top, right, bottom, left).

border-top-width, border-right-width, border-bottom-width, border-left-width

Values:

thin|medium|thick|*length*

Example:

P.sidebar { border-right-width: medium; border-bottom-width: thick }

Applies to:

All elements

Inherited:

No

These properties specify the border widths of the respective sides of an element's box. The keywords thin, medium, and thick will be interpreted by the browser and are consistent throughout the document (i.e., they are not affected by the font size of the element). You can also specify a length unit.

border-width

Values:

thin|medium|thick|*length*

Example:

P.warning { border-width: thin }

Applies to:

All elements

Inherited:

No

This is a shorthand property for specifying the width of the border for all four sides of the element box. A single value will set the same border width for all four sides of the box. More than one value will be interpreted as described for the `margin` property (top, right, bottom, left).

border-color

Values:

color name| RGB value

Example:

BLOCKQUOTE{ border-color: red blue lime yellow }

Applies to:

All elements

No

This property sets the border color for each of the four sides of an element box. A single value will apply to all four borders of the box. More than one value will be applied as described for the `margin` property (top, right, bottom, left).

border-style

Values:

none|dotted|dashed|solid|double|groove|ridge|inset|outset

Example:

P.example{ border-style: solid dashed }

Applies to:

All elements

Inherited:

Yes

This property sets the style of border for an element box. The different styles are illustrated in Figure 23-3. A single value will result in a box with the same style border on all four sides. More than one value will be interpreted as described for the `margin` property (top, right, bottom, left). The following example would create a box with a solid line on the top and bottom and with dashed rules on the left and right sides.

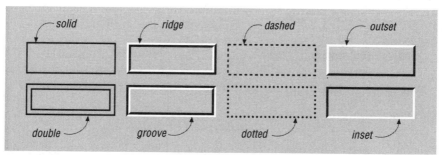

Figure 23-3: Potential border styles

border-top, border-right, border-bottom, border-left

Values:

border-top-width|border-style|border-color

Example:

H1: { border-left: .5em solidblue }

Applies to:

All elements

No

Each of these properties is a shorthand property for setting the width, style, and color of a specific side of a box (as named). The example given would create a solid blue border .5 em thick on the left side of the H1 element only.

border

Values:

```
border-width|border-style|border-color
```

Example:

```
P.example { border: 2px dotted #666633 }
```

Applies to:

All elements

Inherited:

No

This is a shorthand property for setting the border width, style, and color for all four sides of an element box. The values specified in **border** will always apply to all four sides of the box (unlike other shorthand border properties described earlier, which can accept values for separate sides).

width

Values:

```
length|percentage|auto
```

Example:

```
IMG.photo { width: 75% }
```

Applies to:

Block-level elements and replaced elements (such as graphics)

Inherited:

Yes

This property sets the width of the element. It can be applied to text elements or as a way to resize images.

height

Values:

```
length|percentage|auto
```

Example:

```
IMG.photo { height: 75% }
```

Applies to:

Block-level elements

Yes

This property sets the height of the element. The height property can be applied to text elements or as a way to resize images.

float

Values:

left|right|none

Example:

P.sidebar { float: right }

Applies to:

All elements

Inherited:

No

The float property works much like the align attribute for images—it positions an element against the left or right border and allows text to flow around it. Support for the float property is sketchy as of this writing, but it could prove to be useful in the future for creating drop caps and similar effects.

clear

Values:

none|left|right|both

Example:

H1, H2, H3 { clear: left }

Applies to:

Block-level elements

Inherited:

Yes

This property specifies whether to allow floating elements on an image's sides (more accurately, the sides along which floating items are *not* accepted). None means elements are allowed (but not required) on both sides.

Background Properties

Background properties are applied to the "canvas" behind an element. Ideally, background color appears behind the content and its padding, stopping at the border (although work-arounds may be necessary for this effect; see "Style Sheet Tips" later in this chapter). Background properties are not inherited, but since the default value is transparent, the parent's background color or pattern will show through for its child elements.

background-color

Values:

color name or RGB value|transparent

Example:

P.warning { background-color: red }

Applies to:

All elements

Inherited:

No

Sets the background color of the element (creating a colored rectangle). The default is transparent.

background-image

Values:

URL|none

Example:

BODY { background-image: url(stripes.gif) }

Applies to:

All elements

Inherited:

No

Sets a background image for the element. If a background color is also specified, the image will be overlaid on top of the color.

background-repeat

Values:

repeat|repeat-x|repeat-y|no-repeat

Example:

BODY { background-image: url(oldmap.gif); background-repeat: no-repeat }

Applies to:

All elements

Inherited:

No

When a background image is specified, this property specifies whether and how the image is repeated.

repeat
    Allows the image to repeat both horizontally and vertically

`repeat-x`
> Allows the image to repeat only horizontally

`repeat-y`
> Allows the image to repeat only vertically

`no-repeat`
> Displays the image only once (does not repeat)

background-attachment

Values:
> `scroll|fixed`

Example:
> `BODY { background-image: url(oldmap.gif); background-attachment: scroll }`

Applies to:
> All elements

Inherited:
> No

This determines whether the background image scrolls along with the document (the default) or remains in a fixed position.

background-position

Values:
> `percentage|length|top/center/bottom|left/center/right`

Example:
> `BODY { background-image: url (oldmap.gif); background-position: bottom left }`
>
> `BODY { background-image: url (oldmap.gif); background-position: 100% 0% }`

Applies to:
> Block-level elements and replaced elements

Inherited:
> No

When a background image has been specified, this property specifies its initial position relative to the box that surrounds the content of the element (not including its padding, border, or margin).

The CSS methods for specifying position get a bit complicated. Values are given in horizontal/vertical pairs, with a default value of 0%/0%, which places the upper-left corner of the image in the upper-left corner of the element. A value of 100%/100% would place the image in the bottom-right corner of the element.

Length values from the left and top margin can also be specified. Or you can use the keywords, which correspond to the percentage values 0%, 50%, and 100%, respectively. The two examples given create the same result, with the bottom-left corner of the image placed in the bottom-left corner of the element.

background

Values:

background-color|background-image|background-repeat|background-attachment|background-position

Example:

BODY { background: silver url(nightsky.gif) no-repeat fixed }

BODY { background: url(oldmap.gif) bottom left }

Applies to:

Block-level elements

Inherited:

Yes

This is a shorthand property for specifying all the individual background properties in a single declaration.

Classification Properties

These properties classify elements into categories rather than setting specific visual parameters.

display

Values:

block|inline|list-item|none

Example:

P { display: block }

IMG { display: none } *(turns off all images)*

Applies to:

All elements

Inherited:

No

This property defines how and if an element is displayed. A value of **none** turns off the display and closes up the space the element would otherwise occupy. block opens a new box that is positioned relative to adjacent boxes. list-item is similar to block except that a list-item marker is added. inline results in a new inline box on the same line as the previous content.

white-space

Values:

normal|pre|nowrap

Example:

P.haiku { white-space: pre }

Applies to:

Block-level elements

Inherited:

Yes

This property defines how white space in the source for the element is handled. The normal value treats text normally, with consecutive spaces collapsing to one. The pre value displays multiple characters, like the <pre> tag in HTML, except the element is not displayed in a monospace font. nowrap prevents the text element from wrapping unless designated by a <br> tag.

list-style-type

Values:

disc|circle|square|decimal|lower-roman|upper-roman|
lower-alpha|upper-alpha|none

Example:

OL { list-style-type: decimal } *(1, 2, 3, 4, etc.)*

OL { list-style-type: upper-roman } *(A., B., C., D., etc.)*

Applies to:

Elements with the display property set to list-item

Inherited:

Yes

This attribute specifies the appearance of the automatic numbering or bulleting of lists. Values are the same as for the type attribute within a list item (<li>). These numbers/bullets will be displayed when no list-item image is specified or if the image cannot be found.

list-style-image

Values:

URL|none

Example:

UL { list-style-image: url(3dball.gif) }

Applies to:

Elements with the display property set to list-item

Inherited:

Yes

This property specifies a graphic to be used as a list-item marker (bullet).

list-style-position

Values:
>   inside|outside

Example:
>   OL { list-style-position: outside }

Applies to:
> Elements with "display" property set to "list-item"

Inherited:
> Yes

This property specifies whether list items should be set with a hanging indent. The `inside` value makes subsequent lines of a list item wrap all the way to the left margin of the list item (under the list item marker). The `outside` value starts subsequent lines under the first word of the list item, creating a hanging indent.

list-style

Values:
>   *list-style-type*|*list-style-image*|*list-style-position*

Example:
>   UL { list-style: list-item url(3dball.gif) disc inside }
>   UL UL { list-style: circle outside }

Applies to:
> Elements with `display` property set to `list-item`

Inherited:
> Yes

This is a shorthand property for setting the `list-style` type, image, and position (inside, outside) in one declaration.

Positioning with Style Sheets

In August of 1997, the W3C published its working draft of specifications for style sheet properties for positioning HTML elements on the page and in three-dimensional space. This greater control over object placement can be used for more tightly designed static page layout as well as for creating and tracking motion effects with DHTML.

This effort was initiated by Netscape and Microsoft, who began supporting some positioning properties in their 4.0 version browsers. The positioning concepts and properties were picked up and developed further in the CSS, Level 2 specification, which was released in May of 1998.

Style sheet positioning is a rich and complex topic that is beyond the scope of this chapter, however, this section aims to introduce some basic positioning concepts.

For complete positioning information, see the W3C's CSS2 specification online at *http://www.w3.org/TR/REC-CSS2*. A good overview is provided by Eric Meyer in his article, "Playing for Position," in WebReview magazine (*http://webreview.com/wr/pub/98/02/06/feature/index3.html*).

The position Property

The position property has three possible values: absolute, relative, and static.

It works in conjunction with the top and left properties (used for specifying distances from the top and left starting point), and with the width and height properties (for specifying the width and height of the element including its padding and border). Values for these properties can be specified as either length units or percentages.

Relative positioning

Relative positioning places the element relative to its initial position in the flow. Once the element is moved, the space it previously occupied is held blank. The resulting position may cause the element to overlap other elements on the page.

Measurements are relative to the top-left point of the element box. Adding a positive top value moves the element down the specified amount from its initial top position. Adding a positive value for the left property moves the element that amount to the right. You can also specify negative values to move an element up and to the left. In Figure 23-4 and the following code, the emphasized text is moved 20 pixels down and 12 pixels to the right of its initial position.

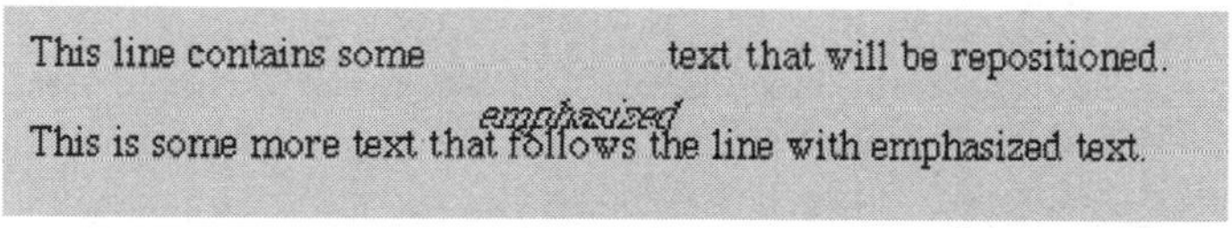

Figure 23-4: Word moved down and to right with relative positioning

```
<HEAD>
<STYLE TYPE="text/css">
<!--
EM { position: relative; top: 20px; left: 12px; }
-->
</STYLE>
</HEAD>

<BODY>
<P>This line contains some <EM>emphasized</EM> text that will
be repositioned.</P>
<P>This is some more text that follows the line with emphasized
text.</P>
</BODY>
```

Absolute positioning

Absolute positioning places the element in an arbitrary position, but technically, it is still relative to the containing block of another element or to the document coordinates (it will scroll when the document scrolls). Measurements in absolute positioning are relative to the top-left corner of the document itself (or the containing block of another element). Again, negative values can be specified.

When an element is positioned absolutely, the space it previously occupied is closed up, as shown in Figure 23-5 and the following code. In its new position, the element may overlap other elements on the page. An absolutely positioned element has no margins—its outer edge stops at the border.

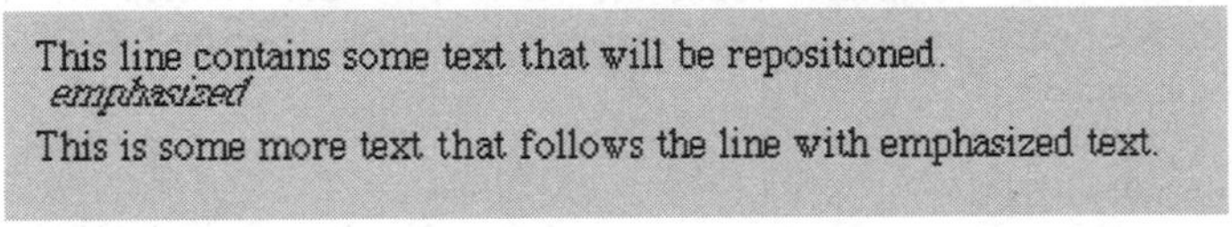

Figure 23-5: Word moved down and to the right with absolute positioning

```
<HEAD>
<STYLE TYPE="text/css">
<!--
EM { position: absolute; top: 20px; left: 12px; }
-->
</STYLE>
</HEAD>

<BODY>
<P>This line contains some <EM>emphasized</EM> text that will
be repositioned.</P>
<P>This is some more text that follows the line with emphasized
text.</P>
</BODY>
```

If its parent element is specified to have relative positioning (whether or not it is actually moved), the absolutely positioned child element will be placed relative to the position of the top-left corner of its parent. One possible application of this is keeping notations nearby their source paragraphs.

Static positioning

Static is the default value for the position property. Static elements can never serve as a context for child element placement (as discussed in absolute positioning above). Static elements cannot be positioned or repositioned.

Z-Order

Z-order refers to the overlapping of elements that can occur when elements are positioned outside of their normal flow. The CSS-P specification provides a special property, z-index, for handling the placement of objects in 3-dimensional space.

Elements with higher `z-index` values obscure those with lower values. When not specified, elements appear from back to front in the order in which they appear in the HTML source.

In Figure 23-6, two ordinary transparent GIFs, *A.gif* and *B.gif*, are positioned using z-index settings. In the top image, *B.gif* is given a higher z-index value and thus overlaps *A.gif*. In the bottom image, the positioning code is the same, but this time, *A.gif* is given the higher `z-index` value and comes out on top.

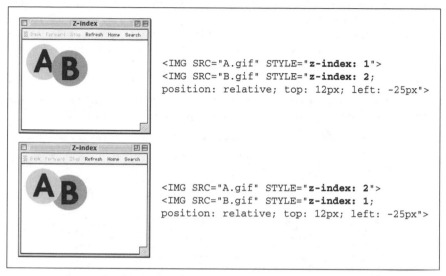

Figure 23-6: Graphic file with higher z-index value is positioned on top

Visibility

The CSS2 specification also includes a new property called `visibility`, which takes the values `visible` (the default) or `hidden`. When an element is hidden, it is not displayed on the page and the space it occupies is held blank as shown in Figure 23-7 and the following code.

This line contains some   text, which will be hidden.

Figure 23-7: Word is hidden using visibility property

```
<STYLE TYPE="text/css">
<!--
EM { visibility: hidden; }
-->
</STYLE>
...

<P>This line contains some <EM>emphasized</EM> text, which will
be hidden.</P>
```

This is different from `display:none` (another method for hiding elements) in that the `display` property closes up the space once occupied by the element. The other difference is that `display:none` only works on block-level items, where `visibility:hidden` can be used on inline elements.

Overflow

Another new property first proposed in the Positioning Specification is `overflow`, which provides alternative ways for handling text that does not fit in the box dimensions as specified. It has four possible attributes: `visible`, which just resizes the bounding box so the whole element can be viewed; `hidden`, which hides from view the portion of the element that does not fit in the box; `scroll`, which places a scroll bar in the box so the user can scroll down to read its contents, and `auto`, which places a scroll bar only when necessary.

Figure 23-8 shows the effects of different overflow settings on a text element specified at 200×100 pixels (`visible`, `hidden`, and `scroll`, respectively).

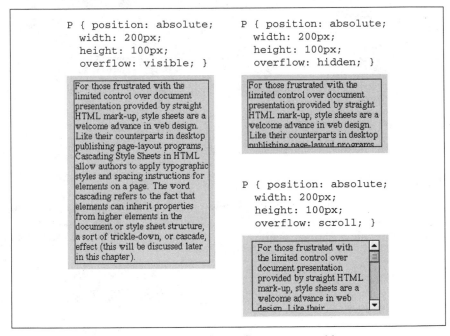

Figure 23-8: Box resizes to fit text when overflow is set to visible

What's New in CSS2

As of this writing, the current specification published by the W3C is Cascading Style Sheets, Level 2 (*http://www.w3.org/TR/REC-CSS2/*). CSS2 expands significantly on the work done in CSS1. Not surprisingly, it includes dozens of new properties (and pseudo-elements), and a fair number of additional values for existing properties (see the following tables).

CSS2 incorporates and refines the set of properties used for positioning to give designers more control over page layout and DHTML authors the ability to create dynamic motion effects.

It provides more controls over traditional typesetting elements such as widows, orphans, and page breaks. This shows that style sheets are being developed with a mind to developing documents for both HTML display and print output.

CSS2 also introduces properties that give additional control over table element presentation.

As part of the W3C's efforts to make web pages accessible to all users, the latest style sheet specification includes a number of new properties that pertain to the nonvisual display of web pages. These new attributes provide controls for speech-delivery and sound controls.

The following list of new CSS2 elements was compiled and graciously contributed to this book by CSS-guru Eric Meyer. It reflects the state of the final CSS2 specification, which was made a W3C Recommendation in May 1998.

New Selectors

The following are the new CSS2 selectors:

Selector	Description
*	Matches any element. Example: `*{font-family:serif;}`
A>B	Matches any element B that is a child of any element A. Example: `DIV.main>P{line-height:1.5;}`
A+B	Matches any element B that immediately follows any element A. Example: `P+UL{margin-top:0;}`
A[att]	Matches any element A that has the given attribute defined, whatever its value. Example: `TABLE[border]{background-color:white;}`
A[att="val"]	Matches any element B that has the specified attribute set to the specified value. Example: `TABLE[border="3"]{background-color:yellow;}`
A[att~="val"]	Matches any element B that has the specified value as one of the values in a list given to the specified attribute. Example: `TABLE[class~="example"]{background-color:orange;}`
A[lang|="val"]	Matches any element A that has the given value as one of the values for the `lang` attribute. Example: `P[lang|="en"]{text-align:left;}`

New Properties

The following are the new CSS2 properties:

text-shadow	top	table-layout
font-size-adjust	right	cell-spacing
font-stretch	bottom	empty-cells
unicode-bidi	left	caption-side
	z-index	speak-header-cell
cursor		
outline	min-width	volume
outline-color	max-width	speak
outline-style	min-height	pause-before
outline-width	max-height	pause-after
	overflow	pause
content	clip	cue-before
quotes	visibility	cue-after
counter-reset		cue
counter-increment	page	play-during
marker-offset	page-break-before	azimuth
	page-break-after	elevation
border-top-color	page-break-inside	speech-rate
border-right-color	orphans	voice-family
border-bottom-color	widows	pitch
border-left-color	size	pitch-range
border-top-style	marks	stress
border-right-style		richness
border-bottom-style	row-span	speak-punctuation
border-left-style	column-span	speak-date
	border-collapse	speak-numeral
position	border-spacing	speak-time
direction		

Font Descriptors

The following are the new CSS2 font descriptors:

unicode-range	ascent
units-per-em	descent
src	widths
panose-1	bbox
stemv	definition-src
stemh	baseline
slope	centerline
cap-height	mathline
x-height	topline

(Note that these properties are only used for font matching and description; most authors will not need to use them.)

New Pseudo-Selectors

The following are the new CSS2 pseudo-selectors:

:after
:before
:first
:first-child
:focus
:hover
:lang
:left
:right

New Functions

The following are the new CSS2 funtions:

@charset
@media
@font-face
@page

New Values for Existing Properties

The following are the new CSS2 value for existing properties:

all properties
inherit

display
run-in, compact, marker, table, inline-table, table-row, table-row-group, table-column, table-column-group, table-cell, table-caption, table-header-group, table-footer-group

font
caption, icon, menu, message-box, small-caption, status-bar

list-style-type
hebrew, armenian, georgian, cjk-ideographic, hiragana, hiragana-iroha, katakana, katakana-iroha

<color> values
(These values are case-insensitive, but use of the capitalization is encouraged for the sake of readability.)

ActiveBorder, ActiveCaption, AppWorkspace, Background, ButtonFace, ButtonHighlight, ButtonText, CaptionText, GrayText, Highlight, HighlightText, InactiveBorder, InactiveCaption, InfoBackground, InfoText, Menu, MenuText, Scrollbar, ThreeDDarkShadow, ThreeDFace, ThreeDHighlight, ThreeDLightshadow, ThreeDShadow, Window, WindowFrame, WindowText

Style Sheet Tips and Tricks

Style Sheet MIME Types

Some authors have reported trouble with gettting their ISPs to correctly serve up CSS files. Apparently, with some Web servers, *.css* is mapped to the MIME-type `x-application/css`, or "Continuous Slide Show," instead of the MIME-type `text/css`. The style sheet gets mangled into something else. If you find you're having this problem, you'll need to contact your ISP and explain the problem. Because *.css* is now an IANA-registered MIME-type, service providers really have no excuse for not supporting it for style sheets. If they refuse to fix it and style sheets are a necessary part of your site, you may have to consider switching ISPs.

Creating a Drop Cap

Although a pseudo-element called `:firstletter` exists, it is not very well supported as of this writing. In the meantime, you can create a drop cap using a `<span>` to isolate the first letter of the paragraph.

The `float` property also has spotty support. The `width` property was added to the following example in order to get float to work with Internet Explorer (and it still doesn't function properly on a Mac). Without the `float` property, the capital letter will stand taller than the rest of the line, which may still be an acceptable effect. Figure 23-9 shows a drop cap created with the following style sheet code.

```
<STYLE TYPE="text/css">
<!--
    .dropcap { font: bold 200% sans-serif;
              color: teal;
              width: 24pt;
              float: left; }
-->
</STYLE>

<P><SPAN CLASS="dropcap">F</SPAN> or those frustrated...</P>
```

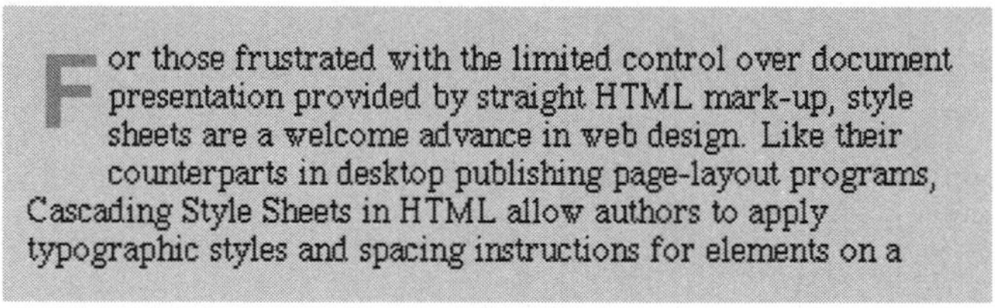

Figure 23-9: Drop cap created with float property

Specifying Text Size in Pixels

One of the great frustrations in designing web pages is that fonts are rendered so differently from platform to platform, especially with regards to point size. The same point size will be rendered much larger on a PC than on a Mac, making it difficult to anticipate how much type will fit on the page. (See "Why Specifying Type is Problematic" in Chapter 3, *Web Design Principles for Print Designers*.)

Style sheets introduce the ability to specify type size in pixels. This translates better across platforms because the size of the type will stay fixed in relation to the other elements (like graphics) on the page. The result is more predictable page layouts.

However, this recommendation comes with a warning: text specified in pixels cannot be printed legibly by Windows machines. Windows maps the pixels directly to laser printer dots, making type too tiny to read. So if your page needs to be printed, stick with point sizes. If the allure of pixel type measurements is too strong, be sure to provide a "print" version of your web page where it can be easily found.

Setting BODY Color

Setting a color for the BODY element will make all the text elements on the page your chosen color, but it will also turn your horizontal rules (<hr>) into solid rules (not 3-D shaded as normally displayed) of your chosen color. This is mostly true for older browsers and is incorrect behavior—color values should not effect <hr>s.

```
BODY { color: green; }
```

Unfortunately, at this point, the only current workaround for this problem is to list every element on the page except <hr>s as shown below:

```
H1, H2, H3, P, UL, OL, PRE, TABLE { color: purple; }
```

Setting BODY Font

Similar to the body color problem, specifying a font and size for the body element will apply to all the elements on the web page contained in it. For example, the following code specifies 12pt serif text for the body font:

```
BODY { font: 12pt serif; }
```

The problem is that in some browsers, this rule will apply to all the H1s, pre text and text enclosed in <font> tags, because they will all inherit the body's values. They shouldn't, but in some browsers, they do anyway.

The only solution is to provide style sheet rules for all the elements on the page, which should override the higher-level body settings. You can specify the type in points, but it is more democratic to use absolute values as shown below:

```
BODY { font: 12pt serif; }
H1 { font-size: xx-large; }
H2 { font-size: x-large; }
H3 { font-size: large; }
PRE, TT, CODE { font-size: medium monospace; }
```

Making Padding Behave in Netscape

Although a background should always fill an element's padding out to its border, Netscape Navigator needs a little extra help to get it right. Anywhere padding is used with a background color, add the following declaration:

```
{ border: 1px solid none; }
```

This will have no visual effect, but in the course of telling Navigator to draw a one pixel, solid, transparent border, padding will suddenly start to inherit the background color. If you leave out this statement, many versions of Navigator will not extend the background color into the padding. (Again, this is just a workaround to compensate for bugs in Navigator—this is *not* how CSS1 is defined to behave.)

Browser Support Charts

Appendix E in this book contains charts with brower support for style sheet properties as of this writing. They were compiled and continue to be maintained by Eric Meyer for WebReview magazine. To get up-to-date statistics on browser support, WebReview's Style Sheets Reference Guide online at *http://style.webreview.com/*.

CHAPTER 24

Introduction to DHTML

Dynamic HTML (DHTML) refers to web pages that move, animate or respond to the user after downloading to the browser. Through DHTML, users get a more engaging and interactive web experience without constant calls to a web server or the overhead of loading new pages or large applets.

DHTML works through a combination of:

- HTML 3.2
- JavaScript—the web's standard scripting language
- Cascading Style Sheets (CSS)—styles dictated outside a document's content
- Document Object Model (DOM)—a means of accessing a document's individual parts

Although HTML pages using one or more of these technologies can be considered "dynamic," the term DHTML generally refers to all of these technologies used together.

Both Netscape 4.0 and Internet Explorer 4.0 support these technologies, but in different ways. This means that web designers whose audience consists of both Internet Explorer and Netscape users (that's just about all of us) must create DHTML pages catering to two different implementations of DHTML. A standard-ized DHTML is in the works, but as of this writing, we're still waiting for the standards to be finalized and for browser makers to implement those standards.

This chapter provides an introduction to DHTML. Before creating your own DHTML pages you may want to read Chapter 22, *Introduction to JavaScript*, and Chapter 23, *Cascading Style Sheets*. Read on if you are simply looking for an expla-nation of DHTML and its uses.

Advantages to Using DHTML

Small file sizes

DHTML files are small compared to other interactive media such as Flash or Shockwave (see Chapter 21, *Interactivity*). Therefore they have a shorter download time and take up less bandwidth.

Supported by both major browser manufacturers

Both Microsoft and Netscape currently support DHTML in some shape or form.

DHTML will be a standard

The World Wide Web Consortium or the W3C is currently implementing standards for DHTML technologies. It has already released preliminary specifications for DOM and CSS (go to *http://www.w3c.org* for more information). These specifications lay the groundwork for more complete standards to come, which both Netscape and Microsoft have pledged to support.

No plug-ins necessary

Plug-ins are not needed to view DHTML files. A visitor to your site needs only a Netscape 4.0 browser or an Internet Explorer 4.0 browser. This puts fewer requirements on your audience; they don't need to download special software to view your site.

Doesn't require a Java Virtual Machine (JVM)

DHTML isn't a Java technology. DHTML provides many functions that can otherwise be attained through Java—a compiled, object-oriented computer language. Pages that contain Java applets require the user to wait for the JVM to start and for Java byte code to download, which takes quite a bit of time and bandwidth. Although Java is good for some applications, DHTML can be an attractive alternative for animations, design issues, and simple tasks.

Disadvantages

Only new browsers support DHTML

DHTML is only supported by Netscape 4.0 or higher and Internet Explorer 4.0 or higher. Many people are still using older versions of both browsers. Web designers using DHTML must choose to provide content for older browsers or eliminate a significant portion of their audience.

Netscape and Microsoft have different DHTML implementations

Two different implementations make creating a DHTML document tedious and complicated task. More information is given in the section called "Browser Differences."

DHTML creation has a sharp learning curve

Because DHTML requires at least partial knowledge of many different web design concepts (HTML, JavaScript, CSS, and DOM) it may take some review before you begin creating DHTML content. DHTML tools go a long way towards eliminating this problem.

Unprotected source code

You may not sweat someone lifting your HTML code, but you may be more leery about giving away your hand-written DHTML application.

Learning DHTML

Because both Netscape and Microsoft have pledged support for the emerging W3C standards, time spent learning DHTML is well spent. Knowledge gained today will not become obsolete and will give you a head start once DHTML is standardized for all browser manufacturers.

In rating the difficulty of all web design skills, DHTML falls somewhere in the middle. It isn't as difficult as Java or Perl programming, but it is more difficult than regular HTML.

You should first experiment with visual DHTML development tools such as Dreamweaver 1.0 or Fusion 3.0 before you begin coding DHTML by hand. A visual tool will allow you to get a feel for DHTML technology rather quickly. Afterwards, if a tool doesn't meet your needs, begin coding by hand.

Tools are discussed again at the end of the chapter. After reading the sections on browser differences and DHTML examples composed manually, it should give you a greater appreciation of the time and effort a tool can save you.

Browser Differences

In order to create DHTML content available to the largest audience, you will need to understand the differences between Microsoft's and Netscape's DHTML. Although both Netscape and Microsoft implement DHTML, they do so very differently.

Both Netscape 4.0 and Internet Explorer 4.0 support the Cascading Style Sheet Positioning (CSS-P) standard as established by the W3C. CSS-P (now rolled into the CSS Level 2 Specification) specifies settings for attributes of distinct objects in an HTML document. These objects are generally words or text. By accessing attributes, objects can be hidden, shown, and layered.

Although both browsers use CSS-Positioning, Microsoft and Netscape have applied this to HTML objects differently. Dynamic objects in a Netscape browser are called *layers*. Netscape has created a `<layer>` tag to add such items to a document. Dynamic objects in Internet Explorer are referred to as *styles*. Web designers must create DHTML documents that utilize both implementations of CSS-Positioning.

The Document Object Model

Many of the differences between Netscape DHTML and Internet Explorer DHTML stem from their incompatible implementations of the Document Object Model (DOM). The Document Object Model exposes every element of an HTML page to a scripting language such as JavaScript. Early iterations of the DOM gave scripts access to only some objects on a page such as forms, frames, and images. Internet Explorer 4.0 and Netscape 4.0 have expanded their DOMs and therefore exposed more objects to scripting.

The DOM begins with a base object called the "window," which refers to the browser window itself. Within the window object is the document object (as well as other non-document objects, such as frames). The document object refers to the

HTML page itself and everything in it. All of the objects contained within the HTML page, such as images and forms, "branch off" from the original HTML page or document, like branches from a tree trunk.

Using JavaScript you can reference these branches by naming each object, from the root to the branch, and separating their names with periods, like this:

```
document.images["image_name"]
```

The HTML code that gives an image its name looks like this:

```
<IMG SRC="start.gif" NAME="start">
```

 While the document object is legally part of the window object (`window.document`), the window object doesn't usually have to be explicitly referenced. Thus we reference `document.images`, not `window.document.images`.

For the most part, Netscape and Internet Explorer use a similar DOM. However, when working with more complicated Web pages—that is, pages with positionable objects placed in a stacking order—Netscape's DOM and Internet Explorer's DOM differ greatly.

Referencing Objects in Netscape and IE

In Netscape, positionable objects are placed in layers with the `<LAYER>` tag or with CSS-P. You access a Netscape layer like this:

```
document."layer_name"
```

A layer is considered a separate document that contains its own objects. In Netscape, JavaScript would reference an object contained in a layer in this manner:

```
document."layer_name".document.images["image_name"]
```

The left-most document object refers to the actual HTML page. Next comes the name of the layer. The second "document" refers to the document contained in that layer. Finally, `images["image_name"]` references the actual image within the layer that you want to access. Thus the image named "start" (remember we use the image's name, specified in the `<img>` tag—not its filename) on the `controls` layer is referenced:

```
document.controls.document.images[start]
```

In Internet Explorer, objects are referred to as "styles." IE's DOM allows you to reference all style objects within the root document. This is done through the `all` property. A named style object looks like this:

```
document.all."style_name".style
```

Thus we would access a style named *controls* like this:

```
document.all.controls.style
```

To access an image object contained within a style object, you needn't reference the style object. You should reference it directly through the image object's name. So, to reference the image named *start*, type:

```
document.all.start
```

Object Properties

Another difference between Netscape and Internet Explorer's implementation of the DOM is in property names.

Every object contains properties. Properties are different for every object but are typically descriptors such as color, size, position, etc. Referencing yet another branch in the DOM can access these properties. Image objects in an HTML page have a source property, which is the image's path or URL. Here's how we would reference the *start* image's source file:

```
document.images.start.src
```

By accessing and manipulating an image's source property, you can create effects such as rollovers (see Chapter 22).

Because Netscape and Internet Explorer don't agree on the names of object properties, you must program for properties that Netscape and Internet Explorer have in common.

There are three properties for positionable objects that Netscape and Internet Explorer share:

- Location
- Visibility
- Stacking order (z-index)

Location

You can control an object's location through its X and Y coordinates. These two properties are named differently by Netscape and Internet Explorer. In Netscape, a positionable object's X coordinate is called `left` and its Y coordinate is called `top`. To access a positionable object's X coordinate in Netscape you could write:

```
document."layer_name".left
```

To access an object's Y coordinate in Netscape you write:

```
document."layer_name".top
```

Internet Explorer's positionable objects have these same properties but they are referred to through different names. In Internet Explorer, a positionable object's X coordinate is called `pixelLeft` and its Y coordinate is called `pixelTop`. To access a positionable object's X coordinate in Internet Explorer you would use the `pixelLeft` property:

```
document.all."style_name".style.pixelLeft
```

To access an object's Y coordinate in Internet Explorer you write:

```
document.all."style_name".style.pixelTop
```

These properties return an integer indicating the number of pixels between the top-left corner of the browser window and the object's position. Thus, the top or pixelTop property of 200 positions an object 200 pixels below the document's top border.

Visibility

In both Netscape and Internet Explorer, a positionable object's visibility property can be set to visible, hidden, or inherit. What the visible and hidden values do are self-explanatory. Setting an object's position property to inherit gives the object the same visibility as its containing object. In Netscape, a positionable object's visibility can be set to "visible" like this:

```
document."layer_name".visibility = "visible";
```

You can do the same in Internet Explorer like this:

```
document.all."style_name".visibility = "visible";
```

Stacking oder (z-index)

Stacking order or z-index works the same way in both Netscape and Internet Explorer: the z-index property of the layer (Netscape) or style (IE) determines the object's place in the stack. Stacking order is set to an integer. A layer or style with a stacking order of 1 will be placed above an object with a stacking order of 0. You can set stacking order in Netscape like this:

```
document."layer_name".zIndex = "1";
```

In Internet Explorer it is set like this:

```
document."style_name".zIndex = "1";
```

Because of these fundamental differences in Netscape and Microsoft's implementation of the DOM, you need to customize your HTML for each of the DHTML-capable browsers; that is, you have to create two sets of JavaScript code. The result is cross-platform DHTML.

Writing for Both Browsers

To write DHTML for both Netscape and Internet Explorer, you must create two sets of JavaScript functions. The user's browser will determine which set of functions to use. If the viewer is using Internet Explorer, then the Internet Explorer-specific JavaScript will be run. If the viewer is using Netscape, then the Netscape-specific JavaScript will be run. See the "Browser Differences" section later in this chapter for more information.

Although this is tedious, it isn't as difficult as it sounds. Code written for one page can be modified and reused for another. Also, if you're really into JavaScript, you can create your own interface for controlling DHTML objects and import them into a document using an external .js file. An example of this is available on the O'Reilly web site at *http://www.oreilly.com/catalog/jscript3/example/text/17-4.txt*. This example is taken from *JavaScript: The Definitive Guide*, by David Flanagan.

In an effort to solve DHTML compatibility problems, the W3C has drawn up preliminary specifications for a DOM for both HTML and XML, but it will be some time before these standards are expanded and become mainstreamed.

DHTML Examples

This section provides two DHTML examples. The first shows how DHTML can be used to hide or show an object. The second example uses DHTML to add motion to a page. In addition, this section discusses the measures that must be taken to make sure the DHTML works with both major browsers.

These examples are intended to introduce you to the basics of DHTML. They are by no means a compilation of all possible DHTML functions and they do not work with or handle Netscape and Internet Explorer browsers below version 4.0. It is possible to detect 3.0 browsers and send them non-DHTML content, but that is beyond the scope of this chapter. If you are interested in learning how to do that, go to the web sites listed at the end of this chapter.

Though the following examples are simple, mixing these different functions or expanding upon them can add a lot to your web pages.

Browser Detection

The examples in this section require that you first check for the user's browser type and version. This allows you to identify the viewer's browser and execute the browser-specific JavaScript code. Each of the example scripts should begin like this:

```
<SCRIPT Language="JavaScript1.2">
var isNet4, isIE4
if ( navigator.appversion.substring(0, 1) >= 4)
{
    if ( navigator.appName == "Netscape" )
    {
       isNet4 = true;
    }
    if ( navigator.appName == "Microsoft Internet Explorer" )
    {
       isIE4 = true;
    }
}
</SCRIPT>
```

This code checks the ID of the browser and sets as true a variable for that browser, either isNet4 (Netscape) or isIE4 (IE).

Now that we have tested the user's browser and set our isIE4 and isNet4 variables, we can create two sets of browser-specific code, but only have the appropriate set execute.

Style Changes

Once you've created your browser detection code, making changes to style sheets is relatively simple. All you have to do is access a style property and change it:

```
document."style_name".visibility = "visible";
```

This line of script changes the visibility property of a Netscape 4.0 layer to visible. Controlling the visibility of an element allows us to have pictures or text appear on demand. The same line for Internet Explorer 4.0 looks like this:

```
document.all."style_name".style.visibility = "visible";
```

To execute either line of code depending upon the user's browser, you would wrap them in conditional statements like this:

```
if (isNet4)
{
    document.hidden.visibility = "visible";
}
if (isIE4)
{
    document.all.hidden.style.visibility = "visible";
}
```

The first if statement checks to see if the browser is Netscape 4; if it is, then the Netscape 4.0-specific code between the curly brackets executes. The second if statement checks the isIE4 variable. If that variable is true then the Internet Explorer 4.0-specific code between the curly brackets executes. In either case, the visibility property of the style or element named hidden is made visible.

If you have a style sheet that looks like this:

```
<STYLE TYPE="text/css">
    #hidden {position: relative; font: 12pt Times, serif;
visibility: hidden;}
</STYLE>
```

 You must specify the position attribute for a CSS object to be accessed by JavaScript. In this case relative means the text appears as positioned by traditional HTML. Designating the position as absolute would put the text identified as hidden in the upper left corner of your browser.

The JavaScript code that accesses the hidden object and changes its visibility property from hidden to visible would look like this:

```
<script language="Javascript1.2">

var isNet4, isIE4
// Variables that you reference for browser type.
//
// Begin the browser detection script.
if ( navigator.appVersion.substring(0, 1) >= 4)
```

```
{
  if ( navigator.appName == "Netscape" )
  {
    isNet4 = true;
  }

  if ( navigator.appName == "Microsoft Internet Explorer" )
  {
    isIE4 = true;
  }
}
// End the browser detection script.

// Function "show" checks for browser type, then executes the
// appropriatecode to change the "hidden" object's visibility
// from hidden to visible.

function show()
{
  if (isNet4)

    document.hidden.visibility = "visible";
  }
  if (isIE4)
  {
    document.all.hidden.style.visibility = "visible";
  }
}
</script>
```

The HTML looks like this:

```
<BODY BGCOLOR="ffffff" TEXT="000000">
We want some text to appear after this text has been loaded.
<br>
<SPAN ID="hidden">This could be used to further define or give
 background information for web content</SPAN>

<br>
<A HREF=javascript:show()>Click here to make text appear.</A>
</BODY>
</HTML>
```

The SPAN tag identifies some text as **hidden**. The **<a href>** tag executes the **show()** function, which makes any HTML between the **<span>** tags visible.

Motion

Creating motion with DHTML is similar to making a style change—JavaScript accesses the position attributes of a CSS object and changes them. Changing an object's position incrementally by one or two pixels creates the illusion of movement. In this example, animated text will move onto the browser window from left to right.

To access a CSS object's `left` property, or X coordinate in Netscape 4.0 write:

```
document."style_name".left
```

To access the `top` property, or Y coordinate, in Netscape 4.0 write:

```
document."style_name".top
```

As with the style change example, Netscape 4.0 and Internet Explorer 4.0 do not agree on how JavaScript can access `top` and `left` properties. To change an object's `left` property in Internet Explorer 4.0 write:

```
document.all."style_name".style.pixelLeft
```

And to change an object's `top` property in Internet Explorer 4.0 write:

```
document.all."style_name".style.pixelTop
```

Be sure to enclose this code in browser detection code as described earlier.

To create the animated text, first, a Cascading Style Sheet creates an object called animate, like this:

```
<STYLE TYPE="text/css">
    #animate {position: absolute; left: -80; top: 10;}
</STYLE>
```

The animate object's `left` attribute or X coordinate is set to -80. Its `top` attribute or Y coordinate is 10. These coordinates set the animate object 80 pixels to the left of the browser window, which is out of sight, and 10 pixels down from the top of the browser.

Now that the animate object is defined, it can be placed into an HTML document using the <span> or <div> tag. The body of the example HTML document looks like this:

```
<BODY onload="counter = setInterval('motion()', 20)">
<DIV ID="animate">Moving text</DIV>
</BODY>
```

The <body> tag contains an `onload` action event, which triggers functions in the following JavaScript.

The JavaScript will increase the animate object's `left` attribute incrementally making any image or text designated as animate by a <span> tag appear to move onto the browser from the left to the right.

```
<SCRIPT LANGUAGE="Javascript1.2">

var isNet4, isIE4
// Variables that you can reference for browser type.
//
// Begin the browser detection script.
if ( navigator.appVersion.substring(0, 1) >= 4)
{
    if ( navigator.appName == "Netscape" )
    {
        isNet4 = true;
    }
```

```
        if ( navigator.appName == "Microsoft Internet Explorer" )
     {
         isIE4 = true;
     }
}
// End the browser detection script.
```

After detecting the browser, we write a motion function, customized for each browser with if statements. This function accesses the animate object and adds 2 to its left attribute. After adding 2, it checks to see if the object's left attribute is greater than 200. If so, the animation stops.

```
// Variable through which timed events will be accessed.
var counter;

function motion()
    {
        if (isNet4)
        {
            // Move the animate object 2 pixels to the left
            document.animate.left += 2;

            // Check to see if the animate object is 200 pixels
            // into the page. If it is, execute the script between
            // the brackets.
            if (document.animate.left > 200)
            {
                // End the animation.
                clearTimeout(counter);
            }
        }

        if (isIE4)
        {
            // Move the animate object 2 pixels to the left
            document.all.animate.style.pixelLeft += 2;

            // Check to see if the animate object is 200 pixels
            // into the page. If it is, execute the script between
            // the brackets.
            if (document.all.animate.style.pixelLeft > 200)
            {
                // End the animation.
                clearTimeout(counter);
            }
        }
    }
</script>
```

The onload event passes the value setInterval('motion()', 20) to the counter. Once this is set, the motion function will automatically execute every 20 milliseconds until stopped with the clearTimeout function.

Changing this example to suit your needs

The previous example can be copied and changed to suit your needs. To slow down the animation, you can decrease the number of milliseconds within the `setInterval` function, like this:

```
<BODY onload="counter = setInterval('motion()', 500)">
```

With the second parameter in the `setInterval` function set to 500, it will wait 500 milliseconds before executing the motion function again.

To make the `animate` object move from top to bottom, you might change the Cascading Style Sheet to this:

```
<STYLE TYPE="text/css">
    #animate {position: absolute; left: 10; top: -10;}
</STYLE>
```

This starts the text outside of the browser page as before, but 10 pixels above the top rather than 80 to the left. Now we can make the text animate downward by changing the `motion` function. Within the `motion` function, change `document.animate.left` to `document.animate.top` and `document.all.animate.style.pixelLeft` to `document.all.animate.style.pixelTop` like this:

```
function motion()
    {
        if (isNet4)
        {
            // Move the object 2 pixels down rather than to the
            // left as before.
            document.animate.top += 2;

            if (document.animate.top > 200)
            {
                clearTimeout(counter);
            }
        }

        if (isIE4)
        {

            // Move the object 2 pixels down rather than to the
            // left as before.
            document.all.animate.style.pixelTop += 2;

            if (document.all.animate.style.pixelTop > 200)
            {
                clearTimeout(counter);
            }
        }
    }
```

To make the animation stop 300 pixels into the document rather than 200, change

```
if (document.all.animate.style.pixelTop > 200)
```

to:

```
if (document.all.animate.style.pixelTop > 300)
```

You could also have the animation start as the result of a button click rather than immediately after the page loads. This can be done by changing the onload event to a function referenced by a web link. To do this, change

```
<BODY onload="counter = setInterval('motion()', 20)">
<DIV ID="animate">Moving text</DIV>
</BODY>
```

to:

```
<BODY>
<DIV ID="animate">Moving text</DIV>
<br>
<br>
<br>
<a href=javascript:start()>Click here to start animation</a>
</BODY>
```

Then add a function to the script section of your page called start:

```
function start()
{
    counter = setInterval('motion()', 20);
}
```

These examples should give you an idea of how Dynamic HTML currently works with both Netscape 4.0 and Internet Explorer 4.0, and how it can be incorporated into your web pages. If DHTML seems complicated to you, remember it is simply a combination of HTML, Cascading Style Sheets and JavaScript working together through the Document Object Model. As you learn more about each of these tools, you will gain more competence in DHTML.

If you feel the need to add functionality beyond what these examples offer, or have mastered them and want to learn more, be sure to read the "Where to Learn More" section at the end of this chapter.

DHTML Tools

Many web designers rely on WYSIWYG tools and editors that make it possible to see the effects of creating and editing immediately. There are many DHTML WYSIWYG editors available today. They may or may not suit your needs.

The previous relatively simple examples demonstrate that hand coding DHTML can be complicated and arduous. Differences between Netscape 4.0 and Internet Explorer force web designers to write two sets of code for each function. This doubles production time and creates code that is difficult to read and maintain.

There are many tools that create DHTML for you behind the scenes. Some of these tools are narrow in focus and provide specific functionality while others such as Dreamweaver and Fusion are full packages with which you can create and maintain whole websites as well as write DHTML code.

It is beyond the scope of this book to provide working details of WYSIWIG DHTML tools. Each of these tools have their own pros and cons. Commercial tools with full DHTML support are likely to provide a more robust implementation and better support to users. However, these software packages require a larger investment. If you only want simple animations or style changes, a shareware tool may be the best way for you to go.

Luckily, most web authoring tools are available for free download over the Internet on a trial basis so you can experiment and choose the one that suits your needs. Please remember to register and pay for any shareware you continue using after your trial period. The fee is usually nominal and goes a long way toward improving the next version of the software and supporting you, the user.

WYSIWYG DHTML tools differ greatly in their operation. They have to allow the user to view and manipulate an animation or style change in a graphical way. You can create animations by dragging objects in the editor, thus eliminating the need to program Javascript that counts pixels, tracks X/Y coordinates, counts, and loops. Dreamweaver, for instance allows you attach a timeline, behavior, or both to a dynamic object or layer.

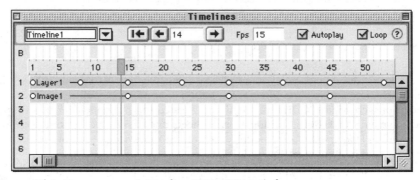

Figure 24-1: Dreamweaver's timeline WYSIWYG interface

Figure 24-1 is a screenshot of Dreamweaver's timeline interface. The numbers on the top of the window represent frames or time. The numbers going down the left-hand side represent layers. According to this timeline, Layer 1 appears as the page loads. Layer 2 appears on frame 10, less than a second after the animation starts. This animation is set to run at 15 fps (frames per second) as indicated by the fps box at the top of the screen. The red line going down through the center of both layers and the number 14 at the top of the timeline indicates that frame 14 is being viewed within the editor.

Advantages of WYSIWYG DHTML Tools

- **There is a shorter learning curve for WYSIWYG editors compared to hand coding DHTML.** Because DHTML is a combination of HTML, JavaScript, Cascading Style Sheets, and DOM, it has a steep learning curve. An editor hides the complexities of DHTML and allows you to manipulate objects through a timeline or other graphic interface.

- **Editors allow you to create effects more quickly.** An effect that may take hours of coding and then debugging may be created on a WYSIWYG editor in a matter of minutes. Editors allow you to create some effects more intuitively. Also, the creators of the tool have debugged a lot of an editor's DHTML code themselves, which means less debugging for you.

- **A large amount of simple DHTML may be easier to implement in a WYSIWYG editor.** If you have a lot of simple effects going on at once on a page, they will probably be easier to create with an editor. If you hand code a lot of simple behaviors, you may get swamped by the sheer amount of code in one document.

- **Cross-browser implementation is less of a worry.** Browser compatibility is less of an issue with DHTML editors. Most of them create cross-browser DHTML. Most will also tell you which behaviors will work with which browsers.

Disadvantages

- **WYSIWYG editors are expensive.** Some of these editors can cost hundreds of dollars. This isn't within every developer's budget. Editors can vary greatly in price, so shop around. Luckily, most software companies allow you to try their editor for free so that you can make an educated decision before buying.

- **Editors may not give precise control over your objects.** Not every editor gives you pixel level control over your dynamic objects and pages. Many designs require precise, pixel-level control of dynamic objects. Also, you are viewing your code as your editor chooses to depict it—if bugs do occur in your DHTML pages, they may be more difficult to fix.

- **An editor may not do everything.** By using a WYSIWYG editor, you are removing yourself from your DHTML code by one degree. If you are dependent upon your editor for DHTML effects, new DHTML features cannot be taken advantage of until the company that creates your editor publishes a version that exploits those advancements for you. Most likely they'll charge for the upgrade. Meanwhile, other designers who can write their own DHTML code are able to exploit advancements as soon as they are released for free.

- **Tools may write unnaturally complex code.** Tools may make some processes more complex than they need to be, for instance, creating custom objects when they're not necessary.

Where to Learn More

This chapter has just skimmed the surface of what there is to know about DHTML. If you want to learn more, see Danny Goodman's book, *Dynamic HTML: The Definitive Reference* (O'Reilly & Associates, Inc., 1998).

The most up-to-date information can be found on the Web. Here are some sites I found valuable:

- CNET: *http://www.cnet.com/* and *http:// builder.cnet.com/*

- WebMonkey: *http://www.webmonkey.com* /and its DHTML specific site called Inside DHTML at *http://www.insideDHTML.com/*

- WebCoder: *http://www.webcoder.com/*
- Macromedia's DHTML Zone at *http://www.dhtmlzone.com/*

Netscape and Microsoft are the official sources of documentation for their respective browsers and the best place to go for current information.

- Netscape: *http://developer.netscape.com*
- Microsoft: *http://www.microsoft.com/* and *http://www.microsoft.com/sitebuilder/*

Go to the World Wide Web Consortium's site, *http://www.w3.org/,* for current information on web standards.

CHAPTER 25

Introduction to XML

XML (Extensible Markup Language) is a new standard that has recently been approved by the World Wide Web Consortium. It is a promising new customizable markup language that will allow for complex information transactions on the Internet. Many companies such as Microsoft and Netscape have developed or are developing XML technologies.

HTML is designed for content being sent to a browser, but isn't good for sending content to other mediums like a printer or a ticker. XML allows developers to create a custom markup language specific to their needs.

Specially coded XML documents reside on a server and can be converted to HTML and read by browsers. Other clients (including future browsers that are XML-compliant) can access the XML documents directly and use the content for a variety of purposes.

Background

Although XML is a markup language like HTML, a common misconception is that XML is HTML on steroids. XML and HTML are related, but through a common parent, SGML, Standard General Markup Language. SGML is a meta-language—a comprehensive set of syntax rules for marking up documents and data. For information on SGML, including its history, see *http://www.www.sil.org/sgml/*, and specifically, *http://www.sil.org/sgml/general.html.#hist.*

When the creators of the Web needed a markup language that told browsers how to display web content, they used SGML guidelines to create HTML. HTML was designed specifically for displaying content in a browser, but isn't good for much else.

Now that the Web has matured and we are using it for more than just viewing text and images, we need to create more versatile markup languages. We could use SGML as we did when creating HTML, but SGML wasn't designed for the Web. It is too bloated in that it has features that are unnecessary and wouldn't be used. Also, SGML documents themselves are too large and would unnecessarily take up much of the Web's bandwidth.

Clearly a more portable, Web-specific version of SGML had to be created. Thus XML is SGML's smaller cousin. XML is SGML with a reduced feature set. It is powerful enough to describe data, but light enough to travel across the Web.

Document Type Definition (DTD)

Another important part of XML is the Document Type Definition (DTD), which defines each tag and provides more information about each tag or the document in general. A DTD can be part of an XML file itself, but it is usually a separate file or series of files. The DTD is what turns XML from a meta-language into a true language designed for a specific task. It's a type of file associated with SGML and XML documents that defines how markup tags should be interpreted by the application reading the document.

The HTML Specification that defines how web pages should be displayed by a browser is one example of a DTD. Other emerging technologies, such as the proposed multimedia standard SMIL and the proposed vector graphics standard PGML (both discussed later in this chapter), use DTDs that were created in compliance with the XML meta-language.

If you were creating recipes that could be accessed over the Web, you might create your own language called RML or Recipe Markup Language. RML would have tags like <title> and <body>, but would also have RML specific tags such as <ingredients>, <prep-time>, and <nutritional-information>.

These tags would be established in a DTD for the new language. The DTD imparts detailed information about what data should be found in each tag. A DTD for Recipe Markup Language might have a line like this:

```
<!ELEMENT ingredients ( li+, text? )>
```

The first line declares an element called **ingredients**. An **ingredients** tag can contain an **li** element and text. The plus sign (+) after **li** indicates that an "ingredients" element will have one or more "li" elements within it. The question mark after **text** shows that text is optional. The Recipe Markup Language DTD would also specify the "li" element:

```
<!ELEMENT li (#PCDATA)>
```

This element contains text only.

XML doesn't have to be associated with a DTD. You can simply mark up a document, and assume the person reading your XML file already has the proper DTD or will make up their own. Because XML doesn't require a DTD, you can turn your existing DTD-less HTML files into XML by making a few changes.

XML Syntax Basics

Browsers will often recover from sloppily written or illegal HTML. This won't be the case with XML documents. A client reading an XML document may be reading tags unique to that document and therefore can't make assumptions about whether or not a tag should be closed. Every XML element must be closed.

Like HTML, XML tags cannot overlap. Overlapping tags look like this:

```
<Element1><Element2>This is content contained</Element1> in
overlapping tags</Element2>
```

In the above example, it is unclear whether the text, "This is content contained" is an Element 1 or Element 2. To avoid such confusion, an XML document cannot contain overlapping tags. The above example should be written like this:

```
<Element1><Element2>This is content contained</Element2>
</Element1><Element2> in overlapping tags</Element2>
```

With this code, there is no question as to which tags or objects are contained within others.

Turning Existing HTML Documents into XML

Because HTML and XML are closely related, it isn't difficult to make an HTML document XML-compliant. You basically have to make sure your HTML is "well-formed."

- Replace the DOCTYPE declaration and any internal subset with the XML declaration. Replace:

```
<!DOCTYPE HTML ...>
```

with:

```
<?xml version="1.0" standalone="yes"?>
```

- Change any empty elements such as <isindex>, <base>, <meta>, <img>, <br>, <hr>, or <spacer> so they end with />, for example:

```
<IMG SRC="this_photo.jpg" alt="Photo"/>
```

These elements may require some experimentation. For instance, some browsers treat </br> or </hr> the same as <br> or <hr>. Others will accept /> if there is a space before it, but not otherwise.

- Make sure that each nonempty element has a correctly matched end-tag; every <p> must have a </p>.

- Escape all markup characters. (< and & should be written as < and &).

- Make sure all attribute values are in quotes.

- Ensure all element names match with respect to upper- and lowercase characters in both start and end tags and are consistent throughout the file.

- Ensure all attribute tags are similarly in a consistent case throughout the file.

- Make sure there are no overlapping tags. Each tag should completely contain any tags within it.

HTML browsers may not accept XML style empty elements with a trailing slash (e.g., <hr/>) and are not backward compatible. If you want your XML document read by browsers, without parsing, you can add dummy end tags to empty elements, so `<hr>` becomes `<hr></hr>`.

Examples of XML Technology

With XML's ability to allow customized tagging systems, it is not surprising it is finding a wide variety of applications. Many XML languages are so specific that they will serve only a particular Intranet of a single business. Other XML technologies might serve a specfic community, as the Chemical Markup Language serves the scientific community but is of limited interest to most publishers.

The World Wide Web Consortium monitors other XML applications that have a greater impact on how media is presented over the Web, thus changing the Web's capabilities. Two such applications are used for the synchronized multimedia presentations and a method for describing vector-based graphics in Web pages.

Multimedia Presentations with SMIL

SMIL (Synchronized Multimedia Integration Language) is a language for combining audio, video, text, and graphics in a precise, synchronized fashion. The SMIL 1.0 specification, released in June, 1998, is one of the first XML-based DTDs proposed by the W3C.

The SMIL file (using tags that follow the XML syntax) instructs the client to retrieve media elements that reside on the server as standalone files. The advantages of SMIL include the ability to:

- Add hyperlinks in a time-based presentation
- Integrate media elements from more than one server
- Reuse media elements in multiple presentations
- Allow users to choose the media tracks they prefer, for example, based on connection speed or language preferences

How SMIL works

The SMIL DTD contains tags that control the presentation's layout and timeline. In the past, timing events over the Web required developers to write in JavaScript, Java, or proprietary development tools such as Flash or Shockwave. With SMIL, developers can experiment with time and space in a declarative, rather than programmatic, way.

Examples of SMIL's powerful declarative syntax are the parallel (`<par>`) and sequential (`<seq>`) tags. Media elements enclosed within `<par>` tags are played in parallel while media elements enclosed within `<seq>` tags are played sequentially. These two tags, used in different combinations, give web developers broad control over a multimedia timeline. For instance, you can have an audio file play while still images are shown for three seconds each in sequential order, as shown in the following code example:

```
<PAR>
<!--audio_file.wav is a 9 second audio file-->
```

```
<AUDIO SRC="audio_file.wav" BEGIN="0s"/>
    <SEQ>
        <IMG SRC="image_1.jpg" BEGIN="0s"/>
        <IMG SRC="image_2.jpg" BEGIN="3s"/>
        <IMG SRC="image_3.jpg" BEGIN="6s"/>
    </SEQ>
</PAR>
```

SMIL resources

The following resources provide useful information on the background, details, and applications of SMIL.

W3C SMIL Recommendation

http://www.w3.org/AudioVideo/

A comprehensive set of links to SMIL information, including the SMIL 1.0 specification, which lists available SMIL tags and explains the rules and syntax for their use.

Just <smil>

http://www.justsmil.com/SMIL.html

A clearinghouse for SMIL content, news, and discussion.

RealNetworks

http://www.real.com/

Many companies are producing tools so that developers can create SMIL presentations today. SMIL's most visible proponent is Real Networks. RealNetworks has already released a SMIL creation wizard that guides developers through the process of SMIL authoring, and the G2 media player, which supports SMIL presentations. Their web site contains tutorials and tools that will get you started with SMIL production.

Vector Graphics on the Web with XML

XML has typically been used to define the structure of text elements within a document; however, many groups are working on ways in which it could be used to define graphical information as well. In fact, there has been a flurry of activity in the vector graphic arena in 1998, and the W3C has established a Scalable Vector Graphics working group to develop a definitive standard.

Vector graphics are mathematical descriptions of the paths (or strokes) that make up graphical images. These differ from bitmap (also known as "raster") graphics, which describe images in terms of a grid of colored pixels.

One of the advantages of vector graphics is that they describe points, lines, and curves with mathematical functions, requiring much less data than describing a shape pixel-by-pixel. With bandwidth a constant concern in web design, vector graphics seem ideal for the transmission of graphical information. Another advantage is that vector graphics are infinitely scalable without loss of quality for display or output at any resolution. Bitmap images get fuzzy and pixellated when resized dramatically.

In XML code, the description of a simple line might include the starting and ending x,y coordinates with an assigned thickness to the stroke, like this:

```
<LINE STARTCOORD="x,01 y,01" ENDCOORD="x,50 y,100"
THICKNESS="2"/>
```

Along with tags defining graphical shapes, an XML language for describing graphics could include additional information that would travel with the graphic such as copyright information, author, title, and printing instructions. Not only would the graphics then be very compact, they would also be more information rich and multipurpose.

Vector standard contenders

There are currently several technologies vying to become the vector graphic standard of the Web. The W3C has acknowledged the following proposals and is working on developing a single vector standard that draws its features and function from the best of the submitted solutions.

PGML (Precision Graphics Markup Language)

This vector standard proposal was developed by Adobe Systems, IBM, Netscape, and Sun. It is based on the PostScript language and Portable Document Format (PDF), a model that has been used for both online viewing and printing of graphical information. Because the tagging is so complex, PGML code would be exported by image creation tools, then copied and pasted into HTML documents. For more information, see the PGML Note submitted to the W3C at *http://www.w3.org/TR/1998/NOTE-PGML-19980410.html*.

VML (Vector Markup Language)

VML is Microsoft's bid in the vector standards race, with development support from Hewlett-Packard, Macromedia, Autodesk Inc., and Visio Corporation. Like PGML, VML would be generated automatically by an image creation application and exported for use in web pages. VML is likely to be supported by Microsoft Internet Explorer 5.0, giving it somewhat of an advantage over competing standards. For more information, see *http://w3c.org/TR/NOTE-VML*.

Web Schematics on the World Wide Web

Proposed by the CCLRC (Council for the Central Laboratory of the Research Councils), a computer science research organization in the UK, Schematics on the World Wide Web is a specification for describing simple flow charts and graphs. Technically, it does not compete with the aforementioned formats, but has been acknowledged by the W3C as a simplified alternative for displaying schematic drawings. For more information, see *http://www.w3.org/TR/1998/NOTE-WebSchematics/*.

Flash (SWF)

The Flash file format (created by Macromedia) brought vector-based animations and interactive movies to the Web via a plug-in. Macromedia is making the Flash (SWF) format an open standard in hopes that it will become the standard vector graphic format for the Web (in the way that GIF has cornered the bitmap market). Unlike the other vector standards, Flash is not an XML text-based solution, but is a binary graphics format that needs to be interpreted and "played" by software on the computer. Macromedia asserts,

---

however, that there is room in the web graphics world for both text and binary solutions, and they are working to keep the Flash file format consistent with developing XML standards. For more information, see *http://www. macromedia.com/software/flash/open/*.

Where to learn more

The article "XML and Vector Graphics" by Lisa Rein provides a thorough background on the emergence of PGML and other vector-based standards. It also includes a detailed comparison of PGML and VML. It is the source of much of the information in this overview and is a good starting place for understanding the development of XML vector standards. Read it at *http://www.xml. com/xml/pub/Graphics/*.

Other XML Applications

Although XML was only recently approved by the W3C, it is already being used in a variety of ways. Microsoft Internet Explorer 4.0's Channel Definition Format is the first widespread use of XML. Other XML initiatives include:

Open Software Description (OSD)

Microsoft and Marimba are working together to create an XML-based software distribution system. For more information, see *http://www.stars.com/ Seminars/Languages/OSD.html*.

Chemical Markup Language (CML)

CML is used for managing and presenting molecular and technical information over a network. For more information, including screenshots of CML in use, see *http://www.venus.co.uk/omf/*.

Open Financial Exchange (OFE)

OFE is a joint project of Microsoft, Intuit, and Checkfree. It will describe financial transactions taking place over the Internet. For more information, see *http://www.ofx.net/ofx/default.asp*.

Extensible Style Language (XSL)

While style sheets are used to display simply structured XML documents, XSL will be used where more powerful formatting capabilities are required, such as formatting structured data. For more information on XSL, read the current proposal at *http://www.w3.org/TR/NOTE-XSL-970910*.

Resource Description Framework (RDF)

RDF is an XML application used to define the structure of metadata for documents, i.e., data that is useful for indexing, navigating, and searching a site. For more information, including a useful FAQ, see *http://www.w3.org/RDF/*.

Where to Learn More

XML is poised to become a major player on the Internet. Companies are excited by the technology and have invested large amounts of time and money in its development.

Some companies have already released XML tools you can download for free over the Internet. A variety of applications exist, ranging from simple XML syntax checkers (programs that make sure your XML documents conform to XML specifications) to XML-to-HTML converters.

The growth and development of XML is well-documented online in resources such as the following:

The XML FAQ

http://www.ucc.ie/xml/

Your first stop in learning more about XML.

The SGML/XML Web Pages

http://www.sil.org/sgml/xml.html

This site contains everything XML—from beginner information through high-level technical analysis.

XML.com

http://www.xml.com

XML.com is a clearing house of great articles and information on XML.

The XML Exchange

http://www.xmlx.com

The XML Exchange is a forum dedicated to the discussion of XML DTDs.

The World Wide Web Consortium

http://www.w3c.org

The World Wide Web Consortium's official web site is the best place to go for the latest news on new XML standards and proposals.

XML INFO

http://xmlinfo.com

A "well-organized and up-to-date" collection of resources on XML.

CHAPTER 26

Embedded Font Technology

Both Netscape Navigator 4.0+ and Internet Explorer 4.0+ support embedded font technology, enabling them to render your web pages with exactly the fonts you've chosen. Although they are called "embedded fonts," the font information is actually in a separate compressed file linked to the HTML document. When the page is downloaded to the client, so is the necessary font information. Although still in its infancy, this is a great breakthrough for designers who want traditional control over type display.

The W3C gave its blessing to embedded fonts by providing a means for importing fonts (the @font-face function) in its Cascading Style Sheets, Level 2 Recommendation.

Not surprisingly, there are two competing embedded font technologies: TrueDoc (developed by Bitstream and licensed by Netscape), and OpenType (developed by Microsoft and Adobe). TrueDoc's "Dynamic Fonts" can be viewed by Navigator 4.0+ and Internet Explorer 4.0+ on Windows, Mac, and Unix platforms. TrueDoc fonts creation and embedding tools exist for both Windows and Mac as well. The current version of Microsoft's OpenType works only with Internet Explorer 4.0 on the Windows platform.

As of this writing, TrueDoc technology is presenting itself as the best solution for embedded fonts. It offers cross-platform viewing on both major browsers, cross-platform creation tools, the ability to compress both TrueType and Type 1 fonts, and better security against font piracy. However, like any young technology, some bugs still need to be worked out of the system.

Using Embedded Fonts

Although the two embedded font technologies differ at the detail level, the general process for creating and importing them is essentially the same:

1. Specify the font document by name in your HTML document using the `<font face>` tag or the `font-family` property in CSS1.

2. Use a special font-embedding tool to create the downloadable font file(s) for your document (note, you need to have the font installed on your machine). The tool compresses the font shapes into a very small file and adds some security features.

3. Include information in the HTML document that links it to the font file.

4. Upload the HTML documents and the compressed font files to your server. If you are using TrueDoc Dynamic Fonts, you need to configure your server to recognize the new font MIME type.

5. The users' 4.0 browser will display the text in the font you've chosen. The font will be anti-aliased to smooth out the jagged edges. (Note, at small point sizes, the anti-aliasing can actually make some fonts less legible. Do some testing first.)

TrueDoc Technology ("Dynamic Fonts")

TrueDoc technology was developed by Bitstream in 1994. Netscape partnered with Bitstream in 1996 to include "Dynamic Font" support in the Navigator 4.0 browser. In 1998, Dynamic Fonts became available for Internet Explorer 4.0 via an ActiveX control. TrueDoc is capable of compressing TrueType and Type 1 fonts, and it is compatible with the Windows, Macintosh, and Unix platforms.

File Format

Portable Font Resource (*.pfr*)

Technology

TrueDoc uses a method called "direct rendering" which means the font information is rendered (by a very compact rasterizer program) within the browser itself without relying on the operating system.

The information for several fonts can be compressed into a single *.pfr* file.

Font Embedding Tool

Eventually, TrueDoc font embedding tools will be built into popular WYSIWYG web-authoring applications. However, as of this writing, the only available tool is HexWeb Typograph 2.0, from HexMac, which works on both Windows and Macintosh. It is available as a standalone product, or as a plug-in to BBEdit for the Mac or FrontPage for the PC.

You can download a free demo of HexWeb at *http://www.hexmac.com/*.

HTML Code

Navigator and Internet Explorer require slightly different methods for attaching Dynamic Fonts to an HTML document.

Netscape Navigator 4.0:

.pfr files are embedded using a `<LINK>` tag, as follows:

```
<LINK rel="fontdef" src="url/fontname.pfr">
```
The `<link>` tag goes between the `<head>` and `</head>` tags at the top of the document.

Internet Explorer 4.0:

In addition to the `<link>` tag, you must add a pointer to an ActiveX control (immediately following the `<link>` tag). The following example points to an ActiveX control on Bitstream's TrueDoc server. You can point to this control from your page or see *http://www.truedoc.com* for more information on putting an ActiveX control on your own server.

```
<SCRIPT LANGUAGE="JavaScript">
if (navigator.appName == "Microsoft Internet Explorer"){
    if (-1 != navigator.appVersion.indexOf ("Windows", 0)){
        document.writeln("<object");
        document.writeln("classid=\"clsid:0246ECA8-996F-11D1-
        BE2F-00A0C9037DFE\"");
        document.writeln("codebase=\"http://www.truedoc.com/
        activex/tdserver.cab#version=1,0,0,5\"");
        document.writeln("id=\"TDS\" width=0 height=0");
        document.writeln(">");
        document.writeln("</object>");
    }
}
</SCRIPT>
```

MIME type

Because TrueDoc font files are accessed via a link, you need to configure the server to recognize *.pfr* requests. The MIME type is `application/font-tdpfr` and the file extension is *.pfr*.

For Windows NT servers, the complete string (including gopher type) is

`application/font-tdpfr,pfr,,5:REG_SZ:`

For more information, see Bitstream's instructions at *http://www.bitstream.com/world/dynamic.htm#forsas*

Security (Protecting Font Copyrights)

–   Bitstream's DocLock is a system for matching a *.pfr* file to a specific domain name. This prevents Portable Font Resource files from being downloaded and used on a server other than the one for which it was created. In addition, web pages on other servers cannot link to *.pfr* files on other servers. This system approximates a typical font "site license" agreement.

–   Because the font information stays within the browser, and is not downloaded to the operating system, it cannot be used for purposes other than viewing that web page.

OpenType (for Internet Explorer)

OpenType technology was developed by Microsoft and Adobe. It was originally intended to combine TrueType and Type1 technologies, however, Type 1 support is lagging behind, and as of this writing, OpenType supports only TrueType fonts (although Type1 capabilities are expected to be added soon). Its other drawback, as of this writing, is it is only supported by Internet Explorer running on Windows machines.

File Format

Embedded OpenType (*.eot*)

Technology

Microsoft has chosen to have the operating system handle font rasterization, font scaling, anti-aliasing, and hinting. OpenType "font objects" are downloaded to the client machine and referenced by the browser.

Font Embedding Tool

Microsoft's WEFT (Web Embedding Font Tool) is a Windows NT application that can be downloaded for free at *http://www.microsoft.com/typography/free.htm*

HTML Code

.eot files are embedded via a special style sheet entry using the `@font-face` function. The following code gives the proper syntax for embedding fonts with a style sheet.

```
<STYLE TYPE="text/css">
<!--
@font-face {
font-family: font name;
src: url(url of the font);
}
-->
</STYLE>
```

In this example, the font object for Interstate Bold (called *interbd.eot*) is embedded in the document via a style sheet.

```
<STYLE TYPE="text/css">
<!--
@font-face {
font-family: Interstate Bold;
src: url(font/interbd.eot);
}
-->
</STYLE>
```

MIME type

Internet Explorer uses the `src:(url)` attribute in CSS2 to access font information, therefore, no new MIME type needs to be established on the server.

Security (Protecting Font Copyrights)

–   OpenType honors TrueType Embedding permissions (`don't embed, print/preview only, editable embedding`, or `installable`) set by the foundry that created the font. (Note, there is no embedding permissions system for Type1 fonts.)

–   Embedded OpenType files contain domain identifiers (same as TrueDoc), which prevent web pages from downloading or linking *.eot* files on other servers.

   Possible security flaw: Because the font information is downloaded to the client's operating system, it was discovered quickly after OpenType's release that any user can access the font and install it for uses other than reading the web page (in other words, font piracy). In late 1997,

Microsoft claimed the problem is in the operating system, not its embedded font technology. To read more about it, see *http://webreview.com/wr/pub/97/11/07/feature/sidebar2.html*.

CHAPTER 27

Internationalization

If the Web is to reach a truly worldwide audience, it needs to be able to support the display of all the languages of the world, with all their unique alphabets and symbols, directionality, and specialized punctuation. This poses a big challenge to HTML constructs as we know them. However, according to the W3C, "energetic efforts" are being made toward this complicated goal.

The W3C's efforts for internationalization (referred to as "i18n"—an i, then 18 letters, then an n) address two primary issues. First is the handling of alternative character sets that take into account all the writing systems of the world. Second, is how to specify languages and their unique presentation requirements within an HTML document. Many solutions presented by internationalization experts in a document called RFC-2070 were incorporated into the current HTML 4.0 Specification.

This chapter addresses both key issues for internationalization, as well as the new character set and language features in HTML 4.0.

Character Sets

The first challenge in internationalization is dealing with the staggering number of unique character shapes (called "glyphs") that occur in all the writing sytems of the world. This includes not only alphabets, but all ideographs (characters that indicate a whole word or concept) for languages such as Chinese, Japanese, and Korean.

8-Bit Encoded Character Sets

Character encodings (or character sets) are organizations of characters—units of a written language system—in which each character is assigned a specific number. Each character may be associated with a number of different glyphs; for instance, the "close quote" character may be displayed using a " or » glyph, depending on

458

the language. In addition, a single glyph may correspond to different characters, such as a comma serving as both the punctuation symbol for a pause in a sentence as well as a decimal indicator in some languages.

The number of characters available in a character set is limited by the bit-depth of its encoding. For example, 8-bits are capable of describing 256 unique characters, which is enough for most Western languages.

HTML 2.0 and 3.2 are based on the 8-bit character set for western languages called Latin-1 (or ISO 8859-1). There are actually a number of other 8-bit encodings, including:

ISO 8859-5	Cyrillic
ISO 8859-6	Arabic
ISO 8859-7	Greek
ISO 8859-8	Hebrew
SHIFT_JIS	Japanese
EUC-JP	Japanese

16-Bit Encoded Character Sets

Sixteen bits of information are capable of representing 65,536 (2^{16}) different characters—enough to contain a large number of alphabets and ideographs. In 1991, The Unicode Consortium created a 16-bit encoded "super" character set called Unicode (practically identical to another standard called ISO 10646-1) which includes nearly every character from the world's writing systems. Each character is assigned a unique two-octet code (2 groups of 8 bits making 16 bits total). The first 256 slots are given to the ISO 8859-1 character set, so it is backwards compatible.

The HTML 4.0 Specification officially adopts Unicode as its document character set. So regardless of the character encoding used when a document was created, it will be converted to the document character set by the browser, which interprets characters with special meaning in HTML (such as < and >), and converts character entities (such as © for ©). In cases where a character entity points outside of the Latin-1 character set (e.g., ϖ for π), the HTML 4.0 browsers will use the Unicode character set to display the correct character.

This is the first step toward making the Web truly multilingual.

Incidentally, Bitstream has created a TrueType font called "Cyberbit" that contains a large percentage of the Unicode character set. For more information about Cyberbit, see Bitstream's site, *http://www.bitstream.com/news/press/1997/pr-mar10. html.*

Specifying Character Encoding

The external character encoding for a document is communicated between browser and server within the HTTP header of the document, as follows:

```
Content-type: text/html; charset=ISO-8859-8
```

To deliberately set the character-encoding information in a document header, use the <meta> tag with its http-equiv attribute (which adds its values into the

HTTP header). The meta tag that corresponds to the above header message would look like this:

```
<META http-equiv="Content-Type" content="text/html;
charset=ISO-8859-8">
```

Note that the browser must support your chosen character set in order for the page to display properly.

Browsers may one day send an `accept-charset` value, specifying their preferred character encoding when requesting a document (currently only Lynx supports this function). The server would then serve the document with the appropriate encoding, if the preferred version is available.

The `accept-charset` attribute is already a part of the HTML 4.0 specification for form elements (although it is not yet supported by major browsers). With the `accept-charset` attribute, the document can specify which character sets the server can receive from the user in text input fields.

HTML 4.0 Language Tags

Coordinating characters sets is only the first part of the challenge. Even languages that share a character set may have different rules for hyphenation, spacing, quotation marks, punctuation, and so on. In addition to character shapes (glyphs), issues such as directionality (whether the text reads left-to-right or right-to-left) and cursive joining behavior had to be taken into account as well.

This prompted a need for a system of language identification. The W3C responded by incorporating the language tags put forth in the RFC 2070 standard on internationalization.

The "LANG" Attribute

The `lang` attribute can be added within any tag to specify the language of the contained element. It can also be added within the `<html>` tag to specify a language for an entire document. The following example specifies the document's language as French:

```
<HTML LANG="fr">
```

It can also be used within text elements to switch to other languages within a document, for example, you can "turn on" Norwegian for just one element:

```
<BLOCKQUOTE lang="no">...</BLOCKQUOTE>
```

The value for the `lang` attribute is a two-letter language code (not the same as country codes). Table 27-1 lists the currently available language codes.

Table 27-1: Code for the Representation of Names of Languages

Code	Country	Code	Country	Code	Country
aa	Afar	ia	Interlingua	rn	Kirundi
ab	Abkhazian	id	Indonesian (formerly in)	ro	Romanian

Code	Country	Code	Country	Code	Country
af	Afrikaans	ie	Interlingue		Russian
am	Amharic	ik	Inupiak	rm	Kinyarwanda
ar	Arabic	is	Icelandic		
as	Assamese	it	Italian	sa	Sanskrit
ay	Aymara	iu	Inuktitut	sd	Sindhi
az	Azerbaijani			sg	Sangho
		ja	Japanese	sh	Serbo- Croatian
ba	Bashkir	jw	Javanese	si	Sinhalese
be	Byelorussian			sk	Slovak
bg	Bulgarian	ka	Georgian	sl	Slovenian
bh	Bihari	kk	Kazakh		
bi	Bislama	kl	Greenlandic	sm	Samoan
bn	Bengali; Bangla	km	Cambodian	sn	Shona
bo	Tibetan	kn	Kannada	so	Somali
br	Breton	ko	Korean	sq	Albanian
		ks	Kashmiri	sr	Serbian
ca	Catalan	ku	Kurdish	ss	Siswati
co	Corsican	ky	Kirghiz	st	Sesotho
cs	Czech			su	Sundanese
cy	Welsh	la	Latin	sv	Swedish
		lm	Lingala	sw	Swahili
da	Danish	lo	Laothian		
de	German	lt	Lithuanian	ta	Tamil
dz	Bhutani	lv	Latvian	te	Telugu
				tg	Tajik
el	Greek	mg	Malagasy	th	Thai
en	English	mi	Maori	ti	Tigrinya
eo	Esperanto	mk	Macedonian	tk	Turkmen
es	Spanish	ml	Malayalam	tl	Tagalog
et	Estonian	mn	Mongolian	tn	Setswana
eu	Basque	mo	Moldavian	to	Tonga
		mr	Marathi	tr	Turkish
fa	Persian	ms	Malay	ts	Tsonga
fi	Finnish	mt	Maltese	tt	Tatar
fj	Fiji	my	Burmese	tw	Twi
fo	Faroese				
fr	French	na	Nauru	ug	Uighur
fy	Frisian	ne	Nepali	uk	Ukrainian
		ml	Dutch	ur	Urdu

Code	Country	Code	Country	Code	Country
ga	Irish	no	Norwegian	uz	Uzbek
gd	Scots Gaelic				
gl	Galician	oc	Occitan	vi	Vietnamese
gn	Guarani	om	(Afan) Oromo	vo	Volapuk
gu	Gujarati	or	Oriya		
				wo	Wolof
ha	Hausa	pa	Punjabi		
he	Hebrew (formerly iw)	pl	Polish	xh	Xhosa
hi	Hindi	ps	Pashto, Pushto		
hr	Croatian	pt	Portuguese	yi	Yiddish (formerly ji)
hu	Hungarian			yo	Yoruba
hy	Armenian	qu	Quechua		
				za	Zhuang
		rm	Rhaeto-Romance	zh	Chinese
				zu	Zulu

Directionality

An internationalized HTML standard would also need to take into account that many languages read from right to left. Directionality is part of a character's encoding within Unicode.

The HTML 4.0 Specification provides the new dir attribute for specifying the direction in which the text should be interpreted. It can be used in conjunction with the lang attribute and may be added within the tags of most elements. The accepted value for direction is either ltr for left-to-right, or rtl for right-to-left. For example, the following code would set a paragraph in Arabic, reading from right to left:

```
<P LANG="ar" DIR="rtl">...</P>
```

There is also a new tag introduced in HTML 4.0 specifically dealing with documents that contain combinations of left- and right-reading text (bi-directional text, or Bidi for short). The <bdo> tag is used for "bi-directional override," in other words, to specify a span of text that should override the intrinsic direction (as inherited from Unicode) of the text it contains. The <bdo> tag takes the dir attribute as follows:

```
<BDO DIR="ltr">English phrase in an otherwise Hebrew text</BDO>
...
```

Cursive Joining Behavior

In some writing systems, the shape of a character varies depending on its position in the word. For instance, in Arabic, the same character at the beginning of a word looks completely different when it is used as the last character of a word. Generally, this joining behavior is handled within the software, however, there are Unicode characters that give precise control over joining behavior. They have zero width and are placed between characters purely as instructions for specifiying whether the neighboring characters should join.

HTML 4.0 provides mnemonic character entities for both these characters, as shown in Table 27-2.

Table 27-2: Unicode Characters for Joining Behavior

Mnemonic	Numeric	Name	Description
‌	‌	"zero-width non-joiner"	Prevents joining of characters that would otherwise be joined
‍	‍	"zero-width joiner"	Joins characters that would otherwise not be joined

For More Information

The following are good sources of information on the internationalization of the Web.

World Wide Web Consortium (W3C): Internationalization and Localization
   http://www.w3c.org/International/

   This site contains excellent technical information, as well as updates on activities surrounding the efforts to make the Web multilingual.

Babel

   http://babel.alis.com:8080/

   Babel is an Alis Technologies/Internet Society joint project to internationalize the Internet.

HTML Unleashed, by Rick Darnell, et al. (Copyright 1997, Sams.net Publishing, ISBN: 1-57521-299-4)

   This book contains an excellent and in-depth explanation of internationalization issues in Chapter 39, *Internationalizing HTML Character Set and Language Tags.* This chapter is available online at *http://www.webreference. com/dlab/books/html/39-0.html.*

PART VI

Appendixes

APPENDIX A

HTML Tags and Elements

(Including the HTML 4.0 Specification of April, 1998)

This appendix contains the master list of HTML tags that appear in this book. It includes all the tags listed in the HTML 4.0 Specification (including the complete list of attributes for each tag), tags in current use that are not specifically mentioned in the 4.0 Spec, and all browser-specific tags and attributes.

Attributes Key

Many of the tags and elements in this appendix are followed by notes indicating their use or exclusive browser support. The following chart provides explanations for each of those notes.

—D	Deprecated in the HTML 4.0 Specification
—R	Attribute is required in the tag
—IE	Tag or attribute is supported by Microsoft Internet Explorer only
—NN	Tag or attribute is supported by Netscape Navigator only
—event	An event used by a scripting language

In the interest of saving space, this appendix adopts the convention established by the HTML 4.0 Specification of using special attribute group names. Each of these names, indicated in italic text in the charts, represents a collection of specific attributes or events, as described:

Core attributes indicates the collection of core HTML attributes:

id	assigns a unique identifying name to the element
class	assigns a classification name to the element
style	assigns associated style information
title	assigns an advisory title/amplification

i18n stands for "internationalization":

lang	specifies the language for the element by its 2-character language code
dir	specifies the direction of the element (left to right, or right to left)

Intrinsic events indicates the events used by scripting languages that are applicable to the elements: onclick, ondblclick, onmousedown, onmouseup, onmouseover, onmousemove, onmouseout, onkeypress, onkeydown, onkeyup.

`<a>` *Chapter 8, page 130*

Description: Anchor (link)

Attributes:

accesskey	charset	coords
href	hreflang	method
name	rel	rev
shape	tabindex	target
title	type	urn
core attributes	*i18n*	*intrinsic events*
onfocus —*script*	onblur —*script*	

`<abbr>` *Chapter 7, page 104*

Description: Abbreviation

Attributes:

title	*core attributes*	*i18n*
intrinsic events		

`<acronym>` *Chapter 7, page 105*

Description: Acronym

Attributes:

title	*core attributes*	*i18n*
intrinsic events		

`<address>` *Chapter 7, page 103*

Description: Address

Attributes:

core attributes	*i18n*	*intrinsic events*

`<applet> —D` *Chapter 9, page 146*

Description: Applet

Attributes:

align —*D*	archive	alt
code	codebase	height
hspace	name	object
vspace	width	

`<area>`
Chapter 8, page 132

Description: Area (in client-side imagemap)

Attributes:
coords	href	nohref
shape		

`<b>`
Chapter 7, page 105

Description: Bold text

Attributes:
core attributes	*i18n*	*intrinsic events*

`<base>`
Chapter 6, page 91

Description: Base URL

Attributes:
href —*R*	target

`<basefont>` —*D*
Chapter 7, page 105

Description: Basefont

Attributes:
color	face	size

`<bdo>`
Chapter 27, page 462

Description: Bidirectional override

Attributes:
core attributes	lang	dir

`<bgsound>` —*IE*
Chapter 9, page 147; Chapter 19, page 340

Description: Background sound

Attributes:
src	loop

`<big>`
Chapter 7, page 105

Description: Big text

Attributes:
core attributes	*i18n*	*intrinsic events*

`<blink>` —*NN*
Chapter 7, page 105

Description: Blink

Attributes: None

<blockquote>   *Chapter 7, page 103*

Description: Blockquote

Attributes:
   core attributes   *i18n*   *intrinsic events*

<body>   *Chapter 6, page 92*

Description: Body

Attributes:

alink —*D*	background —*IE*	bgcolor —*D*
bgproperties —*IE*	leftmargin —*IE*	link —*D*
text—*D*	topmargin —*IE*	vlink —*D*
core attributes	*i18n*	*intrinsic events*
onload—*event*	unload—*event*	

**
**   *Chapter 7, page 109*

Description: Break line

Attributes:
   clear —*D*   *core attributes*

<button>   *Chapter 12, page 226*

Description: Button (form element)

Attributes:

accesskey	disabled	name
tabindex	type	value
core attributes	*i18n*	*intrinsic events*
onblur —*event*	onfocus —*event*	

<caption>   *Chapter 10, page 168*

Description: Caption (of a table)

Attributes:

align —*D*	summary	valign
core attributes	*i18n*	*intrinsic events*

<center> —*D*   *Chapter 7, page 109*

Description: Center

Attributes: None

<cite>   *Chapter 7, page 106*

Description: Citation

Attributes:
   core attributes   *i18n*   *intrinsic events*

`<code>` *Chapter 7, page 106*

Description: Code

Attributes:
core attributes	*i18n*	*intrinsic events*

`<col>` *Chapter 10, page 169*

Description: Column (within a table)

Attributes:
align —*D*	char	charoff
span	valign	width
core attributes	*i18n*	*intrinsic events*

`<colgroup>` *Chapter 10, page 170*

Description: Column group (within a table)

Attributes:
align —*D*	char	charoff
span	valign	width
core attributes	*i18n*	*intrinsic events*

`<comment>` —*IE* *Chapter 5, page 73*

Description: Comment

Attributes: None

`<dd>` *Chapter 7, page 111*

Description: Definition (part of definition list)

Attributes:
core attributes	*i18n*	*intrinsic events*

`<del>` *Chapter 7, page 106; Chapter 23, page 396*

Description: Deleted Text

Attributes:
cite	datetime	*core attributes*
i18n	*intrinsic events*	

`<dfn>`

Description: Defining Instance

Attributes:
core attributes	*i18n*	*intrinsic events*

<dir> —D

Chapter 7, page 110

Description: Directory list

Attributes:

core attributes	i18n	intrinsic events

<div>

Chapter 7, page 103

Description: Division

Attributes:

align —D	core attributes	i18n
intrinsic events		

<dl>

Chapter 7, page 110

Description: Definition list

Attributes:

compact —D	core attributes	i18n
intrinsic events		

<dt>

Chapter 7, page 111

Description: Definition term (part of definition list)

Attributes:

core attributes	i18n	intrinsic events

<em>

Chapter 7, page 106

Description: Emphasized text

Attributes:

core attributes	i18n	intrinsic events

<embed>

Chapter 9, page 147

Description: Embedded object

Attributes:

align —D	alt	border
code	codebase	frameborder
height	hidden	hspace
name	palette	pluginspage
pluginurl	src	type
units	vspace	width

<fieldset>

Chapter 12, page 227

Description: Fieldset (group of form elements)

Attributes:

core attributes	i18n	intrinsic events

`<font>` —*D*

Chapter 7, page 106

Description: Font style

Attributes:

color	face	size

`<form>`

Chapter 12, page 227

Description: Form

Attributes:

accept-charset	action —*R*	enctype
method	target	*core attributes*
i18n	*intrinsic events*	onsubmit —*event*
onreset —*event*		

`<frame>`

Chapter 11, page 206

Description: Frame

Attributes:

bordercolor	frameborder	longdesc
marginwidth	marginheight	name
noresize	scrolling	src
core attributes		

`<frameset>`

Chapter 11, page 207

Description: Frameset

Attributes:

border	bordercolor	cols
frameborder	framespacing	rows
core attributes	onload —*script*	unload —*script*

`<b1...b6>`

Chapter 7, page 104

Description: Headings level 1 through 6

Attributes:

align —*D*	*core attributes*	*i18n*
intrinsic events		

`<head>`

Chapter 6, page 93

Description: Head of document

Attributes:

profile	lang	dir

`<hr>`
Chapter 9, page 149

Description: Horizontal rule

Attributes:

align —*D*	noshade —*D*	size —*D*
width —*D*	*core attributes*	*intrinsic events*

`<html>`
Chapter 6, page 93

Description: HTML document

Attributes:
i18n

`<i>`
Chapter 7, page 106

Description: Italic

Attributes:

core attributes	*i18n*	*intrinsic events*

`<iframe>`
Chapter 11, page 208

Description: Inline frame (floating frame)

Attributes:

align —*D*	frameborder	height
hspace	longdesc	marginheight
marginwidth	name	noresize
scrolling	src	vspace
width		

`<img>`
Chapter 9, page 149

Description: Image

Attributes:

align —*D*	alt —*R*	border —*D*
controls —*IE*	dynsrc —*IE*	height
hspace	ismap	loop —*IE*
longdesc	lowsrc	src —*R*
start —*IE*	usemap	vspace
width	*core attributes*	*i18n*
intrinsic events		

`<input>`
Chapter 12, Pages 228 to 231

Description: Input (form) [Input types: text, password, checkbox, radio, submit, reset, file, hidden, image, button]

Attributes:

accept	accesskey	align —*D*
alt	checked	disabled
maxlength	name	readonly
size	src	tabindex

type	usemap	value
core attributes	*i18n*	*intrinsic events*
onfocus —*event*	onselect —*event*	onchange —*event*

<ins> *Chapter 7, page 107; Chapter 23, page 396*

Description: Inserted text

Attributes:

cite	datetime	*core attributes*
i18n	*intrinsic events*	

<isindex> —D *Chapter 12, page 231*

Description: Searchable Index

Attributes:

prompt	*core attributes*	*i18n*

<kbd> *Chapter 7, page 107*

Description: Keyboard text

Attributes:

core attributes	*i18n*	*intrinsic events*

<label> *Chapter 12, page 231*

Description: Label (forms)

Attributes:

accesskey	for	*core attributes*
i18n	*intrinsic events*	onfocus —*event*
onblur —*event*		

<layer> —NN *Chapter 24, page 432*

Description: Layer

Attributes: None

<legend> *Chapter 12, page 232*

Description: Legend (forms)

Attributes:

accesskey	*core attributes*	*i18n*
intrinsic events		

<li> *Chapter 7, page 111*

Description: List item

Attributes:

compact —*D*	start —*D*	type —*D*
value —*D*	*core attributes*	*i18n*
intrinsic events		

\<link\>
Chapter 6, page 93

Description: Link

Attributes:

charset	href	hreflang
methods	rev	rel
media	title	type
urn	*core attributes*	*i18n*
intrinsic events		

\<map\>
Chapter 8, page 132

Description: Map (client-side imagemap)

Attributes:
name —*R*

\<marquee\> —*IE*
Chapter 9, page 151

Description: Marquee

Attributes:

behavior	bgcolor —*D*	direction
height	hspace	direction
height	hspace	loop
scrollamount	scrolldelay	vspace
width		

\<menu\> —*D*
Chapter 7, page 111

Description: Menu list

Attributes:

compact —*D*	type	*core attributes*
i18n	*intrinsic events*	

\<meta\>
Chapter 6, page 94

Description: Meta information

Attributes:

content —*R*	http-equiv	name
scheme		

\<multicol\> —*NN*
Chapter 7, page 109

Description: Multi-column formatted text

Attributes:

cols	gutter	width

\<nobr\>
Chapter 7, page 109

Description: No break allowed

Attributes: None

<noembed>
Chapter 9, page 152

Description: No embed

Attributes: None

<noframes>
Chapter 11, page 209

Description: No frames

Attributes:

core attributes	*i18n*	*intrinsic events*

<noscript>
Chapter 9, page 152

Description: No script

Attributes:

core attributes	*i18n*	*intrinsic events*

<object>
Chapter 9, page 152

Description: Object

Attributes:

align —*D*	archive	border
classid	codebase	codetype
data	declare	height
hspace	name	shapes
standby	tabindex	type
usemap	vspace	width
core attributes	*i18n*	*intrinsic events*

<ol>
Chapter 7, page 112

Description: Ordered list (numbered)

Attributes:

compact	start	type
core attributes	*i18n*	*intrinsic events*

<optgroup>
Chapter 12, page 232

Description: Option Group (in a form)

Attributes:

disabled	label —*R*	*core attributes*
i18n	*intrinsic events*	

<option>
Chapter 12, page 232

Description: Option (in a form)

Attributes:

disabled	label	selected
value	*core attributes*	*i18n*
intrinsic events		

`<p>`
Chapter 7, page 104

Description: Paragraph

Attributes:
align —*D*	*core attributes*	*i18n*
intrinsic events		

`<param>`
Chapter 9, page 153

Description: Parameter

Attributes:
id	name —*R*	value
valuetype	type	

`<pre>`
Chapter 7, page 110

Description: Preformatted text

Attributes:
width —*D*	*core attributes*	*i18n*
intrinsic events		

`<q>`
Chapter 7, page 107

Description: Short quotation

Attributes:
cite	*core attributes*	*i18n*
intrinsic events		

`<s>` —*D*
Chapter 7, page 107

Description: Strike-through text

Attributes:
core attributes	*i18n*	*intrinsic events*

`<samp>`
Chapter 7, page 107

Description: Sample text

Attributes:
core attributes	*i18n*	*intrinsic events*

`<script>`
Chapter 9, page 154

Description: Script

Attributes:
charset	language	src
type —*R*		

<select> — Chapter 12, page 232

Description: Selection menu (in a form)

Attributes:

disabled	multiple	name
size	tabindex	*core attributes*
i18n	*intrinsic events*	onfocus —*event*
onblur —*event*	onchange —*event*	

<small> — Chapter 7, page 107

Description: Small text

Attributes:

core attributes	*i18n*	*intrinsic events*

<spacer> —*NN* — Chapter 9, page 154

Description: Spacer

Attributes:

align —*D*	height	size
type	width	

<span> — Chapter 7, page 108; Chapter 23, page 395

Description: Span (inline text container)

Attributes:

core attributes	*i18n*	*intrinsic events*

<strike> —*D* — Chapter 7, page 108

Description: Strike-through text

Attributes:

core attributes	*i18n*	*intrinsic events*

<strong> — Chapter 7, page 108

Description: Strongly emphasized text

Attributes:

core attributes	*i18n*	*intrinsic events*

<style> — Chapter 23, page 393

Description: Embedded stylesheet

Attributes:

type	media	title
i18n		

<sub>

Chapter 7, page 108

Description: Subscript

Attributes:

core attributes	i18n	intrinsic events

<sup>

Chapter 7, page 108

Description: Superscript

Attributes:

core attributes	i18n	intrinsic events

<table>

Chapter 10, page 170

Description: Table

Attributes:

align —D	background	bgcolor —D
border	bordercolor —IE	bordercolorlight —IE
bordercolordark —IE	cellpadding	cellspacing
frame	height	hspace
rules	summary	vspace
width	core attributes	i18n
intrinsic events		

<tbody>

Chapter 10, page 172

Description: Table body

Attributes:

align —D	char	charoff
valign	core attributes	i18n
intrinsic events		

<td>

Chapter 10, page 173

Description: Table data cell

Attributes:

abbr	align —D	axis
char	charoff	background
bgcolor —D	bordercolor —IE	bordercolorlight —IE
bordercolordark —IE	colspan	headers
height	nowrap	rowspan
scope	valign	width
core attributes	i18n	intrinsic events

<textarea>

Chapter 12, page 233

Description: Text area (in a form)

Attributes:

accesskey	cols —R	disabled
name	readonly	rows —R

tabindex	wrap	*core attributes*
i18n	*intrinsic events*	onfocus —*event*
onblur —*event*	onchange —*event*	

Chapter 10, page 174

<tfoot>

Description: Table foot

Attributes:

align —D	char	charoff
valign	*core attributes*	*i18n*
intrinsic events		

Chapter 10, page 175

<th>

Description: Table header cell

Attributes:

abbr	align —*D*	axis
char	charoff	background
bgcolor —*D*	bordercolor —*IE*	bordercolorlight —*IE*
bordercolordark —*IE*	colspan	headers
height	nowrap	rowspan
scope	valign	width
core attributes	*i18n*	*intrinsic events*

Chapter 10, page 175

<thead>

Description: Table head

Attributes:

align —D	char	charoff
valign	*core attributes*	*i18n*
intrinsic events		

Chapter 6, page 94

<title>

Description: Document title

Attributes:

lang	dir

Chapter 10, page 176

<tr>

Description: Table row

Attributes:

align —*D*	char	charoff
bgcolor —*D*	bordercolor —*IE*	bordercolorlight —*IE*
bordercolordark —*IE*	valign	*core attributes*
i18n	*intrinsic events*	

`<tt>`
Chapter 7, page 108

Description: Typewriter text

Attributes:
    core attributes   *i18n*   *intrinsic events*

`<u>` —D *Chapter 7, page 108*

Description: Underlined text

Attributes:
    core attributes   *i18n*   *intrinsic events*

`<ul>` *Chapter 7, page 112*

Description: Unordered list (bulleted)

Attributes:
    compact   *core attributes*   *i18n*
    intrinsic events

`<var>` *Chapter 7, page 108*

Description: Variable

Attributes:
    core attributes   *i18n*   *intrinsic events*

`<wbr>` *Chapter 7, page 110*

Description: Wordbreak

Attributes: None

APPENDIX B

List of Attributes

Most HTML tags rely on attributes to modify their behavior and make them more useful. With so many available tags and attributes it's easy to forget which tag goes with which attributes. For instance, you may know that you want to set the padding value for a table, but you can't remember which tag takes the cellpadding attribute (the answer to this one is <table>).

This appendix lists all of the available attributes as listed in the HTML 4.0 Specification, in alphabetical order. The "Related Elements" entry lists the tags that can use that attribute. Also included are:

Accepted values for each tag

In the "Values" list, courier text indicates a literal value that must be typed in as shown; courier italic indicates a replaceable value description, for which you would provide your own value.

Whether the attribute is required

At the right of each entry is an indication of whether the attribute is *Required* or *Optional.*

Whether the tag is deprecated

The word "Deprecated" in parentheses indicates that the tag has been deprecated (discouraged from use in favor of newer tagging solutions) in the HTML 4.0 Specification. To read more about deprecated tags, see Appendix C, *Deprecated Tags.*

A description of the attribute's use

Descriptions of each attribute's function or notes on its use are provided below the attribute.

Note that some attributes appear more than once in the list. This is due to the fact that they may be used differently or may take different values depending on the tag in which they are used.

abbr
Optional

Abbreviated name for table cell

Related Elements: TD, TH

Values: text

accept-charset
Optional

List of supported charsets

Related Elements: FORM

Values: list

accept
Optional

List of MIME types for file upload

Related Elements: INPUT

Values: MIME types

accesskey
Optional

Assigns an access or shortcut key that brings focus (activates) to the element

Related Elements: A, AREA, BUTTON, INPUT, LABEL, LEGEND, TEXTAREA

Values: single character

action
Required

Location of the CGI form processor on the server

Related Elements: FORM

Values: url

align
(Deprecated) Optional

Positions a caption relative to table

Related Elements: CAPTION

Values: top|bottom|left|right

align
(Deprecated) Optional

Vertical or horizontal alignment

Related Elements: APPLET, IFRAME, IMG, INPUT, OBJECT

Values: top|middle|bottom|left|right

align *(Deprecated) Optional*

Positions legend relative to fieldset

Related Elements: LEGEND

Values: top|bottom|left|right

align *(Deprecated) Optional*

Table position relative to window

Related Elements: TABLE

Values: left|center|right

align *(Deprecated) Optional*

Horizontal alignment of rule

Related Elements: HR

Values: left|center|right

align *(Deprecated) Optional*

Alignment or justification of block element

Related Elements: DIV, H1, H2, H3, H4, H5, H6, P

Values: left|center|right|justify

align *Optional*

Horizontal alignment, character alignment, or justification

Related Elements: COL, COLGROUP, TBODY, TD, TFOOT, TH, THEAD, TR

Values: left|center|right|justify|char

alink *(Deprecated) Optional*

Color of active (selected) links

Related Elements: BODY

Values: color

alt *(Deprecated) Optional*

Alternative text if the applet cannot be displayed

Related Elements: APPLET

Values: text

alt
Required

Alternative text that describes image if it cannot be displayed

Related Elements: AREA, IMG

Values: text

alt
Optional

Alternative text for graphic control if it cannot be displayed

Related Elements: INPUT

Values: text

archive
Optional

Space-separated list of preload resources

Related Elements: OBJECT

Values: list of URLs

archive
(Deprecated) Optional

Comma-separated list of preload resources

Related Elements: APPLET

Values: list of URLs

axis
Optional

Names a group of header cells for hierarchical table structures

Related Elements: TD, TH

Values: text

background
(Deprecated) Optional

Location of tiling background graphic

Related Elements: BODY

Values: url

bgcolor
(Deprecated) Optional

Background color for entire table

Related Elements: TABLE

Values: color

bgcolor *(Deprecated) Optional*

Background color for table row

Related Elements: TR

Values: color

bgcolor *(Deprecated) Optional*

Background color for table cell

Related Elements: TD, TH

Values: color

bgcolor *(Deprecated) Optional*

Document background color

Related Elements: BODY

Values: color

border *(Deprecated) Optional*

Width of border around linked images or objects

Related Elements: IMG, OBJECT

Values: pixels or %

border *Optional*

Width of frame around a table

Related Elements: TABLE

Values: pixels

cellpadding *Optional*

Spacing within cells

Related Elements: TABLE

Values: pixels or %

cellspacing *Optional*

Spacing between cells

Related Elements: TABLE

Values: pixels or %

char
Optional

The character along which elements are aligned, such as a decimal point

Related Elements: COL, COLGROUP, TBODY, TD, TFOOT, TH, THEAD, TR

Values: character

charoff
Optional

Distance to first occurrence of the alignment character

Related Elements: COL, COLGROUP, TBODY, TD, TFOOT, TH, THEAD, TR

Values: pixels or %

charset
Optional

Character encoding of the target resource

Related Elements: A, LINK, SCRIPT

Values: character set name

checked
Optional

Sets the initial state of a radio button or checkbox to checked

Related Elements: INPUT

Values: checked

cite
Optional

Location of source document for the quotation

Related Elements: BLOCKQUOTE, Q

Values: url

cite
Optional

Location of document containing explanation for edit

Related Elements: DEL, INS

Values: url

class
Optional

The class (or list of classes) for the element (used with style sheets)

Related Elements: All elements but BASE, BASEFONT, HEAD, HTML, META, PARAM, SCRIPT, STYLE, TITLE

Values: text

classid
Optional

URL for the specific implementation

Related Elements: OBJECT

Values: url

clear
(Deprecated) none

Used to start flow of text after objects or images aligned against the margins

Related Elements: BR

Values: left|all|right|none

code
(Deprecated) Required

Class name of the code to be executed

Related Elements: APPLET

Values: applet file

codebase
Optional

Location of object's codebase (syntax varies by object)

Related Elements: OBJECT

Values: url

codebase
(Deprecated) Optional

URL from which the code is retrieved

Related Elements: APPLET

Values: url

codetype
Optional

media type of the code

Related Elements: OBJECT

Values: MIME type

color
(Deprecated) Optional

text color

Related Elements: BASEFONT, FONT

Values: color

cols *Optional*

List of widths (in pixels, %, or relative * values) for columns in a frameset

Related Elements: FRAMESET

Values: list of numbers

cols *Required*

Width of a textarea form element, measured in number of characters

Related Elements: TEXTAREA

Values: number

colspan *Optional*

Number of columns spanned by cell

Related Elements: TD, TH

Values: number

compact *(Deprecated) Optional*

Reduces interim spacing in a list

Related Elements: DIR, MENU, DL, OL, UL

Values: compact

content *Required*

Content of meta information

Related Elements: META

Values: text

coords *Optional*

List of x,y coordinates used in an imagemap; syntax varies according to a given shape

Related Elements: AREA

Values: x,y coords

coords *Optional*

List of x,y coordinates used in a client-side imagemap

Related Elements: A

Values: x,y coords

data
Optional

Location of the data used for the object

Related Elements: OBJECT

Values: url

datetime
Optional

Date and time of change in ISO format (YYYY-MM-DDThh:mm:ssTZD)

Related Elements: DEL, INS

Values: ISO date

declare
Optional

Declare but don't instantiate flag

Related Elements: OBJECT

Values: declare

defer
Optional

UA may defer execution of script

Related Elements: SCRIPT

Values: defer

dir
Optional

Specifies direction (left to right or right to left) for text

Related Elements: All elements but APPLET, BASE, BASEFONT, BDO, BR, FRAME, FRAMESET, HR, IFRAME, PARAM, SCRIPT

Values: ltr|rtl

dir
Required

Direction for overridden text

Related Elements: BDO

Values: ltr|rtl

disabled
Optional

Makes form control unavailable in a given context

Related Elements: BUTTON, INPUT, OPTGROUP, OPTION, SELECT, TEXTAREA

Values: disabled

enctype
Optional

Defaults to `application/x-www- form-urlencoded`

Related Elements: FORM

Values: Content-type

face
(Deprecated) Optional

Comma-separated list of font names

Related Elements: BASEFONT, FONT

Values: font name

for
Optional

Associates the label with a control

Related Elements: LABEL

Values: ID value

frame
Optional

Which parts of the table frame to render

Related Elements: TABLE

Values: void|above|below|hsides|lhs|rhs|vsides|box|border

frameborder
Optional

Turns display of frame border on or off

Related Elements: FRAME, IFRAME

Values: 1|0

headers
Optional

List of header cell IDs that are related to the cell

Related Elements: TD, TH

Values: ID references

height
Optional

Height of inline frame

Related Elements: IFRAME

Values: pixels or %

height *Optional*

Height of image or object (will resize original to match specified size)

Related Elements: IMG, OBJECT

Values: pixels or %

height *(Deprecated) Required*

Initial height of applet window

Related Elements: APPLET

Values: pixels or %

height *(Deprecated) Optional*

Height for cell

Related Elements: TD, TH

Values: pixels

href *Optional*

Location of target document or resource

Related Elements: A, AREA, LINK

Values: url

href *Optional*

URL that serves as the base for all links in a document

Related Elements: BASE

Values: url

hreflang *Optional*

Identifies language of target document

Related Elements: A, LINK

Values: 2-char language code

hspace *(Deprecated) Optional*

Amount of space held clear to the left and right of the element

Related Elements: APPLET, IMG, OBJECT

Values: pixels

http-equiv
Optional

HTTP response header name

Related Elements: META

Values: name

id
Optional

A unique ID name given to an instance of an element in a document

Related Elements: All elements but BASE, HEAD, HTML, META, SCRIPT, STYLE, TITLE

Values: ID

ismap
Optional

Indicates image is a server-side image map

Related Elements: IMG

Values: ismap

label
Optional

Defines a logical group of options for use in hierarchical menus

Related Elements: OPTION

Values: text

label
Required

Defines a logical group of options for use in hierarchical menus

Related Elements: OPTGROUP

Values: text

lang
Optional

Indicates language used in element

Related Elements: All elements but APPLET, BASE, BASEFONT, BR, FRAME, FRAMESET, HR, IFRAME, PARAM, SCRIPT

Values: 2-char language code

language
(Deprecated) Optional

Predefined script language name

Related Elements: SCRIPT

Values: script language

link

Color of links in the document

Related Elements: BODY

Values: `color`

longdesc
Optional

Link to long description of image contents (complements `alt`)

Related Elements: IMG

Values: `url`

longdesc
Optional

Link to long description (complements `title`)

Related Elements: FRAME, IFRAME

Values: `url`

marginheight
Optional

Height of top and bottom margins

Related Elements: FRAME, IFRAME

Values: `pixels`

marginwidth
Optional

Width of left and right margins

Related Elements: FRAME, IFRAME

Values: `pixels`

maxlength
Optional

Maximum number of characters in a form field

Related Elements: INPUT

Values: `number`

media
Optional

Comma-separated list of media descriptors

Related Elements: STYLE, LINK

Values: `text`

HTML Attributes

method
Required

HTTP method used to submit the form

Related Elements: FORM

Values: GET | POST

multiple
Optional

Allows more than one option to be selected in a menu or scrolling list

Related Elements: SELECT

Values: multiple

name
Required

Names the parameter to be passed on to the forms processing application

Related Elements: BUTTON, TEXTAREA, SELECT, INPUT, OBJECT

Values: text

name
(Deprecated) Optional

Allows applets to find each other

Related Elements: APPLET

Values: text

name
Optional

Names the frame for targetting

Related Elements: FRAME, IFRAME

Values: text

name
Optional

Creates named anchor (for linking to a specific spot on a page)

Related Elements: A

Values: text

name
Required

Names a client-side imagemap for reference

Related Elements: MAP

Values: text

name

Property name

Related Elements: PARAM

Values: text

name
Optional

Metainformation name

Related Elements: META

Values: text

nohref
Optional

Indicates an area of a client-side imagemap that has no associated link

Related Elements: AREA

Values: nohref

noresize
Optional

Prevents users from resizing frames

Related Elements: FRAME

Values: no resize

noshade
(Deprecated) Optional

Turns off 3-D rendering of horizontal rules

Related Elements: HR

Values: noshade

nowrap
(Deprecated) Optional

Suppresses word wrap

Related Elements: TD, TH

Values: nowrap

object
(Deprecated) Optional

Serialized applet file

Related Elements: APPLET

Values: resource name

onblur

When focus is removed from an element

Related Elements: A, AREA, BUTTON, INPUT, LABEL, SELECT, TEXTAREA

Values: script

onchange

When element value changes

Related Elements: INPUT, SELECT, TEXTAREA

Values: script

onclick

When a pointer button is clicked

Related Elements: All elements but APPLET, BASE, BASEFONT, BDO, BR,
FONT, FRAME, FRAMESET, HEAD, HTML, IFRAME, ISINDEX,
META, PARAM, SCRIPT, STYLE, TITLE

Values: script

ondblclick

When a pointer button is double clicked

Related Elements: All elements but APPLET, BASE, BASEFONT, BDO, BR,
FONT, FRAME, FRAMESET, HEAD, HTML, IFRAME, ISINDEX,
META, PARAM, SCRIPT, STYLE, TITLE

Values: script

onfocus

When focus is applied to an element

Related Elements: A, AREA, BUTTON, INPUT, LABEL, SELECT, TEXTAREA

Values: script

onkeydown

When a key is pressed down

Related Elements: All elements but APPLET, BASE, BASEFONT, BDO, BR,
FONT, FRAME, FRAMESET, HEAD, HTML, IFRAME, ISINDEX,
META, PARAM, SCRIPT, STYLE, TITLE

Values: script

onkeypress *Optional*

When a key is pressed and released

Related Elements: All elements but APPLET, BASE, BASEFONT, BDO, BR,
FONT, FRAME, FRAMESET, HEAD, HTML, IFRAME, ISINDEX,
META, PARAM, SCRIPT, STYLE, TITLE

Values: script

onkeyup *Optional*

When a key is released

Related Elements: All elements but APPLET, BASE, BASEFONT, BDO, BR,
FONT, FRAME, FRAMESET, HEAD, HTML, IFRAME, ISINDEX,
META, PARAM, SCRIPT, STYLE, TITLE

Values: script

onload *Optional*

When all the frames have been loaded

Related Elements: FRAMESET

Values: script

onload *Optional*

When the document has been loaded

Related Elements: BODY

Values: script

onmousedown *Optional*

When a pointer button is pressed down

Related Elements: All elements but APPLET, BASE, BASEFONT, BDO, BR,
FONT, FRAME, FRAMESET, HEAD, HTML, IFRAME, ISINDEX,
META, PARAM, SCRIPT, STYLE, TITLE

Values: script

onmousemove *Optional*

When a pointer is moved within the element

Related Elements: All elements but APPLET, BASE, BASEFONT, BDO, BR,
FONT, FRAME, FRAMESET, HEAD, HTML, IFRAME, ISINDEX,
META, PARAM, SCRIPT, STYLE, TITLE

Values: script

onmouseout

Optional

When a pointer is moved out of the element's space

Related Elements: All elements but APPLET, BASE, BASEFONT, BDO, BR,
FONT, FRAME, FRAMESET, HEAD, HTML, IFRAME, ISINDEX,
META, PARAM, SCRIPT, STYLE, TITLE

Values: script

onmouseover

Optional

When a pointer is moved onto the element's space

Related Elements: All elements but APPLET, BASE, BASEFONT, BDO, BR,
FONT, FRAME, FRAMESET, HEAD, HTML, IFRAME, ISINDEX,
META, PARAM, SCRIPT, STYLE, TITLE

Values: script

onmouseup

Optional

When a pointer button is released

Related Elements: All elements but APPLET, BASE, BASEFONT, BDO, BR,
FONT, FRAME, FRAMESET, HEAD, HTML, IFRAME, ISINDEX,
META, PARAM, SCRIPT, STYLE, TITLE

Values: script

onreset

Optional

When the form is reset

Related Elements: FORM

Values: script

onselect

Optional

When some text is selected

Related Elements: INPUT, TEXTAREA

Values: script

onsubmit

Optional

When the form is submitted

Related Elements: FORM

Values: script

onunload

When all the frames have been removed

Related Elements: FRAMESET

Values: script

onunload
Optional

When the document has been removed

Related Elements: BODY

Values: script

profile
Optional

A meta-data profile (dictionary)

Related Elements: HEAD

Values: url

prompt
(Deprecated) Optional

Initial message in an isindex search field

Related Elements: ISINDEX

Values: text

readonly
Optional

Prevents editing of initial value in a form text field (textarea, text, password)

Related Elements: TEXTAREA, INPUT

Values: readonly

rel
Optional

Comma-separated list of forward link types

Related Elements: A, LINK

Values: link types

rev
Optional

Comma-separated list of reverse link types

Related Elements: A, LINK

Values: link types

rows *Optional*

Comma-separated list of heights for the rows of a frameset (in pixels, % or relative * values)

Related Elements: FRAMESET

Values: list of values

rows *Required*

The number of visible rows in a textarea field

Related Elements: TEXTAREA

Values: number

rowspan *Optional*

The number of rows spanned by cell

Related Elements: TD, TH

Values: number

rules *Optional*

Specifies where rules are rendered between rows and columns of a table

Related Elements: TABLE

Values: none|groups|rows|cols|all

scheme *Optional*

Scheme to be used in interpreting the content (varies by context)

Related Elements: META

Values: text

scope *Optional*

Set of data cells for which the current header cell provides header information

Related Elements: TD, TH

Values: row|col|rowgroup|colgroup

scrolling *Optional*

Indicates when a scrollbar should appear (default is auto)

Related Elements: FRAME, IFRAME

Values: yes|no|auto

selected

Optional

Defines initial state of an option as selected

Related Elements: OPTION

Values: selected

shape

Required

Shape description (rect, circ, poly) used for interpretation of coords (for use in client-side imagemaps)

Related Elements: AREA

Values: shape

shape

Required

For use with client-side imagemaps

Related Elements: A

Values: shape

size

(Deprecated) Optional

Specifies thickness of horizontal rule

Related Elements: HR

Values: pixels

size

(Deprecated) Optional

Font size: absolute (1-7) or relative (+1, -1, etc.)

Related Elements: FONT

Values: number

size

Optional

Specific to each type of field

Related Elements: INPUT

Values: number

size

(Deprecated) Required

Base font size for font elements (absolute or relative size notation)

Related Elements: BASEFONT

Values: number

size
Optional

The number of visible rows in scrolling list

Related Elements: SELECT

Values: number

span
Optional

COL attributes affect N columns

Related Elements: COL

Values: number

span
Optional

The number of columns in group

Related Elements: COLGROUP

Values: number

src
Optional

URL for an external script

Related Elements: SCRIPT

Values: url

src
Optional

URL for image used as a form button

Related Elements: INPUT

Values: url

src
Optional

Source of frame content

Related Elements: FRAME, IFRAME

Values: url

src
Required

URL of image file

Related Elements: IMG

Values: url

standby

Message to show while loading

Related Elements: OBJECT

Values: text

start
(Deprecated) Optional

Number an ordered list should begin counting from

Related Elements: OL

Values: number

style
Optional

Associated style information

Related Elements: All elements but BASE, BASEFONT, HEAD, HTML, META,
    PARAM, SCRIPT, STYLE, TITLE

Values: style syntax

summary
Optional

Description of table contents for non-visual browsers

Related Elements: TABLE

Values: text

tabindex
Optional

Position in tabbing order

Related Elements: A, AREA, BUTTON, INPUT, OBJECT, SELECT,
    TEXTAREA

Values: number

target
Optional

Targets the window or frame to load the target document; the predefined
target names are _blank, _self, _parent, _top

Related Elements: A, AREA, BASE, FORM, LINK

Values: window name

text
(Deprecated) Optional

Document text color

Related Elements: BODY

Values: color

title *Optional*

Title for the style

Related Elements: STYLE

Values: text

title *Optional*

Specifies an advisory title that may be rendered specially by non-visual browsers

Related Elements: All elements but BASE, BASEFONT, HEAD, HTML, META, PARAM, SCRIPT, STYLE, TITLE

Values: text

type *Optional*

Advisory content type

Related Elements: A, LINK

Values: MIME type

type *Optional*

Content type for data

Related Elements: OBJECT

Values: MIME type

type *Optional*

Content type for value when valuetype=ref

Related Elements: PARAM

Values: MIME type

type *Required*

Content type of script language

Related Elements: SCRIPT

Values: MIME type

type *Required*

Content type of style language (defaults to text/css)

Related Elements: STYLE

Values: MIME

type
Required

Kind of widget needed

Related Elements: INPUT

Values: text|password|checkbox|radio|submit|reset|file|hidden|i
mage

type
(Deprecated) Optional

Bullet style or numbering scheme for a list item (depending on context)

Related Elements: LI

Values: disc|square|circle or 1|A|a|I|i

type
(Deprecated) Optional

Numbering style

Related Elements: OL

Values: 1|A|a|I|i

type
(Deprecated) Optional

Bullet style

Related Elements: UL

Values: disc|square|circle

type
Required

For use as form button

Related Elements: BUTTON

Values: button|submit|reset

usemap
Optional

Fragment identifier that points to the map element for a client-side imagmap

Related Elements: IMG, INPUT, OBJECT

Values: url

valign
Optional

Vertical alignment in cells

Related Elements: COL, COLGROUP, TBODY, TD, TFOOT, TH, THEAD, TR

Values: top|middle|bottom|baseline

value
Optional

Value of the option when selected; defaults to content of the option container

Related Elements: OPTION

Values: alphanumeric text

value
Optional

Property value

Related Elements: PARAM

Values: parameter value

value
Required

Value of input element passed to the forms processing program

Related Elements: INPUT, BUTTON

Values: value

value
(Deprecated) Optional

Resets sequence number

Related Elements: LI

Values: number

valuetype
Optional

How to interpret value

Related Elements: PARAM

Values: data|ref|object

version
(Deprecated) Optional

Link to DTD for the document

Related Elements: HTML

Values: url

vlink
(Deprecated) Optional

Color of visited links

Related Elements: BODY

Values: color

vspace

Amount of space held clear above and below an element

Related Elements: APPLET, IMG, OBJECT

Values: pixels

width

Length of horizontal rule

Related Elements: HR

Values: pixels or %

width

Frame width

Related Elements: IFRAME

Values: pixels or %

width

Size of image or object. The browser will resize elements to match specified values

Related Elements: IMG, OBJECT

Values: pixels or %

width

Table width

Related Elements: TABLE

Values: pixels or %

width

Initial width of applet

Related Elements: APPLET

Values: pixels or %

width

Column width specification

Related Elements: COL

Values: pixels, % or *

width   _Optional_
___

Default width for enclosed COLs

Related Elements: COLGROUP

Values: pixels, % or *

width   _(Deprecated) Optional_
___

Width for cell

Related Elements: TD, TH

Values: pixels

width   _(Deprecated) Optional_
___

Maximum width for preformatted text

Related Elements: PRE

Values: number

APPENDIX C

Deprecated Tags

The World Wide Web Consortium (W3C) is the organization responsible for setting the HTML standard. The W3C takes HTML advancements into consideration when compiling the new standards. Many once-proprietary tags have been rolled into the standard and eventually find universal browser support. Others go by the wayside.

As HTML advances and improved methods such as Cascading Style Sheets emerge, older tags are put to rest by the W3C. The HTML 4.0 Proposed Recommendation has classified a number of HTML tags and individual attributes as "deprecated." The W3C defines a deprecated element as one . . .

> ". . . that has been outdated by newer constructs. Deprecated elements are defined in the reference manual in appropriate locations, but are clearly marked as deprecated. Deprecated elements may become obsolete in future versions of HTML.
>
> User agents [browsers] should continue to support deprecated elements for reasons of backward compatibility. Definitions of elements and attributes clearly indicate which are deprecated.
>
> This specification includes examples that illustrate how to avoid using deprecated elements. In most cases these depend on user agent support for style sheets. In general, authors should use style sheets to achieve stylistic and formatting effects rather than HTML presentational attributes. HTML presentational attributes have been deprecated when style sheet alternatives exist." *

The tables in this appendix list the elements and attributes that have been deprecated in the HTML 4.0 Spec. Substitute tags or methods are listed when provided by the W3C.

---

* Source: (HTML 4.0 Proposed Recommendation).

Deprecated Elements

The following elements have been deprecated in the HTML 4.0 Specification:

Element	Description	Recommendation
`<applet>`	Inserts applet	`<object>`
`<basefont>`	Sets font styles for subsequent text	style sheets (`color, font-size, font-family, font`, etc.)
`<center>`	Centers elements on the page	`<DIV align=center>`
`<dir>`	Directory List	`<ul>`
`<font>`	Applies font styles	style sheets (`color, font-size, font-family, font`, etc.)
`<isindex>`	Adds search field	`<form>` and CGI programming
`<menu>`	Menu item list	`<ul>`
`<s>`	Strike-through text	style sheets (`text-decoration`)
`<strike>`	Strike-through text	style sheets (`text-decoration`)
`<u>`	Underlined text	style sheets (`text-decoration`)

Deprecated Attributes

The following attributes have been deprecated in the HTML 4.0 Specification.

Name	Related Elements	Comment	Replacement Tag
`align`	CAPTION	Horizontal alignment of table caption	style sheet controls
`align`	APPLET, IFRAME, IMG, INPUT, OBJECT	Vertical or horizontal alignment of element	style sheet controls
`align`	LEGEND	Aligns legend relative to its fieldset	style sheet controls
`align`	TABLE	Table position relative to window	style sheet controls
`align`	HR	Horizontal alignment of rule	style sheet controls
`align`	DIV, H1, H2, H3, H4, H5, H6, P	Horizontal alignment of these block elements	style sheet controls
`alink`	BODY	Color of selected links	style sheet controls
`alt`	APPLET	Short description	`<OBJECT>`
`archive`	APPLET	Comma separated archive list	`<OBJECT>`
`background`	BODY	Tiling background graphic	style sheet controls
`bgcolor`	TABLE	Background color for cells	style sheet controls

Name	Related Elements	Comment	Replacement Tag
bgcolor	TR	Background color for row	style sheet controls
bgcolor	TD, TH	Cell background color	style sheet controls
bgcolor	BODY	Document background color	style sheet controls
border	IMG, OBJECT	Link border width around an image	style sheet controls
clear	BR	Control of text flow	style sheet controls
code	APPLET	Applet class file	<OBJECT>
codebase	APPLET	Optional base URI for applet	<OBJECT>
color	BASEFONT, FONT	Text color	style sheet controls
compact	DIR, MENU	Displays lists with reduced spacing	<UL>
compact	DL, OL, UL	Displays lists with reduced spacing	style sheet controls
face	BASEFONT, FONT	Comma-separated list of font names	style sheet controls
height	APPLET	Initial height	<OBJECT>
height	TD, TH	Height for cell	
hspace	APPLET, IMG, OBJECT	Horizontal gutter	style sheet controls
language	SCRIPT	Predefined script language name	
link	BODY	Color of links	style sheet controls
name	APPLET	Allows applets to find each other	<OBJECT>
noshade	HR	Displays rule without 3-D shading	style sheet controls
nowrap	TD, TH	Suppresses word wrap	style sheet controls
object	APPLET	Serialized applet file	<OBJECT>
prompt	ISINDEX	Prompt message	<FORM>
size	HR	Thickness of horizontal rule	style sheet controls
size	FONT	Font size (based on default)	style sheet controls
size	BASEFONT	Base font size for FONT elements	style sheet controls
start	OL	Starting sequence number	style sheet controls
text	BODY	Document text color	style sheet controls
type	LI	List item style	style sheet controls

Name	Related Elements	Comment	Replacement Tag
type	OL	Numbering style	style sheet controls
type	UL	Bullet style	style sheet controls
value	LI	Reset sequence number	style sheet controls
version	HTML	Constant	
vlink	BODY	Color of visited links	style sheet controls
vspace	APPLET, IMG, OBJECT	Vertical gutter	style sheet controls
width	HR	Length of horizontal rule	style sheet controls
width	APPLET	Initial width	<OBJECT>
width	TD, TH	Width for cell	
width	PRE	Character length for preformatted text	

APPENDIX D

Proprietary Tags

HTML is an ever-evolving language, and progress is spurred forward by tags developed in the head-to-head competition to dominate the browser universe. Although the vast majority of tags work for both major browsers, both Netscape and Microsoft have developed sets of proprietary tags that work only in their respective browsers to gain an edge over the competition.

Despite the acknowledgment of a greater good, dealing with browser differences is the major cause of headaches for web developers. The tables in this appendix list the available HTML tags that are still only supported in either Netscape Navigator or Internet Explorer.

Microsoft Internet Explorer Proprietary Tags

The following tags and attributes are supported only by Internet Explorer. Tags marked with an asterisk (*) indicate the tag has been adopted by the HTML 4.0 Specification, but as of this writing, is not yet supported by Netscape Navigator.

HTML Tag or Attribute	Description

`<basefont>`
　`color=color`
　`face=font face`
	Sets the color and/or font of the entire document when placed in the `<head>` or for subsequent text when placed in the flow of the body text

`<bgsound>`	Inserts an audio file that plays in the background
`<body>` 　`bgproperties=value`	Determines whether background image scrolls with the background

`<body>`
　`leftmargin=n`
　`rightmargin=n`
	Sets the margin between the browser window and the contents of the page

HTML Tag or Attribute	Description
`<caption>` `valign=position`	Sets vertical alignment of table caption
`<col>` *	Indicates a column within a column group
`<colgroup>` *	Groups table columns
`<comment>`	Inserts a comment in the HTML source that does not display in the browser (same as `<!--` and `-->`)
`<form>` `target=name`	Specifies a target window or frame for the output of a form
`<frameset>` `framespacing=n`	Sets the amount of space between frames
`<iframe>` *	Creates a floating frame

`<img>`
  `dynsrc=url`
  `controls`
  `loop=n`
  `start=action`
	Uses the image tag to place video or audio clips

`<isindex>`	Provides URL of the program that will perform the search
`<marquee>`	Places scrolling marquee text on the page

`<table>`
  `bordercolor=color`
  `bordercolordark=color`
  `bordercolorlight=color`
	Sets colors for 3-D table borders in the `<table>`, `<td>`, `<th>`, and `<tr>` tags

`<table>` `frame=value`	Controls the display of the outer borders of a table in the `<table>` tag.
`<tbody>` *	Indicates table body rows
`<tfoot>` *	Indicates table footer rows
`<thead>` *	Indicates table header rows

Netscape Navigator Proprietary Tags

The following tags are supported only by Netscape Navigator

HTML Tag	Description
`<blink>`	Causes text to blink on and off
`<ilayer>`	Inline layer; allows you to offset content from its natural position on the page
`<keygen>`	Facilitates generation of key material and submission of the public key as part of an HTML forms (for privacy and encryption)
`<layer>`	Creates layers so that elements can be placed on top of each other (useful with DHTML)
`<multicol>`	Produces a multicolumn format

HTML Tag	Description
`<nolayer>`	Alternative text for layers; browsers that do not support `<layer>` and `<ilayer>` will display what's between these tags.
`<server>`	Specifies a server-side JavaScript application
`<spacer>`	Holds a specified amount of empty space (used for alignment of elements on the page and to hold table cells open to specific widths)

APPENDIX E

CSS Compatibility

Browser compatibility—or lack thereof—is the biggest obstacle to adoption of cascading style sheets. This appendix provides a comprehensive guide to how the browsers have implemented support for CSS. It lists every aspect of the CSS spec and identifies how well it is supported by Netscape 4, Internet Explorer 3 and Internet Explorer 4 for both Mac and Windows 95. Check this master list to see if the CSS elements you want to use are supported by all the browsers—and whether their support is complete, partial or buggy.

This appendix uses the following key:

Y	Yes
N	No
P	Partial
B	Buggy
Q	Quirky

The data in this appendix was collected by Eric Meyer, BIO, and updated versions of this information will appear on *style.webreview.com* when new browser versions are released.

Table E-1: Basic Concepts

Spec Reference	Property or Value	Windows95			Macintosh		
		Nav4	*IE3*	*IE4*	*Nav4*	*IE3*	*IE4*
1.1	Containment in HTML	P	P	Y	P	B	P
	LINK	Y	Y	Y	Y	B	P
	`<STYLE type="text/css">...</STYLE>`	Y	Y	Y	Y	Y	Y
	@import	N	N	P	N	N	B
	`<x STYLE="dec;">`	Y	Y	Y	B	Y	Y
1.2	Grouping	Y	N	Y	Y	Y	Y
	`x, y, z {dec;}`	Y	N	Y	Y	Y	Y

Table E-1: Basic Concepts (continued)

Spec Reference	Property or Value	Windows95			Macintosh		
		Nav4	IE3	IE4	Nav4	IE3	IE4
1.3	Inheritance	P	P	Y	Y	B	P
	(inherited values)	P	P	Y	Y	B	P
1.4	Class as selector	Y	B	B	Y	B	Y
	.class	Y	B	B	Y	B	Y
1.5	ID as selector	B	B	B	B	B	B
	#ID	B	B	B	B	B	B
1.6	Contextual selectors	Y	Y	Y	Y	P	Y
	x y z {dec;}	Y	Y	Y	Y	P	Y
1.7	Comments	Y	B	Y	Y	Y	Y
	/* comment */	Y	B	Y	Y	Y	Y

Table E-2: Pseudo-Classes and Pesudo-Elements

Spec Reference	Property or Value	Windows95			Macintosh		
		Nav4	IE3	IE4	Nav4	IE3	IE4
2.1	anchor	P	N	Y	P	B	Y
	A:link	Y	N	Y	Y	B	Y
	A:active	N	N	Y	N	N	Y
	A:visited	N	N	Y	N	B	Q
2.3	first-line	N	N	N	N	B	N
	:first-line	N	N	N	N	B	N
2.4	first-letter	N	N	N	N	B	N
	:first-letter	N	N	N	N	B	N

Table E-3: The Cascade

CSS Reference	Property or Value	Windows95			Macintosh		
		Nav4	IE3	IE4	Nav4	IE3	IE4
3.1	important	N	N	Y	N	N	N
	!important	N	N	Y	N	N	N
3.2	Cascading Order	N	P	Y	B	P	Y
	Weight sorting	Y	Y	Y	B	Y	Y
	Origin sorting	Y	Y	B	B	B	Y
	Specificity sorting	Y	P	Y	B	B	Y
	Order sorting	Y	N	Y	B	N	Y

Table E-4: Font Properties

Spec Reference	Property or Value	Windows95			Macintosh		
		Nav4	IE3	IE4	Nav4	IE3	IE4
5.2.2	font-family	Y	P	Y	P	P	P
	<family-name>	Y	Y	Y	Y	P	Y
	<generic-family>	Y	Y	Y	P	P	B
	serif	Y	Y	Y	Y	Y	Y
	sans-serif	Y	Y	Y	Y	N	Y
	cursive	N	B	Y	Y	N	Y
	fantasy	N	B	N	N	N	Y
	monospace	Y	Y	Y	Y	Y	Y
5.2.3	font-style	P	P	Y	P	P	Y
	normal	Y	Y	Y	Y	N	Y
	italic	Y	N	Y	Y	Y	Y
	oblique	N	N	Y	N	N	Y
5.2.4	font-variant	N	N	P	N	N	P
	normal	N	N	Y	N	N	Y
	small-caps	N	N	P	N	N	B
5.2.5	font-weight	Y	P	Y	P	P	Y
	normal	Y	N	Y	Y	N	Y
	bold	Y	Y	Y	Y	Y	Y
	bolder	Y	Y	Y	N	N	Y
	lighter	Y	Y	Y	N	N	Y
	100 - 900	Y	N	Y	Y	N	Y
5.2.6	font-size	P	P	P	Y	P	P
	<absolute-size>	Y	Y	Y	Y	B	B
	xx-small - xx-large	Y	Y	P	Y	B	B
	<relative-size>	Y	Y	Y	Y	N	Y
	larger	Y	Y	Y	Y	N	Y
	smaller	Y	Y	Y	Y	N	Y
	<length>	Y	P	Y	Y	B	B
	<percentage>	Y	Y	Y	Y	P	Y
5.2.7	font	P	P	P	P	P	P
	<font-family>	P	Y	Y	Y	P	P
	<font-style>	P	P	Y	Y	P	Y
	<font-variant>	N	N	P	N	N	P
	<font-weight>	Y	Y	Y	Y	N	Y
	<font-size>	Y	B	Y	Y	B	B
	<line-height>	B	Y	Y	B	B	Y

Table E-5: Color and Background Properties

Spec Reference	Property or Value	Windows95			Macintosh		
		Nav4	IE3	IE4	Nav4	IE3	IE4
5.3.1	color	Y	Y	Y	Y	Y	Y
	<color>	Y	Y	Y	Y	Y	Y
5.3.2	background-color	B	P	Y	B	N	Y
	<color>	B	B	Y	B	N	Y
	transparent	B	N	Y	B	N	Y

Table E-5: Color and Background Properties (continued)

Spec Reference	Property or Value	Windows95			Macintosh		
		Nav4	IE3	IE4	Nav4	IE3	IE4
5.3.3	background-image	P	N	Y	Y	N	Y
	\<url\>	Y	N	Y	Y	N	Y
	none	Y	N	Y	Y	N	Y
5.3.4	background-repeat	Y	N	B	Y	N	P
	repeat	Y	N	Y	Y	N	P
	repeat-x	Y	N	B	Y	N	P
	repeat-y	Y	N	B	Y	N	P
	no-repeat	Y	N	Y	Y	N	Y
5.3.5	background-attachment	N	N	Y	N	N	Y
	scroll	N	N	Y	N	N	Y
	fixed	N	N	Y	N	N	Y
5.3.6	background-position	N	N	Y	N	N	Y
	\<percentage\>	N	N	Y	N	N	Y
	\<length\>	N	N	Y	N	N	Y
	top	N	N	Y	N	N	Y
	center	N	N	Y	N	N	Y
	bottom	N	N	B	N	N	Y
	left	N	N	Y	N	N	Y
	right	N	N	B	N	N	Y
5.3.7	background	P	P	Y	P	P	Y
	\<background-color\>	P	P	Y	Y	P	Y
	\<background-image\>	P	Y	Y	Y	Y	Y
	\<background-repeat\>	P	B	Y	Y	B	B
	\<background-attachment\>	P	N	Y	N	Y	Y
	\<background-position\>	N	N	Y	N	P	Y

Table E-6: Text Properties

Spec Reference	Property or Value	Windows95			Macintosh		
		Nav4	IE3	IE4	Nav4	IE3	IE4
5.4.1	word-spacing	N	N	N	N	N	Y
	normal	N	N	N	N	N	Y
	\<length\>	N	N	N	N	N	Y
5.4.2	letter-spacing	N	N	Y	N	N	Y
	normal	N	N	Y	N	N	Y
	\<length\>	N	N	Y	N	N	Y
5.4.3	text-decoration	B	P	P	P	P	P
	none	Y	N	Y	Y	Y	Y
	underline	Y	Y	B	B	B	B
	overline	N	N	Y	N	N	Y
	line-through	Y	Y	Y	Y	Y	Y
	blink	Y	N	N	Y	N	N

Table E-6: Text Properties (continued)

Spec Reference	Property or Value	Windows95			Macintosh		
		Nav4	IE3	IE4	Nav4	IE3	IE4
5.4.4	vertical-align	N	N	P	N	N	P
	baseline	N	N	N	N	N	N
	sub	N	N	Y	N	N	Y
	super	N	N	Y	N	N	Y
	top	N	N	N	N	N	N
	text-top	N	N	N	N	N	N
	middle	N	N	N	N	N	N
	bottom	N	N	N	N	N	N
	text-bottom	N	N	N	N	N	N
	<percentage>	N	N	N	N	N	Y
5.4.5	text-transform	Y	N	Y	Y	N	Y
	capitalize	Y	N	Y	Y	N	Y
	uppercase	Y	N	Y	Y	N	Y
	lowercase	Y	N	Y	Y	N	Y
	none	Y	N	Y	Y	N	Y
5.4.6	text-align	Y	P	Y	Y	P	P
	left	Y	Y	Y	Y	Y	Y
	right	Y	Y	Y	Y	Y	Y
	center	Y	Y	Y	Y	Y	Y
	justify	B	N	Y	Y	N	N
5.4.7	text-indent	Y	Y	Y	Y	Y	Y
	<length>	Y	Y	Y	Y	Y	Y
	<percentage>	Y	Y	Y	Y	Y	Y
5.4.8	line-height	Y	P	P	P	P	Y
	normal	Y	Y	Y	Y	Y	Y
	<number>	Y	N	Y	Y	B	Y
	<length>	Y	Y	Y	B	B	Y
	<percentage>	Y	Y	Y	Y	B	Y

Table E-7: Box Properties

Spec Reference	Property or Value	Windows95			Macintosh		
		Nav4	IE3	IE4	Nav4	IE3	IE4
5.5.01	margin-top	B	B	Y	Y	B	P
	<length>	Y	B	Y	Y	B	Y
	<percentage>	Y	Y	Y	Y	B	B
	auto	Y	Y	Y	Y	B	Y
5.5.02	margin-right	P	P	P	P	P	P
	<length>	Y	Y	Y	Y	Y	Y
	<percentage>	Y	N	Y	Y	Y	Y
	auto	N	N	N	N	N	N
5.5.03	margin-bottom	Y	Y	Y	Y	N	P
	<length>	Y	N	Y	Y	N	Y
	<percentage>	Y	N	Y	Y	N	B
	auto	Y	N	Y	Y	N	Y

Table E-7: Box Properties (continued)

Spec Reference	Property or Value	Windows95 Nav4	IE3	IE4	Macintosh Nav4	IE3	IE4
5.5.04	margin-left	P	P	P	P	P	P
	\<length\>	Y	Y	Y	Y	Y	Y
	\<percentage\>	Y	Y	Y	Y	Y	B
	auto	N	N	N	N	N	N
5.5.05	margin	P	B	P	P	B	P
	\<length\>	Y	B	Y	B	B	Y
	\<percentage\>	Y	Y	Y	B	B	B
	auto	P	Y	P	N	B	P
5.5.06	padding-top	B	N	Y	B	N	B
	\<length\>	Y	N	Y	Y	N	Y
	\<percentage\>	Y	N	Y	Y	N	B
5.5.07	padding-right	B	N	Y	B	N	Y
	\<length\>	Y	N	Y	Y	N	Y
	\<percentage\>	Y	N	Y	Y	N	Y
5.5.08	padding-bottom	B	N	Y	B	N	B
	\<length\>	Y	N	Y	Y	N	Y
	\<percentage\>	Y	N	Y	Y	N	B
5.5.09	padding-left	B	N	Y	B	N	Y
	\<length\>	Y	N	Y	Y	N	Y
	\<percentage\>	Y	N	Y	Y	N	Y
5.5.10	padding	B	N	Y	B	N	P
	\<length\>	Y	N	Y	Y	N	Y
	\<percentage\>	Y	N	Y	Y	N	B
5.5.11	border-top-width	B	N	Y	B	N	Y
	thin	Y	N	Y	Y	N	Y
	medium	Y	N	Y	Y	N	Y
	thick	Y	N	Y	Y	N	Y
	\<length\>	Y	N	Y	Y	N	Y
5.5.12	border-right-width	B	N	Y	B	N	Y
	thin	Y	N	Y	Y	N	Y
	medium	Y	N	Y	Y	N	Y
	thick	Y	N	Y	Y	N	Y
	\<length\>	Y	N	Y	Y	N	Y
5.5.13	border-bottom-width	B	N	Y	B	N	Y
	thin	B	N	Y	B	N	Y
	medium	B	N	Y	B	N	Y
	thick	B	N	Y	B	N	Y
	\<length\>	B	N	Y	B	N	Y
5.5.14	border-left-width	B	N	Y	B	N	Y
	thin	Y	N	Y	Y	N	Y
	medium	Y	N	Y	Y	N	Y
	thick	Y	N	Y	Y	N	Y
	\<length\>	Y	N	Y	Y	N	Y

Table E-7: Box Properties (continued)

Spec Reference	Property or Value	Windows95			Macintosh		
		Nav4	IE3	IE4	Nav4	IE3	IE4
5.5.15	border-width	B	N	Y	B	N	Y
	thin	Y	N	Y	Y	N	Y
	medium	Y	N	Y	Y	N	Y
	thick	Y	N	Y	Y	N	Y
	<length>	Y	N	Y	Y	N	Y
5.5.16	border-color	Y	N	Y	Y	N	Y
	<color>	Y	N	Y	Y	N	Y
5.5.17	border-style	B	N	P	P	N	Y
	none	Y	N	Y	Y	N	Y
	dotted	N	N	N	N	N	Y
	dashed	N	N	N	N	N	Y
	solid	Y	N	Y	Y	N	Y
	double	Y	N	Y	Y	N	Y
	groove	Y	N	Y	Y	N	Y
	ridge	Y	N	Y	Y	N	Y
	inset	Y	N	Y	Y	N	Y
	outset	Y	N	Y	Y	N	Y
5.5.18	border-top	N	N	Y	N	N	Y
	<border-top-width>	N	N	Y	N	N	Y
	<border-style>	N	N	Y	N	N	Y
	<color>	N	N	Y	N	N	Y
5.5.19	border-right	N	N	Y	N	N	Y
	<border-right-width>	N	N	Y	N	N	Y
	<border-style>	N	N	Y	N	N	Y
	<color>	N	N	Y	N	N	Y
5.5.20	border-bottom	N	N	Y	N	N	Y
	<border-bottom-width>	N	N	Y	N	N	Y
	<border-style>	N	N	Y	N	N	Y
	<color>	N	N	Y	N	N	Y
5.5.21	border-left	N	N	Y	N	N	Y
	<border-left-width>	N	N	Y	N	N	Y
	<border-style>	N	N	Y	N	N	Y
	<color>	N	N	Y	N	N	Y
5.5.22	border	P	N	P	P	N	P
	<border-width>	B	N	P	B	N	P
	<border-style>	Y	N	Y	P	N	Y
	<color>	Y	N	Y	Y	N	Y
5.5.23	width	Y	N	P	P	N	P
	<length>	Y	N	P	P	N	P
	<percentage>	Y	N	P	P	N	P
	auto	Y	N	P	P	N	P
5.5.24	height	Y	N	Y	P	N	Y
	<length>	Y	N	Y	P	N	Y
	auto	Y	N	Y	P	N	Y

Table E-7: Box Properties (continued)

Spec Reference	Property or Value	Windows95			Macintosh		
		Nav4	IE3	IE4	Nav4	IE3	IE4
5.5.25	float	B	N	B	B	N	P
	left	Y	N	Y	Y	N	P
	right	Y	N	Y	Y	N	P
	none	Y	N	Y	N	N	Y
5.5.26	clear	Y	N	P	P	N	Y
	none	Y	Y	Y	Y	Y	Y
	left	Y	N	Y	Y	N	Y
	right	Y	N	Y	Y	N	Y
	both	Y	N	Y	Y	N	Y

Table E-8: Classification Properties

Spec Reference	Property or Value	Windows95			Macintosh		
		Nav4	IE3	IE4	Nav4	IE3	IE4
5.6.1	display	P	N	P	P	N	P
	block	B	N	N	B	N	N
	inline	N	N	N	N	N	N
	list-item	Y	N	N	Y	N	N
	none	Y	N	Y	Y	N	Y
5.6.2	white-space	P	N	N	P	N	N
	normal	Y	N	N	Y	N	N
	pre	Y	N	N	Y	N	N
	nowrap	N	N	N	N	N	N
5.6.3	list-style-type	Y	N	Y	P	N	Y
	disc	Y	N	Y	Y	N	Y
	circle	Y	N	Y	Y	N	Y
	square	Y	N	Y	Y	N	Y
	decimal	Y	N	Y	Y	N	Y
	lower-roman	Y	N	Y	Y	N	Y
	upper-roman	Y	N	Y	Y	N	Y
	lower-alpha	Y	N	Y	Y	N	Y
	upper-alpha	Y	N	Y	Y	N	Y
	none	Y	N	Y	B	N	Y
5.6.4	list-style-image	N	N	Y	N	N	Y
	<url>	N	N	Y	N	N	Y
	none	N	N	Y	N	N	Y
5.6.5	list-style-position	N	N	Y	N	N	P
	inside	N	N	Y	N	N	B
	outside	N	N	Y	N	N	Y
5.6.6	list-style	P	N	P	P	N	P
	<keyword>	Y	N	Y	Y	N	Y
	<position>	N	N	B	N	N	B
	<url>	N	N	Y	N	N	Y

Table E-9: Units

Spec Reference	Property or Value	Windows95			Macintosh		
		Nav4	IE3	IE4	Nav4	IE3	IE4
6.1	Length Units	P	P	Y	Y	B	Y
	em	Y	N	Y	Y	Y	Y
	ex	Q	N	Q	Q	Q	Q
	px	Y	Y	Y	Y	Y	Y
	in	Y	Y	Y	Y	Y	Y
	cm	Y	Y	Y	Y	Y	Y
	mm	Y	Y	Y	Y	Y	Y
	pt	Y	Y	Y	Y	Y	Y
	pc	Y	Y	Y	Y	Y	Y
6.2	Percentage Units	Y	Y	Y	Y	Y	Y
	<percentage>	Y	Y	Y	Y	Y	Y
6.3	Color Units	Y	P	Y	Y	P	Y
	#000	Y	Y	Y	Y	B	Y
	#000000	Y	Y	Y	Y	B	Y
	(RRR,GGG,BBB)	Y	N	Y	Y	N	Y
	(R%,G%,B%)	Y	N	Y	Y	N	B
	<keyword>	Y	Y	Y	Y	Y	Y
6.4	URLs	B	Y	B	B	B	Y
	<url>	B	Y	B	B	B	Y

Glossary

μ-LAW
(Pronounced "myew-lah") UNIX standard audio file format.

accessibility
Refers to making web pages available and readable to all users, including those with disabilities such as sight or hearing impairments.

AIFF
Audio Interchange File Format. Standard audio format originally developed for the Macintosh, which is now supported on PCs as well. It is one of the formats commonly used for distributing audio on the Web.

alpha channel
In graphics, an extra channel for storing information about an image. The alpha channel works like a mask that applies properties (such as transparency) to the pixels in the image. Other channels typically include color value information—as in the red, green, and blue channels of an RGB image.

alpha-channel transparency
The method of transparency used by 24-bit PNGs, which uses an additional (alpha) channel to store variable levels of transparency (up to 256) for each pixel in the image.

animated gif
A GIF89a that contains multiple frames and a "control block" for controlling the animation timing and display.

applet
A self-contained mini-executable program, such as one written in the Java programming language.

ASCII files
Files that are comprised of alphanumeric characters. Some FTP programs refer to ASCII files as "text" files.

ASP

Active Server Pages; the part of Microsoft's Internet Information Server software that allows server-side scripting for the creation of dynamically generated web pages and database functions. Web pages created with ASP commonly have the suffix *.asp*.

audio bit depth

The number of bits used to define the resolution of the amplitude (or volume) of a digital audio waveform—the more bits, the more accurate the rendering of the original audio source, and the larger the resulting audio file.

Some common bit depths are 8-bit (which sounds thin or tinny, like a telephone signal) and 16-bit, which is required to describe music of CD quality.

AVI

Audio/Video Interleaved; a digital video format developed by Microsoft in which audio and video information are interleaved in every frame for smoother playback.

binary files

Files made up of compiled data (ones and zeros), such as executable programs, graphic images, movies, etc. Some programs refer to the binary mode as "raw data" or "image data."

CGI

Common Gateway Interface; the mechanism for communication between the web server and other programs (CGI scripts) running on the server.

character entities

Strings of characters used to specify characters not found in the normal alphanumeric character set in HTML documents.

character set

An organization of characters—units of a written language system—in which each character is assigned a specific number.

client

A software application that extracts services from a server somewhere on the network. A web browser is a client that renders and displays documents on remote servers.

CLUT

Color Look Up Table; a list of colors and associated index numbers used to render eight-bit images.

CMYK

Cyan-Magenta-Yellow-Black—the four ink colors used in process printing. Not appropriate for generating web graphics. (RGB is the color mode for web graphics.)

codec

Compression/decompression algorithms applied to media files.

CSS

Cascading Style Sheets; an addition to HMTL for controlling presentation of a document, including color, typography, alignment of text and images, etc.

CSS-P

> CSS with positioning. Refers to a proposal for adding positioning capabilities with style sheets. The CSS-P proposal has since been rolled into the CSS2 Specification.

data fork

> The portion of a Macintosh file that contains the actual data of the document. See also *resource fork*.

data rate

> In video, the rate at which data must be transferred in order for the video to play smoothly without interruption. The data rate (also called "bit rate") for a movie is measured in kilobytes per second (K/s or KB/s). It can be calculated by dividing the size of the file (in K) by the length of the movie (in seconds).

deprecated

> In the HTML 4.0 Specification, a label identifying an HTML tag or attribute as "outdated" and discouraged from use in favor of newer constructs (often style sheet controls).

DHTML

> Dynamic HTML; an integration of JavaScript, Cascading Style Sheets, and the Document Object Model. With DHTML, content can move across the screen or respond to user inputs.

dithering

> The approximation of a color by mixing pixels of similar colors that are available in the image palette. The result of dithering is a random dot-pattern or noise in the image.

Document Object Model (DOM)

> The browser's internal hierarchical organization of the elements in a document. The existence of a DOM makes page elements available for manipulation via scripting or style sheets. Netscape Navigator's and Microsoft Internet Explorer's DOMs differ significantly.

dpi

> Dots per inch; in graphics, this is the measurement of the resolution of a printed image. It is commonly (although incorrectly) used to refer to the screen resolution of web graphics, which is technically measured in ppi (pixels per inch). See also *ppi*.

DTD

> Document Type Definition; a file associated with an SGML or XML document that defines how the tags should be interpreted and displayed by the application reading the document. As a subset of SGML, HTML has its own DTD.

encoding

> The process of converting an analog source (such as an analog audio signal) into digital format. An encoder is the software that does the converting.

frame rate

> In video, frames per second; used as a measure of video quality.

FTP

File Transfer Protocol; a protocol for moving files over the Internet from one computer to another. FTP is a client/server system: one machine must be running an FTP server, the other an FTP client.

gamma

Refers to the overall brightness of a computer monitor's display. In technical terms, it is a numerical adjustment for the nonlinear relationship of voltage to light intensity.

GIF

Graphic Interchange Format; common file format of web graphic images. GIF is a palette-based, 8-bit format that compresses images with the lossless LZW compression scheme. GIF is most appropriate for images with areas of flat color and sharp contrast. See also *LZW compression.*

hexadecimal

A base-16 numbering system consisting of the characters 0, 1, 2, 3, 4, 5, 6, 7, 8, 9, A, B, C, D, E, and F. (where A through F represent the decimal values 10 through 15). It is used in HTML for specifying RGB color values.

HTML

Hypertext Markup Language; the format of web documents.

HTTP

Hypertext Transfer Protocol; the protocol that defines how web pages and media are requested and transferred between servers and browsers.

imagemap

A single image that contains multiple hypertext links.

indexed color

In graphics, a system for rendering colors in 8-bit images. Indexed color files, such as GIFs, contain an index (also called a palette or color lookup table) of colors and associated index numbers, which is used to render color in the image.

Java

A cross-platform, object-oriented programming language developed by Sun Microsystems. It can be used to create whole applications; however, its primary contribution to the Web has been in the form of Java applets, self-contained, mini-executable programs.

JavaScript

A client-side scripting language developed by Netscape that adds interactivity and conditional behavior to web pages. It has little in common with Java.

JPEG

A lossy compression algorithm developed by the Joint Photographic Experts Group. It is used by files in the JFIF format, which are commonly referred to as "JPEG files." JPEG is most efficient at compressing images with gradations in tone and no sharp edge contrasts. Photographic images are typically best saved in JPEG format.

key frames

In video, master frames placed throughout a video against which the following frames are compared (for use with temporal, or interframe, compression).

Linux

A version of Unix designed to run on PCs.

lossy compression

A method for reducing file size in which some data (usually indiscernable to human perception) is deleted in order to achieve a higher compression rate.

lossless compression

A method for reducing the size of a file without loss of data; in lossless compression, redundant information is removed.

LZW compression

Short for Lempel-Zev-Welch, the names of the inventors. A lossless compression scheme that takes advantage of repetition in data streams (such as a row of pixels of identical color). It is the compression scheme used by graphic files in the GIF format.

MIDI

Musical Instrument Digital Interface. This audio format uses mathematical commands to describe the pitch and endurance of notes that are "played" by available digital instrument sounds.

MIME types

Multimedia Internet Mail Extensions. A protocol that defines a number of content types and subtypes, and allow programs like web browsers, newsreaders, and email clients to recognize different kinds of files and deal with them appropriately. A MIME type specifies what media a file is, such as an image, audio, or video, and a subtype identifies the precise file format.

MPEG

A family of multimedia standards created by the Motion Picture Experts Group, commonly used to refer to audio and video files saved using one of the MPEG compression schemes.

palette

A table in an 8-bit indexed color file (such as GIF) that provides color information for the pixels in the image. See also *CLUT*.

PDF

Portable Document Format; a file format developed by Adobe Systems used for capturing formatted page layouts for distribution. PDF documents, when viewed with the required Adobe Acrobat Reader, will appear exactly as they were intended.

PNG

Portable Network Format; a versatile graphics file format that features support for both 8-bit (PNG8) indexed images and 24-bit images (PNG24). PNGs also feature variable transparency levels, automatic color correction controls, and a lossless, yet highly efficient, compression scheme.

ppi

Pixels per inch; the measurement of the resolution of a screen image.

QuickTime

A system extension that makes it possible to view audio and video information on a computer. It was originally developed for the Macintosh but is now available for Windows machines as well, and has been adopted as the video standard by the ISO in their development of MPEG-4. The term also refers to the file format.

RDF

Resource Description Framework; an XML application used to define the structure of metadata for documents, i.e., data that is useful for indexing, navigating, and searching a site.

resource fork

Extra code added in the Macintosh file format, which is used for storing icons, previews, and file type information. This information should be stripped out when sending the file to a non-Macintosh server. See also *data fork.*

RGB color

A color system that describes colors based on combinations of red, green, and blue light.

rollover

The act of passing the mouse pointer over an element's space, or the events triggered by that action (such as a changing graphic or pop-up message, sometimes called rollover events).

sampling rate

In a digital audio file, the number of samples taken per second.

server

A networked computer that provides some kind of service or information.

Server Side Includes (SSI)

Special placeholders in an HTML document that the server is to replace with actual data just before sending the final document to the browser. Extended SSI (XSSI) (part of Apache 1.2 and higher) provides more advanced command functions, including conditional behaviors.

SGML

Standard Generalized Markup Language; a meta-language that provides a comprehensive set of syntax rules for marking up the structure of documents and data. HTML is a subset of SGML.

Shockwave

Proprietary technology from Macromedia, Inc. for the web delivery of multimedia content.

spatial compression

In video, spatial compression is applied to each individual frame of the video, using compression schemes commonly used on still images (also called "intraframe" compression).

spatial frequency

Refers to the concentration of detail in an image. For example, an image of a blue sky would be considered to have low frequency. A detailed image, such as a close-up of blades of grass, has high frequency.

telnet

An internet protocol for logging into and using a remote system on the Internet. Telnet is a client/server system that requires a telnet server running on one computer and a telnet client on the other.

temporal compression

In video, temporal compression takes place over a series of frames, deleting information that is repeated between frames (also called "interframe" compression).

Unix

A multiuser, multitasking operating system developed by Bell Laboratories. It also provides programs for editing text, sending email, preparing tables, performing calculations, and many other specialized functions that normally require separate applications programs.

W3C

The World Wide Web Consortium; a consortium of many companies and organizations that "exists to develop common standards for the evolution of the World Wide Web." It is run by a joint effort between the Laboratory for Computer Science at the Massachusetts Institute of Technology and CERN, the European Particle Physics Laboratory, where the WWW was first developed.

WAVE

Waveform Audio File Format. This format was developed for the PC but is now supported on Macintosh as well.

Web Palette

The set of 216 colors that will not dither or shift when viewed with browsers on 8-bit monitors.

XML

Extensible Markup Language; a new standard for marking up documents and data. XML is based on SGML, but with a reduced feature set that is more appropriate for distribution via the Web. XML allows authors to create customized tag sets to provide functionality not available with HTML.

XSL

Extensible Style Language; a system for controlling the presentation of complex XML documents and structured data.

XSSI

see *Server Side Includes*.

Index

Symbols

& (ampersand) in form name=value
  pairs, 234
<!-- --> comment tags
  for SSI commands, 253
  for XSSI commands, 256
* (asterisk) for frameset sizes, 213
: (colon)
  pseudo-selectors (style sheets), 397
  style sheet declarations, 392
(hash mark)
  for ID selectors, 397
  in pathnames, 134
-Law (.au) file format, 336
% (percent sign)
  color equivalents, 32, 304
  font sizes, 402
  percentage sizes for framesets, 213
  SSI time formats, 260
  table dimensions, 184
. (period)
  in alternate text, 24
  CLASS selectors, 397
.. for parent directory, 53
/ (slash)
  encoding in URLs, 235
  in URLs, 49, 51

Numbers

3-D shading of horizontal rules, 149,
  156, 497
8-bit character encodings, 458
8-bit indexed color, 266
8-bit palette images, 293
8-bit transparency, 296
16-bit character encodings, 459
16-bit displays, 304
24-bit color, 283

A

<a> tags, 130–135, 468
  linking to audio files, 338, 343–344
  linking to video files, 355
  pseudo-classes with, 398
abbr attribute (<td>, <th>), 174, 484
<abbr> tags, 25, 468
abbreviations, denoting, 25
"above the fold" design, 23
absbottom, absmiddle values (align),
  161
absolute
  font sizes, 402
  pathnames, 51–53
  positioning (style sheets), 420
  URLs, 133

absolute web page control, 20–23
 frame resize, disabling, 216
 frameset sizes, 213
 table dimensions, 184
 two-column layout (example), 199
 style sheets
  (see also cascading style sheets)
accept attribute, 484
 <form> tags, 227
 <input type=file> tag, 229
accept-charset attribute (<form>), 227,
  242, 460, 484
accessibility, 23–26
 internationalization, 458–463
accesskey attribute (<a>), 131, 242, 484
AceFTP utility, 58
<acronym> tags, 25, 468
acronyms, denoting, 25
action attribute (<form>), 227, 234, 484
active hyperlink color, 135
active pseudo-class, 398
ActiveX controls (see embedding
  objects in pages)
Adaptive filtering algorithm (PNG), 294
Adaptive Palette, 305, 310, 326
<address> tags, 468
Adobe
 AfterEffects, 347
 Illustrator, 308
 ImageReady, 203, 267, 271, 311–313,
  324
  creating JPEG images, 286
  creating PNG images, 300
  GIF files, optimizing, 281
  palettes, 305–307
 OpenType technology, 453, 455–457
 PDF, accessibility issues, 24
 Photoshop, 267, 310–311
  alpha channel, 273–277
  CLUTs, creating, 308
  color palettes, 306
  creating JPEG images, 286, 288
  creating PNG images, 298
  dividing images into multiple files,
   203
  GIF files, optimizing, 279
  palettes, 307
AfterEffects (Adobe), 347

AIFF (.aif, .aiff) file format, 336
aliasing, 270–271
align attribute, 484
 <applet> tags, 146, 165
 <caption> tags, 169
 <col> tag, 169
 <colgroup> tags, 170
 <embed> tags, 147, 165, 340
 <hr> tag, 149, 156
 <iframe> tags, 208
 <img> tag, 149, 160–162
 <input type=image> tag, 229
 <marquee> tag, 151
 <object> tags, 152, 166
 <spacer> tag, 154
 <table> tags, 170, 183
 <tbody> tags, 173
 <td>, <th> tags, 173
 <tfoot> tags, 175
 <thead> tags, 175
 <tr> tags, 176
alignment
 centering in window (example), 196
 CSS2 accessibility features for, 25
 form elements, 244
 graphics, 160–162
 horizontal rules, 156
 style sheet properties for, 405, 406,
  413
 tables, 177, 183
 (see also positioning)
alink attribute (<body>), 92, 96, 135,
  485
all value (clear attribute), 162
alpha channel, 273–277, 296, 298, 300
alt attribute, 485
 <applet> tags, 146, 165
 <embed> tags, 148, 165
 <img> tag, 24, 25, 150, 159
alternative graphics text, 24, 25, 159
America Online browsers, 4, 286
ampersand (&) in form name=value
  pairs, 234
Anarchie utility, 58
anchors (see <a> tags)
animation, 321–329
 creating, 324–328
 element motion with DHTML,
  437–441

GIF format for, 267
   GIF87a vs. GIF89a formats, 265
Java applets (see Java applets)
multipart images in tables, 201
optimizing file size, 328–329
slide-show effect, 99
SMIL language, 448–449
Animation compressor, 351
Animation Shop tool, 324
announcement boxes (example), 196
anti-aliasing, 270–271
AOL browsers, 4, 286
Apache servers, 48
Apple "Fast Start" technology, 352
Apple QuickTime, 332, 334, 342, 344,
   348, 351–352
   Sorenson codec, 348, 351
<applet> tags, 146, 164, 372–373, 468
applets on web pages, 146, 164,
   370–373
archive attribute, 486
<area> tags, 132, 137–143, 157, 469
ASCII mode (FTP), 58
asterisk (*) for relative frameset sizes,
   213
attributes, HTML (list), 483–510
   deprecated, 512–514
audience, knowing your, 12
audio, 330 346
   adding to HTML documents,
      338–340, 343–345
   background, 147, 340
   copyright issues, 330–331
   encoding, 333
   file formats, 336
   nonstreaming (static), 333–340
   optimizing for download, 337
   providing transcripts/descriptions, 24
   SMIL language, 448–449
   streaming, 333–335, 341–345
   tools for, 331–332
   (see also accessibility)
author value (<meta name>), 101
Auto option (FTP utilities), 58
autoplay attribute (<embed>), 344, 357
autostart attribute (<embed>), 339
Average filtering algorithm (PNG), 294
AVI (.avi) file format, 353
axis attribute (<td>, <th>), 174, 486

B

<b> tags, 469
background
   audio, 147, 340
   colors, 414
      Flash movies, 363
      GIF animation, 328
      Shockwave movies, 369
      tables, 186
      (see also bgcolor attribute)
   images/patterns, 414
      positioning and scrolling, 415
      tiling, 96
   style sheet properties, 413–416
background attribute, 486
   <body> tags, 92, 96
   <table> tags, 171
   <tr> tags, 176
   <td>, <th> tags, 173
background property (CSS), 416
background-attachment property (CSS),
   415
background-color property (CSS), 414
background-image property (CSS), 414
background-position property (CSS),
   415
background-repeat property (CSS), 414
base attribute (<embed>), 364
<base> tag, 91, 95, 217, 469
<basefont> tag, 469
baseline height, text, 403
baseline value (align), 161
baseline value (valign), 184, 194
<bdo> tags, 462, 469
behavior attribute (<marquee>), 151
bgcolor attribute, 486
   <body> tags, 92, 96
   <embed> tags, 363, 369
   <marquee> tag, 151
   <table> tags, 171, 186, 198
   <td>, <th> tags, 173, 186
   <tr> tags, 176, 186
bgproperties attribute (<body>), 92
<bgsound> tags, 147, 340, 469
Bias Peak, 332
bi-directional opverride, 462
<big> tags, 469
binary mode (FTP), 58

bit depth, 278, 309, 310
  audio files, 333, 337
  GIF animation, 328
  GIF files, 266
  JPEG images, 283
  PNG images, 293
  video clips, 349
Bitstream's TrueDoc technology,
      453–455
black and white, designing for, 16
  (see also grayscale)
_blank target (<a>), 137, 218
blenders, color, 315–317
<blink> tags, 469, 24
blinking text, 24, 405
<blockquote> tags, 470
Bobby validator, 24
<body> tags, 92, 95–98, 470
  background control (see
      background)
  color and font for, 96, 427
  in <noframes> sections, 212
  text and link color specifications, 135
body, document, 95–98
body, table, 172, 180
boldness, text, 401
bookmarks, frames and, 210
border property (CSS), 412
border attribute, 487
  <embed> tag, 148
  <frameset> tags, 207, 215
  <img> tag, 150, 158
  <object> tags, 152
  <table> tags, 171, 182, 188
border-color property (CSS), 410
border-style property (CSS), 411
border-top, border-right, border-
      bottom, border-left properties
      (CSS), 411
border-top-width, border-right-width,
      border-bottom-width, border-
      left-width properties (CSS), 410
border-width property (CSS), 410
bordercolor attribute
  <frame> tag, 206, 215
  <frameset> tags, 208
  <table> tags, 172
  <td>, <th> tags, 174
  <tr> tags, 176

bordercolordark attribute
  <table> tags, 172
  <td>, <th> tags, 174
  <tr> tags, 176
bordercolorlight attribute
  <table> tags, 172
  <td>, <th> tags, 174
  <tr> tags, 176
borders
  frames, 214
  style sheet properties for, 410–412
  tables and, 182
bottom value (align), 160
Boutell, Thomas, 138, 291
box properties (style sheets), 407–413
box rules (example), 197–198
BoxTop Software
  ColorSafe, 315–316
  GIFmation, 323
  PhotoGIF, 268
  ProJPEG utility, 287, 288

 tag, 470
  word wrap with graphics, 162
Braille (see accessibility)
brightness, display, 19, 295
Browser Watch site, 7
BrowserCaps site, 7
browsers
  AOL browsers, 4, 286
  centering in window (example), 196
  client-pull, meta tags for, 98
  color name support, 78
  CSS compatibility, 518–526
  designing for, 9–13
  determining type and version,
      383–385, 391, 435
  DHTML support, 429, 431–435
  feature overview, 8–9
  GIF animation support, 322
  JavaScript support, 383–386, 434
  knowing your audience, 12
  list of, 3–6
  "live space," considering, 16–18
  PNG support, 292
  proprietary HTML tags, 515–517
  status bar text, 136, 381
  style sheet support, 390, 428
  thin client browsers, 27

usage statistics, 6–7
window resizing and page size,
19–23
bulleted lists, CSS properties, 417
Burns, Martin, 245
<button> tags, 470
buttons on forms
<button> tags for, 226
checkboxes, 228, 237
custom, 228, 238
image buttons, 239
radio buttons, 230, 238
submit and reset buttons, 230, 238
buttons, JavaScript-enabled, 143,
373–378

C

caching images, 163
CakeWalk Metro, 332
capitalization and small caps
drop caps, 426
style sheet properties for, 401, 406
<caption> tags, 168, 178, 470
captions for graphics, 24
captions for tables, 168, 178
cascading style sheets, 389–428
accessibility features (CSS2), 25
browser compatibility, 518–526
changing styles with DHTML, 436
CSS2 features, 422–425
fixed page width, 21
how they work, 391–395
conflict resolution, 394
positioning with, 407–413, 418–422
properties, 392, 399–418
background, 413–416
box properties, 407–413
classification, 416–418
CSS2, 424
type-related, 400–407
selectors, 392, 395–398, 423
tips and tricks, 426–428
values for rules, 392, 398–399
XSL vs., 451
cd command (Unix), 54
cellpadding attribute (<table>), 171,
185, 188, 487

cells, table, 173, 177–179
aligning text in, 183
collapsing in Netscape Navigator, 190
coloring, 186
controlling, 179
fonts, 193
size of, 185
(see also tables)
cellspacing attribute (<table>), 171, 185,
188, 487
cellular telephones, 26
<center> tags, 470
CERN servers, 48
cgi attribute (exec command), 257
CGI scripts, 49, 233–234, 247–250
environment variables for, 259
server-side imagemaps, 137, 141
(see also forms)
cgi-bin directory, 49
changePages( ) (JavaScript example),
222, 382
channels, audio, 333, 337
char attribute, 488
<col> tag, 169
<colgroup> tags, 170
<tbody> tags, 173
<tfoot> tags, 175
<thead> tags, 175
character sets and internationalization,
458–460
charoff attribute, 488
<col> tag, 169
<colgroup> tags, 170
<tbody> tags, 173
<tfoot> tags, 175
<thead> tags, 175
charset attribute (<a>), 131, 488
checkboxes on forms, 228, 237
checked attribute, 488
<input type=checkbox> tag, 228, 237
<input type=radio> tag, 230, 238
Chemical Markup Language (CML), 451
chmod command (Unix), 59
Cinepak codec (Radius), 350
cite attribute, 488
<cite> tags, 470
Claris HomePage, 58
class attribute, 397, 488

.class files, 372
CLASS selectors (style sheets), 397
classid attribute (<object>), 152, 166, 364, 489
classification style sheet properties, 416–418
clear attribute (<br>), 162, 489
clear property (CSS), 413
clickable imagemaps, 132, 137–143, 157
  multipart images in tables, 201
  text alternatives for, 24, 143
client-pull, meta tags for, 98
clients, defined, 47
  (see also browsers)
client-side imagemaps, 132, 137, 139–141, 157
  multipart images in tables, 201
  text alternatives, 24, 143
CLUTs (color look-up tables), 308
cmd attribute (exec command), 257
CML (Chemical Markup Language), 451
code attribute, 489
  <applet> tags, 146, 164
  <embed> tag, 148
<code> tags, 471
codebase attribute, 489
  <applet> tags, 146, 165
  <embed> tag, 148
  <object> tags, 152, 166, 364
codecs, video, 350
codetype attribute (<object>), 153, 489
<col> tag, 169, 181, 471
<colgroup> tags, 170, 181, 471
collapsing empty table cells, 190
colon (:)
  pseudo-selectors (style sheets), 397
  style sheet declarations, 392
color attribute, 489
Color Picker (ColorSafe), 316
color property (CSS), 403
colors
  background, 414
    (see also bgcolor attribute)
  black and white designs, 16
  body elements, 96, 427
  borders for elements, 410
  box rules (example), 197–198
  CLUTs (color look-up tables), 308

color blenders (hybrid colors), 315–317
color shift (see dithering)
  CSS2 values for, 425
dithering, 16, 279
  Adobe Photoshop, 310–311
  color names and, 78
  flat graphics, 306
  GIF animation, 328
  photographic images, 306
flat colors, designing with, 278
foreground, for elements, 403
GIF format, 266
  tools for (see specific graphics tool)
hyperlinks, 96, 135
monitor capabilities, 16
names for, 78–84, 399
numbers of (see bit depth)
palettes (see palettes)
photographs (see photographic images)
RGB value representation, 31, 76–78, 304, 399
style sheet specifications, 399
tables, 186
transparency (see transparency)
truecolor images, 293
24-bit color, 283
Web Palette, 16, 32, 78, 303–317
  color names vs., 78
  converting to, 309
  designing with web-safe colors, 307–309
ColorSafe (BoxTop Software), 315–316
ColorWeb Pro (Pantone), 308
cols attribute, 490
  <frameset> tags, 208, 212–213
  <textarea> tags, 233, 239
colspan attribute (<td>, <th>), 173, 179, 490
columns, frameset, 212–213
columns, table, 169
  (see also tables)
  grouping, 170, 181
  sizing, 184, 198
  spanning, 179, 192–193
  two-column page layout (example), 199–201

commands, SSI, 253–254
commands, Unix (list), 54–57
\<comment\> tags, 471
comments, hiding JavaScript with, 383
Common Gateway Interface (see CGI
  scripts)
compact attribute, 490
compatibility, browser (see browsers)
compression
  animated GIFs, 328
  audio file formats, 333
  GIF images, 266, 278
  JPEG images, 283–285, 287–288
  lossless, 266, 293, 350
  lossy, 283–285, 350
  PNG format, 293
  Shockwave file format, 366
  video, 349–351
config command (SSI), 256, 260
content attribute (\<meta\>), 94, 98, 490
content-language value (http-equiv
  attribute), 100
Content-type header, 459
content-type value (http-equiv
  attribute), 99
contextual selectors (style sheets), 396
controller attribute (\<embed\>), 344, 357
controls attribute
  \<embed\> tags, 339
  \<img\> tag, 151, 358
converting graphics
  to GIF format, 266
  to indexed color, 311
  to Web Palette, 309
converting HTML into XML, 447
coordinates in browser window, 433
coords attribute, 490
  \<a\> tag, 131
  \<area\> tag, 132
copying
  files (in telnet sessions), 54
  transparency information, 276
copyright issues, audio, 330–331
copyright value (\<meta name\>), 101
cp command (Unix), 54
CSS (see cascading style sheets)
.css files, 393
current version design strategy, 9
cursive joining behavior, 463

custom form buttons, 238
Custom Palette, 305
Cyberbit font, 459

D

data attribute (\<object\>), 153, 166, 491
data rate (video), 349
data tables, 176
date and time, SSI and, 255
  formatting, 260
DATE_GMT variable, 259
DATE_LOCAL variable, 255, 259
datetime attribute, 491
\<dd\> tags, 471
decimal color representations, 31, 76,
  304
declarations, style sheet rules, 392
declare attribute (\<object\>), 153, 491
decompressing JPEG images, 284
defer attribute, 491
deflate compression scheme (PNG), 293
\<del\> tags, 396, 471
deleting
  files/directories on system, 57
  whitespace from tables, 188–190
deprecated HTML tags (list), 511–514
description value (\<meta name\>), 100
design tips (see tips and tricks)
\<dfn\> tags, 471
DHTML (Dynamic HTML), 429–444
  DOM (Document Object Model),
    431–435
  examples of, 435–441
  tools, 441–443
Digital Frontiers
  HVS ColorGIF, 268, 281
  HVS JPEG 2.1 plug-in, 287–290
digital video (see video)
dir attribute, 462, 491
\<dir\> tags, 472
direction attribute (\<marquee\>), 151
directionality of character encodings,
  462
Director (Macromedia), 308, 366–370
directory structure, Unix, 51
  creating (sub)directories, 55
  deleting directories, 57
  determining working directory, 56

directory structure, Unix (*continued*)
  navigating, 54
  root directory, 48, 51
disabled attribute, 242, 491
display property (CSS), 416
displays, designing for, 14–27
  color capabilities, 16
  monitor resolution, 14–18
disposal methods (animation), 325
DitherBox (RDG Tools), 315
dithering, 16, 279
  Adobe Photoshop, 310–311
  color names and, 78
  flat graphics, 306
  GIF animation, 328
  photographic images, 306
<div> tags, 395–396, 472
<dl> tags, 472
Do Not Dispose method, 325
Doctor HTML utility, 11
DOCUMENT_NAME variable, 259
document object, 431
Document Type Definition (DTD), 446
DOCUMENT_URI environment variable, 259
documents, web (see web pages)
DOM (Document Object Model), 431–435
Dreamweaver (Macromedia), 12, 21, 58, 379, 442
drop caps, 426
<dt> tags, 472
DTD (Document Type Definition), 446
dynamic content (see SSI)
"Dynamic Fonts", 453–455
Dynamic HTML (DHTML), 429–444
  DOM (Document Object Model), 431–435
  examples of, 435–441
  tools for, 441–443
dynsrc attribute (<img>), 151, 358

E

echo command (SSI), 257
8-bit character encodings, 458
8-bit indexed color, 266
8-bit palette images, 293
8-bit transparency, 296

elif statement (XSSI), 256
else statement (XSSI), 256
<em> tags, 472
email
  message links (mailto), 143
  sending form contents via, 248–250
<embed> tags, 147–149, 165–166, 472
  for audio plug-ins, 338–340
  Flash content with, 362–365, 368–370
  for PNG images, 292
  for video plug-ins, 357
embedded font technology, 453–457
embedded style sheets, 393
embedding objects in pages
  audio, 338–340
  <embed> tags, 147–149, 165–166
  Flash movies, 364–365
  object parameters, 153, 164
  <object> tags, 152–153, 164, 166–167
  video, 357
encoded character sets, 458–460
encoding
  audio data, 333
  streaming media, 335
  URLs, 235
enctype attribute (<form>), 227, 235, 239, 492
endif statement (XSSI), 256
ending HTML tags, 390
endtime attribute (<embed>), 340
environment variables, 255, 256, 259
Eriksson, Frederic, 138
errmsg attribute (config command), 257
Exact Palette, 305
exec command (SSI), 257
expires value (http-equiv attribute), 99
Extended Server Side Includes (XXSI), 255–256
Extensible Markup Language (XML), 445–452
  examples of, 448–451
Extensible Style Language (XSL), 451
external style sheets, 393

F

face attribute, 492
Fahrner, Todd, 314
family, font, 400

"Fast Start" technology (Apple), 352
Fetch utility, 58
<fieldset> tags, 227, 472
file attribute
  flastmod command, 258
  fsize command, 258
  include command, 258
file links, 144
file size, graphics
  animated GIFs, 328–329
  Flash file format, 360
  GIFs, 277–282
  JPEGs, 287–290
  PNGs, 301
  Shockwave movies, 367
  thumbnails, 162
files
  absolute/relative pathnames, 51–53
  audio file formats, 336
  copying (in telnet sessions), 54
  deleting on system, 57
  filename suffixes, 57, 61
  file-selection form fields, 228, 239
  Flash format, 359–366
  listing (in telnet sessions), 55
  metafiles, 343
  MIME types, 61–63, 426
  moving (in telnet sessions), 56
  naming conventions, 57
  paging through contents, 56
  permissions for, 59–61
  Shockwave, 366–370
  uploading via FTP, 57–61
  video file formats, 351–353
  virtual includes (example), 253–254
filtering PNG images, 294
financial transactions in XML, 451
Fireworks (Macromedia), 202, 267,
    313–314, 324
  creating JPEG images, 286, 289
  creating PNG images, 299
  GIF files, optimizing, 280
  palettes, 305–306, 307
:firstletter pseudo-element, 426
:first-line, :first-letter pseudo-elements,
  397
fixed page design (see absolute web
  page control)

fixed-width columns, 199
Flanagan, David, 379, 434
Flash file format (Macromedia),
    359–366, 450
flastmod command (SSI), 258
flat color, 278
flat graphics, 306
flexible web page design, 19–20
float property (CSS), 413, 426
floating (inline) frames, 219
  Navigator imitation of, 223
flow control commands (XSSI), 255
font property (CSS), 403
<font> tag, 135, 473
  tables and, 193
font-family property (CSS), 400
font-size property (CSS), 402
font-style property (CSS), 401
font-variant property (CSS), 401
font-weight property (CSS), 401
fonts (typography)
  body elements, 427
  CSS2 descriptors for, 424
  cursive joining behavior, 463
  embedded, 453–457
  internationalization, 458–460
  style sheet properties, 400–407
  tables and, 193
  text size (see type size)
  (see also text)
foot, table, 174, 180
for attribute (<label>), 232, 492
foreground element color, 403
<form> tags, 227, 234–236, 473
formatter value (<meta name>), 101
FormMail script, 248–250
forms, 226–250
  accessibility issues, 24, 25
  appearance of, 242–246
  elements in tables, 187
  elements of, 236–241
    aligning, 244
    sizing, 242
  sending contents by email, 248–250
  tips and tricks, 246
  (see also CGI scripts)
fragments, linking to, 134
frame attribute (<table>), 171, 492

frame delay (animation), 324
frame differencing, 329
frame rate (video), 349
frame size (video), 348
<frame> tag, 206, 211, 473
frameborder attribute, 215, 492
   <embed> tag, 148
   <frame> tag, 206
   <frameset> tags, 208
   <iframe> tags, 208
frames, 20, 206–225
   borders and spacing, 214
   design tips and tricks, 220–225
   frameset structure, 211–214
   hidden, for preloading images, 224
   inline (floating), 219
      Navigator imitation of, 223
   managing with JavaScript, 382
   margins, 199, 216
   nesting, 213
   preventing from loading into, 224
   rows and columns, 212–213
   scrolling, 215
   size and disabling resize, 216
   targeting, 217–219
      multiple from one link, 221–223
<frameset> tags, 207, 211–214, 473
framesets (see frames)
framespacing attribute (<frameset>),
   208, 215
Freehand (Macromedia), 308
fsize command (SSI), 257
FTP for uploading documents, 57–61
FTP links, 144
Furbo Filters's Web Scrubber, 314

G

gamma value, 19, 295
Gaussian blur, 288
Generator (Macromedia), 366
generator value (<meta name>), 101
get method, 234
GIF Animator (Ulead), 323
GIF format, 158, 265–282
   animation (see animation)
   compression, 266, 278
   GIF87a vs. GIF89a, 265
   minimizing file sizes, 277–282

   PNG format vs., 295
   tools for, 267–268
   when to use, 266–267
GIF Movie Gear, 323
GIF Wizard service, 329
GifBuilder program, 323
GifConverter program, 268
GifGifGif (Pedagoguery Software), 324
GIFmation (BoxTop Software), 323
GifSmartsaver (Ulead), 268
glyphs, internationalization and,
   458–460
GoLive Cyberstudio, 12, 21, 58
Gopher links, 145
graphics
   accessibility
      alternate text, 24, 159
      HTML 4.0 attributes for, 25
   aliasing and anti-aliasing, 270–271
   animation (see animation)
   background, 414
      positioning, 415
      scrolling vs. nonscrolling, 415
      tiling, 96
   colors in (see colors)
      dithering (see dithering)
      number of colors (see bit depth)
      transparency (see transparency)
   dividing into multiple files, 203
   GIF format, 158, 265–282, 295
   grayscale (see grayscale)
   how to use, 157
   hyperlinked, 24, 133, 158
   image buttons on forms, 239
   image size, 159–160
      single-pixel images, 190
      thumbnail images, 162
      (see also optimizing images)
   imagemaps (see imagemaps)
   <img> tag, 149–151, 158–164, 358,
      474
   inline frames vs., 219
   interlacing, 268–269, 295, 328
   JavaScript rollovers, 143, 373–378
   JPEG format, 158, 283–290, 295, 306
   list-item markers (bullets), 417
   lossy/lossless compression, 266,
      283–285, 293, 350
   marquees, 151

monitor characteristics and, 14–19
multipart images in tables, 177,
201–205
optimizing (see optimizing images)
PNG format, 158, 266, 291–302
preloading, 160, 224
SMIL language, 448–449
text in, 297
tools for, 310–315, 323–324
palettes and, 306
(see also specific graphics tool)
types of images, 306
vector graphics, 268, 359, 449–451
video (see video)
Web Palette (see Web Palette)
grayscale, 326
designing for, 16
PNG format for, 293
grouping table rows/columns, 180
Gwyn, Philip, 314

H
<h1>...<h6> tags, 473
"halo effect", 269–271
hand-held communications devices, 26
hard value (wrap), 240
hardware
hand-held devices, 26
monitor characteristics, 14–19, 26–27
hash mark (#)
ID selectors, 397
in pathnames, 134
<head> tags, 93, 473
head, table, 175, 180
header, document, 95
headers attribute (<td>, <th>), 174, 492
headers, table, 175, 178, 183
hearing impairment (see accessibility)
height attribute, 492
<applet> tags, 147, 165
<embed> tags, 147, 165, 339, 344,
357, 363
<iframe> tags, 208
<img> tag, 150, 159–160
<marquee> tag, 151
<object> tags, 153, 166, 364
<spacer> tag, 154
<table> tags, 171, 185

<td>, <th> tags, 173, 185
(see also size)
height property (CSS), 412
Heinle, Nick, 373, 379, 385
hexadecimal color representations, 31,
76–78, 304
hidden attribute (<embed>), 147, 165,
339
hiding
frames for preloading images, 224
JavaScript from old browsers, 383
text entry fields, 229, 237
HitchHiker browser, 27
HomePage (Claris), 58
horizontal alignment (see alignment)
horizontal rules, 149, 154–156
in select menus, 245
horizontal spacing (see hspace
attribute; margins; positioning)
hosts in URLs, 133
<hr> tag, 149, 154–156, 474
in <select> menus, 245
href attribute, 493
<a> tag, 130
<area> tag, 132
<base> tags, 91
<embed> tags, 344, 357
<link> tags, 93, 393
hreflang attribute (<a>), 131, 493
hspace attribute, 493
<applet> tags, 147, 165
<cmbed> tags, 148, 165, 340
<iframe> tags, 209
<img> tag, 150, 162
<marquee> tag, 151
<object> tags, 153
<table> tags, 171
(see also margins)
HTML (Hypertext Markup Language)
accessibility features, 25
attribute reference, 483–510
converting documents into XML, 447
deprecated tags (list), 511–514
Dynamic HTML (see DHTML)
ending tags, 390
forms (see forms)
language tags, 460–463
misusing structural tags, 24
proprietary tags, 515–517

HTML (*continued*)
  SSI (see SSI)
  tables (see tables)
  tag and element reference, 467–482
  validation services, 11
HTML Color Picker (MacOS8), 308
<html> tags, 93, 474
HTML Validator utility, 11
.htmlf filename suffix, 254
HTTP_ACCEPT variable, 259
HTTP_REFERER variable, 260
HTTP response headers, 49
HTTP_USER_AGENT variable, 260
http-equiv attribute (<meta>), 94, 98,
        459, 494
Huffman table, 288
HVS ColorGIF (Digital Frontiers), 268
  GIF files, optimizing, 281
HVS JPEG 2.1 plug-in, 287–290
hybrid colors, 315–317

I

<i> tags, 474
i18n (see internationalization)
id attribute, 397, 494
ID selectors (style sheets), 397
IE (see Microsoft Internet Explorer)
if statement (XSSI), 256
<iframe> tags, 208, 219, 474
  faking in Navigator, 223
IIS (Internet Information Server), 48
Illustrator (Adobe), 308
image buttons on forms, 239
imagemaps, 132, 137–143, 157
  multipart images in tables, 201
  text alternatives for, 24, 143
ImageReady (Adobe), 203, 267, 271,
        311–313, 324
  creating JPEG images, 286
  creating PNG images, 300
  GIF files, optimizing, 281
  palettes, 305–307
images (see graphics)
<img> tag, 149–151, 158–164, 474
  inline video with, 358
@import function, 394
importing style sheets, 394
include command (SSI), 254, 258

indentation in lists, 418
indentation of paragraphs, 407
Indeo codec (Intel), 350
index files (servers), 49, 51
indexed color, 266, 293, 311
  transparency and, 269
inherit value (visibility property), 434
inheritance, style sheet, 394
inline (floating) frames, 219
  Navigator imitation of, 223
inline styles, 392
inline video, 358
<input> tag, 228–231, 236–239, 474
  type=button, 228
  type=checkbox, 228, 237
  type=file, 228, 239
  type=hidden, 229, 237
  type=image, 229, 239
  type=password, 229, 236
  type=radio, 230, 238
  type=reset, 230, 238
  type=submit, 231, 238
  type=text, 231, 236
<ins> tags, 396, 475
Intel Indeo codec, 350
interactivity, 359–378
  Dynamic HTML (DHTML), 429–444
  Flash content (Macromedia), 359–366
  Java applets for, 370–373
  JavaScript-enabled buttons, 143,
        373–378
  Shockwave movies, 366–370
interframe (temporal) compression, 350
interframe delay (animation), 324
interlacing, 268–269, 295
  GIF animation, 328
internationalization, 458–463
  character sets, 458–460
  HTML 4.0 language tags, 460–463
Internet Explorer (see Microsoft
        Internet Explorer)
Internet Information Server (IIS), 48
Internet Media Type format, 235
intraframe (spatial) compression, 350
intranets, 391
<isindex> tag, 231, 475
ismap attribute (<img>), 141, 150, 157,
        494
italic font style, 401

J

JASC Paint Shop Pro, 267, 286, 324
Java applets, 146, 164, 370–373
 parameters for, 153, 164
JavaScript language, 379–386
 browser support, 383–386, 434
 controlling status bar text, 136, 381
 Document Object Model and, 432
 Flash format with, 360
 frame management with, 382
 interactive buttons, 143, 373–378
 multiple frames with one link, 222
 pop-up windows, 21
 preventing loads into frames, 224
 rules in select menus, 245
JPEG format, 158, 283–290, 306
 compression, 283–285, 287–288
 creating JPEG images, 286
 minimizing file sizes, 287–290
 PNG format vs., 295
 Progressive JPEGs, 285, 287

K

<kbd> tags, 475
key frames (video), 350
keywords value (<meta name>), 101
King, Andrew, 328
Kirchman, Tom, 329

L

label attribute (<optgroup>), 232, 494
<label> tags, 231, 475
lang attribute, 460–462, 494
language attribute (<script>), 154, 494
language tags (HTML 4.0), 460–463
LAST_MODIFIED environment variable,
 259
<layer> tags, 432, 475
layers of objects, 432
layout (see positioning)
Leave As Is disposal method, 325
left property (CSS), 419, 433
left-to-right directionality, 462
left value
 align attribute, 161
 clear attribute, 162
leftmargin attribute (<body>), 92, 98

<legend> tags, 232, 475
length (see size)
letter-spacing property (CSS), 404
lettering (see text)
<li> tags, 475
line breaks, handling, 422
line-height property (CSS), 403
lines (see rules)
lines of text (see text)
Lingo language, Shockwave and,
 366–367
link attribute (<body>), 92, 96, 135, 495
link pseudo-class, 398
<link> tag, 93, 95, 393, 476
links, 130–145
 anchors and hyperlinks, 130–135
  audio files, 338, 343–344
  linking document fragments, 134
  openWin( ) function (JavaScript),
   380–382
  video files, 355
 colors for hyperlinks, 96, 135
 controlling status bar text, 136, 381
 to external style sheets, 393
 hyperlinked graphics, 133, 158
  captions, 24
 imagemaps, 137–143
  client-side, 132, 157
  multipart images in tables, 201
  text alternatives, 24, 143
 JavaScript rollovers, 143, 373–378
 mailto links, 143
 miscellanous, 144–145
 targeting frames, 217–219
  multiple from one link, 221–223
 targeting other windows, 137
Liquid Music System (LiquidAudio), 341
list-style property (CSS), 418
list-style-image property (CSS), 417
list-style-position property (CSS), 418
list-style-type property (CSS), 417
lists
 files on server, 55
 menus (see menus in forms)
 style sheet properties for, 417
"live space," browser, 16–18
LiveAudio plug-in, 334, 338
logging in (telnet), 50

longdesc attribute, 495
  <frame> tag, 207
  <img> tag, 25, 150
loop attribute
  <bgsound> tag, 147
  <embed> tags, 339, 344, 357, 363
  <img> tag, 151, 358
  <marquee> tag, 152
looping animation, 322, 327
lossless compression, 266, 293, 350
lossy compression, 283–285, 350
lowest common denominator design, 9
lowsrc attribute (<img>), 150, 163
ls command (Unix), 55
ltr value (dir attribute), 462
Lynx browser, 6
LZW compression, 266
LZW interframe optimization, 329

M

Macintosh
  browser live area, 18
  CSS compatibility, 518–526
  Internet Explorer 4.0 on, 4
  MacBinary option (Fetch), 58
  System OS8 palettes, 308
Macromedia
  Director, 308, 366–370
  Dreamweaver, 12, 21, 58, 379, 442
  Fireworks, 202, 267, 313–314, 324
    creating JPEG images, 286, 289
    creating PNG images, 299
    GIF files, optimizing, 280
    palettes, 305–306, 307
  Flash file format, 359–366, 450
  Freehand, 308
  Generator, 366
  Shockwave Audio, 342, 344
mail (see email)
mailto links, 143
.map (map definition) files, 141
<map> tags, 132, 139–141, 476
MapEdit program, 138
MapMaker 1.1.2, 138
margin property (CSS), 408
margin-top, margin-right, margin-
    bottom, margin-left properties
    (CSS), 408

marginheight attribute, 495
  <body> tags, 92, 98
  <frame> tag, 207, 216, 224
  <iframe> tags, 209
margins, 97, 199
  frames, 199, 216
  graphics, 162
  removing from framed pages, 224
  style sheet properties for, 408
  table cells, 185
  (see also hspace attribute; vspace
    attribute)
marginwidth attribute, 495
  <body> tags, 92, 98
  <frame> tag, 207, 216, 224
  <iframe> tags, 209
<marquee> tags, 151, 476
mastersound attribute (<embed>), 340
maxlength attribute, 495
  <input type=password> tag, 230
  <input type=text> tag, 231
media attribute, 495
Media Cleaner Pro (Terran Interactive),
    332, 348
media types, 61–63
  style sheets and, 426
MediaPlayer program, 334
menu attribute (<embed>), 364
<menu> tags, 476
menus in forms, 232, 240, 245
  unconventional use of, 246
<meta> tag, 94, 95, 98–101, 476
  audio via client-pull, 340
  frames and, 221
  specifying character encoding, 459
metafiles, 343
method attribute, 496
  <a> tag, 130
  <form> tags, 227, 234
methods attribute (<link>), 93
Metro (Cakewalk), 332
Meyer, Eric, 428, 518
Microsoft Internet Explorer, 3
  color name support, 78
  coloring tables, 186
  DHTML support, 429, 431–435
  embedded font technology, 453,
    455–457
  feature overview, 8–9

frame borders, 215
FTP via, 58
GIF animation support, 322
JavaScript support, 383–386, 434
live area, 17
Macintosh version, 4
PNG image support, 292
proprietary HTML tags, 515
style sheet support, 390, 428
Microsoft NetShow, 354
middle value (align), 161
MIDI (.mid) file format, 337
MIME types, 61–63
style sheets and, 426
Minimum Bounding Rectangle method, 329
mkdir command (Unix), 55
monitors, designing for, 14–27
color capabilities, 16
size and resolution, 14–18, 22
more command (Unix), 55
motion, with DHTML, 437–441
MouseOver, MouseOut events, 375–377
.mov files, 351–352
MoviePlayer utility (QuickTime), 352
moving files on system, 56
MPEG codec, 351
MPEG file format, 336, 353
-Law (.au) file format, 336
<multicol> tag, 476
multiline text entry fields, 233, 239
multimedia (see animation; audio;
graphics; interactivity; video)
multimedia presentations in SMIL, 448–449
multipart image containers, tables as, 177, 201–205
multiple attribute (<select>), 232, 241, 496
multiple-choice checkboxes on forms, 237
multiple rollovers, 376–378
music (see audio)
mv command (Unix), 56

N

name attribute, 496
<a> tags, 131, 134–135

<applet> tags, 147
<button> tags, 226
<embed> tags, 148, 165, 340, 363, 369
<frame> tag, 207, 217
<iframe> tags, 209
<input type=button> tag, 228
<input type=checkbox> tag, 228
<input type=file> tag, 229
<input type=hidden> tag, 229
<input type=image> tag, 229
<input type=password> tag, 230
<input type=radio> tag, 230
<input type=text> tag, 231
<map> tag, 133
<meta> tag, 94, 98, 100
<object> tags, 153
<param> tags, 153, 165
<select> tags, 233
<textarea> tags, 233
names
CLASS selectors, 397
colors, 78–84, 399
named anchors, 130, 134–135
naming
filename suffixes, 57, 61
files, 56, 57
navigating directories, 54
Navigator (see Netscape Navigator)
NCSA Server software, 48
nesting
frames, 213
style sheets, 394
Netscape Navigator, 3
collapsing table cells, 190
color name support, 78
coloring tables, 186
DHTML support, 429, 431–435
embedded font technology, 453–455
feature overview, 8–9
form element sizes, 242
frame borders, 215
frame margins, 216
FTP via, 58
GIF animation support, 322
inline frames, faking, 223
JavaScript support, 383–386, 434
live area, 17
padding, 427

Netscape Navigator (*continued*)
  PNG image support, 292
  proprietary HTML tags, 516
  style sheet support, 390, 428
  table whitespace, 190
Netscape Servers, 48
NetShow (Microsoft), 354
news links, 145
NNTP links, 145
<nobr> tags, 476
<noembed> tags, 152, 166, 477
  Flash format and, 365, 370
<noframes> tags, 209, 212, 477
nohref attribute (<area>), 132, 497
nonrendering text, 190
nonstreaming audio, 333–340
  adding to HTML documents, 338–340
noresize attribute, 497
  <frame> tag, 207, 216
  <iframe> tags, 209
<noscript> tags, 152, 477
noshade attribute (<hr>), 149, 156, 497
Nothing disposal method, 325
nowrap attribute (<td>, <th>), 174, 497
numbered lists, CSS properties, 417

O

object attribute, 497
object embedding
  alternate content, 152, 166
  <embed> tags, 147–149, 165–166
  <object> tags, 152–153, 164, 166–167
  parameters for objects, 153, 164
<object> tags, 152–153, 166–167, 477
  Flash content with, 362, 364–365,
    368–370
  for Java applets, 164, 373
objects, DHTML
  properties of, 433–434
  referencing, 432
oblique font style, 401
OFE (Open Financial Exchange), 451
<ol> tags, 477
onblur attribute, 498
onchange attribute, 498
onclick attribute, 498
onClick command (JavaScript), 222
ondblclick attribute, 498

onfocus attribute, 498
onkeydown attribute, 498
onkeypress attribute, 499
onkeyup attribute, 499
onload attribute, 499
onload event handler, 438–439
onmousedown attribute, 499
onmousemove attribute, 499
onmouseout attribute, 500
onmouseover attribute, 500
onMouseOver, onMouseOut handlers,
    375–377
onmouseup attribute, 500
onreset attribute, 500
onselect attribute, 500
onsubmit attribute, 500
onunload attribute, 501
Open Financial Exchange (OFE), 451
Open Software Description (OSD), 451
OpenType technology, 453, 455–457
openWin( ) (JavaScript), 380–382
Opera browser, 5
<optgroup> tags, 232, 477
Optimized Colors Palette (ImageReady),
    312
optimizing audio files, 337
optimizing images
  animated GIFs, 328–329
  GIF images, 277–282
  JPEG images, 287–290
  multipart images in tables, 201
  PNG images, 301
<option> tags, 232, 240, 477
  dummy option items, 245
ordered lists, CSS properties, 417
OSD (Open Software Description), 451
overflow property (CSS), 422
overlined text, 405

P

<p> tags, 478
padding, 409, 427
padding property (CSS), 409
padding-top, padding-right, padding-
    bottom, padding-left properties
    (CSS), 409
Paeth filtering algorithm (PNG), 294
paging through file contents, 56

Paint Shop Pro (JASC), 267, 286, 324
palette attribute (<embed>), 148, 369
palettes
    GIF animation and, 326
    grayscale (see grayscale)
    list of, 305
    web-safe (see Web Palette)
palm-top computers, 26
Pantone ColorWeb Pro, 308
paragraphs
    drop caps, 426
    indenting, 407
<param> tags, 153, 164, 478
parameters for applets/objects, 153, 164
_parent target, 218
passwd command (Unix), 56
password text entry fields, 229, 236
pathnames
    # (hash mark) in, 134
    absolute vs. relative, 51–53
Pattern Fill function (ColorSafe), 316
PDAs, 26
PDF accessibility issues, 24
Peak (Bias), 332
Pedagoguery Software's GifGifGif, 324
percentages
    color equivalents, 32, 304
    font sizes, 402
    framesets sizes, 213
    SSI time formats, 260
    table dimensions, 184
Perceptual Palette, 305
performance
    audio sampling rate, 333, 337
    frames, 210
    graphics
        animated GIF optimization,
            328–329
        dithering (see dithering)
        GIF image optimization, 277–282
        interlacing and, 268–269, 328
        JPEG image optimization, 287–290
        PNG image optimization, 301
        reusing graphics, 163
    <img> lowsrc attribute, 150, 163
    lossy/lossless compression, 266,
        283–285, 293, 350
    preloading images and, 160, 224

reducing number of colors, 278, 309,
    310, 328
table display, 194
video data/frame rates, 349
period (.)
    in alternate text, 24
    CLASS selectors, 397
permissions, file, 59–61
pg command (Unix), 56
PGML (Precision Graphics Markup
    Language), 450
PhotoGIF (BoxTop Software), 268
photographic images, 306
    GIF format for, 267
    JPEG format for, 284
    PNG format for, 293
    (see also graphics)
Photoshop (Adobe), 267, 310–311
    alpha channel, 273–277
    CLUTs, creating, 308
    color palettes, 306
    creating JPEG images, 286, 288
    creating PNG images, 298
    dividing images into multiple files,
        203
    GIF files, optimizing, 279
    palettes, 307
physical value (wrap), 240
Piguet, Yves, 323
pixelLeft, pixelTop properties, 433
pixels
    color (see colors)
    measuring text size, 426
    monitor resolution, 15–18
play attribute (<embed>), 363
player, audio, 335
playeveryframe attribute (<embed>),
    357
plug-ins (see embedding objects in
    pages)
pluginspage attribute (<embed>), 148,
    165, 357, 363
pluginurl attribute (<embed>), 149, 165
PNG format, 158, 266, 291–302
    compression, 293
    creating PNG images, 297–301
    minimizing file sizes, 301
pngcrush application, 301

pop-up menus in forms, 232, 240, 245
   unconventional use of, 246
pop-up windows, 21
Portable Document Format accessibility
   issues, 24
Portable Network Format (see PNG
   format)
position attribute, 436
position property (CSS), 419
positioning
   "above the fold" design, 23
   alignment (see alignment)
   background graphics, 415
   box properties (style sheets), 407–413
   coordinates for DHTML objects, 433
   CSS2 accessibility features for, 25
   .graphics, tips for, 162–164
   motion, with DHML, 437–441
   style sheets for, 407–413, 418–422
   tables, 183
   two-column layouts (example),
      199–201
   z-order, 420, 434
post method, 235
<pre> tags, 478
   forms within, 244
precedence, style sheets, 394
preformatted text, forms in, 244
preloading images, 160
   hidden frames for, 224
preview graphics, 162
print impairment (see accessibility)
printenv command (SSI), 259
profile attribute, 501
Progressive JPEG images, 285, 287
ProJPEG utility (BoxTop Software), 287,
   288
prompt attribute, 501
properties in style sheets, 392, 399–418
   background, 413–416
   box properties, 407–413
   classification, 416–418
   CSS2, 424
   type-related, 400–407
properties of DOM objects, 433–434
proprietary HTML tags, 515–517
protocols in URLs, 133
ProxiWeb browser, 27
pseudo-classes, 398

pseudo-elements, 397
pseudo-selectors (style sheets),
      397–398, 425
pull-down menus in forms, 232, 240,
   245
push buttons (see buttons on forms)
pwd command (Unix), 56

Q

Q setting (JPEG images), 284
<q> tags, 478
Qcomp (Qdesign Corporation), 332
quality attribute (<embed>), 363
quality, video, 349
QUERY_STRING_UNESCAPED
      environment variable, 259
QuickTime (Apple), 332, 334, 342, 344,
   348, 351–352
   Sorenson codec, 348, 351

R

radio buttons on forms, 230, 238
Radius Cinepak codec, 350
.ram files, 343
Randers-Pehrson, Glenn, 301
rating value (<meta name>), 101
RDF (Resource Description
      Framework), 451
RDG Tools' DitherBox, 315
read-only attribute, 242
readonly attribute, 501
RealAudio (RealNetworks), 341, 343
RealFlash utility, 366
RealVideo (RealNetworks), 354
RealVideoEncoder (RealNetworks), 354
reducing number of colors, 278, 309,
   310, 328
reference movies (QuickTime), 352
referencing objects (DHTML), 432
refresh value (http-equiv attribute), 99
rel attribute, 501
   <a> tag, 131
   <link> tags, 93, 393
relative
   column widths, 200
   font sizes, 402
   pathnames, 52–53

positioning (style sheets), 419
URLs, 133
REMOTE_ADDR variable, 260
REMOTE_HOST variable, 260
renaming server files, 56
reset buttons on forms, 230, 238
resizable web pages, 19–20
resolution, monitor, 22
unknown, 14–18
Resource Description Framework
(RDF), 451
response headers (HTTP), 49
Restore to Background method, 326
Restore to Previous method, 326
reusing images, 163
rev attribute
<a> tags, 131, 501
<link> tags, 93
Revert to Previous method, 322
RGB values, systems for representing,
31, 76–78, 304, 399
right-to-left directionality, 462
right value
align attribute, 161
clear attribute, 162
rm command (Unix), 57
rmdir command (Unix), 57
robots value (<meta name>), 101
Roelofs, Greg, 301
rollovers, 143, 373–378
multipart images in tables, 201
root directory (server), 48, 51
rows attribute, 502
<frameset> tags, 208, 212–213
<textarea> tags, 233
rows, frameset, 212–213
rows, table, 176, 177–179
aligning cell text in, 183
coloring, 186
controlling, 179
grouping, 180
restraining heights of, 191
sizing, 184, 198
spanning, 180, 195
(see also tables)
rowspan attribute
(, <th>), 195
rowspan attribute (<td>, <th>), 174,
180, 502

royalty-free audio resources, 331
rtl value (dir attribute), 462
rules
colored boxes (example), 197–198
horizontal (see horizontal rules)
vertical (example), 196
rules attribute (<table>), 172, 180, 502
rules, style sheet, 391–392
selectors, 392, 395–398, 423

S

<s> tags, 478
salign attribute (<embed>), 364
<samp> tags, 478
sampling rate, 333, 337
scale attribute (<embed>), 364
scheme attribute (<meta>), 94, 502
scope attribute (<td>, <th>), 174, 502
<script> tags, 95, 154, 380, 478
scripts in web pages, 154
alternate content, 152
CGI (see CGI scripts)
scrollamount attribute (<marquee>),
152
scrolldelay attribute (<marquee>), 152
scrolling
background image, 415
frames and, 215
menus in forms, 232, 240–241, 245
scrolling attribute, 502
<frame> tag, 207, 215
<iframe> tags, 209
search engines
framed documents and, 210, 221
<isindex> tag, 231
<meta> tags for, 100
<select> tags, 232, 240, 479
horizontal rules in menus, 245
selected attribute, 503
<option> tags, 232
<select> tags, 240
selectors (style sheet rules), 392,
395–398, 423
_self target, 218
Server Side Includes (SSI), 251–261
commands for, 253–254
environment variables, 255, 256, 259
Extended (XSSI), 255–256

server software for streaming audio, 335

servers, web, 47–63
configuring for Flash files, 362
configuring for Shockwave, 368
software for, 48

server-side imagemaps, 137, 141, 157
multipart images in tables, 201
text alternatives, 24, 143

set command (SSI), 259

SGML (Standard General Markup Language), 445

shading horizontal rules, 149, 156, 497

shape attribute, 503
<a> tag, 131
<area> tag, 132

shapes attribute (<object>), 153

shifting colors (see dithering)

Shockwave Audio (Macromedia), 342, 344, 366–370

.shtml filename suffix, 254

Siegel, David, 157

sight impairment (see accessibility)

sites (see web sites)

16-bit character encodings, 459

16-bit displays, 304

size
applet windows, 165
audio clip length, 337
browser "live space", 16–18
columns for page layout, 199–201
CSS properties for, 412
embedded objects, 166
font size, 402
form elements, 242
frames, 216
frameset rows/columns, 212–213
graphics images, 159–160
animated GIFs, 328–329
Flash file format, 360
GIFs, 277–282
JPEGs, 287–290
PNGs, 301
Shockwave movies, 367
thumbnails, 162
horizontal rules, 155
length units (style sheets), 398
monitor displays, 14–18, 22
multiline text entry fields, 239

resizable vs. fixed web pages, 19–23

scrollbars in frames, 215

tables, 184, 198
columns, 192–193
restraining row heights, 191

text baselines, 403

text, in pixels, 426

type size, 21

video clip length/frame size, 348

(see also height attribute; size attribute; width attribute)

size attribute, 503
<hr> tag, 149, 155
<input type=password> tag, 230
<input type=text> tag, 231, 236
<select> tags, 233, 240–241
<spacer> tag, 154

sizefmt attribute (config command), 257

slash (/)
in URLs, 49, 51
encoding in URLs, 235

slide-show effect, 99

small caps, 401

<small> tags, 479

SMIL (Synchronized Multimedia Integration Language), 448–449

soft value (wrap), 240

Sol, Selena, 247

Sorenson codec, 348, 351

sound (see audio)

SoundMachine program, 334

<spacer> tags, 21, 154, 157, 479
in table cells, 190

spaces (see whitespace)

span attribute, 504
<col> tag, 169
<colgroup> tags, 170

<span> tags, 395–396, 479

spanning table rows/columns, 179, 192–193, 195

spatial (intraframe) compression, 350

spatial frequency, image, 284

speech (see audio)

speech displays (see accessibility)

speed
audio sampling rate, 333, 337
video data/frame rates, 349
(see also performance)

speed, GIF animation, 324

src attribute, 504
  <bgsound> tag, 147
  <embed> tags, 148, 165, 339, 344, 357
  <frame> tag, 207, 217
  <iframe> tags, 209
  <img> tag, 150, 158
  <input type=image> tag, 229, 239
  <script> tags, 154
SSI (Server Side Includes), 251–261
  commands for, 253–254
  environment variables, 255, 256, 259
  extended (XSSI), 255–256
stacking order, 420, 434
standby attribute (<object>), 153, 505
start attribute (<img>), 151, 358, 505
starttime attribute (<embed>), 340
static (nonstreaming) audio, 333–340
  adding to HTML documents, 338–340
static positioning, 420
status bar text, 136, 381
streaming audio, 333–335, 341–345
  adding to HTML documents, 343–345
streaming video, 352, 353–355
Streamworks (Xing Technologies), 342, 355
<strike> tags, 479
strike-throughs, 405
<strong> tags, 479
structural HTML tags, misusing, 24
style attribute, 392, 505
style sheets, 389–428
  accessibility features (CSS2), 25
  browser compatibility, 518–526
  changing styles with DHTML, 436
  CSS2 features, 422–425
  fixed page width, 21
  how they work, 391–395
    conflict resolution, 394
  link color specifications, 135
  positioning with, 407–413, 418–422
  properties, 392, 399–418
    background, 413–416
    box properties, 407–413
    classification, 416–418
    CSS2, 424
    type-related, 400–407
  selectors, 392, 395–398, 423
  tips and tricks, 426–428

values for rules, 392, 398–399
  XSL vs., 451
<style> tags, 95, 393, 479
  @import function, 394
Sub filtering algorithm (PNG), 294
<sub> tags, 480
submit buttons on forms, 231, 238
subwindows (see frames)
suffixes, filename, 57, 61
summary attribute, 505
  <caption> tags, 169
  <table> tags, 172
<sup> tags, 480
System Palette, 305, 326

T

tabindex attribute (<a>), 131, 242, 505
<table> tags, 170–172, 178, 480
  forms alignment with, 244
tables, 20, 168–205
  accessibility issues, 24, 25
  deleting whitespace in, 188–190
  fonts and, 193
  form elements in, 187
  formatting appearance, 181–186
  forms alignment with, 244
  multipart images in, 177, 201–205
  sizing, 184, 198
  structure of, 177–181
  templates for, 196–201
  text styles in, 187
  tips and tricks, 193–195
  troubleshooting, 187–193
  ways to use, 176–177
tags, HTML (see HTML)
target attribute, 505
  <a> tags, 131, 137, 217
  <base> tags, 91
  <form> tags, 228
targeting frames, 217–219
  multiple from one link, 221–223
<tbody> tags, 172, 180, 480
<td> tags, 173, 178, 480
  extra whitespace and, 188–189
television browsers (see WebTV)
telnet protocol, 50
  basic Unix commands, 54–57
  links for, 145

templates for tables, 196–201
temporal (interframe) compression, 350
Terran Interactive's Media Cleaner Pro, 332, 348
testing web sites, 13
text
  audio transcripts/descriptions, 24
  blinking, 405
    accessibility problems, 24
  capitalization and small caps, 401, 406
  embedding in PNG images, 297
  handling line breaks, 422
  international character sets, 458–460
  line length and window size, 19–20
  line/word/character spacings, 403–405
  paragraph identation, 407
  pixels to specify size, 426
  scrolling marquees, 151
  in status bar, 136, 381
  style sheet properties for, 400–407
  in tables, 187
  type size, 21
  word wrap
    graphics and, 162
    multiline text entry fields, 240
text-align property (CSS), 406
text attribute (<body>), 92, 96, 505
text-decoration property (CSS), 136, 405
text entry fields, 231, 236
  hidden fields, 229, 237
  multiline, 233
  multiline fields, 239
  password fields, 229, 236
text-indent property (CSS), 407
text-transform property (CSS), 406
<textarea> tags, 233, 239, 480
texttop value (align), 161
<tfoot> tags, 174, 180, 481
<th> tags, 175, 178, 183, 481, 183
<thead> tags, 175, 180, 481
thin client browsers, 27
3-D shading of horizontal rules, 149, 156, 497
thumbnail images, 162
tiling background graphics, 96
time and date, SSI for, 255
  formatting, 260

timefmt attribute (config command), 257, 260
tips and tricks
  audio, streaming/nonstreaming, 335
  background tiles, 96–97
  cascading style sheets, 426–428
  designing for multiple browsers, 10
  DHTML, learning, 431
  fixed page design, 20–23
  form elements, 246
  frames design, 220–225
  graphics
    animated GIFs, 322
    color blenders, 315–317
    GIF, when to use, 266–267
    optimizing (see optimizing images)
    unwanted transparency, 271–273
    when to use JPEGs, 285
    when to use PNGs, 294
  graphics positioning, 162–164
  tables, 193–195
  (see also absolute web page control)
title attribute, 25, 506
  <a> tag, 131
  <link> tags, 93
<title> tags, 94, 481
titles, document, 95, 221
top property (CSS), 419, 433
_top target, 219
top value (align), 161
topmargin attribute (<body>), 93, 98
<tr> tags, 176, 178, 183, 481
transparency, 269–277
  editing with alpha channel, 273–277, 296, 298, 300
  GIF animation, 325
  GIF format for, 267
    GIF87a vs. GIF89a formats, 265
  PNG format for, 296
  preventing unwanted, 271–273
  Transparency Index Color, 269
troubleshooting
  Java applets, 373
  tables, 187–193
truecolor images, 293
TrueDoc technology, 453–455
<tt> tags, 482
24-bit color, 283
two-column layouts (example), 199–201

type attribute, 506
  <a> tag, 132
  <button> tags, 227
  <embed> tag, 149
  <input> tag (see <input> tag)
  <link> tags, 93
  <object> tags, 153
  <param> tags, 154
  <spacer> tag, 154
type selectors (style sheets), 395–396
type size, 21
typography (fonts)
  body elements, 427
  CSS2 descriptors for, 424
  cursive joining behavior, 463
  embedded fonts, 453–457
  internationalization, 458–460
  style sheet properties, 400–407
  tables and, 193
  text size (see type size)
  (see also text)

U

<u> tags, 482
<ul> tags, 482
Ulead GIF Animator, 323
Ulead GifSmartsaver, 268
underlined text, 405
underlines for hyperlinks, 136
Unicode character set, 459
Uniform Palette, 305
Unisys company, 266
units attribute (<embed>), 148
Unix systems, 48
  chmod command, 59
  Flash movies (unsupported), 361
  introduction and command list,
    50–57
unordered lists, CSS properties, 417
Unspecified disposal method, 325
Up filtering algorithm (PNG), 294
uploading documents via FTP, 57–61
URLs (uniform resource locators)
  absolute vs. relative, 133
  <base> tag, 217
  encoding, 235
  mailto links, 143
  opening with openWin( ), 380–382

  slash (/) in, 49, 51
  targeting frames, 217–219
    multiple from one link, 221–223
  visible in status bar, 136, 381
urn attribute
  <a> tags, 131
  <link> tags, 94
"Use Compressed Graphics" option, 286
usemap attribute, 507
  <img> tag, 139, 141, 150, 157
  <object> tags, 153

V

validating HTML, 11
valign attribute, 507
  <caption> tags, 169
  <col> tag, 169
  <colgroup> tags, 170
  <tbody> tags, 173
  <td>, <th> tags, 174, 184, 194
  <tfoot> tags, 175
  <thead> tags, 175
  <tr> tags, 176
value attribute, 508
  <button> tags, 227
  <input type=button> tag, 228
  <input type=checkbox> tag, 228
  <input type=file> tag, 229
  <input type=hidden> tag, 229
  <input type=password> tag, 230
  <input type=radio> tag, 230
  <input type=reset> tag, 230
  <input type=submit> tag, 231
  <input type=text> tag, 231, 236
  <option> tags, 232, 240
  <param> tags, 153, 165
  set command, 259
values in style sheet rules, 392, 398–399
valuetype attribute (<param>), 153, 508
var attribute
  echo command, 257
  set command, 259
<var> tags, 482
variables, JavaScript, 380
vector graphics, 268, 359, 449–451
version attribute, 508
versions (browsers), designing for
  current, 9

vertical-align property (CSS), 405
vertical alignment (see alignment)
vertical rules (example), 196
vertical spacing (see margins;
    positioning; vspace attribute;
    whitespace)
video, 347–358
  adding to HTML documents, 355–358
  compression, 349–351
  file formats, 351–353
  Flash movies, 359–366
  Shockwave, 366–370
  SMIL language, 448–449
  streaming, 353–355
  tools for, 347–348
virtual attribute
  flastmod command, 258
  fsize command, 258
  include command, 258
virtual includes (example), 253–254
virtual parameter (SSI), 254
virtual value (wrap), 240
visibility property (CSS), 421, 434
visibility, element (CSS), 421, 434
visited hyperlink color, 135
visited pseudo-class, 398
vlink attribute (<body>), 92, 96, 135,
    508
VML (Vector Markup Language), 450
volume attribute (<embed>), 339
VRML (Virtual Reality Markup
    Language), 13
vspace attribute, 509
  <applet> tags, 147, 165
  <embed> tags, 148, 165, 340
  <iframe> tags, 209
  <img> tag, 150, 162
  <marquee> tag, 152
  <object> tags, 153
  <table> tags, 172
  (see also margins)

W

WAI (Web Accessibility Initiative), 23,
    26
wallpapering (style sheets for), 414
WAVE (.wav) file format, 336
<wbr> tag, 482

Web Accessibility Initiative, 23, 26
web browsers (see browsers)
web pages
  absolute control over (see absolute
    web page control)
  audio with, 338–340, 343–345
  bookmarking, frames and, 210
  cascading style sheets, 389–428
    accessibility features (CSS2), 25
    browser compatibility, 518–526
    changing styles with DHTML, 436
    conflict resolution, 394
    CSS2 features, 422–425
    fixed page width, 21
    how they work, 391–395
    positioning with, 407–413, 418–422
    properties, 392, 399–418, 424
    selectors, 392, 395–398, 423
    tips and tricks, 426–428
    values for rules, 392, 398–399
    XSL vs., 451
  converting HTML to XML, 447
  date and time on, 255, 260
  design tips (see tips and tricks)
  dynamic content (see SSI)
  embedded fonts, 453–457
  embedding objects in
    alternate content, 152, 166
    <embed> tags, 147–149, 165–166
    object parameters, 153, 164
    <object> tags, 152–153, 164, 166
  flexible vs. fixed design, 19–23
  interactivity, 359–378
    Dynamic HTML, 429–444
    Flash content (Macromedia),
      359–366
    Java applets on, 146, 164, 370–373
    JavaScript-enabled buttons, 143,
      373–378
    Shockwave movies, 366–370
  internationalization, 458–463
  margins (see margins)
  marking as searchable, 231
  scripts in (see scripts in web pages)
  structural tags, 94–95
  tables as templates, 177
  titles for, 221
  uploading via FTP, 57–61
  video with, 355–358

Web Palette, 16, 32, 78, 303–317, 326
  color blenders, 315–317
  color names vs., 78
  converting to, 309
  designing with web-safe colors,
    307–309
  tools for, 310–315
Web Schematics on the WWW, 450
Web Scrubber (Furbo Filters), 314
web servers, 47–63
  configuring for Flash files, 362
  configuring for Shockwave files, 368
  software for, 48
Web Shift slider (ImageReady), 312
web sites
  accessibility (see accessibility)
  browser-aware designing, 9–13
  display-aware designing, 14–27
  documents for (see web pages)
  knowing your audience, 12
  purpose of, 13
  rating (kid appropriateness), 101
  testing, 13
Web'able! site, 26
WebMonkey site, 13
WebSiteGarage utility, 11
WebSnap Adaptive Palette, 305
WebTV, 5, 7, 26
weight, font, 401
Weinman, Lynda, 309, 317
Which Browser site, 7
whitespace
  around graphics, 162
  between table cells, 185
  blocks of (<spacer> tags), 154, 157
  encoding in URLs, 235
  in filenames, 57
  graphics for, 157
  indentation in lists, 418
  nonbreaking space, 190
  padding, 409, 427
  paragraph indentation, 407
  in tables, removing, 188–190
  text line/word/character spacing,
    403–405
  white-space property (CSS), 417
width attribute, 509
  <applet> tags, 147, 165
  <col> tag, 169

  <colgroup> tags, 170
  <embed> tags, 148, 165, 339, 344,
    357, 363
  <hr> tag, 149, 155
  <iframe> tags, 209
  <img> tag, 151, 159–160
  <marquee> tag, 152
  <object> tags, 153, 166, 364
  <spacer> tag, 154
  <table> tags, 172, 184
  <td>, <th> tags, 174, 185
  (see also size)
width property (CSS), 412, 426
window object, 431
window, browser
  centering object in (example), 196
  frames (see frames)
  live space considerations, 16–18
  positioning in (see positioning)
  resizable vs. fixed web pages, 19–23
  status bar text, 136
  targeting with links, 137
  two-column layouts (example),
    199–201
  (see also browsers)
Windows OS and CSS, 518–526
windows, browser
  opening with JavaScript, 380–382
  status bar text, 381
word-spacing property (CSS), 404
working directory, determining, 56
wrap attribute (<textarea>), 233, 240
wrapping text
  graphics and, 162
  multiline text entry fields, 240
Wright, Matt, 247, 248
WS_FTP utility, 58

X

Xing Technologies' Streamworks, 342,
  355
XML (Extensible Markup Language),
  445–452
  examples of, 448–451
XSL (Extensible Style Language), 451
XSSI (Extended Server Side Includes),
  255–256

Z

z-index property (CSS), 420–421
z-order, 420, 434
zero-width [non-]joiner characters, 463
‌ and ‍ mnemonics, 463

About the Author

Jennifer Niederst was one of the first designers for the Web. As the designer of O'Reilly's Global Network Navigator (GNN), the first commercial Web site, she has been designing for the Web since 1993. Since then, she has been working almost exclusively on the Web, first as Creative Director of Songline Studios (a subsidiary of O'Reilly) where she designed the original interface for WebReview (*webreview.com*) and as a freelance designer and consultant since 1996. She is the author of *Designing for the Web* (O'Reilly, 1996), and has taught Web design at the Massachusetts College of Art and the Interactive Factory in Boston, MA. She has spoken at major design and Internet events including the GRAFILL conference (Geilo, Norway), Seybold Seminars, and the W3C International Expo. In addition to designing, Jennifer enjoys cooking, travel, indie-rock, and making stuff. You can visit her site at *http://www.littlechair.com/* or send her email at *jen@oreilly.com*.

Colophon

Our look is the result of reader comments, our own experimentation, and feedback from distribution channels. Distinctive covers complement our distinctive approach to technical topics, breathing personality and life into potentially dry subjects.

The animal appearing on the cover of *Web Design in a Nutshell* is a least weasel (*Mustela nivalis*). There are 67 species of weasel, including the mink, ermine, ferret, otter, and skunk. Weasels, who are characterized by long, slender bodies and short legs, are found on all continents except Antarctica and Australia, and in a vast variety of habitats.

The least weasel is the smallest of the 67 species of weasel. Weighing in at approximately two ounces and measuring less than ten inches long, the least weasel is the smallest carnivore on Earth. They are found throughout the world, in northern climates. In warm weather this weasel's coat is brown, with a white underside. In winter it turns completely white. Thanks to its camouflage abilities and its speed and agility, the least weasel is rarely caught.

The diet of the least weasel is made up primarily of voles and mice, which, because of the weasels' high metabolism, they hunt constantly. One family of these little weasels can consume thousands of rodents each year, making them important in controlling pest populations. Because it is so small, the least weasel can follow mice into their burrows and eat them there. Like other weasels, they will occasionally then make their victim's home their own, lining it with the fur of the former resident when preparing to nest. Least weasels can produce two litters a year, with three to five young per litter.

Clairemarie Fisher O'Leary was the production editor and copyeditor for this book; Sheryl Avruch was the production manager; Ellie Cutler and Kim Brown provided quality control. Chris Reilley created the illustrations using Adobe Photoshop 4 and Macromedia FreeHand 7. Mike Sierra provided FrameMaker technical support. Seth Maislin wrote the index. Melanie Wang, Amy Meterparel, and Jeffrey Liggett provided additional production support.

Edie Freedman designed the cover of this book, using an original illustration by Lorrie LeJeune. The cover layout was produced with QuarkXPress 3.32 using the ITC Garamond font. Whenever possible, our books use RepKover™, a durable and flexible lay-flat binding. If the page count exceeds RepKover's limit, perfect binding is used.

The inside layout was designed by Nancy Priest and implemented in FrameMaker 5.0 by Mike Sierra. The text and heading fonts are ITC Garamond Light and Garamond Book. This colophon was written by Clairemarie Fisher O'Leary.

Web Authoring and Design

PNG: The Definitive Guide

By Greg Roelofs
1st Edition June 1999
344 pages, ISBN 1-56592-542-4

Targeted at graphic designers and programmers, *PNG: The Definitive Guide* is the first book devoted exclusively to teaching and documenting this important new and free image format. It is an indispensable compendium for Web content developers and programmers and is chock full of examples, sample code, and practical hands-on advice.

In a Nutshell Quick References

Webmaster in a Nutshell, 2nd Edition

By Stephen Spainhour & Robert Eckstein
2nd Edition June 1999
540 pages, ISBN 1-56592-325-1

This indispensable books takes all the essential reference information for the Web and pulls it together into one volume. It covers HTML 4.0, CSS, XML, CGI, SSI, JavaScript 1.2, PHP, HTTP 1.1, and administration for the Apache server.

AOL in a Nutshell

By Curt Degenhart & Jen Muehlbauer
1st Edition June 1998
536 pages, ISBN 1-56592-424-X

This definitive reference breaks through the hype and shows advanced AOL users and sophisticated beginners how to get the most out of AOL 4.0's tools and features. You'll learn how to customize AOL to meet your needs, work around annoying idiosyncrasies, avoid unwanted email and Instant Messages, actually understand Parental Controls, and turn off intrusive advertisements. It's an indispensable guide for users who aren't dummies.

In a Nutshell Quick References

ASP in a Nutshell

By A. Keyton Weissinger
1st Edition February 1999
426 pages, ISBN 1-56592-490-8

This detailed reference contains all the information Web developers need to create effective Active Server Pages (ASP) applications. It focuses on how features are used in a real application and highlights little-known or undocumented aspects, enabling even experienced developers to advance their ASP applications to new levels.

Perl in a Nutshell

By Ellen Siever, Stephen Spainhour & Nathan Patwardhan
1st Edition December 1998
674 pages, ISBN 1-56592-286-7

The perfect companion for working programmers, *Perl in a Nutshell* is a comprehensive reference guide to the world of Perl. It contains everything you need to know for all but the most obscure Perl questions. This wealth of information is packed into an efficient, extraordinarily usable format.

Internet in a Nutshell

By Valerie Quercia
1st Edition October 1997
450 pages, ISBN 1-56592-323-5

Internet in a Nutshell is a quick-moving guide that goes beyond the "hype" and right to the heart of the matter: how to get the Internet to work for you. This is a second-generation Internet book for readers who have already taken a spin around the Net and now want to learn the shortcuts.

How to stay in touch with O'Reilly

1. Visit Our Award-Winning Site

http://www.oreilly.com/

★ "Top 100 Sites on the Web" —*PC Magazine*
★ "Top 5% Web sites" —*Point Communications*
★ "3-Star site" —*The McKinley Group*

Our web site contains a library of comprehensive
product information (including book excerpts
and tables of contents), downloadable software,
background articles, interviews with technology
leaders, links to relevant sites, book cover art,
and more. File us in your Bookmarks or Hotlist!

2. Join Our Email Mailing Lists

New Product Releases

To receive automatic email with brief descriptions
of all new O'Reilly products as they are released,
send email to:
listproc@online.oreilly.com
Put the following information in the first line of
your message (*not* in the Subject field):
subscribe oreilly-news

O'Reilly Events

If you'd also like us to send information about
trade show events, special promotions, and other
O'Reilly events, send email to:
listproc@online.oreilly.com
Put the following information in the first line of
your message (*not* in the Subject field):
subscribe oreilly-events

3. Get Examples from Our Books via FTP

There are two ways to access an archive of example
files from our books:

Regular FTP

• ftp to:
  ftp.oreilly.com
  (login: anonymous
  password: your email address)
• Point your web browser to:
  ftp://ftp.oreilly.com/

FTPMAIL

• Send an email message to:
  ftpmail@online.oreilly.com
  (Write "help" in the message body)

4. Contact Us via Email

order@oreilly.com
To place a book or software order online. Good
for North American and international customers.

subscriptions@oreilly.com
To place an order for any of our newsletters or
periodicals.

books@oreilly.com
General questions about any of our books.

software@oreilly.com
For general questions and product information
about our software. Check out O'Reilly Software
Online at **http://software.oreilly.com/** for software
and technical support information. Registered
O'Reilly software users send your questions to:
website-support@oreilly.com

cs@oreilly.com
For answers to problems regarding your order
or our products.

booktech@oreilly.com
For book content technical questions or
corrections.

proposals@oreilly.com
To submit new book or software proposals to our
editors and product managers.

international@oreilly.com
For information about our international distributors
or translation queries. For a list of our distributors
outside of North America check out.
http://www.oreilly.com/www/order/country.html

O'Reilly & Associates, Inc.

101 Morris Street, Sebastopol, CA 95472 USA
TEL   707-829-0515 or 800-998-9938
          (6am to 5pm PST)
FAX   707-829-0104

O'REILLY®

TO ORDER: **800-998-9938** • order@oreilly.com • http://www.oreilly.com/
OUR PRODUCTS ARE AVAILABLE AT A BOOKSTORE OR SOFTWARE STORE NEAR YOU.
FOR INFORMATION: **800-998-9938** • **707-829-0515** • info@oreilly.com

International Distributors

UK, EUROPE, MIDDLE EAST AND AFRICA (EXCEPT FRANCE, GERMANY, AUSTRIA, SWITZERLAND, LUXEMBOURG, LIECHTENSTEIN, AND EASTERN EUROPE)

INQUIRIES
O'Reilly UK Limited
4 Castle Street
Farnham
Surrey, GU9 7HS
United Kingdom
Telephone: 44-1252-711776
Fax: 44-1252-734211
Email: josette@oreilly.com

ORDERS
Wiley Distribution Services Ltd.
1 Oldlands Way
Bognor Regis
West Sussex PO22 9SA
United Kingdom
Telephone: 44-1243-779777
Fax: 44-1243-820250
Email: cs-books@wiley.co.uk

FRANCE

ORDERS
GEODIF
61, Bd Saint-Germain
75240 Paris Cedex 05, France
Tel: 33-1-44-41-46-16 (French books)
Tel: 33-1-44-41-11-87 (English books)
Fax: 33-1-44-41-11-44
Email: distribution@eyrolles.com

INQUIRIES
Éditions O'Reilly
18 rue Séguier
75006 Paris, France
Tel: 33-1-40-51-52-30
Fax: 33-1-40-51-52-31
Email: france@editions-oreilly.fr

GERMANY, SWITZERLAND, AUSTRIA, EASTERN EUROPE, LUXEMBOURG, AND LIECHTENSTEIN

INQUIRIES & ORDERS
O'Reilly Verlag
Balthasarstr. 81
D-50670 Köln
Germany
Telephone: 49-221-973160-91
Fax: 49-221-973160-8
Email: anfragen@oreilly.de (inquiries)
Email: order@oreilly.de (orders)

CANADA (FRENCH LANGUAGE BOOKS)
Les Éditions Flammarion ltée
375, Avenue Laurier Ouest
Montréal (Québec) H2V 2K3
Tel: 00-1-514-277-8807
Fax: 00-1-514-278-2085
Email: info@flammarion.qc.ca

HONG KONG
City Discount Subscription Service, Ltd.
Unit D, 3rd Floor, Yan's Tower
27 Wong Chuk Hang Road
Aberdeen, Hong Kong
Tel: 852-2580-3539
Fax: 852-2580-6463
Email: citydis@ppn.com.hk

KOREA
Hanbit Media, Inc.
Sonyoung Bldg. 202
Yeksam-dong 736-36
Kangnam-ku
Seoul, Korea
Tel: 822-554-9610
Fax: 822-556-0363
Email: hant93@chollian.dacom.co.kr

PHILIPPINES
Mutual Books, Inc.
429-D Shaw Boulevard
Mandaluyong City, Metro
Manila, Philippines
Tel: 632-725-7538
Fax: 632-721-3056
Email: mbikikog@mnl.sequel.net

TAIWAN
O'Reilly Taiwan
No. 3, Lane 131
Hang-Chow South Road
Section 1, Taipei, Taiwan
Tel: 886-2-23968990
Fax: 886-2-23968916
Email: taiwan@oreilly.com

CHINA
O'Reilly Beijing
Room 2410
160, FuXingMenNeiDaJie
XiCheng District
Beijing
China PR 100031
Tel: 86-10-86631006
Fax: 86-10-86631007
Email: beijing@oreilly.com

INDIA
Computer Bookshop (India) Pvt. Ltd.
190 Dr. D.N. Road, Fort
Bombay 400 001 India
Tel: 91-22-207-0989
Fax: 91-22-262-3551
Email: cbsbom@giasbm01.vsnl.net.in

JAPAN
O'Reilly Japan, Inc.
Kiyoshige Building 2F
12-Bancho, Sanei-cho
Shinjuku-ku
Tokyo 160-0008 Japan
Tel: 81-3-3356-5227
Fax: 81-3-3356-5261
Email: japan@oreilly.com

ALL OTHER ASIAN COUNTRIES
O'Reilly & Associates, Inc.
101 Morris Street
Sebastopol, CA 95472 USA
Tel: 707-829-0515
Fax: 707-829-0104
Email: order@oreilly.com

AUSTRALIA
WoodsLane Pty., Ltd.
7/5 Vuko Place
Warriewood NSW 2102
Australia
Tel: 61-2-9970-5111
Fax: 61-2-9970-5002
Email: info@woodslane.com.au

NEW ZEALAND
Woodslane New Zealand, Ltd.
21 Cooks Street (P.O. Box 575)
Waganui, New Zealand
Tel: 64-6-347-6543
Fax: 64-6-345-4840
Email: info@woodslane.com.au

LATIN AMERICA
McGraw-Hill Interamericana
Editores, S.A. de C.V.
Cedro No. 512
Col. Atlampa
06450, Mexico, D.F.
Tel: 52-5-547-6777
Fax: 52-5-547-3336
Email: mcgraw-hill@infosel.net.mx

O'REILLY®

TO ORDER: **800-998-9938** • *order@oreilly.com* • *http://www.oreilly.com/*
OUR PRODUCTS ARE AVAILABLE AT A BOOKSTORE OR SOFTWARE STORE NEAR YOU.
FOR INFORMATION: **800-998-9938** • **707-829-0515** • *info@oreilly.com*

O'Reilly & Associates, Inc.
101 Morris Street
Sebastopol, CA 95472-9902
1-800-998-9938

Visit us online at:
http://www.ora.com/
orders@ora.com

O'REILLY WOULD LIKE TO HEAR FROM YOU

Which book did this card come from?

_____

Where did you buy this book?
❏ Bookstore   ❏ Computer Store
❏ Direct from O'Reilly   ❏ Class/seminar
❏ Bundled with hardware/software
❏ Other _____

What operating system do you use?
❏ UNIX   ❏ Macintosh
❏ Windows NT   ❏ PC(Windows/DOS)
❏ Other _____

What is your job description?
❏ System Administrator   ❏ Programmer
❏ Network Administrator   ❏ Educator/Teacher
❏ Web Developer
❏ Other _____

❏ Please send me O'Reilly's catalog, containing
a complete listing of O'Reilly books and
software.

Name _____   Company/Organization _____

Address _____

City _____   State _____   Zip/Postal Code _____   Country _____

Telephone _____   Internet or other email address (specify network) _____

Nineteenth century wood engraving
of a bear from the O'Reilly &
Associates Nutshell Handbook®
Using & Managing UUCP.

BUSINESS REPLY MAIL

FIRST CLASS MAIL   PERMIT NO. 80   SEBASTOPOL, CA

Postage will be paid by addressee

O'Reilly & Associates, Inc.
101 Morris Street
Sebastopol, CA 95472-9902